So Says the Guru

VOLUME I

YodaGuru

2024, So Says The Guru

All rights reserved. No part of this publication may be reproduced, distributed, or transmitted in any form by any means, including photocopying, or other electronic methods without the prior written permission of the author, except in the case of brief quotations embodied in reviews and certain other noncommercial uses permitted by copyright law. For permission requests, write to the author of the address below.

yodaguru77@yahoo.com

Website:
yodaisms.blogspot.com

Visit The Inner Sanctum:
http://yodaisms.blogspot.com

ISBN: 979-8-9900100-0-0

Printed in the United States of America

First printed, 2024

I still go by this message of inspiration that was written by my high school art mentor 27 years ago...

> Dante you have talent & skills AND CREATIVE you don't need anything more to be successful, JUST KEEP GROWING; Mind, Body & SPIRIT ... CREATE... LOOK AND DRAW WHAT YOU SEE.... Have a great Summer C-U-NeXT year
> Rashid

TABLE OF CONTENTS

ACKNOWLEDGEMENTS	xxi
GRADUATION	3
FUTURE	4
THE FINAL FRONTIER	5
INSANITY	6
CHIVALRY	8
KIDS TODAY	9
LIFE IS LIKE A DRAWING	11
BROTHERHOOD	13
SOMEDAY	15
CALM BEFORE THE STORM	16
IS IT WORTH IT	17
GETTING OLDER	19
THE PATH OF LIFE	20
2 IDOLS	21
TAKE NOTHING FOR GRANTED	23
A NAME TO REMEMBER	25
CHECKMATE	26
10 COUNT	27
FULL CIRCLE	29
THAT OLE' FAMILIAR FEELING	31
ARE YOU NORMAL	33
THE FIRE WITHIN	34
FAMILY IS FOREVER	35
WHAT IF	37
END OF THE ROAD	39

WELCOME TO THE DARKSIDE	41
RAINY DAYS	43
THE PERFECT MOM	45
LIKE A KID AGAIN	47
IMMORTALITY	49
WALK-ABOUT	51
REFLECTION	53
SAYING GOODBYE	55
HAPPILY EVER AFTER	57
POTENTIAL	59
FOLLOW YOUR HEART	61
LOST AND FOUND	63
THREE LITTLE WORDS	65
THAT MISSING PIECE	67
DEFINING MOMENT	69
BURNOUT	71
SMILE	73
FAST LANE	75
MY LEGACY	77
MAGIC	79
COME IN	81
CHICKEN SOUP	83
THE BEST MEDICINE	85
THE MOST VALUABLE COMMODITY	87
THAT ONE REASON	89
REALITY	91
HERO	93
LET GO	95
GENERATION TO GENERATION	97

A DREAM COME TRUE	99
KEEP IT REAL	101
WHAT DO YOU WANT	103
WHAT I'VE LEARNED	105
FEAR FACTOR	107
THE HONEST TRUTH	109
TRUST ME	111
PASSING THE TORCH	113
THE LITTLE THINGS	115
TO BE THE MAN	117
WRONG TURNS	119
PERFECT	121
IMAGINE	123
ONE STEP CLOSER	125
W.Y.S.I.W.Y.G	127
PROVE YOURSELF	129
SOUNDTRACK OF LIFE	131
DESTINY	133
JUST A NUMBER	135
INNER VOICE	137
I DO	139
WOULD YOU	141
JUST FRIENDS	143
SKY IS THE LIMIT	145
ONCE IN A LIFETIME	147
100% GUARANTEED	149
FADE TO BLACK	151
MORAL OF THE STORY	153
IT'S SHOWTIME FOLKS!	155

PERSPECTIVE	157
GOT PROBLEMS?	160
CHOICES	162
TO BUILD A DREAM ON	164
JUST AN OBSERVATION	166
WINDOWS TO THE SOUL	168
MORE THAN JUST WORDS	170
LIKE RIDING A BIKE	172
THE BIGGEST IMPRESSION	174
TIME	176
THE SECRET	178
STYLIN' AND PROFILIN'	180
SPEECHLESS	182
LAYERS	184
THE GREATEST DAYS	186
TO WHOM IT MAY CONCERN	188
KEEP THE FAITH	190
LIVE IN THE MOMENT	192
THE CODE	194
THE RIGHT DECISIONS	196
PERFECT HARMONY	198
BLIND	200
MIRAGE	202
THE END	204
CROSS THE LINE	206
CURVE BALLS	208
NEVER A DULL MOMENT	210
THE AGE OLD QUESTION	212
HEART AND SOUL	214

LET IT RIDE	216
BELIEVE IT OR NOT	218
WALK TALL	220
MEANING OF LIFE	222
BALANCE OF POWER	224
ONE	226
THANK YOU	228
ONE THING	230
THAT ONE GREAT POWER	232
ALONE IN THE DARK	234
SECOND CHANCES	236
THE TRUTH IS	238
MAKING A DIFFERENCE	240
FOR BETTER OR FOR WORSE	242
ULTIMATE GOAL	244
DON'T LOOK BACK	246
ONLY HUMAN	248
DOWN HILL	250
KNOW YOUR ROLE	252
PARADISE	254
SPELL RELIEF	256
THE GREATEST GIFT	258
READY TO FLY	260
NEVER GO HUNGRY	262
IT'S OFFICIAL	264
ULTIMATE SACRIFICE	266
ARE YOU HAPPY	268
CLEAN SLATE	270
ON BENDED KNEE (LAST YODAISM OF 2004)	272

FAST AND FURIOUS (1ST YODAISM OF 2005)	274
THE TIES THAT BIND	276
APPLE OF YOUR EYE	278
A GUY THING	280
THAT ONE BRIGHT STAR	282
BREAK THE CYCLE	284
GUILTY AS CHARGED	286
TRAIL OF TEARS	288
RISE AND SHINE	290
SHAPE OF THINGS TO COME	292
SCRATCHING THE SURFACE	294
WHY ME	296
WITH ARMS WIDE OPEN	298
FINAL ANSWER	300
END OF THE LINE	302
THE REAL DEAL	304
GOOD AND READY	306
WORTH WAITING FOR	308
NEVER SAY NEVER	310
A DYING BREED	312
JUST ONE LOOK	314
SINCERELY YOURS	316
A PERFECT FIT	318
A SIMPLE THING	320
BLACK AND WHITE	322
TOP OF THE MOUNTAIN	324
TAKE IT OR LEAVE IT	326
RIGHT ON SCHEDULE	328
HEAD OF THE CLASS	330

WHISPER IN THE WIND	332
YOU GOT SERVED	334
THE HARD WAY	336
YOU NEVER KNOW	338
COOL, CALM, AND COLLECTED	340
FEEL THE HEAT	342
A CHIP OFF THE OLD BLOCK	344
UNSOLVED MYSTERIES	346
STEP BY STEP	348
ROUGH SEAS AHEAD	350
UNFORGETTABLE	352
OFF THE DEEP END	354
THE HARDEST THING	356
THE TOTAL PACKAGE	358
ONE LAST BREATH	360
THEN AND NOW	362
JUST FEEL IT	364
DORKS RULES!	366
A BLIND EYE	368
A CHANGE FOR THE BETTER	370
TO INFINITY AND BEYOND	372
THE GOOD OLE' DAYS	374
SQUARE ONE	376
FIRST TIME FOR EVERYTHING	378
IN ONE PIECE	380
THE KEY	382
MADE FOR EACH OTHER	384
MIRACLES DO HAPPEN	386
HUMBLE PIE	388

JUST GOTTA BELIEVE	390
CRAZY IN LOVE	392
HERE I AM	394
TRUE STORIES	396
THE ANSWER	398
THE WAY LOVE GOES	400
FOREVER AND ALWAYS	402
JUST AROUND THE CORNER	404
BOILING POINT	406
TO YOU	408
THE ONE	410
GO THE DISTANCE	412
THE NEXT BEST THING	414
HEART OF THE MATTER	416
THE PERFECT WAVE	418
DEFY THE IMPOSSIBLE	420
AS DAYS GO BY	422
I DARE YOU	424
YOU'RE HIRED	426
RESISTANCE IS FUTILE	428
YODA OUT	430
EVERYTIME	432
WHO'S NEXT	434
THE PERFECT MAN	436
ISN'T THAT CUTE	438
YOU AND ME	440
IT COULD HAPPEN	442
THE WORLD'S GREATEST	444
LOST IN TRANSLATION	446

WHO I AM	448
TO BE CONTINUED	450
JUST BRING IT	452
YOU CAN'T SEE ME	454
I HAVE A PLAN	456
HERE WE GO AGAIN	458
BEST OF YOU	460
LIKE FATHER, LIKE SON	462
I CAN FIX THAT	464
THAT THING CALLED LOVE	466
OLD SCHOOL	468
LIFE IS GOOD	470
SOMEBODY LIKE YOU	472
WELCOME BACK(3X)	474
GREATEST ADVENTURE OF ALL	476
THE JOURNEY CONTINUES	478
ANALYZE THAT	480
OH, GROW UP	482
FATHER OF THE BRIDE	484
MUST BE DOING SOMETHING RIGHT	486
HERE'S YOUR SIGN	488
AIN'T AS GOOD AS I ONCE WAS	490
THAT'S MY BOY	492
MAY GOD BE WITH YOU	494
OH, WHAT A RUSH	496
ANYTHING HELPS	498
WHERE WERE YOU	500
GOTTA LOVE IT	502
MY 2 CENTS	504

NEVER GIVE UP	506
MY NAME IS	508
I DON'T WANT TO MISS A THING	510
WORDS TO LIVE BY	512
IT'S ALL GOOD	514
STACEY'S MOM	516
HEAVEN SENT	518
PIMPIN' AIN'T EASY	520
BLINK OF AN EYE	522
IS IT JUST ME	524
JUST TOO SWEET	526
A THING OF BEAUTY	528
MOVIN' ON UP (FOR A FRIEND)	530
LAYETH THE SMACKDOWN	532
TRICK OR TREAT	534
PUT UP OR SHUT UP	536
IF YOU WERE MINE	538
SWEET SMELL OF SUCCESS	540
THE HANDS OF TIME	542
CLOUD 9	544
BECAUSE OF YOU	546
WHAT I LIKE ABOUT YOU	548
A GOOD THING	550
GIMMIE A BREAK (FOR ALL MOMS)	552
A WHOLE NEW WORLD	554
WHY NOT	556
THOSE WERE THE DAYS	558
TIME FOR A CHANGE	560
SHE'S THE ONE	562

ANYTHING IS POSSIBLE	564
HERE'S TO YOU (TO ALL MY FRIENDS)	566
CRAZY LIKE A FOX	568
HOME IS WHERE THE HEART IS	570
HERE I STAND	572
LIE, CHEAT, AND STEAL	574
BY THE NUMBER	576
THE BROKEN ROAD	578
IN A HEARTBEAT	580
TO GOD BE THE GLORY	582
TIMES LIKE THESE	584
IT'S ABOUT TIME	586
I'LL BE	588
MORE THAN MEETS THE EYE	590
ONE WISH	592
BEHIND THESE EYES	594
THAT'S COOL	596
WAX ON, WAX OFF	598
STICK WITH YOU	600
BYE BYE BYE	602
THE PERFECT GIFT	604
BELIEVE	606
WELCOME ABOARD	608
MY LIFE	610
JUST A THOUGHT (LAST YODAISM OF 2005)	612
TIME OF YOUR LIFE (1ST YODAISM OF 2006)	614
NO PLACE LIKE HOME	616
NOTHING TO LOSE	618
FOR YOU I WILL	620

DO THE RIGHT THING	622
CLASS DISMISSED	624
YOUTH OF THE NATION	626
BRAND NEW DAY	628
ANYTHING BUT ORDINARY	630
BEST LAID PLANS	632
CAN YOU HEAR ME NOW?	634
IT'S A SMALL WORLD	636
RIGHT HERE WAITING	638
TOUCHED BY AN ANGEL	640
SHOW ME THE MONEY	642
SAY IT WITH A SMILE	644
UNBREAKABLE	646
HEAVEN ON EARTH	648
WALK THE LINE	650
MY VALENTINE	652
YOU DA MAN	654
NEVERMIND	656
BROKEN	658
THE REAL THING	660
I'M FREE AT LAST	662
A SOUL THING	664
A TOUCH ABOVE THE REST	666
GIRL POWER	668
AND THE WINNER IS...	670
THE GIRL NEXT DOOR	672
STAND BY ME	674
BLAZE OF GLORY	676
YOU'LL BE IN MY HEART	678

GO REST HIGH	680
MY TIME	682
THE WAY IT IS	684
I'M STILL STANDING	686
FEARLESS	688
EYE OF THE TIGER	690
OUT OF THIS WORLD	692
YOU'LL THINK OF ME	694
NEVER FORGET	696
X MARKS THE SPOT	698
ALL FOR LOVE	700
MY FINAL THOUGHT	702
DIRTY LITTLE SECRETS	704
BREAK THE WALLS DOWN	706
REALITY BITES	708
BRING ME TO LIFE	710
IF YOU'RE NOT THE ONE	712
ABOUT THE AUTHOR	715

ACKNOWLEDGEMENTS

Thank you to the people, places, and/or things that have helped inspire what I've written and continued to be part of this mental journey. A special thank you to those who have responded in kind to those Yodaisms by sharing their personal stories to the point where those responses have been added to the book. It's considerably humbling how my writing has personally connected to so many people I've met in person and talked to online through social media who I've become friends with. Over the 27 years I've been writing down and then posting my thoughts, I've actually been encouraged publish them in a book. Well, you've got your wish. My writing journey is far from over. It's on ongoing process that is sparked from an initial idea and then a work in progress. I tip my hat to each and every one of you for the unwavering support, encouraging words, and tremendously positive feedback I've received over the years.

So Says the Guru

VOLUME I

GRADUATION
August 2, 1996

Saying goodbye is never an easy thing. Emotions run high as best friends and acquaintances move on to other places. Graduation can be daunting for a kid who is moving to something greater. Within those years close friendships have been made and relationships have been formed, and mentors have been established with teachers.

The memories and places shared together as a whole will never be erased from my mind and well as theirs. Obviously close contacts will be made through email and phone calls, as each of us go our separate ways. Who knows where we will all be in 10 or 20 years.

Parents, CEO's, small business owners, actors or actresses, teachers, it is all unknown for many of us. One thing is for certain, we are a family that is stuck together. Our paths will intersect on day, it is a matter of where and when.

FUTURE
August 25, 1996

What does the future hold for me? It's a question that has been asked by every person in one's own lifetime. But the real question is does anybody want to know their future ahead of time? For one's own curiosity can get the better of him or her, but in reality, a person doesn't want to see their own future.

Someone once said that a person makes his or her own future. You have to take control of your own life, not let your life take control of you. Will I like the person who I will eventually become? It's just a matter of putting things in the right perspective and going down the right path, but every now and then stumbling a few times on the wrong ones.

To be perfectly honest, I don't want to know my future. I would rather be surprised at where I end up. At least I worked hard where I would be rather than just slack off knowing that I would get there. I started this though by asking, what does the future hold for me, and after thinking about it, my answer is I have no idea.

THE FINAL FRONTIER
October 31, 1997

The sailors of the past used the stars to guide them on their way. Scientists use them to chart the wonders of the universe. For many we look upon them to daydream and ponder our own existence. Why are we here? What is our purpose here on this earth? There have been many questions regarding the starry filled universe, but none so asked as, "Is There Intelligent Life Out There?

Though, I truly don't know the answers there are the unexplainable phenomenon such Area 51 and Stonehenge. The questions we seek are easy to come by but getting the answers are hard to find. We may truly never know the answers to the mysteries of the universe.

For we must accept the hand dealt to us and constantly ask those questions for we someday may get the answer. Who knows what is written in the stars, it has the answers we seek. Time will tell as we chart our own path. Reaching for that one bright star that defines how bright we shine.

INSANITY
November 16, 1998

To survive in a place that thrives on those that easily burn out is a job that I love to do. One must have a sense of abnormality or insanity to work in a chaotic environment. Kids can smell fear like a predator to their wounded prey. New employees are considered fresh meat and I often wonder if they will make it out alive from the insane asylum.

Insanity is an artform, an artform that is easily perfected by so many. Many have passed through the hallowed halls of the asylum only to be swallowed up whole by the sheer magnitude of madness. For it's a pressure cooker and one small thing can set off a chain reaction of events that not even Superman can stop.

It's basically a battle of mind games, a strategy like any other. In comparison, it is a game of chess, where each move is critical. We may try to get in their minds and vice versa. See what they see, think how they think, feel how they feel like an FBI profiler trying to catch their elusive criminal.

On the other side of the spectrum, it is the kid's job to push the buttons and totally disrupt order that was one chaos. One must be a little insane, nuts, cuckoo, etc. to work in a place like this. You have to keep them off balance, keep them guessing at what we are going to do next. It keeps the kids wondering, for they don't know what is coming next. Keeping them off guard and without them knowing it, pulling the rug from under them, in a manner of speaking.

Insanity is a state of mind that will get a person through the tough times of life. You have to be a little bit insane in a world that is getting way too serious. Survival is the name of the game that is dominated by kids 24/7. You won't know if you're coming or going, for the straight jacket is always nearby. Welcome to my world, would you like to step into it?

CHIVALRY
December 10, 1998

Chivalry among men has not been forgotten, it is just a matter of restoring it back to the days of King Arthur. Some may say there are ulterior motives for our so-called good deeds, and it may backfire in our faces.

Ulterior motives are not a factor, it is the basic principles of being a gentleman that all men should inspire to be. Such deeds as opening a door for a lady and expecting nothing back except for a smile. The smile a lady gives back is payment enough for a deed that was instilled to me by my own father. If I did not utilize those basic principles of respect, I would not see the light of day seeing that he did train with the NAVY SEALS.

If a lady falls, don't pay attention to it, quickly go and help her up. It is my own belief that one should never hit a lady or disrespect her in any way. In my view, that is the ultimate disrespect.

It's all in how one looks at things, the way one carries himself. Yet there are those that feel it is a waste of time and that the females of today are jaded. Jaded or not, it is the right way to go.

KIDS TODAY
December 15. 1998

ATTENTION* The following views expressed below might offend some people. Do not hold it against me, but if you have another view feel free to email me about it.

Respect has lost its meaning in today's generation of kids. The lessons taught were absolutely vital in the growth of many well-adjusted kids in their early/late 20's and on. Though valued in those that grew up in the past, it has been forgotten in time, a time when kids respected the authority and wisdom of adults.

The wisdom that was shared from generation to generation was kept with great value. Yet, in today's generation it has been lost to deaf ears, in one ear, out the other so to speak. It's like they are totally ignoring anything that is being said to them and only hearing what they want to hear.

The respect that was earned is now being stomped on and kicked to the curb in a manner of speaking. What has happened to these kids of this generation? Have they been jaded by the new wonders of technology being sprouted up every which way?

In the past, kids like me showed respect at the drop of a hat. If disrespect was given in any way, shape, or form, punishment was given swift and hard. Though painful it may seem, it has made me the person who I am today. Whereas, the generation of kids today are totally opposite, and it is evident where I work.

The unorthodox methods of punishment are in, reality, watered down versions, which basically teaches nothing. In the past, picking out your own switch and getting the belt were just the tip of the iceberg for some people. The punishment is the same for all, but the methods are different.

The generation of kids today are turning into nambi pambi whiners who throw a fit when they don't get their way, and that's just my personal opinion from working with kids for the past 8 years. In my view, what this generation needs is just a swift kick in the butt to have their reality checked and checked hard. In the end, the kids of my generation are far more well-adjusted than the kids of today.

LIFE IS LIKE A DRAWING
January 3. 1999

Through thick and thin friends are there for each other through hard times and easy times. We have each other's backs, sort of brotherhood/sisterhood so to speak. If compared to it would be like a clique, the Breakfast Club meets Saved By The Bell mixed in with Beverly Hills 90210. Only we're not actors, or getting paid, or have a hit tv show, it's basically a group of friends that picks each other up when he/she is down, gives advice, listens to each other when one needs to vent.

It's a relationship like no other where stupidity runs rampant in a circle that is considered to be tight as glue. I don't know about the female relationship, but the male relationship is a simple one and doesn't need explaining. Thinking is not a part of our forte for it gets in the way of enjoying things like sports or not thinking at all. Different personalities clicking in one group yet share different points of view, styles, and likes. Yet we all share a common bond and that bond can be tested at any time.

For we all have those unique quarks that can get on people's nerves. It's a quality that friends have learned to live with and even work around. It's a surprise that there hasn't been a homicide of sorts where one or the other hasn't strangled each other. Pushing buttons is always the norm in a clique but there is always a time when one knows when to back off. Long periods of time have been spent chillin' with them and one knows them better than one knows themselves and vice versa.

For there is always one in each group. The loner, the player, the chatterbox, the goofball, the daredevil, the motherly/fatherly type etc, there's always one in each group One may not see it but there are. It's a friendship when one looks back at it and thinks to oneself,

"How did we all become friends?" It's a funny thing about life, the people we meet along our travels can sometimes point you in the right direction. While traveling, you get to know the passengers in the car and a kinship is formed without evening knowing it.

There are times when the bonds of friendship are tested and/or broken. It may take days, weeks, months, years, or decades to repair. It is just a matter of opening the lines of communication back up and it doesn't matter who goes first, it's a matter of being humble and taking one for the team so to speak. What was lost in the past can still be found again both in the present and in the future. I ended a thought before by saying that friends will come and they will go, but family is forever. But it can also be said that even though family is forever, friends will always be there for you when one is in need of help.

Let me leave you with this interesting thought: Friends will help you move, but best friends will help you move your body. Just something to think about.

BROTHERHOOD

December 20, 1998

We all start out our lives as blank pieces of paper waiting to be drawn or written on. The moment a mark is put on that paper our journey of life began. A drawing can show the growth in the past, improvement in the present, and success in the future. Like a drawing the details of our lives are being marked down bit by bit by God. Though the details of a drawing can be erased, the details of our lives can never be. For we can only improve on them and learn from them as we grow emotionally, spiritually, and intellectually.

Like a drawing, our own lives can never always be perfect. For there will always be blemishes that will show when least expected. We all in some ways are perfectionists, yet we aren't perfect. We have our own type of kryptonite so to speak; it's how God made us. One can try to cover up the blemishes of our lives but he sees them all and knows the future blemishes that will show up. A thumbprint there, a water spot here, an accidental bent corner are always inevitable. It's just a matter of accepting what will happen or refusing it all together, which can sometimes have dire consequences.

A drawing can be drawn over and over again, but the original can never be duplicated. In a way, no matter how many times we try to start lives over again, the life we originally led is the one that mattered most. For if we try to correct the past, we run the risk of further putting more blemishes on that piece of paper. We all at one time or another wished we could go back and relive the past. If I could steal a line from one of my favorite shows Quantum Leap, go back into the past and put right that once was wrong. In contrast, a drawing can be thrown away, discarded, or torn in half, and in a way, we can do that with our own lives. Throwing away friends, family, career, the ones we love and care about, and our hopes and dreams.

In the whole scheme of things, God is the artist, and we are the blank pieces of paper that are being written or drawn on. He knows every little detail of our lives and will add them in as time goes by. We may not know what our own picture will look like and in my own opinion, I really don't want to know. I want to experience the details of my own life hour by hour, day by day, week by week, month by month and year by year. Life for most of us is a mix of stress, frustration, humor, success, defeat, and insanity, yet it is that mix that I wouldn't want any other way, for that is what makes life so interesting. Take the good with the bad as it's been said. Though He hasn't completed his masterpieces, the portraits that he will eventually complete will turn out absolutely perfect in the end.

SOMEDAY

February 20, 1999

Each and every person has thoughts of meeting their potential significant other. Who they are, where they are, and when they will come into their lives. It is a matter of patience, for it could take days, weeks, months, years, or maybe even decades.

For some, they have found "the one", the one they are meant to be with, in other words a soulmate. For others it is a continuous search for mr./ms right and it is often compared to looking for a needle in a haystack. A haystack that would be considered the size of the Grand Canyon so to speak.

Many of us have one time or another gazed into the starry filled night sky and contemplated where our potential Mr./Ms. right will show up and interrupt our lives, in a good way of course. With star gazing comes shooting stars and we make a hopeful request of sorts that our wish would come true.
Yet there are special occasions, such as Valentine's Day, which can be tortuous for some but fulfilling for others. It's just a matter of keeping a positive spirit, for God works in mysterious ways.
In the meantime, friends and family will always be there for us through thick and thin. Keeping us distracted from the thoughts of yearning and wanting.
It may not be right now; it may not even be next week. As we look into the starry filled night sky, we continue to wonder which potential bright star will cross our path? Though some have found their bright shining star, most of us will eventually find that one bright shining star to spend our days and nights with……someday.

CALM BEFORE THE STORM
November 5, 1999

Silence, it's a soothing state yet it will be soon disrupted by a stampede. A stampede that has endless pent-up energy and will use that energy to inflict utter chaos.

The calm before the storm as it has been said. The peace, tranquility, and harmony that has embraced my surroundings will fall victim to a chaotic tremor of biblical proportions. A tremor that can be felt and heard miles away. Time is ticking away second by second, minute by minute, and hour by hour.

My thoughts of wanting to go home and sleep run through my mind. The thoughts are then disrupted as the honk of a horn is sounded. The calm has ended, and the storm begins as these words are uttered...The Kids Are Here!

IS IT WORTH IT
December 29, 1999

Is it worth it? The daily grind of set hours day after day after day. It's a constant cycle of headaches, sore throats, and rising stress levels. Why do it every day, come to a place that is filled with high pitched screams and loud yelling. The constant disputes with co-workers that are about a hare away from being knocked out cold. The boss riding one's back, metaphorically speaking, every now and then. Am I making a difference, if any, with these kids?

For it has been said, a person who takes time to listen to kids and ask them how they feel makes a difference in a child's life. In some ways I do, and parents sometimes compliment the way we work with them, but other times they merely find things that are wrong. You have to take the good with the bad sometimes, because these children that stand before us are the future. We can't avoid it, some may succeed, some may fail, it is a matter of keeping the faith.

As years go by, they grow up and they will have kids of their own. They too will someday come to a place of insanity. Will they have the same personality as their father/mother? One can only determine that by careful observation. I often think this will lead to something greater. If and when some of us leave this place one day, will any of us have left their own mark in a place that swallow people whole and burns people out in an instant.

Though the paycheck is an incentive, it's not the main focus, though it pays the bills. It's the smiles and love from the kids whenever I walk through the doors and each of them yell my name. I could compare it; it would be like yelling NORM! when the people see Mr. Peterson walk through the doors of CHEERS. At the end of the day when all is said and done, a hug from any child is the greatest incentive than any paycheck. I started this though by saying is it worth it, and I end it by saying.......Yes It Is.

GETTING OLDER
April 10, 2000

The years have passed by so quickly. As it has been said time and time again, "With age comes wisdom." For every man, from generation to generation, has eventually done "the old man noise." A sound/grunt that all men cannot escape from. Metaphorically speaking, it is a sound that signifies that we're not getting any younger. For many of us have one time or another had this thought, "I'm getting too old for this. A thought that I have said so many times over and over again.

As kids we all felt indestructible, able to take on the world at every turn. As kids we take the bumps and bruises of life. The broken bones we suffer from heal quickly and we're right back in the game so to speak. Now as adults, the bumps, bruises, and broken bones last longer with us and take much longer to heal. The sore backs and cracking knees are just some of the many wonderful things we get to experience as years go by.

As youngsters, eating a meal would be considered a sport. A contest of sorts in which who can scarf down several boxes of pizza. As one gets older a person would be lucky to eat 2 slices of pizza let alone 2 boxes. For a kid can eat a big meal and go on his/her merry way with energy to spare. Yet, as an adult, after eating a big meal one needs a nap, or should I say hibernation. A type of hibernation in which a bear takes during the winter.

Personally, I stand on the cusp of turning 30. My best friend and I tend to say, "It's all going downhill from here", in a joking way. But in reality, our formative years are just beginning and there are events in our lives yet to be experienced. It's hard to tell what the future holds in 10, 20, 30 years from now. In the end, we all will grow old gracefully and during our latter years, we all will pass down our wisdom to the younger generation.

THE PATH OF LIFE
August 26, 2002

25 years have passed thus far. The past 25 years have had its ups and downs and highs and lows. Ultimately the highs have outweighed the lows. Looking to the past there is always the possibility of regrets.

My regrets are none for it was a learning experience, like a ride on a mammoth roller coaster. Like life, there is a fork in the road in which many have crossed paths before. Take the road less traveled and suffer minor scrapes and bruises or take the treacherous road and be prepared for a fight.

Though choosing the easy road would be tempting, I am not one to take the easy road. Challenges have been placed before me and to suffer the proverbial black eye would be worth it. The journey of life is an unpredictable and winding road. There may be U-turns and potholes that will make me stumble but I will stay on the path chosen for me.

To infinity and beyond, what will the next 25 years hold for me in the future? It's a crazy thing about life, you have a front row seat to experience it live.

2 IDOLS
June 3, 2003

Ruben Studdard

205 is where this man hails from. His smile defined him from the very beginning. Grinning from ear to ear, he lit up a room. The velvet Teddy Bear is his moniker.

Though big in size he made up for it in heart. He brought soul back into the music stream. Love him or hate him, he had a magnetic personality. Cool as ice he said little, but he made up for it in song.

It was impossible not to hug this big bear of a man. Consistency was the key in every performance he did. Though many believe he was just all hype, others believed just the opposite and cheered him on.

The man from Birmingham Alabama. Smiling from ear to ear till the end. He represented his city to the fullest. He is America's Idol... FO SHO!

Clay Aiken

True talent over image true to form it was. From first glance we were all befuddled. Though looks can be deceiving, he brought his game. America threw him back into the "fishbowl" so to speak.

Hope was then renewed as he was given a lifeline. America would soon learn what they would have they truly missed out on. The voice of a God, but the body of Martin Short.
Each week we were in awe with his dulcet tones. Lionel Richie said it best, "All that coming from that body!" He amazed the guest

judges and made the ladies swoon. Yet it was his humble attitude that we loved the most.

The man from Raleigh, North Carolina. His passion for singing touched us all each week he performed. His passion for helping special kids touched us even more. True talent over image, America's true Idol.

TAKE NOTHING FOR GRANTED
April 13, 2004

As kids, we often take for granted the little things in life that mean so much to us. Like the clothes we wear, the food we eat, the friends we have made, the wisdom given by teachers and mentors, and the loves we have lost and the loves we have found.

Life is a learning experience where we travel the proverbial road and before us are potholes which may cause a stumbling block. Those potholes may hinder us from getting to our appointed goals.

Each one of us has had true happiness, great triumphs, and have reached highs that we can be proud of. Yet, each one of us has had true sadness, devastating defeats, and have reached lows that we want to forget. You have to take the good with the bad, so to speak, for life won't be as interesting.

It is how you deal with those past experiences, bad or good, that will determine the person who you will become in the present and in the future. Someone once asked, ~Would you live your life over again knowing all the trials and tribulations you are going to go through again?~ Yes? No? Maybe? You, yourself truly know the answer.

There is also the question of regrets. As one looks back at his or her own life do they have regrets? Regrets that warrant a do-over so to speak and fix right that once was wrong. Would you simply accept the consequences of past experiences or continue to wonder what could have been?

In retrospect, the past determines who you have become in the present. The present determines who will become in the future and the future determines who has become by the past and present experiences. So cherish everything that may come your way, bad or good, for it will determine who you are. Will you back up and run away or move forward and hit life head on? Take nothing for granted.

A NAME TO REMEMBER
April 14, 2004

Michael Jordan, Wayne Gretzky, Joe Namath, Cal Ripken Jr. These names are synonymous with greatness and the deemed legends in the annals of sports history. In retrospect, names are merely an identification, putting a name to an identity so to speak.

It distinguishes you from every other Joe and Jane Schmoe out in the world. Yet it is the person behind the name that signifies who he or she is by their personality, heart, and drive. So many have spent a lifetime of blood, sweat, and tears to make a name for themselves either in the entertainment industry or the cutthroat business world. So many succeed and their names are associated with struggle, hard work, and accomplishment. Yet, others may fail, and their names are either forgotten or unfortunately live on in utter infamy.

Proverbs 22:1 states: ~A good name is rather to be chosen than great riches, and loving favor rather than silver and gold.~ No matter the accomplishments made or the riches you acquire, a good name is the biggest investment you will ever have. A name can be used over and over again from generation to generation, but the person behind the name can never be duplicated.

One day each of us will someday leave this hallowed ground we call earth. Those who know us well or have been associated with us will speak of us in remembrance. Whether it be good or whether it be bad, they will speak our names. How will YOU be remembered when your name is spoken?

CHECKMATE
April 17, 2004

The relationship between men and women are similar and yet they are also different. For men, nonverbal communication is the norm and acts of mere stupidity rule supreme and thinking with one side of the brain. For women, verbal communication is constant and always thinking with both sides of the brain.

Both men and women are an enigma, women more so than men. Both are a puzzle of sorts where each side tries to piece together a complete picture of the other. Some pieces may fit perfectly, and some pieces may not fit at all. Some pieces may be missing, and some pieces may be broken or torn.

You just have to work with what you've got. The list of differences outweighs the list of similarities between the sexes. Yet, it is those differences that attract people to each other. In retrospect, the relationship between men and women can be compared to a game of chess. Each move that is made is critical and may determine ultimate victory or ultimate defeat.

It's a matter of making each move count, utilizing sound strategy, and predicting your opponent's next move. In the end, when success is at hand, he or she can claim the right to say.......... CHECKMATE!

10 COUNT
April 20, 2004

Life is like a heavyweight boxing match and your opponent is life itself. Our adolescent years are spent taking hits and jabs in the early part of the rounds. Yet, we recover quickly and get right back into the fight in a manner of speaking. In the beginning, we were all merely rookies, just learning the ropes so to speak. Sometimes, for our own good, the bell is sounded to ensure our own safety. Does it teach us in the long run? That is a question for you to answer yourselves?

As we reach adulthood, the hits we take and the bruises we receive are merely secondary. We are used to it and the adrenaline we feel pumps each of us to not back down and get into the face of life. A throw down if you will, a slobber knocker where teeth get knocked out and each hit feels like a thunderous blow. A blow that would literally shake the earth to its core. We spend our adulthood keeping our guard up, punching and jabbing, losing and gaining momentum. We have the never say die attitude that makes us who we are today.

The latter years of our life means simply surviving the last several rounds. The energy we had at the beginning is slowly fading. The adrenaline that kept us pumped up is now gone and our knees are about to buckle and are up against the ropes. It has now come down to who is going to survive, who wants it more. Our instincts tend to take over and we push ourselves to the limit in mind, body, and soul.

The final round has arrived as we stand in the middle of the ring. Standing face to face with life. We look back and at the life we led in the past up until now. Are there any regrets, if so would you go back and change them? It's a tough call to make but the past is the past, and nothing is accomplished by dwelling in the past. There is no turning back now, for the only way to go is to move forward.

Life can unknowingly give us a blow that will send us down to the mat hard. With all that you have been through, all you have experienced, all that you have strived and worked for within your lifetime. Will you throw in the towel and stay down for the 10 count? Or will you get back up, continue to fight with all your heart and with your last remaining bit of strength give a knockout blow that would make Mohammad Ali proud.

I ask you this question: What round are you in, as you battle life in the boxing ring and have you come close to being counted out?

FULL CIRCLE
April 20, 2004

The bond between parent and child is a complicated yet caring relationship. Both have expectations for each other, a balance of give and take, and most of all equal compromise. For every parent's wish is that their child reach an expected level set for them. Yet, the child wants to reach the level of achievement in his/her own way and in their own time frame. For the parents, they want what's best for them. Who has the correct view? Which side has the better argument?

As the child grows older into his/her teen years, lines of communication are not always connected. For a parent fear, worry, and frustration set in as they realize their child is growing up and trying to find their own identity. Their baby girl is turning into a young woman, and their baby is growing up into a fine young man. The patience of both parent and child will be tested, limitations will be set in motion, and the proverbial line in the sand will be stepped over beyond its limits. In retrospect, that is what being a parent is all about. They keep you on your toes and vice versa, for each will be ready for anything that may come their way.

Eventually the teen becomes an adult and with becoming an adult comes great responsibility. A driving purpose in life and become what you always wanted to be and that is a success. As time goes by love will be found, a marriage forged, and children born into the world. Traits and personalities are passed down from generation to generation as the parent sees a little bit of themselves in their child. The out of the blue realization sets in when giving stern lectures, disciplinary actions, and verbal and nonverbal arguments that you have become your parents. A scary thought as one thinks of it and a thought one never sees coming.

For you see, it's a cycle from beginning to end. A child becomes an adult and then a parent. In the end, as one looks back at the lessons taught, the advice given, the punishments received, and the TLC shared by one's own parents, we realize that it has absolutely come.........FULL CIRCLE.

THAT OLE' FAMILIAR FEELING
April 20, 2004

Each of us at one time or another has had that ole' familiar feeling. A feeling in which a certain vibe/connection that draws us to certain people. It's a feeling best described as seeing someone for the first time and everything around that person is blurry. Time simply stands still or is in slow motion like in a scene from a movie. The question is, is it merely an infatuation or is it something more?

For that person is a bright shining star and yet that star is unreachable. You chase after that one bright star among a sea of stars. For we all have been there as we look from afar and have those uncontrollable nervousness, sweaty hands, and the sleepless nights looking up at one's ceiling. For one often thinks, rethinks, and thinks again of the endless possibilities of might be and what might not be. Should one take the risk and put it all on the line so to speak for one's own happiness? But what of the person, will they feel the same way or merely "shoot" those intentions to the ground and be riddled with bullets.

In retrospect, one or the other may not share the same intentions. For either may have differences in views, differences in entertainment values, and may have differences in one's own thinking. At times it may seem like a lost cause to go with one's feelings because one's own personal baggage we all are carrying so to speak. Our past determines the relationships of the present and into the future. Call it kismet, destiny, or fate, but in my own view it's a matter of chance that certain people meet and have a vibe or connection. Though the vibe or connection may feel strange at first, one must learn to go with one's gut and either do two things:

1. Move forward and see what happens. If nothing comes of it at least an initial response was given.

Or

2. Never go with that gut feeling and always regret never taking that risk. Always looking to the past and wondering what might have been.

In the end, it's just a matter of what one does with that feeling that will determine which road that person will take. I ask you this question, when was the last time you had……that ole" familiar feeling?

ARE YOU NORMAL

April 21, 2004

Are you normal? It's a simple yet complicated question to answer. Everybody is unique in their own way. It's the person's personality that defines us all. If everybody were the same, it would really be a boring world to live in. Someone once stated, "Normal people are weird, weird people are normal". Do you agree or disagree with that statement? Would wearing a sombrero to work be considered normal? It depends where one works, the environment that person is in, and/or how that person deals with the day-to-day stress in his/her life.

For the traits and characteristics of the parents are passed down from generation to generation. Yet it is up to the child to create his/her identity. Finding themselves so to speak and discovering for themselves who they are and what type of personality dwelling inside of them. It is really what makes everybody special in a way. Everybody has that quirky personality that some/most/all people gravitate to. It's who each of us are, in addition, it is how you perceive yourself rather than others perceive you.

For some humor, sarcasm, the way he/she dresses, are just a small piece of a giant puzzle. It may take some people longer than others to figure out where the pieces fit but eventually, they will figure it out through time. Many of us do things that are considered normal to us but weird to others. Look at the little things you do in your life that may seem normal to you but odd to others. In the end, ask yourself this question: Do you consider yourself normal?

THE FIRE WITHIN
April 21, 2004

Each of us has a fire that burns deep within us all. It is the driving force that keeps us moving forward against obstacles, large or small. it can never be extinguished by any conventional means or methods. We all have that inner strength that never lets us throw in the towel so to speak. It's like the saying goes, "We may be down, but we're not out." It is a matter of regrouping, assessing the situation, and going at it at a different angle. Never quitting, never surrendering, always keeping our focus on that "prize" at the end of the rainbow in a manner of speaking.

That fire drives us to be the very best at what we love to do. Though we may make mistakes, it's the person's heart that pumps the flames even higher and hotter. In comparison, it's like climbing to the very top of the mountain and reaching the pinnacle of your career. But to reach the very top, one must endure pain and. In other words, we are willing to give up our blood, sweat, and tears to reach the top. It's a climb that any man or woman would gladly face to get to the richest "prize" in the game, whatever it may be to you. At times, the fire which burns inside us may flicker; it is the people who love, care and stick with us through thick and thin that keeps the embers burning.

All of us have that driving purpose to succeed. It may be different for some, but as the saying goes, "This is where we separate the men from the boys." The fire within us determines whether a person quits because the climb is too hard or moves forward and conquers the steep climb up the mountain. Our will to succeed, our determination, our drive, and our passion for what we love to do are what keeps the fire burning within us. Let me ask you this question: Does the fire still burn within you?

FAMILY IS FOREVER
April 26, 2004

Throughout a person's lifetime friends will come and they will go, but family will always be there for you. The disputes and hectic way of family life are part of what makes a family a strong cohesive unit. Each person with different personalities, views, and styles living under one roof and that can be a pressure cooker so to speak.

For nobody wants to be around when the shiznit hits the fan in a manner of speaking. The pent-up anger that was stored away erupts like a volcano and spews out everywhere. Words are said and sometimes cannot be taken back. The lines of communication are then basically cut off and sometimes ultimatums are given. Ultimatums that are given which aren't thought of because of the heated moment.

"If you live under my roof, you live under my rules." It's a quote that has been said so many times in many households. Many move on with their lives and start a new life and yet others stay and try a compromise between the parental units. It's a give and take between parent and child, a negotiation of sorts. For it has always been said, you can always come home again. For the door will always be open and a place will always be set at the table for you.

As one sits back, one often considers the fact that he/she may be adopted. For each person can agree that in their own way their family is completely insane. One aspect is the family reunion and things can get very interesting at family reunions. It's like your very own Jerry Springer Show, with no studio audience, no Steve, and absolutely no Jerry. In the end, no matter how wacky your family is they will always be there for you.

If I could some this up with a final thought, this would be it.

Sometimes it takes a tragedy for a family to come together, and the lines of communication open up again. No matter how insane your family is, you gotta love them. Though they can get on our nerves at times, we have to remember one thing, friends come and go but Family Is Forever.

WHAT IF
April 28, 2004

There are certain events in people's lives that they often consider what would happen if they took alternate paths. Paths that some or many would describe as the WHAT IF factor. For many of us think of the what if factor every now and then pertaining to our own lives and the people we meet. It's a constant racking of the brain, in a manner of speaking, when one thinks if his or her life would be the same if that event never occurred or he or she never met the people that are in their lives today.

It's a constant guessing game for we all walk the earth meeting new people while we travel the road of life. As said before, life can give us knockout blows that send each of us down to the mat hard. BUT what if that knockout blow never happened and one continued on that path never knowing what could have been and what might have been. It's a crap shoot, so to speak, for we never really know what is going to happen when we get out of bed in the morning. One day we could be hit by a car and the injuries sustained will be well compensated and one can be set for life. For the injuries sustained we will be paid by those at fault.

On the other hand, the accident would have never occurred and life as one would know would still stay the same. The daily grind continues as one burns the midnight oil to get that hard earned and well-deserved paycheck. It's a thought that many think about and yet wonder if they could go back and change certain events. Like Quantum Leap where Dr. Sam Beckett goes back in time and puts right that once was wrong so long ago. Changing the past may solve one's own conscience but would it be right? It's a tough question to answer.

BUT the real question here is, would that person find happiness and/or peace if those events ever happened? Would one continue on that path and later down the road and potentially that particular event would eventually happen. It would be in comparison to the movie Final Destination. Certain events happen for a reason, and the lessons learned from the past can be a guide to what will happen both in the present and future. For it could also be compared to the movie Sliding Doors starring Gwyneth Paltrow. One life, two separate events happen, and one outcome, but which outcome would it be?

One could debate it to the ground but looking to the past solves nothing. It just brings up memories that are near and dear to one's heart. Though a piece may be missing, it is up to the person to move forward and have a sense of closure. For the memories and cherished time spent will always be there in the back of your mind. For if one smiles as he/she reflects then it was worth going through those events. In the end, it is not a matter of thinking in the What If anymore, for that is in the past. For we must eventually move forward in the present/future and live in the here and now.

END OF THE ROAD
April 29, 2004

For many the hours spent on higher learning are coming to an end. The time to move on to much greater things in the real world has now come at last. It is a moment one sees coming, for fear and apprehension takes hold as one analyzes his/her situation. The knowledge, if any, that has sunk in will be used out in a world that eats people alive metaphorically speaking. It's what one has been preparing for since the realization of what he/she wants to do for a profession in life.

The professors/teachers will forever be one's mentors. For they encouraged us to achieve higher excellence when some days we felt like underachievers. It's a profession that never gets well-deserved credit for molding the minds of those that have greatly succeeded in the real world. It takes a combination of brains and street smarts to get to the head of the class in a manner of speaking. One can't rely on one's brains alone and vice versa. It takes both to accomplish goals that may seem impossible to achieve, for one needs MacGyver type knowledge to get past obstacles that seem unmovable.

One can reflect on the long hours of hitting the books, the frustrations, the personal victories, and disappointing defeats for it was a journey that was well traveled. For the blood, sweat, and tears were well worth the sleepless nights as one comes close to walking the path of accomplishment and receives that golden chalice called a diploma. For that diploma is the proverbial knighthood to greatness as one kneels and gets anointed by King Arthur in a manner of speaking. It's a dubious honor and as one savors that moment, he/she will now leave the institution that one entered so long ago.

As one takes the final look back at the past a bit of sadness overwhelms that person. One may think to themselves where each of us will be in the coming years as each separate into individual paths of potential success. Will there be a CEO in the making, a producer, a manager, actor, actress, etc. Who knows what paths each person may walk, it's an unknown that many are excited yet scared about. Nobody wants to see their future ahead of time, for that takes all the fun of finding out what lies ahead.

For some, the ending of one life means the beginning of another. It's a matter of thinking positive and continually reaching for that brass ring and not giving up on one's dreams. One must keep their feet on the ground, stay humble, keep the advice that was given close at all times, and always remember who you are and where you came from. Is it the end of the road? Not by a longshot. It's merely a pit stop from the street to the wide-open road. Hopefully there won't be any stop lights to continually keep you from where you want to go in life.

WELCOME TO THE DARKSIDE
April 30, 2004

Everybody has a dark side that is locked away deep inside one's own mind. For all the anger and frustration that one suppresses over the years builds up and is stored away like old clothes so to speak. It can come out at any moment during one's own lifetime when one least expects it. For we live our daily lives with anger all around us but it is how we deal with the anger that makes us who we are as a person. For friends and family have seen just a glimpse of the proverbial Mr. Hyde as one goes about living like Dr. Jekyll. For they hope they never see that side of us come out any time soon.

For nobody wants their dark side to come out and run rampant among the ones we have gotten to know over the years. The transgression and repercussions that might entail when the so-called "madman" wants to come out and play. It's a thought that scares some because what if the madman comes out and never wants to leave. Would any of us enjoy the feeling of letting go of all emotion and not care about the consequences afterwards. If compared to, it would be like Dr. David Banner turning into the Hulk. Who knows what any of us would do, for the circumstances may vary due to the events of one's own life.

Yet it's there deep inside waiting to come out at any given time, like a supervillain waiting in the shadows to conquer his enemies. If compared to it is somewhat like the struggle Anakin Skywalker goes through as he eventually turns into Darth Vader. He feels the darkness within himself, yet he tries to suppress it and continue the good fight. But some story book endings never have a happy ending. For it may take days, months, years, or even decades to come back from a place that hasn't seen the light of day.

It's like the movie Anger Management, where some have explosive anger and implosive anger. For those that have explosive anger they show it outwardly and have issues with the world. Others have implosive anger where every pent-up rage is bottled up and at any time one could explode like a powder keg. For if one sees the keg about to explode, run for cover because the shiznit is about to hit the fan. For whoever is in the path of the explosion may get hurt or not survive at all. Who knows what any of us are capable of when we let our dark side out to play so to speak.

The question is would we be able to control our dark side or will our dark side control us? A question that many may not have answers to, for one has to experience it for themselves. Each of us has seen our dark side up close and personal, for it is not a pretty sight. The key to coming back to the light, so to speak, is to hold on to that one thing that is near and dear to one's own heart. That one thing keeps one from embracing the darkness completely and turning themselves into something they would never want to be.

It's sort of compared to the movie City Slickers in which Curly tells Billy Crystals' character to think of that one thing that makes him/her happy and hold on to it. Each of us have that one thing in their lives that we hold on to which keeps them from slipping into the abyss. We have all come close to the edge of that abyss and almost fell in but luckily never have. So, I ask you this question. "What is that one thing that you hold on to that keeps you from going into the dark side?

RAINY DAYS
April 30, 2004

As the saying goes, rainy days are here again. For when it rains one's own hectic, chaotic life seems to slow down and take a breather in a manner of speaking. It can be a time of reflection as one thinks about the good ole days when life was much simpler back in the day as a kid. "No Worries, Be Happy". It was an anthem for a kid as he/she plays to their heart's content in the rain and does not worry about the consequences afterwards.

It's often a given that sleep is the number one choice for those when rain can ruin a perfectly good day. Yet, rain is always needed to quench the earth's thirst when the heat can be unbearable at times. For some, rain can be considered the party pooper, so to speak, as certain planned events are canceled and have to be rescheduled. Yet others embrace the rain and welcome it back like an old friend returning home. It can also be a connection to one's own childhood for we all at one time or another played or sang in the rain.

Yet, there are times when the gloom and doom or rain can be considered an omen of bad things to come. It is a sign that their day might be going downhill from that point, and one cannot avoid it no matter what one tries to do. It will be there waiting like a Lion waiting for his potential prey to cross his path. It's just a matter of thinking positive, using MacGyver-like instincts to make one's day interesting. Making up games, cleaning one's house, reading a good book, or taking the day off work and spending time with family. It's the power of choice that makes living in America so great and makes one feel like a teenager who skips school to play hooky.

For each raindrop can be a representation of life. For when each drop hits the ground the ripples that it creates represent the details of one's life. The highs and lows, hopes and dreams, the loves lost, and the loves found, and the journey of life that hasn't been written yet. It's like a window to one's soul for the rain can bring about a sense of peace and can clean out the soul in a manner of speaking. That is what rain does, it is needed to wash away the dirt and grime that life can throw at you when driving down the road of life.

When it rains, it's like getting a fresh new start. Things that couldn't be seen are seen again for the rain has washed the dirt and grime away. For once the rains stop and the skies open up, the smells that it brings forth can send one thinking back to the past. For rain is the psychiatrist of one's life that doesn't need payment in the end. As kids all into adulthood we often repeat this saying. A saying that may vary with interpretation, "Rain, rain, go away come again another day. If you don't, that's okay, I'm just going to sleep the day away.

When the rain stops, the skies open up, the sun shines and a rainbow forms in the distance. For we are often kids at a candy store in a manner of speaking when fun and jubilation are at hand. For it is like the pot of gold at the end of the rainbow so to speak. For the treasure at the end of the rainbow can be different for everybody. What is at the end of the rainbow when skies clear up for you and the rain stops?

THE PERFECT MOM
May 9, 2004

This is basically to all the moms. If you're not a mom, you can give this to your mom.

You have been there for us through the good times and the bad times. You stayed up with us when we were sick, and you knew what made us feel a whole lot better. For you waited on us hand and foot and wanted nothing in return but our love and gratitude. You handled our bumps and bruises with care and used your motherly love to basically kiss them away when we were younger. The tender loving care you gave us made each of us feel special like princes and princesses or kings and queens.
Growing up you have seen us go through every emotion in the book so to speak. You know us inside and out because each of us has a little piece of mom in our DNA. Our quirky little traits and characteristics come from you and a little bit from dear old dad. You have also seen our dark side but never ran away in fear. For you have been there before and the same things we did. The lessons that were taught to you back then are now being taught to us by you. Though we may not listen at times, we hear what you are saying and keep what you say in the back of our minds and in our hearts.

Through our times of heartache, you have stood by our side giving us bear hugs and kisses. You always knew what to say to make our day a little brighter and what to cook when we fell down. A sixth sense in a manner of speaking that all moms have when it concerns their kids. For you act like a superhero coming to save the day so to speak. Whether it is in our professional lives or in our personal lives we can always count on you to be there for us when we are in dire need of advice. You taught us to basically have balance in our lives that tend to be chaotic at times.

You have been there when we succeeded in the things that we strived for. Supporting us with whatever endeavor we wanted to do in life, no matter what. Yet you also be there when we fail, keeping our spirits up, and telling us never to give up on our dreams. Keeping us happy despite the times of sadness and tough times in our own lives. You have sacrificed so much for us and we appreciate that, though we don't show it at times. We are often too caught up with our own lives to give thanks that we have a mom that loves and cares for us so much.

As we get older, you realize your baby boy or baby girl is growing up and is turning to a fine young man or a fine young lady. For one day you hope that we will find the one that we will settle down with and raise our own family. It will basically come full circle for us as it did for you. Looking back, as kids we have made you happy, sad, crazy, angry and everything in between. In the end, no matter what anybody says, each of you are absolutely...THE PERFECT MOM.

LIKE A KID AGAIN
May 12. 2004

Everybody has that inner child within themselves that loves to come out and play. Apparently, my inner child's name is Earl, and he has never grown up. It's like being a kid again, a phrase that has been said by so many adults over the years. Though as we get older, the inner child inside each of us stays young forever. For we often try to keep the spirit alive in us though the energy we have sometimes fades away. It's a matter of having that feeling of excitement that one never seems to lose.

The excitement of visiting new places, watching a movie that one has been dying to see, or trying to see what presents one has under the Christmas tree. It's a feeling that will never go away no matter how hard one tries to keep it held in. Each of us has also had or still has that excitement of waking up on Saturday and watching morning cartoons with a box of cereal in hand. It's basically the kid inside us that makes us who we are and why people like us... sometimes.

At one time or another everybody gets excited when they hear the ice cream truck driving by or is heard in the distance. The inner child wants to basically find the ice cream truck and get that ice cream cone or popsicle. It's part of our childhood which we share with today's generation of kids. Everyone has that urge to play in the rain fearing the consequences afterwards, which is getting sick. It's the inner child mentality we never really grow out of and probably never will.

Each one of us has a job that they really love, or they really hate, there's really not in between. For one must find ways to entertain themselves in order for the time to pass and to make the environment around them enjoyable. Aspects such as swivel chair races, whip cream fights, water balloon fights, copying one's face on the copy machine, these are just some examples of passing the time in one's own way during those days and nights of boredom.

Yet there are those that leave the inner child behind and settle down for a life of responsibility and mediocrity. A person can say that they want to have fun and let loose, but something is holding them back. Call it fear or simply call it being a party pooper, but they need that one spark to completely let loose from the clutches of seriousness. I often say, you have to be a little insane to live in a world that has gotten way too serious. Live a little, throw away the suits and dresses and dress comfortably. Be the leader not the follower in a manner of speaking.

For one can use MacGyver like instincts and look around one's working environment to find ways to amuse oneself. You just have to revert back to the good ole days so to speak and be that kid inside again. In the end, as we get older, we need to realize that each of us needs that kid inside. For if we lose that inner child, we become the old mean neighbor who keeps the sports equipment that lands in his/her years and never gives it back. Let me ask you this question before I end, when was the last time you did something childish, had no regrets and you basically felt like a kid again.

IMMORTALITY
May 12, 2004

Each of us has had the thought of living forever, being immortal in a manner of speaking. BUT what kind of immortality would one seek? The type of immortality of Dracula in which one would not see the light of day ever again? Or the type of Immortality of the Highlander, Duncan McLeod, where there can be only one. A constant looking over one's shoulder as other immortals seek to take your head. There are many types of immortality, but which would one pick if you had the choice?

Never getting sick, never getting old, never getting any broken bones are some of the advantages of being immortal. Living life to the extreme and not caring about the consequences or the safety of one's own health. It's like a kid being in a candy store where all one wants is the rush of adrenaline in your blood. For the world is at your fingertips just waiting to be explored and challenged to its total limits. Climbing the highest mountain so to speak and never coming down from being so high.

Yet there are the drawbacks of having immortality. The ones we love grow older and pass away and we still live as young as can be. The friends made have grown old and withered away like a wilting flower that hasn't had any water to live. For one has to live with the memories of past loves and past friends who one has made over the centuries. One can feel empty inside when the life you once knew is over and you have to start over. It's a constant cycle that will never end, for the people around you will age but you will not

One can go insane at the thought of living forever. For the things they have seen, the people they have met during one's past lives, and the enemies they have made would affect that person physically and psychologically. For one can't be shot or stabbed, for if one suffers a broken bone it heals at an instant. Don't get me wrong, it would be fantastic to have that, but it would mess with the person's mind years or centuries down the road. For one might end up in a padded room, looking at ink blots, and talking to shrinks for the rest of one's life.

In the end, the thoughts of immortality fade when one looks at the aspect of living life to the fullest day by day. Stopping to smell the roses so to speak and basically taking risks every now and then. I ask you this question, would you go through a century of heartache and pain to live forever, or would you accept the life you are living now? Immortality, what a concept.

WALK-ABOUT

May 15, 2004

There are times in every person's life when certain events take place and the only thing that person can do is walk away. Walk away from the friends, associates, and even family that have been there for them through thick and thin. For that person must go on a journey, or in Australian terms, a walk-about so to speak and find themselves. Find the person who they once were and rise back up from the ashes like the proverbial Phoenix.

It's the little things that tend to snowball out of control and eventually become an avalanche. That avalanche has trapped us and the massive weight is smothering us to the point of suffocation. For we sometimes think there is no rescue party coming to save us and the weight of our problems will continue to hold us down. One tends to give up all hope, for one after another, problems seem to stack up and there are absolutely no solutions.

Yes, it is the tough times that we find out who we are when we are backed into a corner. Like the saying goes, "When the tough get going, the going gets tough." Each of us at one time or another has gone on a walk-about and the people we meet along the way inadvertently help us and give us answers to the questions we seek. They see what we don't see and they open our eyes to the truth in a manner of speaking. A spiritual guide who tries to lead that person back to what he/she once was.

Sometimes it takes a tragic accident to see the bigger picture in a manner of speaking. IF each of us have gone walk-about and had to confront the person we are now and the person that we once were. A battle from within in a manner of speaking and we eventually find the answers we seek and what is truly important to us in our lives. It takes a person hitting rock bottom to realize the seriousness of where he/she will be heading. Like a lightbulb turning on above that person's head and seeing what truly means so much in life.

The journey to return is a tough task at hand. There will be blood, sweat, and tears so to speak but that is the price to pay for leaving the life that one once knew and trying to return back to it like nothing happened. The people may still be the same, yet the attitudes have changed. It may take time, but eventually everything will be back as it once was. Let me ask you this question, have you ever come to a point in your own life that a walk-about was needed?

REFLECTION
June 17, 2004

There comes a time in every person's life when they reflect on the life that they have led up to a particular point. For the journey that each of us have traveled on has been a long and tedious road. A road that has many obstacles to overcome which can sometimes make anybody throw in the towel so to speak. A road that has many twists and turns which in the long run one hopes doesn't lead to a dead end. It's just a matter of retracing one's steps and getting back on track to one's intended destination.

When one looks back on our own childhood, we wonder how we survived it in the first place. The bumps and bruises we took during our adolescence seemed like a heavyweight boxing match. Each time we were knocked down we got right back up wanting more, not fearing for our own safety. In a way, we were like daredevils testing the limits of fear and excitement. For when one injures themselves to the point of going on injured reserve so to speak, it's just a setback. For the bones will heal quickly, bruises will go away, but the journey has just begun.

The teenage years represented a time of finding one's own niche. For it is a time of finding who they want to be and what type of person he or she will become. When you look back at their own experiences as a teenager, do you cringe or have a sense of victory? As with being a teenager, the rebellion sets in for those that want to steer clear of their parents' expectations for them in the future. For it's a learning experience for both parent and child, a give and take in a manner of speaking. In a way, our teenage years are just a halfway point to something much bigger and better depending on how one sees it.

For some the crossover into adulthood is like receiving a "key".

That "key" can be represented by certain situations which can lead to bigger and better things. BUT in order to get through, one must find their doors to unlock specific areas in one's own life personally and professionally. Each of us has been given that key to finding success and happiness, it's just a matter of finding the right doors to unlock. Though we may not know what's behind those doors, we just hold our breath, unlock that specific door and walk through.

Each of us reflects on the life we have led so far, do the good times outweigh the bad or vice versa? For if we look back and beat ourselves up, in a manner of speaking, we will drive ourselves to the brink of madness. One has to have a balance, a ying to one's yang so to speak. One must have a sense of satisfaction with what one has accomplished up to a particular point. In the end, each of us will look at our own reflection in the mirror and ask ourselves this question:

Am I going to throw in the towel or am I going to continue on my journey no matter how tough it may be?

SAYING GOODBYE
June 18, 2004

There is a time when a child must leave the roost, so to speak, due to relocation. A path that he/she doesn't choose but a choice that is chosen for them. That's life, for every person will move on with their own personal goals and dreams. Saying goodbye is never really an easy thing to do, for the memories and friendships made can never be forgotten. For the kids that once thought was irritating and annoying are the ones that will somewhat be missed because, in a way, they can make the biggest impression in our lives. The kids you get to know and become friends with over the years are considered to be the ones you truly will never forget. A person can form attachments with these kids which is one of the drawbacks when one works in a place, I like to call the Insane Asylum.

One can consider themselves proud parents/older brothers or sisters as each of us see them move on to something better. As their second parent, so to speak, we hope the lessons taught and the advice given will be used in their own lives later down the road. Though he or she might not take it, one hopes a little bit of the advice given is used. We want them to succeed and return to the place that gave them a chance to shine in their own way. For they will eventually have to go through their own trials and tribulations without us at their side. For someday, the kids we brought up for several years will one day return and have kids of their own. A thought that can somewhat frighten a person but put a smile on one's face as well.

For the headaches, lectures, and insanity that are associated with the kids that leave are the ones that are truly missed and, in a way, we root for them to succeed and consider them underdogs. For we truly never give up on those that have the greatest potential to succeed. We push them to their limit and sometimes they push back, but that's to be expected. One day they will look back at their experiences and realize why we did what we did for them is because we cared. As counselors, we motivate every child to reach a higher level of achievement, but most times, they are not able to reach our expectations. Though they may not reach those expectations, each of us as counselors would be proud to call them "my kids"...most of the time.

As one looks back at the time spent with these kids, one can get somewhat emotional. For one day the journey will end for each of us who work at the asylum to climb our own personal mountain that will lead him or her to one's ultimate goal. By doing that, one will leave behind the people he or she once referred to as co-workers, then friends, and in the end consider them family. For every family has their hardships that can oftentimes be considered Jerry Springer moments. But as a family, we worked through them and hopefully moved on. As each of us looks back at the time spent working in the "nuthouse", we will remember the high points, the low points, the points that made us confused, and the points that made us go absolutely insane.

As I said before, saying goodbye is never an easy thing for anybody to do, for both the child and adult. For we must leave behind all that we once knew and head off into the unknown and I can truly say that my time at the asylum so far have been a crazy, but memorable experience. Once you leave the asylum, you are never really the same person you came in, take it from me. I was very different when I first started almost 8 years ago. In the end, It's just a matter of thinking positive and knowing that a person can make his or her mark somewhere else and succeed. When my time comes to ride off into the sunset, so to speak, it's not a matter of saying goodbye, that's not my style. It's just a matter of saying see you later.

HAPPILY EVER AFTER
June 21, 2004

Most of us have come to the point where the possibility of finding true happiness is just a mere fairy tale. A fairy tale that can either have a happy ending or no ending at all. Though it may be fitting for those that have found their Prince Charming or Cinderella, others are still searching. Ladies wonder if their prince charming will ride in and both will ride off into the proverbial sunset. For guys, it's just a matter of finding that one special person whose foot fits the glass slipper left behind at the ball so to speak.

But the question remains, would a life of solace and wonder be the best alternative as one travels down the highways and byways of life? Who knows, life is all about unpredictability. Someone once said, "In order for one to find happiness, one must suffer a few sorrows. Each of us at one time or another has suffered sorrows which tear at the heartstrings, so to speak. Yet, we persevere and fight the good fight in a manner of speaking. One can call it a setback, but it's a setback that makes every person stronger and able to move forward in their lives.

For we all have looked up at the star filled night sky and pondered if "the one" is out there. It's a constant guessing game of when our day will come and when he or she will cross our path. For those we know and associate with continually find special connections. Connections that may or may not last in the long run, but it's a connection, nonetheless. But do the qualities that make a person who they are count in the end? As the saying goes, Would the proverbial "nice guy" finish last as usual, or does it even matter?

In retrospect, a person must inevitably be comfortable with who they are as a person. The questions come so easily for us but the answers we seek are hard to come by. Nobody knows the outcome of our future and who we will spend it with for the rest of our lives. But if the happiness we seek never turns up, our friends and family will fill that proverbial void. For each of us feel incomplete in a way, like missing a piece in a giant puzzle. It's just a matter of finding that one special piece to one's heart that will complete the puzzle of our lives. IF one wants a more romantic interpretation, that one special person has the key to unlock his or her heart.

In the end, it's just a matter of letting nature run its course. For if our lives were like a Hollywood movie, we could simply write our own happy ending. Prince charming will ride in and the glass slipper will fit perfectly and all is well. On paper it seems plausible, for in reality we are in control of our lives and our futures. Who knows what is down the road for all of us, for each of our stories are still being written. There will come a time and day where each of us will have our own storybook ending. An ending, which is also a new beginning, will hopefully one day will simply read.... Happily Ever After.

POTENTIAL
June 24, 2004

It has been said that patience is a virtue, and it is evident when one works taking care of kids. The unpredictability of a child's mind and actions can be a daunting task to figure out, for one must think like an FBI profiler. In some ways I must think about what that child thinks and see what that child sees. Also predicting their next move before they do it. For some of these kids act like little angels on the outside but deep inside they have the capacity to be like Hannibal Lecter. For they can mess with one's mind to the point of going insane and tearing out one's hair.

One has to remember to keep one's cool as madness surrounds them day in and day out. As the saying goes, "Kids say the darndest things." Sometimes those things that kids say and do can trigger emotions that one can't help bring out. Such emotions as anger, frustrations, sadness, humor, and the ever so popular confusion. It's the weird things that cross our paths on a daily basis that leave me and my friends totally speechless. For I am basically amazed at the depths of insanity that these kids will try just to get any kind of emotion out of us.

Over time one can become a little cynical and have sarcastic wit to them. For one can turn into a George Carlin or a Dennis Miller in which they are known for their sarcasm. Over the years, I have learned that one must not have the mindset that it's not just a job. It's not a job that a person thinks is just for the paycheck or the fact that there are perks to the job. In retrospect, I don't consider it a job, I consider it a place that I come to day in and day out where I can have fun and make a kid's life much more enjoyable. Every day I walk through those hallowed halls and feel like Norm when walking into Cheers so to speak.

They say if you change the life of a child, you change the world. In my own view, I play a small part in something much greater than myself. For a person who seeks to one day become a parent should come to trade places with me and walk in my shoes. For the experiences one will face will change their perspective which some would perceive is "the easiest job in the world." I consider every kid for the last 7/8 years that has walked through the doors of the Youth Center as my own kid. In a way they have somehow given me a better understanding of what it's like to be a parent.

For there will always be whining, crying and temper tantrums associated with my job and that is just coming from the staff. You got to have a little bit of humor in a place that has so much insanity in it. In any case, someone once told me that every person has the potential to be a parent. It's how one uses that potential that separates the men from the boys so to speak. A couple months ago, the question was given to me if I had the potential of being a parent. My answer…I believe I do.

FOLLOW YOUR HEART
June 24, 2004

Matters of the heart can become a complicated subject to deal with as one searches for that one bright shining star among a sea of countless stars. One can never truly know if the feelings one has for another are love or just mere infatuation. But it's the risks we take with our hearts that determine either a newly found relationship or a broken heart. It's a leap of faith so to speak, when he or she puts themselves out there in order to meet that person who could possibly be "the one". It's like having a vibe or connection with someone that you don't even know and yet you are strangely drawn to that person.

The best example I could give is when seeing that person for the very first time. All one sees is that person and everything around that person is blurry. For it can be a magical moment if one considers it like a fairy tale. For that person may be the key to unlocking one's own heart. Take My Breath Away by Berlin, a song that can compare to meeting that special person for the first time. For the physical attraction is there, but in the end, one must find what's most attractive on the inside. Looks or personality, in the end one has to ask themselves which means more to that person.

Both men and women are an enigma, waiting to be solved. For when one thinks he or she has the answers, many more questions pop up. Nobody truly knows all the answers concerning relationships, it is just a matter of taking chances and going with their feelings. For one has to rationalize what one is feeling and find out if those feelings are real. The symptoms are there, for it doesn't take a doctor to figure out what one has. It's just a matter of facing the truth, a truth that one tends to deny until he or she accepts it. For the next move is a critical one and If compared to, it's like playing a game of chess.

But there comes a time when one gets burned, in a manner of speaking, when a relationship fizzles and it's back to the drawing board so to speak. For everybody has a wall that they put up in order to protect themselves from being hurt. A wall that slowly comes down as one gets to know the other personally, emotionally, and intellectually. For it's a matter of trust when one shares a bit of themselves with another person. It's primarily a gamble one takes when rolling the dice on potential relationships. One can often have regrets when one doesn't take that giant leap of faith. It's just a matter of holding one's breath and diving in so to speak.

The possibilities are endless when matters of the heart are involved. If one doesn't try, the "what if" factor can come into play and it can eat that person inside. An optimistic person might say they will someday find happiness and live happily ever after. A pessimistic person might choose to believe that they will never find happiness and live a life of solitude. In any case, it's like looking at a glass half full or half empty. but it's all in how one looks at the situation. One's own heart is like a compass; it can point you in many directions. In the end, you just have to follow your heart and hopefully it will lead you in the right direction.

LOST AND FOUND
June 25, 2004

Everybody at some point in time has lost someone truly special in their lives. For the smiles that once graced their faces are now turned upside down in a manner of speaking. In a way, we can be lost in darkness and never find our way back to the light. The saying goes, that time heals all wounds, but some wounds may never heal. Superficial wounds can be easily treated and healed through time. Time is also a factor when wounds concerning one's own heart come into play. For each of us at one time or another has experienced this and, in a way, lost a piece of ourselves. As said before, when one is "wounded" in the heart, a person just needs time to heal and mourn that person's passing.

For our pain can turn to anger, our anger to bitterness, and our bitterness to utter contempt. In a way, one can feel that one could have done something differently then he or she would be still here. It can be a hard thing to let go of the past, a past when one looks back at it can be joyous and painful at the same time. In one's own mind, nothing can or ever will be the same again. The emotions that one shared with that person will always stay with you and can never be replaced. One often wonders what could have been, what should have been, or what might have been. It can play with a person's own mind to the point that thinking about it will just make one sick.

Emotions can run rampant when someone's heart is on the line so to speak. But oftentimes the emotions one carries is held deep within and not shown outwardly. People sometimes just want to be left alone and deal with the reality that has happened by themselves. For a person can be somewhat of a great actor, in a manner of speaking, when a friend or family member asks if he or she is doing ok. For one can be completely happy on the outside but feeling lost and in pain on the inside. It can eat up a person from the inside out and the emotions that one has hidden can explode like an erupting volcano.

Eventually there comes a time when one must let go of the past and close the proverbial door behind you both emotionally and metaphorically. It's a tough and daunting task to move forward with one's life as one tends to protect themselves. Protecting themselves from being hurt when someone new and unexpected comes into their lives. Life is all about expecting the unexpected, the people we meet on our journey can help us without even knowing it. For the emotional ties that bind one to another will always stay with a person like scars from a battle and in a way, the possibility of someone knocking at the door of your heart will be heard.

In the end, one must simply put himself/herself out there and meet new people. For one day one will find happiness again and the scars that were left will eventually heal up. Though the memories will always stick with a person, it's the time spent talking with him or her that will always be cherished. In retrospect, what a person wants in a potential relationship is for that person to be there without him or her even asking. That's what makes love stronger, showing up when the time is right and being there for that person. Each of us wants to be truly happy in the end and live happily ever after, so to speak. For as the saying goes, what was once lost can be found again.

THREE LITTLE WORDS
June 26, 2004

In the English language there are three little words that have the power to completely change two people's lives. It can be an emotional moment when one truly believes in those three words and expresses it outwardly to another. But one can never be too sure if those words will be said back, and it can be a nerve-racking moment. Silence can be a scary thing as one is waiting for that all-important answer. Though the answer may or may not be the one he or she was waiting for, it's always good to be prepared to be let down.

But the question may be asked whether or not a person can truly say those words and mean it. For many, they can become jaded and somewhat cautious when told those words. Their intentions may be sound, but one often considers what their ulterior motives may be. But for some, it's the first step in a relationship that could flourish and last forever. Oftentimes trying to say those words can be a difficult thing to do. One can repeat it over and over in one's own head but when it comes to the point of saying it, it can't come out.

For fear and rejection can hold back the words that a person has been dying to say to that person. It's the fear of rejection and past breakups that may hinder possibly forging a new relationship. We have all been hurt at some point or another and find it difficult to open one's heart to another. It may be easy for some and yet a difficult and daunting task for others. Nobody really can distinguish the truly "nice guys" from the proverbial "players" so to speak. It's a judgment call that only that person can make with his or her own heart.

One's own instincts must play a part in determining if what he or she says is genuine or merely a way to get into his or her pants in a manner of speaking. For it's those heartbreakers so to speak, that give the people who are looking for long-lasting relationships a bad name. In a previous thought, I compared one's own heart as a compass and it can point you in many different directions. Directions that may lead to a possible dead-end relationship or one that can lead to absolute happiness. It's simply a risk and nobody can ever really know what a person's reaction will be when one decides to tell him or her.

In any case, one just has to put their heart on the line and be prepared for the answer that person will give. For there is no turning back and no rewind button to push if he or she doesn't get the answer they want. It's what life is all about, taking the good with the bad. In the end, it's the little things you do in life for that person that makes him or her feel special. As I have said before, everybody truly wants a person that is going to be there for him or her without even asking. But what makes life worth living is looking into the eyes of the person you truly care about and saying those three little words…I LOVE YOU.

THAT MISSING PIECE
June 26, 2004

A person can spend a lifetime sharing happiness and laughter with others without expecting something in return. For the smiles that one receives back is the absolutely best payment one could offer. Yet the happiness one shares with others is oftentimes missing from one's own life. It's like searching for that one missing piece of an incomplete puzzle. For that missing piece can be considered the key to finding one's own happiness but the question remains, will one ever find it?

We all have walked down the road of life searching for answers to the questions we seek. Such questions as are we alone in the universe, what is the meaning of life, but the biggest question of them all is will we find love? Those questions we seek are hard to find because the road of life is unpredictable, and the people we meet along the way may or may not have the answers. BUT they can hopefully guide us in the right direction and be somewhat of an advisor along our journey.

In some ways, our lives are like a puzzle and every piece shows the past experiences one has had over the years. The happy times, the sad times, and the times in between that one doesn't really want to see ever again. Each puzzle piece represents a time in each of our lives that represents successes, defeats, moral victories, absolute tragedies, loves lost, loves found, loves lost again, and mistakes made in the past which one can learn from in the future. Every piece of the puzzle that fit one to another represented his or her life, which marked a beginning and an ending.

From the very beginning, we were created by the love of two parents. Parents that continued to love each of us as we grew older. In retrospect, our parents are the two most important pieces that keep the puzzle together. For they are the backbone of one's own upbringing and without them, one would not be who he or she is today. It has been said that every beginning must also have an ending. We clearly do not know what each of our endings will be, but do we really want to know? In my own view, I want to be surprised.

Someone once said, ~If you look back at your life and remember the good, the bad, and everything in between, would you smile?~ The answer I came up with is yes, I would. The life I have led so far is filled with family and friends that have my back every step of the way. Yet, that missing piece that completes my puzzle hasn't been found yet, hopefully one day. In the movie Field of Dreams, a voice said to Kevin Costner's character, "If You Build It, They Will Come." Mine would just simply say, "If You Are Patient, She Will Come."

DEFINING MOMENT
June 28, 2004

Every person has a defining moment in which the decision he or she makes can ultimately determine the next step in his or her journey. A journey that involves one's own heart as that person seeks an answer to a question. A question which can either start a new beginning or already possibly ended for two people. It can be a scary thing when a person walks into the unknown and has no control over what is going to happen next. Emotions can run every which way but loose, for that person can be cool on the outside but a total wreck on the inside. Thoughts of doubt and second guessing can come into play but in the end it's an ultimate decision one will make.

For that person can think, rethink, and continue thinking of the repercussions of that decision one has made. It can drive one completely insane to the point where one doesn't want to think about it anymore. It's like standing at a crossroads where one path leads to the happiness he or she is seeking, and the other path leads to a lifetime of wonder and/or regret. Over time, those regrets can ultimately haunt us as one gets older. For every time that person looks in the mirror, one will always see that one chance just slipped by him or her. Someone once said, ~I would rather die knowing I took chances than die with regret that I never tried?~

In retrospect, both men and women were put on this earth to completely drive each other nuts. It's a job that both do equally but some may disagree. As one looks at his or her own past, the moments that they experienced have either taught them life lessons or have not taught them anything at all. There comes a time where one moment in one's own life completely overshadows the others. One could possibly say that the birth of one's own child can fall into that category, nothing else can compare to that. Let me ask you a question, what one moment in your life, bad or good, completely overshadowed the rest and defined your own life?

In any case, every person's one moment is the same, though the situation may differ in his or her own life. Whether it be professionally or personally, it's that one decision that person makes that will determine success or defeat. Yet defeat is such a harsh word, for one can't perceive an outcome that hasn't happened yet. It's like giving up on a battle that one thinks he or she might lose. You can't let one's own doubt control you, it's just a matter of going for it. In reality, it's out of one's own hands and one can only sit back and wait. One just has to close his or her eyes and take that first step into a whole new world.

Follow your heart, a sentiment that holds true for everybody that has or is taking that leap of faith so to speak. I once compared one's own heart to a compass in which it can point you in many different directions. Ultimately, each of us has been or will be pointed in the right direction and will take that leap of faith. A leap of faith in which every guy seeks an answer to the most important question he will ever ask to the woman he loves. For it is when every guy, including myself one day, will get on bended knee, looking into the eyes of the woman he loves, and ask this question…will you marry me?

BURNOUT

June 28, 2004

Every person at one time or another has experienced burnout. Whether it be at the workplace or at home, it can be a daunting task in itself. For each of us we have a job we either love or hate, and the long days and stressful times can cause us to feel like a patient in an insane asylum so to speak. Each of us has a boiling point and when it reaches critical one has to just duck and cover. We all have those days where you just want to call in sick, stay in bed and simply sleep the day away.

When a person reaches burnout, morning people can be annoying to the point of just pimp slapping them out. For they are just way too happy and it's not a good combination when burned out people and perky people cross paths. There can be no middle ground for the two groups, and no amount of negotiations will have either side reach a proposed agreement. It's like setting off World War 3 and the casualties will be high. One little spark could set off a chain reaction of sorts that can't be stopped.

But I digress, for each of us to come to a point of sluggishness. Looking up at the ceiling and pondering whether or not to go to work. It can be compared to my favorite movie Office Space where one day, the main character doesn't care anymore. It's every person's dream to do the things the main character had the cojones to do like ignoring his own boss completely. Saying what's on his mind which could fire any person fired. Though most of us haven't come to that point, it would be a dream come true.

Oftentimes we come to a point in a our lives where the job isn't fulfilling anymore. For we ask ourselves two simple questions. Do I continue to the job that I love doing but without the zeal that I once had? Or do I leave the job knowing that it will make me much happier in the future? It's like coming to a crossroads where there are two paths to choose, but there will always be a third path. No one can say for sure; it is up to that person to figure out what he or she wants to do.

It's just a matter of taking time off, relaxing, and forgetting anything remotely related to work or home. Using one's time to his or her advantage and just resting mentally and physically. A rejuvenation of sorts for when that person returns, he or she will be a new person. For that grumpy and tired person that nobody wants to be around that once roamed the hall is now replaced with the cool, calm and collected laid-back dude. In the end, nobody wants to get burned from a person that is feeling burned out.

SMILE

June 28, 2004

Everybody at some point and time has smiled at somebody, whether it be at a total stranger, or somebody once knows. A smile can be given as a courteous gesture from one person to another. It can also be given as a flirtatious manner in the expressed interest in a particular person. It's how people can communicate with each other without actually speaking to each other as well as show how that person is feeling at that moment and time. In any case, a smile is very powerful for both men and women, but more so for a woman.

Our daily lives are a gamble and the smiles we give consciously and unconsciously to people may determine meeting Mr./Ms. Right or meeting a Dr. Jekyll and Mr. Hyde type. Life is primarily a crap shoot and with every roll of the dice we hope it lands on seven rather than on snake eyes. It's like that with relationships as well, we take the risk of either finding happiness or going back to the drawing board so to speak. One can just continue on the path that he or she is traveling on. For we will all have highs and lows, it's just a matter of smiling when it happens.

We've all had experiences that have turned out bad or good. In retrospect, looking back it was a learning experience. But the question is when one looks back at those experiences does it bring a smile on your face? Would you trade them for other experiences that you regret not doing? The answer may be different for each of us, for one must look at his or her situation and think about it. But one thing is most certain, that a person feels somewhat relaxed and calm when grinning from ear to ear.

Thinking about it, beauty can be seen in many different things. It can be seen in a sunrise as it ascends up into the morning sky. It is seen at night with millions of bright shining stars illuminating the skies above. It can be seen in the birth of a child in which the parents come to the realization that they have created life. It can be seen in a sunset as it descends beyond the distant horizon. But in all honesty, true beauty can be seen in a woman's smile. A smile that can melt the heart of any man and turn supposedly tough guys into gentle teddy bears.

As the saying goes, an apple a day keeps the doctor away. Though I am not a doctor, prescribing smiles is the best way to cure the pangs of daily life. A smile can sometimes cure a broken heart, a stressful day, or the so-called summertime blues. It's like the movie Pay It Forward starring Helen Hunt, Kevin Spacey, and Haley Joel Osmont in which doing a nice gesture for someone, and that person does something nice for someone else. I end this thought by saying, smile because you never really know how you will affect someone in the long run.

FAST LANE
June 30, 2004

Each of our lives are constantly moving on a daily basis. It's basically a constant cycle that repeats itself over and over again which can make any person tear out their own hair. It's a fast-paced world we all live in but there are times we just need to slow down and catch our breath. In between our hectic schedules, appointments, and family obligations, a person needs to live a little and enjoy life. It's an age-old tradition in which everybody has done at one time or another as kids and as adults.

Terms would define it as calling in sick, ditching, cutting, call it what you will, each of us needs a day off every now and then. The constant pressures of one's own life can be a little overwhelming. Sometimes it takes only one day to rest our weary minds and bones to be rejuvenated for the following day. Some may disagree, it may depend on the job and the number of days one seeks to completely feel rested. Each of us will be alot happier, calmer, saner and as the saying goes, it's just what the doctor ordered.

One must stop and smell the roses so to speak and just slow down. Life can be like a lion waiting in the shadows ready to pounce on its intended prey. We've all had those days where the daily grind of going to the same place and seeing the same people every day just makes a person go nuts. The time away from a place that can literally make one go mad is a good way to come back as a new man or woman. In retrospect, if we don't use the opportunity to our advantage, mass homicide will run rampant.

For there is a method to one's madness as he or she uses the tricks of the trade learned over the years. It's a skill that every person uses in one's own daily life to this day. However, one must keep all the proverbial bases covered and not run the risk of being exposed. In some ways, the deception can be somewhat of an adrenaline rush as that person hopes he or she can get away with it. In the back of one's own mind, the repercussions are considered if being caught red handed, so to speak.

In some ways, life is like driving in the fast lane. We spend our days trying to pass every other person on the road to get to where we want to be. One will eventually get to their intended destination, but not after suffering the occasional flat tires, speeding tickets and fender benders. A person every now and then has to stop and look at where he or she is. Ferris Beuhler said it best, ~Life moves pretty fast, if you don't stop and look around once in a while, you could miss out~

MY LEGACY
July 4, 2004

In the latter days of a person's life, one tends to look back at the accomplishments he or she has made. It's like looking back at a timeline of events, for each of us has somehow and in some way made an impact in someone's life. Whether it be good or whether it be bad, it is an impact, nonetheless. One may not consciously know the impact that one is making on others, for it's an impact that will leave an impressionable mark for years to come. It's the things that may or may not seem relevant that determine the legacy a person leaves behind.

People spend much of their lives trying to make a name for themselves and try to build up his or her ego in the process. Every person, whether they want to admit it or not, has an ego and sometimes our egos can get too big for our own good. One has to have an ego, for it's that ego that brings each of us confidence to take life head on. If one didn't have an ego, every person would be the same and that would be just too boring. Sometimes there has to be a limit, if one goes overboard so to speak, then one's own reputation, name, and legacy can be tarnished.

Throughout history there have been many names that have left behind a legacy, a legacy some may have tarnished their reputations and their name. Richard Nixon left behind a legacy in which he was known for Watergate and resigning as President of the United States. O.J. Simpson's legacy will not focus on his great football career, but rather the double murders that he was found not guilty for, a sentence that I highly disagreed with. President Clinton's legacy will be remembered for only one thing and that is the Monica Lewinsky scandal.

It's the legacy that one leaves behind that has some people

questioning the person's ethics and moral standing. Each of us have our own standards of ethics that determine what we stand for and stand against. We have our own individuality that people tend to either hate, like, love, or tolerate. It's that individuality and uniqueness that people will or will not remember years from now when that person passes on into the afterlife. I ask you this, Pete Rose's legacy will be remembered for gambling on baseball. Even though he confessed, should he be inducted into the hall of fame?

Several people such as Ronald Reagan, Bob Hope, Ray Charles, and just recently Marlon Brando left a legacy that was either inspiring and/or influential. Ronald Reagen left a legacy that made any person proud to call themselves an American. Bob Hope left a legacy of smiles and laughter to so many people. Ray Charles brought music to the world that left us waiting for more. Marlon Brando left a legacy that was influential to many aspiring actors to this day. In the end, when it is all said and done, what legacy will you leave behind?

MAGIC
July 5, 2004

Each person has that innate sense of curiosity when meeting somebody for the first time. As the saying goes, curiosity killed the cat, but this sort of curiosity could be worth dying for so to speak. It's that curiosity or feeling that a person can't shake. No matter what you do, one can't seem to get that person out of his or head. Every person has had that feeling before, but somehow it feels different. One can only try to shake it off, but the feeling can be overwhelming at times. But the question is if that sense of curiosity will lead you down the wrong road into disappointment.

We have all been there, for the expectations we have can be cut down to size in a manner of speaking. For our egos can be bruised and the embarrassment one faces can sometimes leave an impression on him or her. As it has been before, if at first you don't succeed, try try again. It's that never say die attitude that keeps on riding that bucking bronco so to speak. In other words, we simply have to pick ourselves up, dust ourselves off, get back on that horse and strap ourselves in for another bumpy ride.

It can take a vibe, feeling, or simply a look to get one's own curiosity into gear so to speak. That overwhelming urge to find out who that person is and figure out what makes him or her tick. It can be somewhat of a mission, a mission impossible if I could put it another way. If compared to, it would be like being in high school or Jr. High all over again. Trying to figure out who likes who and using gossip and word of mouth, which can sometimes be unreliable. It can be a daunting task to figure out what's true and not true, but that's what matters of the heart are all about.

As I said before, everybody will or has received a knock at their door that he or she will know it's the right one. It's the curiosity inside all of us, in which we imagine the perfect man or woman who will be standing there waiting to be asked in. Sometimes, we may be surprised who is standing there waiting on the other side. Truthfully though, there is no such thing as that perfect person, but one can disagree. In one's own mind that person he or she has been searching for is absolutely perfect, faults and all.

One simply has to be himself or herself, being anybody else just complicates things. Nobody wants a potential relationship based on false pretenses and fake personas. Each one of us is attracted to something specific about a person, whether it be their looks, smile, or sense of humor. There is nothing like when two people "meet" for the first time out of curiosity and a spark can be lit between the two. Every person will have or has had that feeling, a feeling that can be only described with one word…magic.

COME IN
July 6, 2004

Each of our lives are somewhat compared to a door that opens and closes when we meet new people. We often tend to be cautious and look through the proverbial keyhole and decide if we want to open the door or not. Every person has trust issues when meeting new people, for we don't know if the people we meet have the best intentions. It's that way with relationships as well, for our hearts can be opened as well as closed permanently and never be opened again. Inevitably, it's a matter of opening the door to new experiences that will bring either joy or sorrow.

Sometimes a person can be afraid to open the door because past experiences have taught us to keep our guard up, so to speak. The wall that comes down from time to time will always be put back up whenever the door to a potential relationship is opened. It's always a risky thing when the door to one's own heart is involved. We risk sharing ourselves to a total stranger that may or may not last in the long run. But that's what life is all about, each door that we open can bring us to new places and new opportunities.

Other times, the door to one's own heart can be closed completely due to constant heartbreak or personal tragedy. Though the opportunities present themselves to find happiness, that person chooses to live a life of solace and wonder. Every person at one time or another has felt that loss which can never be replaced. It's just a matter of re-opening the door that hasn't been opened in a while. For it can take a very special person to bring them back to the light so to speak, a person that is willing to be there without even asking.

One can lose a part of himself and never be the same person he or she was. In some cases, a smile can be lost which may or may not be found again. It's like standing in a hallway full of doors and no matter where you go, you end up in the same place. It's also like walking through a maze, each turn ends up leading to a dead end. For one has to back track, back to the beginning and start over. It can be frustrating, but one cannot give up hope, for that one door will hopefully bring back that smile that once was lost.

Everybody will have or has had a knock at their door and it's a knock that feels right to that person. Though, there have been many times when one opens the door, and nobody is standing there. It can sometimes give someone a sense of false hope. BUT every person has an idea of who will be standing on the other side but can't quite figure out who that person is. In a way, he or she has been standing at the doorway knocking waiting for you to open it. In the end, do you know who will be standing at your doorway and will you ask them to come in?

CHICKEN SOUP
July 7, 2004

Every person has their similarities and differences, but the one similarity that each person shares is the love of music. One can't deny the effect the music industry has on people who listen to music on a day-to-day basis. Much of our daily lives are spent on the road going from point A to point B, but in between we listen either to the radio or our CDs. A song has the ability to transport each and every one of us to the past and open up emotions one thought was long gone. But that's the power of a song, it can bring about the bad times, as well as the good times.

Each and every person has a song that is meaningful. A song that has sentimental value either from a past or current relationship. Though, sometimes hearing that particular song can bring memories that either bring happiness, brings tears or brings memories that a person doesn't want to even think about at all. It's the meaning of the song that tugs at a person's heart strings because it can somehow relate to one's own life. All songs in a way describe a person's life but to what extent?

Songs can remind us of tragic events like 9/11 and the soldiers who died giving their lives for their country. Many songs graced the air waves during those trying times but there was one particular song that people wanted to hear over and over again. It was a song by a band named 3 Doors Down and their song, "When You're Gone." It basically focused on the military and how families coped with probably not seeing their loved ones ever again. But with uncertainty, songs can also bring hope and a sense of peace that each and every soldier will return safe and sound.

In any case, songs also have that innate ability to remind a person of their first kiss and where it happened. It can also have the ability to breathe new life into a person that may be down in the dumps. For the melody or beat can make a person come back from the dead so to speak. It's those certain songs that make a person's toes a tappin' and his or her booty a shakin'. The daily grind can get us all but once the radio is turned on or a CD is put in, a person's stress level can lower considerably.

Ray Charles' ability to bring a person into his world through song was the greatest gift he gave to his fans. He is and will always be considered a class act and can never be duplicated. He was a true performer who sang from the heart and was able to capture the meaning of the song. If a song is able to grab the audience and hold that person's attention, then the artist has done his or her job. Though a person can't actually eat it, one can consider the songs that he or she listens to chicken soup for the soul.

THE BEST MEDICINE
July 13, 2004

It has been said laughter is the best medicine when times of stress, sadness, turmoil, and death cross each of our paths. Laughter can be infectious and when one person gets "infected" it can cause a ripple effect. An effect similar to lining up dominos and when one falls the rest start falling. Each person has the unique ability to make people laugh but it takes a special person that can turn an ordinary chuckle into an all-out gut buster. The type of gut buster in which a person has to change their shorts afterwards.

Every person has a sense of humor, but the question is what type of humor does each person have? It's really an unknown. One just has to find out for themselves. He or she has to find that inner comedian with themselves to share the joy of laughter with others. Such comedians as Jerry Seinfeld, Richard Pryor, Eddie Murphy, Bill Cosby, the list goes on and on and has made it a career making people laugh with their own style of humor. Whether it be crude, sarcastic, slapstick, observational, if it makes you laugh then their job is done.

Each and every person has had those days where everything goes wrong and the times it didn't seem funny to you. Bob Newhart once said, ~Laughter gives us distance. It allows us to step back from an event, deal with it and then move on.~ Anyways, Laughing is like a defense mechanism in which we cover up our fears, sadness, anger, and other emotions. Most of us have learned to hide our emotions through laughter, but as the saying goes, ~What a person keeps bottled up inside, will soon rise to the top and reveal itself.

In any case, every person looks for distinct qualities in a potential relationship. The one thing all or most people are looking for is a sense of humor. One of the questions that has been asked many times is: Will "Ms./"Mr. Right" be able to make me laugh? It's one of the questions that he or she wants answered. It's that "x-factor" in which it can either make or break a person. It's that quality that can turn an uncomfortable situation into a comfortable and pleasant atmosphere where both people can enjoy each other's company.

Josh Billings said, ~Laughter is the sensation of feeling good all over and showing it principally in one place.~ That principal place is in one's own heart and think about this, without laughter we would all go completely insane. Someone once said, ~You can't stay mad at somebody who makes you laugh. Whether you are in a relationship or not, laughter is truly the best medicine.~ I end this thought by saying this: Laugh and the world will laugh with you, cry and the world will just make fun of you and give you an atomic wedgie. :)

THE MOST VALUABLE COMMODITY
July 16, 2004

In a way our lives can be compared to a bank and within that bank is a vault. A vault which protects endless amounts of money and valuable material possessions. Metaphorically speaking, each of us has a vault in which we keep our most treasured and priceless possessions. Possessions that you really can't hold in your hands and those would be one's memories, hopes, dreams, emotions, feelings, and most importantly one's own heart. One has to learn you can't keep your heart locked away forever, if you do, then you miss out on meeting that one special person that one will spend a lifetime with.

The memories that a person holds near and dear to his or her heart will be cherished for years to come. Those memories are like a record of the adventures and mischief one has been on. The places seen and been, the friends that have come and gone, the love lost, and the love found, are all kept in a safe place. For a person can't physically break into that vault and simply take what he or she wants, because the vault each of us has is simply impenetrable. Every person wants to be secure in the fact that their most treasured possessions will be passed on to the next generation as one approaches their golden years.

Oftentimes we closely guard our feelings and emotions to the point where a person can be perceived as greedy. For people can hide how they feel for that one person who he or she feels strongly about and not act on those feelings and emotions. It's one's past experiences that makes someone very protective and have a constant wall in front of them which can never be broken down. For it's a risky venture sharing pieces of one's self to total strangers that he or she hardly knows. Yet, as time goes by, those total strangers will eventually be someone important as both get to know each other personally, intellectually, and emotionally.

Thinking about it, every person wants that special someone to be the first and last face he or she wants to see. From the time one goes to bed and the time one wakes up, one will see that face and it's a face that you never want to forget. In retrospect, when we are born into the world, the first faces we see are the two people who love and care about us. When one eventually passes on, the last face one wants to see is the one person that has meant so much to you. For that last glimpse represents a priceless memory that can never be bought or sold, no matter how much money is waved in one's face.

Ultimately, each of us will have or has had their hearts "stolen" and no amount of security can prevent that from happening. With banks, there are always long lines, it's simply unavoidable. One can sometimes feel that he or she has been waiting in line a lifetime to be called up any time now by that one particular bank teller. In the end, there is one thing that is more valuable than money, less expensive than material possessions and one can be considered rich beyond his or her years. The most valuable commodity is love.

THAT ONE REASON
July 17, 2004

At a certain point in a person's life, he or she will find that one reason to start a brand-new journey. A journey that has always been surrounded by friends and family that have been there for that person. But along the way, a person looks down that particular road that he or she travels on and wonders who is waiting for them at the very end. Sometimes the questions we seek never really have an answer and the only logical step is to continue traveling on the path we choose ourselves until we reach the end.

Sometimes the paths we choose don't necessarily lead to where we want to be in life. For we can oftentimes feel empty inside and that person has to decide for themselves what will truly make him or her happy. Though, it's not so much where a person wants to be exactly but who that person wants to be with. Sometimes a person doesn't need to think with his head but rather think with his or her heart. In other words, what does your heart say, and every person knows what they want in life, it's just a matter of going after it.

We can sometimes feel like a drifter wandering down the highways and byways of life and the cars that pass us by make each of us feel somewhat insignificant. It's like being invisible to the world and the only people that know we are "alive" are family and friends. In a way, we are all searching for that one special person who will pick us up and take us to some new place. It's that one person, who even though he is going on a different path, is heading in the same direction.

One has to come to the realization that you can't go looking for someone that may or may not want to be found. As a matter of fact, that person will find you and it will happen when one least expects it. It has been said things happen for a reason and when it involves a person's heart no amount of explanation can solve it. One just has to go with the flow, so to speak, and let nature run its course. It's just a matter of being at the right place, the right time, and bumping into that right person.

When you think about it, each of our journeys can be somewhat compared to chapters in a book. Each chapter chronicles our own personal history of where we have been and the people we have met along the way on our travels. There comes a time when we meet someone that will inspire each of us to fill the blank pages that are left. Pages that have been blank for quite some time and until now have a reason to be written on. In the end, who will be that one reason to inspire you to write the next chapter of your life?

REALITY
July 22, 2004

Each of our lives can seem to be interesting to others, but as the saying goes, don't judge a book by its cover. What if each of our lives were a reality show and that show would be somewhat compared to that hit MTV series Diaries. Though our lives may not be glamorous, it's our lives, take it or leave it. Oftentimes, the people we talk to sometimes think the lives we lead seem interesting and cool. A person just has to sit back, look, and simply say, "You think you know, but you have no idea."

My life is not so different from the rest of America's. I have a fun and interesting job that I go to each week and have friends and family that have my back. But it's the interesting things that happen in between that can be considered "great television". But what constitutes "great television" when it involves one's own life? For I have spent the last 8 years working at a Youth Center and within those 8 years countless stories can be told. Untold stories that can make a person either laugh or cry upon hearing it.

Tom Hanks' character Forrest Gump once said, "Life is like a box of chocolates, you never know what you are going to get". For that quote is so true, because in my line of work, nothing can truly prepare a person as he or she walks past a bathroom and here these words echoing from within, "See, mine is bigger than yours!" It's totally mind-blowing what kids are capable of doing if left unsupervised for a long period of time. As it has been said, "Now I've heard and/or seen everything" a sentiment that I say over and over again.

Kids tend to fight as they often do and it's my job to step in to cool things down. For I have to be a negotiator, investigator, interrogator, enforcer, referee, judge, jury, and executioner while trying to be a peacekeeper. It can truly befuddle the human mind as the reasons why kids do what they do. Sometimes they don't have a reason and I just have to laugh at the comedy of it all and wonder if I'm being Punk'd. For any minute Ashton Kutcher is going to pop out and I come to the realization that I have just been had.

For a person can discover things about themselves that he or she has never known. Personally speaking, I discovered that I have a lot of patience dealing with kids but I also discovered that I don't make any sense when I get angry with them as well. For a guy's brain can't comprehend emotion and thought at the same time, we can only choose one. That's the life I chose to live folks and you know what, I have enjoyed every minute of it. I wouldn't want to trade my life with anybody else because the kids make it all worthwhile....most of the time. With or without cameras following me around, that's my reality.

HERO
July 20, 2004

A hero is defined as a person noted for feats of courage or nobility of purpose, especially one who has risked or sacrificed his or her life. People such as the police, fire fighters, and the United States military who risk their own lives and truly be called a hero.
But could one consider the regular Joe and Jane Schmo in that particular category? For they can be known as unsung heroes. For its these "impact players", so to speak, that may not know they are making a difference in other people's lives.

Such impact players are teachers, for they mold the mind of future politicians, entrepreneurs, actors, actresses and the list go on and on. Oftentimes the respect that should be received is never given and it's the price they pay for shaping the minds of America's youth. It's these people that push kids to their absolute limits in order to achieve something greater in their lives. Years down the road, that kid turned adult will consider that teacher a mentor and will never forget the valuable wisdom taught to him or her.

Another impact player(s) can be located in one's own home. A parent spends much of his or her life teaching them values that will hopefully one day be passed on to their children and future generations. For a parent can truly say they would literally give up their own life if their child was in danger. It wouldn't be an afterthought to parents for their instincts are to protect what's most important to them and that is their kids. In a way, a parent isn't just a hero, for they can be considered a superhero.

Other impact players are the physically handicapped and how they persevered. Physical handicaps such as blindness, loss of limbs, loss of hearing, and loss of sight. For its these losses that make that particular person more determined to live one's life. That person has to simply adjust and the other limbs or senses kick into high gear in a manner of speaking and get stronger. Someone once said, the greatest obstacle one can face is losing something that oftentimes can be taken for granted but gaining something much greater.

Lastly, the biggest impact player is a person that really doesn't know that he or she is a hero, and that person is us. A hero in the fact that each of us is comfortable with who we are and doesn't listen to what people think about them. Yet there are those that feed off what people think about them, but as the saying goes, be a leader and not a follower. At the end of the day, who are you more likely to listen to, the people or yourself? In the end, I ask you this question, do you consider yourself a hero?

LET GO
July 23, 2004

Each of us carries baggage that can be connected with the past. A person can sometimes keep it close to him or her like a favorite blanket or stuffed animal which can be somewhat compared to a security blanket. In a way, that person holds on to those emotions which are a link to his or past. Emotions that are connected to past relationships and the feelings that stir up. It can be a tough and daunting task to move on with our lives as each of us tries to bring back the smile that once graced our faces.

Death can play a big part in keeping the past close to one's own heart. One can go through many emotions when the person they truly cared about is taken away too soon. Emotions such as denial, confusion, anger, bitterness, utter contempt, acceptance, and most of all regret. Regret, it can always eat a person up inside to the point of going completely mad. For a person can beat themselves up for not saying those three little words that matter, and yet at times we are scared to say them until that person is taken away from us.

A person can metaphorically walk away and close the proverbial door to his or her heart. The wall that was once broken down is back up, but that person's heart is now guarded. He or she can literally feel dead inside as their reason to smile is now gone. It's like being trapped in total darkness and there is no sign of light to walk towards. The life that the person once knew has changed and one can feel lost. For the journey back to the light can either take days, months, or even years.

It has been said that things happen for a reason. Reasons that can't be explained during that particular time but undoubtedly will be answered when the time is right. At the time all a person wants to know is why. It's not so much why but rather why me. A person can oftentimes have that mentality that there will be a price to pay if he or she finds true happiness. One can't think that way, he or she just has to put themselves out there and open the proverbial door that once was proclaimed closed.

Life is all about second chances and surprises that it can bring to one's own doorstep so to speak. A person will eventually start a new life, as well as a new relationship. Though the memories and experiences can never be replaced, he or she can make new ones. Someone once said, ~A person who passes away is never really gone. As long as you have him or her in your heart and in your mind, they will continue to live on.~ In retrospect, we can only do one thing when it comes to the past and our heart and that is simply let go.

GENERATION TO GENERATION
July 24, 2004

Working at a youth center or in the childcare profession, for that matter, can give a person insight. One often thinks about the potential he or she has in becoming a mother or a father. We all have parental instincts, and it has been said that each of us will know what to do when our time comes. The characteristics that are passed down to parent and child can be quite frightening at times. For one day we look at the life that is created, and say in the immortal words of Dr. Evil, "I shall call him Mini-me".

There comes to mind the type of parent one wants to become in the future. Will each of us be the strict disciplinarian that rule with an iron fist? Or will each of us be the laid-back cool parent that goes for the acceptance of his or her child rather than the overbearing parent? In a way, one just has to find a middle ground of coolness and being firm. One tends to think that he or she will never become their parents, but a person has to only look in the mirror to find out that you are them.

It basically comes full circle, everything that one's parents said to each of us back in the day, will absolutely be said to our kids one day. In a weird way, the sayings that were thought would never be uttered from our lips would actually be said. It can be a scary thought as one will eventually wave "the finger" and give "the look" to his or her own kids. For each of us will have that one moment of clarity and in the immortal words of Keanu Reeves' character Neo in the Matrix, we will simply step back and say, "Whoa!"

For one will eventually realize that all the headaches and stress that we gave our parents will be passed on to us. A person has to give credit where credit is due to them as we pushed them to the limit mentally and physically. But they stuck by us no matter how foolish and idiotic we became because they loved us. In retrospect, they deserve our thanks as well as an apology for all the good times and hard times that we have given them. For what they gave up making us happy, we should give back to them tenfold.

Though, those of us who aren't married or have kids of our own, working at a Youth Center, has given most of us, as counselors, somewhat of a hands-on approach of parenting 101 so to speak. In reality, it's not so much telling each of the kids you care, it's just words. It's just a matter of showing them that you care. In a way, I have learned more from them than they will ever know and hopefully the lessons learned will be taught one day to my kids. In the end, the values taught and characteristics we share will be passed on from generation to generation.

A DREAM COME TRUE
July 26, 2004

Every person has at least prayed, wished, and/or wondered when the person of their dreams would come into their lives. For it's that one attainable person that he or she knows is out there, but where is unknown. We oftentimes set a high standard for ourselves for that person who somewhat haunts our subconscious, though we don't know who they are. It's those standards that are a blueprint of the girl or guy that each of us have been waiting for all our lives. A blueprint in which one looks for that so-called perfect person.

Yet, is there such a thing as that one perfect person out there for each of us. That faceless person who one has been dreaming about since the beginning of one's own teenage years. For we see faces every day, nameless faces that we pass by on a daily basis without a thought. It's been said that the eyes on a person's face are the window to one's soul. Can one truly say that just by looking into that person's eyes, he or she is "the one?" Yes or no, that one look may turn that nameless face into a fulfilled dream.

Sometimes the person of their dreams can turn into a complete nightmare. Each of us can have that deluded perception that can actually "blind" a person. Blinded by the superficiality of that person and for whatever reason one can't seem to get past it and it's a mistake he or she regrets. For every person wants something much deeper in a relationship than superficiality which gets old as we get older. If you think about it, a person will suffer several nightmares before having that one great dream come to pass.

As the saying goes, there are two sides to every story which may or may not have a happy ending. One has never really thought about how that person's life was like before each of us entered the picture so to speak. Two people, two stories, two different paths and yet searching for the same thing. In retrospect, we all start out incomplete and our stories are halfway done. But when we meet that one person who will wake us up from the constant nightmares we face, the stories that two people wrote separately will now be written together.

Someone once said, ~A person sometimes gives up what one wants most out of life and that is their dream. Yet, that dream will one day show up at his or her proverbial door and knock on the door whatever or whoever it may be.~ In the song, Unanswered Prayers by Garth Brooks, he says that God's greatest gifts are those unanswered prayers which can sometimes turn out to a blessing in disguise. That blessing in disguise will reveal itself unexpectedly as he or she steps into one's life and you know what, it will forever be a dream come true.

KEEP IT REAL
July 29, 2004

A person can sometimes be someone other than themselves when meeting someone that they are potentially interested in. It's like one's own mental capacity shuts down and for whatever reason their actions do not reflect who they really are. It can also be like that with friends as well. For a person can oftentimes revert back to one's own middle/high school days where stupidity ran rampant back in the day so to speak. Unknowingly, it can follow a person into one's adulthood without him or her knowing about it.

Every person has met that one person that literally made you nervous and speechless at the same time. It can be also said that one's brain completely shuts down and the heart takes over, which is not a good thing. A person can say and do some pretty idiotic things, but when one tries to rectify the situation, it only makes it much worse than it already is. First impressions are that proverbial key, which will either have that person smiling and laughing or have that person frowning and bored to tears.

First impressions are what set each of us apart when one tries asking that girl or guy out on a date. Think back to when you tried to call or talk to someone you liked, how did you act? Every person at one time another has had those first impressions in which the people liked what you were about, and then there were those first impressions that one would rather forget. It can sometimes be an embarrassing moment when a person has egg on their face so to speak, because in a way, it can either make you or break you.

One can sometimes feel that pressure of trying to make our lives interesting for the expressed purpose of impressing others. One will put up illusion after illusion in his or her life until that person doesn't know what's real anymore. A person can literally lose themselves to the people he or she is around. Someone once said, if one looks in a mirror long enough, that person will see his or her true self. He or she must find what's real within your heart and soul, then one can again recognize that person staring back at you.

WHAT DO YOU WANT

July 30, 2004

Each one of us has or has had somewhat of a checklist of what they want in a significant other. It can be either an extensive or short list of qualities that a particular person is looking for. A person can be somewhat picky, and one can oftentimes set his or her standards high in trying to find that one person who fits some or all the criteria. If you think about it, women more so than men, have that long list of specific qualities that she is looking for. In retrospect, every person should set a high standard in order to find that one person who can, in some way, balance you out. It's that balance that will ultimately lead you to that one person who one has been waiting for.

In some cases, looks will always be a constant, when one looks for that diamond in the rough so to speak. A person can sometimes be misguided in what he or she is wanting in a potential relationship. Sometimes, the standards that one has set for one's self can be completely thrown out the window. One can't avoid it no matter how hard he or she tries. For a person's brain can completely shut down when he or she meets that handsome man and/or beautiful woman. It can oftentimes be like High School all over again. In any case someone once said, "A relationship based on superficiality will eventually fade away and what a person will end up with are wrinkles.

In other cases, a person wants something deeper and more meaningful in a potential relationship. Every person has been in a relationship where it didn't feel right, and it was all about him or her. We oftentimes have to ask ourselves will that person be able to make me laugh and when I talk to that particular person will time simply fly by? It's just some of the things a person wants to figure out and one of those ways to find out is through his or her friends.

It has been said that you can know the personality of a person by the friends that he or she has. In a way, a person's own friends know you better than you know yourself.

However, a person will oftentimes ask themselves what they want more looks or personality, or both. Looks and personality, a deadly combination that is rare to find these days. If you think about it, most people truly know what they want out of potential or significant relationships. Others have no earthly idea, and it can constantly change with every new person he or she meets in one's lifetime. Inevitably, a person can ask themselves what they want a hundred times over and still not come up with the right answer. In the long run, a person just has to figure out for themselves who or what will make that person happy.

Over the weekend, my brother and I were talking, and he asked me straight up what I wanted in a relationship. I thought about it for several minutes and I came up with this answer. Basically, I want what everybody wants in a potential relationship and that is a person who I can basically click with. Someone who can be comfortable with being herself and doesn't have to put up an act around me. Someone who has a sense of humor and is able to laugh at herself. Someone who will always light up a room when she walks in and puts a smile on my face every time I see her. In the end, those are the qualities that I want, so, I ask you this, what do you want?

WHAT I'VE LEARNED

July 31, 2004

Over time, a person can learn so much from the past and present that hopefully one will be able to use that knowledge in the future. One can actually grow metaphorically as a person as the mistakes that he or she has made can literally make someone stronger mentally and physically. For the fire within a person's soul will never burn out, it will continue to burn with a passion. Each lesson learned is a steppingstone to something much greater and that proverbial prize that is waiting for each of us is so close at hand.

I've learned so many things as one grows from child to adult. One thing that I have learned is that I have potential to be a father. For as the saying goes "Like father, like son." It's simply the student learning from the teacher, the teacher being my own father. He never gave up on me as I made my own mistakes and continued to have my back until my days as a parent came. It's that gratitude and respect that I show him that will hopefully be given back to me and to generations to come.

I've learned that in my reality, it's all about making the best decisions possible in a place that can burn out a person mentally. Life is all about making important decisions and at a certain point, one will stand at a crossroads in which the decisions he or she makes will determine the rest of that person's life. I've made many decisions within my own life, some good, some bad, and others somewhat questionable. It's my defining moments which taught me that with the decision I make, I must be prepared for the consequences to follow.

I've learned within the past 8 years that I have a connection with kids. It's that child-like mentality that I really never turned my back on, in manner of speaking, that I have a special bond with these kids. They have continually seen me as their friend and not some person who gets paid to take care of them. As I look at them, I can see myself when I was their age. Basically, I'm still a kid at heart, though I am getting older, but getting a bit wiser. For when it's my time to leave, what will my legacy say about me?

Lastly, I have learned that you have to put aside your fear when wanting to seek a relationship with someone; but when you see people around you break up then it gives you second thoughts. Oftentimes, it is hard to walk up to someone you are truly interested in and tell how you feel, which is the biggest problem I have. In all honesty, I don't know if I can ever put aside that fear but if I'm willing to do it for the woman of my dreams someday. In the end, my dream will come true, and that one person will be on the other side of that door, it's just a matter of asking her to come in.

FEAR FACTOR
August 1, 2004

There is a saying that goes that there is nothing to fear but fear itself. Yet there are some fears that a person can't get past which can hinder someone from moving forward on their journey of life. Statistics have shown that the number one leading fear among many Americans is the fear of public speaking followed by death. It's that innate fear of eyes on you and one mistake may cause an embarrassing situation. For the fears that a person has can travel with a person until the latter years of a person's life.

Every person has a particular fear or phobia that will never go away. Some people are afraid of the dark, other snakes and spiders, for many clowns, and in some cases Richard Simmons. There is a plethora of different fears in the world that are too many to mention. Fears such as claustrophobia which is the fear of enclosed spaces. One may have the perception that the walls are closing in on them. It may be only in that person's mind, but that fear can overwhelm a person to the point of extreme anxiety.

In any case, life is all about trying to conquer those fears that seem to beat us, so to speak. For most people, that fear of failure can push a person to reach a standard of excellence that one sets for themselves. In a way, we try to be perfect, but as the saying goes nobody is perfect. Perfection, in most cases, can push that person to the brink or a mental or physical breakdown. But in a way, a person must fail at something in order to prove that he or she is only human after all.

Someone once said,~ That it's alright to be afraid because it shows that we're all human beings. That fear can reveal itself in many different aspects of life such as meeting new people, finding that one who you feel is the right one, and potentially marrying that person.~ It can also be said that one can be afraid of the aspect of being a parent. One just has to trust in their own instincts and not let that fear take over. Not every parent does it the same way, one just has to find their own niche and stick to it.

In a way, life is somewhat compared to the NBC hit show Fear Factor. It's all about facing the tough challenges ahead of us and the fears that go along with it. One can learn that it's ok to be afraid as long as you face those challenges head on and don't back down. Though we don't consume "gourmet" food and win a cash prize, we attain something much greater and that is knowing you conquered your fears. In the end, we want Joe Rogan to say to us that we stared fear in the face and that fear was most definitely not a factor.

THE HONEST TRUTH

August 4, 2004

The saying goes that honesty is the best policy. A policy that one breaks as a young kid, into a teenager, and up into his or her adult years. We've all lied at some point in our lives, whether it be to our parents, teacher or professor, friends, family, significant others, and spouses. A person can't deny the fact that lying is wrong, but one can't really help it. In a way it's oftentimes a matter of sparing someone's feelings, but in retrospect, it's basically part of human nature. A defense mechanism in which one is backed into somewhat of a corner, that person avoids the truth, whatever it may be.

If you observe little kids, they speak the truth whether or not people want to hear it or not. It's just their nature, there is no filter for what the mouth is about to say before the brain is trying to stop him or her from saying it. It can be an embarrassing moment when these kids speak the truth when the time is not right. They speak their minds even though they don't know what they are talking about half the time. It's often fun for us counselors to interrogate kids into telling the truth by means of reverse psychology or by not doing anything at all. They will usually mess it up for themselves and the punishments will be swift, but fair.

Jack Nickolson said in the movie, A Few Good Men, ~You want the truth, You can't handle the truth!~ It's personally one of my most favorite movie lines of all time and it is somewhat related to being an honest person. Each one of us at some point and time had to face the truth concerning our lives either professionally or personally. A person has to sometimes face facts and accept the truth even though we may not like it. It can be somewhat of any eye-opening experience when the reality of what has happened slaps you in the face so to speak. Sometimes, a person has to face the truth even though it may hurt or sting.

The saying goes that the truth shall set you free. Have you ever felt guilty lying to someone and did you ever give it a second thought about lying to him or her afterwards? The lies that a person tells can overlap with each other until one can no longer distinguish which is fact or fiction. The lies that one tells will come back and haunt a person so to speak and no amount of great acting will help him or her out of that situation. In a way, those lies one tells can be a proverbial weight on his or her shoulders that will be dragged around his or her entire life. It's just a matter of telling the truth and one won't have to carry that heavy burden in the long run.

If you think about it, it's that way with significant and potential relationships as well. You have to be honest with yourself and to the person you care about if you want that relationship to succeed. A relationship built on lie after lie will simply fall apart and who really wants a relationship built on that? Working with mostly women in the past 5 years has given me a little insight being that I've been dragged into many conversations about why guys are morons. In any case, the number one quality that women want in a relationship, more so than guys is honesty. If both men and women have that, then a stronger bond will be formed and that my friend is the honest truth.

TRUST ME
August 5, 2004

It's a phrase that can scare a person when those two words are said. Putting your trust in someone one barely even knows or actually knows is a risky venture in itself. It's like gambling with one's own safety on the line and with a roll of the dice, he or she is willing to risk it all. Putting it all on the line if you will and hopefully those proverbial dice will not land on snake-eyes. A person has to be somewhat cautious when meeting new people because you never really know his or her true intentions. It's up to that person's instincts on whether to go ahead and further a friendship or potential and/or significant relationship.

Trust can play a big part in a friendship when total strangers come together and connect in certain ways. One such connection is through mere stupidity which in some ways is always an ice breaker. In any case, there is an unwritten rule among guys that a trusted friend never moves in on one's girlfriend/boyfriend. When that trust is broken, then the friendship is severed, and all lines of communication are broken off. Yet, the trust that was broken can and will be mended, but it will take time and patience. It's just a matter of who takes the first step and part of being a friend is humility and knowing when to say, "I'm Sorry".

Sometimes certain people click and the connection or vibe one feels for another can often be overwhelming. Overwhelmingly enough it's that one particular person he or she can't get out of his or her head. For it's just a matter of putting one's own trust in your emotions and/or feelings which will hopefully either work for you or against you. It's like opening Pandora's box, once he or she opens it, anything and everything inside will come out. Each of us has had that moment or two where one shared their innermost thoughts and feelings with that particular person, only to have those feelings not returned back.

In any case, it's hard really to trust someone when he or she has had it continuously broken. As human beings we can sometimes be too trusting to the point where each of us can have the rug swept from under us so to speak. We've all had people in our lives that we trusted and then stabbed us in the back. That person you once knew is now seen as a person that can't be trusted. It may take either days, months, years, or decades to fix, but oftentimes one may not want to fix it at all. It's an issue that can have a particular person not trust anybody at all and can turn someone totally bitter against the male or female species.

Frank Crane once said, ~You may be deceived if you trust too much, but you will live in torment unless you trust enough. A person has to show that he or she can be trusted in order for a friendship or relationship to progress. There will always be people crossing our paths that will try to pull the wool over our eyes.~ Let me ask you this question: Who are the people that you trust the most and will have your back whenever you need them? For most, the answers come quickly but for others it's an unknown. Who do you absolutely trust to catch you when you start to fall or have fallen? In the end, trust can either kill you or set you free.

PASSING THE TORCH
August 5, 2004

There comes a point in a person's life when one looks back at the years of service that he or she has done and asks, "Is it my time to go?" It's a question one tends to consider when one wants to pursue other aspirations for themselves personally and professionally. All the frustration, stress, and fatigue can add up mentally and physically on a person over the years. In retrospect, one could consider themselves a seasoned veteran due to logging so many hours while acquiring knowledge and experience in the process.

As a seasoned veteran, a person can look at the "rookies" that are wet behind the ears, so to speak, and wonder if they are ready to take on the responsibility that is about to be placed on them. One just has to learn through trial and error, if one doesn't learn the ropes so to speak then it's hasta la vista baby! One can't literally and metaphorically hold that person's hand and show that person what to do, he or she has to do it themselves. In a way, it's like riding a bike, it basically comes natural through practice.

Sometimes there are rules that go with a job, but as the saying goes, "You don't always have to play by the rules." Rules are made to be broken, but yet there are those that stick to them and tend to ruin a good thing. A person just has to remove that stick up their butt and go with the flow. Over time, a person can learn the tricks of the trade, so to speak, after working at a particular place for several years. It's like a handy unofficial guidebook that a person will write themselves and pass down if one wants to.

In any case, he or she can sometimes find that one person that has that burning desire to run with the ball so to speak. It's often been said that one can see themselves in a person that wants to strive to be something better. It's that person that he or she takes under his or her wing and teaches/mentors them like Robin with Batman. Though, there isn't a cool cave to hang around in, or costumes to wear, or the Batmobile to ride in. It's just a matter of the student learning as much as he or she can from the teacher.

Every person remembers that one teacher/mentor that highly influenced their lives and made an impact on them in a big way. It's that one person that took it upon himself or herself to help and guide us, in turn, we help and guide others. It can be somewhat compared to martial arts as the master teaches the student. The skills and training one learns over time will be of great value for years to come. Inevitably, the master will have taught all that he or she knows and, in the end, it's just a matter of passing the torch.

THE LITTLE THINGS
August 8, 2004

If you think about it, it's the little things in life that seem insignificant and are oftentimes the most important things in a person's life. One can often take for granted the things that mean so much to a person that he or she rarely thinks about losing. A person can oftentimes think that they have a nice firm hold on what's important to them, but that mentality can oftentimes bite them in the butt so to speak. One can literally be blind to what a person has in front of them until it's gone.

A person can sometimes take for granted the limbs that he or she has until it is taken away from them. A simple thing such as walking or holding something in one's hand or arms can make a person appreciate what they have. If one loses that ability then he or she simply has to adjust and become stronger physically and mentally. A person who literally turned a negative into a positive is actor Christopher Reeves. Though he isn't able to walk, his spirits are high and he is fighting the good fight.

In some ways, a little thing like friendship can be taken for granted as well. It's been said that one can tell what type of person you are by the friends that you have. Yet, if one doesn't have any friends, it's a safe bet that you don't have any people skills or you're simply a loner. In any case, a valued friendship is one of the greatest assets that a person can invest in because they will have your back through thin and thin. Think about this, who else knows you better than yourself other than your parents?

Have you ever thought about what it would be like to lose any of your five senses? It's those senses a person uses that most that can be taken away in an instant. Even though a blind person has lost their sight, other senses such as touch and hearing will get stronger as time goes by. It's an adjustment that a person will have to make in order to go on with life. Think about this, a person who is blind can see the true beauty of the world better than a person who always has his eyes open and sees nothing.

In retrospect, it's the little things that count in a potential or significant relationship that make life worth living. Little things such as the way that person looks at you, that certain smile that he or she gives, that certain touch that a person gives that makes you feel special like a kiss. There are also those compliments that seem insignificant to you but mean so much to that person which will be remembered for years to come. In the end, keep noticing the little things, if not, then you lose what matters most...love.

TO BE THE MAN
August 10, 2004

There is a saying that goes: ~winning isn't everything, it's the only thing.~ Is that true? Every person has that competitive spirit within themselves, though one may not admit it to one's self or others. In a way, it's like unleashing the beast that one wouldn't want to show like his or her dark side. Yet, it's in our blood and it defines us as human beings. In retrospect, no matter how much one can deny that he or she isn't competitive, that person will face the cold hard truth sooner or later.

That competitive nature can also fall under sibling rivalry which plays a big part in a brother and/or sister relationship. For both would be in competition in sports, academics, and in some cases the attention of one or both parents. It can be somewhat like the Brady Bunch syndrome in which the green-eyed monster of jealousy can rear its ugly head. Hopefully, none of us will come to the point of holding long standing grudges where hand to hand combat is the end result.

As one ventures into the working world, a person will use that competitiveness to make a name for themselves. It can be a cut-throat business and he or she will have to have that mindset of being one step ahead of the competition. It's just a matter of scouting the competition and learning more about what they are all about. It's been said that every strong foundation has a weakness. One has to simply find it and work it to your advantage. It's a dog-eat-dog world out there and hopefully you're not wearing milk bone underwear.

If you think about it, a person can compete with one's self, trying to set a mark of greater achievement and go beyond the limits one has put on themselves. One can oftentimes have that mentality that he or she needs to excel at everything one does. In other words, be absolutely perfect and yet we're not all perfect. We have our flaws and insecurities like everybody else, though we may not show it, he or she can hide it well. A person has to sometimes settle for second best, which one will learn as he or she gets older.

Someone once said, it doesn't matter who wins or loses, it's how you play the game. The pressure to always be number one can be stressful because you will always be looking over your shoulder to see who wants to take your crown in a manner of speaking. In the end, it's not how much a person wins that counts, it's how that person takes a defeat that matters. If one takes defeat with honor and dignity, then that person truly wins. For they win something much greater than money or a trophy, they win respect from their peers.

WRONG TURNS
August 12, 2004

As a person travels down one's road of life, he or she might find that it's not all smooth sailing in a manner of speaking. One can notice that it is somewhat difficult to locate where he or she wants to be and, in the process, get lost searching for that one thing that will make that person truly happy. Yet, the directions one takes can oftentimes lead to nowhere. Sometimes the plans that one intends to go by never work out and it's been said that all roads don't necessarily lead to one's intended destination.

A person, without even knowing it, can wind up on a one-way street. In a way, one can have that perception that the person he or she is interested in is going in the same direction as you are. In reality, that person may be going in the opposite direction and doesn't share the same feelings as you do. One can feel somewhat like a person being hit from behind and the sudden impact causes the wind to be knocked out of you. A person has to just step on the brakes, compose themselves, and wait till the shock goes away.

There can be times when a person ends up going around in circles when one person is interested in another. It can be a frustrating situation in a person's life when one seeks the answers to the question(s) that he or she wants to know from that particular person. One can feel that he or she is in the exact same spot where they themselves began. The attempts that one makes can be considered futile and that one just has to give up the pursuit that has literally wasted much of your precious time.

Dead ends are always inevitable, for one can be constantly in search of that one exit that will lead you to true happiness. He or she may encounter roadblocks, traffic jams, and major vehicular accidents during your travels and detours will have to be taken.

Those detours, though time consuming, are somewhat of a blessing. One has to realize that every person will eventually find that place where he or she always wanted to be. It's just a matter of not having road rage while one experiences these dead ends.

It's been said that life can be considered a one-way street, if you're not paying attention, you will be hit head on. In retrospect, it's that way with the male and female relationship. Nobody really knows how we end up on the same street and click with one another. It's somewhat of a mystery which may or may not be solved in the near future. In the end, a person can go through so many wrong turns within his or her life, until that one wrong turn eventually leads you to the person one has been patiently waiting for.

PERFECT

August 14, 2004

One can say for themselves that the life he or she has led so far has been interesting at best. It's been said that certain events in people's lives that each of us go through can never be undone. Those events can be considered imperfections which can't be erased no matter how many times one tries to sweep it under the proverbial rug so to speak. For we all, in some way, know it's coming but we have some or no idea who, what, where, when and why? It's these imperfections that toughen up a person when life itself can literally give a surprise gift that you really never expected to get or sometimes never really wanted.

A person has to simply grin and bear with what has just happened or is about to happen. Oftentimes one thinks he or she is totally in control of the car being driven down his or her road of life. Inevitably that car, like our lives, can spin out of control and end up crashing hard into life's wall that we have all been against at one time or another. One just has to prepare himself or herself for the impact that is about to occur and hope to walk away unharmed. "Life Stinks", it's a saying that every person has said at some point in time and has seriously meant it. He or she simply has to deal with the awful smells of life that can sometimes make a person wave the proverbial white flag.

It's been said that every cloud has a silver lining. One just has to view the bright side of a potentially bad situation if there is any. A person can somehow feel that the dark clouds that are looming over his or her head will never open up and let the sunshine through. One just has to find that one opening that will let in that one ray of light to brighten his or her day. Though one can't see it, that person simply has to look carefully for it because it is there. For if that person finds that opening then he or she can know that sunny days will be seen again. It's just a matter of trusting God to see you through the tough times of life that each of us will go through.

Many people's lives have been affected by the forces of nature and end up losing everything that they own. It's the people that we hardly know and yet feel for them because they lost homes, businesses, and family members. For each of these people will have to go back and salvage anything that is worth more than material possessions, in other words, a rebuilding process. A process where one starts back at square one when forces of nature such as a hurricane topples everything in front of one's eyes. If you think about it, we all start out with nothing and eventually our hard-earned blood, sweat, and tears turn that nothing into something.

In retrospect, A person will continually fight their way back from darkness and back into the light so to speak. As the saying goes, "We may be down, but we're not out." For a person's home may be broken but the human spirit that lives inside each and every one of us can't. You have to have comfort in knowing that if you leave in God's hands, he will protect you. You basically have to ask yourself what's more important in your life, material possessions which can be replaced or the people that can never be replaced, which do you choose? In the end, if you have your health, friends, and the people you love around you, then life as you know it, is absolutely perfect.

IMAGINE
August 16, 2004

A person's imagination is considered to be one of the single most useful tools he or she can use. It can take someone to far off places within one's own mind without going anywhere physically. As counselors, we often go to a place in our heads where we would rather be but can't go there physically. Inevitably, one's mind will drift to that place where he or she is spending their life with the one person that they feel will offer everything one could possibly imagine. Oftentimes, one's imagination will get the better of him or her and the reality of it all can be somewhat of a letdown in the end.

As kids, we used our imaginations all the time to create people and places that seemed real. In a way, we were like MacGyver, at an early age. Making up our own games with the toys that we had to work with was a challenge back in the day. Sometimes half the activities one planned as a kid would either injure us or almost kill us. It's no wonder how kids like me survived a childhood where using your imagination could be considered the most dangerous weapon indeed. If you think about it, a kid's imagination is endless, and he or she will tend to lose it as he or she grows older.

As counselors, we are surrounded by constant madness and have to think outside the box. But there are times where each one of us just wants to escape the reality of what is happening around him or her by using one's imagination to go into another reality in one's own head. A reality where one is either getting a tan on the beach and the waves are fresh enough to swim in or surf on. Also, one could imagine one's self in the comfort of his or her bed where each of us desperately wants to be as the seconds, minutes, and hours go by which can sometimes feel like an eternity.

If you think about it, women, more so than men, have always

imagined what their lives would be like when or if they met the person of their dreams. The basic idea of an ideal man that all women imagine will sweep them off their feet is tall, dark and handsome. Though it may or may come true, at least she has that one thing that every person has and that is hope. Like an action/mystery movie, there can also be twists that will take her story in a very different direction. A direction in which a woman will find that the man that will be standing in front her will be someone that she never expected to fall for.

William Shakespeare once said, "Love looks not with the eyes, but with the mind. Love doesn't discriminate, it touches everybody in the heart, and you don't need eyes to see that. For each of us has thought about the qualities we look for in that one special person and when we have found it, one just has to hold on to him or her. Think about your first love and how exciting it was. It's that love that can totally take a person by surprise which we never want to go away. Sometimes, finding true love isn't all that a person thought it would be...it's even better than he or she could possibly ever imagine.

ONE STEP CLOSER
August 18, 2004

Each one of us has or has had an ultimate goal in life that he or she has been chasing after since one was a kid. As the saying goes by Kasey Kasem, keep your feet on the ground and keep reaching for the stars. It's every person's dream to make it big in a particular business that can either make you a somebody or yesterday's news in a manner of speaking. It's just a matter of having that fire within yourself to keep burning no matter what. In a way, one has to continue to climb up his or her personal Mt. Everest.

Achieving one's ultimate goal is like climbing a mountain. When one stands at the base, he or she will look up and realize that it's not going to be easy by any means. It will take heart, souls, guts, determination, and that never say die attitude to reach the top of the mountain. It's really unknown how long it will take for one to continually climb that proverbial ladder in order to reach the pinnacle of one's dream. In retrospect, one just has to pace themselves and he or she will get there in due time.

Sometimes one will have several setbacks when climbing the mountain that has their so-called "prize" waiting for them. Such factors are the weather which can blow a person in many different directions and can literally beat down a person into submission. If you think about it, "The Powers That Be," in music and/or entertainment can lead you in every direction but up. A person has to constantly keep that safety line close at hand for at any time his or her rope, like their dream, can be cut off in an instant.

Fame and/or fortune, it's those two things that can drive a person into becoming what they want to be, a celebrity. Yet, does one want to become a celebrity with all the paparazzi hounding you and one's privacy being invaded all year round? It's basically up to that person and it's also the price one pays if he or chooses that life. Let me ask you this question and answer truthfully, would fame and fortune change you if you made it big? One just has to experience it for themselves if or when it happens in the near future.

Last Friday, the Olympics games began and people from around the world came together for the spirit of competition. Though some may or may not achieve that goal of winning gold, they at least climbed their own personal mountain to get there. My goal in life has always been to work for Disney in Orlando, and several days ago I found out my chance is close at hand. I'm still climbing up my mountain and you know what, I'm just one step closer in fulfilling a life-long dream that I have had since I was a kid.

W.Y.S.I.W.Y.G
August 20, 2004

Each one of us has a person or persons that they have known for years or throughout their childhood. In other words, a best friend in which one can consider them brothers or sisters. Though not blood related, he or she can consider them an unofficial member of the family. A person can honestly say that his or her friends can describe and know you better than you ca. Yet, can you really describe your friends that he or she has known for years in depth, rather than going by the generic terminologies? Let me ask you this question: how well do you know your friends or for that matter your best friend?

Oftentimes, close friends can find something about you that one has never known before. Hidden talents that one never really wanted anyone to know about and kept secret, possibly till one reaches his or her golden age. Sometimes, a person can have the mentality that if their friends might find out, then he or she will never hear the end of it. In reality though, they would accept it because they are your friends, but still one would be ragged on, in good fun of course. Someone once said, a person will know who his or her true friends are when one needs them the most.

The funny thing about having friends is that they can describe you in so many ways and most of the time they are correct. Other times you just have to look at each of your friends and wonder if they are just a few McNuggets short of a happy meal. Such descriptions would be weird, funny, loyal, honest, willing to give the shirt off one's back, and much much more. One's own friends can be considered therapists, for they know you inside and out. You can talk with them about your hopes, dreams, fears, loves, and everything in between. When one wants to talk, they lend an open ear without even charging a penny.

Partners in crime and running buddies, are just a couple of descriptions of duos or groups of friends. Different personalities, temperaments, ethnicities, melding into one cohesive unit. Each accepting one's quirkiness and annoying little habits that would make any other person beat the crap out of him or her. For there will be opinions and egos that will clash but that's what makes a friendship unique. Though hand to hand combat may erupt, eventually cooler heads will prevail and all will be right with the world so to speak.

For people who have known me for several years they know I have a wacky side and a serious side. I've been described as shy, quiet, deep, philosophical, an old soul, sarcastic, cynical, weird, strange, laid back, a bit temperamental, wacky, creative, goofy and if you can believe it evil all rolled into one short little package. I really don't count that last one because one of "my kids" described me that way. In any case, a person can sometimes be truly surprised when one is described, it can either be dead on or dead wrong. We are who we are and there is no changing that, and in the end, What You See Is What You Get.

PROVE YOURSELF
August 21, 2004

Throughout our lives each of us will encounter "critics" who will question everything and anything that one does and says. In a way, it's like taking a test in which there are no right or wrong answers. Life itself can be somewhat considered one huge final exam where a person is being tested and he or she hasn't completely studied for it. Nobody can be prepared at what life can throw at you on a daily basis. It's just a matter of relying on one's own instincts and hopefully you will get the answers correct.

Oftentimes, these "critics" are constantly looking over one's shoulder, so to speak, supposedly thinking they have the best intentions for each of us. Such critics one will face are teachers/professors and of the working world his or her boss. One can sometimes feel they're under the proverbial microscope and every little thing that doesn't meet their expectations should be met. It's like having your life on a schedule and one must be on a deadline in order to meet their expectations.

Yet, the two toughest "critics" that a person listens to, most of the time, are one's parents. For they too have expectations that they want to be met and have somewhat of a timeline set for our lives. But sometimes the plans that one's parents have for their lives don't necessarily match up with their own. A parent has to realize that their baby boy and/or baby girl is all grown up and will have to let go. It's their time to make their own mark in life and as the saying goes, you can't hold his or her hand forever.

In any case, the biggest "critic" that a person can listen to is yourself. We can sometimes live our lives second guessing ourselves and come to the point where we can metaphorically beat ourselves up with the decisions we make in life. But that's life, we live with the decision that we make, though it may take a while to get over it. The scars of past mistakes will soon fade. It's just a matter of moving on, not looking back, though one may eventually stumble in the near future, but that is to be expected.

As I said in the beginning, life can be considered one huge test. There will be areas in one's life that he or she may either pass successfully or fail miserably. Life can throw each of us curve balls that either make a person throw in the towel or continue to keep fighting. There is no denying that one will always have "critics" in your ear, but it's been said that critics can always be proven wrong from time to time. Sometimes in order to prove yourself, a person must take a step back to move forward with one's journey of life.

SOUNDTRACK OF LIFE

August 23, 2004

One's life can be somewhat like a movie, though the story may not relate to the music within it. Here's a question, have you ever watched a movie and wondered how they picked the songs for that particular movie? The right script combined with the right songs can either make or break a movie and determine box office success or disaster. But one's life isn't a movie, it's real life with a cast of characters that he or she knows and grew up with. Yet, the songs that are selected which define a movie can also define one's own life.

Life can certainly be one big adventure where a person can oftentimes feel like they're in a non-stop action and or adventure movie. The perfect songs to add in one's library are Bring Me To Life by Evanescence, Sammy Hagar's 55 and White Zombie's Never Gonna Stop. But more than anything, one must simply have in his or her song selection of Steppenwolf's Born to Be Wild in which the opening lyrics open with get your motor running. If you think about it, the minute we are born, our adventures are just beginning.

Our lives can also have tragedies where certain people close to us pass on. Inevitably, the songs associated with that particular person stay with us and have sentimental value. Such songs which can describe this could be My Immortal by Evanescence and Diamond Rio's One More Day. Yet, tragedies not only affect us but people we hardly even know. Take Sept. 11, 2001, and the song that defined everyone's life was Alan Jackson's song Where Were You. Tragedies can make us think about what's more important in our lives and that song proved it.

There will always be that one song that defines a movie, and in a way, will define our lives. Potential/Significant relationships and relationships in general are always the main focus. Countless songs that one could add into their personal library would be Avril Lavigne's I'm With you; Aerosmith's I Don't want to Miss a Thing; Goo Goo Dolls' Iris; Bryan Adams' Everything I do(I Do it For You); Hero by Chad Kreoger and Josey Scott, the list goes on and on. I ask you this, what song defines your life right now?

Thinking about it, some of the songs that describe my life are the following: The Cowboy In Me by Tim McGraw; 55 by Sammy Hagar; Insane In Da Membrane by Cypress Hill; Party Up by DMX(an anthem where I work at); Numb by Linkin Park, I'm With You by Avril Lavigne; Right Here Waiting For You by Richard Marx; I Can't Dance by Genesis; I Don't To Miss A Thing by Aerosmith and to round it off, the song that defines my life at the moment is Feelin' Way To Good by Nickelback. In a nutshell, that is my soundtrack of life, so what is yours?

DESTINY
August 24, 2004

Each one of us has a talent that's considered a gift from God. The abilities that He has given to a particular person as young kids can ultimately entertain, as well as put a smile on people's faces. It's been said that certain people were born to do certain things in life. Yet can a person really determine where he or she is meant solely on one's talent? Someone once said that a person who predicts what one's life will be in the future can sometimes find that there is something much better for him or her elsewhere.

One can make assumption after assumption of what his or her life will be like based on their abilities. It can be somewhat of an embarrassing sight when a person's ego can get the better of him or her. It can be seen in the young, up and coming professional athletes where careers which have just started can end with a snap of a finger. Sometimes a person foresees a future that has never happened yet or probably will never happen. It mainly depends on how one carries themselves as one seeks to fulfill his or her future.

In a way, a person sees the pieces of his or her future and tries to put them together. If compared to, it would be like putting together a jigsaw puzzle that will determine the who, what, where, and when of one's life. But it can be really unclear which pieces go where because like a puzzle, life can get all jumbled up and confusion can set in. One can get easily confused on what path to take because one wrong turn could lead to disaster. It's just a matter of keeping a level head and simply working from the outside in.

Inevitably, a person can change the course of his or her own unforeseen future. Whether it be a tiny insignificant event or something big, it can most definitely change the direction of where one wants to go in life. In a way, it can be decided for you, or you can decide for yourself. In some cases, the other direction that it leads to is something totally different in which one never really expected to go. A destination in which one can end up absolutely happy and content at where he or she has ended up.

One must control his or her path in life, and not let that path control you. It's somewhat like the blockbuster movie The Matrix in which Keanu Reeves' character Neo is told he is not "The One." Sometimes we must hear the supposed truth in order to fulfill what we are meant to do in life. Think about this, one's thoughts will become words; one's words will become actions; one's actions will become habits; one's habits will become character; and in the end one's character will become that person's destiny.

JUST A NUMBER
August 25, 2004

A person will encounter in his or her own lifetime countless numbers that can undoubtedly change a person's life. Whether it be professional or personal, a certain number(s) can make a person ask themselves what one has or hasn't accomplished in one's life so far. In a way, it can also make a person more driven than ever to be in a level of high achievement. It's somewhat like having a mid-life crisis even though one hasn't reached mid-life yet. Each one of us has wondered where one will end up in said number of years.

The number 23, an insignificant number as it may be, but when put on a basketball jersey it is associated with Michael Jordan. A living legend and possibly one of the greatest basketball players associated with the game of basketball. For he is a sure candidate for the basketball hall of fame with the numbers he has racked up over the years. His numbers prove that he deserves to be in the hall of fame, but they are just numbers. It's the man who scored those numbers that basketball fans world over will remember.

The number 3 is how many times it took me to get my driver's license. It can be a frustrating thing when you have to go by the numbers in a manner of speaking in order to get that so-called ticket to freedom. As the saying goes, if at first you don't succeed, try try again. It's also been said that the 3rd time's the charm and it's a statement that holds so true. A person will try several times to attain something that means so much to him or her until that final try will clinch it so to speak.

The year 2000, to some it's a number that signified the future. A future in which every person would be driving flyers cars similar to the Jetsons. Moving sidewalks, teleportation, robot maids/butlers, were on people's expectations but all for not. The year 2000 also supposedly marked the end of the world where everything electronic would be shut down and mass chaos would erupt. One's imagination can oftentimes run wild but to no avail, and in the end, it was a number that thankfully did not live up to the hype.

In life, there will be certain numbers that a person will sometimes look forward to. 8/25/77, numbers which may not seem relevant to you but are important to me. For you see on August 25, 1977, I was born and 27 years later I'm still kickin'. A long time ago, I made 2 very significant wishes which I make every year. One of them you all know will hopefully be fulfilled and I'm still waiting for my other wish to come true. In any case, people will remember you not how old you are and, in the end, age is just a number.

INNER VOICE
August 28, 2004

Have you ever stuck your foot in your mouth and wished you never said what you said?" Every person has done that and each one of us has that inner monologue inside their head which nobody can hear but yourself. Having that argument with yourself inside your own head can sometimes be pure comedy. If life were like a movie or a television show, the viewing audience would supposedly know what one is thinking. Many thoughts can go through a person's head that, if it were possible to hear them, a person would go mad.

As said in the beginning, every person at one time or another has stuck their foot in their mouth and wished he or she never said what they said. Oftentimes, what a person may be saying on the inside can bite one in the butt, so to speak, when it is said on the outside. One's own mouth can overpower his or her brain and that's when the shiznit will start to hit the fan. For the stupidest and craziest things can be said and most of the time it can never be taken back.

Each one of us has been in a situation where one is interested in a particular person. One can have that conversation within themselves as he or she tries to figure out what to say. A person can be cool, calm and collected on the outside as one goes for it, but on the inside, it can be like the Titanic about to hit the iceberg and about to sink into the ocean. In some ways, the imaginary captain of one's brain could jump ship at any time and nobody is in charge to stop what is about to be said.

Sometimes a person has to use that proverbial filter in one's brain that completely stops a bad situation from becoming even worse. The proverbial test is in potential and or significant relationships where a person, mainly guys, will do something that will get him into hot water. It's always inevitable that a guy will say something stupid because the captain of our brain has just jumped ship. The best excuse one can give is that we are guys, and we are sorry. Unfortunately, it's who we are and you have to live with it.

In retrospect, every person will have so many voices in one's head telling him or her what to do and where to go. In times of that proverbial inner struggle over one's personal and professional life as well, a person has to find that one single voice to guide him or her to the right decision, whatever that may be. For each of us will have that voice that keeps us going and pushes us on to our intended goal(s). In the end, one must listen to that one true voice... your inner voice.

I DO
August 28, 2004

There will come a point in every person's life when thoughts of settling down and starting a family run through one's mind. It's somewhat of an uncertainty for both men and women if one will truly find that one person to spend his or her life with. A person can somewhat feel like they are on a game show trying to figure out who will be that one person standing behind the curtain without really seeing his or her face. Each of us will eventually find out who is behind the curtain and hopefully disappointing music won't be played.

Working with mostly women has given me somewhat of an insight of what a woman wants in a guy. For there is an endless list of qualities that women look for in a guy that she hopes meets those specific requirements. The number one quality on top of every woman's list is honesty. Women want a guy that is able to tell the truth when she asks for it. Yet, it can be a double-edged sword when the questions being asked can totally confuse any guy. In a way, it feels like taking a test and the possibility of passing it is an unknown.

For guys, it's just a matter of finding that one person who is willing to tolerate our annoying habits and the stupid things we will do. I can honestly say, as a guy, I know less about women since the day I first started to get interested in them 15 years ago. As it has been said, if one thinks he has all the answers, more questions will pop up. Women are absolutely an enigma, for they are truly the most mysterious and beautiful creatures on the face of the earth that we may never figure out and you know what, I'm ok with that.

In any case, a person can oftentimes feel that being single is the way to go. But on occasion, one will always have that urge to fill a void that is missing in his or her life. A life up to a particular point has been filled with work, family, and friends. If you think about it, nobody wants to be alone, for each of us wants to find true happiness. Some have already found it, many are still looking for it, and others have given up the search for it so to speak. One will find that one person to fill the void, it's just a matter of time.

Several months ago, someone asked me if I had the potential of being a father and my answer, I believe I do. Now, I ask myself this question, do I have the potential of being a suitable husband for any woman one day and my answer is that I have absolutely no idea. Men and women will have doubts and fears when it's their time to walk down the aisle. Fears and doubts will subside as both bride and groom lock eyes. In the end, it's their defining moments as two separate lives form into one as these two words are said…I DO.

WOULD YOU
August 31, 2004

A person never really gets over the loss of someone whom he or she has felt close to over a period of time. Every now and then one has thoughts of that particular person and wishes he or she would be at one's side once again. No matter how many times one wishes for it, it will never come true. Oftentimes, that one person that he or she had somewhat of a connection with is a person that one didn't like but did respect. For the relationship that one has formed with a particular person(s) can never be duplicated.

The relationship between parent and child, particularly between father and daughter, is a strong one. Yet, it can be somewhat of a touchy situation when a daughter loses her father in death at a young age. As the saying goes, life goes one, but it will be hard for her to accept anybody new into her life that isn't the man that raised her. The father/ daughter relationship will always stand the test of time. A time where a father simply wants his little girl to stay young and never ever grow up.

One can also be very close to his or her grandparent(s). In a way, it's like the generation that is just starting life learning from the generation that is soon going to end and is passing the knowledge and experience over the years to them. One such example is John Stevens and his grandparents from American Idol. His grandparents started him on his journey at a very young age by introducing him to old school music. Though they will eventually pass on, J.S. will always have them at his side rooting him on his journey of life.

The best friend relationship is one that can be considered a bond that will never be broken. Yet, a best friend can also be described about one's potential and/or significant relationship. A loss of one's best friend is like losing a part of yourself, like losing the other half of a two-sided coin. Sometimes one tries to find that same relationship in another person but in reality, it's not the same. One has to realize lost relationships can't be willed to happen, it's just a matter of letting time run its course.

If you think about it, if one looks back at the time spent with that person or persons, does it put a smile on your face? Someone once said that in life, we take for granted that one precious commodity when it pertains to people we care about and that is time. Time is always a factor when one wants to say something that one didn't get the opportunity to say. I end this thought by asking you a question:

Would you give up everything you have worked for up to this point, if you could be back with that one person(s)? My answer... yes I would.

JUST FRIENDS
September 1, 2004

It's two words that both men and women hate to hear from a person that he or she is interested in. When a person hears those two particular words it's somewhat like getting punched in the stomach and no matter how much you try to breathe you can't. Every person has at one time, or another yearned to get with that one person who he or she has known for quite some time as a friend or as a co-worker. Yet, one can oftentimes have thoughts of taking that friendship to the next level. A level in which one hopes that person accepts his or her feelings.

One can oftentimes receive mixed signals in which a person can get totally confused. In a way, a person can literally decide that the situation that is before him or her, is a once and ONLY once in a lifetime chance. Nobody really knows what that particular person is thinking and/or what that person might do if he or she finds out about one's intentions. A person has that inner struggle within themselves to tell that person how he or she feels. If you think about it, the decision will always come down to either one's heart or head.

There is that age old question which asks can men and women just be friends? In my own thinking yes, but both men and women have to at least try that one time to find out if there is a slim chance, if any. It can really play with a person's mind when one wants to try to start a relationship with someone one has known and considered a friend. A friend that now for some reason one gets nervous around and blabbers like a complete moron. But there is always that nagging feeling in one's mind that maybe one shouldn't pursue that path.

There will always be that mentality if one does tell that particular person then it will ruin a perfectly good friendship. A person can most definitely count on these two questions popping up: (1) should one hide the feelings that he or she has for that particular person and have thoughts of what if OR (2) tell that person and deal with the repercussions that will follow, and that proverbial weight is lifted off one's shoulders. One just has to hope that he or she survives the aftermath when the dust settles so to speak.

Nobody can predict the reactions that person may have, but the decision that he or she makes will ultimately change lives. One has to think about the people you are associated with because they, in some way, will be affected. In other words, weighing the pros and cons of what might or might not happen if he or she takes that leap of faith. In the end, a person will sometimes decide friendship is more important, and even though it will be painful for that person not to tell him or her, being "just friends" is usually the best decision one will ever make.

SKY IS THE LIMIT
September 2, 2004

Falling in love can somewhat be compared to flying an airplane like in the movie Top Gun. In a way, a person can enter the danger zone as one locks his or heart to one's intended target. It can be sort of a dog fight as so-called enemy aircraft are in pursuit of that same person. Though each of us may not look like or have the financial stability of Tom Cruise, Anthony Edwards, Meg Ryan, Val Kilmer, or Kelly McGillis, one must be comfortable just being yourself and hope things go in your favor.

If you think about it, one can be on his or her proverbial runway, so to speak waiting for a potential relationship to take flight. For any number of things can prevent a person from spreading one's wings and flying up into the wild blue yonder in a manner of speaking. Problems that occur may be that a particular person isn't ready for a relationship or that person is just too immature. Nobody wants a "co-pilot" that doesn't take what one has in front of them seriously. If not taken seriously, then one's plane is grounded permanently.

One will always encounter turbulence when matters of the heart are involved. A person will be in a situation where his or her heart is being played like a violin. For emotions that one feels for that person isn't being reciprocated. It's a sad situation indeed when one can't see what is happening to them but others around you can see clearly on their own radar screens. In a way, one simply has to realize that he or she isn't going up but down. May day will be sounded, and assistance will truly be needed.

For some people that loving relationship can ultimately crash and burn. One can sometimes be cocky as he or she thinks that one's relationship, based on love, will last forever. Want proof, go back and look at your high school yearbooks. Statement after statement can be read of forever with a person they are now longer with in the end. Life just gets more complicated and dramatic when one gets older. It's just a matter of knowing when to pull the proverbial ejector seat when things go from bad to worse.

Love is quite frankly unpredictable, for one never knows who will be showing up at your radar screen. In a way, it's like being shot at, but you have no idea who is shooting at you. If you think about it, a person doesn't find true love, true love will find you and every person will have to learn that. It's just a matter of not continually thinking about when one's Cinderella or Prince Charming will show up. In the end, love is like flying without wings and when you are truly in love, the sky's the limit.

ONCE IN A LIFETIME
September 4, 2004

A person can sometimes sense that something is in the air and for whatever reason it may or may not involve you. For there are certain situations or people who will cross one's own path and somehow affect his or her journey down the proverbial road of life. In a way, it's like having an opportunity knocking and all that person has to do is open the door and either let'em in or you have to walk through it. In any case, the opportunities that are presented to a person can be considered that chance to be happy personally as well as professionally.

One opportunity that can present itself to a person is being offered a job of a lifetime that one feels will help in his or her financial stability. Yet, a person can oftentimes be overly excited and forget to read the proverbial fine print so to speak. For if one does take that job he or she has to relocate to either another state or country and that will mean leaving friends and family behind. A person can be afraid to continue on the next step in one's journey, but yet, he or she feels it's the right time to move on.

Another opportunity that a person can face is owning a business. It's a risky venture when one puts his or her hard-earned dollar into something that he or she believes in 100%. Yet, one has to learn from the failed businesses that preceded yours and turn that failure into a success. It's just a matter of thinking outside the box and having that fire within yourself to compete with the "big boys" so to speak. If you lose it, then one's business venture will go up in flames and all that will be left are ashes.

One of the biggest opportunities in a person's life is marriage. Every person will or has already found that special someone to settle down with and eventually start a family. Sacrifices will be made as husband and wife struggle up the proverbial ladder to keep their heads above water so to speak. Someone once said, marriage is somewhat like a math problem, if you keep communicating with each other plus continually supporting each other through the ups and downs, it equals up to a beautiful and strong partnership.

In retrospect, a person will face countless opportunities in life that will change his or her life, plus the people around that person. One of those opportunities in life that can be considered a defining moment is telling someone you know how you truly feel about them. For each of us will have to make that personal decision whether to reveal our true feelings on our own. If you think about it, saying that one particular person how you truly feel is a once in a lifetime opportunity that should never be wasted.

100% GUARANTEED
September 6, 2004

On a day-to-day basis, a person can have one of those days where life can just literally beat you down mentally and physically. Oftentimes one can ask himself or herself why it's happening to them, and will it ever end? In a way, one can feel like Bill Murray in the movie Groundhog Day, where he wakes up and relives the same day over and over again. If you think about it, there are certain ways one can work out his or her aggressions without resorting to mass homicides running rampant.

One such way to work out one's aggressions is through exercise. Exercise such as martial arts, running, boxing, lifting weights, etc. can, in a way, strip away the frustrations of daily life like tearing a piece of paper in half. For if a person could put a face on life itself, one would put it on a punching bag and continually beat the living crap out of it till his or her hands started bleeding. In some ways, sweating out one's own problems can make you feel better, but they are still with you like a shadow.

A person can also take out his or her frustrations of daily life through art. Art is basically self-expression, a person basically creates something by how he or she feels at the particular time. If you look at certain people's works of art, you can get somewhat of an idea how that person felt creating it. Emotions such as anger, depression, happiness, love, sadness, etc. can be seen in many pictures. Once a person has a pencil, paintbrush, or hammer and chisel in his or her hand, the party is about to begin so to speak.

Music can have a calming effect on a person that was beaten down by life itself. In a way, one can be in the zone as he or she writes and performs songs or listens to them. It evokes emotions that in some way gradually release the tensions that one is feeling. Think about this, once one finishes performing a song that he or she has written or listened to, that person is relaxed and ready to take on the word yet again. In the immortal words of WWE superstar, The Rock, one can say to life itself, "JUST BRING IT!"

In retrospect, there are many different ways for a person to release one's aggressions of daily life. Every person wants that sense of peace when life can just get out of hand. For a person like myself, drawing, listening to music, and writing my thoughts down can put me in a state of calm that only certain people understand. In the end, ways of releasing tension can be like therapy, it's 100% guaranteed that you will feel better than you have ever felt before in mind, body, and soul.

FADE TO BLACK
September 8, 2004

If you think about it, it's easy to fall in love with someone without being committed to that person. Every person has done it in his or her own lifetime with a person one oftentimes can't be with such as a celebrity in sports and/or entertainment. It's somewhat of a fantasy for each of us to meet a certain singer, actor, sports star and marry him or her. One just has to wake up from dreaming and realize that each of us will eventually settle down with that one person who we consider bigger than any celebrity you meet.

It's all about commitment and that promise to keep the fires of love continually burning for his or her true love. It's sometimes not easy for a man or a woman because it means closing one's heart to the possibility of falling in love with someone else more attractive and loveable. As cruel as those sounds, that's how the cookie crumbles so to speak. Love is not easy; it just gets more complicated as time goes by. It's been said, love will make you do crazy things and when you're totally committed, two become one.

Oftentimes, one person is more committed than the other and it can be seen in many relationships. One person gives more of himself/herself than the other person and that love isn't being reciprocated. I once wrote that life can be considered a one-way street, if you're not paying attention, you can be hit head on. A person can never really tell how much a man loves a woman and vice versa. Love isn't an object that can be measured which causes problems. How can a person know if he or she is telling the truth... you can't.

A person can say that he or she is in love with him or her but how far is that person will go to prove it? Courting, which in my opinion is a lost artform and marriage, a sign of full commitment. A person says all the right words and does all the right things in a potential or significant relationship and pledges his or her love forever, but only leaves that person high and dry later down the road, so to speak. The question can be asked: were they in love? Yes, but not enough to hold it together and then the pain of heartache begins.

In retrospect, when two people are in a totally committed and loving relationship, things seem brighter and more colorful. In a way, it's like being on a proverbial high without taking any actual drugs. But one will always get that sinking feeling that something is not right in the relationship. A sixth sense, if you will, that mostly women have and that strong commitment is loosening up and doubt creeps into his or her head. In the end, the once bright and colorful relationship will ultimately fade to black.

MORAL OF THE STORY

September 10, 2004

If you think about it, two people that are in a committed relationship can be somewhat compared to the relationship between a quarterback and a coach of a football team. In a way, the man is considered the quarterback, and the woman is the head coach calling all the key plays. Every person is considered a free agent waiting to be signed or picked up by that key team that will accept him. But the quarterback has to prove to the coach that he will not crack under the pressure when the game is on the line so to speak.

As the season is starting out, mistakes on the field can be made which will hopefully be taken care of as the season progresses. Mistakes such as fumbling the ball will happen from time to time. Being in a committed relationship for the first time can be scary because the quarterback will sometimes say and do things that the head coach may not approve of like calling plays that are not in the playbook. Initially, the head coach will sum it up to mental mistakes for that QB, in a way, has to work out the kinks in the system.

As the season reaches the halfway point, the quarterback may start to lose his edge and reach a stage where he is continually throwing interception after interception. The head coach sees these mistakes and her faith in her star player is slowly beginning to fade. It's the disappointment in her face that will usually make the quarterback check out other teams and talk with other head coaches without her knowledge. Inevitably, the backup quarterback will start to loosen up which is a bad sign indeed.

The head coach will always know where her quarterback is at when her QB is being rushed by the defensive line. For she has the headset on at all times and is always connected to her people giving her the right information to pass on to the head coach.

Ultimately, the quarterback will be traded to another team and the backup quarterback has taken over your spot. As the former QB of the team, one watches the new guy make all the right decisions and moves wherein touchdown after touchdown is made.

Every head coach has confidence in her new star quarterback to eventually lead the team and her to the Superbowl to win the proverbial ring. The QB, who is now traded to another team and is now playing for a coach much different than the one he had before. He has to live with the consequences that he put himself in because he got too cocky. So basically, the moral of the story is: Guys and women too, appreciate who you have in front of you, if you don't you lose that person, and every relationship afterwards is just not quite the same.

IT'S SHOWTIME FOLKS!
September 14, 2004

Every person's journey of life, whether it be professional or personal, will culminate at a certain point. Though one doesn't know where his or her journey will end, in a way, a person's journey never really ends. For it has just begun and those moments in a person's life can be considered events. Events in which everything he or she has worked hard for in the past number of years will come to fruition. An event in which one will consider themselves standing on their own proverbial stage.

As I said before, every ending has another beginning. One such event is when a person graduates from high school to college. If you think about it, each one of us had to prove ourselves and find out who we are. In a way we had to perform in front of our own personal and professional critics in which they will either give us good or bad reviews. As the saying goes, the show must go on and we oftentimes have to ignore the critics and give a performance of a lifetime that hopefully will get a standing ovation in the end.

Another event in a person's life is marriage or getting married. For its every guy's defining moment where the butterflies in the stomach start to stir. In a way, time will stand still as the question he asks will hopefully have the answer he wants. In any case, once the bonds of matrimony are said, both husband and wife will continue to perform for each other. Working hard and giving their all-in marriage. Hopefully, in this particular case, both won't end up having any encore performances if you know what I mean.

The biggest event in two people's lives is when one's child or children are born. For it can be a momentous occasion as a man gets to perform two roles, a father and a husband. It's scary fro any guy to know that life that he helped create is now being held in one's own arms. It can be somewhat compared to getting stage fright as one knows that a specific event, such as the birth of a child, is close at hand. It's just a matter of breathing slow deep breaths and hopefully he won't pass out in the end.

Professionally speaking, an event such as getting that dream job one has been waiting for will become or already has become a reality. For each one of us is climbing our own personal Mt. Everest, in which we hold on to the proverbial lifeline. In retrospect, our whole life is considered center stage. Though marriage isn't written in my program yet, an event somewhat similar is. When I do finally get called up to the big leagues so to speak, I will simply say this with a smile on my face, "It's showtime folks!"

PERSPECTIVE
September 18, 2004

When times of turmoil and devastation occur, a person has time to really think and be somewhat alone with one's thoughts under the star filled night sky. As the dust starts to settle so to speak, and a bit of normalcy starts to get back in the thick of things; you have a sense of peace and calm within yourself. If you think about it, many people will have to clean up the broken pieces of their lives and completely finish, but others the broken pieces are merely superficial. Though not shown on the outside, the wounds that a person can suffer can be mental and need time to be repaired. During these times of sadness, one can witness people coming together and helping people they hardly even know. Being a good Samaritan or fellow "brother" and "sister" and yet in these tough times one can be somewhat uplifted by certain situations that can put a smile on anybody's face.

One situation is that a person can find levity in times of the aftermath of a natural disaster. I once wrote that laughter is truly the best medicine and if one has his or her sense of humor then the times of hardship will be less stressful. My brother and I walked out to minimal devastation outside my house, and we turned around and looked up at the roof and our mailbox was on the roof. I actually turned to my brother and said, and I kid you not, "So I guess we're getting our mail on the roof now, huh?" A person just has to turn the most serious of situations into a situation where one can actually have fun and laugh about it and that is what myself, my brother, and a mutual friend of ours did and it kept our spirits up.

Another situation that can be uplifting is that a family can become even tighter than ever before. With technology such as television and the internet not working, talking with family keeps one's own sanity in check so to speak. In a way, they are the proverbial pick me up and/ or alternative to keep one's mind busy from the proverbial cabin fever syndrome. Plus, going back to school has been somewhat of therapy as well, keeping my mind focused, which hasn't been the case in the past. I had the opportunity to sleep under the stars with the weather being so cool and it was the best experience of my life. No television, just the radio and the stars is just a calming feeling one can feel. One can sometimes take family for granted until a natural disaster brings you together and tightens that loosening bond. Thinking about it, the technologies that we use on a daily basis are somewhat of a security blanket, but in a way, a person can adapt without it and I learned that in these past 7 days.

There comes a point where one is so used to the daily grind such as working in a youth center, that one is temporarily grinded so to speak, that it will make the people around you want to strangle you. My job has been considered a distraction of what has been going on in my life in which I can focus on the kid's problems rather than my own. During these 7 days my parents have witnessed how the kids that I have helped bring up for the past 8 years have had a positive effect on me even though I come home tired and somewhat miserable some of the time. BUT to tell you the truth, I am totally miserable without them and if that is what it is like to be a parent then I have come full circle. It took a Hurricane to open my eyes to that and that revelation has given me that fire back that I once had when I first started working at the Youth Center.

For the past several days, I have really had a lot of time to think and reflect about my life up to this point. There are certain aspects of my life which fear has held me back and that is about to change. In any case, I have been everywhere and met many people all the while leaving lasting impressions on other people that I cross paths with. Whether it be good or whether or be bad, I've made somewhat of an impression on somebody. This situation has shown me how I truly miss my online family as well as my working family. In any case, over the years, I've come across many people during my 27 years of life. I can safely say that I am somewhat of a keen observer of people and I'm a pretty good judge of character. It may be dead on, dead wrong, or somewhere in the middle. But, in retrospect, these past seven days have given me a better perspective on life than you will ever know...but who knows I may feel different next week.

GOT PROBLEMS?
September 26, 2004

Oftentimes a person faces problems in one's own life that can, in some way, pile up on you. It's somewhat like being at the beach and the crashing waves are continually beating down on you so much that one doesn't have time to catch his or her breath. If one doesn't come up for air pretty soon that person will metaphorically drown. In some aspects of life, each of us has been somewhat through the same problems but situations may differ. It's just a matter of having your sense of humor, if you have that, then all is well.

For those that are in pursuit of high learning and wanting to attain that proverbial holy grail called a degree. Yet, there are those tiny glitches that can become overwhelmingly big problems. Problems such as school bills which a person can feel may or may not be paid. Finding the time to do homework, all the while working a job is grueling both mentally and physically. It's the tiny things in the pursuit of higher learning in one's own particular field of interest that can cause problems to the point of giving up.

Another instance is in one's own workplace and the people you work with. It can sometimes feel that when a person immediately enters his or her workplace, the problems just start to mount. It always begins with one's own boss as he or she starts to pile paperwork after paperwork one one's desk. Then there are your co-workers that can get on your nerves and just want to beat the crap out of them. If compared to, it would be somewhat like the movie Office Space, a movie I highly recommend for your viewing pleasure.

One's own love life can suffer problems as a person finds that his or her potential and/or significant other isn't on the same page as you so to speak. There is a saying that goes that the fires that two people once shared are slowly burning out and inevitably one or the other must have that "we gotta talk speech" which is never a really good thing. Every person has problems just finding that one person that he or she can click with. Each of us will meet that one person eventually, we just have to be patient.

In the end, the problems we face along the path of life that each of us are on will come and they will go. One's own family life can be added to the list as well. Let me ask you this, are you the type of person who gives up too easily once those problems pile up or do you tackle them head on? Each of us will suffer problems that will be a thorn in our side, but those thorns can be cut off. In retrospect, every person thinks that they've got problems, but there are those that have much bigger problems than we do, just turn on the news.

CHOICES
September 28, 2004

As an American citizen of the United States of America, one of the greatest freedoms we have is the freedom of choice. Every day, each of us makes choices, whether it be bad, good, small, big, or choices that sometimes don't make any sense at all. Let me ask you this question, have you ever wondered what would have happened if you had made or never made that seemingly all-important choice that somewhat affected your life personally and/or professionally? Regrets or not, it was a choice each of us made.

One of the choices a person can make in life is choosing the friends one wants to hang around with. We've all had friends in our lives that have come and gone, but it's that person's choice to continue that friendship when one leaves. One could call that loyalty, for the bonds of friendship extend beyond state lines as well as the globe. A person has the choice to keep in contact with that person or persons either by email and/or telephone/cell phone. In any case, it's a matter of choice who you feel comfortable hanging with.

Another choice that a person can decide on is saving one's self for marriage. It's an all-important choice that most men and women choose for themselves to wait till he or meets, falls in love, and then marries that one special person. Oftentimes, one can be ridiculed, but yet that decision can be respected by his or her peers. For most people, waiting till marriage is considered to be a romantic display of affection. Though it's a tough choice for any person to make, one's first time with the one you truly love will be that much more special.

One of THE most important choices that a person will make is choosing the next President of the United States. Not only do we have the choice to choose a President, but we also have the choice and right to voice our opinions. For our opinions can swing the tide of who gets into office and who is inevitably kicked out. Myself being from Florida, I hope we don't screw this up again, if we do, our state motto should be changed from Florida: "The Sunshine State" to Florida:" If You Think Hurricanes Mess Things Up, Wait Till You See Us Vote.

In retrospect, the choices that each of us have made over the years can teach us many things. Things which can be considered life lessons, and one of those life lessons is who each of us is as a person. Let me ask you this question, when the choices you made in life didn't pan out, did you learn from the consequences afterwards? I end this thought with a quote by one of the greatest football coaches John Wooden: ~There is a choice that you make in everything you do, and you must always keep in mind, the choices you make, make you.~

TO BUILD A DREAM ON
September 30, 2004

In the song, As Time Goes By, from the movie Casablanca, there is a line that says, ~You must remember this, a kiss is just a kiss.~ Let me ask you this question, is a kiss just a kiss, or is there something much deeper and much more meaningful to it? For it's a special moment that two people share and everything that surrounds you and that particular person fades into the background. If you think about it, a kiss is the most personal form of affection that can never be taken back.

Someone once said, a kiss is something you cannot give without taking and cannot take without giving. Do you think that is true because as the saying goes, it takes two to tango. Women, more so than men, know if there is truly a connection just by a kiss. As said before, it's a very personal sign of affection and that brief moment of vulnerability, two people share a piece of themselves with each other in heart and soul. A special moment that can be considered tender, passionate, and/or romantic.

A kiss can also have a calming effect on a person that is completely stressed out. A woman, more so than a guy, has that power to ease that sort of tension which could be argued over, but not at this moment. In any case, when you kiss someone, all the worries that he or she has seemingly have gone away. A person can somewhat forget what one was stressed about. In a way, a kiss is like a stress reliever that is more potent than headache medicine that is sold and/or prescribed by a doctor.

People tend to remember, if they can, their first kiss and how it felt with that boy or girl back in the day. Answer this question, was the experience worth it or was it that you would rather forget and have that proverbial do-over so to speak. Scary, exciting, new, enjoyable, unforgettable are just some of the descriptions of one's first kiss that you do that another person may or may not have felt. It's just all in how one looks at that particular situation. if the mood, time, and or setting was just right.

Each one of us has dreamed/imagined kissing a certain celebrity, sports star, or that one special person in life. Sometimes one's imagination can get the better of him or her when one does finally give or receive that kiss. One's expectations can be somewhat disappointing, for it was not all that one expected. Yet, a simple kiss can be considered one of the greatest and most personal gifts that can be given from the heart. In retrospect, every person wants a kiss to build a dream on; a dream that nobody wants ever to be woken up from.

JUST AN OBSERVATION
October 1, 2004

Have you ever just sat back and observed people, not in a creepy, stalking sort of way, but in a sort of way where one tries to figure out the type of person certain people are? It can be somewhat interesting just sitting back and learning the different sides and personalities of people that one knows or even doesn't know. In a way, a person can unofficially become a profiler and try to figure out what makes people tick by certain aspects of their life and the way one carries himself or herself.

It has been said that the eyes are the windows to the soul. A person can definitely tell if the person one is talking to is telling the truth, lying, or whether or not he or she really has feelings for that particular person. One who is actively thinking about certain things tends to look to the right. One that is actively looking to the left is basically creating or inventing. Consciously or subconsciously, every person does it and a keen observer can pick up on these things.

A person's body language can also tell a lot about a person as well. The way a person walks can oftentimes tell if one is either laid back or uptight...most of the time. My own brother is a combination of but leans more towards being uptight. If you ever see him walking, he walks like he is getting ready for a fight. Just preparing for any possibility of a throw down that might or might not happen. It's somewhat hilarious when it is pointed out to friends that haven't noticed and they get a kick out of it.

One could also get a feel, so to speak, about a person simply by talking with people. In a sub-conscious or even conscious level, one can get bits and pieces of information about a person that can describe a person without even knowing it. It's just a matter of picking up certain details and REALLY listening to his or her conversation. By doing that, one can be somewhat surprised at either how little or how much one knows about a particular person or person's just by a simple conversation.

In retrospect, every person has the innate ability to somewhat describe the people around him or her. One can meet so many people that oftentimes it can be hard to really figure them out. Yet, every person has made a lasting impression on people that has absolutely intrigued them. For that innate curiosity will make one want to find out more about him or her. In the end, when it is all said and done, all that I have said to you all today in this thought, is merely just an observation.

WINDOWS TO THE SOUL
October 3, 2004

Ralph Waldo Emerson once said, ~A person's eyes can threaten like a loaded and leveled gun. or can insult like hisses or kicking; or it's altered mood, by beams of kindness. It can make the heart dance for joy. One of the most wonderful things in nature is glancing into someone's eyes, it transcends speech, it is the bodily symbol of identity.~ If you think about it, Emerson describes the eyes of a woman and how exotic and powerful they are, but yet it can burn a hole in any person without warning.

In any case, have you ever noticed or at least walked by two people sitting across from each other and they are not saying a word. All those two are doing is basically looking into each other's eyes and letting their facial expressions do the talking. It's somewhat comical just observing that form of affection because one can't help but look. Let me ask you this question and to be honest, have you ever been in that particular situation where it can oftentimes be seen during precious moments such as Valentine's Day.

Someone once said, ~Look into my eyes and hear what I am saying, for my eyes speak louder than my voice ever will. Looking into someone's eyes, all forms of emotion can be expressed without even saying anything such as love, longing, anger, fear, confusion, deep thought, and a plethora of other emotions that reveal things about a person just by his or her eyes. A person can be "blind" when the eyes of interest are focused on him or her and it can simply take a slap in the back of the head to open them up and see clearly.

The question can be asked when you look into the eyes of someone you just met, can you instantly see a future with that person? It's really an unknown, but every situation is different for every person. It may take several gazes to get a better focus of who one is interested in. In some cases, one can look into the eyes of that particular person and see that missing piece of one's puzzle. For nobody wants to close their eyes for fear that he or she will vanish away, and that particular person was merely a mirage.

In retrospect, the true beauty of a woman is not in the clothes that she wears, in the body that she tries to build, or the way she tries to fix her hair. Inevitably, a woman's beauty can be seen from within her eyes because it can be considered a doorway to her heart, a place where love resides. It's not the superficial beauty but rather beauty reflected in her soul. In the end, the passion she shows will keep growing as time goes by and is shown with her eyes which are considered to be windows to the soul.

MORE THAN JUST WORDS
October 5, 2004

In some way, our lives can be somewhat compared to a Hollywood movie that is in post-production. If you think about it, each of us is a writer, director, and lead actor/actress of our proverbial script of life. No matter how embarrassing, corny, frustrating, weird, strange, and/or stupid one's own life can be, we live it day by day. One must accept the responsibility given to us because as the head writer, we are in control of what is written or not being written in the movie that we call our life.

We've all at some point wanted to rewrite certain situations or aspects of our life that were considered unmemorable and never wanted to be relived again. If each of us had the ability to go back in time, we simply would yell "CUT" and talk to ourselves about what we would do differently in that particular situation. One could only dream of that happening, but one just has to realize that the past pages of one's script have already been written and there is no point in trying to rewrite it over again.

Let me ask you this question, if you had the choice to pick a celebrity to play you who would be that one person? For we want that one person who is believable and convincing enough that he or she is each of us and conveys the words written on each page. In some ways, each of us wants to choose that particular actor or actress that best suits our own personality. In some aspect, the decision you make as a director/writer can determine if you have an academy award winning script or one that never sees the light of day.

As each of our scripts are still being written, a person will meet one's potential leading man or leading lady to fill that all important starring role opposite ourselves. If you think about it, each of us is still waiting for that position to be filled. Yet, as each of us meet potential leads to co-star will us, chemistry can oftentimes play a big part. It's that chemistry that can determine whether or not one wants to continue a partnership of sorts, which in the long run, may become permanent as time goes by.

In the whole scheme of things, our lives would be a whole lot simpler if we could continually yell, cut at any time and fix problems with just a simple stroke of a keyboard, pen, or pencil. For good memories would be kept in and out with the bad memories. In one's own mind it would work, but in reality, we have to look forward and keep writing our own personal story. In the end, what's written down on the pages of life are more than just words, they're our past, present, and future that each of us personally lived through or will through.

LIKE RIDING A BIKE
October 7, 2004

William Golding once said, ~The journey of life is like a man riding a bicycle. We know he got on the bicycle and started to move. We know that at some point he will stop and get off. We know that if he stops moving and does not get off, he will fall off.~ If you think about it, what he said can parallel the growth of a person from adolescence to one's latter years of life. In a way, when each of us is born into the world, immediately the training wheels are put on to protect us from the scrapes and bruises we will suffer.

Inevitably, those training will come off as the adolescent becomes a teenager and comes into his or her own way of dealing with the pressures of life. As teenagers, it can be a little scary as one is somewhat set free of the restrictions that hold on back from taking all out risks. Speed is oftentimes a common denominator as one wants to feel the rush of adrenaline as he or she experiences life, but under the watchful eye of one's parents. It's a matter of patience as one's inner daredevil wants to emerge so badly.

As we reach adulthood one starts to learn the tricks of the trades and begins to ride the road of life as if he or she were in the X-games. As said before, one's inner daredevil will begin to emerge and try stunts that no normal person would dare try, just say been there, done that. A person's ego can sometimes get the better of him or her as he or she tries to impress or show off to one's peers or that guy or girl. One will suffer broken bones that will leave scars but that's the price one pays for the thrills of excitement.

For each of us will reach or already have reached the latter days of life; one's ability to stay balanced on the bike of life is becoming harder as time goes by. Each of us knows that if we stop, we will fall and like it has been said so many times before, we've fallen, and we can't get up. One will have the mindset that we're not young as we used to be because the broken bones don't heal as quickly, and we can't keep pace with the younger generation. For one day, we're going to get off that bike and not be able to get back on ever again.

Lance Armstrong spent much of his life on a bike and made a successful career out of it winning the Tour De France 6 times. Through those grueling trials he never gave up the up-hill battle, for he kept pedaling to the finish line. In retrospect, for me personally, it's gonna be an adjustment getting back into the groove of working at the Youth Center after being out of the game for about a month due to Hurricane Ivan. BUT as the saying goes, it's like riding a bike, one's own instincts will kick back in as you get on that proverbial saddle again.

THE BIGGEST IMPRESSION
October 8, 2004

As it has been said so many times before, life can be considered a beach, for the footprints left behind can leave either temporary or lasting impressions. If you think about it, potential and/or significant relationships can fit into this particular subject. Let me ask you this question, how have you ever met anyone that totally made, if any, an impression on you? If he or she did, how long did it last? In a way, it's the things that a person doesn't do that can leave an impression on a person and can bring two people together.

One of those things that a person doesn't do that can make an impression is not forgetting to notice the little things that can sometimes seem insignificant. Such little things as a noticing a haircut, mainly for a woman, and giving a compliment that brings a smile to her face that is considered the best payment a guy can receive. It can also be extended to trying to make her laugh when she feels that life has kicked her to the curb. Leaving those seemingly small impressions of kindness that will never be forgotten as time goes by.

In some aspect, what one doesn't do is in the quality of one's character that makes an impression on a person. One such character quality is never treating a woman with disrespect, for they should be treated with the respect and dignity that they deserve. It's been said that chivalry is dead, which in my opinion, it's just hibernating and waiting for that proverbial wake up call to be sounded. Though rarely seen, but still being practiced it's another seemingly small impression that is left will be remembered as well.

Taking someone for granted is the one thing that a person doesn't do, whether it be a man or a woman. There have been many failed relationships where a guy or girl couldn't hold on to that person because one can become literally stupid for not cherishing what he or she has in front of him or her. Did you or have you known anyone in this particular situation or have you yourself been in this situation? It's just a matter of paying attention on a semi-constant basis which will leave a lasting impression on that guy or girl.

If you think about it, a person can make so many impressions on the sandy beaches of our life, that he or she doesn't realize how significant those impressions are. Each of us met strangers that later down the road became friends, boyfriends, girlfriends, husbands and/or wives and it's one's first impressions that made all the difference. In retrospect, each of us will meet that one person who ultimately will leave the biggest impression in our lives and that big impression will be made and felt in one's own heart.

TIME
October 11, 2004

You have to admit, we as human beings are always watching the clock eagerly awaiting time to either begin or end. One can't really help it because the fact is our lives are based on a planned schedule that can oftentimes not go the way we want. In a way, each of us wants every second that passes by to count, because a person doesn't want to miss anything going on in his or her life. Inevitably, it's a little thing such as time that is considered to be the most precious commodity one never wants to waste when it pertains to a potential and/or significant relationship.

Let me ask you this question, have you ever been in a situation where time just stood still, in a manner of speaking, when that certain guy or girl indirectly entered one's life? It can be somewhat compared to a Hollywood movie where the "scenes" in one's life can play out in slow motion. It's a moment where he or she can literally hear the proverbial ticking of one's own heart as it beats away. In a way, those beats can represent a countdown in which one's heart may burst, not in a heart attack/cardiac arrest sort of way, but in a love at first sight way.

When one does finally establish a relationship of some kind with that particular person, each no longer considers time as a factor. Think about it, when you are with someone you truly care about or love, time can just literally fly by. The moments one spends with that particular person can seem like eternity and the hands of time have just stopped for you two. Every person has been in this situation where it seems there will always be a proverbial time limit set, and if one doesn't use the time he or she has to one's advantage, then one will hear those two dreaded words, "Times Up!"

It has been said that getting together is the hard part, but breaking up is the easiest thing to do. Sometimes in life, we simply don't understand why particular situations happen such as breaking up with someone. In any case, both the guy and girl have all the time in the world to figure out what went wrong in a seemingly tight relationship only to crumble right in front of them. Countless tears will eventually be shed and it's at that point one will hear ticking. Not the ticking of one's own heartbeat, but the ticking of the clock as it metaphorically slaps you in the face as time passes slowly by.

Someone once said, ~Time is a companion that goes with us on a journey. It reminds us to cherish each moment, because it will never come again. What we leave behind is not as important as how we lived.~ In a way, that is true, but when you truly care about or love someone, time is inconsequential and every moment can feel like an eternity, a feeling that one doesn't want to go away. I end this thought by saying, it takes seconds to spot someone, minutes to have a crush on someone, hours to like someone, days to love someone, but in the end, it takes a lifetime to forget someone.

THE SECRET
October 12, 2004

Oftentimes a person can become jaded in his or her profession and/or trade as time goes by. One will tend to lose the desire and focus at one's particular job due to small or big things in his or her workplace. For a person, the cynical side will gradually emerge and take one's personality in a totally different direction. In a way, that particular person will slowly go "blind" as one's cynical side takes over and completely covers up his or her vision. If you think about it, every person has traveled down that path before but never really stayed that long enough to become that person you never wanted to be.

When it comes to one's profession, there will be politics involved that will, in some way, rear it's ugly head. One such aspect is in the working relationship between employees and/or bosses/supervisors. Over a period of time, one can witness the politics start to develop as certain cliques or groups form which can divide a so called cohesive unit. These factions can have an all out battle of words John McEnroe style, in which people start to talk behind each other's back. Inevitably, it can get to the point of becoming a proverbial tennis match of he said, she said, trading shot after shot.

There will always be promises made concerning changes made in different areas in one's job. But as the saying goes, actions speak louder than words. For the veterans that have been there the longest constantly hear time and time again that things will change but they never do. For those that are rookies, they hold on to that sense of hope but for those that have been there before knowing only to believe when he or she sees it. In any case, a person can be a witness to so many broken promises that anything that seems too good to be true is often considered an April Fool's joke.

The basis of a strong cohesive workplace is measure but it's strong leadership. If you have strong leadership plus strong employee commitment it equals a better working atmosphere. Let me ask you this question, have you ever worked or been in a place that defined both strong leadership and employee commitment? One can sometimes feel like Indiana Jones as he or she is looking for the proverbial holy grail. One just has to have hope because even though it is hard to find, one's holy grail is out there, you just have to look hard.

In retrospect, in life there are times where each of us is fed up and has had enough. About two weeks before Hurricane Ivan was going to hit the Panhandle, I seriously contemplated quitting the Youth Center because of the politics and basically just feeling burned out. It took a Hurricane to open my eyes and it gave me three reasons to not quit. Reason one is I wanted to see my friends again and reason two is personal and basically coincides with reason three which I missed "my kids." In the end, the secret for longevity in any profession is that you got to love what you do, if you don't then you have to move on.

STYLIN' AND PROFILIN'
October 13, 2004

It's been said that one of the keys for being a success in life and/or business is how one dresses. Let me ask you this question, do the clothes that a person wears define him or her or is it the other way around? A man that is wearing an expensive suit, tie, and shoes will undoubtedly look much better than a man that is merely wearing normal everyday clothing such as a shirt, hat, jeans, and a pair of sneakers. This can also to females as well. But there is a saying that goes that clothes don't necessarily make a person, it's the person wearing it who brings confidence and a little ego as well.

I know I'm getting old when I start sentences with kids today and I'm only 27. Well, kids today are more fashion conscious and want to pay more for the expensive name brands than the generic brands. Such name brands are Sean John, Tommy Hilfiger, Fubu, Rocawear, and the list goes on and on. My generation wasn't really concerned with fashion, we wore what we felt was comfortable and the only name brands that had our attention were the type of shoes such as Nike, Reebok, Adidas, Converse, and the list goes on and on. The 80's, the era of simplicity and I lived through it back in the day.

In my era of simplicity, ripped jeans, pegged pants, no fear t-shirts, and fanny packs were all the rage. It wasn't so much the name brand but how one looked in the clothes that he or she wore in the 80's and spilling over into the early 90's. Let me tell you something, there are basically two reasons why I stopped pegging my pants in the early 90's because #1 it was too much of a hassle to continually fold them and #2 It started to cut off blood flow to my feet. When I look back at my middle school days, I actually look like a complete dork and ask myself this one simple question...WHY?

In some aspect, it's the trends that seem hip and trendy back then that make people cringe when looking at old pictures of themselves and ask why someone didn't stop us. As I'm getting older, I have to realize that I'm becoming an old fogey searching for comfortability and dependability in pants and in shoes rather than style and flash. I used to buy shoes for the expressed purpose of looking good in them, now I buy shoes for the expressed purpose of finding those gel souls just to be comfortable. One just has to choose either being comfortable or uncomfortable just for the sake of looking good.

In retrospect, a person can be judged by how one dresses, but sometimes the way one dresses can mislead others into thinking who he or she really is. It's been said that you should never judge a book by its cover, because what is shown on the outside is quite different when one opens the book and finds much more than he or she bargained for. If you think about it, clothing can show how confident you are, how trustworthy you are, how much potential you have, and how much respect should be given to you. In the end, if you are stylin' and profilin' you will be able to go places in life you never expected to go.

SPEECHLESS
October 13, 2004

We all will meet or already have met that one person in each of our lives that will absolutely make us nervous and tongue-tied. It's like having your brain going on temporary vacation and the captain isn't manning the proverbial command center that is our head. One will just stand there absolutely dumb founded trying to think of what to say, all the while hoping you don't act like a complete moron. Every person has been in this situation, including myself, when you are interested in a particular person who just absolutely takes your breath away every time you see or around him or her for any given time.

Let me ask you this question, have you ever been standing or sitting next to the person you are truly interested in and wanted to say to that person how you really feel but something stopped you or decided not to? We can sometimes second guess ourselves because one never knows how he or she may react or may not react at all. One has to take into consideration that a person may not feel the same as you or preferably see you as just a friend. One can also have that brother/sister label placed on you which can really sting. It can really play with a person's mind so much that one can start to talk to himself or herself out loud, which can be somewhat embarrassing.

There will be times where one can get bits and pieces to figure out if there is any interest at all from that particular person. It can sometimes be frustrating to distinguish interest because one can receive mixed signals that can totally confuse a person to the point of mouthing words, saying absolutely nothing at all, and throwing one's hands in the air. I've come to the point where I stopped trying to figure women out, it's absolutely pointless. One can continue to try to find those answers to the point where he or she completely takes over one's mindset. A mindset that was completely within all its faculties until he or she showed up unexpectedly and without warning.

For a person like myself, it's hard for me to express vocally how I truly feel about that girl I'm interested in. It's hard for me to go up to her and actually tell her that she is the most beautiful person I have ever come across. Each time I see you, there is always a smile on my face and when I have the opportunity to tell you how I feel, I stop and walk away. I am not the proverbial player or ladies' man that will give you lines to get your interest and/or attention. In any case, I just bare my heart and soul in how I feel writing and It's part of who I am. I can't change that and that is why I have been truly in love once in my life, and had that love reciprocated back 100%

In life we can regret the words that are said, as well as the words not said from our own mouth. Each of us are capable of hiding our feelings for that particular person, but for how long? Someone once said, a person that can touch your soul can, in some way, look past the superficial, a person who is able to tickle your funny bone, and a person who is able to render you not able to form words just because of his or her mere presence, beauty, and overall character as an individual. In the end, each of us will come to a point where we can't even form words and will leave you absolutely speechless.

LAYERS
October 14, 2004

In some aspect, we all have layers which show sides of us which people either see or don't see. These layers each of us have can be compared to an onion. For if a person starts to peel away each layer, one will discover sides of him or her that one never new existed. We've all had at one point a preconceived notion about a person, but once you peel away the superficial covering, one can get a better understanding of who that person is on a deep, personal and emotional level. A level where one can either be friends, despise him or her even more, or completely fall in love with that person.

Personally speaking, the 3 layers which if you peel away little by little, you can get a better understanding of who I am as a person. If you ever meet me in person, you will be introduced to the first layer which will show my quiet, serious, artistic, and somewhat shy side. It takes a while for me to warm up and get to know people, for the simple reason that I am a cautious person. I have that mentality that if I don't know you, I don't trust you and you have to earn my trust. But once he or she peels away that somewhat rough covering, you will find a layer that people will enjoy and grow fond of.

My second layer, my laid-back side, is what people start to see as I gradually feel comfortable around people that I get to know, plus more of my personality starts to show. One will get to see my goofy side in which my more sarcastic and cynical side, add that with my corny sense of humor plus my deep philosophical way of thinking, you got a guy who you can call a friend. A friend that will be there for you to listen, give advice, and talk to when you need some help. But be fair warned, I am somewhat of a practical joker and even though you are my friend you won't be safe, so watch your back.

My third and last layer is a layer that I rarely ever show or share with people that have gotten to know me and that is my emotional/sentimental side. I'm the type of person that has no problem saying how I feel in writing, but when it comes to trying to say it to a girl that I'm interested in, the words can't seem to come out. To be perfectly honest, it's somewhat of a rarity for me to share my feelings with someone that I like and have those feelings returned back, which has happened to me on several different occasions. Hey, I'm just a regular guy living a simplistic but yet complicated life, which is what everybody else is probably living as well.

Let me ask you this question, have you ever tried to figure someone out only to give up on that particular venture because you got nowhere or simply were frustrated trying? In any case, I don't claim to know everything about love, life, relationships and women, but I basically am a person who listens, learns, steps back to get/see the bigger picture and initially come up with these Yoda-isms that I send/write on a semi-daily basis. In retrospect, if you continually peel away layer after layer of a person, one will find his or her heart. A heart that has loved, that has hurt, and has never quit when faced with problems and obstacles that he or she has overcome. In the end, I ask you this question, what are your 3 layers?

THE GREATEST DAYS
October 15, 2004

Throughout a person's life, he or she has been told what to do on a semi-daily basis as kids, as adults, and even as one reaches the latter days of one's existence. One has to accept the fact that he or she will encounter people who have either complete or slight authority over each of us. Though we may not like it, one just has to grin and bear it, knowing that on the inside we're holding back from what we really want to say to that person. At that point, one's proverbial fuse will be lit, but it's just a matter of cutting off that fuse before it ignites one's internal explosive mechanism that no one wants to set off.

As kids, the two most important people that have complete authority over you, well until you reach the age of 18 or 21, are one's parents. For they have devoted their lives to continually preaching to us, but sometimes we tend to not listen or choose not to listen to what they have to say, a tactic that has been done and absolutely perfected by most of us back in the day. In some aspect, each of us were mini-James Deans and considered ourselves rebels but with cause. Let me ask you this question, how far did you stretch the limits of your parents' authority back then and was it well worth it in the end?

The adult years will reveal that authority figures such as professors and bosses will be constantly critiquing one's work and how he or she should be doing his or her job. Every college student has been in a situation where you worked hard on a research paper only to get it back and receive a grade that he or she thought deserved to be higher. It's that way with one's working relationship with one's boss as he or she deserves compensation for the work that his or her boss takes credit for. It's that particular power of authority that can make a person increasingly bitter and not fun to be around.

In the latter days of a person's life, he or she obtains wisdom and knowledge in which they are considered authority figures. As it has been said, one should always respect one's elders because they have the right to say they've been there and done that. It's really amazing what stories one's own grandparents will share if you spend quality time with them. They can create a mental picture in one's own mind that is thought provoking and mesmerizing. Undoubtedly, the respect given to one's elders who have gone through tough situations can be taught and passed to the younger generation.

In retrospect, there will always be authority figures looking over our shoulders and telling us what to do and not to do. But it all comes down to a person's attitude and how one cares for himself or herself when confronted with authority. Each of us have pushed the limits of authority as a kid, stepping up to authority as an adult, and are or will become an authority figure through life experience as one reaches or has reached his or her latter years. In the end, the greatest days of a person's life is when he or she doesn't focus on authority but focuses on living each day to the fullest and simply having fun doing it.

TO WHOM IT MAY CONCERN
October 16, 2004

Every person at some point in his or her life has had a secret admirer or was the secret admirer, who stood back in the shadows leaving a letter or letters that came straight from one's own heart. About 2 months ago, a friend of mine came over to my house and asked me to help him write a letter to a girl that he had feelings for, but here's the kicker: we were friends with her. In some way, I felt like Steve Martin in the movie Roxanne, helping the guy get the girl. In some aspect, I put myself in his shoes and basically wrote what I would say if it were me and this is what I basically wrote for him.

~It's not often that a woman like you can make me absolutely speechless every time I see you. My heart is heavy for the simple reason that you touched it and brought it to life beating harder and much faster. You simply take my breath away and it's not because of your physical beauty but rather the beauty that you don't show that you have inside of you. For those unknown qualities that you may not see in yourself can be seen in my eyes, which puts a smile on my face. There are times where I just wanted to walk up to you and tell you how I felt but I felt it wasn't the right time.

For the light in your eyes shine brightly whenever I look at you and wonder if they will ever burn and shine brightly for me? If you, at some point, ever look into my eyes, you will see all the feelings and emotions that I carry for you without even saying a single word. What I feel for you can't be expressed in mere words and if given the chance I hope to prove my worth to you. You have been a person that I consider a friend but right now, I am taking this leap of faith that I hopefully won't fall hard from. It's basically the risks one takes with one's own heart that make great story book endings.

I am considered a gambler of sorts but I'm not gambling with money. You see I'm gambling with something that means more than any amount of money placed in front of me and that is my own heart. It is my heart that I am metaphorically placing on the table and win or lose I not only took a chance, but I have risked everything to tell you how I feel. For I have already shown my hand to you and all there is for me to do is wait to see how you will respond. In the back of my mind, I know you may not feel the same way I do and that is understandable, but at least you know how I feel, and I have meant every word that I said to you in this letter.

I may or may not be the guy that you want in the end but what matters to me is you being happy. I have always been up front with you in every aspect except when it comes to you. I'm a guy that is truthful and honest when it comes to the heart and have come to a crossroad in my life where I stood in front of two paths. I chose the path that leads to you and not the path that leads away from you. In the end, I don't regret what I said to you because they come from deep within my heart and soul.~ When I gave him the letter, he put it in an envelope and simply wrote these 5 words on it: To Whom It May Concern.

KEEP THE FAITH
October 17, 2004

Percy Bysshe Shelly once said, ~If we reason, we would be understood; if we imagine, we would that the airy children of our brain were born anew within another's, if we feel, we would that another's nerves should vibrate to our own, that the beams of their eyes should kindle at once and mix and melt into our own, that lips of motionless ice should not reply to lips quivering and burning with the heart's bent blood. This is Love~ Every person has been or is in love with someone and there is one day out of the year that he or she can express one's love for that particular person and it is Valentine's Day.

In some aspect, it's a "holiday" that can either bring a good day or a bad day. Think about it, it's only one day out of the year a person, who is single, can get very depressed and somewhat bitter. Thoughts of wonder begin to creep into one's mind as he or she contemplates whether "the one" will step into our lives. For most people, they have already found the man or woman of their dreams. But for some, guys are trying to find the foot that fits the proverbial glass slipper and ladies are still waiting for their prince charming to sweep them off their feet and ride off into the sunset.

As with Valentine's Day, gifts are always going to be a factor, because the gifts one chooses can be a struggle to either find or make. It can get to the point where one gives up and simply goes with the proverbial standby which is usually flowers and chocolate. BUT if one is creative, he or she can express appreciation in a totally inventive, meaningful and thoughtful way like writing this thought for instance. I'm not the type of person who rarely ever reveals his sentimental side, but when occasions such as Valentine's Day rolls around, I can make an exception.

John Alexander Thom said, ~Human affection is like an island of warmth in a sea of indifference, like a campfire in a wintering wilderness. Valentine's Day is simply an occasion set aside for the celebration of that precious affection. We who feel the affection make a move in midwinter to convey some of that warmth; we send a card, write a note, telegraph some flowers, or make a long-distance phone call. It takes off the chill; it gives us a steppingstone to spring.~ A person just has to keep one's heart open and focus on the positive, because one day Cupid will be on target for each of us.

In retrospect, a person doesn't have to spend a lot of money on gifts, cards, stuffed bears, or flowers. If a person creates something that comes straight from the heart it truly is the most special gift one can receive. Thinking about it, a simple smile is considered the greatest gift a person can be given back for giving appreciation to those that are in one's life professionally and personally as well. In the end, I say this to each of you: may the love you have already found last forever; but the love that is so elusive to you, will be found one day, just keep the faith.

LIVE IN THE MOMENT
October 18, 2004

Have you ever been in a situation where a certain moment in your life somewhat overwhelmed you? Of course, everybody has, and it will sometimes cause a person to either freak out, hyperventilate, or babble uncontrollably. For the only way to stop him or her was to either throw water on that person or slap him or her in the face to bring that person back to their sanity. If you think about it, each and every person has a different reaction when a particular moment in one's life stands out than the rest. It's that particular moment that can have a person feel absolutely at ease, all the while, doing the proverbial dance of joy on the inside.

One such particular moment is giving or receiving a kiss that one has been wanting to give to or receive from that one particular person. In some aspect, he or she can have a cool, calm demeanor, but on the inside that person is doing gymnastic type flips. As I once said, in a past thought, a kiss is the most personal form of affection that one person can give another. For when one shares a piece of himself or herself with that person, there is a sense of vulnerability where both people let their guard down. However, once that brief moment of bliss, which seems to last a lifetime, is over he or she can continually repeat it over and over in one's own mind.

A simple embrace from a child, friend, girlfriend/boyfriend. a wife, and/or husband can make a person feel well protected especially for a woman. For in that instance, when she is embraced with open arms all her problems can seem insignificant. For when she is in that embrace, she can feel that particular person's warm touch as he holds that woman tightly but gently in his arms. Each and every woman wants a guy that is able to hold her attention and if he does, then she will never let him go and vice versa. Let me ask you this question, who was the last person that embraced you and is that person an important part of your life and in your own heart?

There is something to be said when two people share a precious moment while dancing cheek to cheek on the dance floor. For both the man and woman, when hand in hand can feel each other's touch as well as each other's heartbeats and both can oftentimes lose themselves in the moment. In some ways, both people can feel like they have reached the highest peak of the mountain when two people have each other's arms around one another. Ultimately, one can have that mentality that the happiness that a person seeks can be found in his or her dancing partner and it can absolutely feel like Heaven.

Think about this, we all will encounter moments in our lives that will truly be memorable. It's those potential memorable moments that will live on in one's own heart, mind and soul which when he or she looks back will put a smile on one's face. It's a moment that a person can't shake and it will never be forgotten. If it were a possibility, those special moments in one's life that he or she will go through, would be placed in a time capsule and stored aways for years to come. In the end, when it comes to precious moments such as a kiss, an embrace, or a dance between two people, a person simply has to close his or her eyes, and just live in the moment.

THE CODE
October 18, 2004

One of the definitions for the word chivalry is the qualities idealized by knighthood, such as bravery, courtesy, honor, and gallantry towards women. It was and still is a basic code of ethics that would bring love, glory, and respect to any lady or one particular lady. In the times of kings and knights, women were treated with honor, respect, and absolute reverence. If you think about it, it's somewhat rare these days for the code of chivalry to be seen and used in the presence of a lady. But the question can be asked, is chivalry dead or is it merely in hibernation waiting for that proverbial wake up call to sound?

In my own thinking, chivalry among certain men is not dead, nor has lost its meaning for guys that believe that being a gentleman is still the way to go. One aspect of the code is holding the door open for a lady, regardless of whether or not a woman has any boxes, bags, and/or packages that she is carrying. Did you know that in some cultures a guy enters the door first rather than the ladder, for the simple reason that if something were to happen when entering into or out of the building, he would be the first to get struck. It's all about honor as the "knight" protects his lady fare which also includes opening the car door as well

The second aspect of the code of chivalry is giving absolute respect to a lady even though there are time when she may not deserve it. Working with mostly women for the past 8 years and being only 1 of 2 guys, has given me appreciation of how important women are. Think about this, if there weren't women around, there would be millions of lost guys driving around who wouldn't stop and ask for directions, I know I would be one of them. In any case, a man should never hit a lady as well which shows complete disrespect and uncalled for. For if a man does continually hitz a lady, every woman in the world has the obligation to kick the crap out of him, the line starts behind me.

The third and final code is showing reverence to a woman. It's the little things in life and love that a guy notices that women remember for years to come. Women have a memory like an elephant, they never forget, unlike guys who can't remember what they just did an hour ago. Little things such as noticing a haircut or hairstyle that she spent hours having done. Another little this is complimenting her on how beautiful she looks. It will not only bring a smile to her face, but it will also bring a smile to a guy's face as well. It's the insignificant little things that man notices that can make a potential and/or significant relationship grow.

In the whole scheme of things, it's the lessons, values, morals, and ethics that my father taught me about honor, respect, and showing reverence to a woman that will be taught to my son one day. It's the basic principles that have been instilled in me and it helps to have a father that I still can go to and ask for advice from time to time. For if I ever break that code, I will not see the light of day, plus he's been in the military and trained with the Navy Seals, so he knows things. In the end, if a guy keeps the code close, and uses it then life, love, and relationships would be a whole lot simpler and less complicated.

THE RIGHT DECISIONS
October 20, 2004

It's a funny thing how certain people make certain kinds of decisions in one's own life. Let me ask you this question, what was the most important decision that you ever had to make in your life and once you made it, did you have any regrets or was it the best one you ever made? In some aspect, we've all come to that proverbial crossroads where each of us stands in front of two paths, but in some cases, there are more than two paths to choose from. One can sometimes feel like standing in the middle of a balance weighing his or her options for the best decision to make. If you think about it, there are several ways a person makes that particular decision in one's own journey through life.

One such way in one's decision-making process is the going by his or her gut, in which a person basically has a particular feeling and either goes with it or doesn't go with it. Every person has been in a situation where you have this funny feeling in the pit of your stomach that something might happen. It's one's own instincts on high alert so to speak and the decision one makes next determines an outcome that may or may not happen. Each one of us at some point, based a decision on a gut reaction whether or not it was the right one to make, it was your call. It's just a matter of listening to yourself and it also helps to have a close friend that you truly trust by your side.

The spontaneous decision is one that a person goes on by a mere whim. There are certain people that will leave everything at the drop of a hat to do things or go places just because one feels like it. In a way, one is a free spirit, for the ties that bind that person are practically loose and one is free to roam around and spread his or her wings so to speak. Every person knows at least one guy or girl who will basically just spontaneously make a decision out of the blue and go somewhere and not take anything with him or her except the clothes on one's back or a friend/boyfriend/girlfriend/husband/wife. A person can admire that person's boldness and it's a trait some people would like to have.

Then there are the decision-making skills which one just has fun with. Non-important decisions that can be decided either a flip of the coin, eenie-mennie-mynie-moe or the ever-popular rock-paper-scissors. Let me tell you something, some of the decisions that are made where I work basically come from the rock-paper-scissors method. Such decisions as where to eat, who's going to drive the van, who's going to ride shotgun in the van, and who's going under the bleachers to retrieve a child that doesn't want to come out, which has happened. Trust me. It's just some of the semi-important decisions that my fellow co-workers and I deal with in a fun and playful way to keep morale up.

In all seriousness, there will be situations in a person's life where prayer is needed to come to an all-important decision. It's that particular all-important decision that one must leave in God's capable hands, for he will give you the answers you need. In Psalms 66:19-29, it says, ~19): But verily God hath heard me: he hath attended in the voice of my prayer. 20): Blessed be God, which hath not turned away my prayer, nor his mercy from me.~ When all else fails, and the advice you are getting doesn't help, turn to God. In the end, God will help you make the most important decisions in your life; all you have to do is bow your head, close your eyes and pray to Him in making the right decisions.

PERFECT HARMONY

October 20, 2004

In some aspect, a person's life can be compared to writing and playing a song on the piano. Let me ask you this question, do you know how to play the piano or at least know somebody that does? If you do, you know it takes skill, patience, proper position of one's body and fingers, plus a total of 100% concentration. In a way, we are the composers of our own piano of life and each key represents something significant in his or her life. From the time we were born, each of us began writing and putting together a composition that ultimately will be heard by those around us in a manner of speaking. Every person has their own blank piece of sheet music, it's just a matter of filling in the blank spaces.

With all compositions, a "composer" like ourselves needs some inspiration to create the music he or she is writing in one's life. Some examples that can bring about inspiration are tragedies such as death, but then there is anger, the creation of life, laughter, family, friends, special events such as a graduation or a wedding, kids, but the best inspiration comes from being in love or being loved by someone such as one's boyfriend/girlfriend and/or husband/wife. It's that specific inspiration that can actually bring the words he or she writes on paper to life on one's blank piece of sheet music. Sheet music that at some point in one's life didn't have any kind of inspiration to write about.

With any composition, a person has to find the words/melody to convey one's message or meaning to the audience or to that one particular person. Oftentimes, the words come instantly, and it flows from one's mind to his or her hands and it basically writes itself, in a manner of speaking. But sometimes, the words are hard to find or write, and it takes something either big or something small to stir the creative juices and let what one wants to sat flow from within one's own heart and soul. It's that proverbial writer's block that every person, including myself, has gone through. Though I don't necessarily create songs but rather random thoughts that can make people really think.

In any case, with any composition, it will sometimes need a particular sound. Every person has a favorite sound in music such as jazz, funk, pop, R&B, hip hop, rap, country, rock, alternative, the list goes on and on. One just has to find that specific sound one wants to play in order for the words/notes to match our own proverbial keys of life. For some people who are musically talented, it's searching for that particular rate, pitch, and tone of the words that one is either playing or singing can determine a grammy award winning song or a song that will never be performed by that particular person. It's just a matter of feeling the music within yourself and simply expressing it outwardly.

Ray Charles once said, ~Reading in braille and playing by ear helped me develop a good memory. I know what the chords are going to be. I know what the structure and sound will be and all that can be heard in my head. So it's up to me to make the decision how I want the arrangement to sound. There's no reason for it to come out any different than the way it sounded in my head.~ Every person will hit a wrong note from time to time, it's simply unavoidable. One just has to continue practicing on one's own piano of life in order to learn from one's mistakes. When we are truly inspired, the melody and sound will come together, and it will create music that is absolutely in perfect harmony.

BLIND

October 21, 2004

If you think about it, a person can walk through his or her own life and not see the opportunities that are set before him or her and just pass it plainly by. A person can completely get caught up in the hustle and bustle of our own simplistic, hectic, and oftentimes complicated lives. In a way it's like walking past something or someone so many times and not realizing that certain person or thing was there. Every person has been in this particular situation when it pertains to either one's personal and/or professional life. There are certain situations where a person can become "blind", so blind in fact that he or she will never be able to see what's in front of him or her for quite some time.

In some ways, one can be "blind" when it comes to situations in the workplace. We've all turned our heads to certain indiscretions, that in our own thinking would consider it none of our business. In a way, we choses to be blind for the simple fact that we don't want to be involved in the drama that might ensue afterwards if found out. Yet, those indiscretions that one didn't want to see may or may not have dire consequences, but it will eat away at you in your heart and one's own conscience, until one can no longer take it and will have to fess up. One just has to step up and be a man, in a manner of speaking, and come clean at what one saw or heard, if that is done, one's vision will become clearer.

Thinking about it, one can become "blind" to the truth that one either doesn't want to hear or reveal. Each one of us at some point closed our eyes and ears to the cold hard truth that life tends to put in front of us so to speak. One will simply choose to either deny all that he or she hears and sees before that person as fact or just completely ignore it if it never was heard or seen. It can be a sad situation indeed when a person can't see that one's relationship is in trouble, and that person simply turns a blind eye, knowing that one's relationship is going to go down in flames. It's a disappointing sight when people around that person can absolutely see it with their own eyes, but he or she can't.

In most cases one can become "blind" when someone is interested in you. For that person can send signal after signal, but for some unknown reason he or she can't seem to see those signals. It's kind of life trying to talk to a person who can't hear or waving to some that can't see; but no matter how hard one tries that person is totally oblivious as to what is going on in front of him or her. Sometimes, it takes a best friend or group of friends who can see it clear as day, to walk up tight behind that person and simply slap one upside the back of his or her head. Once one has gotten that person's attention, they will in some way enlighten you on what you have been truly missing out on.

Personally speaking, I can truly say that I fall into that "blind" category myself. You see, I have been blinded by this deluded perception that I may be out of my league when it comes to a woman that I'm interested in and I lose focus. It has been a thorn in my side which has held me back for a very long time when I want to ask someone out. My best friend simply walked up behind me and simply slapped me upside the head and told me to take that leap of faith. A leap, in which I would either fall hard to the ground below or land safely on the other side. In the end, I took that leap of faith and unfortunately, I fell hard and still unable to see the female in question standing in front of me.

MIRAGE
October 23, 2004

Sir Walter Scott once said, ~A thousand fearful images and dire suggestions glance along the mind when it's moody and discontented with itself. Command them to stand and show themselves, and you presently assert the power of reason over imagination.~ Each of us, who are traveling down our own road of life, in which we have experienced scary situations. Those scary situations, if one looks back on it, gave each of us strength, courage, and confidence that one has always had deep inside one's heart, mind, body, and soul. For that person, it's just a matter of breaking through the facade that he or has imagined and/or built up and simply moved forward in one's own particular venture.

As little kids, what each of us feared the most were the supposed scary monsters that either lived in our closets or under our beds. For our eyes and ears can literally play tricks on us as we are trying to embrace the darkness which will help us head off into that proverbial utopia called slumberland. It's at that point one will start to see dark shapes and hear certain noises in which our minds want to go into maximum overdrive in a manner of speaking. In a way, it's the things we think we see and hear, as a little kid, are in reality simple illusions created by our own imagination. It then basically manifests into something much bigger, but yet it is actually smaller than it appears.

In some cases, a person puts up illusions after illusion pertaining to one work ethic as he or she is talking the talk, but not walking the walk. It's a false perception where a person is not scared to be who they really are, but sometimes who they really are can be a real disappointment. It can be a sad situation indeed when a person claims to have the qualifications to be a potential leader in the making, but yet is still considered a follower that has still so much to learn. What truly makes a potential leader is one that works hard, is able to handle crisis situations under pressure, who is able to delegate authority as well as be a team player, and yet is not afraid to fail and learn from that failure.

Saying "I Love You" can be considered the easiest and/or hardest thing to say to a person. Yet, one has that innate fear that the person he or she is talking to might not say those words back. It can be a scary situation as one awaits those three simple words and have it replaced by a long, drawn out, awkward silence in which it is actually said back or not at all. Let me ask you this question, who was the last person you said I love you to and was it reciprocated back? Thinking about it, when it comes to saying those three words, don't be scared to look that person in the eyes because those two eyes are considered windows to the soul that are a doorway to that person's heart.

Someone once said, ~I have not ceased being fearful, but I have ceased to let fear control me. I have accepted fear as a part of life, especially the fear of change, the fear of the unknown, and I have gone ahead despite the pounding in my heart that says turn back, turn back, you'll die if venture too far.~ Each of us can conquer almost any fear that is placed before out path, it just a matter of putting your mind and heart into it because one's fear doesn't really exist except in our head. In retrospect, the fears each of us have is merely mirage after mirage trying to stop us from moving forward, and it's the things that scare us the most that actually save us in the end.

THE END
October 24, 2004

The journey that each of us are traveling on can be somewhat compared to chapters in our proverbial autobiography of life. Each chapter represents our own personal history of where we have been and the people we have met along the way during our travels. Every aspect of our lives from birth to eventual death will be chronicled as one fills in the blank pages of our book. Let me ask you this question, as the editor of your living autobiography, what type of book are you going to produce in the end when you finally write down the last words in the last chapter of your life?

For some people, they would rather write down the darker side of life and not leave any bit of information out. For that person can have the mentality that the world is against him or her and the only person to trust is himself or herself, which can brand that person a loner. It's their own pessimistic views on life that can give that person the best inspiration when pain, anger, suffering, death, etc. can somewhat bring a person to the edge of insanity. In a way, by lashing out as those that did him or her wrong can be considered the best form of therapy one doesn't have to pay a doctor for.

In some cases, writing about one's own adventures in life can be considered great reading. For the places one has been to can't be explained in just mere words, for a person has to live it personally to know what one is reading about. It's not only the places that one has been to, but also the people that one meets along one's travels that can create bonds of friendships that stand the test of time. Let me ask you this question, who was the last person that greatly influenced/impacted your life and where/when did you meet that person?

Inevitably, one's own living autobiography of life will most definitely focus on one's own love life. The loves found, the loves lost, the loves found again is basically what life is about. Meeting that one person in life that you will share your hopes, dreams, fears and in turn he or she will do the same thing with you. I once said that love is like a battle as it can be confusing, can keep you off balance, and the experience can leave lasting effects, BUT if one doesn't give up on it, then it truly is worth fighting for. In some ways, every person wants to be swept off their feet and have that great ending all people want.

Someone once said, ~Every person's life is like a book, though we may be the author, all the details of our lives are being written by God.~ God is the editor-in-chief and no matter how much we want to revise the past, we must accept it as it is. In retrospect, the story of our lives hasn't been completed yet, for some people they are constantly focusing on the negative side of life. For others, they are embellishing what one has been through over the years. BUT, for most people love is the greatest inspiration to write about and that makes great literature. When it is said and done, all that is left to be said is...THE END.

CROSS THE LINE
October 25, 2004

Every person will or has at some point stood at that proverbial line that is drawn in the sand of life. That represents times in which a person walks up to it, sees who's beyond that line, and one can make that decision to either walk away or step over that line. In some cases, it can also represent a friendship taken to the level of the unknown with that one particular guy or girl one has been friends with for quite some time. In some aspect, each of us, who are primarily single, have always been standing in front of the line that leads to someone; but never really made the decision to cross over it until he or she feels right.

Have you ever been in a situation where you constantly have your foot over the line but never actually stepped over it? Of course, we all have because in some way, we are in a battle with our own mind and heart. It's like doing a proverbial dance back and forth over that potential relationship line in which he or she is so close to that person; one can actually hear him or her breathing. In any case, that inner struggle between heart and mind can ultimately lead to one thing which is writing a letter. A letter in which a person spills one's guts out, in a manner of speaking, and shares all that he or she feels about that person and doesn't regret every word of it.

Let me ask you this question, once that letter is written what did you do with it? For some people they continually revise it to say the right words that are coming from one's heart. For others, they sit holding it and contemplating whether to save it or simply tear it up. But for most people, he or she decides to give it to that person but not actually to that person but in a place where one can find and read it. The last option is usually what one will come to and once that letter is out our hands, then its simply a matter of time. A time in which one bites fingernails, paces up and down, or looks up at that ceiling because that person has affected the way you sleep at night.

Ultimately, when that letter is read, a sense of awkwardness comes about for either one person or both people. In the mind of the writer of that letter, one can literally be freaking out inside and have that somewhat close feeling of how a heart attack feels, or simply beating your head against the wall to the point of either being knocked out or one's head hurts. On the other side of the line, once that reader of the letter has made the decision and knows what to do next. In some aspect, the reader can be considered the judge and/or jury and the writer is the defendant. Inevitably, the verdict will come down and that person's decision will be....

In retrospect, there comes a point where every person makes the decision to step over the line from friends to more than friends. Whether its talking to that person alone or writing a letter and placing it somewhere he or she can find it, it's a decision that nobody can turn back from. We've all been there, done that and even though you received total disappointment for your efforts, as well as a "wounded" heart, you kept going. You learned from what going through that experience taught you as you move on with not only your heart, but your life as well. In the end, for me personally, I have all my life to cross the line; a line that will eventually lead me to that one special person to spend the rest of my days with, whoever she may be.

CURVE BALLS
October 28, 2004

Seeking a relationship with that one particular person, or any person for that matter is like playing the game of baseball. The baseball game of potential relationships, in which there is an infinite number of innings as well as outs. In any baseball game one will encounter several situations where he or she can predict what is about to happen. On the other hand, one can also say that there will be many surprises in store either in the early, middle, and/or late innings of the game. If you think about it, each of us are somewhat like baseball players because we can go through several different phases in the game that is considered to be America's favorite pastime to watch and/or play.

One such phase, we as ball players can go through is encountering a slump. A slump where each of us may his or her concentration and/or focus on what one's goal is. In that slump a person may lose his or her confidence and it will make a person do things he or she would not normally do such as online dating or going on a blind date to get back into the swing of things, so to speak. Things such as on-line dating and going on a blind date, which from what I've heard from friends that it's not a good experience. In any case, it's just a matter of getting that one bloop single in a manner of speaking to start that comeback and slowly but surely one will break out of his or her funk.

Another such phase, in the course of one's season, is going through a streak. A streak, in which one finds himself or herself on the lucky end of the dating scene. One's own little black book is booked solid, and that person doesn't have any worries about finding someone to spend their time with. By continually getting hit after hit after hit, one may feel that he or she may never go into a slump ever again. Yet one's ego can get the better of him or her and it oftentimes needs to be bruised even now in order to bring one back to reality. In some aspect, with every winning streak one must inevitably suffer a loss, but it's how one comes back from that loss that will determine if one is worthy to be named MVP.

Ultimately, baseball is all about establishing rivalries that make the game a nail biter that it is. In a way, each of us are rivals with that one known or unknown person who seeks to have a relationship with that same guy or girl you are interested in as well. It's that competitive spirit that is inside each and every one of us who doesn't like the thought of losing, which will leave a bitter aftertaste in one's mouth. Yet, respect must be given because he or she wanted it even more and it took more than just one's abilities to get where one is today…it took heart. In the long run, if one's heart is still in the game and doesn't quit, then the odds will most definitely always be in your favor.

The Boston Red Sox and New York Yankees, two teams that have established a bitter rivalry that has been going on for years. History has always seen the Red Sox always coming so close to beating them but fall short every time. It has been 86 years since they've won the World Series and last week, they beat their rivals at Yankees Stadium. Now 86 years later, the Red Sox are just one win away from winning it all and breaking "the curse" that has been hanging over them for many years. In retrospect, life can throw each of us curve balls that will keep us off balance when seeking a relationship, but if one doesn't give up, he or she will see that one perfect pitch and hit a home run.

NEVER A DULL MOMENT
October 29, 2004

Working in a place like the Youth Center, one can have either a positive or negative effect depending how long that person has worked there. For a person like myself, it's more positive than negative. Some days it's like working in a nuthouse and the inmates are running the asylum. As one approaches the hallowed halls of the Youth Center, one can hear the echoes of screaming, crying, whining, and mad laughter that is just coming from the staff. A long time ago, I once said that a person will never be the same when you first start till the time you leave, and it still holds true. In some aspect, there are some similarities between working in a youth center and in an insane asylum.

For instance, every insane asylum needs to have their resident oddballs, nutcases, weirdoes, and lunatics. No, it's not the kids I'm talking about; it's the staff because the kids have gotten to us mentally. In my line of work, one will get a handle on which kids are harmless and which kids have that Dr. Hannibal Lecter mentality. It's the mini-Hannibal Lecters that have current and former employees starting to hear voices. But it's those current and former employees that talk back to those voices that one was to worry about. It's just a matter of not showing any sign of weakness in front of these so-called "inmates" because you, they have you in the palm of their tiny little hands.

With every insane asylum, medication is a big part of mellowing out those that may go bonkers and start a rampage of madness that one police in riot gear can stop. Working in a high-pressure job involving kids, one's medication can consist of daily doses of nicotine that help tremendously in one's stress level. Also medications such as coffee can, in some way, have a calming effect though one will be wired and somewhat act like Rain Main for a couple of hours. But the best medication that helps in times of utter chaos is listening to music because it drowns out the madness that surrounds the insane asylum within.

In an insane asylum, you will find an assortment of interesting people who don't think they belong there and believe they are in the right state of mind. In my view, we as counselors don't want to be at work half the time and we're never in the right state of mind due in part to kids constantly in our ear every day. Several months ago, I said you have to be totally insane to work in a place that will mentally eat you alive metaphorically speaking. Fortunately, I am already nuts and even though it's a job that is both mentally and physically tiring, it's a job that I love to be a part of because you never know what is going to happen next.

In life, we will encounter people that think we need to seek professional help because one thinks we're either nuts, crazy, strange, and/or weird. But think about this, there are people out there one knows or has come across that are nuttier, crazier, and/or weirder that each of us. Last night I was to be rewarded with a lap dance by several female co-workers for a job well done putting together a dance routine for "my kids" earlier in the afternoon. There's never a dull moment when a 250-pound man, my best friend, out of nowhere gives me a lap dance that will cause me to have nightmares for years to come and probably have myself committed to the nearest mental institution.

THE AGE OLD QUESTION
October 30, 2004

A wise man once said, ~As a man you have to die once in order to live.~ Most guys never fully understand what that means until he experiences it firsthand. You may be asking yourself what on earth am I talking about and is it relevant. Well, since the dawn of time there have been many epic battles such as Boston Red Sox vs. The New York Yankees, Army vs. Navy, Florida vs. Florida State are just a few battles that are still going on to this day. Several days ago, my best friend and I brought up an age-old battle that has been brewing for a very long time and it is between BAD BOYS and NICE GUYS. It's a subject that both myself and my best friend still scratch our heads over.

The number one thing that bad boys have or pretend to have is confidence. Yet that confidence can be perceived as an arrogant charm that is a defining character trait that these guys share. It's one's arrogance that produces a gigantic, egotistical, all about me attitude whose only interest is the superficiality of a lady. Think about this, that arrogance, which oftentimes brands these guys jerks, doesn't possess a high self-esteem and have a mentality that all women, in their eyes, are merely conquests, These so called "players" or "ladies men" think they are God's gift to women, but that fixation doesn't usually last that long and once her eyes are open, he is kicked to the curb.

There is a saying that goes: nice guys always finish last, and it will always pertain to seeking a relationship with someone you truly like or love. Every man has experienced unrequited feelings of love for someone only to have it spurned or crushed. It's that experience of constant heartache that can make it nice to just wave the proverbial white flag and just give up on ever meeting that one woman to spend the rest of his days with. In any case, it's that knight in shining armor mentality when a certain lady of interest needs a shoulder to cry on and vent about why she isn't able to find the right guy. Primarily what you get from a nice guy is respect and a solid, equal grounded relationship.

If you think about it, it's not only a guy thing it's a girl thing as well with the bad girls and the nice girls. Guys are searching for that diamond in the rough that is the perfect girl, which in reality doesn't really exist but only in mind. It's that weird irresistible attraction that both men and women sense in a proverbial bad boy or bad girl. Ultimately these bad boys/bad girls love the thrill of the chase which means one thing and that it's all about him or her. For he or she isn't the slightest bit concerned about how it is treating that person. In the end, that nice girl or nice guy will be left heartbroken and will start to wonder whether or not he or she is worthy of a boyfriend or girlfriend.

In the whole scheme of things, men and women have no idea what they want when it comes to potential relationships. Women, more so than men, act on impulse and emotion and that is why they pass up the nice guy and go after the dangerous boy thinking she can change him, a feeling I know all too well. In retrospect, nobody wants to get hurt in a potential or significant relationship. Inevitably, both men and women need to look past the superficial and look at what truly matters most in the end and that is a person's heart. It's the age-old question, who do men and women want more, a bad boy/bad girl or a nice girl/bad girl? (Feedback is welcomed on this)

HEART AND SOUL
October 31, 2004

Confucious once said, ~It's true that we shall not be able to reach perfection, but in our struggle toward it we shall strengthen our character and give stability to our ideas, so that, whilst ever advancing calming in the same direction, we shall be rendered capable of applying the faculties with which we have been gifted to the best possible account,~ There comes a point where every person goes through a journey of who they are as a person. Each of us, in some way, tries to be perfect, but in reality, we're not perfect by any means. We're only human and the mistakes we make determine the strength of our character, which in turn reveals our true selves to other people.

For those that have gotten to know me, you know that I'm a straight shooter and there is no BS about me. On a semit-daily basis I send out these Yoda-isms that reflect everyday life. Oftentimes these reflections pertain to situations going on around me while I stand back and merely observe. Other times, these situations have meaning for me and are very personal. In some ways, each time I send out these thoughts, I share bits and pieces of myself in certain aspects of my life. During these moments of vulnerability, I think to myself whether or not to send them out because it comes from a place where people and close friends rarely have ever seen or entered.

By sharing my thoughts that deal with life, love, relationships, etc. there have been times when people ask my advice on certain issues that pertain to one's love life. It's a sticky situation indeed to get involved in because on one hand you want to give that person the best advice possible; but on the other hand, you don't want to be responsible for a broken relationship and be blamed for it. Through my own experience, I simply suggest to that person to follow your heart and hopefully it will point you in the right direction. Each time I faced disappointment, but that hasn't stopped me to keep fighting the good fight because love is truly worth fighting for

I have been the type of person who basically sets myself for a fall when it comes to seeking a potential relationship that I think I may have a chance with. But that's the price one pays for rolling the dice with one's own heart, and if it means I travel alone on my personal journey of life I'll accept it. Potential relationships are a gamble and with every roll of the dice, one hopes it lands on seven and not on snake-eyes. It's just a matter of staying the same person who I am and not trying to be someone other than myself, in other words, keepin' it real. Hopefully, that one woman who I have been patiently waiting for, is placing all her chips on the same number as I am and letting it all ride.

In retrospect, life is all about experiencing the highs and lows that can either make you give up or make you stronger. The subject of love is a common thread that each of us are intertwined in, and we've all been through the highs and lows of it, one more than the other. William Wordsworth said, ~There is comfort in the strength of love: 'Twill make a thing endurable, which else could overset the brain, or break hearts.~ Every person goes through times of heartbreak that leave deep scars within your heart and soul. Ultimately when you read what I write, you don't get "Yoda" and his Yoda-isms; what you get is my heart and soul, but most of all you get me.

LET IT RIDE
November 1, 2004

Sir Hugh Walpoe once said, ~The most wonderful of all things in life, I believe, is the discovery of another human being with whom one's relationship has a glowing depth, beauty, and joy as the years increase. This inner progressiveness of love between two human beings is the most marvelous thing, it cannot be found by looking for it or by passionately wishing for it. It's sort of a divine accident.~ Let me ask you this question, do you think there is someone out there who is meant for every person? It's basically a simple question that people have been asking themselves over and over again on occasion. For some the answers come quickly, yet for others the answer is truly an unknown.

In some aspect, potential relationships are primarily a gamble, and every roll of the dice determines how far or how close each of us will find true happiness. Oftentimes, one may think he or she has either a great role or a great hand that is being dealt to that person. Yet, those proverbial dice that represent a possible potential relationship usually land on disappointment and one's cards will reveal a dead man's hand. Inevitably, each of us loses much more than money and the shirt of our backs so to speak, one loses a little bit of confidence. One just has to keep rolling the dice and hope he or she doesn't go completely broke in the end.

We've all chased after that dream guy or girl who, in some people's mind, is a long shot, but it's a gamble of a lifetime. It's that dream guy/girl who makes your tongue tied and made you somewhat feel like Kramer, a feeling most of us know all too well. It's the random acts of stupidity each of us go through in order to find out if there is a slight chance, if any, of coming up aces so to speak. Though we have left our middle/high school days behind, that juvenile mentality stays with us for years to come and never really outgrows it. The odds of success may not be in our favor, but a person can overcome those odds just by winning back one's own confidence.

In any case, a person that is having this sort of unlucky streak in one's life, it's nice to have that guy or girl friend to be sort of sponsor for one's addiction in a manner of speaking. In some ways, it's easier to talk to that person than trying to talk to that other person who you would risk gambling your whole life for. That one person who is supporting your quest is a friend that will laugh at your corny jokes, be absolutely comfortable around, and just be yourself. Inevitably, it's at that point maybe he or she has been placing the wrong bet on who one wants to be with, and it doesn't take a slap to the back of the head to realize that which every person has come to in the end.

Anna Louise Strong said, ~To fall in love is easy, even to remain in it is not difficult, our human loneliness is cause enough. But it's a hard quest worth making to find a comrade though whose steady presence one becomes steadily the person one desires to be.~ In retrospect, when you do stumble upon "the one" you don't necessarily change you you are, but rather be a better person for meeting him or her. If you think about it, it's the person you least expect that will make you believe that luck is on your side and things are about to change for the better. Ultimately, when you gamble with your own heart, the thing to do is just close your eyes, throw the dice, and simply let it ride.

BELIEVE IT OR NOT
November 4, 2004

Kids can do and say things that are pretty outrageous, take it from me. I've practically heard and seen everything that has crossed my path. It's the totally unbelievable that can make myself and my fellow co-workers put our hands over our faces in absolute disbelief, all-the-while laughing on the inside. Yet, it's those same kids that are part of untold stories that can make any person cry and tug at one's heartstrings. Inevitably, a person doesn't really understand why we do the job that we do until he or she experiences it for themselves. It's a certain unknown connection one has with kids that somewhat determines if that child considers you a trusted friend or a bitter enemy.

In some aspect, the kids are like a pack of wolves waiting for fresh meat to walk through those hallowed halls of the asylum. These mini-Hannibal Lectres will immediately walk up to a newbie and size him or her up and mentally try to figure out what damage he or she can do to this person. In a way, it's like walking through a gauntlet set up by the kids, and if one gets through the day without having a nervous breakdown then one has survived his or her first day. A day, in which one will be mentally fatigued trying to figure which name belongs with which face and which child will take one's patience to the limit and beyond.

As time goes by, one will have to figure out for themselves what kind of counselor he or she will be. I've learned over the past 8 years; one has to have some middle ground when dealing with kids. A person has to have a combination of meanness and coolness, plus an added mix of total insanity sprinkled in. By combining these three qualities, I'm considered on the top four favorite counselors, which can change on a daily basis. One has to understand that a child can love you and think you are cool one day, but then turn right around and simply loathe you and think you need to seek professional help the next day. Kids will be opinionated and will share their thoughts even if one doesn't ask for it.

Ultimately, those who are in the childcare profession will become attached to these kids. In my 8 years working at the Asylum, I have seen every kid grow up in front of my eyes and I feel like a proud parent. It's a tough situation indeed when kids leave the roost, so to speak and venture off to places that are truly unknown to him or her. Yet, what makes it doubly tough is when a child, we as counselors help raise, suddenly passes away. In a way, it's like losing a little bit of yourself and nothing can prepare a person to hear that bit of news. Thinking about it, our paths will cross again one day and as I once said, it's not a matter of saying goodbye, that's just not my style; it's a matter of saying see you later.

Jean De La Bryuere once said, ~Children are contemptuous, haughty, irritable, envious, sneaky, selfish, lazy, flighty, timid, liars and hypocrites, quick to laugh and cry, extreme in expressing joy and sorrow, especially about trivial things, they'll do anything to avoid pain but they enjoy inflicting it.~ A person may ask why do it in the first place and have attachments to these kids that you know don't listen, talk back to you, and on any given day tell you that he or she doesn't like you. In all honesty, I do it because I love "my kids", though they drive me totally insane. Believe it or not, if I had the chance to do again knowing what I'd be getting myself into, I would absolutely do it in a heartbeat.

WALK TALL
November 6, 2004

Each of us has struggled or continues to struggle in certain aspects of our lives. The struggles that we all go through are the same for many, but the situation may be different. If you think about it, as one grows up a person will in some ways be graduating from the school of hard knocks and be initiated in adulthood. A type of initiation, in which he or she will be toughened up as life itself gets tougher and tougher. In a way, these struggles are considered gauntlets and anyone and/or anything will be standing in our way; beating us down as each of us are trying to get to the other side.

Childhood is considered one of the toughest gauntlets one faces because it's basically a search for individuality. In some ways, we battled our way through many obstacles to get to the other side, not emotionally or physically scarred. Remember back in your middle/high school days trying to basically fit in, but yet one felt like you didn't belong. Think about it, our own middle/high school years were tests that took us beyond our limits of mental and physical pain and/or torture in order to find out who will be standing at the end of the gauntlet, and will we like the person we have become in the end.

Potential and/or significant relationships are considered gauntlets as well because one faces tough challenges ahead in order to meet Mr./Ms. Right. Let me ask you this question, have you ever had to go through so many obstacles in order to try to be with that one person you wanted to be with? Let me ask another question, was it worth it in the end going through that relationship gauntlet knowing all that you did to get to that point? We all have a comfort zone that we like to stay in but each of us will step out of that zone and risk being battered and bruised in order to find out if that particular person will be standing at the end of one's gauntlet.

If you think about it, a person faces their own personal problems as one walks the gauntlet of life so to speak. The problems that each of us face can either have a positive or negative effect. One can avoid them but for how long? It's these particular expectations that can beat a person down to the ground where one can either do things: 1.) stay down, give up, and let your own person gauntlet defeat you OR 2.) get up battered and bruised and push yourself to the end with the remaining strength you have. Which do you choose and will you or have you overcome your own personal problems?

Theodore Roosevelt once said, ~A person whose face is marred by dust and sweat and blood; who strives valiantly; who errs and comes short again and again, who knows the great enthusiasms, the great devotions, and spends himself in a worthy cause; who at best, knows the triumph of high achievement; and who, at the worst, if he fails, at least fails while daring greatly, so that his place shall never be with those cold and timid souls who know neither victory nor defeat.~ In the end in the gauntlet that is our life, whether you succeed or fail, keep your head up and continue to walk tall.

MEANING OF LIFE
November 8, 2004

What is the meaning of life? Every person, whether he or she wants to admit it or not, has sat down alone or with a group of friends and pondered this question from dusk till dawn. For most people one immediately knows the answer but for others it's different to figure out. If you think about it, it's a question that has many different answers for each person, but absolutely no wrong answers. Inevitably, while each of us tries to figure out that particular question, we all experience what life has to offer while traveling on our proverbial journey. A journey in which we ask ourselves what is life really all about and what's our purpose for being here?

For some people the meaning of life is attaining as much knowledge as possible. It's been said that knowledge is power and is the key for certain people who spend their entire lives searching for answers to questions that have been asked and debated on countless times. Such questions in particular are: What do women want? Is there another form of life out in space than our own? Is there an afterlife? Does God really exist? One may not even come up with the answers, but for that particular person it is a challenge to figure it out. Let me ask you this question though, when a person does finally come up with the answers to these questions, what's next?

In some cases, what brings meaning to a person's life is making that all mighty dollar. Every person wants to be secure in the fact that he or she has enough money to be set in the latter years of one's life. Yet, there is a saying that money is the root of all evil. For particular people, money can consume him or her and ultimately it can change a person's personality. A change in which one becomes someone that one's friends and family don't recognize and may not want to be around. The material things that one wants in life are semi-important; but when it becomes all about the benjamins so to speak, he or she will sacrifice the most important thing he or she has and that is one's family.

Ralph Waldo Emerson said, ~The purpose of life is not to be happy. It is to be useful, to be honorable, to be compassionate, to have it make some difference that you have lived and lived well.~ In a way what he says is true, BUT a person doesn't have to give up one's happiness in order to find meaning in one's life. One can absolutely go through life spreading happiness to others even though one's own personal happiness hasn't quite been fulfilled. Ultimately one can stumble upon it because the answer to one's purpose in life has always been staring that person in the face. Call it an epiphany or an eye-opening moment, one's meaning/purpose of life will be eventually realized.

I started this thought by asking the question: what is the meaning of life? The better question to ask is what is the meaning of your own life? You basically have to ask yourself who or what makes you happy in life? About 2 months ago, without power for seven days after Hurricane Ivan, I reflected on what has meant most to me and does it give me purpose. After 6 nights looking up into the stars I came up with this answer. In the last 8 years I have connected with so many kids that I realized I was miserable not being in a place that drove me nuts. In retrospect, what has given me meaning and purpose has been "my kids" because they make me happy...most of the time.

BALANCE OF POWER
November 9, 2004

As a guy, I've accepted the fact long ago that women have "the power". Every guy may think he is in control but in reality, there is a woman lurking in the shadows running the show so to speak. It's really no big secret, for the proof is in the pudding because when kids ask their father for something fairly semi-important, he would primarily tell him or her to wait for one's mom and see what see says. The power a woman has is simply unexplainable and can't be figured out. For if it could be compared to something that a guy would understand, it would be compared to the power of the force, which a jedi master would yield.

Looking at it from a guy's perspective, the influence that a woman has over a man is unbelievable. That basic influence doesn't come from a wave of the hand, it comes from her smile and the way she looks in one's direction. A woman's smile and certain look that she perfects should be outlawed because guys will turn into mindless zombies that will say yes to anything. Every guy has been in a situation where he refused to do something that would compromise one's own masculinity but would soon find himself doing it because it made her happy. It's that certain quality that makes women special, even though they drive us nuts.

In my own thinking, "the power" would balance out if guys and girls correctly picked that one person who truly makes one smile as well as your heart smile too. Each of us has had moments in life where you wanted our dream to come true when it concerned someone that you knew one wouldn't have a chance with. A dream where anything was possible and the chances one had were endless because in reality each of us had only one life and one chance to do and say all the things with that one person. Inevitably each of us must make the most of the opportunities that are placed in front of us because second chances are sometimes hard to come by.

In the whole scheme of things, each one of us wants a relationship that is well balanced. A balance of friendship, romance, conversation, respect and love. It's been said that love begins with a smile, grows with a kiss and ends with a tear. The brightest future is oftentimes determined by a painful past and sometimes a person can't move on to the future until one let go of past failures and heartaches. Ultimately, telling someone that you care about and/or love him or her is never 100% guaranteed that he or she will return those feelings back. We're human and like the saying goes, what doesn't kill us will only make us stronger.

Someone once said, ~ Relationships are like roses with endless beauty. To enjoy its beauty one must love and care for it. Give it the things it needs to bloom. The feeling is much greater than to be pricked by its hurting thorns.~ In other words, both men and women have to be prepared to work hard to keep the roses from losing all its petals. Petals epresenting the true beauty of a person, and that beauty comes from a person's heart and in the end, nobody wants to be left with a stem full of thorns. In retrospect, every person will find that one person who will bring a harmonious balance of power to a seemingly unbalanced life.

ONE
November 10, 2004

Someone once said, ~Life is divided into 2 parts, what is and what should be. And that with a lot of effort, some hard hard work, and maybe a little luck, there are moments in your life when the two parts touch. When what is and what should be are one in the same.~ In some aspect, it can also describe love as well, because each of us knows what love feels like and it only takes a feeling/vibe/connection to have an attraction to that guy or girl. Think about this, we all know what each of our lives is like, but what about the life of that unknown person. A life that is shrouded in mystery and will he or she somehow and/or someday intersect with ours?

Our lives are our own, and the reality of it is, that when it comes to life and love nobody has a clear perspective on the situation. Each of us continues to experience the highs and lows of love when it pertains to potential and/or significant relationships. Oftentimes, life and love somewhat parallel each other to a point where a person simply stands back and just lets out a giant size sigh of disbelief. For that person ultimately asks WHY ME when things don't necessarily go in our favor. Inevitably, life can give each of us the hardest reality check that nobody wants to face when it comes to finding that one person who has that proverbial last puzzle piece to one's heart.

Let me ask you this question, are you or should you be at a certain point in your life where the goals one has set for yourself have been fulfilled? It's the ultimate goal of every person to meet, fall in love, and settle down with that guy or girl who is the last remaining key to achieving one's goal. The path of life and love that each of us are traveling on to reach one's specified goal isn't as straight and smooth as one thought it would be; but rather it's a long, winding road that can sometimes lead a person to become completely lost. A feeling every person has had when he or she just wants to be taken by the hand and led in the right direction to where one's goal is located at.

We all want to meet that one particular person who each of us wants to build our world around. In some aspect, it's a world that one has seen but only from his or her own perspective. Traveling the world, seeing the sights, experiencing the different cultures which can have a positive and/or negative effect on a person. In a way, when each of us has met or will finally meet that one person, he or she will metaphorically take our hearts on a magic carpet ride so to speak. Show us a side of ourselves that we necessarily never knew existed, and most importantly that one person will teach us that love is a powerful thing and it can hit you when you least expect it.

Michael Dorris said, ~At different stages in our lives, the signs of love may vary: dependence, attraction, contentment, worry, loyalty, grief, but at heart the source is always the same. Human beings have the rare capacity to connect with each other, against all odds.~ Every person has a motto in life, mine happens to be -Live life one day at a time, if you go through it too fast, you miss out on the special moments that make life interesting.- In retrospect, what are the odds that two people accidently meet as each travels on separate journeys. In the end, two lives that traveled separately will be intertwined and merge into one.

THANK YOU
November 10, 2004

As Thanksgiving approaches, one starts to notice a change in the weather, as well as a person's demeanor. He or she realizes that we all will soon celebrate and enjoy the festivities of consuming mass quantities of food and then passing out later while watching the Dallas Cowboys and Washington Redskins battle it out over supremacy. A battle that has been waged since the days of the old west, but now waged on a football field, and the weapon of choice is a football. In any case, Thanksgiving is about fulfilling time honored traditions in which families institute customs that have been either going on for years or just newly started.

Let me ask you this question, when your whole family gets together, is it a time of togetherness where people come share embarrassing stories about one another? A time where lost connections of certain family members such as an uncle, aunt, brother, sisters, cousin, mother, and/or father connect once again. OR is it a time of togetherness where old wounds are opened up again that were once healed. In a way, it's like having one's own personal Jerry Springer Show even though there is no studio audience, no Steve, and most definitely no Jerry. Though, on the outside, it seems dysfunctional, it's one's own family and family is forever.

If one's life were a Hollywood movie, as director, one could absolutely choose who you want to play as your family. But one's life isn't a movie, and we have to accept the ties that bind us to family, which is blood, no matter how strange, weird, screwed up, and totally embarrassing you consider them to be. Have you ever just looked at your own family and thought to yourself that there might be a possibility that you were adopted; for his or her real family has been searching for you. Of course, everybody has, and nobody wants to be around when the shiznit hits the fan, as one's family frustrations get the better of him or her before, during, and/or after the day of thanks.

Thomas Moore once said, ~Family life is full of major and minor crises--the ups and downs of health, success, and failure in career, marriage, and divorce--and all kinds of characters. It is tied to places and events and histories. With all of these felt details, life etches itself into memory and personality. It's difficult to imagine anything more nourishing to the soul~ The resiliency a family has is not determined by how rich and physically strong they are but by how they continually hold on to hope and always come together when a member of the family is in dire need of help, even though he or she doesn't want that help.

In retrospect, family is the link to our past and inevitably a bridge to his or her future. It's the memories that are both forgettable and unforgettable that each of us will always cherish and keep with us in our hearts and minds. We all will meet people that we will let into our lives gradually but surely. These people will become friends and then become a second family. A family that has had its dysfunctional moments, but that is to be expected. Personally speaking, though I haven't met any of you in person, I am glad that I have crossed paths with each and every one of you. In the end, I thank you for taking time to read what I write and letting me share a piece of myself with you.

ONE THING
November 14, 2004

Someone once said, ~We are all a little weird, and life's a little weird, and when we find someone whose weirdness is compatible with ours, we join up with them and fall in mutual weirdness and call it love.~ It's a rare and little bit scary when you meet someone that you truly click with and have certain things in common with that person that can make one just do the proverbial dance of joy. In some aspect, it's like putting together pieces of a puzzle and those pieces represent a complete picture of that particular guy or girl who one thinks will fit perfectly in his or her life. It's just a matter of getting to know that person both personally, intellectually, and emotionally.

The key to completing a puzzle is to locate the outside edges which is a good starting off point; by doing that one can work from the outside in. If you think about it, we all have to start from square one when seeking a potential relationship with that particular person of interest. First impressions are a big part of the puzzle because it's a proverbial ice breaker that can determine if he or she likes you just for being yourself. One way to find that out is to say something that is either stupid, funny, or stupidly funny that it actually makes that person genuinely laugh. By making a person laugh, you have your basic start-off point to get to know that person one on one.

As that potential relationship hopefully starts to progress nicely, he or she will get a better understanding of who that person is. Such as what are his or her likes and dislikes, favorite authors, and other aspects that particular people want to find out. By doing that, it will somewhat determine if one's relationship puzzle will start forming a complete picture. It's been said that a picture can say more than mere words ever can say. One of the qualities that every person is looking for in a person is intelligence. Not too smart or not too dumb but exactly right in the middle, a criteria which most people look for and for the most part have found.

Inevitably, one of the major pieces to complete one's puzzle is the heart. To truly get to know a person is if you can touch him or her emotionally in one's heart. Emotions such as happiness and confusion are just a few aspects of what a person will go through when one's heart is touched. It's been said that you can never really fall in love with someone until you find out what makes that person cry. Each of us have suffered heartache and those emotions stay with us and never really go away. In any case, when you stumble on a person that you start to fall in love with, you will get up every time; but when you fall completely in love with that person, you will never be able to get up ever again.

Natalie Clifford Bailey said, ~When you're in love you never really know whether your elation comes from the qualities of the one you love, or if it attributes them to her; whether the light which surrounds her like a halo comes from you, from her, or from the meeting of your sparks.~ It's truly amazing how people stumble upon each other by accident and find qualities in that person that he or she is absolutely looking for. It's like finding that perfect diamond among many, but that one particular diamond happened to find you. In retrospect, in order to complete one's puzzle that pertains to a potential relationship, a person has only to do one thing….just simply say, Hi.

THAT ONE GREAT POWER
November 18, 2004

Henry Miller once said, ~Every day we slaughter our final impulses. That is why we get a heartache when we read those lines written by the hand of a master and recognize them as our own, as the tender shoots which we stifled because we lack the faith to believe in our own powers, our own criteria of truth and beauty. Every man, when he gets quiet, when he becomes desperately honest with himself, is capable of suffering profound truths. We all desire from the same source. There is no mystery about the origin of things. We are all part of creation, all kings, all poets, all musicians, we have only to open up, to discover what is already there.~

Oftentimes, this so-called power each of us possess can sap us of the strength we need to move forward in our intended goals. It's somewhat like Superman losing his own strength when he comes in contact with Kryptonite. The kryptonite in our own lives can be considered the "critics" and obstacles that can hinder one's quest, so to speak. In a way, these critics and obstacles can ultimately make us second guess ourselves in the decisions we make to the point where it saps our strength both mentally and physically. The strength, which comes from within ourselves, helps us believe that each of us can make it to that proverbial finish line.

Yet, there are times when a person has attained a little or too much at that power and becomes arrogant and/or cocky. Athletes, for example, are a prime example, because their abilities either on the baseball diamond, football field, basketball court, and many other areas make their particular sport what it is today. Such athletes that exude arrogance are Barry Bonds, Deion Sanders, Terell Owens, Dennis Rodman, the entire New York Yankees, and many others; but it's that particular power that has them achieving their ultimate goals and that is winning championship titles. He or she just knows when to turn it on and off like a light switch when the time is right.

Let me ask you this question, is there someone in your life that helps you build up your power to the point where you are back in the game so to speak? It could be a friend, family member, teacher/professor, boyfriend, girlfriend, husband, wife, or even a complete stranger. Sometimes each of us has to hit rock bottom in order to get back on that proverbial horse even though we may get thrown off that horse several times; but that is to be expected. For it's a particular person or group of people who will have your back cheering you on and one's power will start to build up. One just has to look in the mirror each day and in the words of Adam Sandler say to yourself, You Can Do It!

In retrospect, a team that personified this so-called power are the Boston Red Sox. After being three games down in the American League division series and almost being eliminated yet again from possibly going to the World Series. For these underdogs, it wasn't time for them to hear the fat lady sing and they fought for that decisive victory in game 4 which swung the moment back their way. The Yankees never really recovered after that and the Red Sox made history, in a good way of course. If you think about it, it takes small victories in certain areas of our own lives that will inevitably swing good fortune our way; it's just a matter of having that one great power…confidence.

ALONE IN THE DARK
November 21, 2004

Each one of us, while traveling down our proverbial journey of self, can become somewhat frustrated at certain aspects of one's life. The one aspect that every person can agree upon that can totally frustrate a person is seeking some kind of relationship with someone or being in a meaningful and significant relationship. Let me ask you this question, have you ever met someone that makes you so crazy and frustrated, but yet are attracted to him or her at the same time. I'm truly convinced that men and women were put on this Earth to mess with each other mentally to the point where we can go completely insane, but in a good way.

In some aspect, every person has hit that proverbial wall in which certain obstacles just get in the way. High hopes and/or great expectations are somewhat a given when a person thinks maybe that once lost smile can permanently stay on his or her face. Yet, one's high hopes and/or great expectations turn into disappointment when that one particular person you are interested in lets you down. It's like having the door of opportunity slammed or closed in your face without ever actually stepping through it. BUT the question is, how long should a person stand at the door of opportunity before he or she should decide to walk away completely?

Women are truly an enigma, for they are mysterious and beautiful. Yet, they can be totally confusing at the same time which is like trying to put together a complete puzzle, but some of the pieces are missing. As a guy, we are gluttons for punishment because even though we know we may suffer hurt and disappointment, continue to try to walk through doors of opportunity knowing that it may or may not be closed. Doors of opportunity will open again, but the question remains, will that door of opportunity ever open if I close my eyes and step towards it? In a way it's like putting your finger in a light socket, you know you are going to get shocked, but you do it for the simple reason that the socket is there.

Cy Eberhart once said, ~It is a fact of life that we find ourselves in unpleasant demoralizing situations which we can neither escape nor control. We can keep our morale and spirits high by using both "coping" and "hoping" humor. Coping humor laughs at the hopelessness in our situation. It gives us the courage to hang in there, but it does not bring hope. The uniqueness of hoping humor lies in its acceptance of life with all its dichotomies, contradictions, and incongruities. It celebrates the hope in human life. From one comes courage, from the other comes inspiration.~ Think about this, a person can continue to find humor in one's own situation until he or she stops laughing completely.

About 8 years ago, if you had asked me if I was ever ready to be in a relationship I would have laughed in your face. Since then, I have done a lot of growing and basically matured over these past 8 years. I've said before, I was a very different person than I was 8 years ago and for the most part, it was a change for the better. I clearly know that I have the potential to be a father, it's just a matter of finding that one missing ingredient, a woman to share my life with. In retrospect frustration is like being alone in the dark; you have no idea where you are, but it only takes that one ray of light to lead you in the direction one wants to go. Who is that ray of light for you?

SECOND CHANCES
November 23, 2004

It's been said, ~Chance is mere chaos or an order that escapes our understanding? Chance can be experienced only in a total surrender to the unconscious. Enter a world of very real uncertainty. We live in close proximity with chance. Because it dwells inside of us no less than our intentions, we ARE chance - chance and intention. Inexplicable reasons. Some of the so-called greatest works of art were found by chance. To delve into the unknown and unexpected gives an opportunity for unseen creativity to present itself that might have gone unrecognized if searched for while under certain commands to find. True chance and intention can be the most beautiful and inspiring work because it was not searched for. Its innocence makes it original and unique within our organized world.~

We've all taken chances that have pertained to one's own personal and/or professional life. Yet, more often than not, each of us have taken more chances personally putting ourselves out there in order to be seen and inevitably meet that one person who we will spend a lifetime with. Someone once said that it's better to regret something you've done than something you didn't do because one doesn't have another chance to do it again. In other words, it is better to have been given the answer to what one has been interested or wondering about than to continually have to wonder whether or not he or she should have asked that particular person, which will be a regret that will surface in the back of one's own mind from time to time.

If you think about it, it's rare to be given another chance when it pertains to finding love again. Every person has been at that proverbial rock and a hard place when he or she wished for that do-over after saying or doing something stupid that either put you or that particular person in an awkward position that you never really intended to be in. One's intentions were purely from the heart, but the timing was way off and in turn, one's hopes and/or expectations can be dashed in an instant. In a way, it's like running with that person but unsure where he or she is running to. Once one's momentum is pushed forward, it's hard to stop until we hit that proverbial wall of embarrassment and/or disappointment.

Let me ask you this question, if you had that one chance to turn back time and be with that one person that truly made you happy, would you do it? It's that one person, who you considered a best friend, the one that got away, and he or she absolutely knew the real you. He or she is that one person who saw through the façade, all the BS, knew you inside and out, plus found things about yourself that you didn't know you possessed. On a subconscious level, it's that one person who one often tries to find in another person, but as the saying goes you truly can't replace that one person who you loved with all your heart. Oftentimes, one wonders why certain things happen and never really see coming, but that's life and we have to deal with it.

In retrospect, a person can have that mentality that when it comes to love, there will be only ONE chance at ever finding true happiness. It's that true happiness that will never be able to be duplicated because it was different, unique, and special. What made it different, unique, and special was that particular individual who one happened to cross paths with by chance. When you take a chance with you, it's the biggest gamble one will ever make in life. Though you might roll snake-eyes, at least you gave it your best shot. In the end, second chances come once in a lifetime; cherish it, don't throw it away, you only get it once and if you don't take advantage of whom your heart is leading you to, then it will truly be crushed.

THE TRUTH IS
November 25, 2004

Ralph Waldo Emerson once said,~The soul is the perceiver and revealer of truth. We know truth when we see it, let skeptics and scoffers say what they choose. Foolish people ask you, when you have spoken what they do not wish to hear, 'How do you know it is true, and not an error of your own?' We know truth when we see it, from opinion, as we know when we are awake.~ Think about it, when one finally meets that one particular person that you truly know is right for you, one can oftentimes feel he or she is in a dream world. A dream world, in which a person thinks is absolutely too good to be true and hopes he or she doesn't wake up from it ever.

If you think about it, men and women deserve to be truthful and honest, even though he or she may not want to hear it. It's those two that are considered the best one-two punch combos when it comes to meeting and keeping that potentially new and hopefully lasting relationship. It's those two combos, so to speak, that will ultimately give a person the courage to face the possibility of defeat that may occur in an unknown and unpredictable area that is love. Let me ask you this question and be truthful to yourself. Have you ever been in a relationship where you knew the fire wasn't there anymore; but told yourself that it could be rekindled? What did you do, and did you face the truth?

Someone once said, ~The TRUTH, it may not lead you to where you thought you were going, but it will always lead you somewhere better. When ignored, it will eventually show itself. The closeness of your relationship is directly professional to the degree to which you have revealed the truth about yourself. It can be painful.~ Each one of us has had to endure some painfully hard truths when it comes to life, relationships, and especially love. In a way, it can be a great learning experience even though at the time one heart was going through a downward spiral of emotions. It's at a person's lowest point that he or she will inevitably see who one really is.

Every person is in pursuit of finding the truth when it pertains to their own heart. It's that particular truth that will, in some way, set him or her free from the bonds of self-doubt that will hold back a person from doing or saying something to that one person of interest. In a way, it's like having that dream where you are running towards something or someone, but you can't seem to get there. It's simply unattainable because something in your subconscious is holding you back from completely opening one's proverbial floodgates of emotions. It's those particular emotions, which can be compared to a rollercoaster, that can either be one's downfall or one's saving grace.

In retrospect, when you look into a person's eyes and that person looks back into yours, an unexplainable truth will be revealed. When one looks into each other's eyes, you look into each other's soul and what you find is something absolutely truly amazing. It's something that isn't quite right because you feel weak and scared but at the same time you feel stronger and excited. In the whole scheme of things, it's a totally confusing feeling; but it's a feeling in which you absolutely know that you want to be a better person than you want to be for him or her. The truth is, in the end, it's like reaching the top of the highest mountain, but you weren't quite ready for the climb up.

MAKING A DIFFERENCE
November 25, 2004

Every person comes to a point in one's own profession in which he or she wonders if there is anything being accomplished at all. I've often asked myself if there is any self-gratification for working in a place that will contribute to his or her hearing loss, add to the growing number of gray hairs, and possibly reconsider having kids in the near future. Working at the asylum for a long period of time will turn any happy-go-lucky person into a cynical and sarcastic person, a transformation that doesn't happen in an instant, but through time. It's a combination of broken promises, friction amongst friends and/or wo-workers, and seemingly long hours doing the same thing over and over again.

It's that constant cycle that can make a person feel edgy and somewhat frustrated that things, in one's own mind, will never change. In a way, it's like being stuck in the middle of a deserted island and you have no way of getting off it. Each one of us has a routine that one goes through and if that particular routine is broken then the shiznit hits the fan, in a manner of speaking. In some way, a person welcomes the mediocrity that is oftentimes a seemingly never-ending cycle of telling the same kids to do the same thing time and time again. One can get somewhat stuck and in order to get out of it, something has to happen to pull that person out of that particular rut.

Inevitably, it will spill over into one's personal life as well. For some people, one's journey, though adventurous, has been considered a lonely road indeed. As he or she travels down that road of life, it seems that one has been passing the same signs, billboards, and places. One can have that feeling, that one has been completely going around in circles and there is absolutely no opening to get out. To venture off the beaten path, in a manner of speaking, and meet new people that will peak one's interest. One starts to feel invisible and has that mentality that he or she is truly missing out on that one great adventure that one should be a part of.

In any case, the pressures of dealing with kids on a daily basis can take its toll on a person. You spend countless hours telling them what they should and shouldn't do; but it can be quite clear that it's going in one and out the other. Oftentimes there is a skewed line in which one can't distinguish if there is absolute success or absolute defeat when trying to get through to kids. One's ego can take the brunt of it; but ultimately what it boils down to is the absolute challenge to getting through to a child by any means necessary. For me personally, it's the challenge of connecting with kids in several different ways that the kids have responded in a more positive than a negative way.

In retrospect, you know you are making a difference in a child's life when they have seen you completely angry, frustrated, and totally stressed out; BUT at the end of the day, they still want to give you a hug and that is the best reward I can ever receive. I end this thought with a quote by George Bernard Shaw and he says, ~This is the true joy of life, the being used up for a purpose recognized by yourself as a mighty one; being a force of nature instead of a feverish, selfish little clot of ailments and grievances, complaining that the world will not devote itself to making you happy. I am of the opinion that my life belongs to the community, and as long as I live, it is my privilege to do for it what I can.~

FOR BETTER OR FOR WORSE
November 28, 2004

Anthony Storr once said, ~A happy marriage perhaps represents the ideal of human relationship - a setting in which each partner, while acknowledges the need of the other, feels free to be what he or she by nature is: a relationship in which instincts as well as intellect can find _expression; in which giving and taking are equal, in which each accepts the other, and I confronts Thou.~ Many topics that have come to my mind and in turn have been formulated into Yoda-isms. The one topic that I have somewhat avoid, due to my *poptomistic view on it, and has gotten my gears a movin' in the old noggin' is the topic of marriage. *poptomistic- a combination of pessimistic and optimistic.

In some aspect, marriage is like building a house, because if you think about it, it takes the right kind of materials to build a strong, sturdy, house that will not fall down or be destroyed by elements such as anger, resentment, jealousy, etc. In a way, both a husband and a wife can be somewhat compared to building contracts. Together, they have a floor plan/blueprint of a union that will continually change as time goes on. It's a change that is hopefully for the better, rather than no change at all, which can sometimes be a bad sign indeed. In today's society, some people give up so easily on marriage; but it's nice to see couples who have stuck with it and lasted more than 40 years.

Primarily what holds a house together is the cement and/or nails depending on what type of house the two are building. Think about this, what continually holds a marriage together is the keeping the romance alive and keeping the passions within that marriage burning. Ways to keep the romance alive is continually noticing the little things, which women will remember and never forget about. Other ways are giving flowers just to show that one's thoughts are always on his or her spouse. Another way to keep proverbial fires burning within is taking one's spouse on a date, which shows that one still knows how to be romantic. Ultimately, what will continually keep the romance alive is looking deep into your true love's eyes each day and saying these three little words, I LOVE YOU.

With every house, in order for it to be built, it needs a solid foundation. That solid foundation in building one's house is communication, because it takes two people to talk to each other and work out problems that will either patch up the damages or make the damages even greater. It's a sad situation indeed when you see a house that is poorly built because the romance has faded, the passion has burned out, and there is no longer communication between the contractors. Inevitably, what is needed is an extreme makeover: home edition; in which both spouses go back to square one and build back up what they gradually lost

Someone once said, ~The easiest part of marriage is falling in love and walking down the aisle. The most difficult part of marriage is 10 years later when the problems have ensued, and issues have come about and still find love. Marriage is not about the beginning, marriage is about the process and still being able to love through all things.~ In retrospect, two separate souls walking the earth but are intertwined and it only takes a small tangle in the thread of life to have two souls meet, fall in love, and get married. For better or for worse, till death do you part, as long as you both shall live; a vow that each of us is holding true or will someday hold true.

ULTIMATE GOAL
November 30, 2004

Claude M. Bristol said, ~The person with a fixed goal, a clear picture of his desire, or an ideal always before him, causes it, through repetition, to be buried deeply in his subconscious mind and is thus enabled, thanks to its generative and sustaining power, to realize his goal in a minimum of time and with a minimum of physical effort. Just pursue the thought unceasingly. Step by step you will achieve realization, for all your faculties and powers become directed to that end.~ Every person from the time that he or she was a teenager has had or still has an ultimate goal in life. A goal that is a burning desire in one's mind, heart, and soul; and though it's far off in the distance, one can clearly see it from where he or she is.

Let me ask you this question, what is your ultimate goal in life and have you achieved it or are you still trying to achieve that particular goal? It's somewhat of a great motivator for a person as he or she wakes up each morning and strives to be the very best at what one does and in turn one's specific door of opportunity will be opened. Yet, for some people short cuts are the way to go as one wants to find that back door in; but what will that accomplish? It's just a stepping stone to nowhere that will be locked out of the house, in a manner of speaking. For that person didn't earn the blood, sweat, and tears that other people worked their tails off, so to speak, to get to the pinnacle of one's personal and/or professional life.

In a way, each of us can be considered Indiana Jones trying to attain that proverbial Holy Grail. That Holy Grail, which is different for each of us, can somewhat signify making a mark in one's personal history book of life. Though it may not mean any importance in the annals of what is going on in the world today, it is important to each of us who wants to prove something. In some aspect, it's not so much proving it to others, it's proving it to yourself that if you set your mind to it, work hard, and not give up one's ultimate goal will be achieved. It's just a matter of having that one basic commodity that is precious to each and every one of us and that is patience.

Sometimes a person can literally be obsessed with attaining that ultimate goal, as well as achieving it. If compared to, it would be like the Lord of the Rings' character Smeagol who couldn't live without having his one and only precious thing which would be the ring. He would do anything to have it back in his hands because it contained absolute power. That obsession, as you know, was his downfall because it overtook his mindset. If you think about it, each of us can be like Smeagol in a way, because one's absolute power is our own ambition which can either attain absolute victory and/or absolute defeat as one tries or is trying to achieve his or her ultimate goal, whatever it may be.

In the whole scheme of things, the ultimate goal or goals that we have set for ourselves will always be there. It's not going to simply walk away or disappear when you close your eyes or turn around. Ultimately, the best course of action for each of us is to continue on our own personal journey of life. A journey, in which you will experience what life has to offer, seeing the world and what it has to offer, as well as, meeting that one special person who will make an unknowingly definite impact in one's seemingly complicated, yet simplistic life. I'll end this Yoda-ism with a quote that best sums up this particular thought which is: ~Never be consumed with goal that you fail to enjoy the journey.~

DON'T LOOK BACK
November 30, 2004

In some aspect, life can be considered a relay race in which each of us is preparing to run the greatest race of our lives. Yet, there will be circumstances that will hold us back from either finishing the race or crossing the finishing line and attaining a medal. One such circumstance is the past because, in a way, it's a giant weight that will slow us down and keep us from moving forward with the present and into the future. Someone once said, ~What you need to know about the past is that no matter what has happened, it has all worked together to bring you to this very moment, you can choose to to make everything new, right now.~

If you think about it, from birth to our teenage years our parents are immediately training and guiding us to something much greater in life. As one's proverbial track coaches, they push us to excel even though experience has somewhat taught that parents tend to relive their past youth through their kids. Oftentimes, the training and guidance that they give can bring resentment, as well as pain, both mentally and physically; but that's the past. For the expectations that were pushed beyond one's limits, are put to the test as the gun sounds. One must continue to look straight ahead as one will eventually pass the baton, which signifies a handing over of a childhood that is past to adulthood that is present.

As one runs straight forward into adulthood, he or she will hopefully not drop the baton, a mistake that can sometimes haunt a person. It's a matter of keeping focus on the task at hand but sometimes pictures of the past will tend to pop from time to time. Images, which represent certain people that have made an impact in one life both personally and professionally, will flash in one's mind. Yet, if one remenices too long, a person will become distracted and lose focus on where he or she is. Inevitably, all that one has worked hard for will be lost, for a great deal of time and effort will be wasted as the baton is passed from the present to the future.

Joe Henderson once said, ~Your toughness is made up of equal parts of persistence and experience. You don't so much outrun your opponent as outlast and outsmart them and the toughest opponent of all is the one inside our head.~ In a way, as the baton is passed on into our latter years, the past mistakes and pain that we have endured and/or inflicted, both mentally and physically, will be forgotten. It's just a matter of taking each step stride by stride, as one is getting ever so much closer to that finish line of life. Ultimately, it's not about winning that matters; what matters is that you were prepared to win and never gave up on the relay race of life.

In retrospect, as one gets older the race of life, though strenuous; is the most rewarding experience a person will ever be a part of. Though, one's time will become slower as one gets older in mind, body and soul; the experiences of the racing is simply unforgettable. Each step in the race represented our own personal drama that each of us endured, challenges that pulled us in ever possible direction or another, but most of all it helped us learn more about us and others. In the end, our greatest rival when running the relay race of life will always be the past; so when it comes to the past, don't look back because you may just stumble and/or fall.

ONLY HUMAN
December 2, 2004

Rainer Maria Rilke once said, ~ Be patient toward all that is unsolved in your heart and try not to love the questions themselves like locked rooms and like books that are written in a very foreign tongue. Do not seek the answers, which cannot be given you because you would be able to live them. And the point is, to live everything. Live the questions now. Perhaps you will them gradually, without noticing it and live long some distant day into the answers.~ Through one's travels down the road of life, a person will take a journey into one's own being and in turn, will try to find that proverbial key that will unlock specific "rooms" in one's own heart and soul that have never been completely open.

In search of the answers one seeks, a person will come to a point where he or she asks a question that one is afraid to tell himself or herself. It's those specific questions that are stored away in the back of one's mind that you never really want to answer. In a way, it's like running away from ourselves because once you come face to face, the truth will be clear as day. In some aspect, every thought that has crossed my path, either intentionally or by accident, has been a Yoda-ism that told the truth in my own unique perspective on life. It's these truths that, in a way, have somewhat brought me closer to the key that will hopefully unlock all the doors to my questions.

Consequently, what you read can mentally captivate and stimulate one's mind, as well as one's own imagination. For it can give you a sense of what is seen through my eyes; yet it can be seen through every person's eyes as well. Every word, excluding the quotes, comes from a place that I look deep within and that is my heart and soul. It's in these two places that I seek solace in and consider it a comfort zone, which I have slowly ventured out of when I share pieces of myself with you. If you think about it, there is essentially a deep wisdom in the thoughts that I write and then send out; though one may not sense it, you can somehow feel it by way of its emotional aspect.

One such emotional aspect is the feeling of love and/or unrequited love. Oftentimes one's heart can play tricks with you and inevitably leads you to the person you want to be with who is simply out of reach. Sometimes, one's head and heart can be in a proverbial dual. A duel in which the head thinks who one will fall in love with; and with the heart, it knows who you will fall in love with. Every person, including myself, has gone through it and more often than not my head has gotten the better of me. For it's the schoolboy/schoolgirl crushes that can get a person absolutely nowhere leading him or her down dead ends every time; ultimately, it's the one truth that I couldn't avoid facing any longer.

In any case, each of us goes through pressures in life that will bring us to different areas of emotions. I've often been able to hide my emotions, as well as the pressures of life through sarcasm, laughter, and cynicism. It's somewhat of a poker face that I show and working at a Youth Center one has to suppress those emotions because the kids will be affected by it. Every person comes to a breaking point where pressures of life can get the better of you. Yesterday it happened to me, and I had somewhat of a meltdown; in a way it revealed an all-important truth. In retrospect, that truth is that a person can have that perception of being invincible; but when the pressures of life catch up to you, it shows that each of us is, of course, only human.

DOWN HILL
December 3, 2004

There comes a point in every person's life when one's mind and body start to break down. Let me ask this question, have you ever walked into an area of your house or workplace and totally forgot why you were there in the first place? It's just one of the signs of things to come as one gets older. It's simply unavoidable as time passes by at a seemingly slow, but yet fast pace. We've all stopped dead in our tracks, so to speak, and simply asked ourselves where has the time gone? With time comes change; for the changes we all go through as we get older can have a person either denying that it's going to happen to that person or accepting and welcoming it in with open arms.

In a way, getting older can absolutely hit a person without any warning. It can somewhat be considered like a well-trained sniper concealed out of sight, who is about to hit his or her target. If you think about it, the one part of the body that after being hit and is never the same again is one's back. I don't know about women, but for guys it's the second sign that old age is upon us; the first sign being memory loss. Working at a Youth Center, a person's back will be greatly affected as kids will jump on you constantly. As with one's memory, trying to remember names with faces has been at times daunting; and the best solution, in my opinion, is to call every kid dude or dudette.

Think about this, as young kids we couldn't wait to reach two fairly important stages in our lives. The first stage is the teen years which can signify big things such as learning to drive, then entering high school, and ultimately graduating. The second stage is reaching that ever-so-popular age of twenty-one; but as soon as you reach it, you realize it's really nothing to jump up and down about and nothing hasn't really changed except one's expectations. Yet there is a third stage, which kids never thought one would actually see coming and that is turning thirty and I am about 3 years away from it. It's a somewhat exciting but somewhat depressing thought indeed.

In any case, the saying "I'm not as young as I used to be" holds true, as I find myself not being able to stay up past midnight anymore. More and more, I hear my bones cracking and certain bones that haven't healed due to a particular injury have now aided me in determining what the weather is like. It's somewhat of a trade-off as a person loses something, but yet gains something in return. For me, the old dude. has now settled in and made himself comfortable. For he is no longer a simple guest, he's now a permanent resident. The gray hairs have already shown up, which shows that with age comes wisdom; and the wisdom that I have shared has hopefully helped you in a way.

Charles Dickens once said, ~Father Time is not always a hard parent, and, though he tarries for none of his children, often lays his hand lightly upon those who have used him well; making them old men and women inexorably enough but leaving their hearts and spirits young and in full vigor. With such people the gray head is but the impression of the old fellow's hand in giving them his blessing, and every wrinkle but a notch in the quiet calendar of a well-spent life. ~ In retrospect, I may not live to the ripe old age of one hundred as my fictitious Star Wars namesake Yoda, but sure as heck going to try. In however long I live, I don't consider it an ending and all going downhill. As a matter of fact, this is just the beginning of my journey.

KNOW YOUR ROLE
December 8, 2004

Mignon Mclaughlin once said, ~Tough and funny and a little bit kind; that is as near perfection as a human being can be.~ Working in the childcare profession, you can get somewhat of an idea of what role one will play as time goes on. In some cases, that particular question can be immediately answered or not answered at all. For some people it takes a while as he or she tries to find one's particular niche when dealing with kids. One has to have a balance of meanness and coolness; but there are those days where one trait outweighs the other. Over the 8 years I have worked at the Asylum, I have been put in several different roles that in some way, shape or form have taught me some life lessons.

Someone once said, ~Every leader needs to look back one in a while to make sure he has followers. Being a leader is an important responsibility because the people one works with look to you for answers. In some aspect, I consider myself a veteran and sometimes the solutions to problems and/or questions that relate to the job come easily. Yet, there are the times where blame for something one did or didn't do is placed squarely on one's shoulders; but it comes with the territory when working in the childcare profession. I've learned that being a leader doesn't necessarily mean taking on all the responsibility, it means delegating some of the responsibility to one's co-workers; in other words, teamwork.

Another role that I feel quite nicely is the role of mentor/big brother. Though, I don't know what it's like to have more than one sibling; but I can imagine. Yet, it's somewhat of a nice feeling to make an impact, if any, in these kids' lives. I've been a person who likes to draw and from time to time try to teach the kids step by step to draw whenever an opportunity for a drawing class is scheduled.

About 4 years ago, a parent came up to me and told me that their child has been drawing a lot and it was due to my influence and how fun I made it for him. A person never really knows the impact that one can make on a child until the child's parent informs you; it can be an ego boost, but it's just part of the job.

Though I don't have any kids myself, the role of parent is one I have somewhat eased into being that I have learned from the best which are my parents. One can have that mindset that he or she will never say or do the things that his or her parents did; ultimately you will be in for a rude awakening. For the phrase "BECAUSE I SAID SO" has been permanently integrated into every response that pertains to a child when he or she simply asks why. I never thought a day would come when those 4 words would come out of my mouth after arguing with a child about sitting in someone else's seat. If you think about it, we spend our lives trying not to be our parents and yet, we are our parents.

In retrospect, the people I work with are considered family and every family member has a role. After 8 years, I finally realized what my role actually is, and you know what, it actually suits my personality. I will forever be by the crazy uncle who visits the house; but in this case I clock into the asylum. I make the kids laugh when they need cheering up, get them and myself into trouble when things get a little rowdy, and promise them treats and sometimes don't deliver on time. I then do it all over again the next day; it's that inner child you never leave behind that helps you when the aspects of the job get you totally stressed out. So, when it comes to your own job, do you know your role?

PARADISE
December 10, 2004

Every person has that one place where he or she can get away to. A place where one can just hang, chill, and get away from people and the daily trappings of life that tend to just overwhelm you. In some aspect, when you are at this particular place one can feel a sense of calm because it's a place that hopefully nobody really knows about. For you claimed it as your own and yet if there is any kind of disturbance, that peaceful harmony will absolutely be ruined. It can be somewhat like Superman's fortress of solitude, though it may not be a grand or spectacular place to look at, it's a place where you can simply gather your thoughts and drift off in your own little world, nonetheless.

Oftentimes, one's fortress of solitude isn't located at a place where a person can physically go to. If you think about it, each of us have easy access and all you have to do is simply close your own eyes. A person can somewhat think outside the box as he or she creates from one's own imagination a place in which he or she can get away to. A proverbial happy place that you feel comfortable in, and you can be absolutely content in exploring one's own past, present, and possibly the future without ever really going anywhere. For all the worries that he or she has are left at the front door, so to speak, and that do not disturb sign is placed on one's doorknob.

As kids, a place such as the playground or clubhouse was sort of, in a way, holy ground so to speak. Nobody could tell you what to do and you could push the limits of stupidity beyond its limits. For it was a way to let out one's own aggressions, if any. As you got older other places such as the mall, Wal-Mart, the movie theater, Starbucks, a certain restaurant or drinking establishment, and even one's own car were ways to take yourself out of the reality that has somewhat slapped you in the face into another reality that you can better control of. Let me ask you this question, when was the last time you basically had time by yourself, just relaxed and didn't think about what is happening around you?

Inevitably, it doesn't have to be a place, but rather a person that one can talk to about life's most difficult problems. It could be a friend, mentor, parent, grandparent, a potential or significant other, every person has someone different. It's that particular person who is considered the go to person for the answers that he or she is seeking. Yet, it's not so much talking but hanging with that person that is considered the best therapy you don't have to pay for. That one person will always be there for you whenever you need to talk and get things off your chest, but when you are good and ready. Each one of us knows a person like this and values the advice given, though we may not want to hear it at times.

Jeffrey Kotter once said, ~There is convincing evidence that the search for solitude is not a luxury but a biological need. Just as humans possess a herding instinct that keeps us close to others most of the time, we also have a conflicting drive to seek out solitude. If the distance between ourselves and others becomes too great, we experience isolation and alienation, yet if the proximity to others becomes too close, we feel smothered and trapped.~ In retrospect, each of us need a balance of space and closeness when times of stress go to all of us. For when each of us go to that one place or to be with that one person, it can be a feeling that can be described with only one word...paradise.

SPELL RELIEF
December 15, 2004

Douglas Pagels once said, ~Sometimes it's important to work for that pot of gold. But other times its essential to take time off and to make sure that your most important decisions in the day simply consists of choosing which side to slide down on the rainbow.~ For most people, attaining that all important degree is serious business, but you have to have fun in between all the hard work one does. The decisions one makes will determine if he or she will encounter constant setbacks that will hinder a person from walking down the aisle and proclaiming what one truly earned. It's that proverbial pot of gold, so to speak, that is considered the most valuable document that one will ever have in one's own life.

In some aspect, the pursuit of higher learning in college can somewhat be compared to the story of the tortoise and the hare. On some days or everyday, one can feel like the tortoise and things just seem to pass you by and you can't get motivated to do anything. Let me ask you this, have you ever had one of those days where the time was just going way too slow? It's those particular days in which the sluggishness, combined with the long hours will have one's energy slowly fade away. Inevitably, it's more of a mental game than a physical one, and in a way, you have to constantly motivate and repeat to yourself I KNOW I CAN. It's just a matter of keeping that slow and steady pace to win that race, in a manner of speaking.

On the other side of that coin, one can also feel like the hare. As a college student, he or she has to run from point A to point B, all-the-while, grabbing something to snack on when one can't find the time to eat a big meal. It's the life of a college student, for one can be so focused and/or determined to get to the finish line that a person will run on adrenaline or sheer will power. For one's gas tank is running on empty, so to speak, and all that person is running on is fumes. Every person comes to a point either in the middle or late stages of the semester where he or she kicks it into a higher gear. A gear, in which a person taps into some reserve fuel, in other words inner strength that is both mental and physical.

Consequently the moral of the story is that slow and steady wins the race. One has to realize that a diploma will be there waiting; even though it may take longer than expected to get it, at least you took your time. Within that time, one hopefully will never take for granted the people who helped and guided you through one's own journey. A journey that consisted of uncovering hidden lessons and lessons that you had to learn first hand. If you think about, it's the people that you unknowingly cross paths with are the ones you will always remember most. It's those people who see the person you really are; and what they see is a person who never quit when the going got tremendously tough.

In retrospect, every person goes through drama during his or her years in college, it's simply unavoidable. It may pertain to one's personal or professional life; but if those two separate entities merge into one, then the shiznit will hit the fan, in a manner of speaking. A person has to have his or her sense of humor in tact, when it comes to college life. If you don't have it, then you will literally go mad; for me personally I went off the deep end but I didn't drown. An old commercial asked the question, How do you spell relief? When I am handed that diploma, all the long, stressful nights will truly be worth it; and in the end, this is how I will spell relief.....S-L-E-E-P.

THE GREATEST GIFT
December 15, 2004

It's beginning to look and feel a lot like Christmas as the decorations are hung in the house, as well as on the tree. For Jack Frost is nipping not only at your nose, but every other major body part depending on where you live. It's one time out of the year where every person feels a certain energy i the air that can turn you back into a wide-eyed little kid again. It's that innocence that is seen through our eyes way back when that makes the holiday season so festive. For that proverbial countdown has already started and the days on the calendar are being crossed out as we speak. Let me ask you this question, do you still get excited when Christmas time comes around or do you gradually turn into an Ebeneezer Scrooge?

Oftentimes, a person will become jaded as the holiday season rolls around. He or she will focus on the negative aspects such as the long lines in stores and in airports, plus encountering people who are absolutely rude. For that person's focus isn't on building up a memorable Christmas that will be enjoyed by all; but rather tearing down of it. We all know a person or crossed paths with someone like this and even though you try to be friendly with him or her, they will still have a crabby attitude no matter what one does or says. It's these scrooges that have lost the spirit of Christmas and that wide-eyed little kid that they used to has been replaced with a nasty Grinch.

In any case, Christmas presents are just one of many aspects that most people really enjoy. Every person's eyes light up when he or she receives a gift from someone or sees some under the old Christmas tree. Each of us at some point, as young kids, tried to sneak a peek at his or her gifts and either got caught in the act or not at all. Personally speaking, I never was caught, and I had a sneaky way to find out what I got. Depending on what type of package it was, I would poke a hole at the bottom, shine the Christmas light in it and see what I got. Of course, it ruined the mystery; but think about this, it was the mere challenge of not getting caught that made it absolutely such a thrill to do.

Inevitably, as one grows older, the perception of Christmas tends to lose its spark. For one realizes that Santa doesn't exist and eventually finds out that in fact one's own parents are Santa Claus, which was somewhat disappointing. Yet it's that solid belief, as a kid, that it's an absolute possibility that a man flies all across the world bringing presents to little children. You can't help but smile when someone mentions the name Santa Clause, because the name takes you back to your own childhood. A childhood where you stayed up and tried to see if he would come to your house and leave presents. Though one may not believe in jolly old Saint Nick anymore, his essence still lives on in each of us.

Someone once said, ~The universal joy of Christmas is certainly wonderful. We ring the bells when princes are born or toll a mournful dirge when great men pass away. Nations have their red-letter days, their carnivals and festivals, but once a year and only once, the whole world stands still to celebrate the advent of a life. Only Jesus of Nazareth claims this worldwide, undying remembrance. You cannot cut Christmas out of the calendar, nor out of the heart of the world.~ In retrospect, Christmas isn't about getting or giving gifts that may or may not be returned. For you see two thousand years ago, Jesus Christ was born in a manger, and He is the greatest gift ever given from the heart to mankind from God.

READY TO FLY
December 18, 2004

Patrick Overton said, ~When we walk to the edge of all the light we have and take a step into the darkness of the unknown, we must believe that one of two things will happen: there will be something solid to stand on or we will be taught to fly.~ In some aspect, each of us can be compared to an eagle that is about to spread one's wings for the very first time. It can be a scary thing when you can't control what might or might not happen when one takes that leap of faith with your heart. In a way, each one of us can be cautious as we walk to the edge and have these two options: either back away from the edge and not fly at all or take that step off the edge and soar to new heights.

If you think about it, when a person backs away from the edge, he or she tends to push away that one person that essentially you are interested in or vice versa. It's that one person who when you first meet or see, one absolutely forgets how to breathe; also, one seems to forget his or her own name, which comes with the territory. In any case, each time one continually backs away from the edge, a person will lost that window of opportunity to actually feel the wind beneath your wings. It's a matter of psyching yourself up even though you, and that person as well, are absolutely scared out of your mind. One just has to let go of that fear, walk to the edge, spread your wings, and fly.

Unfortunately, for some people taking that first step off the edge to fly towards that particular person can oftentimes leave a person with a tremendous headache, in a manner of speaking. We've all experienced that awkward and sometimes embarrassing situation where one thought you were flying to someone that he or she may have a chance with; but crashed into that proverbial invisible glass window which happens to all of us from time to time. For each one of us has suffered a broken wing, which is a representation of our own heart, and it can keep us from being able to fly once again. Consequently, it's that self-doubt that will keep one from stepping into the unknown phenomenon that is love.

Ultimately, falling in love or being in love is an experience that can be best described as soaring above the clouds with or towards someone you would risk life and limb for. Let me ask you this question, with the eyes of an eagle who was or is that one person that caught your attention and initially he or she captured your heart? I once said that love is like flying without wings, but when you are truly in love the sky is the limit. To be perfectly honest, when you are in the air flying high, the answers you seek sometimes become much clearer than when you are simply standing at the edge rather than wondering whether or not you should have at least tried and live with that regret for years to come.

In retrospect, love is about hoping, dreaming, continually believing and taking that step to the edge without fear, and never looking down no matter what happens below you. It's that Superman/Supergirl mentality that one will always have because love is considered kryptonite; it will bring you down to your knees and can either make you lose the strength you have or make you stronger. Someone once said, ~May you soar like an eagle and shine like the sun.. and may your spirit and heart join together with someone as one.~ Every person will step or has stepped off the edge and flew high; but suffered or will suffer a broken wing that may or may not heal. In the end, a person will ask yourself this question when it comes to falling in love again, am I ready to fly?

NEVER GO HUNGRY
December 22, 2004

Guisseppe Mazzini once said, ~The family is the Country of the heart. There is an angel in the family who, by the mysterious influence of grace, of sweetness, and of love, renders the fulfillment of duties less wearisome, sorrows less bitter. The only pure joys unmixed with sadness which it is given to man to taste upon earth are thanks to this angel, the joys of the family.~ When you are part or become a part of Filipino American family you not only have your own family, but one also has an extended family as well. In some aspect, it's an extended family that is well connected and informed than the FBI, CIA, and Al Qaeda, without the violent terror related tendencies.

Thinking about it, time is inconsequential for a group of people that never really arrive on time. Being an hour or two hours late for that matter is practically expected and one shouldn't expect anything less. In some ways, a person set their watch on when we will arrive depending on whether or not food will be involved with this particular function. In any case, making an entrance is somewhat similar to when a person or a family is making his or their departure. It can be disappointing, as a young kid, to leave a party that one is really enjoying; but not when you are on Filipino time. It's that proverbial Filipino time, where young kids can enjoy several more hours of fun when parents say they are about to leave in a couple of minutes.

In some instances, being part of a culture that expresses itself in dance or song, one will get roped into doing certain dance or singing related activities that he or she doesn't want to do as a young kid. It can be either a win-win or win-lose situation depending on how one looks at it. On one hand, you can simply refuse not to do that particular activity and suffer the biggest guilt trip that a parent will hand down on you to the point where you agree to do it. On the other hand, you can do it, get it over with while you're young, and not do it ever again…most of the time. A line from a movie that escapes me right now best sums up how one can feel at times: ~Just when I think I done, they pull me back in.~

It can somewhat boggle the mind that cooking food comes a close second to the one thing Filipino-Americans love to do the most and that is singing Karaoke. One can be absolutely drawn to it like senior citizens to a lunch buffet; though he or she may not want to sing, that person will have the microphone in his or her own hands. It's truly uncanny the power of a karaoke machine can hold over a Filipino because it turns a fairly normal person into a singing machine that will either make a person be perceived as the next American Idol or the next American Idol reject. Ultimately, whether you are making a fool of yourself or not, one will have absolute fun doing it; even if you can't sing worth a lick like myself.

In any case, a person can be unofficially adopted into the Filipino American family that will absolutely welcome you with open arms. There is no background check, and you don't have to wait months or even years to get on a waiting list. Personally speaking, over the years there have been a number of friends from college that are considered part of the family. Though not related by blood, it's the ties that bind that make a person feel like a brother and/or a sister. For them it's like a second home where they can get away from the college food and eat food they can actually taste. In the end, there is one absolute fact that when you are accepted into a Filipino American house that considers you part of the family, you will never go hungry.

IT'S OFFICIAL
December 23, 2004

There comes a point in any person's job that there are certain tell-tale signs and/or realizations that one has been working at his or her particular establishment for a long period of time. Working in the nuthouse for the last eight years, there can be several aspects of the job that can cross over into life outside the asylum. In some aspect, they tend to sick with you and never really go away; though you may not want it to happen, it happens, and you can't stop it. It's kind of like taking your work home with you, which is actually a frightening thought indeed having over a hundred kids who one watches over on a semi-daily basis knowing where you actually live.

One tell-tale sign that a person has been working for a long period of time is wanting to use a whistle. There are certain days I find myself in a crowded and loud area where I wanted to use my whistle to tell people to quiet down; but when I reached for it, I simply grabbed air. It's kind of like an off-duty cop trying to grab for his or her gun when a crime is about to be committed or being committed. Yet, if I actually were to have used my whistle, people would either stare at me, ignore me, or do both. Working in an environment that just exudes loudness, having a whistle is the best "weapon" to calm down a group of kids that have endless amounts of energy that they want to burn off.

One realization that a person can come to is that wherever you go these kids will follow you. It's like they are the FBI, they know their whereabouts 24 hours a day, seven days a week. Going out of town is an impossibility as well, for they are everywhere. It's simply unavoidable and no matter how hard one tries to get away from these kids they will find you. Inevitably there is one place that is an absolute guarantee a person who works in the asylum will run into these kids and that place is Wal-Mart. Let me tell you something, having your name yelled out loud in a Wal-Mart store can be a very humbling experience, which has absolutely been done to me on many occasions.

In some instances, one will realize that certain kids live near you, which is either a pleasant or unpleasant thought. It really depends on which particular kid or kids, who you absolutely like or tolerate, to keep the location of one's house on the downlow. Oftentimes it can be a surprising situation when there is a knock at my door and standing there are the asylum kids who want you to solve their arguments for them. Fortunately, it hasn't happened yet, but if it did happen it would be an awkward situation which can be handled in two ways: 1.) scream and slam the door OR 2.) talk to the kids. Ultimately, you are never really off duty when they need someone to listen and talk to.

Last weekend, my best friend and I came to one huge realization, and it came to us while standing in line to see the movie, Blade Trinity. You see, we ran into a former teenager that used to go to the asylum and he grew up. As we were talking about old times, we asked what he has been up to lately and he mentioned that he got married and his wife was with him. It was a nice surprise, and we gave our congrats, as well as giving him a few parting shots to embarass him in front of his wife. In the end, as we were standing in line at the concession area I turned to my best friend and told him this statement which he agreed wholeheartedly with: ~It's official, we're old.~

ULTIMATE SACRIFICE

December 26, 2004

Love. It's a word that can oftentimes be difficult to define. It can mean so many different things to many people. If you ask someone to define it, he or she may have a different interpretation of what it is. Yet, it is really hard to zone in on a simple definition or statement of what love actually means. If you think about it, we are in search of someone to fill the void that is missing in one's heart. For some people, that void has already been filled, but for others, he or she is still in search of that one person who can fill that empty spot in their own heart. Every person wants that type of love that will last a lifetime and not the type of love that is temporary, which makes that void in his or her heart even bigger.

Thinking about it, love is a word that certain people hate to hear due to his or her past experiences. When one hears that word that person associates it with betrayal and/or dishonesty. It's from there a person will inevitably hold back and/or limit just how much he or she will allow feelings of love for the particular person to surface. It basically comes down to trust issues with one's own heart and primarily taking that wall down, which will leave a person truly happy or sad in the end. Though a person can hide the love that one feels for someone, it can't be suppressed, or it will burst like a volcano. Love will make you sick and no matter how hard you try to avoid it, a person will get bitten by that proverbial love bug.

Let me ask you something, do you absolutely know the feeling of true love? That type of true love where you are with someone, you feel like there is no one else in the world but you and that person. For one's surroundings are inconsequential and merely a part of the background to your own fairy tale setting, so to speak. We've all had that feeling and its that whirlwind roller coaster that can bring either bliss and/or insanity to this sometimes-confusing phenomenon known as love. It's truly unpredictable and it can strike any time, any place, and anywhere. Ultimately, each of us will hold on to that feeling and never want to let it go; but no matter how tight one holds on it can slip through our fingers like grains of hands.

Although love is painful and sometimes you just want to give up on ever finding it, it doesn't die. Crushes, infatuations, lusts, adoring someone from afar do die and are types of feelings that will fade away like a sunset. Yet, the one thing that never fades away or dies is true love; for it is never ending. It's subsequently infinite and it's been said when you are there for someone without him or her asking you to be there, it shows a strong bond of affection for that person or vice versa. True love is giving yourself up to him or her even though that person may push you away at first either physically or emotionally. In the end, you have to realize sometimes one must give up our own happiness in order to make someone else happy and that my friend is an act of selflessness that is considered to be the ultimate sacrifice.

I end this with a quote which says~ "Love and relationships are truly one of the most paradoxical aspects of being human. For it is in love that we find the greatest of strengths and the deepest of sorrows. Love can seem to be so fleeting and unachievable yet it remains well within our reach if we only learn how to embrace its power. To experience true love, we must be willing to open ourselves up and sacrifice part of our heart and part of our soul. We must be willing to give of ourselves freely, and we must be willing to suffer. It is only when we expose our inner selves to the white hot flame of rejection, that love can burn so brightly as to join two souls, melding the two into one, creating a bond that joins forever. It is from this bond that we draw strength eternal and power everlasting. It is in this thing that we call love that we find the means to achieve greatness, both in ourselves and in our lives.~

ARE YOU HAPPY

December 27, 2004

William Lyon Phelps once said, "The happiest are those who think the most interesting thoughts. Those who decide to use leisure as a means of mental development, who love good music, good books, and good pictures, good company, good conversation, are the happiest people in the world. And they are not only happy in themselves, they are the cause of happiness in others.~ Every person has come to make the most of their own situation, a situation where if life gives you lemons, simply make lemonade. Inevitably, it's one's own situation where friends, family, or colleagues ask you that proverbial question which primarily asks about your own happiness.

Essentially what makes a person happy is that he or she has something to do to distract one from his or her life. A person will oftentimes keep himself or herself busy and with one's particular job, that person can take the time to focus on something else. In some aspects, accomplishing a task that seemed utterly impossible can give you a sense of achievement, which can boost one's spirit. It's that sense of achievement that can also boost one's confidence and in turn give a person a better night's sleep. For me personally, it's an achievement in itself to be still working in a place that even though it makes me totally insane, actually brings a smile to my face.

For most people, what makes one happy is that one tangible thing that he or she can continually hold on to and that is hope. Each of us hopefully has something to hope for in life; for it's that proverbial holy grail that one keeps focused on as he or she continually climbs that ladder of success. Yet, one will come across those Al Bundy types where all their hopes are crushed, and all their happiness is replaced by broken dreams with an added mix of miserable complaining. Though you may not be an unhappy shoe salesman, one can rest in the fact that you put your nose to the grindstone, in a manner of speaking, then that something you have been hoping for will one day come true to life.

In some cases, to be happy means to have someone to love and that someone to love you back. Oftentimes, when you do meet someone, one doesn't want to mess it up to the point where you spend time analyzing what went wrong. Just move forward because he or she may not be "the one" for you. For a person to risk falling in love, then being hurt, then falling in love again can be considered the thing a person can do. For that person should feel happy because all the heartache that one went through culminated into eventually leading you to meet that one special person. In other words, a person has to have a balance of sadness and happiness and for you, which side weighs more?

C.P. Snow said, ~The pursuit of happiness is a most ridiculous phrase: if you pursue happiness you'll never find it.~ Let me ask you this question, are you searching for happiness or have you already found it standing right in front of you all along? In some aspect, it's like sitting or standing in one spot for a certain period of time and familiar faces cross your paths. In a way, a person just has to sit or stand in one spot and happiness will find you, whoever he or she may be. For the most part, I am happy because I have my family, my friends, something to do to keep me busy, something to hope for, but that someone to love that's a big question mark. In the end I ask you this simple question, are you happy?

CLEAN SLATE
December 28, 2004

Thomas Mann said, ~Time has no divisions to mark it's passage, there is never a thunderstorm or blare of trumpets to announce the beginning of a new month or year. Even when a new century begins it is only we mortals who ring bells and fire off pistols.~ As we start to turn the last page of 2004, we inevitably start a new one as 2005 approaches in a couple of days. Within this past year, we've all been through many experiences that were considered memorable and unforgettable. Yet, whether they were bad or good, it's those experiences that are now in the past; though not forgotten it will stick with us. When one looks back at 2004, did you make every moment count or was every possible moment thrown out the window?

If you think about it, each year we are given equal amounts of time for the opportunity to implement what one has learned over the last twelve months. It's within those twelve months that he or she has hopefully made every effort to make or reach his or her goals. As one goes for the gold, so to speak, the knowledge one attains while going through one's own professional or personal experience will hopefully give a person some newfound insight. Insight in which a person asks himself or herself whether or not the time one has used was completely wasted or not. Initially, time can be either your best friend or your worst enemy and it's the one thing that you can never stop.

In this last year, each of us have experienced all sorts of emotions that have lifted one up, brought one to his or her knees, or brought one to places in between. For our emotions can be associated with time because once you have a particular emotion such as anger, it's gone...for the most part. It's considered yesterday's news, in a manner of speaking, but tomorrow is an uncertainty, because one's anger may return like an unwelcome houseguest. Consequently, a person has no real guarantee that the emotions that he or she has carried in the past year will disappear. It's just a matter of knowing that it will probably happen all over again but under new circumstances.

Over the last twelve months, each of us has gone through our ups and downs when it comes to love. For some people the downs outweigh the ups, for others it's vice versa, but for most people it was more of a balance. Subsequently, we can either waste and worry with the remaining time one has dwelling in ourselves or simply share the love; though it may not be reciprocated the way he or she truly wanted. Thinking about it, one can't slow time down, turn it off, or adjust it and when it pertains to love, time ultimately marches on. It's basically a part of life and the past mistakes and successes will unfortunately linger on in our hearts, as well as in our minds for years to come.

In retrospect, it's truly amazing how quickly the year has passed us by. In some ways, as you get older time just seems to go much faster than usual. One moment you turn 21, then the next moment you are 30 years old, and then you ask yourself what happened to those 9 years in between? Let me ask you this question, does it feel like you've missed out on life, or do you feel that you're keeping pace with it? As we make our new year's resolutions for 2005, one will attempt to keep them, but for how long? It will be 12 months, 52 weeks, 365 days, 8,760 hours, 525,600 minutes, 31,536,000 seconds to 2006 so make the most of it; because when the clock strikes midnight, each of us will have that proverbial clean slate all over again.

~Have A Happy New Year Folks!~

ON BENDED KNEE (LAST YODAISM OF 2004)

December 30, 2004

It's a funny thing about life, you never really expect to meet anyone that one thinks he or she might match up perfectly with. A person can oftentimes come close but no cigar, in a manner of speaking, because each of us tend to be somewhat picky. We all tend to look for qualities that will hopefully match with every criteria in which he or she is or could be considered a potential relationship in the making. For when one does choose that one particular diamond in the rough, so to speak, it's from that point on to unravel the mystery of who that person really is. In some aspect, both people must find their way through a proverbial smoke screen to truly know whether or not each is truly compatible.

Every person has that innate ability to read people as one could be dead on, dead wrong, or somewhere in the middle. Yet, when it pertains to someone that you might, probably, or could spend the rest of your life with it's really an unknown. In some ways, it's like playing a game of Russian Roulette with your heart and you absolutely don't know if you are going to make it to the end. It's that type of thinking, for myself anyway, that can make any person feel somewhat afraid of actually letting someone gradually know the real you. It's one's true self as he or she reveals one's own fears, as well as insecurities and once shown that person may either turn and run away or stay and stand by your side.

Let me ask you this question, what is your deepest fear in life? For most or all people it's dying alone and not having someone at your side to share memorable experiences with. Every guy comes to a point in his life when he wants to settle down and start a family. It can be somewhat of a depressing situation for any person to hear that close friends have gotten engaged and oftentimes one after another. It's even more depressing when those same friends and even family members ask when one's time of holy matrimony will be, which may or may not happen. Consequently, its that optimistic attitude that can truly surprise a person when he or she stands or walks down the aisle and gets married.

Ultimately, that proverbial smoke screen will start to clear, and one will get a clearer picture of the person who one wants to be with. Sometimes one, the other, or both will pass each other, but that is to be expected because every relationship a person is involved in is considered a test. A test of patience, in which he or she will encounter faults that a person will get past and if you do, then it's just one less hurdle for a person to deal with. It makes the ties that bind one to another stronger as the love for each other grows even bigger. For each hurdle that one jumps over, it simply makes knowing each other emotionally, intellectually, and personally even more exciting.

In retrospect, I spent some time searching for quotes from Shakespeare to Socrates; but in all honesty the words that someone else said can't compare to what two people find within each other who will one day embark on a new journey together. Every person travels down the lonely road of life, but undoubtedly all roads lead to someone that you somehow know is the one for you. It's that one person you take a chance on, risking your heart and soul to be with. When you know you have it, don't let go of it, and for every guy out there, including myself, will one day let our heart guide us to make an all-important, scary, as well as life changing decision. It's that particular decision where a guy will speak from his heart, look deeply into her eyes with love, and when down on bended knee ask this question: Will you marry me?

FAST AND FURIOUS (1ST YODAISM OF 2005)

January 2, 2005

Every person feels somewhat at ease when behind the wheel of his or her car. Each of us can be in our own world as rubber meets the road as we venture off into our intended or unintended destination(s). If you think about it, each time a person gets in his or her car you have no idea what to expect when one leaves the driveway. Yet, it's that unknown that makes getting behind the wheel and putting the pedal to the medal such an adrenaline rush. In a way, it's like having that exciting feeling as one sits in the driver's seat for the very first time minus the occasional speeding tickets and minor or major fender benders that may or may not happen when one is driving.

When we receive our drivers' licenses, it can be considered an absolute right of passage. A rite of passage in which he or she may or may not push the limits of speed. As young kids, the view from the back seat, as well as the passenger seat is not all that interesting or entertaining as a person tends to get cabin fever, so to speak. Looking out the window can be pretty boring after ten minutes and the only options were to either mess with your sibling(s) or fall asleep, which wasn't all that bad to do. In any case, the days of being driven to the mall, Wal-Mart, the beach, or a friend's house are over as his or her time to feel the wind in one's hair begins, in a manner of speaking.

When it comes to cruisin' a person must have the tunes cranked up to make the duration of one's car ride enjoyable. Let me ask you a question, are you the type of person who sings out loud in your car whether or not there are passengers in it? Music is essential and it's the one common denominator that each person shares though the type of music one blares through his or speakers may differ but as the saying goes, ~To each his own~. In some aspect, each of us can be ourselves as we listen to our favorite songs on the radio and/or CD. It's within the confines of one's car that our inner dork tends to reveal itself as we try to sing along with the best of our ability.

For some or most people, road rage is a part of hazards when getting behind the wheel of a car. Whether it be minimal or excessive, each of us have certain pet peeves that tend to annoy, anger, or slightly perturb a person. Personally speaking, what gets me slightly perturbed are people who leave their turn signals on and they seemingly have no idea that it is still on and blinking. Yet, one has to know because you usually hear clicking sounds but I digress before I go off on people who tailgate, which my brother does often. Ultimately, when it comes to road rage, one just has to keep repeating to one's self this phrase which comes from a Seinfeld episode which is, ~Serenity Now!, Serenity Now!~

Dave Barry once said, ~The one thing that unites all human beings, regardless of age, gender, religion, economic status or ethnic background, is that, deep down inside, we ALL believe that we are above average drivers.~ Each of us know the feeling of being a passenger as well as the driver, and when you become a passenger again it feels kind of weird not being able to drive. When it comes to driving, each of us feels we know what we are doing even though our passengers oftentimes feel like they need to write and sign a will. In retrospect, it's a fast and furious world out there where people tend to do crazy and stupid things; but in the end be safe, buckle up, and try not to drive like you're competing in the Indianapolis 500.

THE TIES THAT BIND
January 2, 2005

Erica E. Goode once said, ~Sibling relationships...outlast marriages, survive the death of parents, resurface after quarrels that would end any friendship. They flourish in a thousand incarnations of closeness, distance, warmth, loyalty and distrust.~ The bond between siblings is a strong one because no matter how annoying one becomes he or she will always be there to have your back. Other than our best friends who would know us better than our own brother and/or sister whose initial job is to torment us or vice versa. In a way, it's like having a houseguest who never really leaves the house and although you try to get rid of that person you are stuck with him or her......unless you're an only child.

The one thing that is scary to a sibling is his or her bedroom. In some aspect, it's a safe haven where a person can express their own personality. Yet, it's hard to do that when you share a room with a brother and/or a sister that has several annoying habits and will drive you crazy. We've all at some point, in our younger days, had to share a room with a sibling that you somewhat tolerated. Being temporary or permanent roommates, you find out what type of person your brother and/or sister is, which is a slob or a neat freak; somewhat compared to that popular television show The Odd Couple. It can be a comical situation as two people with totally different personalities try to coexist in a small, enclosed space and hopefully not kill each other in the process.

Let me ask you this question, what type of relationship do you have with your brother(s) and/or sister(s)? Depending on how many siblings one has and the brother to sister ratio, added with that the bathroom or food situation it be considered survival of the fittest. I don't know anything about the relationship between sisters, but a relationship between brothers is often filled with torture and scars which result in battles that have either been won or lost. Personally speaking, my younger brother and I have had our battles, but it really hasn't come to hand-to-hand combat in years. It's just a matter of having respect for each other even though at times you just want to know his or her block off.

Like it's been said before, other than our friends who know us better than our very own siblings. Whether you are the youngest or oldest, it's an absolute that a brother and/or a sister will be there to cut you down to size. If you think about it, he or she can bring you back to reality when your ego can get out of hand. In a way, it's like having your very own conscience living with you because in the snap of a finger they will slap you upside the head and tell you what they really think of you, but in a loving way. Essentially, it's that same brother and/or sister that even though he or she can make one's life a living nightmare, that person will absolutely be at your side when times of strife occur.

In retrospect, when you look back at your childhood, was it a relationship of distance or closeness? Let me ask you this, when was the last time you talked to your brother and/or sister on a personal level and asked how he or she is doing? As we grow older, we tend to drift away from the one person that absolutely knows us inside and out. When each of us lose the unbreakable common bond that holds siblings together, we lose certain pieces of the puzzle that keep it incomplete and in turn, a rift is formed. Ultimately, it's the blood that siblings share and run through their veins will forever be the ties that bind brother to brother, brother to sister, and sister to sister.

APPLE OF YOUR EYE
January 5, 2005

Robert Frost once said, ~How many apples fell on Isaac Newton's head before he took the hint? Nature is always hinting at us. It hints over and over again. And suddenly you get the hint.~ In some aspect, a woman is like an apple growing from it just waiting to be picked. It can be frustrating for a woman as she contemplates why the right guy hasn't come along to pick her. Oftentimes when one thinks she is going to be or about to be picked, her expectations lead from hope to disappointment. For the disappointing experiences a woman can have will subsequently make her assume that all guys are immature, moronic, egotistical jerks which is absolutely true, for the most part...but not all guys.

In any case, some guys are just afraid of climbing up because when he stands at the base of the tree and looks up, his fear will start to kick in. A fear, in which he might slip and fall hard to the ground below as one attempts to reach from for that one beautiful apple. It's that mentality that not all guys have, which can have a guy not want to reach for the absolute best of the bunch. It's from that mindset that a guy will metaphorically kick himself in the butt for not risking life and limb to climb to new heights for love. For that particular guy, in the back of his mind, will always wonder if he had at least tried harder. Maybe he wouldn't care how high the apple tree is and he would be at the top in a heartbeat.

Essentially, a guy settles for the apples that have fallen on the ground. In a way, if a guy chooses that particular apple, he is settling for second best. It's these apples that have fallen on the ground that don't seem to have any blemishes on them on the outside, but on the inside, they're completely rotten depending on how long it's been on the ground. For as the saying goes, ~It's easy pickings hold true~ as some guys just don't want to make the effort to climb straight to the top which is a sad situation indeed. One just has to put into consideration the type of guy that would rather settle for second best and not climb up which would lead him to that one absolute flawless apple.

Inevitably, every apple at the top of the tree tends to think there is something wrong with them as they wonder why guys are completely passing up a good thing. It's not always the case because in reality, it's not the woman's fault. In fact, it's that particular guy's fault and his own stupidity. It's that stupidity which makes a guy fall head over heels from a woman over and again for the wrong apple, in a manner of speaking. It can really turn a woman bitter and completely give up on the male species. For when a guy falls, he will fall hard and the injury he suffers to his heart will heal with time. Undoubtedly, the apples at the top of the tree are truly amazing and with time and patience she will one day be picked by the right guy?

In retrospect, when it comes to picking the right apple, guy or girl, you have to ask yourself a couple of questions such as: Will that person be able to make me laugh? Will that person be able to keep a smile on my face? Will that person like me for just being myself? Will that person be everything that I ever wanted and more? All perfectly good questions that will be answered in due time and each of us will have answers to those questions ourselves when one meets that right person. As said before, it's a matter of having patience because the right person will come along for each of us; for when that person finally arrives that particular guy or girl will absolutely be the apple of your eye.

A GUY THING
January 9, 2005

To understand a guy, you don't have to really think that hard to figure us out. The male species is considered more basic than complex because we are all about simplicity. We thought about it and then moved on and that is why man invented instant replay. For when something semi-important happens we have a referee to check and tell us if the play was correct or not. When it comes to using the most powerful muscle in the brain, it's not one of our strong suits because when we start to think we usually get into hot water afterwards. Inevitably, when it comes to using brain power, women have us beat hands down. There is no denying it because quite frankly we don't like to think, it hurts our head.

When it comes to fashion, guys rarely don't have that eye for style as women do. It's that attention to detail that we don't have the time and patience for because as long as our clothes fit, we will wear them. For when it comes to buying clothes, we tend to use a military-like strategy. When we go into the store, we seek out our objective and when our objective is met it's a job well done. Let me tell you something, if you asked us to describe what we are wearing from the neck down our response would be a shirt, pants, and shoes. Plain and simple, nothing to go into detail over and we get straight to the point. For it's our mentality that if it absolutely feels comfortable, we will wear it even if it doesn't match.

The one thing that every person shares in common is that each of us has a butt. Yet a guy will not worry over the size and/or shape of his rear end because in the whole scheme of things, we really don't care what it looks like as long as we know it's still there. There are occasions we oftentimes don't realize we have one until it itches, or a potentially potent gas is released due to eating foods that involve using salsa on it. It's been said that a guy's rear end is connected to our brain and when we scratch it, it helps in the thinking process, which hasn't been scientifically proven to be fact. In any case, when it comes to the buttocks, as long as we can still sit on it we're still happy campers.

As said before, guys are known for random acts of stupidity that would cause absolute embarrassment, bewilderment, and/or bodily harm. Every guy knows or is friends with that one person who will do something so outlandish that stupid isn't quite the word you would look for. Personally speaking, I have a friend who stopped his car in the middle of traffic, went out, ran around it, got back into his car and drove off. His honest to goodness explanation was that he just wanted to do it which to me was the most dangerous and stupid thing to do; but he had the cojones to pull it off. When it comes to doing something before ever thinking about it we win hands down and usually we end up paying for it in the end.

Someone once said, ~Men are like a fine wine. They start out like grapes, and it's our job to stomp on them and keep them in the dark until they mature into something you'd like to have dinner with.~ We may be grown up and matured, but on the inside we're still little kids at heart. Personally speaking, I'm 27 years old and I still get excited whenever I hear the ice cream truck roll around. For we will still make up secret handshakes, have burping contests, pull practical jokes, do prank phone calls, play video games into the wee morning hours, and say and do stupid things. Though idiotic it may seem, it's a guy thing and in the end you gotta love and accept us for being who we are.

THAT ONE BRIGHT STAR
January 11, 2005

Someone once said, ~If you could reach up and hold a star for every time you've made me smile, the entire evening sky would be in the palm of my hand. We've all at some point in our lives gazed at the stars. It's a pastime that can have a calming effect on a person as one looks up at the vastness and beauty of the infinite universe. It's up in that so-called final frontier where a person almost sees every single star that is unique in their own way. Those particular stars illuminate the skies above and tend to show the way to one's intended destination. In some aspect, there is one star that shines brighter than the rest and it's that one particular star each of us gaze at that we make our personal wish on.

In a way, each of us can be somewhat compared to Fievel from American Tail as we sit amongst our thoughts and ponder whether or not that one special person is somewhere out there. Though separated by miles, one can't help but feel that he or she is close by, which is a feeling most people have encountered. The one person, who may be saying the same prayer and wishing on that same star, which is sometimes considered a fool's hope. Yet, even though it is a fool's hope one continues to look up at the sky on a semi-nightly basis and make that prayer and/or wish for love to come his or her way. It's that one wish that oftentimes will or won't come true, but it's just a matter of believing it will happen.

Undoubtedly, there will be times where we will have stars in our eyes and be either temporarily or permanently blinded by a particular person's glow. It's a glow that totally mesmerizes a person until the focus in one's eyes becomes much clearer. Like stars burning out from the night sky, the light that shined brightly on one's eyes for that particular person, who one has been chasing after slowly burns out as well. It's that proverbial high that one experiences when meeting someone that he or she is infatuated with. For when it wears off, a person can only stand back and realize that he or she has just been getting totally lost. One just has to let go and watch it return to that celestial sea of light that is in the night sky.

Let me ask you this question, when was the last time you looked up at the stars and were you with someone that you really cared about? Think about this, it's when we look up at the stars that we dream of where we want to go and who we want to be with. We've all had that spark from within get extinguished when we suffer heartbreak; but somehow it tends never to die because the fire within keeps burning even though we may suffer some failure at times. One can come so close and yet fall short in finding true happiness. A person just has to ground themselves and have patience because one's true star will shine their way. For it was Kasey Kasem who said, ~Keep your feet on the ground and keep reaching for the stars.

Eric Clapton said, ~If I could reach the stars, pull one down for you, shine it in my heart, so you could see the truth, then this love I have inside is everything it seems, but for now I find it only in my dreams.~ In retrospect, each of us are stars among a billion others stars that shine brightly with the rest. Oftentimes, one may feel that he or she may not be twinkling brighter than the others which can make us feel unworthy to be looked at from a telescopic lens. One just has to remember we're part of something that is bigger than all of us. In the end, it's truly amazing that there are billions of stars that haven't been seen; but it's when one sees into the eyes of that one bright star you truly love, you have a billion reasons to smile.

BREAK THE CYCLE
January 12, 2005

Frank B. Gilberth said, ~We're worn into grooves by time-by our habits. In the end, these grooves are going to show whether we've been second rate or champions, each in his way in dispatching the affairs of every day. By choosing our habits, we determines the groove into which time will wear us; and these are grooves that enrich our lives and make for ease of mind, peace, happiness, and achievement.~ If you think about it, we're all creatures of habit that tend to predict our actions in the way we do things. Whether or not one acknowledges or refuses to acknowledge it, our habits somewhat define who we are. It's these particular habits that people consider annoying, humorous, strange, and/or interesting.

The one habit that people tend to share is biting his or her fingernails which is annoying to most people. We all do it either when we are stressed out, worried, or in a thinking mood that will oftentimes leave one's fingernails almost chewed completely off. Nobody is really immune to it and to tell you the truth I do because, in a way, it helps me think up new topics to write about which never come easy. I'm the type of person who thinks way too much and you can imagine how my fingernails look. Oftentimes biting one's fingernails is considered a lazy alternative to finding nail clippers and cutting them neatly. Unfortunately, one will pay for it in the end as you unintentionally expose the skin under the nail which is not a pretty sight indeed.

Some habits can be a combination of interesting, strange and humorous. Yet, it's not so much a habit but rather a ritual one goes through like a person knocking on wood for luck. Personally speaking, I have a ritual that I go through when I adjust my hat and the way I do it would be best described as how a baseball manager gives signs to his players from the dugout. I tend to get strange and humorous looks from "my kids" when they proceed to ask me what in the world I'm doing. In any case, it's these particular rituals that a person does over and over again that can slightly border on obsessive compulsiveness. One such example is washing one's hands. When it comes to working with kids, you have to wash your hands on a regular basis because they can spread germs quickly.

Let me ask you this question, are you a person or know a person who is a sleepwalker? It is a very interesting, humorous, and yet dangerous habit as one does or says things that one will not remember in the morning, unless blackmail is involved but that's a whole other subject that I won't get into. Anyways…in some aspect, it's somewhat like a person drinking way too much, passing out, waking up with a hangover and absolutely doesn't know what happened to him or her the previous night. Let me tell you something, it can be a strange experience waking up in a place that is not your own room like the garage or the back seat of your car for instance, which has happened to me a number of times.

Frank A. Clark once said, ~A habit is something you can do without thinking - which is why most of us have so many of them.~ During my tenure in Youth Center or the Insane Asylum as I like to call it; I used to have a habit of giving three basic responses whenever I get called into the office. Response #1: Whatever it is, I didn't do it; Response #2: Whatever happened, I was nowhere near it because I have an alibi; and Response #3: Am I fired?, which doesn't get used that often. In any case, we all have habits that one needs to take care of; for it's an endless cycle that a person will continue to keep into the latter years of one's life. For it's a new year, one must take up the initiative and simply try to break the cycle.

GUILTY AS CHARGED
January 14, 2005

Charles Stanley once said, ~Romantic love reaches out in little ways, showing attention and admiration. Romantic love remembers what pleases a woman, what excites her, and what surprises her. Its actions whisper: you are the most special person in my life.~ The word romance is defined as an ardent emotional attachment between two people. In some aspect, when a person hears the word romance, he or she can have a sour look on one's face, so to speak, because that person doesn't believe in it due to that person's past experiences. Every person has a different interpretation of what romance means and yet the concept of what it is remains the same.

Let me ask you this question, what does romance mean to you? When it comes to romance between two people, it doesn't necessarily mean the physical aspect is always involved. We all know someone or were involved in a significant relationship that was based solely on the physical and even if there was love, the passion that was shared is missing. Inevitably two people can create a romantic atmosphere with the surroundings that have and bring back that passion. One just has to simply improvise, and one can do that by either talking to each other, going to a movie that she would like, a candlelight dinner, going out dancing, or simply sitting on the beach at night and looking up at the stars.

Yet, for most guys and women as well, the fear of intimacy can sometimes come into play when one wants to be in a relationship or already is in a significant relationship. It's basically that fear every person has of completely letting down their guard that he or she has built up. For it's that mentality that if you let go and completely fall in love with someone, you run the risk of getting your heart broken. But that's part of life as some of us, who are single, travel the lonely road that hopefully leads into the arms of that one special person. Subsequently, it's one's basic fears of love brought to the surface by that one person who you want to put your trust in and can be absolutely comfortable just being yourself.

Oftentimes, giving someone that you truly care about flowers is considered a romantic gesture from the heart. Undoubtedly, roses are the choice flowers to give when showing absolute affection to someone that you probably would imagine spending the rest of your life with. Whether the cost is a dollar or fifty dollars, does it really matter when it comes to giving something that will put a smile on someone's face and make one's day? Yet, one can be romantic even though there isn't any personal connection at all. On such a day is Valentine's Day, which my best friend and I are planning to have roses delivered to the asylum for the female co-workers. A token of appreciation from two guys who want to do something nice.

About 2 days ago, I received an email from a friend that kind of surprised me. She said that I was romantic after she read a particular Yodaism. To be perfectly honest, I don't really consider myself romantic, I'm just a person who writes what he feels. For if it tugs at a certain emotion for particular people then that is an added bonus. In a way, when I write on topics such as love and relationships, I tap into something from within my heart and soul that I hope one day to fully express to that special lady in person. You see, I'm a person who believes in "the one", wishing on that one bright star, and love that lasts forever. In retrospect, that type of person is considered a hopeless romantic; well, if that be the case, then I'm guilty as charged.

TRAIL OF TEARS
January 17, 2005

Una Stannard said, ~Men are no more immune from emotions than women; we think women are more emotion because the culture lets them give free vent to certain feelings, "feminine" ones that is, no anger please; but it's okay to turn on the waterworks.~ People tend to cry for several different reasons and oftentimes no reason at all. Every person has a complicated and/or stressful life; even though one seems to be put together on the outside, on the inside he or she can be mentally break down. Each one of us isn't immune and it basically shows that we're only human and no matter how tough one is, you sometimes have to let it all out to feel a whole lot better.

Let me tell you something, guys don't really want to admit they cry because, in our own thinking, it will bring down our masculinity. For the male species, we were taught since we were little kids not to cry. For at some point in our lives, if we ever hurt ourselves, we would hear these words coming from our father's mouth, ~You're ok, just shake it off.~ It's a guy thing and we only cry when our favorite sports team wins a major championship like the Boston Red Sox. Red Sox fans have an obligation to cry after finally winning a championship after 86 years and have the curse of Babe Ruth lifted. They can now die happy knowing that the tears that they have shed through the years came to fruition in 2004.

It's truly amazing how women can cry in a snap of a finger. It can be somewhat comical as when guys encounter women or young ladies who are bawling their eyes out. In some aspect, to a guy it's like stumbling on a really sensitive explosive and we have no idea how to turn it off. In my case, working with kids, especially little girls, I've found that a way to comfort a crying child who is either having a really bad day or just missing their parent(s) is just to make them laugh. For its when you see that big and bright smile beaming from a 6 or 7 year old's face, you not only have a warm fuzzy feeling inside you; but you also, in a way, feel like a father comforting a daughter.

D.H. Mondfleur once said, ~I like the snot to run a little, the tears to accumulate a bit before reaching for the handkerchief. Then I know I'm really crying. Crying just isn't crying unless it's messy.~ Let me ask you this question, when was the last time you cried? Certain situations can make a person start to tear up and such examples are watching a certain movie or television show, listening to a song, losing a friend or family member, and most often suffering heartbreak that causes one to go through endless amounts of tissues. Personally speaking, the last time I really cried that I could remember was when I was a kid watching the movies Charlotte's Web and Savannah Smiles.

In retrospect, there are many types of crying such as sympathetic, whining, manipulative, sensitive, and that ever popular temper tantrum. Someone has done these types of crying as a kid or even as an adult. Whether it be years, months, weeks, days, or just recently a person will be in a situation where one just needs to open up the floodgates. Inevitably, one's friends, family, or loved one will help comfort you when one most needs it. Thinking about it, each one of us has the right to let out all the emotions he or she has kept inside when times of tragedy, strife, or even joy for that matter come our way. In the end, it's the trail of tears that one sheds from childhood to one's latter years that make you stronger as time goes by.

RISE AND SHINE
January 17, 2005

Groucho Marx once said, ~Each morning when I open my eyes I say to myself: I, not events, have the power to make me happy or unhappy today. I can choose which it shall be. Yesterday is dead, tomorrow hasn't arrived yet, I have just one day, today, and I'm going to be happy in it." Waking up can be the easiest or toughest thing a person can do when one has to go to work or go to school. It often seems like as one gets older it gets harder and harder to motivate oneself to get out of bed. In some aspect, we all don't want to be awakened from that deep slumber that transports us to a place that nobody else can physically be. So then, let me ask you this question, are you a morning person?

We all know someone or are that person that is just way too happy in the morning and it can really be annoying to some or most people. It's that type of person that springs out of bed, who has that early to bed, early to rise mentality and watches the sun rise as he or she sips one's morning coffee. It's a person's chipper attitude combined with that proverbial kick in his or her step that can make any "normal" person either knock that person out or turn right around and go back into one's warm, comfortable bed. Yet, it's that same person who can absolutely motivate a person and jump start one's day like a dead car battery that is out of juice in one's car.

On the other side of that coin, you have a person like me who is totally the opposite. It's that type of person who when he or she opens one's eyes, looks straight up at the ceiling, and has to negotiate himself or herself to get up. When one does finally get up, a person is still trying to get his or her bearings straight and words are either mumbled or all connected together to make one long totally non-understandable word. It can be quite comical as you pass by someone who has been up for a while, and they have to figure out what you just said to them. In any case, it's really hard to comprehend anything when one's mind is still in la la land and probably will be there until one fully wakes up, which for me is around noonish.

For some people, being a morning person is considered an inherited gene such as with a person who is a night person; in other words, it's in one's blood. It's basically the type of person who can be best suited to working in the daytime or nighttime, also added to that the mood he or she is in. Personally speaking, I am a person who goes to bed around 1am and gets up before my alarm clock turns on at 6am. It's just one of those things that no matter what I do, I wake up right before the time I should get up even though there are days where I don't have to go to work or class which ticks me off. Inevitably, it's that internal college clock that will always stay on and will never be able to be turned off.

In retrospect, for some people being a night person means more excitement and having more creativity. On the other hand, being a morning person, you can be up all by yourself and gather your thoughts for the day. One can completely argue or debate it to the ground but the one thing that can be agreed upon is that each of us have either been or still are a night person, a morning person, or have switched sides. In the whole scheme of things there isn't really much of an advantage or disadvantage of being a person who is an early bird or night owl, so to speak. In the end, as long as a person gets some sleep, he or she will be able to rise and shine and get one's day started whenever that may be.

SHAPE OF THINGS TO COME

January 19, 2005

Louis L'Amour once said, ~Up to a point a man's life is shaped by environment, heredity, and movements and changes in the world about him. Then there comes a time when it lies within his grasp to shape the clay of his life into the sort of thing he wishes to be. Only the weak blame parents, their race, their times, lack of good fortune, or the quirks of fate. Everyone has it within his power to say, "This I am today; that I will be tomorrow."~ At some point every person looks back at one's life up until now and does a self-evaluation. A self-evaluation in which he or she ponders if the mistakes that were made or not made would have put him or her in the position that one is now in life.

As it has been previously said, our lives are like a piece of clay that we can shape it to be as we wish it. In some aspect, it seems simple enough to mold our lives the way we want it to be. To direct certain important or unimportant details to or away from us. The imperfections, whether they be big or small, basically smoothed out so that no bumps or cracks are shown. It's within those bumps and cracks that a person tries to be as perfect as one can be and have that so-called perfect life. A life in which there are no worries and every problem that one faces is solved in an instant. But the reality of it all is that one has to keep in mind that like life, a person isn't as perfect as one thinks or hopes to be.

Think back to your own childhood when you were in preschool or in elementary school and you made something out of clay for your mom or dad. It was usually a plate that really didn't look like one but more resembled like an ashtray; yet it didn't matter because to you it was a masterpiece. One's parent(s) didn't care what it looked like because it was made from the heart and the imperfections were insignificant. For it was one's hard work into shaping something that somewhat resembled a particular object that was made out of love that much more special. As a person who works with kids, it feels good to get something from the heart from them because they took the time to make it especially for you.

Undoubtedly as adults we have an obligation to mold a child's mind in today's society into respectable young men and women. Oftentimes the clay we are given doesn't want to be shaped and one basically feels that there is no hope for him or her. Yet, it's that pessimistic attitude that can totally surprise a person when that same child is seen again as an adult and changed immensely. Though one didn't fully mold the clay, the impressions that he or she made on that child made somewhat of an impact. It's that particular person who started the process and it was up to that child to finish it by flattening out the rough spots in his or her life. A life in which he or she just required some much-needed encouragement.

In retrospect, each of us is still being molded today and what will be the end result is anybody's guess at this point. Every mistake, heartbreak, victory, setback, failure, tragedy, and triumph happened for a reason. But the question still remains, would one be at his or her particular point in one's life if those things never happened? Who knows, one just has to work with the clay that he or she has and find out for yourself. Eventually the life you always wanted will come to fruition, it just takes time and patience for one's piece of clay to turn into something spectacular. Inevitably, we all don't know what tomorrow brings and yet it's the shape of things to come that makes life absolutely interesting.

SCRATCHING THE SURFACE
January 21, 2005

If you think about it, love can take shape in many different forms, big or small it really doesn't matter. For it's been said that if you stop looking then that will be the time it will show up at your doorstep so to speak. Do you think this is true? Let me ask you this question, when one is in search of that so-called perfect person, he or she will sometimes settle for someone that doesn't really make him or her happy. One can witness so many relationships fail and in turn second guess your own potential relationship that will one day become a serious relationship. As it has been said before, a person can have a sense of false hope that will have a person get one's heartbroken every time.

Every guy at some point has tried to hook up with a female friend, but in the end, it is the decision to be "just friends" in her eyes alone. Though that unrequited love was never reciprocated, that friendship is still intact. Yet, it can be truly disconcerting when you become the proverbial shoulder to cry on when dates or that significant relationship didn't work out well. The go-to-guy to hear all the qualities that didn't necessarily make that particular guy the prince charming that he turned out to be, which was known all along and warned about about several times. It can be a frustrating situation indeed when she says she wants someone like you, but not you and that can be taken as a compliment, as well as an insult.

In any case, life can be considered great, but when that one person you fall in love with shows up, life just gets even better. It's that one person that you unknowingly send a vibe that sends a message to him or her that you are absolutely comfortable with yourself to be around that person. He or she is the one that will tell you to continue to be who you are, which makes you unique and distinguishable among the rest of the pack. A person has to learn to be able to accept one's idiosyncrasies, however strange or annoying it may be to me, which shows a growing love for each other. Inevitably, that person will absolutely appreciate and hopefully not take for granted what one has in front of him or her.

Undoubtedly, each of us would like to think that the person we fall in love with is the one that we spend the rest of our nights and days with. It can be a daunting task to keep wasting one's time opening up one's heart to that guy or girl and just have that person break it all over again. It basically comes back to the issue of trust as you are placing your heart in that person's hands. A person just has to learn from experience and hopefully one's heart doesn't turn black as night to the possibility that he or she will find true love. Though the pain we each suffer at times is disguised as that so-called handsome guy or beautiful woman, one will ultimately get stronger in mind, body, soul and especially in your heart.

In retrospect, I don't claim to be an expert in these matters. I just say what I feel and observe what is around me on a semi-daily basis. The past Yodaisms that I've written and sent out are thoughts written down on paper to help grasp a sometimes confusing thing such as life, love, family, and/or relationships. Oftentimes, when it comes to love you have to give a little to get more back. Ladies will encounter jerks and guys will cross paths with that heartbreaker, it's a given. One just has to truly see the person who is standing in front of you and what you might find can scare you, but make you smile. In the end, a person just has to keep scratching the surface until what is revealed underneath is the guy or girl one has been waiting a lifetime for.

WHY ME
January 22, 2005

Someone once said, ~Momentum is largely a matter of perception, and therein lies its power. When two or three disagreeable things happen, you suddenly see yourself having a bad day, it truly becomes a bad day, not because of some outside force or twist of fate, but because of your own chosen perception.~ Every person has had at some point one of THOSE days that tend to make one's day seem like it was never going to end, We've all woken up and as soon as you got out of bed you had that proverbial gut feeling and something told you it wasn't going to be a good one. In some aspect, it's like having somewhat of a sixth sense that can sometimes be wrong.

Oftentimes the weather can play somewhat of a key role in one's day of dread. It can be an absolute test in one's patience as his or her day with a forecast that calls for rain. In some ways, rain is the quintessential kryptonite for regular people who don't have superpowers because we don't want to get sick, but yet we do. Each one of us has been in a situation where we had to either walk or run in the rain because one left his or her umbrella either at home or in the car. Let me tell you something, it can be an absolutely uncomfortable experience sitting in a cold classroom and shivering due to one's clothes being completely soaked from head to toe.

Getting a ticket or getting into a car accident can most definitely ruin one's day. Let me ask you a question, have you ever tried talking your way out of a ticket and did it ever work? I don't know about guys, but women can use their charms to get out of it...most of the time. If we ever tried it, we would just get ticketed twice and that means more money to pay. Getting into a car accident, on the other hand, can mess up one's day immensely because your basic mode of transportation is either slightly or severely damaged. It can be a real bummer not being able to drive for several months after getting into an accident in the rain, which is a double whammy, take it from me.

There comes a point where one's bad day can turn even worse, and I've experienced it to the fullest working in the asylum. There are some days I love going to work and interacting with "my kids." Then there are days where I consider some, but not all of them, children of the corn. As I've said in the past, they may look like sweet little angels on the outside, but on the inside, there are mini-Hannible Lectre's lurking in each of them just waiting to come out. I kid you not, there are days where I ask my friends and parents as well, to take a particular foreign object that I hand them and knock me completely out so the day will be over. It really hasn't happened yet, but one day it will.

In the long run, a person can have that mindset that his or her day will continually worsen as the day progresses. Or one can have the mindset you will see the tides turn in your favor, he or she just needs to have a positive outlook. Ultimately when one's day is finally over, a person will either spend time alone, listen to music, watch tv, make it a blockbuster night, go to the movies, or the best alternative is to sleep it off. It's just a matter of finding what works for you to not remember one's painful experience. In the end, every person's bad day will culminate by hanging his or her head, then looking up to the skies above, and ask the big man upstairs this question, why me?

WITH ARMS WIDE OPEN
January 24, 2005

Jacques Prevert once said, ~Millions and millions of years would still not give me half enough time to describe that tiny constant of all eternity when you put your arms around me and I put my arms around you.~ Let me ask you this question, when was the last time you hugged someone or someone hugged you? If you think about it, a hug can be very therapeutic because it can either take the pain away from heartbreak, ease the tension in a seemingly stressful day, or just show a sign of affection from one person to another. Yet, it can be just a simple greeting between two people or a group of people that haven't seen each other in days, weeks, months, or even years.

When it comes to giving someone a hug, men and women do it differently. Subsequently, there are two styles, which are the regular way and then there is the guy way. Women tend to react differently than guys when they haven't seen someone for quite some time. It's a level of excitement that somewhat overflows to a point where warm, friendly embraces run amuck. On the other hand, for guys, it's totally the opposite as we take that level of excitement down several notches. It's usually a head nod, then the obligatory handshake, which then leads into the shoulder bump, and ends with the proverbial pat on the back. It's that solemn and usually reserved greeting that again deems it another guy thing that we just do.

Working with kids for the past several years, I have received countless amounts of hugs from kids that genuinely like me for who I am. For in their eyes, I'm a weird, wacky, strange, sometimes mean, fun-loving counselor that takes their abuse and torture day in and day out; but I love them anyway. Let me tell you something, it's quite an event when you are unknowingly tackled to the ground by forty potential mini-linebackers who all at once are attempting to give you a massive group hug that will knock a person down. In any case, it is reciprocated as I give them bear hugs and oftentimes hug them when one is sad or injured themselves to take their mind off what just happened to them.

In some cases, when a person is locked in the arms of someone who cares for him or her either as a friend, family member, or one's potential and/or significant other you feel absolutely safe. It's that mindset that nothing will ever harm you when you are in the arms of the one you love or at least care about. While embracing, the beating of two hearts can be absolutely felt, as well as, heard depending on the size differential. Anyways, just like a kiss, a hug can most certainly determine one's intended interest in that particular person and it's all in how he or she holds him or her. Whether you are big, small, short, or tall, a hug coming from someone that means so much to you, whoever that may be, is worth receiving and giving back.

Someone once said, ~Hugging has no unpleasant side effects and is all natural. There are no batteries to replace, its inflation-proof and non-flattening with no monthly payments. It's non-taxable, non-polluting, and is of course, fully refundable.~ In other words, what is received can be given back as well. In the whole scheme of things, it doesn't cost a dime, and you can freely give it to anyone you want. It would be an interesting concept if someone went out and gave hugs to people that they absolutely needed, like people who are really having a bad day and just hugged him or her. Though awkward at first, it's with arms wide open that a hug can make a person's day, as well as your day seem that much special.

FINAL ANSWER
January 27, 2005

Leo Buscaglia once said, ~Most of us are pawns in the game of love we don't understand.~ Every person oftentimes feels like the rules are constantly being changed on each of us. it can get to the point where one can get completely confused when there is the slightest hint of a possibility one might fall in love with someone. Life would be much simpler if love came with an instruction manual. For it would tell us where to place ourselves on the board game of life and where specifically we would meet that one special person. In some aspect, when it comes to love, we're all on that proverbial hot seat trying to answer the tough questions somewhat like on that popular game show Who Wants To Be A Millionaire.

In some aspect, the beginning of the game is always easy because the questions asked are simple to answer. The proverbial no brainers that don't need any brain power to figure out. For it's that one simple question that asks what type of person are you looking for in a potential mate? Some, maybe most, of the female population is looking for the stereotypical tall, dark, and handsome kind of guy. Whereas, for the guys, it's just a matter of finding that so-called diamond in the rough who is willing to put up with all the stupid things we eventually do and say somewhere down the road. For it's when each of us thinks we have the answers all figured out, the questions will become harder as time passes on.

Inevitably, there will come a point where each of us will call for a lifeline. One such lifeline is asking the audience, which primarily is one's friends and family. A person will sometimes seek their guidance in order to advise him or her on the best alternatives in seeking a possible relationship with that particular person. Yet, most of the time, one ignores the advice given due to conflicting answers to which he or she must leave it up to one's capable hands on who is right for him or her. Oftentimes, that choice has either substantially gained quite a bit more or absolutely bottomed out in which he or she ultimately ends up with nothing but one's high expectations being deflated.

Consequently, that proverbial 50/50 shot is given to every person when one is in a dilemma in deciding who one wants to be with when it involves either two guys or two girls. A person just has to weigh the options between the person you are absolutely attracted to visually and makes your heart melt or the person who has been or will always be there for you without ever asking. For some it's a tough decision that will make any person sick to their stomach. One just has to come to a realization in which he or she has to ask himself or herself this question: Who couldn't I ever imagine my life without him or her in it? For he or she is the person that unquestionably will always be the one that truly made your heart smile.

In retrospect, each of us may or may not have the chance to ever sit across from Regis Philbin and possibly have our dreams of a stable financial future come true. Yet, each of us sits or will sit across from that one person, who is considered bigger than any celebrity one will ever meet in his or her life. For that stable financial future has or will come true because true happiness makes two people rich beyond their years. In the end, it's that million-dollar question for those that haven't found that someone special, yet which asks: Will you ever find true love? For one's choices are: A.) Maybe B.) Someday C.) Never D.) I Don't Know. Speaking for myself I choose B) Someday, and yes, that is my final answer.

END OF THE LINE
January 28, 2005

Let me ask you this question, were you the type of child that always wanted to be first in line? For it's within a child's mind that if he or she is first in line one will get some type of special reward handed to him or her. Working with kids over the years, I witnessed countless kids scratch, claw, push, shove, trip, and elbow their way to get to that number one spot. Once the dust settles, so to speak, kids are either on the floor crying due to being knocked to the floor, some are having pushing and shoving matches to be behind the number one girl or boy, and others are complaining that he or she is cutting in front of him or her in line. *Sigh* Welcome to my world folks, would you like to come in and stay for a bit?

It can truly befuddle the mind of a full-grown adult that kids are fighting for a spot in line that will take each and every child both in front, middle, and back to the same place. In some aspect, it's a whole lot safer to be in the middle or somewhere in the back rather than in the front. In a way, it's that power to be the leader of the pack that you have to deal with another child trying to steal your spot and take over one's leadership position away from him or her. Though it may sound funny to each of us who have hopefully outgrown these childish antics and/or behavior and matured, to a child it's that competitive spirit that will probably help him or her in the real world one day.

Yet, each of us may not want to be first in line anymore; but a person does want to be the first to attain the finer things in life such as a car, house, spouse, or that successful job one dreams about. Inevitably, one just wants to be either two steps in front or beyond his or her competition, which oftentimes is one's own friends. For each of us can be somewhat green with envy as we see close friends or associates getting ahead of the line or completely cutting it. We've all heard of people making it big who didn't want to take the road less traveled and just tried to keep cutting in line to get into a spot that might possibly get himself or herself in or near the front of the line.

In any case, as each of us grow up and get into the groove of the daily grind, we will find ourselves stepping into many lines. Lines that either flow smoothly or take forever to move such as the back, doctor's office, dentist, or the post office. It can really test a person's patience standing or waiting in line for minutes or hours on end waiting for something to someone and not go completely insane. As young kids, we learned that patience is a virtue, but for some patience is not one of their strong suits as they want to be at the front of the line as soon as possible because he or she has things to do and people to see. For it's just a matter of keeping one's composure when the line of life isn't moving quickly enough.

It's been said that the shortest distance between two points is a straight line. In the whole scheme of things, a person has to try to keep on the straight and narrow to avoid being sent to the back of the line, so to speak. It's at the back of the line that a person actually has time to see the bigger picture of one's own mistakes that he or she has made. Thinking about it, being number one isn't all that it's cracked up to be as you spend time constantly wondering who is going to take your spot away from you. In retrospect, each of us are all heading in the same direction as we fight to be on top of that proverbial totem pole to one's goal; but it's from the end of the line that we all started our journey to our intended goal.

THE REAL DEAL
January 29, 2005

P.T. Barnum once said, ~You can fool some of the people some of the time, and you can fool all the people some of the time, but you can't fool all the people all of the time.~ In our own pursuit of happiness, whether it be person or professional, one tends to sometimes be fooled by the outside appearances of certain people, places, or things. It's not until we find out during or at the end of one's seemingly drama-filled life that we tend to give a premature verdict when we, as the saying goes, judge a book by its proverbial cover. What may look too good to be true in the beginning ends with a painful price, which is utter heartbreak. Ultimately, when it comes to potential relationships, it's just a matter of distinguishing fact from faction.

The one basic fact that every person can agree on is that love can and does oftentimes stink. We've all experienced the pratfalls of either being turned down, dumped, having one's feelings not returned back by that particular person, unrequited love, or been cheated on. Though cold and heartless it may see, that's life and we just have to roll with the punches, so to speak. In a way, it's like being in a heavyweight boxing match in which there are times where we want to throw in the towel and give up. Though we are physically and mentally drained, our own heart will drive us to keep on going and going and going. For its one's own heart that doesn't want to be counted out because it still has some fight left in it.

Most or some women believe that all guys have a hidden agenda when they meet someone, he is interested in which is purely fiction. True, some guys, who are the self-proclaimed "players" and/or "ladies' men" who basically give every other decent guy in America a bad rap because we're basically guilty by association. Working with mostly women for the past several years has given me somewhat of an inside scoop into what women want, like, and dislike. From my own perspective, a woman should be treated like a lady, and she should be treated with the same respect as if a guy were dating my own mother. Yet, it will always be a Catch 22, when something such as love gets involved.

For it's definitely a fact that the human condition in all guys are basically hunters. From a philosophical standpoint, it's that thrill of the hunt or chase that is always flowing in our veins and it will never go away. Unfortunately, particular guys have this sophomoric and deluded ideology that women are merely conquests to brag about and add to one's little black book. To some guys, the hunt is just a game that ends up hurting someone that doesn't deserve to be hurt. Anyways, personally speaking, I have temporarily given up on the so-called hunt because in the back of my mind, I think she will catch me. Let me tell you something, I don't like playing games and I'm not that hard to find.

In retrospect, a person can be fooled once, possibly twice, but never a third time because one will be cautious as matters of the heart will be temporarily or permanently closed due to trust issues. The question can be asked, how do you know if that person who is interested in you is telling the truth? You can't, you just have to go with your instincts. Inevitably, each of us will meet someone that will slip past one's proverbial radar screens and that is a fact. But not ever opening up your heart and not falling in love again is fiction. In the end, whether it be fact or fiction, when you finally meet that one person who is genuinely the total package, he or she will truly be considered the real deal.

GOOD AND READY
January 30, 2005

What is real love? That my friends is the million-dollar question that hopefully might get answered. Love means so many different things to so many people and yet it is the one thing that everyone wants in his or her life. But the funny thing is, that when it comes one's way, a person can totally mess it up by trying to relive the past. Getting back something that he or she had and relieving it through someone else that one is interested in. In any case, when each of us suffers heartbreak, one has to re-learn what leave means for ourselves all over again. For it's a work in progress that constantly keeps changing and quite possibly a person might not even know for sure what love is.

Undoubtedly, people are attracted to each other by the physical aspects, its what keeps life interesting at times. We've all been attracted to someone that piques our interest only to find that he or she didn't live up to one's expectations. Yet, it's that so-called rush one gets when meeting someone new as two eyes are locked on one another and some kind of connection is formed. Every person has heard the phrase, love at first sight, but is it really love? I don't think so, it's more of an infatuation than actually being in love where a person simply is initially attracted to the attractive outside covering. It's not until one metaphorically strips away that outside covering that he or she will truly see the real person inside.

In some aspect, real love doesn't go away or vanish into thin air, but it does change. Each of us can remember a time when you were happy with someone but now you are even happier and committed to someone else. In the whole scheme of things, life would be so much simpler and less crazy if a person had only one true love for life. But, life isn't that simple and oftentimes it doesn't work the way we want it to. Ultimately one just has to keep going through the bad experiences until that one great experience will keep you, as well as your heart smiling. Though each of us may fail at times, it's not really a failure but rather a success as you keep trying until you get it right.

Falling in and out of love is something some people are good at, and usually certain celebrities are very good in that department. As glamorous as their lives are, they can't quite seem to grasp what love really is and it's proven by break-ups, multiple marriages, and divorces. We all know friends that fall in love every other day of the week. Does he or she truly know what love is? I don't think so, for you see each and every person is uniquely different from each other. What may be right for one person, isn't really your cup of tea, in a manner of speaking. Our job is to find out who is right for ourselves and not compare what our friends are supposedly right for them which one may never find out.

I started this thought by asking what is real love? In my opinion, real love is between two people who have a deep friendship who truly know and care unselfishly for one another. Though it's not easy, which it will never be, it's the most valuable commodity that can ever be bought or sold. A friend recently said to me, ~Love can be forever or temporary, it's all in what you make of it. It is something that has to be conditioned, tuned up, updated, and revamped. It's not just something you can take for granted and that will always just be. Love knows where you are ready, even if you don't think you are.~ In retrospect, what does real love mean to you and will you be good and ready when it finds you?

WORTH WAITING FOR
February 3, 2005

There is an old Zen saying which says, ~Watch water drop onto the rock beneath it. One drop does nothing but many drops over time creates a hole in the rock. Such is the power of patience.~ When it comes to wanting someone to share his or her life with, a person will tend to get very impatient. It's that yearning to be with someone or anyone for that matter who fulfills one's desire to feel wanted even if it is for a short period of time. Every person has experienced at one time or another that exciting, yet oftentimes desperate attempt at forging a relationship that one knows is probably not going to go anywhere and usually one ends up falling flat on his or her face in the end.

We all know or are friends with someone that doesn't want to wait for Mr./Ms. Right, but rather wants Mr./Ms. Right now. In some aspect, that person is tired of being alone and constantly seeing those around him or her in a dating, potentially committed, or committed relationship. It can get really frustrating when one thinks there is an absolute possibility that a connection has been made that could change for the better. Yet, its that connection that one interprets as something more, is actually interpreted as just purely friendship by that particular person. It's a position that somewhat stings, as certain people have to realize that it's not one's time. One just has to be patient and let it happen on its own.

If you think about it, sometimes the idea of being in a dating, potential, or committed relationship is what one really wants. It's that misguided perception that if a person has someone in his or her life then all is well with the world, so to speak. There comes a point in every guy's, as well as a woman's, life where one feels that nobody will truly see the person that is either standing beside or in front of him or her. That untapped potential which will never see the light of day, in a manner of speaking. In a way, it's like being completely stuck in the "just friends" mode which can get pretty old and tiresome. Even though one's patience is starting to wear thin, one will handle his or her situation with dignity...well most of the time.

Someone once said. ~Wait for that person who pursues you, the one who will make an ordinary moment seem magical. The kind of person who brings out the best in you and makes you want to be a better person. Wait for that person who will be your best friend. Wait for that person who makes you smile and when that person smiles back, you know it's for real. Wait for that person who is confident and confused, the type of person who wants you to understand one's own world. The whole picture is family, friends, and God. But most of all, wait for that person who will put you at the center of one's universe because that person is obviously the center of yours.~

In retrospect, the water that drops onto a rock represents one's own feelings for that person as well as that person's heart. Initially, it will take patience for one's feelings to penetrate that person's heart as one gets to know him or her. Hopefully, that particular person will open his or her heart and something will build from there. The physical aspect of a relationship will or will not always become an issue. For it's this much I know, it takes a man to say that he will wait for you, but it takes a real man to prove it. I made a promise long ago that I would wait for the right women to come along and I'm still sticking to it. In the end, the right woman will come along and she will absolutely be worth waiting for.

NEVER SAY NEVER
February 3, 2005

Jan Mydail said, ~Traveling is not just seeing the new, it is also leaving behind. Not just opening the doors, also closing them behind you, never to return. But the place you have left forever is always there for you to see whenever you shut your eyes. And the cities you see most clearly at night are the cities you have left and will never see again.~ Being a military kid was an experience that I wouldn't want to ever have missed. Though I didn't consider myself a military brat, there were certain kids that absolutely fit the bill. In any case, being part of the military family, moving from place to place is always the case, which can have some distinct advantages, as well as disadvantages.

One advantage is going to new places and whether it was in the states or overseas, every person gets that excited feeling. A feeling somewhat compared to the day before Christmas as one anticipates waking up and finally opening up his or her presents. In any case, living overseas can be an absolute culture shock as one will encounter and/or experience first-hand the food, language, and lifestyle that a person will call home even if it is on a temporary basis. It's been said, home is where the heart is and sometimes the place we are is not really where one wants to be. Let me tell you something, of all the places that I have lived, I have to say living in Puerto Rico was considered a tropical paradise.

The one basic disadvantage, though English is spoken on the navy base, was learning a new language that hopefully would be used down the road. It was a basic necessity as trips taken off the base would put one's own Spanish speaking skills to the test. Of my 2 1/2 years there and 2 spanish classes this is what I am able to say. Buenos Días, ¿Cómo te llamas? Me llamo Dante Abundo. You soy vente siete años. Yo voy al colegio como estudiante. Que? Si, soy muy loco en mi cabeza. Si senor, yo tengo un gato en mi pantalones. Si, la comida está bien caliente. Tolo lo menos mi tang y van me loco. Yo quiero Taco Bell, and last but least, Senor/Senora, Donde están los baños por favor?

As with all High Schools, there will inevitably be cliques that will segregate only with each other. Yet, the advantage with an overseas high school is that the cliques tend to merge within one another because basically everyone knows each other and practically are neighbors. Living on a military base, there isn't much of a clique where jocks, cheerleaders, etc. only hang out with each other. For it's a mixed group of jocks, cheerleaders, stoners, loners, troublemakers, freaks, geeks, class clowns, brainiacs, and artists that share a common bond. Of course, there will be altercations but that is to be expected due to living in such a confined area where you will bump into classmates on a seemingly regular basis.

J.R.R. Tolkein once said, ~The Road goes ever on and on, Down from the door where it began. Now far ahead the Road has gone, And I must follow, if I can, Pursuing it with eager feet, Until it joins some larger way, Where many paths and errands meet. And whither then? I cannot say."~ In retrospect, military life will always lead you away from one place to another, which may seem fun, but it can be considered an endless cycle that will keep on going until one's parent(s) decide to retire from the military. Ultimately, one may think the friends that one has bonded with and even tolerated over the years will never be seen again as he or she travels the road to some new place; but never say never because being in the brotherhood that is the military, that person will absolutely be seen again.

A DYING BREED
February 5, 2005

Ellen Key once said, ~For success in training children the first condition is to become a child oneself, but this means no assumed childishness, no condescending baby-talk that the child immediately sees through and deeply abhors. What it does mean is to be as entirely and simply taken up with the child as the child himself is absorbed by his life.~ A person who works with kids, like myself, will tell you it is not easy, for it can be a thankless and yet fulfilling job. One has to find his or her own niche in relating to a child, which can be either an easy or difficult task indeed. For it's the smiles, hugs, and respect given back that makes it all well worth the headaches and frustration that is oftentimes received from them.

As said before in a past thought, there will be certain realizations that will set in that will leave a person stupefied. Just recently, my best friend and I came to the realization that we're at the age where we consider the kids at the asylum our sons and daughters. For most the parents that pick their children up are near or close to our age, which is a sobering thought. Thinking about it though, we've helped raise them, comfort them when they were sad or injured, tried to instill right and wrong, lectured on seemingly daily basis, so in the whole scheme of things we are parents. For they will and always be considered "my kids" even if they have grown up, got married and have children of their own.

Working in a youth center/insane asylum, countless kids have walked through the hallowed doors and either made my job quite difficult or absolutely easy. Yet, it's those kids that are considered "children of the corn" that you will never be able to forget, trust me I've tried. In any case, there are times when you think just when you've seen or heard it all from a child, he or she will do or say something that will make us as counselors ask each other or ourselves, 'Tell me I did not just hear or see that?' Sometimes it can be a serious moment where the safety of a child takes precedence, but other times it's a moment where you just burst out laughing because of that particular situation that happened to him or her.

For it's not only countless kids that have passed through those doors, but it's countless employees as well. Young and old, each person with his or own unique style of dealing with and caring for a child. Of the many orderlies or patients, depending on the day, only three people have lasted the longest and that is myself, my best friend, and a female co-worker who I consider my mentor. Thinking about it, if one were to add our combined work experience it would total 31 years. In some ways, we consider ourselves the triad because we have been through so much crap together that it takes a bulldozer to haul it all away. Consequently, it's those two people and several others that I trust to have my back and I for them.

Over the years, the male presence in the asylum has been noticeably decreased rather than decreased. There was a time when the male ratio outnumbered the female ratio but through time that has undeniably changed. For the brotherhood, as I like to call it, desperately needs new members to join the fold; but as of now we are holding down the fort, so to speak. In some aspect, we're like Gilligan and the Skipper, Laurel and Hardy, Batman and Robin....for we are Yoda and Biggie, a dynamic duo who have been through thick and thin for 8 years. In retrospect, we're a dying breed of guys that enjoy working with kids because in the end, they need a strong male presence that ultimately may be missing from one's own family.

JUST ONE LOOK
February 6, 2005

Someone once said, ~The power of a glance has been so much abused by love stories, that it has come to be disbelieved in. Few people dare now to say that two beings have fallen in love because they have looked at each other. Yet it is in this way that love begins, and in this way only. The rest is only the rest and comes afterward. Nothing is more real than these great shocks which two souls give each other in this spark."~ We've all at some point in our lives done that proverbial double take when we either knowingly or unknowingly spot a particular person of interest. It's in our human nature to be curious of who that person is and it's from a simple look or glance that the proverbial ball will start rolling.

Let me ask you a question, have you ever been in a situation where a particular guy or girl looked either directly or indirectly in your general direction? What is your first reaction or instinct to do? For me personally, it's to always look behind me because every person has been in that awkward and somewhat embarrassing position of thinking that a window of opportunity might possibly open one's way. For our own ego can get the better of us as a person tends to not see the whole picture because one's peripheral vision is only seeing what he or she wants to see. It can be a truly humbling experience when one thinks the window of opportunity is about to be opened, but in fact it was actually closed all along.

Every person has either looked at someone or has had that look done on one's self with the expressed interest of hopefully establishing a relationship of some kind. It's a look that every person knows because it's been seen on our friends' faces and even on our own face. It's that undeniable look of happiness and confusion when you think you might have met that special person but aren't quite sure if that person is interested in you. For there will be subtle clues left here and there, but won't be seen, which as a guy, will always be our fault for not seeing the signals and picking up on it. Ultimately, every guy wants a woman who makes him happy and without a doubt accept us for who we are faults and all.

Undoubtedly, a woman wants a guy that will love her for what he sees from deep within her heart and soul. It's a love that has a deeper meaning that some, not all guys, never can seem to quite grasp. For it takes that one-of-a-kind guy, so to speak, to show it to her, which is a rarity to find these days. Inevitably, it's a woman's inner true beauty that will shine forth that makes her absolutely beautiful when you start getting to know her. It's from there you find things that you have in common and also things you don't have in common, but the end result is that a stronger bond is formed. For it can be a disappointing situation indeed when a relationship fades because the guy didn't take the time to truly see what was in front of him.

There will come a point in every person's life where each of us will meet someone that will capture our attention. Whether or not that person will give each of us the time of day is really unknown as a person will have to find that out on one's own. It's just a matter of having the confidence to be yourself and not put up a persona that doesn't really fit you. For it's been said that if a person is genuinely interested in you after only knowing you for only a short period of time, that while walking away he or she will take a look back and smile. In retrospect, sometimes it takes several glances/looks to see the one person who truly makes you happy, but other times if we're truly lucky, all it takes is just one look.

SINCERELY YOURS
February 7, 2005

As Valentine's Day approaches, a person tends to wonder if one will ever meet that one special person and end his or her time of being a single bachelor or bachelorette. One's time of constant availability can make a person believe he or she will end up alone, which is a mindset that nobody should have; but oftentimes does. It's simply unavoidable as you ponder what might, could, or should have been in one's past. Inevitably, there comes a point where just writing a heartfelt letter to that unknown person will, in some ways, ease the frustration one has been feeling. In some ways, it's like a message in a bottle being thrown into the sea and falling into the hands of someone unknown. For my letter would go something like this:

~To whom it may concern, You have been in my thoughts for quite some time and even today I think about you as I am sitting here alone with my thoughts. For I dream of the day that we meet each other and forge a future together. It's a future that hopefully we both can make things work out, yet in my heart of hearts I know that it will work out for the best with you in my life. There are times when I think of the day we meet, I will smile both on the outside and on the inside, for I truly know you bring out the best in me. It's when my day becomes absolutely unbearable, that I close my eyes and see your face in my head. Though the image of your face is unclear, it's enough for me to make my day happier and brighter.

You have the qualities that make my heart melt for you. It's in your smile that will bring me to my knees and your laugh that I will get to know and love. Even though certain people can't see it, I can see your beauty shining from within. For it's in your personality that we may or may not click, but hopefully we can come to an understanding. For you will forever be my best friend, as I know that I won't be afraid of sharing certain aspects of my life with you that I don't normally share with other people. For you will have the courage as well to open up to me about anything and everything. Ultimately the love that you share for me is a testament that tells me I am the guy you truly want to spend your life with.

For you will give me so much and because of this I will give up my life and my heart to you as we both take this leap of faith together. In some ways, writing this letter has eased my loneliness and the words that I am saying to you are coming so easily now. Each time my thoughts turn to you, I get that feeling that you are the woman that will absolutely complete the last puzzle piece of my life, as well as my heart. I have no idea when or where we will meet, but I do know one thing for sure, on that special day you will make me a happy man. For I thought I met you once, but I guess it wasn't meant to be. But I do know this much, things happen for a reason and that one reason will hopefully lead to you.

In retrospect, I'm a simple man, who doesn't have much to offer you except my heart which I give to you. I'm not rich, but I make enough to keep me financially stable. I'm quiet and yet I will shout my feelings for you on top of the highest mountain. I will take each day with you one day at a time, because I don't want to miss each and every moment of it. In the end, all I can ever offer you is my love which may not seem like much, but I have a lot to offer you if given the chance. Well, that's all I can really say to you, I just wanted to let you know what has been on my mind and how I feel for you. So I say this, I will meet you someday and you know what, I can't hardly wait till it happens. Sincerely Yours, Dante.~

A PERFECT FIT
February 10, 2005

Let me ask you this question, if I asked you to describe yourself would you be able to do it? In some aspect, when it comes to describing either total strangers, colleagues, friends, and/or family members each of us can come up with so many things to list down without even thinking about it. Yet, when it comes to describing ourselves, it can be considered the most difficult thing to do, depending on whether or not one has the patience to sit down and make a list that can either be true or not. In some ways, it's like trying to figure out which clothes that a person will be able to fit in; but in order for him or her to do that, he or she has to try each article of clothing to test it out, which we all have done at some point in our lives.

The one underlying trait that most people describe themselves as is that they tend to dislike being told what to do by an authority figure or anyone for that matter. From the time we were little kids, to our adulthood, and into our latter years we will have someone telling us what to do, where to go, and so on and so forth. It's a never-ending cycle really because even if we are in a position of authority, one will have to answer to the proverbial powers that be, which look over our shoulders on a semi-daily basis. It's what each of us metaphorically signed up for as we clock in and out of the daily grind that each works hard in. Though we may not like being told what to do, one just has to grin and bear it.

Oftentimes, one will describe themselves as a people person who can easily get along with others. We've all come across that one person or that one person who just has that magnetic personality and can make friends in an instant. It's a quality that is very admirable and makes the experience of meeting him or her a memorable one. For one never forgets the people who come into our lives directly or indirectly that have made a difference in it. Yet, much can be said for those that caution themselves when faced with meeting someone new either as a friend or a potential relationship. For it takes some people time to warm up and figure out whether or not that person is either dating or friendship material.

Inevitably, each of us can describe ourselves as particular objects or food items that usually can or can't be seen in that particular person. The one object that a person tends to use when he or she talks about using the talents that God has given to him or her to be a potential success in a particular business is a star. For each of us can be considered shooting stars going after our dreams that can either continue to shine or burn out completely. For when it comes to describing a person as a particular food, such examples would be pretty as a peach, one hot tamale, spicy as a jalapeno, cute as a cucumber, the list can go on and on. It's a description that can be considered flattering, but it can get old quickly.

About three days ago, my Advertising Design professor gave us a creative concept in which if we were to walk into Wal-Mart, what object or food item would describe us the best. He then proceeded to tell us to make a word list and describe ourselves, which sounded easy but in fact it was hard. For the past three days, I've been racking my brain trying to figure it out and it's been said that the answers we seek come to us when we least expect it and it came to me today when I stopped off to get some Chinese food for lunch. In retrospect, I would best describe myself as a fortune cookie. For it's a perfect fit, because the outside may look plain, but once opened the information found inside can not only make you think but can quite possibly be helpful as well.

A SIMPLE THING
February 15, 2005

Someone once said, ~Sooner or later we begin to understand that love is more than verses on valentines and romances in movies. We begin to know that love is here and now, real and true, the most important thing in our lives. For love is the creator of one's favorite memories and the foundation of our fondest dreams. Love is a promise that is always kept, a fortune that can never be spent, a seed that can flourish in even the most unlikely of places. And this radiance than never fades, this mysterious and magical joy, is the greatest treasure of all-one known only by those who love.~ Valentine's Day gives an opportunity to give something from the heart that is considered a generous token of appreciation from one person to another.

Think back to your childhood as you randomly signed and gave out Valentine's Day cards to your friends and classmates. You really didn't think anything of it at the time because as a kid, love was a word that you had absolute deniability to. Back in the day, one's mentality was the girls, as well as the boys, had cooties and if one ever caught it, you were going to infect other people you came in contact with. It's a phase that every person has gone through as a kid and that mindset is somewhat still going on with today's generation of ankle biters. For it's an amusing aspect of one's childhood that has given each of us fond memories and hopefully we have all outgrown that cootie phase in our lives.

As we get older, Valentine's Day cards will take a back seat as one will take it to the next level when it pertains to that special someone or potential special someone in one's life. It's a level in which guys will make Valentine's Day a day that she will truly remember and show her that she is the most special person to him. Oftentimes jewelry, a romantic dinner date, roses, etc. will be given to show that money is no object when it comes to her happiness. Yet, when it comes to her happiness you can't put a price tag on it, because love is absolutely priceless. Whether its considered romantic or thoughtful, it's a gift from the heart that one can appreciate even if it's from a person that you hardly know.

Sometimes a person will find himself or herself alone in a day that whenever you turn around it's constantly in your face, seemingly laughing at or mocking you. It can make a person slowly lose that sense of hope that tends to keep a person optimistic and that the so-called proverbial silver lining will be seen one day. For some, it's a position that he or she has been used to for quite some time but for others, one is always in the arms of someone only after a short period of availability. A person can be truly envious of that type of person; but if you think about it, he or she just doesn't want to be alone as well and basically forms an attachment even though it's just for a short period of time.

In retrospect, Cupid is never really off duty after Valentine's Day is over, he continually does his job metaphorically shooting arrows of love at specified targets. Unfortunately, sometimes one may think those arrows are missing or must be bent because when someone of interest comes his or her way, there isn't that spark/vibe/connection one feels for that person or vice versa. Yet, when you least expect, one of his arrows will be right on target and hopefully it will never be removed. In the end, it's a simple thing such as love that every person wants in his or life and yet it's the most complicated thing to ever come one's way; but once one truly experiences it, you never want it to end.

Happy Valentine's Day To One and All!

BLACK AND WHITE
February 15, 2005

Someone once said, ~Falling in love is easy, it involves only the senses. Staying in love and growing harmoniously with another is truly where love begins. Learning how to love brings us to the happiness and fulfillment we are seeking, because we share and give from what we have, what we feel, when we accept this, we can begin to heal from the past, and start building a loving foundation that won't be destroyed by what others have done to us, that won't be crushed because we haven't the best partner. Finding a true love means we must become a true lover, a knower of love, giver of love. Then we will attract them to us, just like bees are attracted to a beautiful flower.

In some aspect, when each of us is truly in love, things seem much brighter and full of color when you are with that particular person. For one can have an extra kick in his or her step, one's demeanor changes, and the frown that he or she usually has is now proverbially turned upside down. But the question is, for how long? Does it really matter though because one doesn't want to think about whether or not his or her relationship will last. It's a mindset that will, in some cases, ruin a perfectly good relationship in which friends and family are genuinely rooting for it to grow. In a way, every potential relationship starts off in somewhat of a gray area, but through time, hopefully colors will start to be seen clear as day.

Yet, some people can be totally color blind to the fact there is a person right in front of him or her that is trying to paint a colorful picture of a potential relationship. It can be a frustrating situation indeed for some people when you want that particular person of interest to see the same-colored picture you want him or her to see. Though one may be seeing colors that represent a warm tone for that person, he or she may be seeing something different as that person only sees neutral colors, which is otherwise called "just friends." Initially it may take a while for that guy or girl to see those colors, especially guys because you know we are slow at figuring things out.

Every relationship goes through hardships and one of the things that can make it difficult is the green-eyed monster known as jealousy. It can be a person's worst enemy when it pertains to having a relationship with someone that, in your own mind, other people want what you have got. One's imagination can get the better of him or her when a platonic relationship between a girl and a guy is totally innocent. For it takes only one seed to be planted and inevitably it can either be uprooted immediately or let it continually grow, at which point trust becomes an issue. It's just a matter of keeping that green-eyed monster in check and having total faith in that person or the colorful picture will turn into something totally unrecognizable.

When you think about it, there are millions of books that teach people how to keep the love going in a relationship. A person, like Dr. Phil, who I respect, talks to people who are in troubled relationships and tries to break through the wall to find some kind of common ground. In reality, it doesn't take a rocket scientist to know that the most important part of a relationship is communication. Without it, a relationship that started off colorful will slowly fade to black and nobody wants that to happen. In retrospect, relationships aren't always solved simply by reading what's in black and white; you simply have to read from the one place that when it is pierced it bleeds crimson red and that is each other's heart.

TOP OF THE MOUNTAIN
February 16, 2005

Someone said, ~People are unreasonable, illogical, and self centered. Love them anyway. If you do good, people will accuse you of selfish ulterior motives. Do good anyway. If you are successful, you will win false friends and true enemies. Succeed anyway. Honesty and frankness make you vulnerable. Be honest and frank anyway. The good you do today will be forgotten tomorrow. Do good anyway. The biggest people with the biggest ideas can be shot down by the smallest people with the smallest mind. Think big anyway. People favor underdogs but follow top dogs. Fight for some underdogs anyway. What you spend years building may be destroyed overnight. Build anyway. Give the world the best you've got anyway.

If you think about it, in our own ambition to succeed in certain aspects of life, a person will go though many peaks and valleys in order to get where one wants to be. It's within those peaks and valleys that he or she will find out if what one is really doing will matter in his or her own future. For it will also determine what type of person you are as life's most greatest challenges will be put in front of us. A person can either do two things when faced with those particular challenges which are: 1.) back down, give up, and be labeled a quitter or 2.) continue to climb up that mountain that stands before you and try to conquer it. Let me ask you this question, what has been your toughest challenge to climb, or has it even happened yet?

We've all suffered many disappointments in our lives which cause us to doubt whether or not we will be able to get through it both emotionally and physically. For each of us we tend to physically push ourselves to our limit and sometimes it can take a toll on our bodies, as well as our minds. It's within the valley of our minds that we tell ourselves that we can handle the responsibility and pressure, but in reality, we are just adding on to it. We are all only human and the pressure that we tend to put on ourselves will most definitely boil over and erupt. Inevitably, one will have to try to climb up and past the point where one fell from, which will be the toughest valley he or she will have to go through and experience.

Yet, when we do go through the valleys of life, one will encounter several peaks that will uplift a person's spirits. It can be said that people along our journey can, in some way, help and guide us to where we want to go. Sometimes, the destination we want to go will oftentimes take a detour and end up in an area that we didn't want to be but are absolutely happy that he or she ended up there. It's from these particular people that we get emotional support as they lend an open ear as we spill our guts, so to speak, to get what's been bothering us off our chest. Whether it's total strangers, close friends, or even your worst enemy that they, in some ways, can be considered one's strong support to climb up with when life simply gets rough.

In retrospect, there will be people in one's life that will absolutely doubt that one will ever make something of himself or herself and become a success. Yet, it's these particular people that tend to fuel the fires within to burn even hotter to go after our dreams and aspirations of doing and being what we want to be in life. In some ways, proving that person wrong would be considered sweet retribution and to see the look on his or her face when you've made something of yourself would be absolutely priceless. Life is basically one big mountain that each of us climbs in order to reach new heights in success or failure. In the end, we all may not reach the top of the mountain, but we can surely try our best, which is all we can ever really give.

TAKE IT OR LEAVE IT
February 17, 2005

Wilford Peterson once said, ~The art of being yourself at your best is the art of unfolding your personality into the person you want to be...Be gentle with yourself, learn to love yourself, to forgive yourself, for only as we have the right attitude toward ourselves can we have the right toward others.~ Thinking about it, myself and every red-blooded male never really knows if a female is truly interested in who we really are. It can be difficult to figure out as we meet and talk with a potential female of interest that one has been getting to know or just getting to know. Inevitably, we try to be ourselves as our personality shines through and hopefully that particular female will not be blinded by who she sees in front of her.

Women are an absolute mystery because, as a guy, we have no idea if any of us fit the endless list of qualities that they are looking for in a potential mate. In a way, it's like trying to create a formula, which will inherently bring one to the answer that leads her to that so-called perfect guy. It's within this formula/list that the question can be asked whether it's looks or personality or both that matter to a woman in the end. Consequently, it's up to her to proverbially weed out the egotistical jerks and find a guy who is absolutely worth giving her heart to, which is hard to find these days. It's just a matter of looking in the right places rather than looking in the wrong places.

Let me ask you this question, what attracts you most about a person when you first meet them? Is it the outward appearance or the inward appearance that compels you to strike up a conversation and in turn become truly interested in him or her. Oftentimes, there is no attraction at first only until he or she gets to know that particular person and gets a better understanding of who he or she is. In some ways, that attraction can be infected by that person's presence and will leave a lasting impression, in a good way of course. As a guy, it takes me a while to figure out if I am really attracted to someone and if I truly am I will take time to get to know her. The old school ways of courting a woman still work in my book.

In any case, each of us can sometimes have personality issues as we meet someone new that we want to get to know. It's simply part of being human as one tends to have that mindset that we want to meet someone that basically has the same interests. A person with an easy going, laid back attitude who doesn't take one's self too seriously and can laugh at the stupidest and craziest things that happen in life. A person one can absolutely call a best friend but knows that sometimes space is needed to grow even closer. In some ways that is who I'm looking for and hopefully if she is out there that particular person will one day stand at my door, knock, and will ask to come in.

Last Friday, I sent out a personality test which compares certain personality traits with a certain animal type. I'm a Golden Retriever, but I have a little lion and otter in me as well. As a Golden Retriever, I tend to feel deeply for certain things or people which comes with working with kids, but I don't have difficulty saying no to them. I'm an introverted person who likes being by myself at times. I'm also a person of habit and I don't like breaking a set routine that works. I'm a calm, reserved, even keel person which "my kids" might disagree with, but I do know when to let my hair down, so to speak. Ultimately, do those personality traits consider me an interesting and/or attractive person for any female out there? Who knows, but she has to either take it or leave it because that is who I am and I'm comfortable being myself.

RIGHT ON SCHEDULE
February 19, 2005

If you think about it, each of us live our lives on a set schedule that at times will or will not be met. It's the constant daily grind that a person will go through to do things and meet certain people that will have him or her feeling both physically and mentally fatigued. Have you ever been in a situation where you had a million things to do in one day that when you first look at that seemingly endless list, one's reaction is either to cry or scream out loud. Oftentimes in life, the things we plan in the present or the road ahead don't necessarily correspond with who or what might come one's way. In some ways, it will throw a proverbial monkey wrench into the works and have one's schedule all out of whack, so to speak.

There are times on those very rare occasions where that proverbial monkey wrench is a person that you never expected to walk into your life without being scheduled or asked to make an appointment. It's that one particular person who you would completely clear and/or cancel everything that he or she has on one's calendar just to meet him or her. Each of us is walking our personal journey of life and at times, we will or have come across someone on our journey that just takes us totally by surprise. It's been said that a person who initially isn't looking for love will find it and will soon realize it at some point in time. Yet, it doesn't start off as love but rather a friendship that grows after time when two people get to know each other.

In any case, we all make appointments to be somewhere or to meet someone in order to fulfill a specific obligation to be met. Sometimes it can be a mandatory meeting or a meeting that is considered special where time is spent together. Yet, it's those same appointments which can be broken or not met at all and seemingly its certain people that he or she puts one's friendship, trust, faith, and/or love into being there but never fails to show up. Let me ask you this question, is there a person in your life who has always shown up either in person or in spirit when life just gets rough? In a way, that person somehow knows when you are having a bad day or just needs some encouragement to make a person feel better about themselves.

Oftentimes, it seems that a person spends so much time meeting his or her schedule and appointments that there isn't time for a social life, if any. It's one's co-workers and classmates that tend to be the only faces he or she sees on a daily basis, which tends to make a person feel sick, tired, and a little restless. For the little amount of free time, one has it ends up spending with friends, a significant other, or in some instances going online and surfing the web. It's within instant messaging and/or email that one will socialize with people or someone that peaks his or her interest. Though it may not seem like much, when you receive an email, you know that someone thought about you which can make your day.

Someone once said, ~A relationship is like a train. If one passes, then the next one will come. I'm sure and if you get off the train, you'll realize that everything is the same.~ For it can be that way with love, but more meaningful as a person tries to run after it. Sometimes, one feels as though his or her timing is completely off as a person stands on the platform of life and sees the opportunity to start a potential relationship roll away. In retrospect, you can't predict when love will stop at our platforms as we metaphorically stand there waiting for that one specific train to arrive. In the end, that one train which carries that someone special is never really late; as a matter of fact, it will be considered right on schedule.

HEAD OF THE CLASS
February 21, 2005

Ralph Waldo Emerson once said, ~Most of the shadows of this life are caused by standing in one's own sunshine.~ I've come across this quote many times and never really could understand what it meant until now. In some aspect, each of us is attending the school of life and the world we live in is one big classroom. For the lessons of life are constantly being taught by each and every person one meets who are somewhat considered teachers. Whether it be directly or indirectly he or she can open your eyes and reveal things from a totally different perspective. It's not until we find the answers, which will shed light on our particular situation, that we will continue to stay in the shadows and question everything.

Let me ask you this question, when it came to choosing your seat in the classroom what seat did you pick? For some students, they would choose the back because it represents a place that one can disappear from and hide in the shadows, so to speak. In a way, that is how some people are as they don't want to be noticed and live a life of obscurity. It's a mindset in which a person thinks if he or she is safe in a sea of faces that one will hopefully never be seen and called upon to answer the questions that are either important or unimportant. Yet, life doesn't work that way as there are certain things in life that can't be avoided and solved just by disappearing and hiding.

For other students, they thoroughly enjoy sitting up front and soaking up the knowledge that the teacher is giving to him or her. It's these particular people that stay out of the shadows and are in constant view of the teacher, which can be labeled a teacher's pet. A label that usually comes with consequences as he or she lives a life of torment and ridicule. It's from that person's perspective that if he or she is constantly heard and seen then one will always be remembered, but that is not often the case. Undoubtedly, they may know all the answers to the questions that will be asked, but when it comes to answering questions that concern one's life in general, one usually doesn't have the answer to it.

In any case, for most students, the middle of the classroom is chosen for the simple reason that even though one wants to be seen and answer questions from time to time, he or she doesn't necessarily want to be hidden completely from the world. Initially, a person has that mindset that one can have the best of both worlds, in a manner of speaking, as he or she has one foot in the shadows and the other in light. In a way, it's like a proverbial balance and on any given day one can tip the scales as he or she can be a person who wants to be seen and noticed or the person who wants to disappear. It's within this place, which is considered neutral ground or comfort zone, that he or she is absolutely comfortable in.

As JayZ put it, people can live a hard knock life and in the whole scheme of things we have to go through the school of hard knocks to find out what we are made of. In retrospect, each of us may or may not have all the answers that life puts in front of us, but it will be a challenge to try to figure them out. When it comes to life, there are no right or wrong answers; you just go figure it out for yourself. The questions may be the same, but the answers may have a different meaning for each of us. In the end, it's the teacher who usually decides whether you are up front, in the middle, or in the back of the class; but when you finally decide to completely step out of the shadows, then you've finally graduated to the head of the class.

WHISPER IN THE WIND
February 23, 2005

Someone once said, ~Who knows what true loneliness is, not the conventional word, but the naked terror? To the lonely themselves it wears a mask. The most miserable outcast hugs some memory or some illusion. Now and then a fatal conjunction of events may lift the veil for an instant. For an instant only. No human being could bear a steady view of moral solitude without going mad.~ There comes a point in every person's life where you start missing someone that you never even met or only met just once. It's an unmistakable feeling that grows with time and no matter how hard one tries to take it off it will still come back. One surely suppresses that feeling but it will, in a way, come back and haunt a person.

Each one of us has spent periods of time alone during our lives. If you think about it, there are others out there who feel lonely, which is good to know because at least you are in the same boat, so to speak, with many other people. It's never really easy to meet someone who you can genuinely talk to and not act like a complete idiot or dork around him or her. It's especially tough when one's shyness can get in the way, or one isn't much of a talkative person. Initially, we're all social beings who feel the need for human contact and whether it be physical, emotional, spiritual, or metaphorical, it leads us to someone that one can hopefully share his or her thoughts and feelings with.

Yet, it's hard these days to know what to say when you meet new people who may or may not have anything in common. For it is in the technological age we live in where meeting new people is just a click away with email, online dating, instant messaging, and chat rooms. Though these are great alternatives to "meeting" people, absolutely nothing can replace the feeling of a human touch where one can actually see someone smile at you, feel a hug that is given back, a hand stroking one's cheek, and taste that kiss that is considered passionate when one's lips touches another will love. In the whole scheme of things, the internet can either bring a positive or a negative in one's life, it all in how one perceives it to be.

Let me ask you this question, have you ever thought to yourself that you aren't worthy or interesting to be noticed? For me personally, I can honestly say that I feel that way most days BUT I surround myself with great friends that continually keep me uplifted and encourage me that my day will come. In any case, a person will oftentimes think that he or she will be alone for the rest of one's life, which would be a fate worse than death. Every person wants to be and feel loved by that one guy or girl who one can spend all his or her days with. Inevitably, each of us, who are living the single life either by choice or unfortunate circumstance, want an honest to goodness real relationship.

In retrospect, it's within our dreams that each of us are never alone. For the pain that one can suffer in his or her heart will never be felt, but in reality, it's still there eating away at each of us. In a way, it's a burning sensation that can't be extinguished by pouring water on it; it needs words of hope and love that will most definitely breathe new life into a seemingly dying soul. Ultimately, it's in our dream that Ms./Mr. Right loudly calls out our name as he or she seems to be getting closer in one's echo filled mind. In the end, as with all dreams, they end. For that loud echo of your name that was heard so very clearly is now just a whisper in the wind as you sit up in your bed and find yourself all alone.

YOU GOT SERVED
February 23, 2005

Without a doubt music plays a big part in expressing one's self through dancing. For our inhibitions can be thrown out the window, in a manner of speaking, as you completely let yourself go to the rhythm, beat, and sound of the music that plays. Depending on how fast or slow the song is played a sort of Pavlovian reaction takes place when a certain song comes, and one immediately heads to the dance floor. Let me ask you this question, do you feel like you are in a whole other world as you or your dance partner(s) tear it up? If you think about it, when a person is on the dance floor busting a move, one's problems seem to take a back seat. For it gives an outlet to release one's frustrations of the day or week.

When a person gets his or her groove on, that person doesn't care what other people think. For as long as one is having fun, the opinions of others, who believe that he or she is dancing like a fool, doesn't mean anything. Initially, it's those that dance like a fool who create spectacular dance routines and moves that wow the crowd. It's the type of move that when you see it, you're amazed at the skill and talent that these individuals have. It can simply boggle the mind in the creativity that certain people have who can take one's body too the limit and not wind up in a recovery room suffering from hyperextension or broken bones. In my opinion, it's an artform that so few can accomplish but many want to try.

We've all done or at least tried to do the moonwalk, which is Michael Jackson's trademark move. BUT did you know that many of the dance moves of the 80's 90's and today are either updated, added to, or borrowed and originated in the late 60's and early 70's? Michael Jackson's moonwalk wasn't his, its original name was the Goodfoot and the man who performed was the Godfather of Soul James Brown. You see, you learn something new every day and you thought this would just be a regular Yodaism. One has to give respect for the pioneers of dance moves of years past that originated from the late 60's by people who simply danced in the ghetto streets of NYC.

Growing up in the 80's, breakdancing was the thing to do for young kids like myself who wanted to try it. Moves such as the robot, headspin, windmill, the worm, and flaring were considered movies that looked simple to do if one practiced to perfect it. Young school kids, like myself, would try moves that the older kids saw in the movies and were taught to us in our school playgrounds. It was a way to make friends and bond with kids that now you shared something in common with even though one was in a different social circle. Now that I am older, there are some moves that I can still do such as the moonwalk and robot; but moves such as the worm, if I tried now, I would not be able to get back up again.

About 2 weeks ago, the Youth Center held a Valentine's Day dance for the kids and we chaperoned it. The teenagers really enjoyed themselves as they hung out with their friends, listened and danced to their favorite songs such as Ciara's 1,2 Step. During the festivities, a dance battle between the girls and boys happened in which I subsequently became the MC to it. Both the girls and boys traded dances moves back and forth to each other. The dance skills were impressive as they performed moves that absolutely no words could describe, you just had to see it to believe it. Even though the girls gave their all, the boys were proclaimed the winners. In the end, they turned to the girls and said all together, You Got Served!

THE HARD WAY
February 26, 2005

Someone once said, ~Life isn't supposed to be an all or nothing battle between misery and bliss. Life isn't supposed to be a battle at all. And when it comes to happiness, well, sometimes life is just okay, sometimes its comfortable, sometimes wonderful, sometimes boring, sometimes unpleasant. When your day's not perfect, it's not a failure or a terrible loss. It's just another day.~ Oftentimes life doesn't coincide with one's own expectations of how it should go. In our own ambition to see things that bring joy and pleasure into each of our lives we tend to ignore the things that make one's smile turn upside down. In a way, it's like signing a contract and every now and then, the fine print will show up and bit you in the butt.

Growing up is hard enough as it is without having to deal with trying to figure out one's own identity in life. From the minute we are born and into our teenage years, one will try to carve out a niche in life for himself and herself by establishing one's individuality. It's our own individuality that sets us apart from every other person who wants to be like or dress like the other kids. It's that inner struggle within ourselves that we can sell out and try to be someone whose family and friends will not be able to recognize and probably not like. In some aspect, as kids, we can go through so many contract negotiations with our parents to try to find absolute common ground and be content with the finality of what both have agreed upon.

Undoubtedly, when each of us enters adulthood, the conscious choices one makes will be, at times, costly. For our stress level will go through the roof, in a manner of speaking, when certain obstacles are knowingly or unknowingly put in front of us. It's at this stage of our lives that we learn what it's like to be a responsible adult and when we have those big mess ups, we not only mess it up for ourselves we can mess it up for other people as well. It's these mistakes in life that one has to simply deal with our transgressions with the utmost dignity and grace. If not, one will create an even bigger hole for one to climb out of and that's a part of life which isn't found in one's contract of life; we just have to figure it out on our own.

Consequently, when it comes to falling in love, there is no absolute guarantee that the contract will be with you and that special someone will last. We all tend to ignore the fine print when one falls in love and we're just happy; but when one gets burned that happiness turns to sadness and that fine print will seem clear as day. It's within that metaphorical document written in small bold letters that life is not responsible for one to become angry, bitter, lonely, and depressed when a feeling such as love doesn't quite work out. Initially, it can leave a big hole in one's heart to the point where it hurts when the wind passes through and every time there is even a slight possibility of falling in love again one will keep in mind the fine print.

In retrospect, a person tends to think that he or she has life's most difficult problems solved. For it's in one's contract that a person can try to find loopholes to get something more out of life. Without a doubt, each of us wants the simple life where we don't have to continually worry where the money is going to come from. Yet, life doesn't work that way as we just have to work with the contract that life gives us, which isn't much. We may not have all the things that life has to offer such as materialistic possessions and someone to share our lives with, but it's a work in progress. In the end, life without question is hard and sometimes it doesn't take the easy way to figure that out, you have to figure that out the hard way.

YOU NEVER KNOW
February 28, 2005

Emanuel Swedenburg once said ~Kindness is an inner desire that makes us want to do good things even if we do not get anything in return. It is the joy of our life to do them. When we do good things from this inner desire, there is kindness in everything we think, say, want, and do.~ Every person has the ability to be kind, it's just a matter of finding it within ourselves. Let me ask you this question, have you done anything that was out of the goodness of your heart for someone and expecting nothing in return? Or did someone do something for you out of the goodness of his or her heart that warranted the same result? Initially, it's from these so-called good Samaritans that they perform random acts of kindness.

If you think about it, a person can't give what he or she doesn't have due to one's own personal experiences of being hurt emotionally and/or personally. We've all come across certain people that if you genuinely do something nice, that person thinks there is a hidden agenda. Far from it, for it is the mindset of that good Samaritan that doing one kind thing for one person will have somewhat of a ripple effect. In other words, what was done out of kindness for that person will hopefully be done by other people as well. Initially, a person can be an inspiration just by sharing one's joy of life by doing something that can sometimes be lost, which is to smile.

Undoubtedly, when someone smiles at you your initial reaction is to smile back, which is a common courtesy. Yet one can be a bit weary of that person's smile because he or she can't determine his or her true intentions behind that smile, but I digress. At some point in time, each of us will meet or come across someone that when you have a conversation with him or her, either through email, instant message, or in person you smile and laugh because of the vibe that particular person exudes. It's from interacting with that person that there is a smile in their heart which is made of gold. Kindness can absolutely change the complexity of a person's demeanor or attitude just by giving someone some much needed kind words.

Mark Twain once said, ~Kindness is the language which the deaf can hear and the blind can see.~ A person can do something nice without even knowing it and though he or she can't see or hear it, other people can. In the whole scheme of things, kindness costs nothing and it never wears out. For when something such as a kind smile is gen away, it is usually returned back; but when you lose it, someone will come along to help you find it. You never really forget someone who somehow knows when you need to cheer up at a time in your life when things aren't going so well. It can open your eyes, as well as your heart, to know there is a person out there who is always thinking about you, which is a comforting thought indeed

Since graduating from High School in 1996, I have been writing my thoughts down and it wasn't until 2 years ago that I decided to share these Yodaisms with other people. Whether or not I have made an impact, if any, or your lives is inconsequential because each and every one of you have made an impact on me. Sending out Valentine's Day, Woman's Day, and Birthday e-cards, for the ladies, were done not because I had to, but because I wanted to. For if it put a smile on each of your faces and made your day then that is just an added bonus which tells me that I'm doing something right even if I don't know it. In the end, you never know what a kind word or gesture will get you unless one tries, you may actually like it.

COOL, CALM, AND COLLECTED
March 2, 2005

Someone once said, ~There is no doubt - we face trying times at work, at home, and with those who are tested by factors beyond their control. Some days it's hard to get out of bed, much less "leap tall buildings with a single bound!" Yet, there are also the times to discover what "stuff" we are made of and to fulfill a purpose that is often bigger than ourselves.~ Working in a place that is nicknamed the insane asylum, there are days that I love coming to work, there are days I don't, and some days it's in between. Over the past 8 years, I've been involved or associated with situations that are either expected or unexpected, and it's within those particular situations that are considered the good, the bad, and the ugly.

The Good - Every person has been in a situation where as soon as you walk through the doors of your workplace a certain energy is felt from within. For it's not only the energy that one is giving off, it's the people around you as well that makes it a fun and/or memorable experience. During my tenure in the insane asylum, I have had some fun and wild times to the point where I tend to forget that I'm in a position of authority and rather than helping to squash the mischief; I'm actually contributing to it. A person can't help but feel like a kid again due to being surrounded by so many kids that have endless amounts of energy, which can rub off on adults who need the energy during a hectic day.

The Bad - Let me ask you this question, have you ever walked through the doors of your workplace and felt the tension within? A type of tension so thick that you can cut it with a knife and if one pushes the right button or buttons Armageddon will ensue to the point where words or fists will fly. Every person has their limits when it comes to pushing his or her buttons; the consequences can either be expressed outwardly or not at all. It's all in how one deals with the particular situation at hand. From personal experience, I've had my buttons pushed many times, but one time in particular had my fellow co-workers see a side of me that they had never seen before, which in reality needed to come out and I'm glad it did.

The Ugly - With kids they go through the usual bumps and bruises, which are dealt with the proverbial tender loving care. Yet, nothing can prepare a person when a child breaks a particular body part, such as an arm, or gets one's head busted open doing something totally foolish. I've witnessed both of these and much more than one could possibly imagine as one minute they are fine and the next minute they are down for the count, in a manner of speaking. For that's when our training kicks in and we respond with professionalism...most of the time. In a way, it's like being in a real-life emergency room because at any given time a child, as well as an adult, will need emergency assistance.

In retrospect, you can't prepare for what life will throw at you, so to speak, each and every day. You simply have to adjust for whatever comes your way whether it's planned or unplanned. In some aspects, going through the experiences that I have gone through has somewhat prepared me for when I become a father one day. In a way, life is like a small child, you never know what he or she might do to either embarrass you, make you angry, make you laugh, make you cry, make you smile, or make you absolutely proud to be where you are. In the end, when you have days that are considered good, bad, and ugly, a person needs to keep a level head and just stay cool, calm, and collected.

FEEL THE HEAT
March 3, 2005

Martial arts legend Bruce Lee once said, ~Love is like a friendship caught on fire. In the beginning a flame, very pretty, often hot and fierce, but still only light and flickering. As love grows older, our hearts mature and our love becomes as coals, deep burning and unquenchable.~ Men and women, who want to seek a potential relationship with each other, should start as friends. It can truly be a dicey situation when two people fall in love too quickly and yet do not know who each other is. It's a sad situation indeed when hearts are broken and the emotions that come along with it take its toll and burn people out. In some ways, love can be compared to three things: a match, a candle, and a piece of coal.

Every person at some point has used matches to light something, hopefully for legal reasons. Anyways, a match can be very unpredictable because you never know how many times it will take to get the spark one actually wants. If you think about it, that is how love usually is as a person can try to continually create a spark with someone of interest and absolutely nothing happens. It's a situation that each of us has been in, whether one wants to admit it or not. What one ends up doing is throwing away match after match until he or she has wasted so many that a person is left with one. Initially, the harder one tries to get a spark going, more often than not he or she will end up with a match that will never light up.

Consequently, it can be at times like a candle burning into the night. Let me ask you this question, have you ever played with a flame that is burning on a candle? By playing, I mean running your hand through it or keeping your hand above it until it gets too hot and painful to keep it there. There is a saying that goes, if you play with fire you get burned and when it comes to having your heart played with, it is absolutely true. In some aspect our heart, as well as our emotions can be played with and inevitably one will get burned by that person's false flames of love. Like a candle, love can burn brightly but there are times when it can be easily blown out without a single thought or care in the world.

For it's a proven fact that after being exposed to pressure and heat over time, a piece of coal becomes a diamond. In some aspect, the same goes for two people who are truly in a loving relationship. For it takes a lot of heat and pressure(work) to make something that will turn out absolutely beautiful in the end. As each of us grow older and hopefully a little wiser, each of us seeks someone that will have that burning desire to be the person who one always wanted in his or her life. It's that one person, that even though the scorching hot flames have gone away, his or her warm feelings of love will never die. Ultimately, it's within our proverbial inner fireplace that love continually burns for that person and that fireplace is in our own heart.

Bradley Trevor Grieve said, ~Love, in all its fragile forms, is the one powerful, enduring force that brings real meaning to our everyday lives...but the love I mean is the fire that burns inside all of us, the inner warmth that prevents our soul from freezing in the winters of despair.~ Each of us, who are single, feel absolutely cold within our souls and no matter how warm we can feel on the outside, we can still feel cold on the inside. It's just a matter of rekindling a flame that was unfortunately extinguished but hopefully can be lit again by someone truly special who does exist. In retrospect, a person will feel the heat of love again; it's just a matter of getting back the spark which ignites an eternal flame that will last a lifetime.

A CHIP OFF THE OLD BLOCK
March 5, 2005

For those that are living the single life, there comes a point where one ponders what it would be like to have kids of his or her own. Women, more so than men, have that proverbial biological clock that can oftentimes have them yearning for an offspring to call one's own. Yet, in today's ever changing world countless stories can be told of kids, who without question, disregard a parent's authority and the parent's response is simply to throw his or her hands in the air. In some ways, witnessing it or hearing about it can make a person rethink the possibility of having kids or wanting kids one day. But one can't base his or her decision on that; it's just a matter of having a style all your own that balances meanness and coolness.

Up until now, I've never really thought about what it would be like to have a son, but I technically have over 30 of them at work who I consider absolute daredevils. When it comes to boys, a person in profession tends to keep repeating this same sentence, "If he jumped off a bridge would you jump off as well?" Let me tell you something, on any given day working in an asylum you will find at least one of "my boys" trying to do some kind of crazy stunt that involves jumping off something high. It usually ends up with me standing over him and lecturing about why that wasn't a very good idea. Hey, boys will be boys, but like my dad told me when I got hurt, I now tell them which is, just shake it off.

Undoubtedly, nothing will prepare a guy more than having a daughter because there are several things that go through our minds. All these things involve her starting to get interested in boys and boys getting interested in her. I can already tell that my daughter will have me wrapped around her finger because "my girls" in the asylum have me wrapped around theirs. Thinking about it, I feel more protective of them than the boys because I know what boys are thinking because I used to think the same way. For it's my job, any obligation to scare away the boys and tell each of "my girls" not to date until they are 35 years old. Though they aren't my daughters, I will and always be a father figure to them.

Someone once asked me several years ago if I would ever take a bullet for "my kids" and without hesitation I said yes. Though I am not a parent, the parental instincts are in me, as well, as in each of you. Let me ask you this question, if someone harmed or was trying to harm your child would you stop at nothing to get your hands on him or her? Hopefully your response would be a definite yes because the safety of your child is all that matters to a parent. Over the past 8 years I have seen a number of kids grow up before my eyes. Even though most of the kids have outgrown the asylum, there is a side of me that still sees them as that little boy or girl who thought cooties were contagious.

Someone once said, ~Any man can be a father, but it takes a special person to be a dad.~ I don't know what it is about me that kids gravitate to. Doing some research, I have learned they like me because I'm sarcastic, weird, funny, strange, altogether kooky, but most of all I found that they like me because I talk with them on their level. For most of the kids, they don't just see me as their counselor, they see me as their friend who he or she can absolutely feel comfortable to be around and talk to one on one. In retrospect, someday I will have children of my own and they will inherit certain personality traits, which is a scary thought indeed; but in the end, he or she will be a chip off the old block.

UNSOLVED MYSTERIES
March 5, 2005

How do you know when you are really in love? That is the sixty-four million-dollar question that every person has trouble answering. To be quite honest, I don't think anybody knows for sure including myself because, in a way, it's like trying to solve a mystery that concerns one's own heart for that particular guy or girl. Every potential relationship starts off as a friendship but determining whether or not you actually love that person is in that proverbial gray area called love limbo. In some aspect, each of us can be considered amateur detectives as one searches for that all important answer. It's just a matter of asking questions and looking for clues that will hopefully blow the case wide open, so to speak.

Undoubtedly, love is a powerful feeling as the emotions can be intense to the point where you feel scared and excited at the same time. Yet is it really love one is feeling or just mere infatuation because the only thing that is affected is a person's emotions which is based solely on the outward appearance. During one's investigation, a person has to question if he or she can be totally real around that person. Little by little the time spent around him or her will bring down one's own wall to the point where personal information is shared. Information such as long-term goals, family, and career in great detail that one wouldn't necessarily share with someone else if he or she felt there was absolute trust.

Someone once said, ~Spiteful words hurt your feelings, but silence breaks your heart.~ Let me ask you this question, have you ever hurt or been hurt by someone, not physically but verbally? Words do hurt and whether it is intentional or just in a joking manner, a person can be offended to the point where he or she is affected emotionally. We all say things we tend to regret and when it involves someone that you're probably in love with, the relationship will either be severed completely or temporarily depending on how harsh the words were. Consequently, one just has to admit being in the wrong by giving that sworn statement/(apology) in which he or she swallows one's pride and says, I'm sorry.

One can truly have a better understanding when you interview parents and grandparents as they share their experiences of how as soon as he or she saw that person, one absolutely knew it was love and both of them were going to get married. But the question is how does one truly know? As far as knowing whether or not you are really in love, it comes down to putting the needs of that guy or girl before yours. Giving encouraging words, lifting that person up, respecting one's feelings and emotions, as well as being that person who takes great joy in making you smile and laugh. In other words, putting one's own happiness aside means that person is the center of your world rather than the world centered on you.

In retrospect, it's when a person says "I love you" that he or she has to find out if it is the love that the person wants to give you rather than the love that has a hidden agenda behind it. It's that kind of love that just wants you physically and nothing else. Women hear those three little words so often they really don't know whether to believe what a guy is telling her is actually true. If only love came with a lie detector to find out the truth, but it doesn't. Ultimately, when it comes to knowing if you're really in love it can be an absolute mystery. In the end, no matter how many answers a person comes up with, it's a question that will always be considered one of those unsolved mysteries that one may or may not be able to figure out.

STEP BY STEP
March 6, 2005

Salvatore Satta once said, ~The birth of thought in the depths of the spirit, the shaping and ordering of it in periods, the translation into signs, and above all the transference of it from one spirit to another, the communication of that is, if only for an instant, the meeting of two beings, with the unforeseeable consequences that such a meeting always causes, is in fact a miracle; except that the moment one stops to think about it one can't even write a letter.~ People often ask me how I come up with these thought provoking Yodaisms that can somehow dig deep into a person's soul which can relate his or her life. For it's within these Yodaisms that I go through a process which I'm going to be sharing with you today.

The title often plays a big part in many of the thoughts which are good starting off points. When a certain thought comes to mind the first thing that has to be worked out is the title. Every Yodaism that has been written and sent has had several different working titles which are changed sometimes at the last minute. Undoubtedly, it is what piques your interest, as well as grabs your attention to where you are naturally curious to read what has been thought about in the course of a couple days. Inevitably, when it comes to the title a person will always find it in the ending of the thought rather than the beginning, because it usually ties together what I have been trying to say.

Quotes are regularly used to aid in what is being said and all it takes is someone to say or read something interesting that the proverbial gears in my mind start to turn. Finding the right quote is key because it has to convey or at least parallel the thought that is going to be written. There have been times where a particular quote was chosen, and it didn't quite come together when the thought was finished. It can be a frustrating situation when you're searching for that so-called perfect quote that may or may not be able to be used and because of that many unfinished thoughts are either scrapped or never completed. In any case, whether it be from Ralph Waldo Emerson or from a total stranger, if it's interesting it might or will be used.

The key ingredient of many of the thoughts that are sent out is the mood, which can affect a person emotionally. Let me ask you this question, what emotions, if any, have you experienced reading a particular thought that made a kind of lasting impression within your heart, soul, or mind? Moods such as happiness, sadness, loneliness, frustration, anger, etc. are what every person goes through and in some ways, you can see yourself in that exact position that you are either in now or in the past. For it can be a tough situation not to reveal too much in what I'm feeling at the time, such as loneliness, because if I completely let go of my emotions, then I lose control of who I am and that absolutely scares me.

In retrospect, every potential thought that comes to mind is like a jumbled-up jigsaw puzzle. For I have all the pieces in front of me and the next logical step is figuring out which piece goes where which can be a difficult thing at times. There are also times when certain pieces don't exactly fit and will have to be reshaped in order for it to fit properly. Let me tell you something, it can be mentally draining to think of the words that I want to say. Sometimes it comes to the surface without really thinking about it and other times I have to metaphorically dig deep until the words are finally found. In the end, it's a systematic step by step process that I go through, and so far it's a system that has been an absolute success for me.

ROUGH SEAS AHEAD
March 8, 2005

Edmond, from The Count of Monte Cristo said, ~Life is a storm, my young friend. You will bask in the sunlight one moment, be shattered in the rocks the next. What makes you a man is what you do when that storm comes.~ Life, for each and every one of us, is never smooth sailing as we pull up anchor and set sail on our own personal journey through the high seas. As one looks across the open waters, he or she contemplates all the possible destinations where one can drift away to. For we all have that metaphorical map set in front of us as we chart the rest of our lives. Yet, it is sometimes not used at all as one simply relies on where the winds of fate will take him or her

In some aspect, each of us is in a small boat trying to explore a very big ocean. An ocean that swallows people whole both in a literal and metaphorical sense, which can change a person. For it is when we get farther and farther from shore the waters of life start to get treacherous. The bright beautiful blue skies have now been replaced by the dark ominous clouds, which is never a good sign. Whether one is prepared for it or not, it can make any person scared to be out there as you find yourself experiencing the calm before the storm. It can be a truly uneasy feeling as you look around your surroundings and think to yourself why is this happening to me of all people.

Oftentimes, we may feel like we're up a creek without a paddle, in a manner of speaking. Initially, there comes a point in one's life where he or she thinks, is gaining mileage but is actually not going anywhere at all. It can be a frustrating situation for any person to be in as the waves toss and turn you in every different direction, which can alter the course of one's destination and become absolutely lost. It's at that point we try to figure out whether or not the journey that one set on was actually worth traveling in the first place. It's just a matter of conquering the forces of nature by looking in the one place that has a fighting spirit to keep on going when the mind wants to give up and that place is in your heart.

If you think about it, it's that way when it comes to love and relationships as well. Each of us, at one time or another, has experienced the somewhat disorienting effects of being thrown in every different direction but in the direction one wants to go. One can go through a whirlwind of emotions as a person's mind, body, and soul can undergo a so-called perfect storm that no human alive would ever survive from. Let me ask you a question, have you ever felt lost in the sense that by seeking out that beacon of light he or she will somehow rescue our heart from sinking into that deepest, darkest depths of the ocean where wreckage of past relationships and heartbreak now reside.

In retrospect, we have to learn not to be afraid of what is in store for each of us as we go through our own particular storms. Yet, it's within these storms that a person grows, learns, receives blessings from it and in turn gives thanks for them. For it is within that non-fearful attitude that we see the beauty of all things that were created and start to appreciate what life has to offer. Undoubtedly, there will be times where we want to jump ship because certain aspects of our lives are simply overwhelming but that is to be expected from time to time. In the end, there will be undoubtedly rough seas ahead for each of us, which can't be avoided; but if we keep our faith in God, then He will help see us through life's most difficult storms.

UNFORGETTABLE
March 8, 2005

Someone once said, ~There are certain words which are nearer and dearer to a man than any other. And it often happens that in some remote corner of the country, in domed deserted spots, you unexpectedly meet a man whose warming words make you forget yourself and the impassibility of the roads of the noisy contemporary world, and the deceitfulness of the illusions that lead mankind astray. And an evening spent in that way will be forever imprinted on your mind and your memory will retain everything: who was present and who sat in what place and what was in his hands-the walk, the corners, and every trifle in the room.~ Let me ask you this question, have you ever felt moved by the words that you either read or heard by someone you know or don't know?

Without question musicians (group singers/solo artists) have that innate ability to move a person simply by singing words that were either written by that person or by other people. Yet, it is merely words at first, but when it is sung with meaning, heart, and passion behind it you will most definitely get a song that means something special to many people. It's when one listens to those written words in musical form that we can feel several different emotions such as love, sadness, anger, frustration, happiness, heartbreak, etc. Whether a person is married, single, or divorced, if the words to a song speaks to you and moves you to the point where you start crying then it has done its job.

Oftentimes, a person can be moved without even a word being said. Two people, either married or in a dating relationship who absolutely know each other for a said period of time, can communicate emotions and feelings without saying a word to each other. For it's all in how he or she looks at that person that reveals a kind of hidden communication that only two people who truly know each other can share. Let me tell you something, just from an observational standpoint I've witnessed guys and girls use more non-verbal than verbal to communicate to one's potential or significant other. Initially, it's just a matter of interpreting those non-verbal words, which guys figure out…most of the time.

In any case, we all communicate our feelings in different ways, but it's the way we say those particular words to people or that one person that can redefine its meaning. We've all said I love you before to friends and family members; but when it comes to saying it to someone that one truly and deeply cares about, it takes on a whole new meaning. It's basically three little words that can make an enormous impact on a person that may or may not share the same sentiments as you do. For most people, it's a statement of affection or adoration that is freely given back to that particular person. Yet, for some it's just three words that one doesn't believe in saying unless he or she is absolutely sure that the person standing in front of him or her is worth saying it to.

In retrospect, there are certain people you meet along your journey that have a way with words. It's a God given talent that creates emotional word pictures in which a person sees/imagines what is being said or read. Several months ago, a friend of mine told me that I've been causing him to have a lot of headaches. The reason… well the Yodaisms that I've sent to him cause him to feel, as well as think more and he blamed me for it. To be quite honest I didn't know whether to take it as a compliment or as an insult; but in the end, he gave me mad props for bringing to life words that capture a person both intellectually and emotionally, which to him was an experience that he simply described as unforgettable.

OFF THE DEEP END
March 13, 2005

Jane Wagner once said, ~See, the human mind is kind of like...a pinata. When it breaks open, there's a lot of surprises inside. Once you get the pinata perspective you see that posing your mind can be a peak experience.~ Every person has experienced the feeling of losing their mind to the point where he or she isn't able to find it again. Yet, when a person is able to find it, parts of it are missing as if it went on an extended vacation and lost key pieces of luggage. Working in the asylum is a truly mind-blowing experience for any new employee who doesn't expect to lose their mind on the first day, but they do. In some warped aspect, it's like going through an initiation and if they return then next, they have passed with flying colors.

If you think about it, losing your mind isn't such a bad thing because it helps a person release pent up anger and/or frustration that has been building for quite some time. Being a youth program specialist, you lose your mind on a semi-daily basis and no matter how in control of your emotions you are, one will lose it. For it is simply unavoidable as kids will test the limits and boundaries of a person's sanity to the point where he or she enjoys seeing a counselor break under the pressure. Undoubtedly, we all have a breaking point and kids have that ability to find it, exploit it, use it to their advantage, to where we will scream out these six words: Have you all lost your minds!?

Working with kids, especially 6- and 7-year-olds, repetition is part of my job that tends to get extremely boring and old. On any given day, words will be repeated over and over again, which usually never get heard. A person can literally tear out their own hair trying to get through to kids who sometimes don't want to listen. There are days where I just want to come to work with a tape record and just play the most repeated things that I have to say on a regular basis. Such things are stop running, get down from there or you will get hurt, tie your shoe before you crack your head open and bleed all over the place, and my personal favorite which is stop yelling when you are talking to me, I'm two feet away from you I can hear you just fine.

Let me ask you this question, have you ever been in a situation where you started to lose your mind, have lost it, or came close to losing it? Oftentimes it can involve family, friends, life, love, school, but more often than not one's own workplace can bring about craziness, as well as madness. Every person deals with the pangs of potentially slipping into complete madness in different ways when it comes to kids. For a person like myself, I use sarcastic humor as a response to either a totally off the wall question that "my kids" ask me or something that happens that is considered funny which merits a sarcastic response. It's just a matter of keeping a sense of humor about it, when things just get too serious.

In retrospect, we've all met people that are either one chicken McNuggets short of a happy meal or their lights are on but nobody's home. Ultimately, the world is one big insane asylum in which we have to figure out who is out of their mind or who doesn't have a mind to lose. Personally speaking, I'm about 75% insane and you know what I'm enjoying the experience of being the counselor that is considered kooky. Hey, I embrace my kookiness because it shows that the kids like me even though I lose my cool sometimes. In the end, every person has the right to go off the deep end every once and awhile; it's just a matter of not staying in the pool of insanity too long or you will be lost in it forever.

THE HARDEST THING
March 14, 2005

C.S. Lewis once said, ~Love anything and your heart will be wrung and possibly broken. If you want to make sure of keeping it intact you must give it to no one, not even an animal. Wrap it carefully round with hobbies and little luxuries, avoid all entanglement. Lock it up, save it in the casket or coffin of your selfishness. Put it in that casket-safe, dark, motionless, airless- it will change. it will not be broken, it will become unbreakable, impenetrable, unredeemable. To love is to be vulnerable.~ The most fragile part of the human body is a person's heart because it can easily be broken or torn apart. Initially one can be fooled so many times by love that a person considers it an illusion too good to be real.

Oftentimes, when a person checks into the proverbial heartbreak hotel, he or she tries their best to repair the remaining pieces of one's heart. If you think about it, a person can physically, as well as mentally exhaust himself or herself trying to figure out the answer to the one question that keeps popping up: Why does this always happen to me? Inevitably, that reserve inner strength that a person could always count on may not always be there to comfort you. It's when one begins to put together the shattered hopes and dreams that were taken away, one tries to hold back the emotions that are starting to fester within.

During one's time of painful reflection, a person will go through a gambit of real emotions that can hit a person hard like a ton of bricks. Emotions such as confusion, sadness, yearning to be back with that guy or girl, bitterness, but most of all anger. One can feel absolutely betrayed for letting himself or herself open up one's heart only to have it close back up again either temporarily or permanently. For it's when we share the most intimate details of your life to someone, we feel comfortable around that the illusion of love becomes real and it's never easy getting over someone who meant so much to you at the time.

Let me ask you this question, who was that one person who broke your heart and truly affected you both mentally, physically, as well as personally? It's that one person who when you start letting other guys or girls get close, you start pushing them away which can be a scary feeling for each of us. Consequently, a person can put a strong facade for friends and family, but deep down inside we are all fragile. In a way, our hearts can suffer so many cracks that it could possibly shatter into a million pieces. Yet, we risk it day in and day out as we meet that guy or girl who makes our heart skip a beat whenever you see or talk with him or her.

Someone once said, ~My heart is all black and blue from all the abuse it has been through. No more abuse, no more shame, all because my love for you isn't a game. I'm tired of all your lies, and all the crap you say. As I leave my love for you behind, my heart is screaming YAY. Yay for no more abuse, no more pain, and no more sorrow, now my heart can heal, but it won't be healed by tomorrow. How could I have been so blind to see how much loving you was hurting me? I don't care anymore because I am free from all the pain that your love has caused me.~ In the end, the hardest thing to ever protect from being hurt is our very own heart, which keeps on beating as each of us keeps moving on with life.

THE TOTAL PACKAGE
March 17, 2005

Every person, whether he or she is in a dating relationship of a single person, ultimately wants to find that one perfect person to be with and eventually marry. Yet, one can find himself or herself in relationships that don't meet a person's expectations, which he or she can find out too late in the game, in a manner of speaking. It's at that point, a person goes back to that proverbial drawing board where he or she goes through some deep re-evaluation of who one ultimately wants to happily settle down with. Inevitably, we have to ask ourselves three key questions that will hopefully determine if the qualities we are truly looking for in that so-called perfect person have matched up with certain relationships of the past.

The first question that has to be asked is, does that guy or girl have the ability to truly open my eyes? Undoubtedly, each of us is physically attracted to one another, but it takes someone truly special to hold our attention to where you don't focus on that person's outer beauty at all. One attribute that can be an eye opener, so to speak, is how modest he or she is in appearance. You basically have to ask yourself; would that person still be attractive in your eyes if he or she dressed down and didn't seek to be the center of attention? It's when a person starts to genuinely see what's truly attractive about him or her that the physical aspects are simply inconsequential.

Secondly, does that person open your mind to where he or she can make you think either intellectually all-the-while be a person who you can absolutely talk with one and one. Let me ask you this question, have you ever met or talked with someone who you were comfortable with, and time just flew by because you enjoyed his or her company? Primarily, each one of us wants someone that is a balance of book smarts and streets. For it's a good combination to have because you don't want someone who is smarter than you and yet you don't want someone who is dumb as bricks either. Even though it's a rarity to find that type of person, he or she is out there and hopefully that person will step into one's life someday.

The third and final question to ask ourselves is whether or not that so-called perfect person can open our hearts and keep it open for good. We all know the pain of heartache, which shows that we are human beings with genuine human emotions. Yet, life can lead us to someone who has that hidden gift to re-awaken our hearts to reveal that one is not alone in the feelings he or she is experiencing. It's when we are truly comfortable within ourselves that we share our fears, past heartaches, as well as our negative attitude about ourselves and others. What that means is one is stepping in the right direction for love to possibly bloom and ultimately what it comes down to is change; but only if you really want it.

Jason Jordan once said, ~True love does not come by finding that perfect person, but by learning to see an imperfect person perfectly.~ Let me tell you something, each and every one of us isn't perfect; for we all make mistakes in life that become learning experiences. When it comes to finding the right person you have to stop and realize that you are the right person. For that someone special will find you and God knows who each of us will spend the rest of our lives with, its just a matter of waiting patiently for our time to come. In the end, that guy or girl, who can truly open your eyes, open your mind, open your heart and still love your imperfections is considered to be the total package.

ONE LAST BREATH
March 18, 2005

Every person, whether he or she wants to admit it or not, thinks about their own mortality. You never really know how long a life one can lead as the sand in our proverbial hourglass runs out or continues to fall. Undoubtedly, death or dying changes a person to the point where one doesn't take life too seriously, but instead lives it to the fullest. Yet, it's when someone such as a friend and or a family member passes away unexpectedly that one learns to cherish the time he or she has left on this earthly plane of existence. Depending on how long each of us has left, which is unknown, a person has to go with living. Let me ask you this question, how would you spend your last days and what would be your last words?

For some people, traveling the United States, even possibly overseas and seeing the sights and/or landmarks, can give a person a sense of achievement by simply taking the initiative to pack one's bags and just see the world by either land, sea, or air. Sights and/or landmarks such as Mount Rushmore, The Grand Canyon, The Great Wall Of China, The Taj Mahal are just a plethora of attractions a person should see and experience up close and personal. It can be a truly awe-inspiring experience to just be there because you may never be able to have a chance to come back ever again. Inevitably, where there is nothing left to see, one's last words are, I've been there and done that.

Without question, we all have certain fears that one has been able to conquer. Yet, a person can't stop time from counting down, but only uses it to one's advantage by facing fear eye to eye, so to speak. In a way, its like going through one's own personal fear factor; but we're not doing it for the money, we're doing it for ourselves. Doing something such as skydiving, bungee jumping, deep sea diving, climbing Mt. Everest, running with the Bulls in Spain can be scary but it can give a person such an adrenaline rush that it makes a person feel more alive and could possibly add a little more time to one's clock of life. Initially, when one's time is almost up his or her last words are. I did that and I absolutely conquered my fear.

Without a doubt, each of us would like to spend our last remaining days on God's green Earth with friends and family. If you think about it, that is the time when a person truly knows how many people care about him or her and how great of an impact/influence one has made on that particular person or persons. As embarrassing and unforgettable stories are told/shared, one will cherish it for all its worth as memories will start flooding back. Some good, some bad, some in between, but undeniably they were memories that were shared with the people who would give up their own life just to let you live. Consequently, before the party is over, one's last words are, I came into the world loved and left the world loved.

Someone once said, ~Love is stronger than death even though it can't stop death from happening, but no matter how hard death tries it can't separate people from love. It can't take away memories either. In the end, life is stronger than death.~ Ultimately each of us want to spend the last remaining days with that one special person in our lives. A person who you would die a thousand deaths for and though I haven't found that one special person to spend my last days, I eventually will. In retrospect, before we are physically separated from each other my last words will be, the first time I saw you I smiled, for as I am about to breathe my one last breath and see you for the last time, I smile again because I know we will see each other again.

THEN AND NOW
March 19, 2005

George Eliot once said, ~There are various orders of beauty causing men to make fools of themselves in various styles...but there is one order of beauty which seems made to turn heads not only of men, but of all intelligent mammals, even women. It is a beauty like that of kittens, or very small down ducks making gentle ripping noises with their soft bills, or babies just beginning to toddle and to engage in conscious mischief - a beauty with which you can never be angry, but that you feel ready to crush for inability to comprehend the state of mind into which it throws you. It's truly amazing how a baby or child under the age of 4 can have such a Pavlovian effect on a person to where he or she flocks to that child.

Without a doubt, women will flock at the sight of a baby, especially if he or she is a newborn. Undeniably, when a baby is seen the first thing usually uttered from her mouth is one word which is aaawwwweeeee. I can't count the number of times a parent has walked in with his or her baby and almost immediately a female co-worker has that child in her arms. Whether or not she is a mother is inconsequential because that child brings a smile on her face as he or she is rocked back and forth in her arms. Let me tell you something, you don't want to ever be in the way of a woman who sees a baby walk through the hallowed halls of the asylum. Trust me, I have the bumps, bruises, as well as scars from past experiences.

Guys, on the other hand, don't necessarily flock to a baby, but rather mosey on over there and take a gander on what all the hubbub is about. Now, for some reason from a guy's perspective we have this mentality to try to make a baby smile or at least laugh by any means possible. In some aspect, once we put our minds to something then we will not quit until that objective is met. Though we may fail the first or second time, usually the third time's the charm. It can be a comical situation when you see a group of guys try to do this and absolutely nothing happens, but it doesn't faze us as we continue to make faces and stick things up our noses to see any _expression of happiness form on his or her face.

Working in the asylum, you don't get a chance to take care of the babies, but rather their big brother(s) and/or sister(s). Initially, when they jump ship from daycare to the youth center, its a whole new ballgame with a different set of rules to play by. As a person who takes care of 6- and 7-year-olds, we consistently tell them that they aren't babies anymore and they should act like big boys and big girls who don't need to be always picked up or babied. Over the years I have been able to see kids grow up, but it's a rare occasion indeed when you get the chance to see him or her grow up in front of your eyes starting as a baby, which I have been privileged enough to see happen.

A couple of months ago I found out that a guy who works at the asylum knew my brother and I when we were practically babies when he was stationed with my dad in Adak, Alaska. It's basically a surreal experience knowing that someone kinda helped raise you and knew how you acted back in the day. Whether it can be considered a good thing or a bad thing, he basically told me I've grown up to be a fine upstanding young man. In retrospect, we're all still cute babies in the eyes of our parents, but they have to see that we have grown up even though our parents don't want to see that. Looking at photos I can honestly say that my brother and I were cute and hopefully we still are, just look at these two pictures of us then and now.

JUST FEEL IT
March 21, 2005

Richard Bach once said, ~A soulmate is someone who has the lock to fit our keys, and the keys to fit our locks. When we feel safe enough to open the locks, our truest selves step out and we can be completely and honestly be who we are; We can be loved for who we are, and not for who we're pretending to be. Each of us unveils the best part of one another. No matter what else goes wrong around us, with that one person in our lives, we are safe in our paradise. Our soulmate is someone who shares our deepest longings. Our sense of direction. When we're two balloons and together our direction is up, chances are we've found the right person. Our soulmate is the one who makes life come to life.~

Let me ask you this question, do you believe in soulmates? Whether or not you believe in it, every person is connected to each other in some way, shape, or form, though it may or may not be a romantic connection, it's a connection, nonetheless. A kindred spirit who cares about you, understands you, and what you are going through. In a way, it's like that person can tune into the same frequency that you are in and yet others before that person have never been able to come close to getting a clear reception. It can be an exciting and somewhat scary situation when you talk with some and find out that you have the same interests as that guy or girl. For it's a rarity to find someone who you can truly connect with in mind, body and soul.

Every person has experienced talking with someone either online or face to face for the first time and when you go your separate ways, their presence haunts you. Yet, with only that one meeting it's like one has known that person forever. Let me ask you this question, have you ever had that feeling of being drawn to someone that you don't even know; but for some reason you feel absolutely comfortable talking with that person about important issues and beliefs which wouldn't normally be shared with someone so quickly. Personally speaking, I've had that feeling only once in my life and I felt excited and scared at the same time to the point where I basically asked myself, is she "the one"?

In any case, there will always be that one person who will always be there in our dreams, thoughts, and heart, even though he or she isn't in our lives personally. It's that one person that you could be open, honest and not shy with, but with anybody else it's impossible. Yet, when things in life seem dark and dreary, he or she will step into it and brighten your world with either an email, phone call, or a surprise visit. In some aspect, it's like meeting an old friend that you haven't seen in a very long time and both of you need to make up for lost time. Inevitably, when a person is about ready to give up on ever finding love and happiness, somehow through pure luck it will show up.

Someone once said, ~Sometimes, if you're lucky...you get close enough to a person (usually the opposite sex) to see beyond the immediate physical features and "touch" what may be the soul. Obviously, if both experience this at the same time its effort is greatly magnified. The entry point(for me) is the eyes...and although I'm trying now to put feelings into words I know that it's really beyond description...beyond words...And yet maybe one word comes a little close...Love.~ In retrospect, whether or not you believe in soulmates, you have to admit love is a powerful thing which can transcend even death. Ultimately, you can't explain how a deep love between two people who have such a strong connection, in the end you just feel it.

DORKS RULES!
March 23, 2005

Someone once said, ~Embrace the total dork in yourself and enjoy it, because well, life is too short to be cool.~ We've all met people who have this persona of being a cool or absolutely stunning person; but yet when you ask him or her about their persona, one's perception of himself or herself is totally the opposite. Every person has a tendency to reveal how dorky they are when he or she is around friends, family, and even co-workers. For it can also pertain to certain situations or events that a person can really get excited about to the point where people either look at you funny and tell you that professional help is needed immediately. Let me ask you this question, do you consider yourself a dork?

If you think about it, what makes each of us "cool" is the way one takes particular situations in stride with a sense of humor. In some aspect, a sense of humor can go a long way for a person that can somehow make life just a little bit bearable. It's either the way a person laughs, which can be truly infectious and who among us hasn't laughed to the point where one snorted; but you didn't care who noticed because you were happy and having fun. Though, you have to admit, we're all a little strange in our own unique and dorky way and that's why people like us or at least tolerate us. In most cases, it's the people who know us best who wouldn't want us to change because they respect who each of us is as an individual.

For it's not only a person's sense of humor, it's also how a person reacts to certain things that can consider him or her a dork. Without question, there are certain songs that when one immediately hears it, you start to get up and dance or at least move your head in every direction possible. Personally speaking, several days ago some kids were sitting beside me on the gym stage, and we were listening to the radio. At one point, a song came on where all the kids started to shake their groove thang; but my dorkish self sat on the stage, put on my sunglasses, and started to act like Stevie Wonder with the clapping hands included. I haven't had so many people stare at me since I walked in one day wearing a sombrero.

In any case, a person can consider themselves a complete and total dork when it comes to that certain guy or girl. It's that person who can not only smile but make you act like you're back in middle school. Essentially, it can't be helped because there are certain people in this world who have that innate ability to turn a calm, reserved person into a bumbling, dorky person. I can safely guess that many of you and I have been in a particular situation like this and would gladly try to forget. But the question can be asked, does the quality of being a dorky person add or subtract to one's criteria in who one is looking for in a potential relationship? Who knows really, it's all in what he or she likes in a person.

In retrospect, a person has to take pride in his or her dorkiness. Inevitably, we're all a bunch of dorky people living in a crazy world and yet we're more alike than different. Nobody is better than anybody else and if people accept who one truly is then life gets a little less complicated. When it comes to friends and family, we just accept them for who they are and they are with us, which includes the emotional and personal baggage that is carried around. Ultimately, who cares what others think about you because if you are comfortable with yourself then that's the only opinion that matters. If you were once or are a dork, be proud and stand tall because I'm a dork and in the end Dorks Rule!

A BLIND EYE
March 24, 2005

Each of us have our own opinions on politics, issues of the world, as well as what one thinks is either ethical or unethical. In this day and age of political correctness or incorrectness, there are certain issues, whether they be political or not, that a person feels strongly about. One can go through so many emotions when a particular issue affects him or her such as sadness, anger, happiness, confusion, down and out contempt, and sometimes, it can be all rolled up into one massive indescribable emotion, which may not have a name. For if one agrees or disagrees is inconsequential because he or she has the right to voice one's opinions that can oftentimes bring about heated words and worldwide debate.

A hot topic such as abortion can really bring about heated debate to the point where people go to extremes. We've all heard stories of abortion doctors being killed by an individual who took it upon himself or herself to become a sort of vigilante for the rights of unborn children. There has been this growing consensus on whether life starts at conception or does it start at birth. I don't know about you, but I truly think life starts at conception because you can't tell me that a tiny human being is made with a heart that can be heard beating. Initially, my stance is that I'm Pro-Lifer, but I do feel that a woman has the right to choose, which primarily puts me between the proverbial rock and a hard place. In other words, I'm basically neutral.

When it comes to the issue of Michael Jackson, there is a fine line between pop music legend and supposed child molester. Michael Jackson has done a lot in his career musically with chart topping songs and revolutionary music videos such as Thriller, which is my all-time favorite. As a musician, he is a genius; but as an individual his life beyond music is truly questionable when it pertains to the issue of his fondness for young boys. In my honest opinion, there is something wrong when you perceive yourself as Peter Pan who doesn't want to grow up and would rather spend time in the company of young boys. Inevitably, whether he's found guilty or innocent, he will be judged by God and his verdict is final.

As many of you, who watch the news on a semi-daily basis, there has been an ongoing case here in Florida involving Terri Schiavo. In summary, her husband has refused medical attention for her to the point that he has asked the feeding tube to be removed so that she can starve to death. This man, who supposedly loves her, and he's been quoted as saying that is what she would have wanted; but there is a twist to this because he stands to inherit a lump sum of money when or if she dies. From an ethics standpoint, how can he say that she is a vegetable when she is within all her faculties and responds to everybody and you want to pull the plug, it's totally unethical? Doctors say with treatment she could possibly eat and talk on her own and like many other people I'm pulling for her and her family.

In retrospect, there are many other issues out there such as gun control, same sex marriage, steroid abuse in major league baseball, and last but not least is the war on Terror. Essentially, my views on the war are neither here nor there, I'm basically supporting our troops. Each of us have friends and/or family members that we hope to come back home soon safe and sound. I have a good friend in Iraq who used to work at the asylum. He has two kids and a wife, who also used to work at the asylum as well. Both of them are considered family and we hope he comes home soon safe and sound. In the end, we can sometimes be so self-involved that we can turn a blind eye to certain issues; but when it hits close to home, our eyes as well as our ears are wide open.

A CHANGE FOR THE BETTER
March 26, 2005

Someone once said, ~If I can endure for this minute whatever is happening to me…No matter how heavy my heart is or how dark the moment might be…If I can but keep on believing what I know in my heart be true. That darkness will fade with morning and that this will pass away too…Then nothing can ever disturb me or fill me with uncertain fear. For as sure as night brings dawning, my morning is abound to appear…~ Each and every one of us tends to like change because it breaks up the mediocrity that one is somewhat used to. It's that mediocrity that we are in control of what we say and do in our daily lives; but when it comes to love the biggest fear one can ever face is change.

If you think about it, that one guy or girl can put a person in an awkward position where there is an inner struggle, if any, to change. Initially, for guys, it's a step in the right direction where a mature relationship will be forged, though he might resist at first. From a guy's perspective, it's that vulnerability that we rarely acknowledge because we're so used to showing our tough exterior that if we show the slightest bit of weakness that control is lost. It's that innate fear of being allowed to step out of one's comfort zone where one can do two things: 1) Push that person away because he dislikes the feeling of vulnerability OR 2) accept the vulnerability and let that person care for you.

It's a tough situation indeed opening your heart to someone that may or may not wound it later down the road, so to speak. Every relationship has that sense of unpredictability because they have no idea what his or her next move might be or what he or she is thinking. In a way, its like playing a game of Russian Roulette and the barrel of the gun is aimed directly at your heart. With every click of the trigger, a person will hold their breath, close their eyes, and hope things don't turn ugly, which is how love can be at times. In inevitably, that one pull of the trigger will find one's self shot through the heart and to be quite honest no amount of defibrillating or chest compressions can revive it to beat the way it used to.

Oftentimes, when relationships don't work out and both people go their separate way each person tries to change back to the person who he or she was once before. It's a tough task indeed because that particular person initially opened one's vault of vulnerability wide open in his or her heart to where it can't be closed. For it can leave someone completely unprotected from having your heart taken advantage of where misguided love happens. Love definitely hurts and essentially, we all want love without fear of being hurt and rejected; but life doesn't work that way. The fear of anything and everything that can go wrong, will go wrong in love will always be there. We just have to accept it, deal with it, and hopefully move past it.

There is a quote that says, ~To succeed in relationships we must be humble enough to admit our mistakes, smart enough to learn from them, and committed enough to correct them.~ In retrospect, when it comes to relationships, potential and/or significant, a person can continue to make the same mistakes to where one will be considered absolutely foolish. Life gives each of us opportunities to make personal changes so that one won't ever make those same mistakes with someone new. It's when one strives to change for that particular person by sacrificing/compromising certain aspects of our life, we find what love really means and, in the end, it will ultimately be a change for the better.

TO INFINITY AND BEYOND
March 27, 2005

William James once said, ~Most of us can learn to live in perfect comfort on higher levels of power. Everyone knows that on any given day there are energies slumbering in him which the incitements of that day do not call forth. Compared with what we ought to be, we are only half awake. It is evident that our organism has stored-up reserves of energy that are ordinarily not called upon — deeper and deeper strata of explosible material, ready for use by anyone who probes so deep. The human individual usually lives far within his limits.~ If you think about it, whether a person knows it or not, there's a level of achievement that one puts his or her heart and soul into which is considered a journey that begins with that first initial thought or step.

From the beginning, the things one achieves in life start off as a single positive thought. For each of us tends to focus on our vision of where we want to be and who we want to be with; and in some aspect a person will become what he or she thinks about. In other words, thinking about certain outcomes or goals that have already been achieved, but only in our minds. Yet, it can be a catch 22, when one's own thoughts can focus on the negative nature such as doubt or failure which is an end result that nobody wants. Consequently, we're human beings and despite the fact we can succumb to those negative thoughts, one will persevere as he or she doesn't give up and tries to achieve something great and/or spectacular.

Oftentimes, the road to achieving something great and/or spectacular can start off with many potholes, bumps, detours or roadblocks. Thinking about it, a person is primarily getting his or her feet wet, so to speak, as one is trying to settle in a proverbial groove. It's within one's early stages of accomplishing personal and/or professional achievements that a person searches for that right style, voice, or system that will eventually become somewhat of a trademark of who or what each of us are. Though it didn't have that cohesiveness in the beginning that it now does, it showed that there was potential within the mistakes that are made early on. Let me ask you this question, have you made mistakes trying to achieve certain accomplishments that were undoubtedly tough?

Cal Ripken Jr., a hall of fame shortstop/third baseman for the Baltimore Orioles, achieved many great things in his 20-year career. He will always be considered an ambassador for the game of baseball. For many up-and-coming rookies, they should learn, study, and have the work ethic that he had both on and off the field. For baseball fans, such as myself, the most memorable career achievement that he accomplished was on Sept. 6, 1995, when he surpassed Lou Gehrig's unbreakable record of consecutive games played as he played in his 2,131st game. Now retired, with 2,632 consecutive games played it is a record that may never be matched. From his first step into the major leagues, Cal Ripken Jr. would unknowingly make history and be forever known as The Iron Man.

Rose Fitzgerald Kennedy said, ~Life isn't a matter of milestones, but of moments.~ In retrospect the milestones of my life, whether they were good, bad, or in between. have been memorable ones and it took that first initial thought or step to experience it. On August 2, 1996, I started on a journey that prompted my first initial thought, not knowing where it would lead or take me. Though it's on a semi-daily basis, I've been consistent and from what I've been told is that I am a master at making things make sense. For you see, on this day, March 27th, 2005, marks the 200th Yodaism and ultimately, I have to ask myself this question: How high of a number can I go to and how far can I take my thoughts? My answer......hopefully to infinity and beyond.

THE GOOD OLE' DAYS
March 29, 2005

Jeff Salz once said, ~The most exotic destinations of all is the one to be found within your own adventurous spirit--after you've put yourself to the test and found hidden reserves of creativity, resourcefulness, and perseverance.~ Working in the asylum, especially during the summer, you get to go on many road trips that not not only the kids get to look forward to, but the also the employees as well. I can safely say that on certain road trips one can have an extra kick in his or her step because quite frankly being stuck inside all day will actually make a person go absolutely mad. While on these normal as can be road trips, one finds yourself in a crazy situation somewhat like being in a National Lampoon's movie.

Personally speaking, there have been many memorable road trips that have happened over the past several summers; but one particular trip sticks out in my mind occurred a couple years ago. *Flashback sequence and before I start, keep in mind that it was an extremely hot day which will be relevant later on.* It started as a normal day, but as soon as I walked through the hallowed doors the craziness would start to unfold. Have you ever had that feeling something was going to happen, but you didn't know what? For it was when I stepped through the front doors, I was asked to go with another group on a road trip, which was fine with me because my group was indoors all day, so I welcomed the invitation.

As we pulled off, I would unknowingly have the ride of my life, so to speak, as we set forth to our intended destination, which was a train museum. Thirty minutes into the trip we got lost and at one point made several U-turns in the middle of traffic. It was somewhat embarrassing as cars behind us and in the other lanes were looking at us seeing that there were two vans that were doing this which made it doubly embarrassing. Consequently, we stopped at three gas stations and me being a sarcastic person said, 'If we end up in Canada, drop me off at the border, so I can call a cab and then meet you there.' We eventually made our intended destination, and all was thankfully well.

Now remember in the beginning I said it was extremely hot, well I wasn't really dressed for going to a road trip and after 20 minutes there, I was soaking wet from sweat. Due to the fact that I was wearing jeans and a kinda heavy shirt. Now imagine this, my jeans hiked up above my knees and my shirt sleeves rolled up kinda like The Fonz from Happy Days. So, I can honestly say, I looked like a complete dork. To make matters even more discomforting the kids kept on hanging me on as myself and my fellow co-workers were trying to feel some cool air that was flowing around the open area in the outdoor train museum. To make a long story short, I lost several pounds due to being in that sauna type environment.

The road trip ended with everybody getting ice cream, which was a good ending for an unforgettable trip. Oh did I forget to mention, a possible hit and run of a public park tree that was witnessed by several people? The kids kept asking us "Are we going to get arrested?" My response was no; but I said a silent prayer just in case. Over the past 8 summers, that right there tops my list, but that could change it all depending on how this summer goes. In the end, when I take a look back at the good ole' days and consider all the road trips that I've been a part of, I realize it's not just a job; in my opinion, it's an adventure.

SQUARE ONE
March 30, 2005

Steven Rodgers once said, ~Beginnings are often scary, endings are often sad, buts its the middle that counts. You should remember that when you find yourself at the beginning.~ Without a doubt, love is the scariest and most complicated thing that a person can and will ever go through because there are certain aspects of it that one never really wants to see or experience. In some aspect, we tend to look the other way and don't acknowledge the possibility of it being taken away from us because quite frankly we can be scared of facing the truth, which one can't run away from. The truth can be a hard concept to grasp, which is that each of us will go through emotional pain and suffer extreme heartache that one doesn't want to experience but that's how life is no matter how hard you want to try to avoid it.

When it comes to love in a relationship, it can be quite scary in the beginning because you don't want to say anything that would jeopardize what could possibly be a lifelong partnership. Guys have that innate ability to proverbially stick our foot in our mouths and sometimes we can do it without even knowing about it. Primarily it's because women are so complicated and frustrating to figure out, BUT that is what partly makes a woman have such an attractive appeal about her. When you get right down to it, the wrong words we oftentimes tend to say seem to be the right ones which every guy has fallen victim to when in the company of a woman that we truly would like to get to know on a deeper level.

Let me ask you this question, have you ever thought to yourself when meeting someone new that he or she will never be that kind of person who would ever break my heart into a million pieces; yet, in the end that person does? Every person has had those thoughts and to be perfectly honest I think we avoid that scary and painful thought because we tend to put that person on a pedestal. For it is what we imagine that person to be that can overshadow or mask who he or she actually is once you sit down and get to know that person. Each and every person, including myself, has fallen victim to it and there comes a point where a reality check of one's heart needs to be given by those who care about us the most.

For it can be a sad situation indeed at the possible end of a relationship whether it be a breakup or divorce. It's at that point where one or both people try to recapture what each seemingly had in the beginning and middle of the relationship which was a strong loving bond for each other. Yet, when it comes to recapturing the past, one can find yourself running away from the problem rather than running to it and confronting that problematic situation. Undoubtedly, one wants something to happen so badly that it would merit a reconciliation of the relationship which he or she may not want just yet. It's just a matter of having patience and letting that person have time to himself or herself; for whatever he or she decides one just has to respect it because you love that person enough to let him or her go.

In retrospect, there are no magical buttons to push or levers to pull that can fix or solve one's love life. There are times where a person can get it right one time and one time only; but there are times where a person gets it wrong several times before he or she will get it absolutely right. No matter how scared you are of love, if you continue to move forward rather than backwards then you've already won. If only love came with an instruction manual to show us how to properly assemble each of our hearts that have fallen apart due to the wrong directions being given. In the end, it's not until we find the right directions that we will have all the pieces of our hearts in place that, like an instruction manual, we simply have to go back to square one.

FIRST TIME FOR EVERYTHING
April 2, 2005

Someone once said, ~Falling in love for the first time is easy. It's the second time around, after you had fallen and trusted someone to catch you for the first time and they didn't, when it becomes difficult to let yourself fall in love again.~ Essentially, we really never forget that guy or girl who started one's heart beating harder and faster to the point where it will be changed for better or for worse. If you think about it, it's that guy or girl that is usually the basis for one's timeline of either successful or failed relationships. Did that person ever change your perspective on other potential and/or significant relationships after being with him or her? Let me ask you this question, do you remember your first love?

It's a funny thing about a first love, one tends to never really get over that person because he or she was a very instrumental part of your life. It's that first guy or girl who opened your eyes to a whole new world; a world that one has never been or has been in, but not fully experienced it. It's a dynamic that is somewhat uncomfortable at first, but you get used to it because he or she, in a way, helped bring you out of your shell. Due to his or her influence, you tend to give specific guys or girls with that person's hair color a second look. We all have our preferences as some like blondes, other redheads; but for a person like myself I'm a brunette/dark black hair kind of guy because it brings out the mysteriousness in a woman.

Yet, as with first love, things will happen that will have two people grow apart, but it's because of that person you, in a way, can thank him or her for helping you cross over into the next stage of your life with someone else. A sort of steppingstone, in a manner of speaking, from a young, immature kid to a mature, grown adult where you will learn what being in a relationship is truly all about. For its within that relationship, you couldn't say anything bad about him or her because that person helped you grow within yourself. Each of us has someone like this in our lives that one can call, email, instant message, or personally talk to who you share a special and valuable friendship with.

Undoubtedly, we all have a story of the one that got away. It's that person, who when one spends time with you basically imagining yourself growing old and having kids with him or her. Initially, it's that guy or girl who you spent more time with than your friends and family combined to the point where both of you were absolutely inseparable. Thinking about it, it's that person who is oftentimes portrayed as "out of your league" and yet he or she ends up with you, which can be mind-blowing for you and anyone else. Consequently, he or she will always be in your thoughts, and one will be reminded of how he or she made life that much more livable. For a special place will and always be made in one's heart for that person who when you reflect back, you think to yourself what could have been.

Rosemary Rogers said, ~First romance, first love, is something so special to all of us, both emotionally and physically, that it touches our lives and enriches them forever." In retrospect, when it comes to first love, one rarely ever focuses on the bad memories but rather the good ones. Though it may hurt to look back, it's a good kind of hurt that makes you smile, laugh and cry all at the same time. Nobody will ever compare with your first love as you experience a plethora of emotions and situations that were absolutely new to you. Ultimately, there is a first time for everything as you experience all the same emotions and situations that come with falling in love; but with someone new and under a different set of circumstances.

IN ONE PIECE
April 5, 2005

When you work in the asylum, you expect to take the occasional bumps and bruises that are associated with the job. For those that are in the childcare profession, especially in the youth division, one will suffer some wear and tear in mind and in body due to working there for so many years. Oftentimes, I share my experiences working with kids and what affect, if any, they had on me emotionally, physically, and mentally. Essentially when you apply for a job like mine, you primarily apply to be a human punching bag for kids, which says something about me…I'm a glutton for punishment. Let me just share the hazards of my job and initial brutality I have experienced over the past 8 years shall we.

One of the aspects of the job that, as a guy, you never really see coming is either getting hit, punched, kicked, or kneed where the sun doesn't shine. Sometimes it's an accident but other times it's intentional and unfortunately, I have suffered fairly the most pain; but my best friend would beg to differ on that. In any case, when it comes to a recreational sport such as dodgeball these kids can oftentimes be downright sadistic as they aim for either the face or below the belt. Let me tell you something, it's not a good day when you are hit in those areas…at the same time. Though it may sound funny, it's a situation that I tend to go through on a semi-daily basis to the point where wearing a cup is a much-needed alternative.

During the summer, the swimming pool is one of the activities that every kid, as well as counselors, love to do because it cools each of us down from the hot weather. Yet, as a counselor, we primarily have to watch our backs due to kids wanting to drown the living daylights out of us. In all honesty, every summer there's a bunch of kids that have made it their mission to try to drown us, but not intentionally. Thinking about it, over the years it happens more to the guys than the girls primarily because, in the past, the teenage boys have had crushes on the female counselors. So, if you guys don't get any emails from me over the summer, then their mission was a success, but hopefully that doesn't happen. *knock on wood*

When I first started at the asylum, I never had any back problems; but when that first child jumped on my back 8 years ago, a downward spiral started. These kids thrive on jumping on our backs and trying to take us down in the process. I can't tell you the number of times kids, out of nowhere, have taken me down and when they have me down a massive dog pile ensues. It's not a pretty picture as you see 6- and 7-year-old bodies just jump on top of a 28-year-old man with the expressed purpose of either bodily injury or knocking the wind out of him. In some aspect, they are little like mini-ninjas who are getting ready to pounce on their intended target and they do it with such cat-like stealth which is very impressive.

In retrospect, when I take a look back at what the kids have done to me, I laugh and smile. Why you may ask? Well, because in a weird way, I know that the kids still like me because they care enough to check how I am doing afterwards when I'm face down or up on the ground. Things have changed over the years since I started back in 1999, but the one thing that hasn't changed is the spirit of fun. When I first started my job, I was a young 19-year-old kid that felt no pain the next day after a basketball game with the kids. Now as a 28-year-old man, I'm in pain before, during, and after the basketball game with the kids. In the end, after 8 years of taking the best these kids had to offer, I'm still in one piece physically but mentally…not so much.

THE KEY
April 7, 2005

Someone once said, ~There is a place you can touch a woman that will drive her crazy and that place is her heart.~ Let me ask you this question ladies and feel free to respond back, what sort of things will a guy genuinely do for you that will put a smile on your face and make your heart melt? For it's one of those so-called "it" factors in which you put your proverbial stamp of approval on that particular guy who you hopefully believe is worth completely opening your heart to. Yet, for some guys, they believe that to truly touch a woman's heart you basically have to give her bad pick-up lines, wear flashy clothing, drive a fast car, which ultimately isn't the way to go.

Initially, you have to be observant and pay attention to certain things about a woman that make her uniqueness such an attractive quality. Such unique qualities are the certain way she smiles, laughs, gives that trademark look that she has perfected, and/or twirls her hair when she is truly interested in a guy. For when these qualities are combined it's a deadly combination that no guy in the world can ever ignore or resist…unless they are really stupid. It's that attention to detail that women have down pat and yet some guys choose to ignore those character traits that make her special. Consequently, it's just a matter of simply reciprocating back what a woman goes through just to keep us happy, and for that I salute you ladies.

Without question, each of us has what is considered most valuable and that is time. When it comes to a woman, guys will be absolute boneheads for not spending quality time with the one person who he supposedly cares about. It's a sad situation indeed when a relationship is in turmoil all because time wasn't set aside to spend together. In any case, time spent together doesn't always have to be face to face, for it can be through a phone call, email and/or, instant message, to simply say he or she was thinking about that person. For a heartfelt I love you that is said with meaning, shows that even though we are constantly shown masculinity on seemingly constant basis, we actually do have a sensitive side.

Undoubtedly, a gift from the heart is worth giving to someone that you are truly interested in. It's a gift in which there are no strings attached and there are no ulterior motives behind it. A gift such as a simple rose placed in a box that is wrapped nicely with a bow, shows that she is absolutely worth being with. Unfortunately, there are guys who have the stupidity gene where one doesn't take the time to give a gift such as a romantic candle lit dinner and the end result is both eating at a fast-food restaurant. It's within these bad experiences of failed gift giving that all women will remember and share through the grapevine, which many of you may or may not have experienced over the years.

In retrospect, it doesn't take pick-up lines, wearing flashy clothing, driving a fast car, or having that perfect physique to touch a woman's heart. It's just a matter of showing how you truly feel about her from deep within your heart such as putting a hand on her cheek. Or merely in the embrace of each other's arms as both watch the sun rise and/or sunset as you take in that precious moment together without saying anything. Being a guy who is very observant, I take into consideration every quality that makes a woman unique and special; but I still don't know what women are thinking and probably will never know. Personally speaking, the key to touching a woman's heart, in my opinion, is to look at what's in a guy's heart and hopefully she likes what she sees and finds inside.

MADE FOR EACH OTHER
April 9, 2005

Men and women are, without a doubt, on a different level of thinking when it comes to all aspects of life. In theory, I believe all women think the same; but guys, on the other hand, don't think like women because quite frankly we'll be too confused than we already are. Essentially, there are basic truths about guys and girls in which both see the world from a different perspective that hopefully doesn't offend anyone. It's just a humoristic look at the basic and simplistic style of guys against the detailed and analytical style of women. When you think about it, it's the challenge of both men and women to try to understand each other even though we can drive each other absolutely up the wall.

When it comes to shopping men treat the experience like a battle plan. For if something doesn't fit or is torn to the point it can't be worn again our objective has been initiated. Once we get to the store, absolutely nothing will hinder us from our target unless a new video game has just come out or we're hungry. In our own thinking, spending more than an hour just walking around, buying and accomplishing nothing is a waste of time. For a woman, on the other hand, spending more than an hour just walking around is considered window shopping because in their own mind they are just getting warmed up. When it comes to shopping, women just take it more seriously than we do because it's in their blood.

Doing the laundry is something that both men and women do differently as well. For a woman, she will wash clothes at the end of every week because she doesn't want to run the risk of being seen wearing the same thing. For their process of separating articles of clothing are colors, whites, darks, and delicate, which is a system that is absolutely foreign to guys. For a guy, we'll wear every article of clothing we have until we need to do laundry, or we just reuse certain articles of clothing such as pants and shirts, which we just turn inside out. As a guy, we have just two piles, dirty and funky; dirty we can wear again and funky...well, we have to actually wash because the smell will seriously knock someone out.

The relationship between guys and girls is completely different because quite frankly we don't get emotionally attached to each other. The male relationship is considered very simplistic, and I'll give you a perfect example: A group of guys are hanging out and one of them announces that he is breaking up with his girl or getting a divorce. The basic response for a guy is, "Sorry dude" and we'll go back to whatever we were doing before he said that. Now, when a group of women are gathered around bonding and someone announces a breakup or a divorce, an emergency style meeting ensues where they analyze what went wrong point by point. In all likelihood, tears will be shed, and that guy will be ostracized from pictures, as well as not be acknowledged by her friends.

In retrospect, there are so many things that we're on a different level of thinking on such as shopping for food, asking for directions, certain kinds of movies, farting in public, what's considered funny, how many shoes a person needs, what guys are thinking which is NOTHING at the moment, and the list goes on and on. If you stand back and take a really good look at what we do as men and women, it is quite humorous. Thinking about it, men and women make each other feel like they want to kill themselves when things go wrong but yet, make each other feel alive when things go absolutely right. Ultimately, even though the things that both sides do make no sense at all, you have to agree on one thing, which is that men and women are made for each other.

MIRACLES DO HAPPEN
April 10, 2005

Someone once said, ~What is needed, rather than running away or controlling or suppressing or any other resistance, is understanding fear; that means, watch it, learn about it, come in direct contact with it. We are to learn about fear, not how to escape from it.~ Oftentimes, the emotions that are being felt for a guy or a girl can cause a person to become scared. Every person has been in a situation where, from within their heart, someone has clutched it to the point that it gets harder to breathe. For there is absolutely no medical treatment or any science textbooks that will explain what is happening to you. For you see, it doesn't take a rocket scientist to know its love, which can hit a person out of nowhere hard.

For when one is in that early stage of self-denial a person will give reason after reason as to why love doesn't appeal to him or her. For it is in that person's mindset that he or she wants to focus on himself or herself first and doesn't want the headaches that love causes. Due to love, one's thinking process will be all out of whack and he or she will eventually have that goofy looking grin plastered on one's face. Yet, it's that same person who professes that he or she will never fall in love and never go through those experiences will be, in fact, that person. A person that one desperately never wanted to be, which is a lovestruck fool who then must decide to either act or not act on those feelings.

In any case, it's that fear of love that grabs each and every one of us by the proverbial heartstrings and pulls our emotions in every different direction. Yet, we can deny ourselves from having someone to love or being loved by someone by continually witnessing broken relationships. In some cases, a guy or girl fears being in a relationship due to seeing their own friend's breakup, as well as one's own parent's marriage ending in divorce, which thankfully hasn't happened to my parents. *knock on wood* For one has that mindset that he or she doesn't want to be another statistic on love's journey to the deep dark abyss where pain and sorrow reside. Yet, it will always be there in the back of your mind, waiting in the shadows as potential relationships come about.

Subsequently, that fear of love leads a person to just run away or hide from that person, which in his or her mind solves the problem. Let me ask you this question, have you experienced an overwhelming sense of emotion for someone that you basically walked away not knowing what the outcome could have been? Essentially, a person figures that by running away or hiding from the so-called "problem", you can run away or hide from the feelings that he or she has for that particular person. A person will find out that it's just not that simple and the only way to confront what you are feeling is to talk to that person. It's a scary situation indeed, but it's one of those life lessons that you have to learn on your own.

A wise man once said, ~Sometimes you just gotta let your heart lead you even if its to someone you may never be with.~ In retrospect, there comes a point where you have to just stop running from that fear and finally accept what you have been feeling for that particular person is real. You can never tell what that other person is feeling because he or she could be experiencing the same kind of emotions that have him or her running or hiding scared as well. Someone once told me never be afraid of love because that person, who you will fall in love with, will be considered a miracle sent by God. In the end, one can safely say that miracles do happen for everybody and hopefully I will look into the face of my miracle that God will send me.

HUMBLE PIE
April 13, 2005

Phillip Brooks once said, ~The true way to be humble is not to stoop till your smaller than yourself, but to stand at your real height against some higher nature that shall show you what the real smallness of your greatness is.~ We've all been cut down to size, so to speak, when one tends to think too highly of himself or herself. It's one of the drawbacks of being human as our ego can get the better of us, which can be built up by our own doing or by other people. Each of us primarily takes pride in knowing or doing something that one excels in either mentally or physically. Working with kids, a person will learn that oftentimes you have to keep your own ego in check and ask yourself this question, what does humility mean to you.

In my line of work, humility means several different things such as cleaning up vomit after a child throws up coming from a field trip to a restaurant. Yet, it doesn't have to involve food as he or she is just plain sick. Knowing what the child is feeling at that point, it's essential to just put aside one's own reservations of gagging yourself and getting someone else to clean it up, which has been done by a former employee who I didn't see eye to eye with; but I digress. One just has to swallow your pride for the sake of the child who is scared, crying, and wants to go home asap. Here is a helpful tip to know: Dumping sand on vomit will deaden the smell, help in easier clean up, and most of all take away the gag reflex due to the smell.

Essentially, humility means accepting victory or taking defeat with honor and dignity. Over the past 8 summers the teens and counselors have had an epic battle of supremacy on the basketball court. As far as the record is concerned, we have won 4 out of the 7 games that have been played so far and hopefully this year we can add another win. Yet, as summers have come and gone, the teens have progressively been getting better and better to the point where they are taking us to school and teaching us a few things. It wasn't too long ago that we let them have the ball to shoot, now they're fighting for the ball and shooting 3 pointers in our faces like it was nothing. One just has to accept, as aging counselors, we're losing our edge; BUT what we lose in speed and quickness we make up for in devious tactics.

Without question, what humility means to me is admitting to the kids when I am wrong which can be a catch 22 at times. Kids, as they do, will harp on the fact that we messed up and will not let you forget about it as they dangle it in front of your face like a worm for a hungry fish. However, 99% of the time kids are always in the wrong; but it's that 1% that they are right due to us not getting the full information needed to determine an accurate judgment call. I'm not the most rule conscious employee seeing that I've almost been fired 4 times for doing stupid things; but when it comes to the safety of "my kids" I will enforce them. When it comes to kids, whether you are right or wrong, you have to be willing to save face and be a better person, which makes for a better relationship with one's own kids someday.

Over the past 8 years, I've received countless compliments from parents about how I have influenced their child's life in some way, shape or form. Unfortunately, there are also parents who just see you as a babysitter so he, she, or both can go out and have a good time. Working in the asylum, I've learned you can't please every parent who walks through those doors and trust I've tried to. In some aspect you primarily have to have a balance of parents that love you and parents that think you are incompetent workers who like to write up kids for fun. It's just a matter of not letting it get to you because you won't have fun doing your job and right now I'm having a blast. In the end, sometimes you just have to eat a slice of humble pie every now and then to know that not all people think the work you are doing matters in the long run.

JUST GOTTA BELIEVE
April 15, 2005

Let me ask you this question, have you ever felt insecure about yourself when situations in your life tend to embarrass and overwhelm you? Each and every one of us has our own insecurities to deal with that one doesn't want to reveal to friends, family, and/or significant other because it might give a whole new perception of how they see you. If you think about it, we all have perceptions of people who we know or are in the public eye and think he or she doesn't have any insecurities; but that thought is oftentimes dead wrong. Initially, every person struggles with certain insecurities that every person goes through in life and, in a way, its nice to know that its just not you who feels the same way.

Unquestionably, the underlying insecurity most women have is the issue of weight. You see, there has been an overwhelming focus, especially in Hollywood, to be a thin which drives women and even young girls to go to extremes to attain the body they truly want. On such extreme is anorexia, which is an unhealthy and dangerous eating disorder that causes serious damage both mentally and physically. For the seeds of insecurity are planted by reality television, Hollywood, rail thin models, magazines which promote perfect bodies with no imperfections. It's a sad situation indeed when a woman looks in the mirror and sees an overweight person; but when other people look at her, she's in perfect shape.

In any case, there comes a point when a person's height can become an insecurity and more often than not, guys feel they can never measure up, in a manner of speaking. It's another deluded mindset that all women are looking for tall, dark, and handsome guys, which is a criteria that the vertically challenged may fall short when interested in a particular female. Personally speaking, I'm 5 '3 and I used to feel that I would never be seen as boyfriend material because of my short stature. It wasn't until a good friend of mine told me this statement: ~A woman, who is truly interested in you, won't see how tall or short you are; but rather how big of a heart you have inside which, in turn, will have her seeing a giant among men.

Without a doubt, a person can have insecurities about love, falling in love, and being in love. There are countless insecurities that both guys and girls have, such as bad breath. Good smelling breath is always key for two people who spend much of their quality time with their faces two inches from each other. Another insecurity which women, more so than guys, feel insecure about is releasing a potentially potent gas from one's rear end. Women, we'll hold it and not release that bad boy until she isn't in the proximity of people she knows. Guys, on the other hand, have no insecurities about it and will do it in front of people, which is a quality that makes us moronic, but you love us anyway even though you are embarrassed.

Audrey Beth Stein once said, ~Deep down, beneath all our insecurities, beneath all our hopes for and beliefs in equality, each of us believe we're better than anyone else. Because its our beliefs that are right, our doubts that are allowable, our fears which are legitimate.~ For the most part I don't necessarily agree that we are better than anyone else. What I do think is that each of us shares the same insecurities but have different reasons as to why he or she feels that way about himself or herself. In retrospect, whether it's weight, height, or love there will always be something in life that will cause us to be insecure. In the end, you just gotta believe that you will be strong enough to get past those insecurities that hold you back from someone you want to be with or the person you always wanted to be.

CRAZY IN LOVE
April 17, 2005

Someone once said, ~Meeting you was fate, becoming your friend was a choice, but falling in love with you I had no control over.~ Let me ask you a question, can you control love? In my heart of hearts, you can't because quite frankly it's impossible to figure out, to break down, and to try to analyze the mystery that is love. It doesn't have a physical presence and yet it can be felt by millions of people every single day. Each and every person has felt that loss of control when experiencing love; but one also has felt that control destroys you from the inside out. If you think about it, it's the price one pays for either expressing or keeping in the emotions he or she feels in a relationship, whether it's good or bad.

Essentially, a person can't control what he or she has no control over. Oftentimes we say to ourselves that I am not going to fall in love because it's just going to complicate my life even more. One can also add to that the emotions that are felt will become too strong for us to handle to the point where we're completely at the mercy of something that one swore never to be, which is a lovestruck fool. A fool that finds himself or herself saying things that one never thought he or she would never utter. For we've all fallen victim to having that control, which one worked so hard to keep at an even keel, slip through our fingers because that guy or girl got in our head and eventually in our heart.

For the question can be asked, why do we torture ourselves when it comes to love? The feelings we have for someone that has touched our hearts never really go away and can't be shut off in an instant. In some ways, it's like a dial that has no off and on switch and you have absolutely no control over it. It's a tough situation indeed meeting someone that you start to feel deeply and yet you choose to suppress the overwhelming emotions because you don't want to ruin what both of you have by revealing how you feel for him or her. It's kind of like being a prisoner of your own emotions and no matter how badly you want the words of love for that person to escape your mouth, you keep it under lock and key for one's own protection.

In some aspect, we are in complete control when we are in an environment that one knows how to fix. It's within that particular environment, such as work, you know what is about to happen and can adjust to any possible scenarios that could come from it. BUT, when it comes to love, the environment that it has placed you in with that guy or girl can't be controlled because anything and everything can and will go wrong. Every person has been in a situation where one felt like a fish out of water as you were in an environment that felt foreign to you and you had no idea what to do, what to say, or why you are even there in the first place. It's not until you take a close, hard look at that person that you realize that even though you feel uncomfortable, being with him or her makes it all worthwhile.

In retrospect, the one place that we are in control of is in our thoughts because in there everything goes as planned. For the scenarios that are going in our head are executed to perfection and the glitches that usually happen in reality, don't come to fruition in one's mind. Yet, when love enters a person's heart and mind it's a double whammy that nobody can recover from because it has captured two places that will never be the same again. Someone once told me that it's better to lose control of your heart than lose control of your mind because it's within your heart that you realize how crazy you are for that person. In the end, it's better to be crazy in love than to be just plain crazy, don't you think?

HERE I AM
April 18, 2005

Someone once said, ~In the end, it's still best to wait for the one we want rather than settle for what is available. It is still best to wait for the one you love rather than settle for the one who is around. It is still best to wait for the right person because life is too short to waste on the wrong person.~ Let me ask you this question, how do you really know if the one you have been waiting for is the right person? It has been said that the person one has always been waiting for is never the one you expect to fall in love with. For it's simply an unknown because each and every one of us have an idea of who that right person is and what considers him or her to be that so-called diamond in the rough.

For the most part, that unknown person one has been waiting for, oftentimes doesn't have that certain electricity he or she feels at first like in past relationships. In some cases, that electricity that he or she expects to feel in an instant may not be felt right away. For it is gradual, as it slowly surges through one's soul and starts to jolt every part of one's body from the top of one's head to the tips of his or her toes. It's that undeniable energy you feel from that particular person that you can't quite figure out; but it's a familiar feeling that excites you and scares you at the same time. An energy that may take days, months, or even years for it to be felt and when it is finally felt, one will be "shocked" at who will be standing there.

Essentially, the one you have been waiting for all your life may not give you that spine tingling chill that makes you shiver when you talk about him or her. In many happy relationships, the guy or girl didn't really like that person at first. For it wasn't so much of chill that he or she felt for one's future girlfriend/boyfriend/spouse, but rather a feeling of being ignored. In a way, meeting someone after waiting for so long is like setting off fireworks. Without a doubt, you can feel an immediate spark to the point where emotions just illuminate the night sky for all to see; but sometimes, it takes time for that fuse to ignite the fireworks of love which, in all intents and purposes, will provide a light show that is well worth waiting for.

There comes a point when waiting for the right person, you don't necessarily know if he or she will be the one that will complete you. Completing you in such a way that he or she will be the one and only person you fall in love with forever and that love will hopefully have no ending in sight. For he or she is not only the one you love, but also your very best friend who you can trust and are absolutely compatible with in certain aspects of your own life. It's within that person that you receive strength from even though at times, you didn't have the courage to stay on course; but you did. Without question, that person will consider you his or her North Star, which he or she will use as a guide to connect one's heart to yours.

In retrospect, it's painful to wait for someone that may or may not come into your life. Many of us, who are living the single life, have been waiting patiently for months and even years for that right person to show up at our doorstep. Undeniably, the anticipation of when that person will arrive can make us either impatient or sick to our stomach. For it can also bring a person to the brink of insanity as he or she questions what hasn't his or her time to be happy arrived yet? Ultimately, its put in God's hands as he directs that special someone into our awaiting arms. In the end, it's when we look up at the starry filled night sky that we find ourselves saying telepathically to that person: Here I am, where are you?

TRUE STORIES
April 20, 2005

As I said before, there's never a dull moment when you're working in a place that is nicknamed the asylum. More often than not the craziness that goes on in the looney bin either involves the kids or doesn't involve them. You see, as much as these kids get into trouble on a semi-daily basis, we can get in hot water ourselves. Working in the asylum you are expected to act professionally and do your job with the deepest and utmost respect for yourself, the parents, and the kids who look up to us, as well as respect is...most of the time. BUT once you step through those hallowed doors one's professionalism can be forgotten sometimes and yet we do our job with respect to ourselves, the parents and the kids.

Most of the time, the madness that goes on happens when the kids are not around and that when we turn in troublesome, hyperactive adolescents. Let me tell you something, it's never really a good idea to leave seemingly full-grown, well-adjusted adults alone with certain equipment that can cause bodily harm. Certain equipment, such as-I don't know-let's say a laundromat dryer and getting into that dryer, turning it on, and seeing what it's like to be spinning around in there. Personally speaking, even though I almost broke my neck going upside down, it was a fun experience. This basically proves one thing, when employees have too much free time on their hands, we will do some crazy things.

Essentially, what's so great about being a counselor is that one can easily form friendships with parents. A friendship that allows us to beat down their child and are willing to help in the beat down process. Last Friday, my best friend and I were constantly being annoyed, chastised, and patronized by this particular teenager who at one point in the afternoon called both of us grandpa. We chased him around the asylum, cornered him, got him on the ground where I got him in a headlock which then turned into the crippler crossface. My best friend got some parting shots in and all the while his mom was laughing at the whole thing which tells you that we have, bar none, the coolest parents. Though it started as a mediocre afternoon, it ended pretty crazy.

Initially every person who works or has worked at the asylum is considered a few McNuggets short of a happy meal without the toy inside. What job that you know of you can have the most absolute fun in and get paid for doing it. I've had a blast going to places such as Waterville where I basically got paid to simply float down the lazy river. Thinking back, there have been times where spontaneous limbo lines have formed, water balloon fights have broken out, and hordes of kids chase counselors to the point where a massive dog pile ensues and I have been under many of those dog piles. Over the years, I have done and been associated with so many crazy and insane moments that its hard to name which one tops the list.

Albert Einstein once said, ~The definition of insanity is doing the same thing over and over again and expecting a different result.~ In retrospect, you have to have a break in the monotonous and seemingly repetitive aspects of one's own job. One has to either make it happen or it will happen all by itself. In some ways, working in the asylum is like being in a weekly tv series with a cast of characters that changes every season. Though the premise of this weekly series is about kids, it's also about the people who work there. For the drama, action, and hilarity that ensues will never disappoint you because in the end, they're all true stories of my reality and those who are along for the ride with me.

THE ANSWER
April 21, 2005

The one basic truth about love is that the answers never come easy. Oftentimes, each of us have this preconceived notion that we have it all figured out as to who we want to spend our life with. However, what one preconceived never turns out the way you want to go as the questions one continually asks on a day-to-day basis primarily stay the same; but the answers keep changing. It's a frustrating situation indeed for every person to experience disappointments that cause a person to become absolutely jaded to the point where love is simply a four-letter word that has no meaning behind or emotion behind it. Let me share something with you that you may not know, it's not just you that feels that way; everybody feels that way.

There comes a point for every person, including myself, that maybe life would be better off single because you have absolute freedom to do what you want and go wherever you want without answering to someone else. For one can say that life is a lot less stressful without having to deal with someone else's wants and needs. To be perfectly honest, it's hard enough trying to fulfill your own wants and needs but it's doubly tough when you are trying to fulfill someone else's wants and needs that you are trying to get to know. Yet, when one witness couples walking hand in hand and giving each other that look of peaceful contentment it makes any person yearn to have someone in his or her life.

Essentially, for any woman, the commonality that each share is finding all the answers in that one guy who is everything she ever wanted and more. It's that guy who will actually sit and listen to everything that you say. It's that guy who treats you how you should be treated, which is a lady. It's that guy who will talk to you and treat you like one of his friends. It's that guy who will give your personal space knowing that you had a whole other life before you met him. For it is a quality that shows a deep and utmost respect for you as he lets you live your own life, plus it's essential for your own sanity that being together all the time can make you want to kill each other.

Undeniably, I want nothing more than to be seen as the guy who hopefully has all the questions answered for some women out there. I want to be that guy who sends flowers to her at work just to show how I am thinking of her. I want to be that guy who tells her she is absolutely beautiful when she doesn't think so. I want to be that guy that will look into her eyes and say, meaning behind it, I love you. I want to be that guy who will stay with her when she is sick knowing that I may get sick myself. I want to be that guy who knows the feeling of having someone love me back. But most of all, I want to be the guy who can truly say that just to my friends that I have found "the one" that completes me, and I am going to marry her.

Someone once said, ~Love is the answer to the final question you ask.~ In retrospect, when someone asks you life's most simplest questions, the best response is to give simple answers. Yet, when it comes to love the most simple question of whether you are falling for someone can get pretty complicated to answer. Each and every one of us has been in a situation where you have this inner struggle between what your heart says and what your head says. A friend recently told me when it comes to love, don't let your head decide for you, let your heart decide for you and it will make all the difference. In the end, after looking into my own heart the answer to the final question that I have continually asked myself is…that I have no clue what the answer is and I may never know.

THE WAY LOVE GOES
April 22, 2005

Without a doubt, not knowing how another person feels about you can be, at times, emotionally draining. It's that constant wondering, worrying, and wishing to have those feelings reciprocated back from the one person you appreciate and like. We've all felt, at one point or another, the need to figure out where one stands in that person's life. A life can hopefully be a part of, if given the chance; but ultimately what one wants to know is whether that particular person simply sees you as a brother/sister or does he or she feel the same way you do? Though complicated it may seem, it would be a whole lot simpler if potential relationships were solved by doing certain things that one used to do as a child.

Wouldn't it be great to go back to a time where giving that boy or girl half your dessert or any food for that matter meant that you really liked him or her and was willing to share. For its that particular child who you would sit next to either on the bus, lunch table, or on the school playground and would give him or her an extra dessert that he or she brought especially for that child. Let me ask you this question, did you ever share food with someone who you considered to be your "boyfriend" or "girlfriend" when you were a little kid? If you think about it, it takes a special girl for us to give up what we most love in life, which in this case is food; but most importantly our dessert.

Boys and girls chasing each other is really nothing new and doesn't say a whole lot. Now chasing each other and beating the crap out of each other is something that speaks volumes. Working in the asylum, I see so many little boys chasing after the girls and all too often I hear them complain that they are hitting them. My usual response is that they like you, which is a sign of affection for a boy, and if they really like you, they will knock you down. Personally speaking, I was never the chaser or the type to hit a girl, but rather the one being chased and hit by the girls. According to my mom, I had something that attracted girls in my direction when I was little and that something were my dimples which they wanted to pinch all the time.

Undeniably, it would be more uncomplicated if men and women went back to the old standby of wanting to know if you wanted to be in a relationship and that was by writing and sending a note to that person who you were interested in. We've all done that when we were kids and it was a system that worked for practically every kid and all you had to do was simply check two boxes or circles, yes or no. It was that easy and you went on with your day knowing you now have a "friend" that you can play with until he or she dislikes you for whatever reason and then finds someone else to be "friends" which was cruel but that was what being a kid was all about.

Glen, age 7, said, ~If falling in love is anything like learning how to spell, I don't want to do it. It takes too long.~ In retrospect, love is a lot like learning how to spell because it takes time and patience. Inevitably there will be errors made that will cause a person to have to keep writing or saying the word over and over until he or she gets it absolutely right. Sometimes it can be so hard to learn and correct the mistakes that are made that we just want to give up. BUT when you have someone to help you learn and correct those mistakes then it won't be long before you can spell perfectly all because of that person sticking by you when it got tough. Ultimately, as a kid, that's the way love goes as we gave, chased, and wrote back in the day; but now as an adult, we are giving, chasing and writing for that one specific special person.

FOREVER AND ALWAYS
April 23, 2005

Sir Pavio Writesalot said, ~Love is the binding that holds to your dreams. Love does not come over, rather you choose to love. Only when you choose to love one forever and you stand by that dedication of love will you truly love for life and live happily ever after.~ Let me ask you this question, does love last forever between two people? If you think about it, as each of us go through life and love, one oftentimes wonders if he or she will have that kind of love that one's own parents have. A love that is so deep and strong that it feels right to show how much you love that person in a personal sense; but also in a spiritual sense as you love from within your heart and soul.

Essentially, before ever attaining that forever love, one must have appreciation for that person who is kind and considerate enough to go out of his or her way to do something nice and in the process put a smile on your face. It's a rarity these days to find that guy or girl who appreciates all you try to do for that person and yet, he or she expects nothing in return which shows a selfless love that is an attractive quality for both men and women; but more so to a woman in my opinion. For every one of us can agree that its nice to know that someone is thinking about you and greatly appreciates who you are as a person, which makes you feel special and in turn makes that person special.

There will come a point where appreciating that person turns into liking that particular person. Genuinely liking him or her for who they are inside and not how they physically look on the outside. Most definitely, it's what first attracts you to that person but if he or she is beautiful on the outside, but yet is ugly on the inside then that person is not worth liking and not worth your time. We all have specific qualities you like about a person that makes you want to hang around him or her and get more acquainted. It's that person who can make a deep impression on you; an impression that other guys or girls have failed to put on you. Someone once told me, never feel guilty or ever apologize for liking someone because they may actually like you back.

Ultimately, that like you have for a person turns or hopefully turns to love for that guy or girl. What I have come to learn is that every person is capable of loving someone with every fiber of their being; but to smother that person with love can cause a person to want some space. Yet not too much space that one thinks that he or she has taken him or granted. How many of you can honestly say that you are, were, or have been truly in love with someone? To be truly in love, you sacrifice what you held most dear to in your heart and refocus it to that one person who you gladly give it up for...but not entirely. Let me tell you something, when you know you have it, hold on to it, and never let go because if it slips through your fingers, one may never get the chance to experience it ever again.

For 29 years, my parents have been happily married and have two sons they are both proud of. Within those 29 years they have had their share of rocky moments, which my brother and I have been a witness to; but through it all they still loved each other enough to work it. One reason their marriage is strong is that my dad takes my mom out on dates, which shows he still has what it takes to keep the bond of love forever tight though the good times and bad. I look at both of them and think to myself, that is how I want my marriage to my future wife to be as we go through our own triumphs, trials and tribulations. Forever and always, till the day I take my one last breath I will love her unconditionally and she for me.

JUST AROUND THE CORNER
April 25, 2005

Essentially, for guys, when it comes to aging, we have three specific categories which are young, middle aged, and you look good. In pasts Yodaisms I've joked that I've considered myself old but in reality, I am actually middle aged. For guys, we reach a certain point where we can't do certain things like we did when we were young and yet we're not at that point where we're going to stop either just because that fire is still felt inside. But the question can be asked how does one know when one reaches middle age? Thinking about it, there are tell tale signs that will reveal a person's crossover from young man to a middle-aged dude. A middle-aged dude that will come to realize that change comes whether you like it or not.

Listening to music is fundamentally a staple of many people's lives, it keeps us sane from our own lives that we live on a daily basis. When I was younger, blaring music that would shake, rattle, roll a person's windows was part of what being "cool" was all about. Now that I'm reaching the age of 30, I find myself wanting to hear music at a respectable level. A level in which it's not too low where you can't hear it; but not too loud that it makes your ears bleed. Working in the asylum, I've been told that I'm not cool anymore and that I'm not hip and happening. Whether or not I know what's hip or happening is inconsequential; as long as their song that I like to hear, understand, and has a nice beat I'm a happy camper.

Someone once said, ~It's frustrating when you know all the answers, but nobody asks you the question.~ To tell you the truth, I don't have all the answers and if I did it would be shared with everybody. Unfortunately, I ask the same questions you do as its put down in these Yodaisms on a semi-daily basis and many of you have taken it to heart. For its the wisdom that I have gained over the years I find myself taking aside particular kids in the asylum and sharing what I know. In a sense, I'm kind of like Yoda, though I'm not a green, 900 years old, or have the powers of the force. Initially, its a funny thing when they roll their eyes at me because I used to do the exact same thing to someone who was around the same age as I am now.

There comes a point when a person is about to reach his or her 30's, one takes a look at his/her friends and realizes that things do change. The one underlying change in any person's life is marriage and it starts to have a domino effect amongst your friends. Personally speaking, some of my friends are mostly single but the majority of them are either engaged, getting married, already married, but thankfully not divorced. Let me ask you this question, are more of your getting engaged/married or getting divorced rather than hooking up or breaking up? It's that realization that you have crossed over into a place of maturity in which there is absolutely no turning back.

My motto has always been ~Take life one day at a time, if you go through it too fast you will have no idea where you will end up.~ Whether or not every person takes life one day at a time, you have to admit that life can move very quickly. So quickly that it all becomes one big blur to where one says an all too familiar phrase when looking back at the past which is, it seemed like yesterday. Looking back at the first 27 years of my life I have had setbacks, disappointments, heartbreak, triumphs, defeats, dreams fulfilled and/or dreams crushed. Yet, there has been one constant that has been keeping me going, which is my desire to keep moving forward in life. In the end, I don't know what's in store for me when I turn 30; but I do know one thing though, it's up 2 street and just around the corner.

BOILING POINT
April 27, 2005

Albert Smith once said, ~Tears are the safety valve of the heart when too much pressure is laid on it.~ Each and every one of us feels as if the weight of the world rests entirely on our shoulders. We all have or are experiencing certain pressures in our personal, academic, or professional lives to the point that it most certainly affects us physically, mentally, and emotionally. Let me ask you this question, if I asked you if you are currently dealing with pressure what would you say? I would assume that you all are probably nodding your head yes because, in some aspect, like can be considered one big pressure cooker. A pressure cooker, that if left on the stove too long, will explode and the shiznit will hit the fan.

For the most part, certain people thrive on pressure because it essentially gets a person more focused on what he or she has to do. For the adrenaline rush that one feels can give each of us that added boost to accomplish certain tasks that one's heart may not be in. Speaking for myself, I'm at times a procrastinator and will wait till the night before to complete something that is due the next day. Yet, when the pressure is on, my focus is to get my project accomplished and not let any distractions get in the way. Personally speaking, when the chips are down on the proverbial gaming table of life, do you keep folding or do you keep raising the stakes in your favor?

Without a doubt, telling someone how you feel for him or her is considered one the greatest pressures in life to go through, trust me I know. Without a doubt, a person can't eat and will lose so much sleep that he or she continually looks up at the ceiling debating on whether or not to tell him or her how you feel. Whether it's loving someone or liking someone, not being able to share your feelings with that person can be a tough situation due to one's own past heartaches that tend to stay with a person. Inevitably, it's that added pressure on one's already heavy-laden shoulders to speak from one's heart and reveal how you feel about him or her and not have that same person tear your heart in half.

Thinking about it, there is a certain amount of pressure that I put on myself to try to top every Yodaism that is sent out to you all. In some way, I'm pushing myself to keep coming up with topics that generally every person goes through on a semi-daily basis, which puts pressure on me to keep what I write and send to you fresh and not have it sound like you've read the same thing over and over again. Essentially, I've done a good job trying to convey my thoughts into words, which are then sent to you guys. Hopefully, it makes sense to you because half the time it doesn't make sense to me; but whether or not you don't understand the words, the message is loud, clear, and touches your heart and soul.

In retrospect, the pressures of life that each of us go through tests the limits of how much we can take until we crack. In some ways, we are like a pinata, and life is just continually hitting us with a stick to see what emotions will fall out. Undoubtedly, there will come a point where life will push the right buttons and have one just fall apart mentally, emotionally, and/or physically. Yet, the only person that knows our limitations and how far we can physically and mentally go to the point where we don't go postal due to the overwhelming pressure is ourselves. In the end, when the pressures of life have reached a boiling point, simply let out some steam(crying, screaming, breaking stuff, etc.) and you'll feel a whole lot better.

TO YOU
April 30, 2005

Let me ask you this question, when was the last time you sat down and just looked through your old yearbooks? When you take a look at the past you essentially look back at the person you once were as a kid to the person you are now as an adult. Yet, you not only look back at yourself, you also look back at the people who you associated with who either had direct or indirect contact in your life. The memories and moments shared throughout the years of your life, as well as the lives of others who were a part of it are captured live and in living color. For it can be said that a picture can say a thousand words but quite frankly it can't reveal thoughts or emotions that nobody really knows except for you at that particular time and place.

Each and every one of us tends to cringe when one looks back at pictures of ourselves in a book that is a representation of a time capsule. A time capsule that represented your own humble beginnings as a young adolescent trying to find one's own identity all the while trying to fit in a particular social group. Its within one's own personal time capsule that it had such remarkable individual, duo, or group shots of particular people who were considered most likely to succeed, most athletic, most witty, most attractive, best all around, best dressed, most intelligent, most friendly, most flirtatious, most talkative, best personality, most friendly, and most likely to end up on an episode of cops. So the question can be asked, were you ever any of the above mentioned?

Without a doubt, some of the funniest, weirdest, saddest, funniest, and craziest times are captured and forever cemented in one's own history of life. However, those captured still shots can never compare to the actual atmosphere and energy of where one was and who he or she was with, which is why it's considered such a memorable one. Oftentimes, a person can over exaggerate what happened during that particular moment in time to the point where he or she actually believes the tales he or she is spinning. Whether or not it was with friends or with a boyfriend/girlfriend that one may or may not be with anymore it was a priceless memory that one hopefully still treasures to this day.

In any case, when you take a look back down memory lane and see certain individuals what emotions do you get when you look at his or her picture. For some people, the two basic emotions that tend to stir up are infatuation and love because that particular guy or girl had some type of effect on you that when you look at his or her picture one's emotions still run deep for that person Unfortunately, for other people, emotions such as anger and bitterness can bring about resentment due to how he or she was treated by that particular person or persons. For its when you see or bump into these particular people do you still feel the same emotions for that person, or have you matured enough to move on with your life?

In retrospect, I attended school overseas in Ceiba, Puerto Rico from 1994-1996, I considered my classmates not just friends, but family due to being part of the military. Looking back in my yearbook, I had countless friends; but there were 7 of us who hung out together and were known as The Slackers. Though it absolutely had nothing to do with being lazy, it was just a name that stuck when my art teacher kept preaching to us about not being slackers. It was that same art teacher, Mr. Rashid, who wrote in my yearbook that art is life; create, look, draw what you see and what I can conceive can be. In the end, I say this to you as my friends wrote this to me 9 years ago: stay sweet, stay cool, and don't ever change.

THE ONE
May 2, 2005

Nancy Reagan once said, ~Love means giving one's self to another person fully, not just physically. When two people really love each other, this helps them to stay alive and grow. One must really be loved to grow. Love's such a precious and fragile thing that when it comes we have to hold on tightly. And when it comes we're very lucky because for some it never comes at all. If you have love, you're wealthy in a way that can never be measured. Cherish it.~ There comes a point where a person just gets tired of the dating scene which can oftentimes be considered a lost cause. We all want to find or already have found that one person who brings one's soul to life. For it's that person who makes you want to keep reaching higher and without a doubt gives you peace of mind when things just don't make any sense.

Undeniably, whether it's guys or girls, a person eventually wants more substance rather than style in a significant other. Most certainly, each of us has fallen into the pitfalls of falling for someone based on the way he or she looks. For its that outer beauty that makes him or her, in one's own words, "HOT", which can have you absolutely spellbound. However, it can get old pretty quickly as you find yourself in unfulfilling relationships that made you happy in the beginning; but you still find yourself feeling empty in your soul, as well as, in your heart. It's that mistake that one doesn't realize until the end when the love you give to that person isn't fully reciprocated back which is a sure sign that you deserve better than him or her.

For the most part, one just has to keep in mind that love is faith, and you have faith in that person who truly knows what love is all about. In some ways, it's like planting flowers; for it takes time and patience for the love between two people to grow. Essentially, you can't make it grow to where you want something to happen right here and right now which isn't the way love goes. You primarily have to let it grow on its own by just being there as a friend, even though you so desperately want to be in his or her arms. Whether or not you know the person you want to be with, there can be circumstances that tend to prevent you from being with him or her. Circumstances such as death, distance, and/or working through feelings for someone else.

Speaking of feelings for someone else, both guys and girls will get into a situation where one's heart will be in a proverbial tug-of-war between a person who makes one feel good inside and one who also makes you feel good inside; but tends to disappoint you when you need him or her the most. It can be a tough situation indeed as the decision to who one wants to be with comes down to several different factors. Factors that can cause a person to go through an emotional rollercoaster as he or she tries to figure out which path to take on the road to only his or her happiness but that person's happiness as well. Even though the decision is squarely on one's shoulders, it doesn't hurt to seek guidance every now and then from someone you know and trust.

Garman Wold said, ~When love is your greatest weakness, you will be the strongest person in the world.~ If you think about it, it's not every day that a person steps into your life who is absolutely genuine and worth crying over. Though you may have reservations about taking that next step, that person doesn't and is willing to be there for you no matter what, unlike others before him or her. Initially, a person can have the mindset that maybe he or she isn't strong enough to put one's heart out there because you are scared of getting hurt; but guess what that person is scared of as well. Ultimately, you just want to take him or her by the hand and simply say from the heart, Let me be the one to give you strength because you make me stronger each and every time I'm around you.

GO THE DISTANCE
May 6, 2005

Someone once said, ~Distance never separates two hearts that really care, for our memories span the miles and in seconds we are there. But whenever I start feeling sad, because I miss you, I remind myself how lucky I am to have someone so special to miss.~ Let me ask you this question, do you believe in long distance relationships and whether or not it has longevity between two people? Without a doubt, being in a long-distance relationship is the hardest thing for people to be in because your miles away from the one you love. For the temptations of straying to someone other than one's significant other tend to show itself; but not succumbing to those temptations make the relationship two people have stronger.

Trust, above all else, is the most important thing between two people who are head over heels for each other. Though oceans or states separate you physically, which can be a painful feeling, it can't separate the emotional bond you have and feel for that particular person. For no matter how hard you try not to think about him or her, you end up thinking about that person even more and that can tear you up inside. But the question can be asked, if it hurts so bad, why does it feel so good? If you think about it, it doesn't make any sense at all, but in all honesty nothing absolutely nothing about love makes sense. A person can try to understand it all he or she likes, but in the long run, one will just get more and more confused.

I once said that it's a simple thing such as love that every person wants and yet its the most complicated thing to come one's way; but once you truly experience it, you never want it to end. Undeniably, you know how you feel for that person and have no doubts that he or she is the one you have been waiting your whole life for. Yet, it's easy to say you want to be with that person but when you can't physically be there next to him or her, it can be a frustrating situation indeed. Life would be great if we simply had the ability to think about that person or wish for that person to be at your side and within a blink of an eye, he or she appears in front of you. Initially, one just has to be there for him or her in spirit and as the saying goes, distance makes the heart grow fonder.

Essentially, the key factor and most important aspect in long distance relationships is communication. However, one of the biggest mistakes guys, as well as girls, make in a long-distance relationship is usually not communicating with the one he or she supposedly loves and is committed to wholeheartedly. For it doesn't necessarily mean contacting him or her every single day of the week, but rather on a semi-daily basis, which in my opinion is every 2 or 3 days. Staying in contact with that someone special shows that you truly value the loving relationship that is shared between each other, which shows a level of progression that could possibly lead into the next level of one's relationship whatever that level may be.

Someone once said, ~Though the miles between us are many, the heart is a bridge that can span the largest oceans. Thus, we shall always be close, as long as we are in each other's hearts."~ I started this thought by asking the question, do you believe in long distance relationships and does it have longevity between two people. In my opinion, if it is built on faithfulness, trust, honesty, and communication I would say yes; but for some people if it isn't, then you and that person will have to re-evaluate the relationship at hand. In the end, when it comes to keeping a long-distance relationship between you and the one you love that stands the test of time, are you willing to go the distance?

THE NEXT BEST THING
May 9, 2005

Charlotte Davis Kasl once said, ~Whether or not you have children yourself, you are a parent to the next generation. If we can stop thinking of children as individual property and think of them as the next generation, then we can realize we all have a role to play.~ One of the greatest responsibilities in life for a person is the rearing, well-being, and safety of a child or children. Whether its your own or someone else's, people will undeniably take stock in one's own social interaction, temperament, and disciplinary action which gives people a preconceived perception of the type of parent you are or potential parent you might become one day. Let me ask those that don't have kids yet, do you think you would make a great mother or father?

In some apsect, depending on one's own upbringing, each of us wants to someday be the parent who wants to be either close or at least the same level of one's own parents. Yet, one can never match the skills one's own parents attained; you just have to live and learn like they did with their own parents who, like us, made them crazy, angry, and frustrated to the point they too pulled out their own hair. If you think about it, anybody can have kids; but it takes two special people to be a mother and a father. For its those qualities that aren't really revealed at first but as time moves on friends, family, and possibly co-workers will see the hidden potential slowly rise to the surface.

In any case, we've all heard of or seen stories of deadbeat dads, as well as, moms that don't care about their family, For it's a sad situation indeed when a father and a mother walks away from one's family and refuses to take responsibility for the life or lives he or she has helped bring into the world. Much can be said for a person who is a single father or mother as the added pressure of providing for them as he or she is also trying to spend as much time with them as possible. One can give thanks to him or her for what one had and hopefully you grew up to be a well-adjusted kid(s). Essentially, the question can be asked: are you a part of a single parent household or did you have both parents firmly in your corner?

Ultimately, if you take a step back and look at what one's parents have done for us over the years which shows how they truly love us. Despite the punishments, which were either deserved or undeserved, it helped us become the well-adjusted, respectful, polite, and well-mannered adults we are today. Nowadays, you can't even punish your kids in public. For its truly amazing to witness when a child, not a parent, is in control of the situation at hand and all she does is let him, her, or them express themselves. Let me tell you something, I had everything thrown at me except the kitchen sink whenever I acted up and to be perfectly honest, I'm glad they did it when I was young because it knocked some sense into me.

In a past Yodaism, I said I believed I have the potential to be a father and I still stand by that statement. Yet, to become a father would mean I have to get married first, which I hope to one day, but in the meantime I'm at least a father figure to "my kids" in the asylum where I work at, but I digress. Over the past couple of months, I've been bonding with a friend of mine's baby son. The parents, over those couple of months, apparently saw how that bond grew and last Sunday, I was given a possible offer that I couldn't refuse. Undoubtedly, it's an honor and privilege just to be asked and this past Sunday I was officially made Godfather and even though I may or may not be a father one day, being Godfather is the next best thing.

HEART OF THE MATTER
May 11, 2005

John Dewey once said, ~Every closure is an awakening, and every awakening settles something.~ We all can agree that breaking up with someone is never really easy and undeniably the hardest thing a person can do or try to do. Essentially, the feelings that you, as well as, that particular person shared for each other were strong, however, feelings fade at some point; but not entirely. For a piece of you still feels for that person and yet one wants to move on with his or her life without deliberately hurting that person causing him or her bitterness and/or utter resentment. Subsequently, one must go about in an entirely mature manner rather than an immature manner, which brings not only closure for you but closure for that person as well, if any.

Let me ask you this question, how many of you have gone through a really bad break up where it left you with unanswered questions and a feeling that certain areas of the relationship were not handled properly by either you or that guy or girl? Unquestionably, the blame game can come into play; but blaming each other for the faults and mistakes basically solves nothing in a relationship that was once based on trust and dependability. It's within that proverbial he said/she said conference style atmosphere that hurtful words may or may not be said, which is never a good thing when trying to end a relationship on preferably good terms with that person who you have spent considerable amount of time with.

Without a doubt, there is only one way to break up with a person which is face to face and if done cleanly it will not come back to haunt you in a future relationship. Oftentimes, a person makes the mistake of breaking up with someone through email, a Dear John/Jane letter, though a friend, and more often than not through a phone call, which is unfair either for you or that person because one is absolutely thrown off guard. In my opinion, doing it face to face shows that you were willing to sit down and explain why the relationship didn't work, hopefully in a calm, rational, and civilized manner. In other words, an amicable split on both sides where each still remains friends as you and that person emotionally go your separate ways.

If you think about it, closure doesn't always necessarily have to deal with the ending of a relationship, but rather the beginning of one where a person has to make things right with himself or herself than with someone else. We've all known someone or are that person who finds excuses and/or reasons to break up with someone which leads people to believe that you are either indecisive about who you want to be with, or you just don't want to get too close to anyone emotionally. For if he or she does get too close, one instigates a breakup; but what a person ends up doing is hurting himself or herself because you never really find out if he or she was truly the one who is worth going the distance for.

Tigress Luv said, ~When we live resentment towards another our hearts close down. Letting go of our resentment frees us from placing blame on them and allows us to look towards ourselves for peace.~ In retrospect, it's all about forgiveness even if that person doesn't want to forgive you or be forgiven, at least one knows you can live without that person. Ultimately, in order to move forward with a present relationship a person must first make things right with a past relationship, which can be a tough task indeed. In the end, once you get to the heart of the matter with that person and lay it all on the table, one won't feel things are unfinished or have any regrets whatsoever as you move into a new relationship.

THE PERFECT WAVE
May 12, 2005

Someone once said, ~I have seen and felt all sides of it. I've been on the top of it and had the best feeling of my life. Been thrown down by it and been crushed on the bottom. Love is like the ocean. No matter what you do, the waves keep coming in. You can ride them, enjoy them, duck under them, go over them..they're big or small.. sometimes one right after another..sometimes you have to wait for a good one. If you don't keep your eyes open and your lungs full of air then any one of those waves will crush you..just like in love. It's not up to you whether you sink or swim. It depends on the wave. But all I can say is..never get out of the water...you might drown but its better than never getting wet at all.~

Let me ask you this question, what is the one activity you love to do at the beach that thrills you to no end and can give you an adrenaline rush? If you hopefully answered surfing, you are absolutely right. For if you really think about it, surfing and love can parallel each other. Stay with me on this because the more I think about it, the more it makes sense to me and it will surely make sense to you...I hope. Essentially, the thrill of surfing and love coincide as you feel so excited to embrace, both metaphorically and literally, something that makes you feel good inside. It's that feeling every person has felt, as well as, experienced and we absolutely never want it to go away.

As it has been previously said, love is like the ocean and each of us are like surfers surfing the unpredictable waves that will keep a person guessing as to who, when, and where the waves will lead you. Without a doubt, we've all metaphorically stood and gazed at the majestic beauty that is the clear blue ocean. An ocean that has swallowed and spit out surfers that have tried to surf those waves but end up continually wiping out. For its within the ocean of love that even though relationships have been badly broken apart, kept people apart for reasons known and unknown; but it most definitely has brought two people together to where they both surfed off into the sunset hand in hand.

If you think about it, whether it's a person's 1st time or 101st time, he or she will get swept into unpredictable waves which will cause a person to be utterly confused as one tries not to freak out. It's a scary situation indeed when you have no idea where you are at first, and when one thinks you're swimming towards the surface you're actually swimming to the bottom. Let me tell you something, nobody is ever prepared for that feeling of drowning when you might not know if one will get his or her head above water to get some much-needed air. Undeniably, that's a lot like love or falling in love because someone will come along that completely knocks you off your surfboard and all you want to do when you resurface is find out who that person was.

Baroness Orczy said, ~It is only when we are very happy that we can bear to gaze merrily upon the vast and limitless expanse of water, rolling on and on with such persistent, irritating monotony, to the accompaniment of our thoughts, whether grave or gay. When they are gay, the waves echo their gaiety; but when they are sad, then every breaker, as it rolls, seems to bring additional sadness, and to speak to us of hopelessness and of the pettiness of all our joys.~ In retrospect, as "surfers" each of us are waiting for that one wave which represents that guy or girl to take us somewhere new. In the end, the question can be asked: are you still waiting for the perfect wave, or have you already found him or her?

DEFY THE IMPOSSIBLE

May 14, 2005

Someone once said, ~Love is a strong wind, easy to spell, difficult to define, impossible to live without.~ Oftentimes a person completely shuts love out of his or her life due the fact, that in one's own mind, its impossible to find or have it show up on one's doorstep, so to speak. Yet, no matter how many times one faces sorrow and/or utter disappointment, we continually put ourselves, as well as our heart out there. Although the human heart is considered the most fragile part of the human body, in an emotional sense, it can most definitely withstand a lot of punishment. Essentially, there are so many impossibilities concerning love that it can make a person throw in the towel and remain single for the rest of his or her life.

For it's impossible to verbally describe how a person feels for another because the words that you want to say come out all wrong and you wind up sounding and looking like a complete dork. For there is so much going on inside one's head that it's hard to really focus on one thought which can cause a person to say things that he or she may regret or feel absolutely embarrassed about. We've all been in a situation whether alone with someone one is interested in or hanging with friends, we can be intensely focused trying to figure out what to say to that particular person. For its when a question is directed towards us by him or her, comedy will ensue as one will say the first thing that pops into his or her mind, which is usually something totally off the wall.

If you think about it, it's impossible to love someone without first having love for yourself. Let me ask you this question, are you somewhat self-conscious about your appearance that it affects your self-esteem? Women, more so than guys, are caught in the appearance aspect of potential relationships, which unfortunately is caused by guys who solely base relationships on the superficial. Subsequently, it can cause women to wrap themselves in a metaphorical cocoon. In turn, if a guy, who is absolutely genuine, tells her she is absolutely beautiful she'll refuse to believe it. One life/love lesson is that if you like who you are and don't feel the need to change then that person will love you just the way you are.

You know, it's most definitely impossible to trust your feelings for someone you have only met once and have only known for a short period of time; but one's heart skips a beat whenever you think of him or her. One can say its simply a phase that he or she is going through, an initial crush which will wear off as time passes on; but it doesn't. For the question can be asked: do you trust your own feelings enough to tell that person how you feel and run the risk of being rejected, which is not a good feeling for anyone to go through; or do you hold back knowing that the chance to tell that person may never come again. It's a tough decision indeed as there is an inner struggle going on between what one is thinking and what one is feeling.

In retrospect, when it comes to potential relationships, its impossible to know how that person may or may not react. For it one's of those unknowns that a person will never be prepared for as the decision rests in his or her hands. Initially, there are so many impossibilities that are associated with love, there is one absolute possibility a person can rely on and that is the love you have for a person will never fade even though he or she may never love you back. Ultimately, when it comes to love, falling love, or figuring out the love you have for a person, you just have to defy the impossible and a song that best reflects this sentiment is The Look by Ryan Tedder.

AS DAYS GO BY
May 18, 2005

Erna Bornbeck once said, ~One thing they never tell about child raising is that for the rest of your life, at a drop of a hat, you are expected to know your child's name and how he or she is.~ As a youth development specialist, which is better than the title of counselor or recreational aide, you're always going to be remembered by the kids as an influential part of their lives even though you may forget who they are at times, especially former asylum kids. It can be a truly embarrassing situation when former asylum kids see you or walk up to you and say do you remember me? Let me tell you something, being put on the spot to try to remember one child out of hundreds can put any person in a tight spot.

Working with kids for an extended period of time can really affect your mental status and attitude, which can rub off on the kids in the asylum. We've all had our bad days, we've all had our good days, and there are those particular days that are somewhere in between. Initially one seemingly good day can either turn weird or bad because quite frankly, working in the asylum as long as I have, you begin to have somewhat of a sixth sense as to what might be on the horizon, in a manner of speaking. Several factors can play into it such as the weather, how many employees have or haven't shown up for work, and with a doubt waking up on the wrong side of the bed.

Undoubtedly there are days where you just feel like crap and coming to work can oftentimes raise one's "I've had it up to here level" to the breaking point. To be perfectly honest, I am a pacifist, which basically means that I'm a laid-back dude; but if my buttons are pushed the wrong way expect to see another side of me no one has ever seen before. However, you have to admit when kids see or feel that something is wrong, they will help you in some way, shape, or form. Perfect example, last year I had somewhat of a breakdown due to stress and the kids were so concerned that they hugged me, as well as, sat down to talk with me. I will forever be in debt for those specific kids who got me through that particular tough day for me.

Anyways, for the most part one can have a handle on the kids you know or are getting to know while on the job. Yet, it's the kids that I don't know that for some reason I attract when I'm out and about. Let me ask you this question, have you ever felt like you were being watched or stared at? Whether I'm in line at Wal-Mart or just going out to eat, kids come up to me, who I don't even know stare at me and usually it's kids that are under the age of 5. So I do the most logical thing I can think of and that is smile, make faces, and hope they smile rather than cry. For it can be a truly awkward moment to explain to a parent why I made their child cry and have it all end up with me getting arrested, which hasn't happened yet. *knock on wood*

Last Friday, a birthday luncheon was held at Barnhill's buffet, which is a home away from home for the asylum staff. At that birthday luncheon, a parent whose kids used to go to the asylum showed up, which was a nice surprise for all of us. After everybody ate, the traditional speeches were made to the birthday girl, who I considered my mentor for training me for the past 8 years. When it reached that particular parent, he said something that truly stuck in our minds and touched us to no end. He said the reason his kids are so well behaved and turned out so good was due to our influence on them. In retrospect, as days go by many things have been said to us by the kid's parents, whether it was good or bad, what was said by that particular parent made each of us proud to do what we love to do...most of the time.

I DARE YOU
May 19, 2005

In some aspect, life can be compared to a playground, which was the funnest part of being in school or for just recreational purposes. Personally speaking, I liked art class because the teachers were usually a little out there, but I digress. Whether or not one remembers your childhood, the playground can represent certain areas of life that each one of us tends to go through on a seemingly day-to-day basis. Think back to a time when you had no worries, and all problems were simply left behind like articles of clothing or books at a school's lost and found. Let me ask you this question, what area of the playground did you like playing on and what area of life does it represent for you?

The merry-go-round, the bucking bronco for younger kids, somewhat represents our competitive spirit, depending on if you have one or not. Each and every one of us grab hold or try to grab the handle bars of possible success as life itself spins us around as fast it can. Undoubtedly, there will be times where someone will try to push, knock, or kick you off; but as long as you have that fighting spirit to hang on, then success will hopefully be in your grasp. Unfortunately, it's every kid for himself or herself as one holds on for dear life trying to keep his or her hold on the proverbial prize at the end, which is being the number one guy or girl left standing and/or sitting.

If you think about it, the monkey bars represent life in general as you swing from one rung to the next, not knowing what will happen next. Oftentimes, while swinging one decides to do something out of the ordinary such as hang upside down, which we all have done when we were kids. It's when we're looking at the world from a different vantage point that the best memories, as well as experiences are made or shared either by yourself, with friends, family, or your significant other. Yet, it's also on those rungs of life that a person can just hang there and completely decide to let go because life is just too difficult and/or unbearable to live through. For it's a sad situation indeed when someone gives up swinging too early and doesn't fight tooth and nail to get a better grip when he or she feels that one is slipping off.

Without question, the swings represent the one thing that each of us would swing high for and that is love. Initially, it takes a person to have momentum to get the desired height one wants, which is as high as possible. In some ways, each of us is swinging to someone that is out of reach and hopefully with an added push by friends or family one will get to his or her intended destination. Without a doubt, jumping off the swings is considered mandatory. even though you may end up falling flat on your face, which happened to me last week. Unquestionably, that is how love is as a person risks injury to one's self to try to jump into the arms of that one person who may or may not catch you.

In retrospect, you are never really too young or too old to play on certain playground equipment, unless its the teeter totter because you'll feel not only awkward, but you'll also feel like a complete dork. In any case, when it comes to the playground of life do you see it with fresh eyes or have you become so jaded that it doesn't have that fun factor that it used to back in the day. Inevitably, we all grow up, but that doesn't mean we don't outgrow having fun once in a while. Ultimately, I am challenging you to have fun by going to a playground near you, to have fun, plus bring friends and family with you. In the end, I dare you…no I double dare you… actually scratch that I double dog dare you not to have fun because trust me on this, it will bring back great memories, as well as create new ones for you.

YOU'RE HIRED
May 23, 2005

Donald Trump said, ~Experience taught me a few things. One is to listen to you gut, no matter how good something sounds on paper. The second is that you generally better off with sticking with what you know. And the thing is that sometimes your best investments are the ones you don't make.~ In some aspect, whether it's guys or girls, potential relationships are complicated to get off the ground, in a manner of speaking. One has to listen to your own instincts to figure out if that person meets the standards that you have set forth. In a funny and interesting kind of way, its like potential relationships are like going through a job interview somewhat compared to the popular show The Apprentice; but one doesn't receive a job at the end, on the contrary he or she receives that person's heart, which is the best prize one can ever be given.

If you think about it, each of us start out with anonymity as, in some aspect, hide in the shadows and wait for the right time to reveal ourselves. It's sort of like the dark side of the force finally overwhelming the Jedi in episode 3, which was an awesome movie, and it answered many questions that Star Wars fans wanted to know; but I digress. In any case, a person steps out of the proverbial crowd and stands front and center hoping that particular person who has the so-called power either accepts you or denies you. Let me ask you this question, when you finally decided to step out of the crowd and revealed yourself to that particular person, was his or her reaction happiness, shock, or utter disappointment?

More often than not, whatever potential "employer" looks at are our own individual resumes which determine if you fit some, most, or all of the qualifications that he or she is looking for. For women, there is an endless list of qualifications that they look for in a guy;

but for guys, that list of qualifications can be counted on one hand, maybe two. Yet, when it comes to a potential relationship, there is an absolute unknown as to who that person will choose in the end because quite frankly the time spent proving and/or explaining why one should be accepted to the position that will hopefully have you side by side with him or her. Oftentimes it can work for you and unfortunately it also can work against you as well.

Without a doubt, a person can be considered "overqualified" for the position and that type of person I am speaking of is the supposed nice guy and/or nice girl. It's truly amazing when a seemingly qualified "applicant" gets turned down only to have a less qualified person be chosen, which can be a frustrating situation indeed. What's most undoubtedly frustrating is that even though he or she has initially turned you down, that person wants you at one's side, not in a personal way; but rather a "just friends" way. For it is that all too familiar secondary position that guys, as well as girls, end up filling and to be perfectly honest nobody wants to ever be put in it; but one humbly accepts the job and does his or her duties as if one were chosen by him or her.

In retrospect, you never really know who lies on their resume in order to get their proverbial foot in the door so to speak. Ultimately, it's better to be honest from the beginning than to continually cover up lies and certain indiscretions that will eventually be found. For it's just a matter of time. Essentially, it's that arrogance or overconfidence which can bite a person in the butt and inevitably that person will hear the words that were made famous by Donald Trump with hand gestures included…You're Fired! In the end, whether it takes several interviews or just one interview, when you finally meet the perfect candidate for the job you can say this with an absolute smile on your face…You're Hired!

RESISTANCE IS FUTILE
May 27, 2005

Nicholas Follansbee once said, ~Collecting, like most other human activities has both very positive and, potentially, negative aspects. The latter may include obsession or over-involvement that leads to financial hardship or the neglect of responsibilities and loved ones. Many of us prefer to keep those who are nearest and dearest in the dark about the extent of our spending. And sometimes-friendly competition for treasures can turn not so friendly. I think we all sometimes feel deep down like our hobby is a guilty pleasure, and we may sometimes wonder at the madness of spending small (or maybe not so small) fortunes on pieces of colored paper or hunks of hardened mud.~ Let me ask you this question, do you collect certain kinds of things and if so, what are they?

Baseball cards are considered a piece of Americana that will always and forever be a part of every young child's life. Essentially, collecting baseball cards is generally done by guys and to be perfectly honest girls, mainly moms, think it's simply a waste of time and money. Anyways, for some it's a hobby that one will eventually grow out of, like myself, whose cards are now collecting dust under my bed and on top of my closet shelf. Yet, for other people collecting these seemingly worthless cards can oftentimes pay big dividends as he or she finds or buys one that can be considered a lucrative investment, which will most definitely be protected to keep it in perfect condition.

You wouldn't think collecting toys would be considered a hobby, but it is, and many collectable toy shops make a living buying and selling certain kinds of toys whether they're broken or not. Classic toys such as Barbie, Star Wars, Care Bears, He-Man, Dukes of Hazzard, and Gobots are just some of the valuable merchandise that certain people would give their right arm for, in a manner of speaking. Let me tell you something, if I knew now what I didn't know back then the toys that I grew up playing with, such as transformers, G.I. Joe, and M.A.S.K, would stay in better condition and not be thrown against the wall, stepped on, buried in dirt, or given away when a person outgrows them.

When it comes to foot apparel women, as well as some guys, buy shoes to either show off to other people or to match the clothes that he or she is wearing or is going to wear. It can be a truly amazing sight indeed to see the average woman's shoe collection and then compare that to the collection of a sports figure, Hollywood celebrity, and singers. Singers such as Mariah Carey, who has a room full of shoes that have their own shelf and I know this by watching MTV cribs. From a guy's point of view, we only need three pairs of reliable shoes that will sustain us throughout our own lifetime, and they are a good pair of sneakers, durable yet comfortable work shoes, and dress shoes.

Personally speaking, I am a person who collects two things which are hats and Yoda merchandise. The particular hats that I like to purchase are ball caps and those fisherman type hats that have cool designs in the front or all around. With the Yoda merchandise, I basically started collecting them off and on over the years and as of right now the collection stands at 22, which will keep growing. Oh, if any of you guys out there come across some Yoda stuff would you be able to hook a brotha up? In retrospect, whether a person collects stamps, coins, cars, shot glasses from all fifty states, etc. a person won't be able to resist buying that particular item to add to one's own collection and a famous line from tv/movies says it best…resistance is futile.

YODA OUT
May 29, 2005

Let me ask you this question, when I say the words American idol who or what immediately comes to your mind? For if you have been living under a rock for the past 4 years, American Idol has been and still is a proverbial monstrous phenomenon that every person anticipates to watch or audition for. Without a doubt, it makes stars out people who have the potential to become great recording artists; but it also makes stars out of those that have horrible voices. Voices that would make your ears bleed and yet, we keep watching /listening because quite frankly we love a good train wreck, which has given us memorable people such as Leroy Wells and "Mr. She Bangs' ' himself, William Hung.

So, what makes American Idol such a popular show is that it can literally bring families together or divide them apart, in a good way of course. For most people it's the judges and it's one judge in particular that we've all grown to like or at least tolerate, and that person is Simon Cowell. He's a man that has made critiquing/insulting people have little or no singing ability an absolute artform. Whether you agree or disagree with what he says, you have to admit he has the cojones to say it to your face and not get beat up for it. As egomaniacal as he is, the show wouldn't be the same without him or Randy "The Dawg " Jackson and Paula "Clap Happy" Abdul judging right alongside him.

Most definitely, the contestants themselves unite complete strangers and form fan clubs for talents such as Kelly Clarkson, Tamyra Gray, Ruben Studdard, Clay Aiken, George Huff, LaToya London, and for this season it's Carrie Underwood and Bo Bice. If you think about it, every season there is one guy or girl who stands out among the rest and we root for him or her until the end, which can oftentimes label a person a fanatic or die-hard fan. For me personally, I wasn't instantly hooked when the first season started and yes, I freely admit as a guy I watch American Idol. It wasn't until the second season that two people caught my attention, who were considered "average joes" and they were Ruben and Clay. Since then, I've been an avid watcher and every now and then vote for my favorites.

As many of you may or may not know, Carrie Underwood won the title of American Idol over Bo Bice. In my own mind, I wanted a guy to win to bring some continuity to a guy/girl winner. Unfortunately, it wasn't meant to be and despite the fact that Bo didn't win the title of American Idol he did get the admiration of people all across the world. Inevitably, this year's competition has been deemed a Ruben Vs. Clay matchup, which everybody wanted. Like Clay, Carrie was never in the bottom 3 and gave strong performances throughout the entire season. Though Clay did not win, which is still debated to this day, he won in the long run. For Carrie, as well as for Bo, they both will have successful and bright futures ahead of them.

Ultimately, what makes American Idol such a juggernaut is due the support of the fans not just in the United States, but also around the world. Think about it, each and every person is part of something special when they vote for someone to be the new American Idol. In a sense, the heart of the show is the fans that cheer, scream and holler for their favorite contestants, who keeps the show beating every year despite the controversies. When or if, the heartbeat starts to fade, that is when American Idol should ride off into the sunset, so to speak; but I don't see that coming any time soon. Well, until next season this has been another semi-daily Yodaism and in the end, all there is left to say is...Yoda Out!

EVERYTIME
June 1, 2005

Someone once said, ~Why do we close our eyes when we sleep? Why we cry? When we imagine? When we kiss? This is because the most beautiful thing in the world is unseen.~ If you think about it, that previous statement is true indeed because it's oftentimes better to have one's eyes closed because it opens up a whole new world that a person has never been able to fathom. In some aspect, a blind person can see and hear things better than a sighted person could possibly ever comprehend. Though we all can see, we're actually blind and can't see what's in front of our face till its too late. Essentially, there are certain areas of life that closing our eyes initially helps us get a better understanding of who or what is placed in front of us.

For the most part, music is a part of every person's life that one can never escape from. On a seemingly regular basis we watch and/or listen to our favorite artists perform live, on television, or on the radio. Yet, the question can be asked, does closing your eyes when you are listening to him, her, or them sing their songs help? In my own opinion, yes because you get a better vibe, sense, or feel of the song by that particular person or persons. Without question that's how love is as you try to feel, not see, the beat of the music coming from that one special person. It's what a person doesn't see that makes a song special and if two people can connect on a deeper level with that song, then they're absolutely just made beautiful music together.

Without a doubt, trying to figure out the feelings you have for someone can oftentimes be solved by simply closing your eyes and imagining your life without that person in it. For it can be considered the best problem solver when one is in a situation where he or she is torn between two people that has his or her in a proverbial tug-of-war. It's within one's own drama-filled world that it's nice to know that you have friends and/or family members that will help you decide one's dilemma of love by weighing the pros and cons of that particular person. Whether or not, an actual decision is made concerning who one's heart lies with at that exact moment; it at least helps free you from distractions that may be hindering your decision process.

However, when it comes to love or falling in love, a person doesn't want to close his or eyes for the simple reason that if one opens them up that person will be gone. We've all been at a particular place in life where you meet someone, who is or was everything you always wanted in a significant other. One hopes its not an elaborate illusion set up by life itself to mess with you, which can be viewed as cruel and inhumane torture. Yet, you still want to be assured you aren't dreaming and a simple request such as being pinched will squash one's worries. For its one's so-called dream come true that keeps that person's eyes wide open and no matter how badly he or she wants to blink, one doesn't want to miss the experiences that one will enjoy to the fullest.

In retrospect, when it comes to love, a person can have his or her eyes opened and closed so many times that it swells shut. For it can be a frustrating situation indeed for any person to try to see who is standing in front of him or her only to have one's vision impaired. In a way, it's like something has been covering one's eyes and you can't remove them no matter how hard you try. Yet, we have some idea who is standing there even though we can't see him or her. In the end, everytime you close your eyes, who do you see that brings a smile to your face to the point where you think he or she can truly open your eyes for good.

WHO'S NEXT
June 5, 2005

Someone once said, ~What "geek" seems to mean in this context is "I am incredibly passionate about something trivial, and I can tell you every tiny detail about that subject, and I'm kind of embarrassed at how much I know...and yet...here goes."~ Essentially, every person in the world, though they don't admit it, is considered a geek no matter how "cool" and/or "hot" one perceives themselves or is perceived to be. Though one can try to hide one's geekiness from others, it will be revealed in due time. If you think about it, we all tend to get fired about certain things and that's when one's geek side comes out. So, let me ask you this question and be honest with yourself, do you consider yourself a geek?

When it comes to video games, a person's geeky side will tend to show. Usually playing video games is a male dominated activity that starts basically from infancy till the day we die. No matter what type of game it is, as a guy, we consider it a challenge to beat that particular game without looking through any game guides or using cheat codes, which generally gives us a sense of pride and accomplishment. Let me tell you something, every guy knows that self-gratification of beating a boss and/or level that has one frustrated to no end. Undeniably, all guys are stubborn and when it comes to video games we will not rest until we feel vindicated and if that means not sleeping then so be it.

You would never expect to be a geek when it relates to sports or sports related activities, but you do. Every person has their favorite sport/team and without a doubt one knows the lingo, personal and professional information, and history of the specific team of that sport. For no matter how long one has been a fan, a person will continue to keep track of a team progress, as well as the progress of its individual players because quite frankly if there is a weak or struggling player on that team, he or she must be traded for a stronger player; but I digress. Thinking about it, whether it's baseball, football, hockey, basketball, football, Nascar, surfing, skateboarding, cheerleading, etc. your geeky side will reveal itself when things start to get intense and that is usually when the fun begins.

Personally speaking, I consider myself a geek when it pertains to professional wrestling. First off, it's not fake its predetermined to the point where they actually choreograph every move they both make to ensure they don't really hurt each other, which wrestling fans call an oops. Knowing wrestler's real names, former personas, how many titles they've won, and other trivial information is just a part of what makes a wrestling fan. I have been and still am a wrestling fan since the NWA days with such wrestlers as Jimmy "Boogie Woogie" Valiant and The Road Warriors, the question I have to ask myself is will I lose any major "cool" points after revealing this bit of info. My answer is who cares because, as a guy, professional wrestling is considered a male soap opera where we tune in to figure out story lines, angles, and watch grown men hit each other over the head with chairs.

In retrospect, just like embracing your inner dork you also have to embrace your inner geek. Look back at your middle/school high school days, were you a member of the band or any clubs such as the drama club, which were considered the geekiest school activities to be a part of. For me, I considered myself an art geek and I spent my time creating and making stuff up in my mind and drawing them on paper. In a sense, you can't escape how people knew you back then and to be perfectly honest you can't hide who you truly are. For it's those people that are truly your best friends and will love you for who are inside, not the outside. In the end, I have told you what kind of geek I am and to what extent the level of my geekiness is, all I have to say now is...who's next?

THE PERFECT MAN
June 9, 2005

Someone once said, ~ I am no one special, just a common man with common thoughts. I've led a common life. There are no monuments dedicated to me, and my name will soon be forgotten. But in one respect, I've loved another with all my heart and soul, and for that has always been enough.~ Undeniably, that's how every guy feels as one says that while looking into the eyes of that special someone. For its that sensitive side that every guy rarely reveals to anybody and yet, when it is shown by someone who is truly genuine then he is considered a keeper. There comes a point where we know there is a chance that the common man can find true happiness just look at Lyle Lovett who at one time married Julia Roberts. Who'd a thunk it?

In some aspect, it actually gives hope to the so called "average joes" out there that one might have a chance after all. For it's the "nice guy" that tends to receive the short end of the stick, in a manner of speaking, but yet end up in very happy relationships with a woman that he never imagined spending his life with. For its that proverbial long and winding road that guys, as well as girls, travel on until it straightens out and leads to that special someone. It can be a frustrating situation indeed for the "nice guy" to compromise one's own morals and integrity to become someone that would break a girl's hopes, dreams, and inevitably her heart, which doesn't fit one's true character and/or personality.

In any case, every guy has made a fool of himself since the discovery that girls don't have cooties and it's not contagious. Much can be said for a guy who knows that he doesn't have a chance with that particular girl but still tries like fictional character Steve Urkel did with Laura Winslow from the television show Family Matters. However, what about the guy who has absolutely no idea what his chances are with that particular girl of interest. As a guy, there comes a point where it feels like one is completely fooling himself to where the things that he does seem thoughtful and sweet but maybe it's just annoying in her eyes. Inevitably, one tends to think about giving up; BUT as stubborn as we are, giving up is never an option.

Let me share something with you ladies, guys go through quite a bit of self-analysis when we are interested in a girl or that particular girl is interested in us. Initially, we go through so much to figure out our true feelings and ride an emotional rollercoaster as well. Emotions such as innate fear that we may have in which we may never fulfill the expectations you are looking for in that so-called perfect guy. Though it is considered a myth, there is such a thing as perfect and when you find him or when he finds you don't overthink/over analyze the day when you may lose him or her; but rather think about what you both will have gained that puts a smile on both your faces.

In retrospect, the quote that started this thought is a true statement indeed for a guy who truly believes that all you can ever give a woman is two things: your heart and yourself. Thinking about it, that's all any guy can ever give and if that isn't enough for her then she isn't worth pursuing. Without a doubt, there is a guy out there who will truly care and love you with all his heart and soul, which you really don't have to look hard for. In some aspect, he has always been right in front of your face either standing next to you, right beside you, or been with you in spirit and you have been too busy to notice him. In the end, once you have your heart truly opened, then you will finally see what you haven't been seeing all this time and that is the perfect man.

ISN'T THAT CUTE
June 12, 2005

Let me ask you this question, have you ever had a crush on someone or did someone, that you know of, have a crush on you? Of course, we've all had or still have a crush on someone you know, but never told that person. Plus, knowing whether or not that guy or girl has a crush on you can be considered flattering and yet it leaves one in an awkward position. Without a doubt, it's part of what being a human being is all about and no matter how hard you can fight it, it's simply an unavoidable feeling. A feeling that can absolutely overwhelm you to where you can't eat, sleep, and think straight. Although it's an overwhelming feeling, one can control your emotions and not have one's emotions take control over you.

For the most part, each of us may or may not have had a schoolboy/schoolgirl crush on a teacher. From preschool to college, at some point in the past or present, a person has had or may still have that special feeling for him or her. Think back to the good ole' days, if you can, and try to remember that one teacher that made your heart skip a beat. For me personally and every other adolescent guy in Bellview Middle School, it was Ms. Cook, who is probably now married by now. For the life of me, I can't remember what class she taught, but I do know one thing though and that is every guy paid attention to her which can either be a good or bad thing depending on how you look at it.

Having that office crush on a particular co-worker will happen from time to time, which has happened to me on occasion; but I'm keeping my lips sealed on who those specific female co-workers were. Anyways, when it comes to that office crush, a person essentially wants to have a sense of professionalism and not have it affect his or her own work. Most of the time it can be squashed; but when you work together on a semi-daily basis something is bound to happen that one or both people act on his or her feelings. However, it can backfire, and that awkwardness ultimately prevents a smooth working relationship that once was there; now utter silence and constantly avoiding each other is there, which nobody ever wants to happen.

Undeniably, people have crushes on certain celebrities, sports figures, singers, and even political figures if you can believe it. For it can be a perfectly harmless crush that one outgrows through time. Unfortunately, though, a simple crush can turn into an obsession where a so-called "fan" stalks or harasses him or her. We've all heard sad stories such as John Lennon of the Beatles and Rebecca Schaeffer of the one-time popular show My Sister Sam who so called "fan" gunned them down. It's truly unfortunate indeed that there are these types of "fans" that can take a simple crush and escalate to a whole new level. A level to where it is perceived as sick and twisted by other people who know where and when to draw the line.

Working in the asylum for the last 9 years now, I never had "my girls" have a crush on me because they're too busy either hating me or beating me up. It wasn't until the second week of summer camp that I thought a 6-year-old girl had a crush on me. I'm not telling you this to boost my own ego but there are signs such as every time I walk anywhere, she is right behind me, smiling at me, and she always wants to hold hands. To be perfectly honest, it's flattering but I would be the last person to have a crush on because quite frankly I consider myself the biggest goober working there. Listen, if any of you guys can tell me the qualities that would consider me a crush worthy then I'll accept it. Ultimately, whenever I share this bit of news, particularly with females, their basic response is an awwww and these three words...isn't that cute.

YOU AND ME
June 14, 2005

Someone once said, ~We all want to fall in love. Why? Because that experience makes us feel completely alive. Where every sense is heightened, every emotion is magnified, our everyday reality is shattered and we are flying high into the heavens. It may only last a moment, an hour, an afternoon. But that doesn't diminish its value. Because we are left with memories that we treasure for the rest of our lives.~ Nothing is ever really the same after the first time really falls in love because the memories that you take with you with that particular person helps you gain somewhat of a perspective as to who your heart began with years ago and to who you finally now share your heart with for a lifetime.

We've all had people catch us at a moment where a smile, a laugh, or a tear was witnessed and oftentimes it's due to either a past or current memory shared with someone special. It's within that moment of vulnerability, people see how truly of an effect that person had or has on you. Let me give you this particular challenge which is to think of someone that gave you great memories in a past or current relationship and try no to smile. I'll give you time to think...so, how did you do on the challenge? Did it answer any questions that you have been wondering about or did it give you more questions to ask, which is without a doubt what love can undeniably give to every person.

For the most part, the memories that are captured in photos can essentially tell a timeless story that can absolutely touch the human heart. Take a look at your parents/grandparents photo albums and within each picture countless stories can be told behind them. For it's when they reflect back, you can see and feel the love they have for each other. It's a loving bond that you don't see too often due to marriages lasting only a couple years rather than a marriage that has lasted 30 plus years. It can be truly a touching situation for any person to lose their best friend and all he or she has left of that person are the memories, either photos or keepsakes, that in some way keep him or her alive in one's heart.

Let me ask you this question, when it comes to a past or current love, do you keep close to your heart the memories that you cherish for all time or do you keep the memories that metaphorically leave scars that either stay on the surface or run very deep into the core of your heart? For some people, keeping the cherished memories shows that you have a caring heart and a part of you still loves and/or cares for that person. Yet, for others he or she would rather keep the unwanted memories close to one's heart because it shows that past hurts were real; but the strength it gives helps you to continue on the path of life. A path that will lead you to eventual true happiness or sadness where more scars will suffer.

In retrospect, when it comes to love, the memories that a person can attain can either be satisfying or absolutely disappointing. For it really depends on the person who he or she spends time with and if the memories that were shared are worth reliving over and over in one's own mind. Whether or not you find that one person or that one person finds you, the memories that are or will be shared with him or her will be a great story to tell one's own grandkids someday. Ultimately, every person wants to say to that someone special that I want you and me to make a lifetime of memories together.

IT COULD HAPPEN
June 16, 2005

Filipinos are without a doubt some very interesting people, trust I personally know this to be a fact. For its our culture that people seem to enjoy and find interesting. For the food that is either made, cooked, or baked can most definitely fill empty stomachs. The traditional dances that are performed are not only entertaining but also historical. We are a singing people and whether or not it's karaoke, we sing our hearts out. When it comes to acting, my people tend to be on the overly dramatic side, and I know this by watching Filipino movies on occasion even though I have no idea what they are talking about. Now with that said, do you think there will ever be a Filipino as President of the United States. My answer is no and there are several different reasons, but I will focus on the following three below.

It's a well-known fact that my people aren't the most punctual group, so what makes you think a Pinoy President will be on time for any particular events. Events such as his own inauguration to be formally sworn in, his State of the Union Address, and White House Press Conferences are just some of the important events that would cause some concern if he weren't on time. Thinking about it, it would truly be disappointing for the first Filipino President of the United States to be late for his own swearing ceremony. So, my solution to his dilemma is to either schedule important events one hour later or tell him that food will be served afterwards which usually gets any Filipino to come early.

Speaking of food, Cabinet Meetings, as well as White House Dinners would be pretty interesting. Like a true Filipino, whatever kind of meeting it is, food will be brought whether you're hungry or not and you can't refuse the President on what he wants you to bring. Essentially, when it comes to Presidential dinners, I don't think senators, foreign dignitaries, corporate bigwigs, and others will not be able to handle a President that eats with his hands, but that's the Filipino way. As for the dinner itself, we're not the type of people to waste food and have it thrown away; so every person, by order of the President and First Lady, receives "To Go" boxes wrapped in tin foil to take home and eat later.

As many of you know, one of the jobs as President is to pick people for Cabinet positions. Now if he chooses a fellow Pinoy or Pinay as a cabinet member, things will get most definitely interesting. Positions such as secretary of education will get all out of whack because Filipinos are notorious for switching P's with F's or vice versa. As for the issue of gender, a Filipino will have the slip of the tongue and call he a she or him a her, which could cause an international incident if he were to pick a Filipina as Secretary of State. For the secretary of transportation would take all the unused military hummers, paint them yellow and turn them into jeepneys, which will replace taxi cabs. It would make for a better cab ride wouldn't you think?

In retrospect, I don't think America would be ready for a Filipino as President of The United States. The secret service will not be able to handle the President getting their attention by saying pssst... pssst or hoy! Visitors to the White House would have to take off their shoes before entering a Filipino's house, a law that's put into effect by the First Lady. The presidential limo will not be able to get a good parking space with the Hondas, Toyota Celica, and Vans taking up all the room. There will be disputes over in-laws fighting over who gets the Lincoln Bedroom and don't get me started on Air Force One. Ultimately, a Filipino as President is just a fleeting thought, but hey it could happen.

THE WORLD'S GREATEST
June 18, 2005

Someone once said, ~ A father is someone that holds your hand at the fair, makes sure you do what your mother says, holds back your hair when you are sick, brushes that hair when it is tangled because mother is too busy, lets you eat ice cream for breakfast, but only when mother is away, he walks you down the aisle, and tells you everything's gonna be ok.~ It's true indeed that fathers tend to take the proverbial back seat to moms in the so-called parent totem pole. Yet, even though its mothers who give the tender loving care and tend to get much of the attention, it's the fathers who can be given credit where credit is due when one calls for some much needed, as well as, best advice possible.

As little kids, we've all had those petty arguments about whose dad was better and it eventually turned into my dad can beat up your dad scenario, which my dad can beat up all you dads...just kidding or am I? In any case, it's that superhero mentality we placed on him due to the fact that in our young adolescent eyes he was an invincible man like Superman. Though we never saw him leap tall buildings in a single bound or used heat vision that came from his eyes, one practically looked up to him as a role model to one day grow up to be as. Yet, as we got older one started to figure out that he wasn't a superhero, just a regular man; but a man that each and every one of us hopefully still love and respect, nonetheless.

A father expects so much from the oldest son, like myself, who is to one day take care of the family if something unfortunate ever happens to him, which hopefully doesn't occur any time soon. *knock on wood* It's a father's obligation to push and mold a son/sons, whether he's the youngest or oldest, to be the man that he can be proud of. A son that he can see with his own eyes that he has grown up into a fine upstanding man who still has the values and manners ingrained into one's own being. At times, a father will be disappointed and frustrated with a son; but that is to be expected because of course, he too disappointed and frustrated his own father many years ago.

When it comes to a daughter or daughters, a father will absolutely feel overprotective. Can you blame him because he knows that there are young men out there who are just waiting to date his precious little jewel(s). At that point, a father will go into a mode where potential young suitors will have the fear of God into them somewhat like in the movie Bad Boys II; but with not so much of the humoristic side used because he knows what they are thinking. Working in the insane asylum, I honestly feel protective of "my girls" not only as a big brother but also as a father due to the fact that I've seen each of them grow up from little girls to not yet a woman. Essentially, a father will always and forever be seen as daddy's little girl(s) even if she is married and all grown up with her own kids.

In retrospect, there are several different names that a child can call a father such as dad, pop, papi, tatay, old man etc. If you have a father or at least a father figure in your life, tell him that you love him and thank him for all that he has done for you. For if that relationship has been severed years ago, then at least make the effort to try to set things right that were once wronged in the past. Through all the disappointments and mistakes that a father will see, hear and experience from his child, he will always still love you no matter what. Even though he may not be in your life physically he's always in your heart or if you don't want him to be in your life personally, he will always be your father. Ultimately, it takes a certain kind of man to be a father that will always be there for his family and in the end, that man will truly deserve to be called The World's Greatest.

Happy Father's Day Folks!

LOST IN TRANSLATION
June 24, 2005

Someone once said, ~How many languages are there in the world? How about 5 billion! Each of us talks, listens, and thinks in his/her own special language that has been shaped by our culture, experiences, profession, personality, mores and attitude. The chances of us meeting someone who talks the exact same language is pretty remote.~ Trying to talk to a child or a group of children, particularly if they are where I work, is a lot like being a teacher for the Peanuts characters because all "my kids" hear from us is a lot of muffled sounds. Initially, there comes a point where you just look at and say to them, Do you understand the words that are coming out of my mouth?

Working at the asylum, there are essentially three different levels of language that the kids have grown to understand from each of us over the years. The first level is clear and concise verbalization with a little bit of excitement. The second level of language is in the afternoon which is considered choppy but still can be understood verbally and with mild elation. Then there is the third language level near the end of the working day where it basically turns into grunts and pointing, which most or all of the kids at the asylum either do or don't understand. For it's just a matter of them opening their ears wide open, not halfway, and listening to us very, very carefully.

Yet, it's not so much them understanding us, it's really us trying to understand them…. hopefully. Let me ask you this question, try to figure out what a child is trying to say to you when he or she is either way too hyper or is crying to no end. In some ways, it's like trying to decipher a cryptic language that you hopefully can interpret to the best of one's ability in order to rectify his or her particular situation. It's just a matter of calming the child down to get the child or group of children to father himself, herself, or themselves so we can properly assess their situation at hand. Hey, it's a tough job, but somebody has to do it and you thought we just sat around and basically goofed off.

In any case, when it comes to following instructions, such as cleaning up, lining up, washing hands, etc. its seems to us like we're completely speaking a foreign language. Though it's really unclear for me, after 9 years working there, what specific language "my kids" think I'm speaking; but as far as I know it's English. Let me tell you something, it's truly amazing to me, as well as my fellow co-workers when we repeatedly tell the same things over again and without failure, they come back to ask us the same question again. For its that communication barrier that apparently, as a youth program specialist, that we're not in tune with and that is why kids tend to hate us when we continually say no on a seemingly constant basis, which is just now a reflex action that we have grown accustomed to.

In retrospect, working at the asylum you would never expect to have to speak another language seeing that it's a naval base and most of the kids there speak English, which primarily makes our job easier. However, this past Monday a child came into the asylum that made myself and my comrades a little weary at most because you see he spoke fluent Italian. Now, imagine three guys, kinda like the 3 stooges, trying to break the language barrier with an Italian dictionary and sometimes failing miserably at it. In that child's eyes, he must have thought we were complete morons; but the following days we started making progress and by the time this summer is over myself, my fellow co-workers, as well as the kids will be speaking Italian. Ultimately, we were thrown off our game plan on that Monday because everything we tried to say to him or he to us simply was at times lost in translation.

WHO I AM
June 25, 2005

Last Saturday, I watched the new Batman Begins movie and it got me thinking, which I don't necessarily like to do when I'm watching a movie, but hey what can you do. Anyways, in some ways, each of us can be compared to the fictional character Bruce Wayne and his menacing alter ego the caped crusader Batman. Whether or not you are a comic book fan, watched the old school television show, and/or seen all trilogies you know, next to Superman, he is considered an icon. An icon that we've all grown up with and probably, if you are a little boy, dressed up in a costume for Halloween. Essentially, he's two sides of a very complex individual character and if you think about it, we can see a bit of ourselves in him.

In a sense, even though we all aren't rich or fight crime, each of us have two sides to us that people either see or you don't want them to see. It's that proverbial mask that one puts on in order to hide something such as anger and pain, whether it's physical or emotional. For some people can mask it through humor, smiling, or simple sarcasm and initially nobody would know something is wrong. In some aspect, people have seen or felt a small portion of what one tries to keep hidden from people; but inevitably he, she, or they will eventually find out. It's at that point where a person will learn if the people that have stuck by you will continue to stick by you no matter what.

In any case, we all have a Bruce Wayne side to ourselves that represents the sociable aspect of our life. It's that need or want for companionship, whether it's a person or friendly interaction, we all crave to be around people because we don't want to feel left out of the so-called party of life. It's within that party of life that one mingles with people to where we find potential friends and possibly someone special who you either do or don't hit off immediately with. For its basically the confidence we oftentimes exude that attracts people in our direction, which can either work for us or against us depending on the level of confidence. Let me ask you this question, does your confidence make you an enjoyable person to be around?

On the other hand, there is that Batman side which represents our anti-social aspect of our life. Without question, we all want to be left alone when we're surrounded by people in our ear on a seemingly constant basis. For we all hide within our own metaphorical bat cave where we sit and mull over our thoughts. For it is in that deep dark cave of our own minds that we look deep into our heart and soul. A journey that each one of us has gone on and the answers we sometimes are looking for are found or not found at all when reflecting back at our lives then till now. For the most part, it can at times be a depressing journey and yet when we step out of our metaphorical bat cave, we can feel a whole lot better.

In retrospect, there will always be that inner struggle to find out who we truly are as a person and whether or not we will like who we find at the end of our quest. As I said before, we all wear a mask, but the question is, which mask reveals the real you? Is it the mask that people see every day or is it the mask you tend to hide from people? For that particular question will have to be left up to you to figure out because you only know the answer to that. It can either be difficult or easy and it's just a matter of how truly comfortable you are with yourself on the inside, as well as out. There comes a point where you just have to either accept or deny who you really are and not run away from it. In the end, if you are truly honest with yourself and choose the right mask, then you can most definitely say that is who I am.

TO BE CONTINUED
June 29, 2005

For the most part, I'm usually one step ahead of possible topics for a potential Yodaism that may or may not be in the works. It really depends on the subject matter at hand and whether or not it can keep me interested to tackle it head on. Believe me there have been times where I've been in the middle of a possible Yodaism and just completely scrapped it due to lack of inspiration or it didn't make any sense at all. Oftentimes the inspiration can come in an instant and other times it doesn't come for days, but the question can be asked what/who keeps me motivated/inspired to keep doing what I do. In a sense, it has been fun in an intellectual sense in opening my mind, as well as yours, which I do apologize for ahead of time.

One of the sources of inspiration is experiencing life as it happens and each one of us has a front row seat to it. In some aspect, we all go through the same crap on a semi-daily basis, though the situation may be different, it's crap, nonetheless. Such crap that I'm referring to are relationship problems with either your family and your potential or significant other, your job, money, whatever the case may be. You are not alone in this department because life does sometimes stink and it can make your day, in a way, knowing that other people are going through what you are going through as well. It's a unifying commonality that bonds every human being on the planet and it never seems to end for some of us

Believe it or not, all things entertainment such as music, movies and/or television can give that much needed inspiration to get me motivated to write something that can either tickle the funny bone, make you think, or make you shed a tear or two. It's really an unknown what effect it will have until someone emails me telling me he or she really needed to read that due to something one was going through at that particular time. Initially, all it takes is simple words, lines, or quotes and the proverbial gears in my ole noggin start to turn. Let me ask you this question, what song, movie, or television show is your absolute favorite, and do you have a particular line or quote that sticks with you, which keeps you, as a fan, listening for more.

Without a doubt, my job is considered to be one of the best sources of inspiration due to the fact you can always count on kids to give you great material. As I said before, I'm usually one step ahead of possible topics and what I will probably be working on after this, unless another topic piques my interest, is one that is entitled "Just Bring It." It's primarily about seeing and experiencing the violent tendencies kids have, which can be humorous at times depending on the particular child. Anyways, it's those bundles of joy(said with a sarcastic tone) that makes my job interesting each day because quite frankly you never know what "my kids" will say or do when working in the insane asylum where madness runs 24/7.

In retrospect, I never really know if this will be the last Yodaism or not but what keeps me motivated are the responses I get every now and then which I really appreciate. Hopefully you've enjoyed the misspelled and oftentimes confusing rantings of a guy that really needs to have his head examined after working with kids for 9 years now. In any case, I've often wondered if you guys are thinking if I should quit sending them to you OR what possible topic have, I come with this time, and will you like it? In some aspect, every Yodaism is somewhat like a cliffhanger in which you basically ask yourself will there be another one coming? In the end, it's when you read the last words of every Yodaism there are three additional words that you never actually see and read which are...To Be Continued.

JUST BRING IT
July 3, 2005

Keri Smith said, ~Children possess this divine awareness. They are naturally joyous and passionate. They also instinctively know what they want, and they find ways to act on their instincts, doing exactly what they want.~ Working in the asylum, you can most definitely see, hear, and/or experience the best of children; but one can also see, hear, and/or experience the worst. It's one of the aspects of the job that a person will become used to because you get somewhat of a crash course in parenting 101, which can prepare one to have kids someday. Essentially, kids have a violent side and when it comes to "my kids" they can show it to the fullest extent in three ways: verbally, nonverbally, and most of all physically.

Without a doubt, when a child doesn't have one's own way, he or she will give you a verbal attitude to the utmost degree. It's that kind of verbal attitude that if you ever mouthed off to your own parents that way back in the day one would not see tomorrow. Yet, it's not so much the verbal attitude that is tossed at us by the kids but rather the kids towards each other when it pertains to something he or she wants. The insults/threats that come out of these seemingly innocent children towards each other can either make you laugh, completely dumbfounded, embarrassed, or absolutely speechless to the point where you think to yourself or say out loud, Tell me I didn't just hear that particular child say that.

Kids can show you emotion without even saying a word and it's all in their nonverbal body language towards each other and towards us. We've all made that "I want to hurt you" face which is a face that primarily stares a hole right through you or that particular child. It's primarily in that child's eyes that you either see or look for ahead of time so the fight potential fight can be squashed before it ever happens. However, there are times when you just look into a particular child's eyes and see that the lights are on but nobody's home. It's at that very point you turn to your fellow co-workers with a worried look on your face and say to them these words which are be afraid, be very afraid.

Let me tell you something, kids play rough, and they do it to the point where one, the other, or both get hurt. On any given day at the asylum, you will find yourself in the thick of things trying to stop a fight that may or may not have you getting beaten up as well. Personally speaking, there have been times where I, the proverbial peacemaker, have been punched and kicked separating two kids. To be perfectly honest, even though I am considered the peacemaker there are times when being a referee crosses my mind so both of them can learn a valuable lesson. Unfortunately, its a lesson that the kids in the asylum don't at times follow and they continue to go after each other despite the consequences they will suffer in the end.

In retrospect, the violent tendencies that kids have aren't just seen and/or experienced by kids 6 years old and older. For it can also be seen and/or experienced by babies as well, particularly by my own godson who I'm predicting might grow up to be a professional wrestler someday. Several months ago, I was holding him and to be playful I gave him a light headbutt to his forehead. Well, he looked at me, smiled, and then proceeded to give not 1, not 2, but 7 consecutive headbutts to my nose and the side of my head. I can freely admit that I was almost knocked out by my own godson who was laughing the whole time he was doing it. Anyways, there will always be a power struggle of wills between kids and adults to where both sides will look at each other and, in the end, say these three words...JUST BRING IT.

YOU CAN'T SEE ME
July 5, 2005

Ralph Waldo Emerson once said, ~Within man is the soul of the whole, the wise silence, the universal beauty to which every part and particle is usually related, the eternal one. When it breathes through his intellect, it is genius; when it breathes through his will, it is virtue; when it breathes through his affection, it is love.~ When you meet me in person I tend to be man of very few words; but when I get a pencil and paper in my hand I have a lot to say. Essentially, everything that is written and eventually sent to you guys is primarily all seen through my own perspective; yet, in some aspect, you can see yourself going through or have gone through those same things even though your situation may be different.

For the most part, you're metaphorically walking a journey in my shoes even though you aren't physically in them. A journey in which each and every one of you have been on, but the only difference here is that it's partially my life that you are reading. In some weird way, it's like you've been given a key that opens a small door into my own mind and practically reliving certain aspects of my life have happened to me or people around me. It's kind of like that movie Being John Malkovich, though there isn't an actual doorway that leads into someone's mind...at least I hope not. Although enticing as it sounds, it's merely a fantasy and besides reality is much more interesting, as well as entertaining, don't you think?

There comes a point in these Yodaisms, there is a wise silence in which you kind of feel like you're going for an intellectual ride. A ride in a submarine to be exact and you basically start off on the surface then as you eventually descend deeper and deeper into my heart, mind and soul. For one can be amazed at what truths can be discovered when you yourself go on a voyage to find what lies beneath the surface of your own heart, mind, and soul.

Undoubtedly, it can be a scary situation to look deep into your own heart and not drown in all the emotions that you go through when it comes to love. Initially, you have to work through it slowly, and resurface too quickly or you will suffer the bends, which every person has gone through one time or another.

Speaking of love, the affection you have for that particular guy or girl can leave you, at times, trying to get his or her absolute attention. Let me ask you this question, have you done something so out of the ordinary or genuinely nice/sweet to get that particular person's attention and see you? How many times were you unsuccessful and how many times were you successful? Hey, oftentimes the good outweighs the bad and it can also be the other way around; but the unsuccessful times in your life will prepare you for true success in love as seen through your own eyes. Personally speaking, when it comes to the subject of love as seen through my own eyes, it's honest and truthful to the point where it can be perceived as totally irrational.

Someone once said, ~Rationality does not reside in love; it can't and it never will, because love is all about being irrational; doing things for people that most would consider foolish, giving up things and dedicating yourself to the one you love.~ In retrospect, when it comes to the human heart, irrationality happens to everyone including myself and whether or not I'm considered the biggest fool or a fool worth giving a chance for, it's all in how she truly sees me. Anyways, there will be guys, as well as girls, who are unable to look deep into a person's heart and see someone worth loving. In the end, if he or she can't see into that then in the immortal words of WWE Champion John Cena, you simply say to that person face to face...you can't see me.

I HAVE A PLAN
July 7, 2005

Mark Twain once said, ~If I were required to guess off-hand, and without collusion with higher minds, what is the bottom cause of the amazing material and intellectual advancement of the last fifty years, I should guess that it's the modern-born and previously non-existent disposition on the part of men to believe that a new idea can have value.~ Working at the asylum, otherwise known as the Youth Center, you have to be able to think of ideas and oftentimes do it on the spur of the moment. Yet, it's during those times of brainstorming for good ideas, there comes a point where we start formulating other ideas that technically aren't worthy or should I say ready to be implemented...yet.

One such idea that usually comes up around the ole' water cooler, so to speak, is the "take your child/children and as many other kids home with you" plan. Its a simple plan really in which a parent arrives to pick up his or her kid/kids and when they ask for their whereabouts, we direct them to where he, she, or they are. BUT, before doing that we greet them, schmooze with them, and then spring the plan into action. It's that particular plan we do on a seemingly regular basis and to be perfectly honest it has never really worked to perfection. Essentially, its just a matter of time until a parent actually says yes and then the other plans, we have in store will come to fruition...hopefully.

Another idea that needs to be tweaked around a bit more before it is perfected is the youth center child exchange program where you send several of our children of the corn to another youth center and we receive their children of the corn. It's a month-long program where we see if a change in environment helps them or a particular child and if there is any that the youth center keeps that child or children; somewhat like a trade in baseball only there is no money involved. Again, it's one of those ideas that needs to be tweaked to where documents need to be signed, parents' permission must be needed, several lawyers present, and probably a judge to see if things are legit; but other than that it could possibly work.

When it comes to the mother of all ideas, this one takes the cake in a manner of speaking and all we need is the parents', as well as the military's permission. The plan, called Operation Oompa Loompa, is to ship every asylum child to Iraq, drop them off, and there they will be given a mission to find Osama Bin Laden. You basically have to know the mindset and mentality of the kids at the asylum because quite frankly they scare us at times and there are particular few that we actually fear for our life. I'm not kidding. Think about it, they can blend in, the Taliban won't suspect a thing, and let me tell you something "my kids" will fight dirty and when I mean dirty..lets just say one of the kids at the asylum is a biter.

In retrospect, when it comes to thinking up crazy ideas that deal with the kids of the insane asylum, we can be a little twisted at times; but we do love all of them…well some of them. In any case, the ideas we do come up with are usually put into two categories which are: Ready To Go and the other is Are You Out Of Your Mind? Most of the ideas we do come up with on our own or as a group sometimes fall into the Are You Out Of Your Mind category due to the fact we might either get fired, sued, or arrested. Thankfully, nobody has gotten fired, sued, or arrested…not that I know of anyway. In the end, when or if you ever get the chance to work at the asylum be fairly warned when you hear the following words coming out of our mouths which are I have a plan.

HERE WE GO AGAIN
July 9, 2005

Dennis "The Menace", a once popular television show from one's childhood, but not such a popular name given to a Hurricane. As many who live in the Gulf Coast know that even the possibility of a Hurricane can change one's plans in an instant. For those who are old pros at this, so to speak, can oftentimes reassure the ones who are going through it for the first-time tips and pointers to get through the storm. Essentially, it's just a matter of keeping a positive outlook even though past storms such as Ivan "The Terrible" didn't give people of the Gulf Coast a reason to smile. For the most part, keeping yourself distracted and/or busy can hopefully get one through the storm we're going to experience.

Undoubtedly, it can be tough to distract yourself mentally from the carnage that is going on all around you. With all the sounds and debris that one hears, especially at night, can make a person jump and/or a little edgy to the point where paranoia can set in. The tapping of branches on a window, or the howling winds pushing against one's house can make you somewhat feel as if you're in a movie somewhat like The Wizard of Oz; but what Dorothy went through in the movies can't compare to what people are going to go through in real life. Nobody can fathom the thoughts and feelings a person goes through and yet one can fairly have a good idea what those thoughts and feelings are.

There comes a point when the Hurricane is over and one witnesses the aftermath of what it has done, you now find yourself without the necessities that you are so used to. Necessities such as hot water, air conditioning, and most of all electricity, which in all honesty one wants back on when Hurricane Dennis is over. However, it doesn't work that way and one has to endure what everybody else has to endure for the period of time the storm lasts and how fast the power companies can save the day, in a manner of speaking, by turning on the power quickly. Let me tell you something, a person will actually do the happy dance when the power cuts on and my dance is somewhat uncoordinated, as well as a little dorky.

Keeping yourself entertained can be a tough task indeed. One can most definitely have cabin fever being stuck in one place for quite a bit of time with people who you generally get along with but will knock out without hesitation if one spent more time with them. In any case, doing activities such as listening to CD's, playing board games, writing, drawing, and playing ping pong can help with the boredom of not having power, as well as not going postal on your friends or family. Fortunately, my brother's ping pong table arrived a couple of days ago, so he and I know what we are doing when the power goes out, plus it gives a chance to see who wins the title of champ for ping pong supremacy.

In retrospect, it's all in God's hands now as the storm gets stronger and stronger by the minute. Who knows what the Gulf Coast will be in store for as Hurricane Dennis slowly but surely approaches. Keeping my sense of humor though all this, here is the plan just in case I land on your doorstep or in your tree. First off, check to see if I'm ok and If I am, take me to the airport or put me in a taxi for home, depending on how far Dennis throws me. If I'm not ok, take me to the hospital, then to the airport or taxi. Anyways, as of right now this is my last Yodaism, but I'll be back when the power is on. So, in the end, the people of the Gulf Coast batten down the hatches and all there is left to say is here we go again.

BEST OF YOU
July 12, 2005

Someone once said, ~The power of love can bring a grown man to his knees in tears, can bring an icy woman to melt down. The power of love can bring light to the darkest night and soothe the beast. The power of love is binding and can make the world tight and make the weak strong.~ One of the greatest mysteries about love is that it brings out qualities in a person who either hasn't shown them at all or hasn't shown at all due one's social status and has someone fall for you. Every person has those unique qualities within themselves that make us absolutely special and attractive in our very own way; but it takes that one truly special someone to bring it completely out in the open for him or her to see.

Yet, it can sometimes be intimidating to a person to strike up a conversation with someone who he or she is attracted to at first. Why is that? For the most part its due to our own fear; but the question is what are we so afraid of in the first place that we don't risk walking up to someone that you don't know or telling someone that you've known for quite some time that you would like to go out with that person or better case scenario tell that person you love him or her. For the most part, its better to risk your heart and show the qualities that will gradually reveal themselves through time, which will show how truly special one is, than to never have taken the risk and kept hidden the qualities from that guy or girl. In the long run, the greatest reward that is ever exchanged is two human hearts that are in love with each other.

Essentially, it's within those qualities that you tend to act and feel like a kid again. For it can bring someone new life, new energy, as well as a new attitude when you are around or with that certain someone. Who among us hasn't acted hyperactive that one is perceived as a complete dork to where we probably smacked our heads against something without even looking. Hey, its that adrenaline rush that gets you pumped up and makes you do wacky things. It's kind of like how Tom Cruise is when he is around Katie Holmes or when her name is mentioned to him; but it's a little more toned down than that and whether or not you jump on top of furniture is all really up to you.

Let me ask you this question, what qualities make you a prime candidate to be a great boyfriend or girlfriend for someone out there who wants to be or maybe looking to be attached? Oftentimes with that question being asked so many times its somewhat like going through a job interview, only its not your qualifications that he or she is actually looking at. For its what you can fully give with your own heart added with that the trustworthiness, honesty, affection you continually give to that person, plus dependability, openness of mind, a pinch of humor and what you have is an equation to a formula of an outstanding relationship tat exceeds far beyond you and that particular person's expectations.

In retrospect, its not so much the qualities that you bring to the table, so to speak, that make you worthy of that guy or girl's heart or attention. As a matter of fact, it's the way you use the qualities that keeps a smile on his or her face through the good times and through the bad times as well. We all have our own special qualities about ourselves; but the ones that we don't see are seen by people or by that one person who sees who you truly are deep inside your heart. Without a doubt, love has that special power to change people, change lives, and change the way he or she feels about love. In the end, when it comes to love it's the ties that bind one heart to another and what the eyes of a person's heart will see through time is the best of you.

LIKE FATHER, LIKE SON
July 14, 2005

Someone once said, ~Friends are like television. Some are like PBS and always asking for money. Others are like the news, with sad tales to tell everyday, some are like that one station with the foreign language; you don't understand a word of it but you listen and watch anyway. And then there are the ones like the commercials, always changing, ever-so-annoying and only seem to be there when you are bored. But every once and a while you meet someone who's like a really good movie of the week or that one tv show you hardly ever get to see anymore because you're so busy. My point is hold on to the friends you care about and since we don't have a remote control to mute someone or just change the channel, pick your friends carefully.~

Let me ask you this question, how long have you known your partner(s)in crime who you can basically consider them as your brothers and/or sisters. You know, the funny thing about the friends that we run with either from childhood or over the years is that we oftentimes don't see them as the people they are now or vice versa. It's that underlying truth we all can try to hide from or escape from but can't. Without a doubt, they change on the outside, but they don't change who they are on the inside. If you think about it, they can become an important and/or successful person in a particular field and despite that fact we still treat them as if they never made it big for themselves.

Each and every one of us will and forever be a part of a group of friends that has their own individuality. It's those same friends that you can fight with on a semi-daily basis and yet can keep that bond of friendship intact...most of the time. Essentially, they can give you the biggest headaches by doing things that can totally embarrass you to the point where you just can't believe that you are associated with them. On the other hand, they can give you that much needed source of entertainment when life just gets a little bit boring. Hey, you may not be able to see eye to eye with them at times, but the one thing you know for sure is that when you need a friend or friends you can count on to be there for you and you for them.

As with life, friends move on and have their own lives to lead either on a professional or personal level; but one will try to stay in contact. For its nice to read an email or get a phone call from a friend that you haven't seen or talked to in years and find out what they have been up to lately. In some cases, it can be a sad situation to hear that he or she has fallen on hard times and is just trying to keep one's head above water. However, it can be a great situation indeed to run into a friend who you haven't seen in years and find out they got married and have a family of his or her own. It can be news that either does or doesn't surprise you, which really depends on the friend in question.

Several weeks ago, on a field trip at a bowling alley, I ran into 2 old friends and a former co-worker that I haven't seen in quite some time. Though I have seen his wife out and about, her husband, my old running buddy from the asylum days I found out, was on leave from Iraq for about 2 weeks. For the most part, he hadn't changed a bit because he was the same goofball, but one thing had changed he was a father, which I could never grasp that concept around my head. You see during his asylum days he was the biggest hyperactive kid working there and now he has 2 kids of his own. From what I could see his son looked like his mom. but the hyperactivity that I saw was exactly just like his dear old dad and in the end, what I thought was true saying indeed which was like father, like son.

I CAN FIX THAT
July 17, 2005

Leo Buscaglia once said, ~The heart is the place where we live our passions. Its is frail and easily broken, but wonderfully resilient. There is no point in trying to deceive the heart. It depends upon our honesty for its survival.~ Every person has had or will have their own heart broken which you can't avoid. Essentially, nobody is immune to it and the experience can leave a person confused, angry, sorrowful, as well as depressed. It's those experiences that we don't feel, but we do due to the fact that we can't help those who our own heart likes, is attracted to, or falls in love with. For its when we are left holding or looking at our broken but beating heart, we slowly try to fix the pieces that are left back together again.

In some aspect, the times one suffers heartbreak are the times when you tend to look back and contemplate what you either could, should, would have done or vice versa. For when we are left alone with our thoughts, a person can initially fix the problem and hopefully not let what happened happen ever again. However, one can't really ever know if the mistakes of the past will be fixed and come back to haunt a person in the present when you are forging a potential or in a current relationship. Undeniably, one can beat himself or herself up mentally for not fixing or going overboard in fixing the problem such as communicating by way of sharing one's feelings, listening to that person, or showing affection.

For the most part, women can't go back and fix the times they cried themselves to sleep because of a particular guy. A guy that either didn't notice her, didn't give her much attention, gave her too much attention, or spurned her to the point where he swears off all guys for good. For it can take either a guy who is a real jerk or someone that is really special to have a woman become absolutely emotional over. Think about these real hard ladies, how many times have you truly cried your heart out over a guy that meant something special to you that you thought he could actually be the one, but in the end turned out to be the wrong one who completely wasted your time and patience?

Without a doubt, both men and women can't go back and fix the things they said wrong at the right time or the wrong things at the wrong time. In a sense, every time we stick our foot in our mouths a metaphorical truck smashes into our heart, as well as that particular person leaving behind tire tread marks that leave a lasting impression. Depending on how many times we say the wrong things can either greatly lessen or add to one's chances of having that truck miss one's heart or completely smash it to pieces. Oftentimes, the wrong things that are said can actually help in fixing a potential/significant relationship or end one which inevitably needed some much-needed truth even though he, she, or both don't want to accept it.

In retrospect, the human heart is like a house that needs to be fixed after suffering some damage to it. The foundation of one's own heart can no longer support the many times it has been broken. For its one's own heart that will sink lower and lower with every heartbreak until he or she can't see or feel the beat of it any longer. Unquestionably, the tears that one sheds can represent a leaky roof that has been leaking for a said period of time. Whether or not its tears of joy, anger, or sadness it's only that person who really knows for sure. In the end, someone truly special will come along who will gently lift your head up by the chin, look into your eyes, wipe those tears away and simply say I can fix that.

THAT THING CALLED LOVE
July 18, 2005

Someone once said, ~When you love somebody, you should follow your heart. Sometimes when you are with the person you love the most, you feel confused. You don't know who you are or what you want but that is totally understandable. Its is natural to let go of a part of yourself to be with that person but the important part is that you don't lose your own identity in the process.~ The chances each and every one of us take when we follow our heart can have a person sometimes not know where and who it is leading us to. For the most part, our own heart can lead us in many different ways emotionally and physically to the point where we can become absolutely lost, as well as, confused.

It can truly be a confusing feeling when you have absolutely no idea what to do or say as you decide to follow your heart towards someone that may or may not feel the same way. For its a physical journey towards possible happiness a person also takes an additional journey of the emotional kind. It's within that emotional journey where a person goes through many different reasons, in one's head, as to why he or she gives one a chance of a lifetime, in a manner of speaking. Yet, even though we have many different reasons for that particular person to be given a chance, in the back of one's mind there are many different reasons that he or she may have for you not to be given the chance, which you do unfortunately take into consideration.

Without a doubt, every person has been in this type of situation and if you haven't...just wait you will be. When one is following his or her heart, you basically are letting go of a part of yourself that you try to keep in control. A part of yourself that can have you not remember your own name and it's that part that you try to keep in control. A part of yourself in which you can be scared to be yourself because quite frankly you can say or do some stupid things at the wrong time or right time depending on the atmosphere you both are in. To be perfectly honest, there is no telling how much of yourself you are letting go and once its let go you may not be able to get it back again.

However, it's that type of situation that has made some people turn their back on the word itself and any possibility of ever coming his or her way. In their own experiences, following one's heart is a journey they have taken so many times before and so many times afterwards he or she has ended up with a broken heart. If you think about it, you can lose your own identity in the process of an unmistakable smile that can most definitely brighten a room or bring a smile to other people's faces. You can also lose that one-of-a-kind sense of humor which can make a person's day that much more enjoyable. Whatever you may lose, it inevitably takes someone special to give a simple word such as love to bring back meaning and feeling behind it for you.

In retrospect, every person has a story to tell in which they followed their own heart to be with someone that they truly cared for. Stories that either had one traveling great distances, in competition with another guy or girl, etc. Whether there is a happy ending is that particular person's story to tell and share. For the question can be asked, why do we continue to follow our heart when there is a great risk of heartbreak. My answer is you have nothing to lose by trying and at least they know how you feel, which does count for something. In the end, its that thing called love that makes each of us insane, foolish, cynical, frustrated, say things that make no sense at all; but you know what I wouldn't have it any other way, how about you?

OLD SCHOOL
July 21, 2005

As kids we've all heard our parents, grandparents and every other grownup go on with their rants and raves of how easy modern life is for us. In a sense, we did actually have it easy unlike them who supposedly traveled to school each day by walking through a snowy blizzard, rainy monsoon, or whatever catastrophic weather conditions they endured. Now that I'm reaching thirty, I'm now realizing that these kids today are really living the good life and to tell you the truth I wish I could be a kid again. Essentially, with every generation there is one phrase that gets metaphorically passed down from adult to child and solidifies you as a grownup which is back in my day.

Let me tell you something, back in my day there weren't any emotional teen angst television shows like the O.C. that the younger generation is crazy about now. Growing up, it was about action shows like the A-Team where you had endless amounts of bullets flying everywhere and yet nobody got hit or hurt. We had 6 Million Dollar Man, Battlestar Galactica, Buck Rogers, and Knight Rider, in which a guy drove a pimped out black trans am which talked and made wisecracks. But most of all we had Miami Vice where two cool looking guys wore expensive trendy looking clothes and drove fast cars. This was the show that gave guys the idea that wearing pastel colors and wearing shoes with no socks was a cool fashion statement.

Back in my day, we didn't have cell phones to carry around and different ringtones to figure out who was calling you. Initially, you had to be at home if you were expecting an important phone call or kept calling that person to get in touch with him or her. Half the time, it was a complete surprise who called you and also as a kid, there were no buttons to push due to the fact you had to physically dial the numbers yourself. For it was a prehistoric device called a rotary phone that you had to dial with your finger in either a clockwise or counterclockwise motion. For its hard to fathom for the kids of today how we were able to manage and to be perfectly honest, we managed just fine.

Game systems such as PSP, PS2, XBox, Gamecube, SNES, NES were nothing if you first didn't have an Atari system. You weren't a real gamer unless you were holding a black plastic joystick with only one button that made your whole hand cramp up unlike today's controllers that have so many buttons to figure out and only made your thumbs hurt. When it came to beating games there were no cheat codes or strategy guides, we just used patience and our own instincts to beat the game. Speaking of games, PACMAN was THE game to have and to tell you the truth I was the master at it. Who knew that a little yellow face who chased ghost and was being chased by ghosts around a maze would be hours of fun for a kid like me.

Looking back, there was no internet and the way to look up the information you needed were in actual books. When it came to watching television there were no remote controls and what you actually had to do was get up and physically change the channel yourself. When it came to burning CD's, we simply had a double cassette player that would record our favorite songs on cassettes and play such classics as Jessie's Girl by Rick Springfield, Celebration by Kool and the Gang, 867-5309 by Tommy Tutone, and Billy Jean by Michael Jackson. In the end, if you remembered certain shows, a time without cell phones, and had calluses because of the Atari controller then my friend you are most definitely old school.

LIFE IS GOOD
July 24, 2005

Elias Canetti once said ~Adults find pleasure in deceiving a child. They consider it necessary, but they also enjoy it. Then children very quickly figure it out and then practice deception themselves.~ Working in the asylum, deception is sometimes the name of the game when you deal with kids who physically, mentally, and emotionally break you down. It's that kind of deception where you pay them back, in a fun way of course, for all the times they don't listen to anything you say, don't tell the truth, and most definitely throw temper tantrums when they don't get their way. It's basically sweet retribution for basically losing your mind to where you and/or your fellow co-workers plan or do something on the fly merely for entertainment purposes.

One such thing that isn't considered deception but rather something fun to do is announcing to the kids that you've changed your name. Although you haven't legally done it, there comes a point where having your name said repeatedly over and over again can make you lose your mind. It's like a child repeating "momma" and without a doubt moms have a limit to the number of times it is said and so do we. Anyways, it's that proverbial go to name that usually is well thought out or picked out at the spur of the moment. Personally speaking, I've changed my name several different times over the years and the name that I've told "my kids" to call me this time is Mr. Ziloolee.

In any case, there comes a point where we will find it necessary to deceive them and simply say three words that come in handy when a question is asked which are I don't know. It's primarily a reflex response that comes second nature when you don't have an answer to give to them. Although we may know the answer, we don't want them to know that we know because if they know that we know they will hound us to tell them, and you know that is opening up a pandora's box that should be left closed. When you work with kids, especially 6- & 7-year-olds, you come across questions that tend to be left to the parents to answer such as the one pertaining to the circle of life and that is all that I am saying.

There comes a point where...I don't want to say we lie but rather give something that seems fairly close to the truth. One such example is canceling a field trip due to unforeseen circumstances and when the kids ask where they are going the response is Disneyland. Let me tell you something, no matter how many times I give that response "my kids" actually think they're going until they find out where they are really going. Another example would be giving something as a reward for doing what we ask them to do; yet we don't specifically say what the reward is and its usually a well-deserved handshake for a job well done. Hey, it only seems fair as they tend to stretch the truth a bit, so why can't we?

Last Friday, two co-workers and I deceived the entire 6 & 7 group by merely making up a whole scenario where something happened, and every child was involved somehow. We interrogated every child on what they knew, and the funny thing is that they had no idea what they knew and started thinking. What made it even more hilarious was we gave them names that were supposedly involved like Toucan Sam, Snap, Crackle, and Pop, and many more that I can't think of right now. Ultimately, it was a success deception even though three kids did cry, but they laughed afterwards and were part of the lynch mob that beat me up. In the end, when you've successfully had a bunch of 6- & 7-year-olds get punk'd, you simply say to yourself or to your co-workers around you that life is good.

SOMEBODY LIKE YOU
July 27, 2005

Someone once said, ~Opening your heart to someone isn't always the easiest thing to do, but giving your heart to someone is about a million times harder.~ If you think about it, it's within our own heart that we can feel safe, secure, and where you can truly be yourself. Undeniably, there will always be someone looking into your heart and wishing that he or she sees himself or herself in there. It's an aspect of love that will never change because it's a place that guys and/or girls want to be and only one person can fit perfectly in it, so to speak. For its the attention one receives that can inevitably leave one trying to read what's really true or false in that person's own heart.

Without a doubt, a person can have doubts as to why there is a certain amount of attention directed in one's way which can have you closely guard your heart. It's those doubts that can lead you to ask three questions or more depending on how big they are and reasons, if any, as to why you're not throwing caution to the wind. Those three questions that a person can ask himself or herself are: 1.) Does that person have an interest in me because I am easily approachable? 2.) Is that person only interested in me because of how I look? 3.) Is that person interested in me for me and not with me just for ulterior motives? Whatever question you have, trust your own instincts and the answers will reveal themselves in due time.

Yet, in the meantime, you simply go with the flow, even the feelings you have for that particular person may be unclear to understand. However, it's not being able to understand that makes you a better person which is witnessed by the smile on his or her face. A smile that can represent sunshine beaming down on you to where you actually feel that person's love. It's like a feeling of a warm embrace which can tell you there's nothing in this world or the next that you can't handle. Unfortunately, before ever reaching that point of euphoria one must take a few steps back in order to figure out if you both are heading in the right direction or merely going around in circles.

Essentially, what it comes down to is trust; the trust that you have within yourself to take that so-called leap of faith for love and completely let go of your heart, which is a gamble that every person has taken. In some aspect, its like jumping out of an airplane without a parachute and the only thing that will prevent you from ending up six feet under is having him or her be your cushion and safely catch you. To be perfectly honest, there is no telling if one will get badly hurt or not because quite frankly nobody can ever prepare for how big of an impact you may or may not suffer. Let me ask you this question, is there someone who you have been thinking about lately that you would gladly jump out of an airplane without a parachute on?

Roberta Sage Hamilton said, ~In our deepest moments of struggle, frustration, fear, and confusion, we are being called upon to reach in and touch our hearts. Then, we will know what to do, what to say, how to be. What is right is always in our deepest heart of hearts. It is from the deepest part of our hearts that we are capable of reaching out and touching another human being. It is, after all, one heart touching another heart.~ In retrospect, there will be someone who you'll want to fully open and ultimately give your love and heart to. In the end, if that person accepts your loving heart, you can thank him or her by simply saying it's somebody like you that I can now finally feel the way I do and song that somewhat reflects this thought is Somebody Like You by Keith Urban.

WELCOME BACK(3X)
July 30, 2005

Ada Louise Huxtable said, ~Summer is the time where one sheds one's tensions with one's clothes and the right kind of day is jeweled balm for the battered spirit. A few of those days and you can become drunk with the belief that all's right with the world.~ Essentially, a person has to sober up to the fact that all things must come to an end and unfortunately, though you want it to keep going, the end of summer is at hand. Let me ask you this question, when you look back at it, were your experiences memorable or would you rather forget them altogether? Personally speaking, my experiences of summer 2005 have been filled with absolute craziness and looking back there are things that I miss, as well as not miss.

One of the things that I will miss is antagonizing/messing with all the kids who have antagonized/messed with us. Unlike past summers, this particular one has been absolutely for the simple reason that there is a cast of characters that truly make us laugh and have made our job very interesting. There is one child that we love to antagonize/mess with due to his name which is associated with a chipmunk's cartoon character and whenever we call him, we say the other two names too. As wrong as those sounds, it's quite entertaining even though we may be responsible for him going into therapy later down the road. For the most part, it's all in good fun and the kids know that...at least I hope they know that.

Another thing that I will miss is the field trips that we don't have to pay for ourselves and some that are just free to go to. It's just one of the perks that my fellow co-workers and I have enjoyed going over the past years and won't take for granted. Field trips that have involved food, such as pizza, have been particularly enjoyable because the tab is picked up by the asylum, which isn't a bad thing, it's a good thing. With this summer being such a scorcher, going to the swimming pool has never been so good although one can get sick from swimming 2 or 3 times a week. It's simply one of the drawbacks of going to the swimming pool, but hey it's part of the job that you have to deal with.

Without a doubt, the things that I will not miss are things that can get under a person's skin when it involves kids, especially 6- & 7-year-olds. Having the same question asked over and over again such as: 1.) When is snack time? 2.) Where are we going? 3.) Are we there yet? It's those kinds of questions that will make you go into a dark room to either cry, break things or go completely insane. When it's not the questions, it's dealing with the constant complaining, whining, and fighting that happens every day by the same usual suspects, who seemingly enjoy what they do. It's evident on the smiles on their faces and to be perfectly honest we might testify against them after we first join the witness protection program and I'm not kidding on this.

In retrospect, I have loved...liked...spending time with "my kids" over the summer, BUT they have to go back to school. Can I get an Amen from the parents and to those that work with kids! Let me tell you something: I need another vacation from my working summer vacation. I'm ending this thought with a greeting to a teacher named Mr. Kotter from a popular television show from the 70's that introduced to us a young actor named John Travolta a.k.a Vinny Barbarino, who is now a meg movie star. So, in the end, with a sigh of relief/disappointment I say see you later to summer 2005 and to the returning school year I simply say welcome back, welcome back, welcome back.

GREATEST ADVENTURE OF ALL
August 3, 2005

D.H. Lawrence said, ~One must learn to love, and go through a good deal of suffering to get to it, like any knight of the grail, and the journey is always towards the other, not away from it... To love you have to learn to understand the other, more that she understands herself, and to submit to her understanding of you. It's damnably difficult and painful, but it is the only thing which endures.~ Every woman has that proverbial fantasy of her knight in shining armor sweeping her off her feet and riding off into the sunset. Unfortunately, in this day and age it's rare for a woman to meet a so-called "knight" who exemplifies what she is looking for. It's at that point, metaphorically speaking, a guy will go on a so-called quest to prove that her "knight" is absolutely real.

Without a doubt, for a guy, it's that first initial step on his quest that will lead him on a journey, in which the first few steps are viewed as easy due to the fact that one's spirits are high. It's one's own heart that is guiding him towards his destination and not knowing what will happen shows that he is willing to prove his worth to her no matter what the consequences may be in the end. What I mean by this is actually doing the following things that some, most, or all guys should do, which are: 1.) Know her deep inside, not just in the physical sense; 2.) Hear every thought that she is expressing from deep within her heart and soul; 3.) See every dream she wants to come true; and 4.) Be her wings when she wants to fly high and reach for those dreams. If that's not what love is about, then tell me what is.

Yet, there comes a point within a guy's quest where he thinks that maybe he's getting in over his head about what he is doing. It's that seed of initial doubt that turns into a subsequent obstacle which grows with every fear that creeps into one's mind. Undeniably, whether its guys or girls, we all have that basic fear of being hurt emotionally either from not having one's feelings returned and/or being lied to or cheated on. Essentially, it will have a person push a possibly great relationship away because of being hurt in the past or not wanting to show the real you, which that person might not like. That fear will inevitably turn into confusion to where one's self confidence is totally shot and the quest, which one was so fired up for in the beginning, is now either temporarily or permanently put on hold.

In some aspect, love is like falling in quicksand which is considered an obstacle that a "knight" may face on his quest. When a guy or a girl follows his or her heart, it seems as if everything is going, but then one thing goes wrong, and you fall in. It's that one thing that seemingly turns into a million other wrong things. For its one's own instincts that tell you to get out but the more you try and the harder you try the deeper you sink. You sink until you come to a point where you basically can't move, you can't speak, you can't scream, and finally you can't breathe. Let me ask you this question, have you ever felt this way at times or are are feeling this right now

Johnny Depp's character Don Juan Demarco said, ~Have you ever met a woman who inspires you to love? Until your every sense is filled with her? You inhale her. You taste her. You see your unborn children in her eyes and know that your heart has at last found a home. Your life begins with her, and without her it must surely end.~ For some guys they have found a woman like that and yet others are still searching. Ultimately, there are guys who say that the journey/quest to meet that someone special is an adventure in itself, which might be true. BUT getting to know her on a deeper, more intimate level by looking into her eyes and seeing what she sees, in my opinion, is the greatest adventure of all.

THE JOURNEY CONTINUES
August 7, 2005

Someone once said, ~The path of a relationship with true love is like a trip together down an old dirt path in the woods. Sometimes it'll be beautiful and easy, other times it will be a rough walk with its ups and downs, turns and twists. But when you're out of the woods and you look back, you are glad the journey took place, and in all, you are glad you and your special someone took it together. But the journey is not over, you only have just begun. So don't lose faith, keep on walking. If your love is true, the path you two take will never end.~ Before ever taking that trip, both guys and girls do some "exploring" in which they try to find out if both share any common goals or interests, which makes love and relationship that much more interesting.

Who likes to have a good laugh? I know I do, and it's a common interest that basically everybody shares. Yet, when it comes to the funny guys and girls walk seemingly different paths as to what is funny and what is just plain stupid. Let me give you an example, every red-blooded guy loves the three stooges, who are in my opinion comedic geniuses. It's their brand of comedy that we find hilarious and to be perfectly honest we've probably tried a move or two on each other at one time or another growing up. Girls, on the other hand, watch the three stooges, scratch their heads, and wonder why squeezing a guy's head in a vice or hitting someone over the head with a wrench can be considered funny? My answer is…it just is and there is no logical explanation either.

Without a doubt, it's hard enough meeting someone that you can truly click with, but it's even harder to meet someone who enjoys the same things you do. For a woman, the path that they are walking on will always lead to guys that supposedly are interested in the same things that they are into. It's no secret that there are guys who will say anything to get their proverbial foot in the door and work their so-called mojo as they continue to tell lie after lie of how they both are so alike. Essentially, it's that smoothness that is exuded which can shield her vision to the point where he is leading her off the beaten path, in a manner of speaking, and getting her metaphorically lost in her own emotions.

For most single women, having kids is a goal that they would like to have someday; but it's just a matter of finding the right guy who truly has that same goal and will walk that path with you side by side. But the question can be asked, how do you know if that particular guy wants to have kids or is just saying that just to be with you? What it comes down to in looking for that husband/father-to-be is that genuine vibe between guy and child/children, which can't be faked. Its that rare vibe in which a guy will hold a baby or step into a room and an immediate connection is witnessed by how he interacts with him, her, or them. Trust me ladies, that guy is out there somewhere and when you meet him don't let him go.

Someone said, ~As you journey through life, choose your destinations well, but do not hurry there. Wander the back roads and forgotten paths. Seek out new voices, strange sights, and ideas foreign to your own. Such things are riches for the soul.~ In retrospect, there is no rush to get to one's intended destination; for its the journey that will enlighten us as we meet new people, discover common interests/goals, and make any kind of impact on their lives, as well as ours. In some aspect, we're kind of like the fictional character Kwai Chang Caine as we travel on our individual paths to true love. Ultimately, for some, their travels have ended and a new path with that someone special has opened up; but for others who are still traveling like myself, the journey continues.

ANALYZE THAT
August 9, 2005

Erich Fromm once said, ~We all dream, we don't understand our dreams, yet we act as if nothing strange goes on in our sleep minds, strange at least by comparison with the logical purposeful doing of our minds when we are awake.~ Did you know we have at least 5 dreams a night when we sleep? For the dreams we have can be weird, strange, and downright confusing, but they can have a deep hidden meaning to them. Without a doubt, the experiences we all go through on a day-to-day basis will manifest itself into something symbolic and it's up to us to figure out what they mean. Let me ask you this question, do you remember dreams when you wake up and do you dream in color or in black and white?

Essentially, every person has had that somewhat embarrassing dream of being in his or her birthday suit at the one place you never want to be seen in the buff, which is in a school and/or college classroom. It's one of those situations in life or in your dreams that you don't want to be in or have happened to you unless you are an exhibitionist and love the attention, but I digress. In any case, when it comes to finding yourself in that type of vulnerable position the reasons may be something such as anxiety over performing an important speech, which can make anybody freak out. Personally speaking, I can talk to a room full of kids with no problems but put me in front of a room full of my own peers. I'll freeze up, as well, as go completely blank out at what I'm about to say.

For the most part, a person's job and those associated with that particular job will oftentimes affect what goes on in one's own dream world. Working in the asylum for the last 9 years, my dreams have been invaded by "my kids" who somehow find a way to beat me up even when I'm away from work and trying to sleep off the day I had with them. I'm doomed to live my waking and dreaming life as a proverbial punching bag, but you know what I'm their punching bag because I know they at least care about me and I with them. Primarily, it's a no win situation for those working with kids as you can't get away from them physically because they will find you no matter where you go and you can't get away from them mentally due to the fact, they make you absolutely crazy.

Undeniably, each and every one of us has had that same ongoing dream that you could never quite figure out. It's a dream where you are the main character and a cast of characters who you either know or don't know lead you on an adventure without leaving the comfort of your own bed. Although you may feel comfortable, the type of dream you're having will most definitely leave one drained to the point where it's hard to function and keep focus on the tasks at hand the next day. For the question can be asked, when was the last time you had a dream like this and who was part of it that when you woke up the next day you had to share it with him, her, or them?

For the past several months, I've had this same ongoing dream involving the one thing I hate the most in this world and that is clowns. I can remember it vividly, it's in color, and it starts off with me walking around in an airport and all of a sudden, I start running after something or someone. That something or someone has a sheep under his or her arm, which isn't that weird until I look back a whole bunch of clowns are chasing after me with nerf bats. So, I try to lose them by going through doors, gates, bathrooms and inevitably the chase turns into something you would see in a Scooby Doo cartoon. My dream ends when I catch someone or something with the sheep under his or her arm; but I get tackled by the clowns, a dog pile ensues and that's when I wake up. In the end, analyze that and help me figure out what it all means.

OH, GROW UP

August 11, 2005

Emmanuel Kant once said, ~Enlightenment is man's emergence from his self imposed immaturity. Immaturity is the inability to use one's understanding without guidance from another. This immaturity is self imposed when its cause lies not in the lack of understanding but in the lack of resolve and courage to use your own understanding.~ Undeniably, love is something that most people take for granted and of the reasons why there is such an immature attitude towards its is due to the fact that a person has some unresolved issues or feelings to work through. Whether or not those issues or feelings will be resolved, there will always be a big question mark above that potential or significant relationship.

Essentially, relationships are hard enough without a person doing something totally immature and embarrassing that it hurts him or her in the end. Let me ask you this question, have you ever seen, heard, or been in a relationship where a person's immature side is shown by doing something such as flirting with someone right in front of one's own eyes, which can most definitely wound a person's heart. For its loving one person and yet selfishly wanting to be with other people, which every person felt at one time or another. Primarily, love is strong, driving, and very powerful, which makes it such a deadly force. A force that can build you up and break you down either gradually or in an instant.

For the questions can be asked, who is more immature or mature when it comes to love and relationships, guys or girls? To be perfectly honest, I am not going to answer those questions for fear I might get beat up if I do. For the most part, guys and girls can be immature when put into the position of opening their heart to someone that he or she truly feels comfortable being himself or herself with. It's that capacity to actually let someone get to know us not just on the outside but on the inside which can be considered scary. So scary in fact, that feelings are put on hold and distance is put in between for the simple reason that if we fall in love with that person, we fall hard and...if we ever fall in love again, we may fall harder and quite possibly not survive the impact, so to speak.

Unfortunately, immaturity can be taken to that proverbial next level which most of you have either been in, done, or witnessed to some extent. It's that immaturity where a person makes that particular guy or girl jealous by hooking up or messing around with someone else just to make him or her mad. It's that deluded perception that if one messes with that person emotionally then possibly, he or she will realize that they are better off together than apart, which can backfire on him or her. Initially, playing head games is considered the most immature thing guys, as well as girls can do to each other, which shows that he and/or she isn't ready to be in a real relationship just yet.

In retrospect, it's all about commitment and being mature enough to handle the emotions and everything else that comes with being in a lasting relationship. A person has to keep in mind that there are two people in the relationship rather than just one and without a doubt, tough times will be encountered to where it will test how far both the guy and/or girl are willing to go. When it comes to committing yourself to someone a person has to get away from the "all about me" mode and get into the "all about we" mode. For it's the mutual trust, respect, honesty, understanding, and love for each other that flourish and in turn the relationship flourishes. In the end, if you are with someone who is emotionally mature and committed to you congrats; but for those that tend to keep meeting the emotionally immature and are commitment phobic, three words come to mind for them, oh grow up!

FATHER OF THE BRIDE
August 13, 2005

George Banks aka Steve Martin said, ~You fathers will understand. You have a little girl. An adorable little girl who looks up to you and adores you in a way you could never have imagined. I remember how her little hand used to fit inside mine. Then comes the day when she wants to get her ears pierced, and wants you to drop her off a block before the movie theater. From that moment on you're in a constant panic. You worry about her meeting the wrong kind of guy, the kind of guy who only wants one thing, and you know exactly what that one thing is, because it's the same thing you wanted when you were their age. Then, you stop worrying about her meeting the wrong guy, and you worry about her meeting the right guy. That's the greatest fear of all, because, then you lose her.~

Working in the asylum, a person pretty much gets a front row seat on the discipline and raising of other people's kids. When it comes to kids, especially girls, you feel obligated to keep a close eye on them due to the fact you consider them like your very own daughters. It's an aspect of the job that one will never be able to outgrow because you spend time getting to know them not only on a professional level, but also on a personal level as well. For the most part, through time they consider you a father figure and to be perfectly honest it's a role I gladly accept. It's that so-called father-daughter bond/relationship that grows over the years as you witness then grow up in stages from little girl, to teenager, and into a woman.

Like any father would with his own daughter(s), he would be concerned with how she/they dance. Essentially, there are three words that are generally used on a seemingly constant basis when it comes to "my girls" style of dancing and those three words are just wrong. One day they're on your feet as you dance with them and the next thing you know you turn around and they're dancing like they're in a 50 Cent video, which in my eyes is unsuitable at their young age. It can be an embarrassing and uncomfortable feeling seeing them do that type of dancing to where you seriously contemplate telling them or making a rule, they can't dance like that until you're over the age of 18.

When it comes to dating, it's usually treated the same with dancing only the age limit is hiked up tremendously. There have been many one-on-one conversations with my 6 & 7 girls that they are not dating at all or they're not dating till they are 45 years old. It's basically one of the things that you can't help but do because you want them to stay at that age and not lose their innocence. For the most part, we can't be personally for them when they suffer their first broken heart from a guy that she really liked. We can't be there when they pass their driving test and see the smile on their face being witnessed by mom and/or dad. Though, I may not be there for those specific events in life, I'm there for the events in between and that's ok with me.

In retrospect, all guys will always have those initial fears instilled into our being when we have a daughter or daughters of our own. It's that scary realization that she will someday meet the right guy and you will no longer be her/their # 1 guy, but rather her # 2 guys. For me personally, I will put the fear of God into each and every boy that stands in front of my door asking to take my daughter(s) kind of like how Martin Lawrence and Will Smith did it in Bad Boys 2. Ultimately, she will meet the right guy and hopefully it's a guy that will treat her with the respect and dignity that is deserved for my daughter(s). In the end, it's when the preacher asks who gives this woman to this man I will reluctantly but proudly say…I do, the father of the bride.

MUST BE DOING SOMETHING RIGHT
August 16, 2005

Billy Currington said, ~A woman is a mystery. A man can't just understand. Sometimes all it takes to please her is the touch of your hand. At other times you gotta take it slow, and hold her all night long. Heaven knows there's so many ways, a man can go wrong.~ As a guy, one of the greatest mysteries that is most oftentimes difficult to solve and/or unlock, other than love itself, is a woman's love. For the most part, every guy has been or still is trying figure out a woman's love due to the fact that some, not all, don't take the time to get to know them and what's in their heart. In my honest opinion, a woman's love is boundless, extends far beyond words can ever say, and reaches within the deepest parts of her heart and soul.

Let me ask you this question ladies, was there ever a guy in your life, past or present, who you thought could not only feel but also see the love you had/have for him? Essentially, it's that guy who got "it" and knew what the love of a woman meant to him. It didn't mean just in the physical sense, but rather in emotional, spiritual, and intellectual sense as well. For he saw or sees the true beauty behind the everyday and simple things in life when shared in your company. Such beauties in life, which can pretty much be taken for granted at times, are things like a sunrise, a sunset, watching falling rain, a nice quiet dinner for two, sleeping under the stars, and/or dancing barefoot on the beach together under a moonlit starry night.

In some aspect, a woman's love can be tender and warm as she gives you hugs and kisses that have meaning behind it. It can be flirtatious as she acts shy around you knowing that there is nothing for her to be shy about. It can be friendly as she hits you as hard as she can in the arm and then apologizes for it...sometimes. It can be compassionate as she pours her heart and soul out to you in which tears may or may not be shed. It can be dark and scary as you say or do the wrong things which can cause you to risk serious mental and/or physical injury of some sort. But without question, a woman's love can be absolutely priceless due to the fact that no amount of money can, could, or will never match the love she has for you.

Without a doubt, there is truth in a woman's love and in that truth she reveals to a guy a comfort factor. It's within that truth there comes a creative atmosphere where reason and rational thinking get thrown out the window, in a manner of speaking, and is replaced with something strong, yet fragile which is trust. For the question can be asked, how long does it take for you to be so comfortable around a particular guy that you start to reveal something about yourself? Inevitably, its putting faith in something such as trust where truth and love can either do two things for a woman and they are: 1) bring her sadness and emptiness or 2.) bring her happiness and contentment.

Andrea Dworkin once said, ~For a woman, love is defined as her willingness to submit to her own annihilation...The proof of love is that she is willing to be destroyed by the one whom she loves, for his sake. For the woman, love is always self-sacrifice, the sacrifice of identity, will, and bodily integrity, in order to fulfill and redeem the masculinity of her lover.~ In retrospect, the love of a good woman can be found by guys and it's just a matter of truly opening their eyes to finally see who they have in front of them. In the end, every guy comes to a point where he thinks to himself as he looks at his girlfriend/wife and says I don't know what I did to deserve you in my life, but whatever it is I must be doing something right.

HERE'S YOUR SIGN
August 19, 2005

Someone once said, ~The problem with America is stupidity, now I'm not saying there should be capital punishment for stupidity, but why don't we just take the safety labels off everything let the problem solve itself.~ If you think about it, there people you meet along your journey of life who have a good head on their shoulders and seem quite intelligent. Yet, there are some people who you meet that really need to get their head examined due to the fact they do or say things without being properly supervised. On any given day you could be standing next to or talking with someone who has the capacity to do or say something stupid; but the decision of when and where to show that particular act of stupidity rests on his or her capable shoulders.

Let me ask you this question, what was the most stupidest thing you ever saw, heard, done, or were involved in that when you look back you asked this simple question, why? For the most part, it seems harmless enough until one realizes there are consequences for his or her actions and the so-called "victims" suffer from it. In some ways, it's like catching a disease which there is no known cure for because quite frankly nobody is immune to random acts of minor or major stupidity. Yet, is it stupidity, a lack of common sense, or is it both that can get the better of a person? Case in point, there are a lot of stupid criminals, and one particular criminal robbed a taco bell but instead of fleeing the scene he placed an order to go. The criminal was arrested at the scene.

Whether or not any of us wants to admit it we all go through spurts of stupidity every now and then. A perfect example is when we're in an elevator, there is a tendency to jump the gun, so to speak, and get off on the wrong floor. For its that realization that lets the people know of your minor act of stupidity, which they help to rectify your situation by letting you back in... sometimes. It's that split second decision to play it off as if you did get on the right floor that can be considered great acting on your part. Unfortunately, our own pride and stubbornness can get the better of us to the point where we will not allow ourselves to get back on knowing they have already been amused at your faux pas.

Without a doubt, love and stupidity go perfectly together like a peanut butter and jelly sandwich. People can't help but be stupid when you're with, near, or around someone you like or in with. For some unknown reason, the rational parts of our brain simply shut off and the irrational part turns on and takes control which is oftentimes never a good thing. For the question can be asked, were you ever in a past or in a present relationship where you saw and/or experienced total and utter stupidity either on your part or by that particular person. Undeniably, love can be or get stupid with the person you're with; but if you can't be stupid with the one you love, then who can you be stupid with?

Working in the asylum for the past 9 years, I've seen, heard, been involved in, or done acts of stupidity that would make you either shake your head or roll on the floor laughing. One such act of stupidity involved my co-workers, a dare, a laundromat dryer, and me getting into that dryer. Needless to say, I almost broke my neck doing something that seemed fun at the time, but it would have suffered some serious injury such as not being able to walk. Anyways, acts of sheer stupidity will always happen, that's why we have the Darwin Awards to keep us informed and entertained all year round. In the end, comedian Bill Engvall said it best when he suggested that stupid people should wear signs and if you ever come across a stupid person, you can simply walk up to him or her and say here's your sign.

AIN'T AS GOOD AS I ONCE WAS
August 25, 2005

Robert Louis Stevenson once said, ~We advance in years somewhat in the manner of an invading army in a barren land; the age that we have reached, as the saying goes, we but hold with an outpost, and still keep open communication with the extreme rear and first beginnings of the march.~ Essentially, a person can't stop birthdays from coming no matter how many times you try to deny it, the fact is they will happen. Women, more so than guys, oftentimes don't acknowledge the concept of actual age to the age they really are and that is why lying about one's age is so widely done which just seems pointless to do. In some aspect, it's like an ongoing battle against the biggest adversary we all face sooner or later...Father Time.

Without a doubt, there are certain things from our childhood that a person just can't do no matter how hard he or she tries to do it. Certain things such as playing with a hula hoop and making it stay around your own waist which looks easy enough when you see kids do it. Plus, you did it as a kid, so it will probably come naturally to you and you'll show these young kids how its done. Unfortunately, for some adults we tend to lose that ability and we tend to overthink what we're doing wrong to the point where you can totally be frustrated. So frustrated in fact, one will throw the hula hoop away because you can't seem to master it whereas kids will go for it and succeed, which kinda hurts one's own pride as we are defeated by a simple round object

You would think getting out of bed would be considered something that a person would easily get the hang of. Think about it, when we were younger we would generally spring out of bed, do our morning routine, put our clothes on, eat breakfast, get your stuff ready and then face whatever battles that one was going to face or be put in front of us. Now as an adult there isn't much of a spring anymore when one gets out of bed but rather more of a fall out of bed roll type maneuver, which every person will do eventually. In all honesty it will happen to you in an instant with absolutely no warning as Father Time sneaks past security and metaphorically grabs your youth like a well trained Navy Seal.

Working in the asylum, a person's back will never be the same again as kids will ambush you from time to time which is never a good feeling. Whether it's a forward assault or from behind, they have that no mercy, take no prisoners attitude. When it comes to bending down it can be truly an event in and of itself, as you will find yourself tying shoes, picking up, pushing, or pulling stuff which one will truly feel later or the next day depending on how many times you do it. Let me tell you something, when I first started there I walked normally and could bend down with ease; but after 9 years there I have developed the old man walk and whenever I bend down I make the old man noise/grunt, which is at times very amusing to the kids of the asylum.

Today is my 28th birthday and when you reach a certain age such as 28, there are just some things you are never meant to do or try to attempt again. A couple of nights ago, I was entertaining my Godson and I had the bright idea of doing a breakdance move somewhat like WWE wrestler Booker T's spin-a-roonie. On a side note, my break dance moves were good/ok back in the day, nothing that really wows the crowd, but I digress. To make a long story short, I ended up hurting my lower back. For the next five minutes I was on the floor looking up at the ceiling and telling myself never to do that again. In the end, when it comes to trying to perform break dance moves now, pardon my grammar when I say I ain't as good as I once was and its a song by Toby Keith that everybody can literally or figuratively relate to.

THAT'S MY BOY
August 28, 2005

Essentially, there are moments in life where a person looks back and smiles. For its that particular moment of one's life that brought you joy, happiness, plus some tears as well, and it was something to be proud of. Proud not in an arrogant/egotistical way, but proud in a sense that you were glad you experienced and/or witnessed something special live and in living color, so to speak. Let me ask you this question, was there a particular moment in life in which you were proud to have gone through your experiences even though the situation was a tough/difficult task to accomplish? For the most part, there are many things to be proud of in our lives, but the main three things are the following: graduation, marriage, and kids.

Without a doubt, graduation is a momentous occasion for students who worked their butt for 4 years or more. Whether it's high school or college, a person gave their blood, sweat, as well as tears plus a lot of sleepless nights to stand on stage with their classmates and friends to finally receive that all important document. A document that seemed out of reach in the beginning, but as you metaphorically climbed that tough academic ladder, it slowly but surely was within reach. In some aspect, the weight of the world on one's shoulders will be lifted off and a much deserving big sigh of relief is given once that diploma hits your hand. For the question can be asked, how did it feel for you as you finally walked across the stage and were handed that proverbial holy grail?

When it comes to marriage, it's a proud moment between you and your significant other to be in. However, the road to the altar can have several or many setbacks such as a bride/groom having substantial doubts or cold feet. Other factors that could complicate things are the potential in-laws not getting along and most definitely the planning of the wedding itself can cause friction.

Friction not only between families but also between the bride and groom to the point that the wedding is either postponed or called off entirely. Every person has either been in, been involved or witnessed that particular situation, but if you have an excellent support system backing you up they will hopefully be well.. For when you look at each other from the aisle and face to face at the altar, everything beforehand is inconsequential.

Working in the asylum for the past 9 years, there have been many proud moments I've experienced, and one particular proud moment happened on the day of my birthday as "my kids" and fellow co-workers showed me some love. If you are wondering, yes, I did work on my birthday and I'm glad I did because I would have missed out on something special, but I digress. In any case, a card was made by "my kids" and every kid plus staff signed it. I also received individual cards with gifts that they made especially for me which I gave them a big bear hug in return. The gift giving ended with two birthday cakes that were from a friend/ fellow co-worker and one from one of "my kids", which gave me a warm feeling inside knowing they cared...it was that or indigestion...just kidding.;)

In retrospect, every person will experience proud moments and those proud moments will be overshadowed by other proud moments. When it comes to looking back at those moments in your life are they worthy to be rated or do they stand alone as one moment you will always remember? For it was about a week ago, when I realized I wasn't able to do a particular break dance move for the expressed purpose of entertaining my Godson and in the process, I hurt my lower back. Well, it was on that same night I was able to see my Godson walk a few steps, which was an extremely proud moment for me. In the end, even though I wasn't his dad, I felt like a proud dad and at that particular moment these three words came out of my mouth... that's my boy!

MAY GOD BE WITH YOU
September 1, 2005

Without a doubt, there have been times that in the middle of writing a Yodaism, I've stopped to do a new one. Monday afternoon I was halfway done with a Yodaism entitled "In A Heartbeat" when Hurricane Katrina hit the Gulf Coast, mainly Mississippi, Louisiana, and Alabama, plus Southern Florida. Watching the news for the past 4 days has been one of absolute disbelief as you witness homes either underwater or destroyed completely and it got me thinking. Yet, what makes this catastrophe so unbelievable is that an entire city, New Orleans, is no longer livable. For many of its surviving citizens they have only but the clothes on their backs and treasure keepsakes, if any, that were taken that meant so much to certain people.

It's so surreal to know that parts of Alabama are without power, probably for several weeks or months. New Orleans, a place where people and many college students like to party, as well as celebrate Mardi Gras, is now considered a ghost town. If you think about it, Mardi Gras is a staple of Americana just like apple pie and the late Peter Jennings. It's not only New Orleans, but parts of Mississippi such as Biloxi where millions of people have trekked to have a good time and hopefully win some money instead of losing it. It's basically the luxuries, which deal with fun and entertainment, will be temporarily or permanently closed. Let me ask you this question, when was the last time you stopped by the French Quarter of New Orleans and the Casinos/Shows of Biloxi?

Unfortunately, when a natural disaster such as a Hurricane occur, the so-called Mr. Hydes tends to reveal themselves in people when desperate times call for desperate measures. Measures such as breaking into stores and stealing/looting food and/or clothing. It's a sad situation indeed as you witness seemingly levelheaded, law-abiding citizens run rampant in a city, such as New Orleans, where fighting has been reported and shots are being fired at helicopters who are trying to save/help these people. It's understandable that sometimes you have to fight to survive but doing something such as firing at people who are trying to help is just plain stupid. For the question can be asked, would you resort to looting and/or stealing if you were in their shoes?

For there is a saying that goes with every dark cloud there is a silver lining. Essentially, the silver lining to this is that all across the United States from New York, Texas, California, etc. and even overseas are wanting to help. Help by providing some much-needed services like getting food, clothing, blankets, and even electricity to people as best they can. You hear good Samaritans opening up their homes and even baseball stadiums such as the Houston Astrodome to refugees. People helping people out of the goodness of their own heart who genuinely want to give or do something to help their fellow Americans and neighbors who have nothing to go back to.

In retrospect, for a person who lives in Pensacola, Florida you feel happy that it missed you; but at the same time, you feel guilty. Guilty because you see so much suffering there and yet we're watching all this in the comfort of our air-conditioned homes, sleeping in our warm beds, with plenty of food to eat. Initially, it makes you sick to your stomach to see people go through this as you find yourself crying but also you find yourself wanting to help in some way, shape or form. Where I work, we're talking about putting together a drive to give food, blankets, clothes, and letters of encouragement to the people from the kids, which will hopefully lift many spirits. In the end, to all the refugees we will keep you in our prayers and may God be with you.

OH, WHAT A RUSH
September 5, 2005

Someone once asked, ~Did you ever put your arms out and spin really fast? Well, that's what love is like. It makes our heart race, it turns the world upside down...but if you're not careful, if you don't keep your eyes on something still, you can lose your balance...you can't see that you're about to fall.~ When it comes to love, it can throw us, as well as our own heart, in a proverbial tailspin in which you can be literally or figuratively disoriented to the point where you have no idea what just happened. For its a slow and/or sudden fall that one will or has experienced and you will never see it coming until the very last second, unless you are paying close attention, which nobody rarely ever does; but that is what makes it so exciting.

Let me ask you this question, have you ever seen someone or been that someone who had one's world totally spinning that it actually made your head hurt because of a guy/girl who you have known for a while or just met for the first time? It can oftentimes be a comical situation as you either find yourself or a friend totally messed up mentally in the head and the only thing one can do is laugh. Laugh, not in a side splitting, out loud kind of way; but in a frustrated, about to lose one's mind way, which probably every person has gone through a time or two or three. For its simply a part of love or falling in love as a person will never get used to it due, in part, of a certain high you feel, without the use of illegal substances of course.

For the most part, when we experience the so-called high from being spun around by that particular person our instincts initially tell us to close our eyes, which is not a really good thing to do. There are many different reasons for not closing your eyes, but the one main reason is that it will give you a chance to focus and focus on that particular someone of interest. In some aspect, that person you are focusing on, in some way, will stabilize you so that you don't lose your concentration. In other words, he or she is that person who hopefully will keep you balanced when things around you are spinning out of control in one's personal, professional, and/or family life, which is what every person is looking for and wants in a relationship.

Without a doubt, there have been many strong relationships that ended up broken because the guy, girl, or both didn't catch that person and inevitably the trust, which was there, is now gone. If you think about it, the sometimes-dizzying relationship, if there was one to begin with, can spin both people so hard that they both have no idea where they have ended up. Initially, it can be a difficult task indeed to pick yourself back up when the impact of the fall leaves you absolutely numb in your heart and soul. However, it really depends on how hard one falls which determines if a person bounces back immediately or takes several weeks/months/years to recover from someone who you thought truly made the world stop spinning on its axis just for you.

In retrospect, each of us has met or will meet that person who makes our heart race faster, slower and sometimes both at the same time. It's that one person when you touch his or her hand you somehow know that he or she is the one for you to spend the rest of your days with. It's when you start to feel everything around you just go out of control, being in that person's warm embrace makes everything around stand still or merely seem insignificant. It's that person who somehow knows when a kind word or gesture is needed when you have been going through some trials and tribulations. In the end, when you do finally meet this person, who has metaphorically stopped your world from spinning, and you look into his or her eyes as he or she holds you up so that you won't fall, you will say either in your head or out loud oh, what a rush.

ANYTHING HELPS
September 9, 2005

Buddha once said, ~Let us rise up and be thankful, for is we didn't learn a lot today, at least we learned a little, and if we didn't learn a little, at least we didn't get sick, and if we got sick, at least we didn't die; so let us all be thankful.~ Hurricane Katrina devastated many lives by leaving people homeless, sick, separated from, looking and grieving for lost family members. Yet, within the ashes of tragedy there comes the joys of hope as domestic, as well as foreign aid pour in without even an afterthought. With so much that many families have lost from Hurricane Katrina, it's nice to see on the news and in person people contributing whether it's digging deep into one's pockets or giving their free time to help in any way.

All across the United States, people are opening their homes to complete strangers even though they themselves may or may not have the space for them to reside. Personally speaking, a friend/co-worker of mine has 17 displaced family members, from her husband's side that lived in New Orleans, living with them, which truly has been a test in patience for her, her family, and the family dog as well. However, the funny thing that was mentioned to me was that it's humorous to see the sibling interaction between her husband and his family, which shows her husband in a different life. Anyways, in the whole scheme of things, it doesn't matter because people are not just opening their homes but also their hearts as well.

With so many displaced families, there are also many displaced family pets, which are considered part of the family who practically grew up with the family. Without a doubt, it's a difficult decision indeed to leave one's pet(s) behind to weather the storm, so to speak, by themselves. For some, most, or all pet owners they consider their pets as one of their children, an absolute best friend, or both. Fortunately, many pets did amazingly survive and were eventually reunited with their family, which some saw rescued on the news or other television programs such as Oprah. Let me ask you this question, if the choice had to be made by you and you alone, would you leave your pet(s) behind when or if a Hurricane is approaching?

Unquestionably, the entertainment industry and sports entertainment is doing all it can to help in any way by donating thousands/millions of dollars to bring food, water, medical help, and clothes to those that need it. New Orleans' own Harry Connick Jr. almost lost his voice trying to give a voice to his hometown and its people. Due to this, he has agreed to be honorary chair of Habitat for Humanity's "Operation Home Delivery" and in his own words Connick said, "It is hard to sit in silence, to watch one's youth wash away," said Connick. "Everything that I have professionally, and so much of what I have personally, is because of this great, fair city … to see it being drowned like this is almost unbearable."

As said before, many displaced families are located all across the United Stated getting good meals to eat, clothes to wear, and a warm bed to sleep in. One of the places is in my backyard of Pensacola, Florida, mainly Naval Air Station Pensacola. Over Labor Day weekend, myself and my best friend had the opportunity to open the asylum to the displaced families, mainly the kids. Let me tell you something, it's a humbling experience to see those kids happy and playing together with seemingly insignificant toys such as a hula hoop or frisbee, which "my kids" tend to fight over on a constant basis. Ultimately, I am thankful for the several hours I spent with those kids because it was truly an eye-opening experience. So, I urge you to do whatever you can to contribute in any way because in the end, anything helps.

WHERE WERE YOU

September 11, 2005

Someone once said, ~Tragedy carries a tremendous power within it. Power to cause grief, power to cause mourning, power to cause sadness, and power to cause upset. It also carries power to cause closeness, power to cause reflection, and power to cause change. A tragedy can become a positive reference or a negative reference depending on the meaning one attaches to it. the more powerful the tragedy, the more powerful the reference. Understand the tragedy and its potential power to change you for the better.~ For my generation, September 11th, 2001 will and forever be ingrained in our minds as it is compared to the attack on Pearl Harbor on December 7th, 1941, which was an attack that changed all our lives from that moment on.

For the name Osama Bin Laden will be synonymous with 9/11 and each one of us would gladly beat the living shiznit out of him for it. For a line would form stretching around the world and its probably a line people wouldn't mind waiting hours on end for. However, there is an uncertainty as to whether or not he is alive due to his health as he is/was using a dialysis machine. How hard is it to look for a guy who is 6'6, lanky, sickly, ugly and transporting a dialysis machine wherever he goes? For its truly amazing that a man, who looks as if Italian actor Roberto Benigni and British actor Rowan Atkinson aka Mr. Bean had a child, can wield/has wielded some major stroke among people that would absolutely die at his word.

Essentially, there have been many questions people have asked, but the main question is why? Why did it happen and why did it happen to New York? For some, most, or all people believe that America considered itself invincible and nobody could touch us in our backyard, so to speak, but they were wrong. In one split second, everyone's seemingly normal Tuesday morning was turned upside down as each one of us experienced confusion, disbelief, shock, anger, as well as, retribution all in one balled up emotion. So why did it happen to New York and not to California, Illinois, Missouri, Nevada, etc.? In my opinion, New York is considered the hub where every person of every walk of life comes to visit and quite possibly make it big.

Without a doubt, the glue that held New York together during its time of crisis just went by one name...Rudy. Despite what he did as mayor before 9/11 was wiped clean and after the senseless tragedy he would be known as the man who stepped up and took control of a perilous situation. He literally became the voice of New York as many New Yorkers looked to him for information and most importantly comforting words, which would hopefully heal in mind, body, and soul. In his very own words that evening Rudy Giuliani said, ~It's going to be a very difficult time. I don't think we yet know the pain we're going to feel. But the thing we have to focus on now is getting the city through this and surviving and being stronger for it. New York is still here.~

In retrospect, it has been 4 years since that tragedy and yet its seems it was only yesterday that it happened. For the many people who valiantly risked their lives, such as the NYPD and NYFD, we will always keep them in our hearts and never forget what they did for those people. For the husbands, wives, brothers, sisters, cousins, friends, and co-workers, they have a piece missing from their heart but eventually they've moved on as best they can. On that day, I was getting ready for class while I was watching the Today show and as I turned around that's when the second plane hit the Tower. In the end, I ask this question where you when the world stopped turning on that September day?.

GOTTA LOVE IT
September 13, 2005

I am a child of the 80's and undeniably, it was the best time of my life bar none. For a person like myself, who grew up in the 80's, it was a decade that defined my childhood and hopefully yours as well. Let me ask you this question, when it comes to the 80's, do you feel somewhat or absolutely nostalgic that it brings a smile to your face when you think back, or do you cringe? For it was a fun, interesting, and sometimes embarrassing time indeed as music as well as fashion ruled the era, but what ruled in my honest opinion back in the day was television. So, boys and girls, I ask you to join me as I reflect back on when television was television and please buckle up for your own safety.

When it comes to educational shows back in the day, nothing compared to shows such as Reading Rainbow and Schoolhouse Rock, which had 3-minute series called Conjunction Junction and I'm Just A Bill. For the question can be asked and to be honest, how many of you still remember the songs and can you sing it? As kids, Sesame Street and Mr. Roger's Neighborhood taught us some very valuable life lessons such as friendship and helping our neighbors. However, the show that made science fun and exciting, which paved the way for Bill Nye the Science Guy was Mr. Wizard's World. Mr. Wizard, Don Herbert, was kind of the MacGyver of science and many people were truly influenced by him.

Without a doubt, family and/or family related shows were part of our upbringing as they taught us about serious issues such as sex, drugs, drinking, racism, etc. Such shows were Growing Pains, the Facts of Life, Punky Brewster, Full House, Cosby Show, Different Strokes, Gimme A Break, Webster, etc. Who could forget memorable characters such as Alf, Alex P. Keaton from Family Ties, Buddy from Charles in Charge, Mork(Robin Williams) from Mork and Mindy, The Fonz from Happy Days, Ricky Stratton from Silver Spoons, and many more. BUT the one show that probably had a huge impact on every kid's life was the Wonder years with Winnie and Kevin. In some aspect, you saw yourself in either Winnie or Kevin or Paul unless you were Wayne in which I raise my fist to you...just kidding.

Essentially, when you talk about the 80's you have to talk about the cartoons of that time. Cartoons that defined the era such as G.I. Joe where we learned something new at the end of every show and knowing that particular bit of information was half the battle. Transformer, not the updated version one, but the original where more than meets the eye and the names actually went with the character. Let me tell you something, when Optimus Prime died by the hands of Megatron I cried, but I digress. I grew up on shows like Silverhawks, GoBots, Voltron, He-Man, She-Ra, and yes even Jem and The Holograms. Yet THE cartoon for me was and still is Thundercats with the most coolest way to call for help by way of the sword of omens which is....THUNDER! THUNDER! THUNDER! THUNDERCATS! HOOOOOOOOOOOOOO!!!!

In retrospect, as these people who show up on our television screens grow up such as Fred Savage(Kevin) and Danica McKellar(Winnie), who are practically the same age as me. In a sense, you can say each of us grew up together with that particular show and actors as well. For the most part, when you talk with people about certain cartoons of the past one will occasionally get some blank stares as they have no idea what you are talking about. However, shows like Inhumanoids, Pole Position, Wuzzles, Turbo Teen, C.O.P.S, Shirt Tales, Galaxy High, Dungeons and Dragons, Mysterious Cities Of Gold, Jayce and The Wheeled Warriors, B.O.T.SMaster, Captain N: The Game Master, were all real. In the end, these shows were awesome and all I have to say about 80's television is, you gotta love it.

MY 2 CENTS
September 16, 2005

There comes a point, every now and then, when a person gets on and stands on that proverbial soapbox to speak his or her mind, which is what I am doing right now. You see, there are certain things in life that gets you either annoyed, frustrated, confused, and/or leaves you speechless to the point that it irritates you like an itch that you aren't able to reach and scratch. We've all had those moments where we bit our tongue and wanted to say something but it wasn't the appropriate time to say it. Let me ask you this question, is there anything that has been bugging you to no end that you just want to get off your chest and simply vent it out? Personally speaking, there have been many things that have bugged me, but the three main things are: The Tooth Fairy, MTV's Laguna Beach, and Kanye West.

The Tooth Fairy, otherwise known as mom and dad, would secretly exchange their child's/children's tooth/teeth for money. In some aspect, it would be a stealthy maneuver that a Navy Seal team would do in the silence under the cover of night. Now with that said, I'm asking this question, when did receiving money for teeth from the so-called "Tooth Fairy" get so profitable? For the past several months, I've been hearing news from "my kids" that they received mucho dinero for their teeth. Teeth that are apparently worth 5, 10, and/or 20 dollars all together or individually, which absolutely blows my mind. Back in my day, depending on how many teeth I lost, I received either a quarter, 50 cents, or a dollar and you know what, I felt jipped and a little jealous.

When it comes to television, MTV is a worldwide phenomenon that aired old shows like The Real World and Punk'd. However, the one show that bugs me to no end is the show Laguna Beach for the simple reason that every person on that show, with the exception of LC aka Lauren, are morons. This particular show proves that relationships don't work, that guys such as Jason and Stephen or complete douche bags, and girls such as Kristin are why guys are so messed up in the head, which is how Stephen is. Speaking of Stephen, he should choose Lauren plain and simple. This show is a trainwreck and I don't want to watch it, but you can't help but watch. Essentially, you lose two things when you watch this show which are brain cells and intelligence.

Kanye West, the man of the hour, so to speak, and the guy I eventually would voice my opinions about. For the most part, the man is an accomplished singer and he, like the rest of America, has the freedom/right to voice his opinions. Yet, when it came to Hurricane Katrina he used that opportunity to speak his mind at the one place that he shouldn't have and that was at a television special to help the victims of Katrina. Several alternatives could be sending out a press release or writing/singing a song about it but to do it in a controversial way while raising money for the Gulf Coast was totally out of line. Whether his opinions were right or wrong, his decision to express himself on the air to millions of people watching was wrong and should have been handled differently.

In retrospect, that's just the tip of the iceberg folks as there are many other things that get my goat in a manner of speaking. Such things are certain celebrities who get caught with someone other than their wife/girlfriend. Case in point, Hugh Grant and Jude Law are total boneheads who messed it all up with Elizabeth Hurley and Sienna Miller, who are two absolutely beautiful ladies. As a guy, I would just like to go up to both of them and slap them upside the head. Other things are slow drivers, people who don't do the old school ways of disciplining their kids, and spamming. Ultimately, I feel better now that I've gotten that off my chest as I put my 2 cents on what's been going on and I hope you have something to get off your chest as well.

NEVER GIVE UP
September 18, 2005

Someone once said, ~You live and you breathe and then you die. In between, if you're lucky, you fall in love. Some loves stay forever, others are lost in only a day. But it's still there, underneath all the hurt and pride and years. If it's true love, it's never forgotten. So when someone says they're in love, don't tell them they can't be. Don't say they're too young, or it's too soon. Love knows no age or length of time. Love is a feeling, deep in your heart, that squeezes you tight and makes you never want to let it go.~ In some aspect, love/and/or falling in love is like the cycle of life as a person goes through 3 stages with someone that he or she is interested in. A cycle in which one will experience or has experienced birth, growth, and most certainly death.

Without a doubt, love can be born in an instant but true love is gradual through time. It sometimes takes that one initial feeling to make you feel alive to the point where you're acting like a teenager again and have those teenage, related tendencies. Such tendencies are physical play fighting, insulting each other in a sometimes non hurtful way, writing each other notes, and most certainly of all waiting to see who hangs up the phone first. For its that proverbial breath of life that fills not only your heart and soul but also that person's heart and soul as well. Let me ask you this question, have you already met that someone special who truly gave you fresh eyes to see him/her/each other somewhat like a newborn baby seeing the world for the very first time.

As a person grows, so does in fact the love that two people share who keep working at it and not just give up easily when the relationship either gets too complicated, frustrating, confusing, and/or drama filled. Essentially, its that growing mature love that works and survives the immaturity that some, most, or all guy/

girls experience when in a potential and/or significant relationship. One such immaturity that oftentimes has been the downfall of relationships is the so-called green-eyed monster known as jealousy. Whether it's being jealous of not spending enough quality time or jealous of a friendly relationship your bf/gf has with a particular guy/girl, it's the growing trust that hopefully both of you have within each other to keep the love growing stronger every day.

Like a person, love can die in the metaphorical sense as the trust that was established through the course of a relationship is broken either temporarily or permanently. In a sense, when a person breaks your heart ones like that he or she has just died or is dying as that particular guy/girl holds your beating heart in the palm of one's hand, points a gun at it, and then pulls the trigger not once but several times. It's an unfortunate situation indeed as that mostly everybody has been in and quite frankly nobody wants to go back and relive or remember. For the question can be asked, was there ever a guy or girl from a past or even a current relationship where you felt that person treated you as if you never even existed; like you died and didn't really care about you at all?

In retrospect, though a person may die, love can be brought back to life but it takes time, patience and without a doubt a buildup of that key word trust. Yet, how many times can a person's trust be broken by oftentimes the same person until one gets it through his or her head that one's so-called special someone is not worthy of your time and love. Thinking about it, our own pride can get in the way as one doesn't want to admit that they have failed in love, which not only hurts your ego but your heart as well. We've all been there and despite that fact we still keep moving forward even though our hearts are metaphorically battered, bruised, and scarred. In the end, hold on to the feeling that there is someone out there who truly loves you, never let go of it, and the best advice I can possibly give to you is never give up.

MY NAME IS
September 21, 2005

When I say the name Eric Bishop, would you be able to figure out who this particular person is. Now what if I told you that Eric Bishop is in fact otherwise known as Jamie Foxx then would you recognize the name of an Oscar winning actor who played the late Ray Charles brilliantly. Essentially, a person's name is their whole identity and, in a way, describes the person they are or was when someone mentions him and/or her by name. Let me ask you this question, do you like your name, or would you rather change it to something that best suits your personality if the choice was yours and yours alone. In some aspect, it's like a certain kind of clothing being able to fit on certain kinds of people and that goes for a person's name, which can be amusing at

Without a doubt, people have names that are the same as a famous/infamous celebrity, musician, politician, and/or sports athlete. It can sometimes be a living nightmare to share the same name with that particular person depending on whose name one has. One can't even imagine the possible ridicule and scorn he or she went through growing up, if it even happened to him and/or at all. On the other hand, it can probably work to one's advantage, which a person can be sued for if taken too far. Such names that people and stars share are Martha Stewart, Matt Damon, Ben Affleck, Jennifer Lopez, and many more. For the question can be asked, do you hang out or at least know someone who shares a name with a certain famous person?

Being a guy, I like watching sports such as baseball and my favorite team has always been the Atlanta Braves, but I digress. What I also like watching is sports related shows such as Sportscenter on ESPN. Here's a little-known fact, ESPN has been a name that many parents over the years have been choosing for their child, boy and girl. For the most part, it's a pretty unique name that is associated with a sports network that mainly men and some women watch either on a semi-daily basis or religiously. There are several different variations in the spelling of the name and how to say it, but one thing is perfectly clear and that is ESPN is part of pop culture to the point where future generations of kids are being named after this show.

When it comes to naming their child/children, parents must really sit down and carefully think about it unlike certain celebrities. Celebrities who are out of their mind and unknowing are going to have their child/children mentally tortured to where he and/or she needs countless hours of therapy. Such celebrity baby names are Pilot Inspektor, Audio Science, Apple, Rain, Cash and other strange/weird names that boggle the mind. However, if you're George Foreman, former heavyweight boxing champion and creator of an awesome grill, you can simply name all your children George including your daughters, with some changes of course. Hey, it probably saves on trying to remember different names but who am I to judge?

In retrospect, there are unusual names that celebrity parents give to their child/children that basically pass such as Frank Zappa's kids and their names are Ahmet, Moonunit, and Dweezel. When or if I have kids someday and I've thought long and hard about this. For my son(s), it would be Alexander, Romeo, and/or Romero after my grandfather who passed away before I ever met him. For my daughter(s) it would be Gabrielle, Isabella, and/or Kari, which is a name that means something special to me. Ultimately, the name that my parents gave to me, I didn't like at first but have grown to get used to. So, for those who don't know me let me introduce myself, my name is Dante Tejada Abundo Jr. but you can call me Yoda and may I ask what your name is?

I DON'T WANT TO MISS A THING
September 24, 2005

Someone once said, ~Sometimes you don't know what you're missing until you reach out to touch it. Sometimes you can't see how beautiful something is until it steps back into the light. And sometimes you miss a love you almost didn't lose. But when you need beautiful dreams and love the most, you find them taken away from you. And when someone is drifting away from you, you feel it screaming inside your chest. Your heart feels numb and ignorant because the truest of love isn't easy. It's the worst thing in the world. True love breaks you, but you become real. When you are real and in love you will never be unhappy. You are only unhappy when you deny the truth held in love.~

Let me ask you this question, has there ever been a person in your life, whether in the past or in the present, that you thought missed out on something really special in you. It's the qualities that make you absolutely special, seemingly not seen by that particular person who somehow lost his or her sight either gradually or in an instant. In some aspect, it's as if somebody walked up from behind, put blinders on that person's eyes, and is stumbling about and trying to figure out where his or her heart lies. For the mistakes that person made is not oftentimes fixable and undeniably it can be the biggest regret that he or she will have to live with as it consequently haunts that person every waking day, as well as, in one's dreams.

Essentially, every person has struggled deep within his or her own heart the feelings that he or she has for a particular person of interest. Feelings that each of us get when someone passes or walks into our life to the point where we've all done that proverbial double take at a particular guy/girl who has caught our eye. Personally speaking, I've done many double takes in my lifetime to the point of suffering whiplash, which probably won't be covered in my medical insurance any time soon. Yet, if you think about it, love can turn anybody's head and heart in many different directions; but when it comes to true love your heart and head will be turned for you without you even knowing about it.

Without a doubt, true love brings out the real you, which is a side that some, most, or all people are scared to show. Why? In my opinion, it's because we don't want that particular person or other people for that matter to see you at your worst, as well as, your most vulnerable moments. For its that mindset, if he and/or she sees that side, the control that you thought you had is now out of your hands and in the hands of him or her, so to speak. In a sense, a person will metaphorically grab one's heart and step back from the emotions that one is feeling to figure out if revealing the real you to that guy/girl is absolutely worth it, which in most cases has been the best choice he and/or has ever made.

Someone said, ~Sometimes you're afraid to become a couple because you are afraid of losing what you already have with that person. But life is all about risks and it requires you to jump. Don't be a person who has to look back and wonder what they would have, or could have had. No one waits forever...~ In retrospect, a person ultimately doesn't want to miss out on finding true love and sharing moments that make you smile from ear to ear. Special moments like a comforting hug, a kiss, etc. Ultimately, it's within those treasured moments, bad or good, you say you would rather keep your eyes open than closed because if it were all a dream, then I don't want to miss a thing, which is a song by an iconic band known as Aerosmith.

WORDS TO LIVE BY
September 26, 2005

Willard Gaylin once said, ~English is such a deliciously complex and undisciplined language that we can bend, fuse, and distort words to all our purpose. We give old words new meaning, and we borrow new words from any language that intrude into our intellectual environment.~ Without a doubt, as a society, we are influenced by the words we hear, read, or said by other people. It's the popularity of a word or words that determine whether it has longevity or dies out due to it becoming so overused. Case in point, "that's hot" made popular by Paris Hilton is not turned into the two most annoying words uttered by a human being. Let me ask you this question, is there a word or words that you unknowingly or knowingly say that is part of your everyday speech?

One of my favorite words to say to my friends back in the day was the word psyche. As a matter of fact, we've all used that word at some point in our childhood and it's like the equivalent to being punk'd without the elaborate setups planned by one's friends, family, and/or co-workers. For the most part, it was mainly all you as you knowingly led someone to believe something to be true only to pull the rug out from under him, her, or them and nobody got hurt physically, as well as mentally. Unfortunately, psyche is no longer in circulation as a word that today's generation of kids which, in my honest opinion, should make a comeback and be put back into circulation. So, if you ever have the opportunity, say it to someone to keep the word alive.

You would never think that three normal words such as yeah, okay, and what would become so popular that it's basically part of pop culture. Essentially, the man responsible for influencing this 3 word phenomenon is the man known as Lil John. You know you've made three simple words popular when comedian Dave Chapelle impersonates you and takes those words to a whole new level of popularity. Working in the asylum, it can oftentimes be amusing but also frustrating trying to talk to "my kids" and he or she is basically repeating those words just to be annoying. So annoying in fact, that I realized why most parents have become crazy, which includes my own parents as well.

Undoubtedly, the one man who teaches us new words to learn on a seemingly daily basis is Snoop Dogg. Such words from the Snoop Dogg dictionary are: chuch, crackalackin, and fshizzle mnizzle mdizzle which has been said not only by young kids but also by senior citizens. You can't turn on the radio, television, or even watch a movie and not have some kind of Snoopism reference in there somewhere. Snoop makes the words he says fun to say and most of the time you don't feel like a complete dork saying it no matter how old you are. Distinguished rapper, clothing designer, actor, football coach, car designer, and now added to the list, creator of words.

If you ever meet me in person, there is one word that I tend to use on a regular basis and that is dude. If you think about it, it's a word that has a universal meaning which can describe emotions such as anger, confusion, happiness, etc. Personally speaking, I call every one of "my kids" dude because quite frankly trying to remember 100 names can be quite difficult at times especially during the summer. In retrospect, words such as bling and crunk will and forever be part of the mainstream. If you don't believe me, open your dictionaries. In the end, there will be plenty of new words created that will be heard and said in our lifetime, and you know what they will primarily be words to live by.

IT'S ALL GOOD
September 28, 2005

Margaret Oliphant once said, ~Perhaps, on the whole, embarrassment and perplexity are a kind of natural accompaniment to life and movement; and it is better to be driven out of your senses with thinking which of two things you ought to do than to do nothing whatever, and be utterly uninteresting to all the world.~ We all go through our fair share of embarrassment growing up as kids, through our adult years, and into the latter years of our lives. It's part of life each of us signed up for, in a manner of speaking, as we humiliate ourselves either by choice or by accident. When it comes to embarrassment and/or being embarrassed, you can't go wrong when it involves childhood pictures, dating, and love.

Let me ask you this question, do you have any embarrassing pictures of yourself growing up that you wouldn't want anybody to see and kind of consider them tools for blackmail? For the most part, parents(MOM) love to dress their kid(s) up in some type of clothing that, in her own words, would look cute in. One of those types of clothing to be dressed in, if you were a little boy, would be the sailor suit which I unfortunately wore at the age of 3 years old. Hey, since my dad was in the Navy at the time, it was only natural that I would wear it to be just like him because I considered him my hero. Let me tell you something, I have those pictures and nobody will ever see them, not even if you ask me nicely.

If you think about it, dating and embarrassment/being embarrassed go hand in hand like mashed potatoes and gravy. Every person has those proverbial horror stories in which they suffered minor or major embarrassment due to the person he or she was going out with, which can also include blind dates as well. 99.9% of the time, the guy is at fault due to something he said or did that cause you to either hide your face or end up walking out on the date. For the question can be asked, when was the last time you had a date that ruined the entire evening to the point where you either went home and made it a blockbuster night or just hung out with your friends to talk about your horrible date?

Without a doubt love can cause totally normal, level headed people to become insane and embarrass themselves to no end. Whether it's guys or girls, a person's sense of reasoning will completely shut off as he or she will risk one's dignity to take that so-called leap of faith into the arms of that particular person of interest. It's a sad but also embarrassing situation indeed as he or she is in pursuit of that one special person as he or she is repeatedly turned down. Its kind of like how Steve Urkel professed his love for Laura Winslow in different ways and kept asking her for a date, which in turn she repeatedly turned him down. However, through all the embarrassment Steve never gave up and finally won the heart of Laura.

In retrospect, everybody will go through embarrassment and no matter how hard you try to avoid them, they will happen. About three years ago, I suffered one of many embarrassments working at the insane asylum and it involved me being late for work. Well, I was approaching a stop light that was on yellow about to turn red and instead of stopping I drove past without really thinking about it. I was busted big time but that wasn't the embarrassing part, because you see I was stopped near the bus stop where "my kids" were happening to get at that particular moment and let's just say, word spread in the asylum and I was ragged on by the kids. In the end, if you can laugh at the embarrassment you have gone through then you can say either to yourself or to the people around you, hey it's all good.

STACEY'S MOM
September 30, 2005

First off, before you begin reading let me apologize ahead of time if this particular Yodaism offends you as I will handle this particular subject matter with the respect and dignity that is deserved. Now with that said, there is a select group out there that guys generally talk about around the ole' water cooler, so to speak. The select group that I'm referring to are the attractive looking moms or if you want to put it more bluntly, MILFs which is a term you know so I won't go any further. Anyways, it's this select group that has guys the world over debating, as well as, choosing who they would have relations with if the opportunity ever presented itself. Though it's considered a fleeting fantasy, which changes over the years as we grow up, it is a fantasy we keep till the time we're born till the time we die.

As a guy, there are many attractive single females out there who can turn our heads no problem at all. However, there is also the attractive looking mom's, single and/or married, that can turn a guy's head to the point where we turn into either Wayne or Garth from Wayne's World and simply say schwing. Hey, as stupid and immature as that sounds, it's a guy thing which some, most, or all guys will never outgrow. Yet, the question can be asked: do women do this as well with fathers who are either single and/or married, which may be the single most stupidest question that I have ever asked. Yet, in all honesty, its not wrong to be attracted to this select group of people just as long as you don't act on it because it will potentially open up a Pandora's Box one will never be able to close.

Without a doubt, there are slew of celebrity moms that some, most, or all guys want to hook up with. It's these particular moms that guys know they don't have a chance with, but it doesn't hurt to dream that it could happen. Such celebrity moms that are on any guy's proverbial list to hook up with are of course Angelina Jolie,

Britney Spears, Pamela Anderson, Jenny McCarthy, Heidi Klum, Brooke Burke, etc. However, though attractive they may be, my list is a bit different as my picks are of the following ladies such as Reese Witherspoon, Michelle Pfeifer, Catherine Zeta-Jones, Demi Moore and Julia Roberts. Let me ask you this question ladies, which celebrity dads would you like to hook up with if the opportunity presented itself?

Over the past 9 years, there are or have been kids who have attractive moms, and you can't help but notice them. Its oftentimes hard not to notice as you see them on a regular basis when they drop off in the morning and pick up their child/children at the asylum in the afternoon. Guys, as well as girls, have an unspoken signal when an attractive mom/dad is seen. For myself and my best friend, I usually just look at him and give a head nod to look in the particular direction that I am motioning to or I walk over and tell him. Not only do you see them, you talk with them and get to know them, but it has never gone beyond the professional level and it will always be kept that way.

In retrospect, moms can take it as a compliment that guys think of them in an attractive way. In a sense, moms every now and then want some reassurance that they still got it and have what it takes to attract a guy. Essentially, it gives a woman an ego boost that guys, especially young guys find a particular mom hot, fine, and/or phat, which is totally wrong in the eyes of her child/children. Whether or not you agree, I am simply stating my opinion on this particular subject matter, which I hopefully kept on a respectable level. In the end, if I could be perfectly honest to all the ladies who will be a mom someday, you might be or will be considered to be a Stacey's Mom.

HEAVEN SENT
October 1, 2005

Someone once said, ~Everytime God creates a soul in Heaven, He creates another to be its special mate. Once we are born, we begin the search for our soulmate, the one person who's the perfect fit for our mind and body. The lucky ones find each other.~ In some aspect, God is considered the perfect matchmaker who sets you up with that one true special mate that every single person wonders about since they were a kid. Without a doubt, it can be frustrating to constantly meet Mr./Ms. Wrong to the point you just want to give up on dating entirely and just be happy living the single life. Let me tell you something, it's not just you that may feel that way because all single people feel that way and it can make a person lose faith that his or her prayers aren't being answered.

For the most part, we all pray to God a somewhat similar prayer when it pertains to one's so-called perfect match. A match in which we give Him the 411 on the type, personality, and description of who each of us are basically looking for in a potential/ significant other. Yet, while people tend to lie, leave out, and/or exaggerate certain details on one's bio and info, God knows every detail that a person hides. Essentially, He will not only take into consideration the positive aspects but also the negative aspects which in His own way will turn it into some kind of positive in the eyes of that particular bachelor or bachelorette. Let me ask you this question, are there any negative qualities you have that you try to keep on the down low?

If you think about it, the dating service industry is a business that thrives on people helping you find a guy or girl that meets the standards, qualities and interests one is looking for. Its these traits that can have a person either knowingly or unknowingly share which can match two people who are total opposites or who are eerily the same. It's primarily a service that either fulfills a person's every expectation or gives countless disappointments. It's this type of service that certain people constantly put their entire faith in and yet seem to never find happiness. However, when you put your faith in God's flawless service, he will be able to connect you with someone that can truly make and keep you happy for a lifetime.

Personally speaking, when it comes to that special soul, I know God will direct me to her or both of us towards each other. Without a doubt, He knows who my perfect match is, which is a comforting thought indeed. Yet, there are times where I want to sit down with Him face to face and ask him straight up who she is, but that would take all the excitement out of it? But the question I have to ask myself is what woman would want a guy who is at times serious, hardheaded, tends to overthink certain situations, and a bit of a procrastinator. However, I'm laid back, a nice guy, caring, thoughtful, driven, and relatively smart. Plus, I genuinely like kids, have a sarcastic sense of humor, and if you ask me what I'm thinking I will actually tell you, which is hopefully qualities that some woman out there is looking for.

In retrospect, God works in mysterious ways and his methods to bring two people together, who are perfect for each other, can never be questioned. It's a matter of having absolute faith that He has chosen the right one for you and doing it on His own timetable. A timetable where some, most, or all people can get pretty impatient. Whether or not a person will rely on God's will or rely on dating websites such as eHarmony or reality shows such as The Bachelor/The Bachelorette, its really up for him or her to decide. Many lucky people have found each other, are happily in love, and have raised a family to be proud of. In the end, the special matches God created for each of us will absolutely be considered angels and my angel will truly be Heaven sent.

PIMPIN' AIN'T EASY
October 3, 2005

The Jigga Man Jay-Z once said, ~If you feelin' like a pimp, go and brush your shoulders off. Ladies is pimps too, go and brush your shoulders off...don't forget that boy told you. Get, that, dirt off your shoulder.~ Let me ask you this question, do you consider yourself a pimp when it comes to the male and/or female persuasion? When I use the term pimp, I mean do you get a certain amount of attention to the point where you have to beat guys/girls off with a stick? Who wouldn't want attention from the opposite sex, which can boost a person's ego unless the attention one receives makes you uncomfortable. In any case, the question can be asked, were you a pimp growing up back in the day and did you or did you not know it?

As a little kid, the thought of girls or boys liking you would cause widespread panic. In one's own adolescent mind, girls or boys had a contagious disease that would spread like wildfire and that disease was known as cooties. In a sense, you didn't have to go the doctor to have it treated because quite frankly all you had to do was walk or run up to another child and just touch him or her and they had it. However, the only guy or girl that you liked was mom and dad, who would take away those cooties in an instant. For the most part, it was a harmless game that we all played and is still being played as a kid, which goes to show that some things never really change.

If you think about it, you may or may not have realized that you had the Austin Powers mojo going and, in some aspect, you were considered a P.I.T, which is a pimp in training. It's really unclear who tends to get the most attention when you're considered a cute kid, boys or girls. One can or could debate that particular topic but it will probably turn into a stalemate. Essentially, its that pimp status that can be seen early on by grown-ups who just think it cute unless you're a father who is getting an early glimpse at what he is in for with his daughter as boys are starting to notice her. But the question can be asked, does it wear off or does it stay with as one grows older?

Working in the asylum over the years, kids tend to proclaim themselves pimps, particularly the boys. It's a funny situation indeed when they try to mack on one particular female counselor who has all of them struck with puppy love. To her it's flattering as she just laughs it off, but in a kind of way lets you down easy so as not to hurt their feelings. When it comes to the girls, on the other hand, I treat them as if they were my daughters even though I don't have any kids of my own. Just last week, one of my 6 & 7years girls told me that 4 boys were interested in her and a part of me went into protective second dad mode. In a sense, I can't keep them from growing up, but I sure as can help put the fear of God into any guy that goes near them.

Suffering from a bit of insomnia, I was looking through some old photo albums late last night and I found something out that I never really knew. What I found out was that I was a pimp and there were six pictures in which I was either holding hands with or standing next to a little girl. There was only one picture that I actually knew the name of, which oddly enough I keep in touch with every now and then. Now that I'm older, wiser, and hopefully cuter, the mojo that I had back then is kind of on the fritz but hopefully I can kick back in high gear, so to speak. Check out those six pictures and please don't laugh at the clothes that I'm wearing. In the end, I was pimpin" back in the day and you know what they say, pimpin' ain't easy.

BLINK OF AN EYE
October 5, 2005

Someone once said, ~Who says love has to make sense? Whoever said that at all? But what I do know, what I HAVE heard, is that men are bastards. Oh yes they are, and age doesn't matter. Age doesn't matter one bit because they learn how to destroy what bit of compassion, love, and hope that women hold inside.~ Not all men, as so bluntly put it, are considered bastards. There are guys out there who women are looking for that are truly genuine and have the qualities to be the man they have always wanted, which some have already found. Working with mostly women for the past several years, you tend to be the proverbial punching bag as to why guys are jerks. For women, there are 3 types of guy to be careful of and one of them is considered the most dangerous.

Unfortunately, women will fall for the Dr. Jekyl and Mr. Hyde type of guy in which he is one way and then another. Its this split personality where a woman tends to see the side of a guy she really doesn't want to see and experience things such as physical and/or mental abuse. Every woman wants a guy who acts the same way when he is around you and with his friends, but that's often not the case. It can be a sad situation indeed when a woman doesn't realize that there is a proverbial red flag warning her that her man may not change how he acts and its time to leave for her own good. For the question can be asked, were you ever or have ever seen someone in this type of relationship?

Essentially, women will sometimes gravitate towards the so-called smooth operators that say and do all the right things to touch a woman's heart. Let me ask you this question ladies, when was the last time you went out with a smooth operator and was temporarily blinded? These guys generally fly under a women's highly tuned radar, which can detect if a guy is full of it but unfortunately their looks or body, or both can have them be temporarily blinded. One guy who is considered a smooth operator in my book and all women seem to be absolutely in love with this man is Jude Law. It's really unclear if its his James Bond looks and/or his body that women love or the fact that he talks with a British accent which would make any woman swoon.

Without a doubt, women tend to fall for the bad boys, which is most definitely the nice guy's worst enemy. For it's these guys who are considered untamed free spirits who live hard, party hard, and take each day to the limit. Some well known celebrity bad boys are Colin Farrell, Dennis Rodman, and of course Tommy Lee who personified the bad boy lifestyle with sex, drugs, rock & roll, as well as some stints in jail. However, there is one bad boy that did turn his bad boy membership and settled down with one of the most beautiful women in Hollywood Denise Richards and that man is Charlie Sheen. Some, most, or all women know what they are getting into and yet, in their minds, they want to try to tame the untamable.

In retrospect, women basically know what they are getting into when it comes to the bad boys and the Dr.Jekyll/Mr. Hyde type. Thinking about it, who knows what kind guys women like because quite frankly it tends to change on a semi-daily basis. All I know is that most women are looking for a guy who has a great sense of humor, is honest, can get along with everybody, and hopefully not a guy who is one Mcnugget short of a happy meal. So, the question was who is the most dangerous guy to be careful of? In the end, the smooth operator is considered the most dangerous because within a blink of an eye a woman will end up heartbroken for a man that she loved who not only walked away with her heart, but walked away with her trust and she didn't even see it coming.

IS IT JUST ME
October 6, 2005

Let me ask you this question, do you consider yourself either slightly or majorly obsessive compulsive? For the most part, its a disorder that can affect a person mentally to the point where it takes complete control of one's life and can sometimes ruin a relationship. If you think about it, we all have our own quirks that some, most, or all people tend to see as either reasonable, weird, or strange. It's the things we do on a semi-daily basis that are deemed as normal by our standards. Here is a little-known entertainment fact: Did you know Marc Summers, who was the host of a widely popular television show, Double Dare and Family Double Dare, is obsessive compulsive about cleaning, which probably wasn't good thing when hosting a show that was all about being messy.

Without a doubt, each and every one of us likes to feel clean and smell fresh for not only ourselves but for other people as well. When it comes to one's cleanliness, it can be taken to the extreme to where a person can become like Tony Shalhoub's television character Monk or Jack Nicholson's character in the movie As Good As It Gets. Personally speaking, I'm a person who washes my hands constantly due to the fact that I'm around kids on a semi-daily basis. It can be an unfortunate situation indeed when the cold/flu season rolls around, and you have a building full of runny noses. Kids that will use anything but a tissue to wipe their noses clean and then want to hang on you, which is always a bad thing.

We all have bad habits that tend to be either compulsive or obsessive compulsive. The one habit that people generally share is biting one's own fingernails which can be considered annoying to some, most, or all people. Essentially, it's something we don't realize we're doing until someone points it out to us or one almost makes one's finger(s) bleed, which I have done on occasion. Again, personally speaking, I tend to bite/chew my fingernail(s) when I'm worried about something or thinking about something to write for a potential yodaism. A yodaism that can either take minutes, hours, or days to think up and then write about. In a sense, if I don't do it then ideas won't be able to flow smoothly in my head.

For the question can be asked, do you consider yourself a superstitious person? Countless stories can be told of athletes, celebrities, musicians, and people like ourselves doing certain rituals over and over again. For some people, they certain rituals before ever boarding an airplane such as stepping on the plane with their right foot and touching the top of the entrance. For a person like myself, whenever I enter or leave a room I have to knock on wood and its something I've been doing for years. In some aspect, I do consider myself superstitious because 1.) I don't walk under any ladders whatsoever and 2.) I have a green rabbit's foot on my key chain.

In retrospect, whether it's a person's handwriting, cleaning the house, making one's bed, taking a shower, alphabetizing one's CD/DVD collection, etc. a person will have some idiosyncrasies that people will find peculiar. People who know, know that I like to draw, and they have seen my drawings, but what they don't know about me is that I throw away perfectly good drawing that are in my mind stink and draw them until they look perfect which can be frustrating from my standpoint. When it comes to drawing a character that I have made up, I tend to be a perfectionist. In the end, a person will ultimately ask this question either to one's self or to others and that question is do other people do these things or is it just me?

JUST TOO SWEET
October 9, 2005

Garrison Keller once said, ~Nothing you do for children is ever wasted. They seem to not notice us, hovering, averting our eyes, and they seldom offer thanks, but we de do for them is never wasted.~ Working in the asylum, you sometimes get the impression you're never appreciated or liked be the kids, who I like to refer to them at as the children of the corn. At times, I sometimes wonder if "my kids" only see me as someone who provides the fun and entertainment by just snapping my fingers, which is a delusional point of view on their part because quite frankly they don't deserve it most of the time. Let me ask you this question, is it me or are kids now a days getting bored too easily and want to be entertained 24/7?

In any case, I'm a guy that has pretty much lost most of my marbles, so to speak, from having my name called out every single for petty arguments that could have been solved by themselves. As I said before, I'm not just a counselor, I'm also a negotiator as well and there are times where that part of my unofficial job description comes into play in which I will make him/her/them and offer/solution that couldn't possibly ever be refused. Unfortunately, those offers/solutions tend to be thrown back not only in my face but the faces of my fellow co-workers who worked hard o put particular events/projects together. For they simply want a better deal that they can be happy with, but the thing is when attitude is given there are no deals.

Without a doubt, a person like myself can sympathize with what a parent or parents go through, especially out in public. We've all witnessed kids going ballistic either at a restaurant, fast food places, stores, and primarily any place that is out in public with people watching. Kids who, in my opinion, have absolutely lost their minds as they run and scream at the top of their lungs with the parent(s) frustrated and embarrassed to no end. Personally speaking, I can honestly say that over the past 9 years, I've been embarrassed by "my kids' countless times and yet the great thing about my job is that I can embarrass them back. Embarrass them not in a cruel, sadistic way, but more of a respect my authority in front of your friend's kind of way that a child should have for an adult, as well as their own parent(s).

However, there are times where kids can truly surprise you to where a a high five or hug is given either by you or by the child. It's those times that you can see and be proud of a particular child or group of children as he/she/they do something thoughtful and don't expect anything in return...most of the time. I have been privileged to have experienced many situations in which "my kids" did something for me or my fellow co-workers and it made me smile. For the question can be asked of you, have you witnessed and/or experienced the kindness, thoughtfulness, adoration, and love of a child who not only thinks of you as a friend, but also as part of your family.

As many of you know, many kids were out of school and had a week of sleeping, having fun, as well as going on vacation. The asylum prepared a week line involving skating, movies and pizza. Well, last Wednesday "my kids" went to Chuck E. Cheese had a blast. I had only 1 token left so I asked one of my 6 & 7 girls if she wanted to take a picture with me and she said yes. The picture was taken, and she asked me if she could have it, which I gave her and thought nothing of it later. The following day I asked what she did with it thinking she probably lost it or was thrown away by her mom/dad, but she said she put it in a frame and is hanging above her bed. I end this thought on what she did with a catch phrase made famous by a former WCW organization known as NWO Wolfpack, which is that she was just too sweet.

A THING OF BEAUTY
October 11, 2005

Edith Wharton once said, ~A classic is classic not because it confirms to certain structural rules or fits certain definitions (of which its author had quite probably never heard). It is a classic because of a certain eternal and irrepressible freshness.~ Let me ask you this question, in your own mind what do you consider a classic. Essentially, one of the definitions of a classic is having lasting significance or worth; enduring. For its a person, place, place or thing that stands the test of time and can be considered meaningful to some, most, or all people. I can safely say probably each and every one of you has already thought of something that is a classic and if you can't then you're thinking too hard.

When you talk about a classic, there is a plethora of reading material that we all have read in school growing up and in college as well. Curious George, Lord of the Rings, Romeo and Juliet, The Scarlet Letter, Huckleberry Finn, etc. are just a handful of works that were written by established writers such as Margret Rey, J.R.R. Tokein, William Shakespeare, Nathaniel Hawthorne, and Samuel Clemens aka Mark Twain. For its not only the books we read, but the poetry that was written as well by such linguistic writers such as E.E. Cummings, Edgar Allen Poe, Walt Whitman, Emily Dickinson and Ralph Waldo Emerson who is my personal favorite because I tend to use his quotes and/or poems in my Yodaisms from time to time. Out of curiosity, who is your favorite writer/poet and what are your favorite works to read from him or her?

If you think about it, classics and cars go hand in hand like maple syrup to a stack full of pancakes. Guys, more so than women, appreciate classic cars and will spend countless hours, as well as money to build/restore classic cars. Actor/Comedian/Tonight Show host Jay Leno has a warehouse full of classic vintage cars that he collects which to my knowledge is over a thousand but I could be wrong. For those who live in California, particularly in the Los Angeles area, you probably have seen him drive around in his cars such as a 1933 Roadster, a 1959 Chevy Corvette, and the list goes on and on. Personally speaking, the one car that I dreamed of owning one day would be a 1967 Ford Mustang with its original interior but have the sound system updated and pimped out.

Without a doubt, each of us grew up watching classic Disney movies such as The Jungle Book, Dumbo, Alice In Wonderland, Snow White, and Cinderella. What made Cinderella a classic is that every little girl wanted to be like her and dreamed that one day her prince charming would come holding that proverbial glass slipper in his hand. As a guy, in a metaphorical sense, I'm holding that glass slipper to put on that special someone's foot. Anyways, within those animated features were classic songs that we all loved, still loved today, and probably sang along with. For the question can be asked, what Disney animated movie and song still gets to you emotionally even though you are grown up, which for me is The Jungle Book and The Bear Necessities.

In retrospect, there are many things that are considered classics such as the classic Christmas movie It's A Wonderful Life or the classic 1939 film which won 8 Oscars Gone with the Wind. Yet, within every classic movie there are classy actors such as Jimmy Stewart, Fred Astaire, Bob Hope, James Cagney, Clark Gable, etc. and for the classy actresses they are Katharine Hepburn, Lucille Ball, Grace Kelly, Bette Davis, Judy Garland, etc. For the most part, you have to appreciate the styles, movies, songs, cars, and people that personify the word class or classic. Ultimately, the classics never really go out of style, grow old, or even get boring because in the end, they can be considered a thing of beauty.

MOVIN' ON UP (FOR A FRIEND)
October 12, 2005

Dan Carter once said, ~Every monring is a fresh beginning. Every day is the world made new. Today is a new day. Today is my world made new. I have lived my life up to this moment to come to this day. This moment--this day--is as good as any moment in all eternity. I shall make this day--each moment of this day--a heaven on earth. This is my day of opportunity.~ There comes a point in every person's life where change happens. Initially, it can be a much-needed change where you literally and metaphorically leave part of your past behind to move forward to your anticipated present/future. A present/future where not only you get a new lease on life but also the people who are close to you as well.

Oftentimes, the changes a person experiences can be well worth the pain and tears suffered as a new path opens up, but yet still on the same journey. One of those experiences in life is when a divorce happens that may or may not affect children/parent inwardly and/or outwardly to the point where unresolved issues/feelings, if any, are or have been expressed. However, it can be truly a liberating situation indeed as you feel one of the many dramas in your life come to a close and the pressure has been lifted off your shoulders, which can make one's journey a bit more tolerable. For the circumstances which led up to the divorce is really no one's business except your own and those who were closely part of one's inner circle who have been there for you through good times and bad.

With a newfound sense of freedom, one leaves behind a place that you once called home that gave you lasting memories for another home to make new memories in. Though you leave behind a place that you practically grew up in and physically take with your possessions. For it's not only the material possession you take along, you also metaphorically take certain unforgettable memories with you that made you laugh, cry, and smile. Let me ask you this question, what were your absolute best memories that you took with you to your new home, and did you leave any unwanted memories behind in a place that you once hung your hat in, so to speak.

Without a doubt, you can be absolutely nostalgic as you begin a new life/path to some new surroundings. Surroundings, in which you personally made that particular home your own and decorated it with one's own style and personality. Yet, if you think about it, the new path that you and your family is traveling on will fork off as each of you individually live your own lives. Subsequently, a new chapter is created in each of your autobiographies, in which the details may or may not be exaggerated. For each chapter in your proverbial life story have pages that haven't been written in yet and you get the chance to fill those pages with new memories, experiences, and most all friends both current and new.

In retrospect, you never really know what other people are going through and the situations that they may be facing until you find out for yourself. In a sense, other people may be going through the exact same thing, but the situation is a bit different, which unknowingly bonds people together. Ultimately, whether its down the street, up the street, across the street, miles apart, or across the sea, any place you live in is considered home once you make it a home. I end this thought with a pop culture reference with one of my favorite shows as a kid The Jeffersons, which is you're movin on up to something better, even though you are moving down the street.

LAYETH THE SMACKDOWN
October 16, 2005

Don Marquis said,~Many a man spanks his children for the things his own father should have spanked out of him.~ In this day and age, punishing a child by way of the physical means is deemed wrong and if caught doing it in public you could be sentenced to several years in jail or even in prison, which in my opinion certain parents don't deserve. For its the new school way of parenting that some, most or all kids behave in a way that is not only embarrassing to the parent(s) its also embarrassing to others as well. Let me ask you this question, how many of you grew up with the old school way of parenting and are you the respectful, well-adjusted man or woman you are today?

Working with all types of kids from ages 6-17, you primarily witness firsthand kids who have been raised new school and those who have been raised old school. For those kids who are/were raised new school tend to be the proverbial wild stallions in which nobody, not even their own parent(s) can try to settle/tame him or her down. Its a truly amazing situation indeed when you witness a child mouth off to one's parent and when you think that a beatdown is about to happen to him or her, the parent does nothing. However, for those that are/were raised old school their parent(s) broke them down early and even though there may be a few moments of wildness, once something is said or "the look" is given you know it's time to straighten up and fly right.

The time out vs. the knockout, it's two styles of parenting that have every person debating which is more effective to use. In a sense, what you get with the time out is a child who doesn't really get the point from what one did wrong. What it actually does, it gives him or her time to figure out what mischievous acts he or she can think up next. Speaking from experience, I've put plenty of kids in time out and it doesn't do anything but get them hyped up. BUT what you get from the knockout is a well-trained child who is well behaved, well mannered, polite, respectful, courteous, not a brat will say Yes Sir/Yes Ma'am, No Sir/No Ma'am, which people will compliment you about and it put a smile on your face.

Personally speaking, I wasn't considered a bad due to the fact that I was a quiet child who sat in front of the television quietly watching cartoons while eating my favorite breakfast cereal Froot Loops. However, I did have my fair share of hyperactivity and stupidity growing up where punishment was given. Its unclear if other parents do this but for a Filipino, particularly moms, will uses something other than a belt or hand to pass down judgement, so to speak. Let me tell you something, there's nothing like being punished with certain household objects such as a fly swatter, shoe, slipper, ruler, stick broom, wooden spatula, back scratcher, and basically anything not bolted down would be or has been used and you know what I'm a well-adjusted child because of it.

In retrospect, every person remembers the worst punishment handed down by their parents growing up and if you can't then you've probably blocked it out of your memory. For the question can be asked, if one is able to remember will it cause you to become somewhat or majorly emotional to the point of tearing up? In any case, on the bright side when you did suffer that punishment the rest that you got afterwards was absolutely the best you have ever had because you had built up tension, combined with trying to stay calm, added with that worrying if you might or might not wake up from it for days or weeks. Ultimately, every parent back in the day layeth the smackdown on their kid(s) and in the end they all say the same thing when it's over which every person knows by heart, so say it with me kids...you know I did it because I love you.

TRICK OR TREAT
October 17, 2005

Twisted Sister front man Dee Snider said, ~Halloween is huge in my house and we really get into the 'spirits' of things. A few years back, my wife was frustrated with the same old stupid sound effects tape we would play which ends with the theme from 'Ghostbusters' and 'Monster Mash'. I told her that Halloween is way too cool a holiday to suffer though this year.~ Well folks, it's the one holiday that kids as well as grown-ups look forward to because it's one night out of the year you can be and act immature. Though Halloween is two weeks away, many people have already decorated, bought tons of candy, and plan elaborate setups to scare kids. Essentially what makes Halloween so enjoyable are the following three things: candy, costumes, and haunted houses.

Without a doubt, the cady given out on Halloween is considered the proverbial holy grail to every child and its their mission to fill one's bag till it can't be filled anymore. A mission in which a child uses a military-like strategy either solo or with friends to hit every house that one's legs could take him/her not once, not twice, but as many times one can possibly push himself or herself. Oftentimes, if one were going in groups your "team" would suffer casualties in which friends went missing in action due to being tired whereas you shut out the fatigue for your soul objective. Unlike the Marines where they go by the creed nobody gets left behind, you went by a different one which was every boy/girl for one's self.

Let me ask you this question, do you still dress up for Halloween or have you outgrown it? The costumes you either buy or create can make or break you to where you not only try to outdo yourself each year but also outdo your friends, if there was any competition in it. We all remember or choose not to remember the costumes each of us wore back in the day, which one can either be proud of or absolutely cringe due to how extremely unoriginal/lame it was. For the question can be asked, how many of you already know what you are going to be/wear for Halloween and how many of you are just going to wait till the last minute to create.

The haunted house. It's a staple of Halloween and for some, most, or all people when it comes to haunted houses the scarier the better. Back in the day, were you the type of kid who got scared easily and nobody could be able to convince to go in even when someone told one would go with you? OR were you the type of kid who wasn't scared of anything and went into the haunted house balls to the wall by going by yourself, which you couldn't due to the fact that an adult had to go with you, but I digress. For the most part, we all probably have been or will be participants of a haunted house in our high school or college days, which was/is/will be an experience that gave you such a thrill because it gave the chance to scare the living shiznit out of people you either know or don't know.

In retrospect, Halloween will always bring out the little kid inside each of us and the memories connected to it will forever be remembered. Whether its egging someone's house, stealing someone else's candy, watching horror movie marathons, or having parties that may or may not involve either police, paramedics, or someone running naked down the street unforgettable memories will be made this year. Unfortunately, I am officially retiring from the game, so to speak; in so doing I turn over my bag and flashlight to the next generation of candy seeking kids, but that doesn't mean I'm not going to dress up. In the end, on October 31st, 2005, kids of all ages will be knocking on doors and saying those three familiar words which are trick or treat.

PUT UP OR SHUT UP
October 19, 2005

E.E. Cummings once said, ~To be nobody-but yourself-in a world which is doing its best night and day, to make everybody else-means to fight the hardest battle which any human can fight; and never stop fighting.~ For the most part, each of us live a hard knock life in which we either metaphorically or physically fight certain situations we all have been or are going through. Its the unpredictability of life that we instinctively keep our guard up at all times in order not to get knocked out, in a manner of speaking. You never really know what is in store for each of us as we wake up, get ready for the day, and step outside one's door each day. Let me ask you this question, whether its metaphorical or physical, what throw downs have you gone or are going through in your life?

In our daily lives, we metaphorically fight to survive in order to get to the next day. For some, most or all of us struggle to keep our head above water as we all battle to get that mighty dollar into our individual bank accounts. It can be an embarrassing situation indeed when one receives a "black eye" due to the fact that you don't have enough money or no money at all to pay the bills. Bills that have the power to take away your electricity, house, car, material possessions, and even yourself either temporarily or permanently. When it comes to money, are you financially set for life to where you have absolutely no worries or are you in a constant face off with others who say the same thing you do which is, Show me the money!

Essentially, a person can both metaphorically and physically fight for someone who one absolutely feels strongly for. For some, most, or all women, it can be considered romantic and a bit comical when a guy or group of guys fight not only for the attention of a particular female but also for her heart, which can also happen the other way around as well. In sense, it's like the NBC show Average Joe or MTV's hit dating show Next, where guys and girls vie for the attention of one man and one woman. Oftentimes, the metaphorical fight can turn nasty to the point where it becomes physical; as emotions run so high that words are said, fist fly, teeth are lost, hair is pulled, and what was considered a romantic situation is now a situation that's completely out of hand.

Without a doubt, we've all been in a physical fight that you either won, lost, or nobody won at all. Every person tends to remember a fight that sticks with them and for me personally it was back in my middle school days and to this day that fight is being talked about, which shows that particular fight had staying power. In any case, fighting can be considered a rite of passage, mainly for guys, as cuts and bruises received from that fight were seen as a badge of honor depending on if it was one's first fight or not. For the question can be asked, when was the last time you had a fight, who was it with, what/who was it over, and do you remember where you were when the fight happened?

Working in the asylum, you're not just a counselor; you're also a profiler, referee, judge, jury, negotiator, detective, and add to that list a cooler. Early Monday morning, a couple of "my teenage kids" were talking smack to each other, and it got to the point where they were about to throw down, which I immediately got in between them. Now imagine a 5'3/155 pound 28-year-old guy trying to hold back/cool down a 5'7/190 pound 13-year-old teenager who could have easily picked me up and used me as a lawn dart, but he didn't. The potential of a fight was squashed because cooler heads prevailed and quite frankly nobody wanted to get written up because of it. In the end, when you're talking smack about somebody and a fight might happen, there comes a point where you have two choices which are put up or shut up.

IF YOU WERE MINE
October 21, 2005

Someone once said, ~He'd only break your heart you know? Rip it up into pieces and watch you as you cry. He's done it before you know? Played with girl's emotions and laughed at them as they die. He's no good for you, you know? Every look in his eyes, every touch of his lips, are just a lie. He's not the one for you, you know? But even though, your heart still can't say goodbye.~ Without a doubt, every woman wants a guy that will treat them the way one wants to be treated. Treated with tender loving care like a flower and it doesn't always involve the physical aspect of love. Essentially, when it comes to love women will encounter guys who will or have treated them with disrespect in three ways: psychological, verbal, and/or physical.

The psychological mistreatment of a woman can most definitely have either short- or long-term effects. Thinking about it, saying I love you to a woman and to truly mean it can deeply touch her within her heart and soul. However, it can truly be a sad situation indeed when a guy doesn't express those three little words to a woman and there is no meaning behind it. It can get to the point where she will wait to hear those three important words but unfortunately, they're never uttered from his lips, which can hurt a woman not only emotionally but also psychologically as well. Let me ask you this question ladies, how many times a day does your significant other express his love for you and is absolutely lucky that you're in his life?

When it comes to the verbal mistreatment of a woman, it can deeply affect her to where one's self esteem is lowered tremendously. Every woman wants a guy that genuinely compliments her on the way she looks, which puts a beautiful smile on her face and makes her day that much brighter.

Unfortunately, there are guys who will verbally assault women to no end on their looks and it can psychologically affect the way they see themselves or how they think others perceive them to be. One such verbal assault can be on he issue of weight, which can create a deep psychological impact on women to the point where she starves herself to death because of what guys or others say about them. For the question can be asked to you ladies, has this particular situation ever happened to you?

We've all either read, seen on the news, witnessed firsthand, or know/knew women who went through the physical mistreatment from a man who supposedly loved her. In all intents and purposes, a man is not considered a man once he physically puts his hands on her no matter how much she verbally and physically provokes a guy, its just not cool. Yet, countless stories can be told of women in abusive relationships who will not leave due to the fat that she still loves him, which is considered a deluded love that can oftentimes lead in death. Subsequently, the physical and verbal abuse suffered can undeniably leave scars both physical and psychological to where a woman will take drastic measures to ensure that abuse never happens again or to anybody for that matter.

In retrospect, whether its psychological, verbal, and/or physical no woman deserves to be mistreated in any way, shape, or form. For its been said, treat a woman as you would want your own sister to be treated; but if a guy doesn't have a sister, then place one's mother into that spot. Working with mostly women for the past 6 years, I've being dragged into conversation where you hear countless complaints of how there aren't any guys who are considered mature gentlemen who treat women like ladies. Let me tell you something, there are guys like this out there who are real, like myself, who will treat you like a lady and, in the end, say to you if you were mine, I'll make you believe that you are truly special in every way.

SWEET SMELL OF SUCCESS
October 23, 2005

Ralph Waldo Emerson once said, ~To laugh often and much, to win the respect of intelligent people and the affection of children...to leave the world a better place...to know even one life has breathed easier because you have lived. This is to have succeeded.~ It's a funny thing about life, it gives each of us the opportunity to meet new people, get to know them, and hopefully form a friendship. There is an uncertainty as to how long that friendship will last due to the period of time, you're able to get to know him, her. and/or them. Essentially, we all want to succeed in making friends with people one hardly knows and it can, without a doubt, be a challenge to do so; but it's a challenge that can unknowingly give you countless stories that are memorable to look back on.

If you think about it, we meet hundreds of thousands of people who may or may not become either our acquaintances, friends, and/or homies. In a sense, all the people we meet growing up and in life are a part of our own history and vice versa. Each of us has childhood friends who we either remember or don't remember and they are connected to our past, which begs the question: do you remember that person's name? Like life, we move on and forge new friendships but the connection with that person is still there. For the laughter that was shared back then can inevitably be shared again when he, she, or they step back into our loves to talk about the good ole' days which can most definitely involve looking at old videos and pictures.

Let me ask you this question, how did you meet your partner(s) in crime you hung out with and was it a successful interaction? For its these people, who are now in your inner circle, were at one time strangers that you either vibed gradually with, in an instant, or not at all in that first initial meeting. For some, most, or all of us can be considered shy, standoffish, and/or quiet at first but once that proverbial ice breaker is given the comfortability level rises and so does one's personality as well. It's unclear though whether it is easier for guys to click with each other than women due to the fact that we generally form an instant friendship by either taking sports, particular hobbies, through a spirit of competition, or something that involves sheer stupidity, which is usually the case for us.

Working in the asylum for the past 9 years, I've hopefully succeeded in earning the respect of not only my friends/co-workers, past and present; but also countless kids who have come and gone. Kids who have grown up before my eyes and hopefully have had a positive influence on each of their lives to the point where I'm not just a friend to them, but considered a big brother even though most of them are taller than me. When it comes to kids, it's not an easy task to earn the respect or affection for that matter of kids who will disrespect you at a drop of a hat, in a manner of speaking. BUT that's the challenge one is given for a person who works in the childcare profession and I'm loving every minute of it even though I've lost most of my marbles doing it.

Last month the asylum opened up its doors for the kids who were displaced by Hurricane Katrina, which my best friend and I were able to meet in person if it was for only a brief period of time. Let me tell you something, it was truly a humbling experience as we gave them a chance to have fun, laugh, and to be entertained for several hours, which was a once in a lifetime opportunity that will truly be remembered where we made some new friends. However, life can unknowingly give you second chances to bring fun, laughter, and entertainment to displaced kids again which happened Saturday night with myself and best friend. In that brief time, the laughter heard throughout the night is considered to be, in the end, the sweet smell of success that stays with you and will be remembered for years to come.

THE HANDS OF TIME
October 25, 2005

Khalil Gibran once said, ~The things which the child loves remain in the domain of the heart until old age. The most beautiful thing in life is that our souls remain over the places where we once enjoyed ourselves.~ Without a doubt, a person's childhood is one of the things each of us cherish because we can all look back on it and hopefully smile. Smile for the simple reason that you had no responsibilities placed upon you except to do two things which are listen to our parents and be a kid. It's unclear whether or not each of us actually listened to our parents back in the day, but what each of us absolutely knew to do was be a kid. For it's our so-called good ole' days that we all, at times, wish to be like a kid again.

Essentially, the art of mocking someone was something that every one of us did as young kids. It was primarily done when you were having an argument with another kid/adult and just to mess with him or her when you repeated everything he or she said. Whether it was to our teachers, parents, brothers, sisters, friends, pets, etc., practically nobody was safe at being potentially mocked. For it was a totally harmless thing to do due to the fact nobody got hurt unless you took it too far and you yourself got hurt. Working in the asylum, you get mocked by kids on a regular basis, which really doesn't faze me because the fun part of my job as a counselor is mocking the kids back. Hey, one never really outgrows mocking someone because quite frankly it give each of us a chance to act totally immature for a moment or two.

When it comes to playing kids games, the one underlying truth is that the rules can change at any time if you feel like it. You have to admit, we've all done it when playing such childhood games as tag, freeze tag, hide and go seek, etc. For it was in the middle of the game that you would basically change the rules if it wasn't going in your favor, which didn't go over too well with our friends. Let me tell you something, I've played countless kids at pool and when they know they're losing or about to lose they suddenly change the rules so that he or she can try to beat me; but I win anyway...most of the time. If you think about it, as adults one could only wish we could change the rules by just announcing it so that life and/or love can go in our favor.

Undeniably, whining/complaining/throwing temper tantrums was what each of us did as kids to get something or go somewhere that was considered important/matter of life and death, which if you deny then you are lying. For if we didn't get our way or what we wanted, the whining/complaining/throwing temper tantrums would begin and if "PLAN A" didn't work "PLAN B" would be implemented... holding one's breath. It would probably be safe to say "PLAN B" never really worked out and the question remains who does it better, boys or girls. In my opinion girls, because no man alive is safe from it being done to him and they inevitably cave in. In some aspect, it would be interesting and comical to see grown adults do this when they either don't get a parking space, job promotion, etc.

Bill Cosby said, ~The essence of childhood, of course, is play, which my friends and I did endlessly on streets that we reluctantly shared with traffic.~ In retrospect, you never really leave behind the little inside you because that inner child is always eagerly waiting to make an appearance when the time is right. An appearance that, in some ways, feels liberating when doing something totally out of character and acting like Pee Wee Herman before the unfortunate theater incident, of course. Though it's unclear if each of us as kids went around saying to other kids I know what you are but what am I, you just had fun being a carefree kid with no worries whatsoever. I end this thought by asking you this question, if life were able to turn the hands of time just for one day for you to be a kid again, would you take it?

CLOUD 9
October 27, 2005

Annie Sullivan once said, ~Love is something like the clouds that were in the sky before the sun came out. You cannot touch the clouds, you know, but you feel the rain and know how glad the flowers are to have it after a hot day. You cannot touch love either; but you feel the sweetness that it pours into everything. Without love you would not be happy or want to play.~ Essentially, there is an oftentimes certain calm you receive when you stare/gaze at clouds that are in the so-called wild blue yonder. If you think about it, one receives that somewhat same calmness with a guy or girl you are either in love with or falling in love with as you stare/gaze at him or her even though your own heart may be beating a mile a minute.

We've all at one time or another in our lives sat/laid down in a very comfortable grassy area and basically watched the clouds roll by. It was and probably still is an activity that kids as well as grown-ups of any age enjoy doing due to the fact that you're outside feeling the breeze and soaking up a little bit or a lot of sun in the process. For it when we continue to gaze at those particular clouds, one can start to see shapes that look like somewhat familiar images one may or may not recognize at first. In a sense, when a person is in love or falling in love, he or she can see the all too familiar face of that guy or girl whom you are thinking about. Let me ask you this question, whose one face, guy or girl, do you see when you gaze up into the clouds

Yet, there comes a point where those proverbial dark clouds cover what was once a majestic looking scenery. In a sense, those dark clouds represent heartbreak which can metaphorically cover one's own heart to the point where it is lost in darkness either temporarily or permanently. It's a sad situation indeed when guys and girls can't seem to pull their own hearts from under their own dark cloud of sadness due to the impact that he or she has faced from being in a relationship with someone who basically was rolling steadily away rather than towards you. There is an old saying which goes that every dark cloud has a silver lining and it can brighten not only a person's day to the point where his or her heart smiles. So, who is considered to be your silver lining?

Without a doubt, each of us as kids have tried to reach up and touch/grab the clouds which in all intents and purposes was an absolute impossibility. In a way, that's how love is as each of us have tried or are trying to reach higher and higher for the person you love as one pushes himself or herself, as well as our hearts to the limit just to feel that high one gets when a person is in love or falling in love. In some aspect, if each of us had the abilities of Superman or Supergirl, we would simply fly up and away high above the clouds. For the question can be asked, which has both men and women asking themselves, how high are both willing to go for the one he or she loves?

In retrospect, I said in a past Yodaism that love is like flying without wings; but when you are truly in love the sky is the limit. To be perfectly honest, when you are in love or falling in love with someone, you feel strong/invincible like the man/girl of steel to where you feel like you can take on the world. However, that person is also considered to be your kryptonite because he or she makes you feel weak in the knees; BUT he or she makes your heart beat stronger and stronger as you both spend time with each other. Every person wants a guy or girl like this who will not only take you higher than you ever wanted to go in your heart and soul, as well as, far beyond the clouds you see above you, which is a feeling that we all know is like being on Cloud 9.

BECAUSE OF YOU
October 28, 2005

Someone once said, ~Friendship is a dangerous thing. Like when you get that those with someone, to a point where you can feel that you can talk to them about almost anything, then it is just natural to want to take the relationship to the next step. That is what love is all about, friendship. And then you realize that it is more than that, something that you can't even describe with words, because words only seem to reduce the power you feel.~ It's rare these days for a person to meet someone who is genuinely real and one can feel comfortable in the fact that he or she has no intentions of breaking your heart. Though one may be skeptical of that happening, it's considered absolute truth rather than pure fiction.

If you think about it, we live our lives trying to figure out what's fact or fiction when it involves someone who may be potentially "the one." For some, most, or all people they can easily distinguish what's fact as he or she gets to know the person inside and out. However, for others the fiction that he or she hears can sound totally believable to the point that you metaphorically hand over your heart to that person. To be perfectly honest, when you are in love, fact and fiction can be totally unrecognizable to where one tries to sort out whether what that person is saying to you is either true or untrue, which is a tough task indeed. Let me ask you this question, have you ever been in this particular situation before?

In any case, people who are living the single life by choice, like myself, you witness/hear about many relationships falling apart over a period of time that can affect you mentally to the point that being alone is the best choice possible. Whether it be acquaintances, friends, and/or family you have that mindset where you don't ever want that situation to happen to you because one doesn't want to endure that kind of pain, suffering, and inner turmoil due to it. For it can be rough for any person to hide the feelings he or she has for someone because of certain personal issues that one is going through and metaphorically battling yourself to tell or not tell that person. For some people, that's the life he or she chose, and it can be a living nightmare that you truly want to be woken up from.

However, there are people out there who are living the single life by choice as well, but for an entirely different reason. For it was a particular situation in question that caused one to not only closely guard their own feelings but also keep his or her heart at a distance from ever being broken again. It's an oftentimes sad situation indeed when it happens to people you know, care about, and/or love such as acquaintances, friends, and/or family. In some aspect, that person didn't choose to go through those unbearable moments of life for himself/herself and unfortunately, he or she is living a somewhat similar nightmare that one wants to be woken up from as well.

In the movie Batman Begins the question was asked, why do we fall? The answer to that question was so that we can learn to pick ourselves back up again. In retrospect, that is how love/friendship is as a person can fall so hard that impact leaves deep scars that are either gradually healing or haven't healed within one's heart and soul. Without a doubt, it takes a lot of inner strength to not only pick ourselves up but also our own heart as well. Ultimately, it takes someone who is really special to pick you up and not let you fall ever again. In the end, whether it's to that person or to each other, one will say it's because of you that I'm taking this chance and if you or I fall, we will be there for one another to pick each other up.

WHAT I LIKE ABOUT YOU
October 29, 2005

Someone once said, ~Every now and then, we find a special friend who never lets you down, who understands it all, reaches out each time we fall. You're the best that I have found, I know that you can't stay, but part of you will never go away. Your heart will stay. I'll make a wish for you and hope it will come true, that life will be kind to such a gentle mind, and if you lose your way, think on yesterday; remember me this way.~ There is no denying the feeling you get when you meet someone that you feel comfortable with and yet scared at the same time. Scared, not in the sense of turning around and running away, but rather facing that person's direction to where you simply face the fear that feels good within you.

There comes a point in life where you think nobody understands the particular situations one is going through. However, there is somebody out there who somehow knows what you are going through and reassures you that you are not alone, even though you may feel like it at times. Fortunately, you have friends that you absolutely trust to have your back and comfort you when one needs them the most. In some aspect, that loneliness you feel is like being in the ocean and the so-called waters of past hurts, as well as the emotions that go along with it tend to be at times overwhelming to the point you feel like you're drowning, in the metaphorical sense of course. For everywhere you look there is no sign of help to throw you a life preserver to pull you out of the water and take you to safety.

Primarily, it takes someone who not only will reach out to you when you are "drowning" but also get into the water as well. The key factor in all this will and always be trust as you show that person that you're not just going to stand there and encourage him or her but physically be there at one's side. Oftentimes, those who supposedly encouraged you in the past and put your trust in to stay at your side turned their backs on you leaving not only you to "drown" in your emotions but also your heart to "drown" in sadness as well. It's that particular time when you are treading water, one wants to simply let go and sink within yourself and not come up; but there will be someone who will come along that won't give up on you and prevent you from "drowning" ever again.

Let me ask you this question, has there been or is there a person who you feel helped you or is helping you from sinking and consider him or her special in your life? It's that person that even though you only see him or her for either a brief moment of time or on a daily basis part of that person stays with you. A part of him or her that makes you smile when you think about that person to the point where acquaintances, friends, and/or family catch you at your most vulnerable. A vulnerability that at first you want to deny your experiences, but soon realize you can't help but feel that way and accept the truth within your own heart. Let me tell you something, every person has felt or is feeling that way and hopefully it's a feeling you never want to go away.

In retrospect, whether you know it or not there will be someone who wishes for you the happiness that you seek in hopes that it will come true for you. For it may be that someone who is standing in front of you, and you don't even know it. Unfortunately, it's unknown when the happiness you seek will eventually come and he or she will metaphorically throw that proverbial life preserver towards your heart which arrives just in time for you. Ultimately, it's that person whose selfless acts of kindness such as being there for you as a friend, making you laugh just to see that smile on your face, or simply spending a brief moment in with time with you just chillin' and hanging out with each other, which in the end, you say to that person or to each other that's what I like about you.

A GOOD THING
October 31, 2005

Arthru C. Clarke once said, ~New ideas pass through three periods: 1.) It can be done. 2.) It probably can be done, but it's not worthy doing. 3.) I knew it was a good idea all along.~ Now as you may or may not know, working in the asylum ideas pop in our heads on a semi-daily basis to where we can be considered creative or out of our minds due to when we say these four words out loud which are I have a plan. However, it's the kids of the asylum that are out of their minds when they have ideas/suggestions that either involve the rules, the asylum itself, or the staff who work there such as myself. Let me tell you something, a person can either laugh, be concerned, or be very afraid at what "my kids" come up with.

For the most part, I'm the type of person who's not a stickler for the rules, but when it comes to the safety and well-being of "my kids" they will be enforced. It can really be a frustrating situation indeed when the rules one enforces don't necessarily fly with them and suggestions are made to change those rules. Rules they don't like abiding by then we suggest that he, she, or they shouldn't come back or go somewhere else if you don't like the rules. I've basically said in the past, that you're considered #1 in a child's list of favorite counselors unless you say or do something they don't like due to the rules, which has happened to me over the past 9 years. Let me tell you something, If I had a penny for every time a child asked me to bend/change the rules just for them, I would be a very rich man.

Fred G. Smalley Youth Center aka The Insane Asylum hasn't really changed that much on the outside in the past 9 years but on the inside changes have been made over the years. Many of these changes have been suggested by not only staff but by kids as well who without a doubt have a say in their house, so to speak, which they hang out in before and after school. If compared to it would like an extreme makeover: home edition type change in which a new floor for the gym, new games as well as game systems such as XBOX, PS2, Gamecube, etc, sound resistant barriers added to the game room ceiling to greatly reduce noise, and finally new furniture that truly needed to be updated with the times.

When it comes to suggestions/ideas there is one that tends to be repeated over and over again by the kids to me. What suggestion you may be asking...well lets just say its about me growing taller, which you would think would get under my skin to the point where I turn into and/or act like Joe Pesci's character in Goodfellas and start laying the smackdown. BUT I'm bigger than that...nahhh not really... because you see, experience has taught me that its best to fight fire with fire and use what comes natural to me which is sarcasm. Essentially, when they throw the height issue in my direction, I primarily retaliate back as to why they don't listen/behave and why I should not give the lowdown to one's parent(s) as to their misdeeds that I chose not to report to them. *sinister grin* Hey, this is what I go through folks almost every day

In retrospect, the suggestions that are made by "my kids" can either be reasonable or unreasonable. It really depends on the suggestion at hand which can be pretty out there when you hear them. Yet, the one thing that staff and kids of the asylum agree on suggestion wise is that the vans/bus needs to be majorly altered. Undeniably, the suggestion by the kids, as well as a few staff is to put together a tape to send to Xzibit and West Coast Customs to pimp our rides. Suggestions as pimp out the sound system; add flip down monitors to the ceiling plus monitors to the backs of the seats for long road trips of course; spinners for the wheels, a kickin' paint job that reflects the asylum's personality, and finally hydraulics so that the vans/bus' front end rise up and down low rider style. In the end, that particular suggestion right there by the kids is not considered a bad thing, it's most definitely considered a good thing.

GIMMIE A BREAK(FOR ALL MOMS)
October 31, 2005

David O. McKay once said, ~The noblest calling in the world is that of mother. True motherhood is the most beautiful of all arts, the greatest of all professions. She who can paint a masterpiece or who can write a book that will influence millions deserve the plaudits and admiration of mankind; but she who rears successfully a family of healthy, beautiful sons and daughters whose immortal souls will be exerting an influence throughout the ages long after painting shells have faded, and books and statues shall have been destroyed, deserves the highest honor that man can give.~ Let me ask you this question ladies, how many of you are moms to beautiful kids, whether you're single or married?

Essentially, the key to motherhood is patience because it takes a lot of that to keep a handle on your kids whether you're a single mom or a married one. Though dear old dad may be in charge of the family, it's ultimately the mom who has the final say. We've all asked our dads for something fairly important in our minds to where he proceeds to tell us to wait and asks one's mother, which is somewhat comical because I may do that someday with my kids, but I digress. For it takes a lot of patience to deal with one's child/children when they throw fits/temper tantrums in public and not let the full fury of one's anger run rampant to the point one child may or may not return home." For the question can be asked, have you ever done that to your kids or was that ever done to you?

Motherhood can oftentimes be a thankless job as moms take on so many responsibilities and roles that she can be absolutely confused at where she is. It's truly amazing that a mom can handle so many things on her plate, in a manner of speaking, as she is able to keep at times her own thoughts in order. Thoughts that are probably exhausting to even think about from a guy's perspective because we can only focus on one thought at a time unlike women who have many thoughts running through their head. Whether it's what food to repair, paying the bills on time, what you're going to do the next day or next week even, helping your kids with homework, and most certainly worrying about the safety as well as well-being of one's kid(s)/spouse, which they do with military like precision.

Without a doubt, moms can truly be considered the general of the family as they try to keep order in a sometimes unorderly home. It can be a daunting task to be strong not only for yourself, but also for your kids because if they see you fall physically and/or emotionally then, in a sense, you've failed. Yet, it's not considered a failure because you sacrificed so much to keep him, her, them happy even though you yourself may not be. Whether you're single or married, it's a tough job to raise children either by yourself or with help of family due to breaking up, divorce, and/or by one's spouse in the military. Inevitably, it's just a matter of receiving the strength you need from not only those who love/care about you, but also from God through constant fervent prayer.

In retrospect, when you are a mom, every day should be Mother's Day, which dads would disagree with due to the fact that they seemingly receive the same gifts every Father's Day such as ties, shirts, tools, and mugs with the world's greatest dad on it. It's the go-to-gifts that, in some ways, make it easy for mom and the child/children to buy for. However, if you think about it though, moms go through so much more and yet ask for so little that they deserve to be pampered every once in a while, or practically every day, which I bet every mom would love to have happen to her. In the end, there comes a point where moms basically need a time for themselves and say to themselves or to the big man upstairs, oh please gimmie a break.

A WHOLE NEW WORLD
November 2, 2005

George Elliot once said, ~What greater thing is there for two human souls than to feel that they are joined together to strengthen each other in all labour, to minister to each other in all sorrow, to share with each other in all gladness, to be one with each other in the silent unspoken memories. I like not only to be loved, but to be told that I am loved.~" Living in a world that has billions of people on it, you can't help but sometimes feel alone even though you may be surrounded by friends and family who care about you enough to help you through the tough times. Times, in which world you're living in, as well as the world in your heart can spin out of control to a point where you're left with torn pieces that may or may not be repaired.

Without a doubt, a person who you once considered you're everything, your world suddenly stops turning. For the world that you once knew metaphorically crumbled from underneath/around you as that once stable foundation, which solidly supported your heart, now lies in rumble with your own heart underneath. Yet, even though that particular guy or girl no longer has you in his or her heart, you have unwanted emotional pieces of him or her still within your heart. It's truly a sad situation for a woman, as well as a guy, to let go of the love one has for that guy or girl who now has turned one's heart against you, which can totally stop your world from turning on its axis, so to speak.

For the most part, it takes a while for your world to rebuild to the point where your own heart can be supported again. It's in that rebuilding stage you find reasons not to fall in love with someone who knowingly or unknowingly walks into one's life. Without a doubt, the pangs of a past hurt or past hurts left a person with empty spaces in his or her heart that when a possibility of love might touch it again, those empty spaces cause you pain as you try to breathe in that person, in a manner of speaking. In some aspect, its like soaring higher for someone you want to be with, but the higher you keep going the more pressure builds up and it gets harder and harder to breathe, which is how love is at times as one wants to go to new horizons within your heart.

If you think about it, it's not only the pressure you feel to try to breathe in someone new, but also the pressure that causes your own heart to have an emotional connection as well. It's a tough task indeed for some, most or all women to re-open one's vault of feelings and emotions that you so wanted locked away in order not to be toyed with ever again, which is most definitely understandable. For it takes someone who one feels absolutely comfortable with and is able to make you not only breathe easier but also brings back that once lost smile that was not only missing from your face but from within one's heart and soul. Let me ask you this question, how long did it take before you let your emotions that you felt within your heart and soul take over with a certain guy or girl after suffering a really hard breakup with someone you truly cared about/loved.

Someone once said, ~To the world you may be one person, but to one person you may be the world.~ In retrospect, a person will think that his or her world will never change as one will continue to let one's head decide instead of his or her heart due to past pain(s). However, that special someone will show up and take you on a so-called magic carpet ride to where your heart and soul has been before, but never stayed long enough to touch the stars, as well as see the points of view that weren't able to be traveled until now. In the end, that guy or girl will ultimately take you out of a world once filled with sadness and heartbreak to one filled with love and happiness that is considered to be for you a whole new world.

WHY NOT
November 3, 2005

Arthur Christopher Benson once said, ~Because of a friend, life is a little stronger, fuller, more gracious thing for the friend's existence, whether he be near or far. If the friend is close at hand, that is best, but if he is far away he is still there to think of, to WONDER about, to hear from, to write to, to share life and experience with, to serve, to honor, and to admire, to love.~ If you think about it, there are many things to wonder about that you just have to ask those tough questions. Questions such as: Why is the sky blue? What is the meaning of life? Where does your lap go when you stand up? Why do hot dog buns come in a package of 6 when hot dogs come in a package of 8? BUT the big question to wonder about is why does liking/loving someone feel so good and yet hurt so bad?

Essentially, when it comes to liking or loving someone, you wonder why we go through what each of us go through. Undeniably we're all gluttons for punishment when you're taking the chance to put not only yourself out there but also to put your own heart out there as well. In some aspect, one's heart can take hit after hit, somewhat like a pinata, from people who one thought cared enough about them not to metaphorically stick a knife in their own heart. For when he or she walks away, you are left with your heart bleeding with emotions that you try to stop/ control but can't and the only thing left to do is let the tears fall where they may, which is the best thing a person can possibly do in that particular situation.

For those who are living the single life, like myself, you tend to wonder if there is someone who is thinking about you, which can be considered somewhat egotistical on one's part. When it comes to potential relationships, if any, there is an uncertainty as to whether or not that a particular person is thinking about you. Without a doubt, we all have been or are going through situations where you wonder what thoughts are going through the mind of him or her to the point where you start to drive yourself completely crazy. In all honesty though, knowing or finding out that someone is thinking about you, in a non-creepy sense of course, gives a person hopefully a special feeling inside to where he or she is truly flattered.

Unfortunately, that uncertainty one experiences, is experiencing, or will experience keeps a person continually wondering/guessing what that person's life was before you met him or her. For the question can be asked was his or her life filled with seemingly great relationships or relationships that left a person burned to the point he or she is scared to open one's heart again. It can work both ways as a person takes a chance with one's heart and wonders if that door of opportunity will either be opened or closed shut. Essentially, it's something that everybody wonders about when we meet someone who totally intrigues us to where you genuinely want to get to know more about that person on a more personal, emotional, spiritual, and intellectual level.

William H. Sheldon said, ~There are those much more are people who never lose their curiosity, there almost childlike wonder at the world; those people who continue to learn and to grow intellectually until the day they die. And these usually are the people who make contributions, who leave some part of the world a little better off than it was before they entered it.~ In retrospect, there will always be wonder/curiosity as to why liking and/or loving someone can be considered easy, but in reality, difficult. Ultimately, a person will oftentimes ask and wonder why liking/loving someone has to hurt, has to be so frustrating, has be so complicated when its someone you like/love; but then you stop asking why and realize why not because in the end, it gives you that sense of purpose to not quit and to go for it will all your heart.

THOSE WERE THE DAYS
November 4, 2005

Ann Fairbairn once said, ~A man cannot cast aside his childhood, though he ran from it as he would the devil. He may make of it a burden under which to stumble and fall, or a shield to hide behind, or he may make of it a tool. One of the best things to keep close and look back on is our own childhood as we remember certain aspects of it that you really enjoyed. As said before, television was a big part of my childhood that ruled in the 80's, which I would gladly relive again if it were humanly possible, but I digress. When it comes to our childhood, a person can talk with others and find out if he, she, or they did the same things you did, but in a different way. Things that if you suggested that person do now either with you or alone, he or she may actually do it.

Let me ask you this question, did you ever in your childhood wear a fanny pack? For it was considered a fashion accessory for girls, but for boys it was something to keep their junk in like pencils, cards, and stuff. Essentially, it was a portable storage unit in front that fit around your waist that you could wear either in front of you, to the side, or the back of you. Personally speaking, I have one somewhere collecting dust, a black Nike fanny pack that was used consistently back in the day when no fear t-shirts were the thing to wear, and BMX biking was the extreme sport to be in or watch. To be perfectly honest, I had one because everyone else had one so basically, I was considered a follower, and I would probably wear it again just to do it.

Without a doubt, each of us wore friendship bracelets and the more bracelets you had on your wrists the more friends you supposedly had. For the most part, you either knew someone or were friends with someone who made them and got the proverbial hookup, so to speak. Personally speaking, my friend back then Stacie Allen made a black and white one for me that I wore and never took off. Initially, the only way for it to come off was either it was old and fell off or your mom told you to cut it off due to a pungent odor coming from it. For the question can be asked to the ladies, did you ever make them and if so, did you make any profits to those that weren't considered your friends?

One of the best recreational activities that mainly boys like myself participated in back in the day was pencil fighting. It was considered a sport of champions which tested the durability of one's pencil against the durability of another kid's pencil. There was strategy and a bit of underhandedness to the whole thing as you would try to get the upper hand by doing things such as taking the eraser out, flatting the metal end, and using it to your advantage which I did. Hey, it got the job done and to tell you the truth it was a lot of fun even though I did suffer many pencil casualties playing the game. Let me tell you something, if someone challenged me to a pencil fight right now, I would do it in a heartbeat.

In retrospect, there are just some things in our childhood when we look back on them the kid inside us just smiles. Just go back, look at your middle school yearbooks, and have a fun time looking at what fun you hopefully had back then with the people who are either were or still are friends. Hey, you may even find out that your future best friend of 9 years went to the same middle school you did and not even know it. For the nostalgic feeling you get when looking back at good times with your friends makes you wish that the hands of time could turn back for either a day or a week and relive it with one's current memories included. In the end, when you take a look back at the things you wore or did back then, you simply sigh and say with a smile on your face, those were the days.

TIME FOR A CHANGE
November 4, 2005

Someone once said, ~Dependability is being trustworthy. If you are dependable, you are believable and reliable. A dependable person persists or endures in a responsibility until the job is complete.~ In life, whether its personal or professional, dependability is key when it involves the people we know, hang with, care about, are involved with, are related to, and/or work with on a semi-daily basis. Essentially, it's that keyword called trust that you have with a person or a group of people who will not let you down when life gives you tough challenges. Let me ask you this question, who do you know that is absolutely dependable to help you in any way, shape, or form at a moment's notice?

Without a doubt, dependability and friendship go hand in hand as you trust that friend or group of friends to have your back. Yet, that dependability can be tested as one can be taken for granted for being the go-to-person when someone needs or wants something. Such needs or wants are many and a ride which are the two most significant things that a friend can overstep on. We all have friends that borrow money who we trust/depend on to pay back the amount in due time, which he or she can try to avoid depending on the type of friend one hangs with. This can also pertain to a person's ride as well to where a friend/friends continually take advantage of your generosity, which can be limited.

When it comes to potential and/or significant relationships you want a person who one can depend on to be there for you even when that person is there without even being asked. For it's that selfless act of kindness/love that is rare to find these days in someone who you want to spend the rest of your life with and yet you somehow find the Mr./Ms. Wrongs of the world. It's a sad situation indeed for a woman when a guy she trusts/depends on to be her steady anchor and to catch her when she falls doesn't, which can mentally and emotionally bruise her deep within her heart. For the question can be asked, when it came to bad past relationships, who was that person or persons that you thought you could depend on to be there for you but failed you.?

When talking about dependability it can oftentimes be associated with a certain well-known establishment and the employees who work there, which includes management. Whether its services such as car repair, fast food, construction, accounting, etc., whatever the case may be, we all want the absolute best from them as possible. For a company such as Enron, which was billed by Fortune Magazine as 'America's Most Innovative Company' for 6 straight years(1996-2001), had many investors trusted and depended on them to keep their money safe and well protected, but unfortunately that did not happen as Enron managers/executives took the money, retired early, and sold company stock before it went belly up. Many jobs were lost, and a sizable portion of people's retirement funds ruined all because of greed.

Working at the asylum for the past 9 years, I along with my best friend have been considered the two most reliable and dependable guys working there. Guys who primarily break our backs for the asylum day in and day out and we don't ask for the recognition for it because in our minds we do it for the kids. Not to sound egotistical or anything, but for the most part, we're the backbone of the asylum and whenever there is some event, such as The Blue Angel Air Show, the two people that management usually come to first are us. For they think we will always say yes, but not this time due to the fact we feel burned out and overworked. In the end, you sometimes just have to put your foot down and say enough is enough, it's time for a change.

SHE'S THE ONE
November 5, 2005

Someone once said, ~Throughout life you will meet one person who is unlike any other. This one person one could forever talk to. They understand you in a way that no one else does or ever could. This person is your soulmate, your best friend. Don't let them go, for they are your guardian angel sent from heaven about.~ It's a funny thing about life, we meet so many people in our lifetime that we may or may not remember the names that go with the faces. It's those faces that we all pass by on a semi-regular basis whether it's a complete stranger or the people we know, care about, and/or love. There comes a point, while on our journey, where you will meet that one person who will, has given, or is going to give you a reason to smile and keep that smile on your face.

Let me ask you this question, have you met or encountered someone who totally gave you or is giving you a new and/or different perspective on the way things are seen. Seen through the eyes of that person who somehow can see not only through your eyes, but also see into your heart as well. It's that person who can share, reveal, and/or bring to surface certain truths about yourself, life, and love that we all have or are going through, but really couldn't put it into words. It's a rarity these days to meet someone like this who is truly genuine that you don't question the smile he or she gives you, which is oftentimes cause for concern due to the fact you don't know what that person's true intentions are.

For a woman, it's hard to meet a guy that sets your own doubts aside when bad past relationships have them playing it safe with their own heart. Essentially, it's hard to trust themselves in opening up to a guy that quite possibly could possibly bring her to that deep dark place within one's heart and soul that has been like a sanctuary which keeps not only her anger, frustration, and bitterness but also the love she wants to truly shar with someone, but is afraid to. For it is her own heart and soul that isn't fully whole as there are missing pieces that have been metaphorically taken away by a guy or guys who at one time gave a reason for her to smile only to give her a reason to have that smile, as well as her heart and soul die.

Without a doubt some, most, or all women have that empty feeling inside that it probably makes them sad/miserable to see people she knows and is friends with have relationships that are filled with friendship, love, communication, and that key word again trust. Let me tell you something, its not only women who feel this way, but guys feel this way as well and its a feeling that can make you sick to your stomach and no amount of Pepto Bismol will make it ever go away. In a sense, women can feel like she has lost her way by forgetting how to love again and come to the point that she is no longer able to shed anymore tears. For the question can be asked of you ladies, how many of you have felt or are feeling this way, how has that feeling lasted, and is there a guy in your life right now that has your heart potentially smiling again?

There is a thought that I probably would be safe to say that a woman wrote which says: ~Find a guy who calls you beautiful instead of hot, who calls you back when you hang up on him, who will stay awake just to watch you sleep. Wait for the guy who kisses your forehead, who wants to show you off to the world when you are in your sweats, who holds your hand in front of his friends. Wait for the one who is constantly reminding you of how much he cares about you and how lucky he is to have you. Wait for the one who turns to his friends and says, "...that's her.~ Ultimately, every woman will meet or already has met that guy who sees what she doesn't see or want to see about herself and in the end that guy will say either in his head or to his friends she's the one.

ANYTHING IS POSSIBLE
November 6, 2005

Someone once said, ~There are 3 great things in the world. The first thing is for you to love someone. The second great thing is for someone to love you back and the third greatest thing is for the first and second thing to happen at the same time.~ Without a doubt, love is considered the single most powerful entity that one person can have for another. It's the driving force that keeps a person going even though one may not physically be strong enough. If you think about it, the power it has, whether it is given or received, can and/or will make a person physically, mentally, and emotionally stronger when it comes from someone that truly and genuinely loves/cares for you. Let me ask you this question, how many of you have someone in your life that loves/cares about you with all your heart and vice versa?

We all have people that we love such as family and friends, but when it comes to that someone special there is a much greater love for him or her. A love that oftentimes can't be explained and yet no amount of explanation can describe how a human being feels for another. Usually, there are no words to explain/describe how you feel for that particular person, you just go with what's in your heart and soul to where you let it speak for you. Each one of us have talked with people or someone who when asked about him or her, one's facial expressions just brighten up and they witness this firsthand. Let me give you this challenge, if you truly love somebody try not to smile when you talk about him or her and see how you do.

Essentially, it's quite easy to love someone with all your heart but to have that someone love you back can be considered at times difficult. For those who are living the single life, like myself, you want to meet that one person who will love you unconditionally with every fiber of one's being. Yet, that love can't be forced to where you make that person love you which is a deluded perception that can be taken too far, but I digress. For the love I'm speaking of has to be reciprocated back and all a person has to do is be there for that person as a friend first. Eventually that friendship turns into appreciation, that appreciation turns into like, that like turns into the love you always wanted not only in your life, but in your heart and soul as well.

For some, most or all people it took only one shot for love to come his or her way, which can also be said for the other person as well. Unfortunately, for others it has taken several shots to find/meet the love that is absolutely perfect, even though it isn't at times considered perfect. It's a whole lot of hard work, patience, communication, commitment, trust, honesty, but most of all a sense of humor when things in life just seem overwhelming that you can simply laugh at it together, which I was recently told. In a sense, that is the beauty of a long-lasting love that is found in someone you call your best friend when no matter how mad, frustrated, crazy, insane you get with each other he or she will be at your side forever and always, till death do you both part.

This past Sunday, two couples celebrated the bonds of marriage as well as the bond of friendship as well. The first couple celebrated their 44th wedding anniversary and the second only a mere 40 years together, which to me is longevity my friend. As to be expected, there was not a dry eye in the house as the couple who celebrated their 40th anniversary renewed their vows with not only the eyes of the Fil-Am Church family watching but also with eyes God watching as well. How many people can truly say that they've found the person they're going to spend the rest of their lives with and like I said in a past Yodaism, all it takes if you are truly lucky is just one look. In the end, if two people can meet each other, fall in love, and have love last 40 years or more, then anything is possible for a guy like me and for you as well.

HERE'S TO YOU (TO ALL MY FRIENDS)

November 8, 2005

What's up boys and girls! Let me first say that this won't be your typical Yodaism that I usually send out because I'm directly speaking to you guys. Secondly, this won't be "Yoda" speaking to you, it will be me, plain ole' Dante that you've gotten to know and grown to love...hopefully. Anyways, about 9 years ago I started a journey that began after I graduated High School in 1996 and it wasn't until 2 years ago that I started sharing my thoughts with friends and so far, you've enjoyed them. Why am I telling you this? Well because after the 1st Yodaism there were 298 that came right after that and now this Yodaism marks the 300th edition. So, what better way to say thank you than to give a shout out to all my friends.

To my friends in myspace and Friendster: Thank you for not deleting me from your friends lists and may we have a great cyberspace friendship for years to come. To Ed, you and I have known each other since back in our Bellview Middle School, as well as the Fil-Am days. Now that you're retiring from being a publicist, come back to the place where it all began for you which is Pensacola. To Michelle Haro, I wish you best of luck in finding the guy that will make you truly happy one day, plus I stick by all that I said about you whether it be mostly right or wrong. To Ashley, I'm glad you found the guy of your dreams and may it last a lifetime. Oh, one more thing keep on writing because a piece of me truly rubbed off on you.

To the asylum crew past and present. You guys have not only been my friends and current/ former employees, but you've also been like family. When I first started at the asylum 9 years ago, I was a quiet, wet behind the ears 19 year old kid. BUT that all changed after a verbal fight between 3 former co-workers who had me so angry that my best friend had to take me outside and cool me off. From that point on, I changed, and it was a change for the better. To Germaine, Val, and Rose you ladies brightened up the asylum. To Ms. Angie and Ms. Cindy, I consider you two mentors who taught me to be a leader. To Cheryl, a big oohra to you. To the asylum brotherhood knuckle ups and heads to you guys. But most of all to Ducky and Biggie, my running buddies from the start, you both are and will always be my bros.

To the PCC filipino posse: ka guys ay pag-araal mag-anak. Frank, ako pag-araal iba kapatid na lalaki at Rebecca, ako pag-araal ka ang maliit kapatid na babae atipan ng pawid akin kapatid na lalaki at ako lagi magkulang. sa ang pinoys maibigan Frank, Alex, Dave, Jepoy, Jahmai, Bryan, busbusin panguluhan nods at buko ng daliri ups sa ang kapatiran. sa ang maganda pinays maibigan Maiza, Jek, Airish, Barbie, Blessing, Joy , at ang lalong nakararami lahat Lyrisse; ako naisin ka talunin naisin at true happiness sa lumapit mo daan. ang pinto ay lagi buksan at akin bahay I'll iwan ang sindihan sa dahil sa ka. pagayon ako sabihin kumuha a malaki puso, marami ibigin at mayo ang panginoon basbasan bawa't isa at bawa't isa ng ka. kapayapaan lumitaw!

Special shout outs to the S4LP, GH Nation, and to "my kids". To the S4LP, you guys are a part of my past, which has seen its good times and bad times. To the GH nation, you were guys that actually read what I wrote/sent to you two where many of you actually printed them out and kept them which I do greatly appreciate. To "my kids", thanks for giving me great stories that have made people laugh and cry. To everybody, I've said many times before to those who are asking and have asked for my advice, when matters of love/life get complicated simply follow your heart and it will hopefully lead you in the right direction. To all my friends, as well as those I forgot to mention, here's to you and in the immortal words of 90's pop culture icons Bartles and James I simply say thank you for your support.

CRAZY LIKE A FOX
November 10, 2005

Charles and Ann Morse once said, ~The history of our grandparents is remembered not with rose petals but in the laughter and tears of their children and their children's children. It is into us that the lives of grandparents have gone. Its is in us that their history becomes a future.~ Without a doubt, the cornerstone of one's family is the grandmother and/or grandfather because they are considered to be the matriarch/patriarch who have been through and seen it all. Some amazing stories can be told by one's grandparent(s) as they share/reveal things that can either make you laugh, cry, or become totally speechless to where you not only learn something new but get closer to him, her, or them. Let me ask you this question, when was the last time you spent quality time with your grandma, grandpa, or both?

Big momma/poppa, Nanay/Tatay, Mammy/Pappy, Grams/Gramps etc. whatever the case may be, people from every walk of life call their grandparent(s) by a certain name that one either distinguishes him, her, or them by as a child growing up or through tradition. It can be somewhat of a comical situation to not only hear people say it but also witness firsthand the way a person acts around their grandparent(s) depending on whether or not they hear or have heard some upsetting news about their grandchild/grandchildren. If you think about it, parents can be disappointed in their kid(s) and he, she, or they would probably shrug it off in a nanosecond. However, to have one's grandparent(s) be disappointed in you can be a tremendous blow to not only you but to him, her, or them as well.

When it comes to one's grandparent and/or grandparents there should always be absolute respect shown towards them because they truly deserve it. In my own thinking, if a person shows respect, that will carry over when each of us become grandparents as they show respect towards us, which is what you want to teach your kids when or if you have some someday. Being part of a Filipino family and the culture, as a kid, or in your 20's, or in your late 40's when you see a grandparent the proper respect given is to take that person's hand and touch it to your forehead. Yet, it's not limited to blood relatives, because I've seen my own friends do it with my own grandmother and that's simply cool in my book.

One of the many advantages of being a grandchild is receiving money for such events as one's birthday, graduation, or just because he, she, or they love us. It can warm and touch a person's heart that a person who may or may not have much to give is willing to give out of their own pocket because they love us and that makes him, her, them happy. Though one may not at times show that love due to one's own hectic life, it's nice to reciprocate that love back by doing something special back such as giving a card, a dinner on you, or just simply a hug, which can be considered the best gift a person can ever give. For the question can be asked, when was the last time you gave your grandma and/or grandpa a hug and is it a hug that has been long overdue?

In retrospect, I never really had the chance to meet both my grandfathers due to their passing away, but my dad's mom I got the chance to spend a month with her before she passed away due to cancer. It was a sad but happy time because she accepted God as her Lord and savior before she passed away My grandmother, my mom's mom, is 83 years old, had 10 wonderful kids, and is the one of the craziest/funniest people I know because you see every time she sees either me or my brother she is shaking us down for money(quarters) as if she is in the mafia. Do you have a grandmother like this? In the end, whether it's your grandparent or mine, in our eyes they're crazy like a fox; but it's a good kind of crazy because when they eventually pass on, he and/or she will be remembered with laughter rather than sadness.

HOME IS WHERE THE HEART IS

November 11, 2005

Rainer Maria Rilke once said, ~Believe in love that is being stored up for you like an inheritance, and have faith in this love that there is strength and a blessing so large that you can travel as far as you wish without having to step outside it.~ In some aspect, love can be considered a destination in which every person is traveling or has traveled to and for some its a destination that one has been traveling on for quite some time. For its when a person finally reaches their intended destination, it sometimes or oftentimes seems as if there is nobody truly genuine to greet not only yourself, but your own heart as well. In a sense, its like you're stranded in a foreign, but oh so familiar territory with your passport(heart) in hand.

If you think about it, a passport is considered one of the most important documents to have because it identifies who you are when entering/leaving a country. We've all traveled or planning to travel to places known or unknown and myself being at one time a military kid my passport was stamped traveling to such places as to the place of my birth the Philippines and Puerto Rico. In any case, like a passport, our own heart identifies who each of us truly are on the inside and no amount of physical changes to one's own face can hide your true identity from people who know, love, and care about you and I. For its those people who have stamped your heart in some way, shape or form that had or still have an impact on your life.

Without a doubt, a person can rack up some major frequent flier miles to new, interesting, and exotic places. In a way, our own heart can rack up some major frequent flier miles, in a manner of speaking, as one metaphorically travels or tries to travel a whole new world in a place that is oftentimes or sometimes difficult to open up. Yet, its within our own heart that one has always been ready to venture to something or to someone but for reasons known or unknown there are or were problems that prevented you from boarding, so to speak. Let me ask you this question, is there a person who is potentially holding your passport that you truly want to get his or her stamp of approval and have him or her enter your heart?

Unfortunately, though, there are times where one's passport gets rejected not once but several times to where it can make a person lose interest in never seeing what is in his or her heart. For it can also come to the point where the decision is made to put away one's passport to never be used again, like your heart. Essentially, the feelings and emotions one has for a particular either in one's past or present, can be either stored or hidden away, which can be the most difficult thing a person can ever do when someone he or she is truly interested in. For the question can be asked, how many times have you put away your passport never to be used again, but as the saying goes never say never.

Marvin J. Ashton once said, ~Love is a vehicle allowed to travel without limitations.~ In retrospect, when it comes to the love you have in your heart, one should never hide it or put it away for safekeeping like a passport. The reason why is that you never know when you will meet someone that will take you on a journey that you weren't prepared to go on, which nobody ever really is. Ultimately, it's just a matter of showing/opening your passport(heart) little by little until you truly feel comfortable completely opening it. In the end, when you do finally open your heart to someone without any limitations holding you back, that once foreign territory in your heart is now a place you can truly feel comfortable living in, which feels like home and as the old saying goes home is where the heart is.

HERE I STAND
November 13, 2005

Someone once said, ~Friendship is the bridge between lonely and loved, between a glance and a gaze. It stretches from the fog into sunshine, hopelessness into faith, between despair and joy. It crosses the chasm from hell to heaven, from God to man, and from you to me.~ Essentially, there is an in between place that every person has been in before or is in now, which like the above quote is considered a bridge where we basically stand smack dab in the middle. For that metaphorical bridge can most definitely represent a person's heart as it "stands" there in the middle deciding on which direction to take when it pertains to a special someone. Let me ask you this question, how many of you are standing in the middle of your own personal bridge as we speak?

If you think about it, a person can spend so much time walking/running one's metaphorical bridge that he or she has no earthly idea where they are going. It's like chasing after a dream, so to speak, that has seemingly gone on for a lifetime. We all know or have some idea who we want to be with and yet there is that relentless voice in the back of one's mind that is telling you it's a bad idea. For those initial seeds of doubt can lead a person to go back and forth not only within your heart but within your emotions as well. Let me tell you something, it's not a fun experience whatsoever being in that kind of endless wandering back and forth leading to absolutely nowhere, which is a place that you never want to be in, trust me on this.

Without a doubt, when it comes to potential and/or significant relationships the bridge that every person is standing on can be a long tedious trek as we look at the vastness of an ongoing road. For there are primarily two directions in which we all have looked or are looking at and it's those two directions that are a representation of the past and future, with ourselves standing in the middle which represents the present. A present, where each one of us is teeter tottering within our own heart to either stay back or move forward but due to one's fears it makes you stay back not letting you move forward to whoever that person may be that is either standing up close or far beyond the road ahead.

There comes a point when you stand on your own individual bridge, certain things tend to mean a lot more than it did in the past. We've all simply glanced at the water reflected sun when crossing a bridge but never really took the time to really look at it. However, when you start gazing into that water reflected sun you start seeing the calming beauty of it all as things start to make sense for you, which makes one's journey that much more enjoyable. For the heavy fog that's been clouding one's direction and mind has initially been lifted to where the hopelessness and despair that you feel eventually turns to faith and joy. Yet, the question remains: does that person feel the same way or is he or she on a different bridge and going in a different direction?

Gillian Anderson's character Dana Scully(X-Files) once said, ~Well, it seems to me that the best relationships--the ones that last-- are frequently the ones that are rooted in friendship. You know, one day you look at the person and you see something more than you did the night before. Like a switch has been flicked somewhere. And the person who was just a friend is...suddenly the only person you can ever imagine yourself with.~ In retrospect, I've stood on my personal bridge many times before, but I found myself simply walking away knowing who was beyond it due to my own fears. In the end, I find myself standing at that bridge again in which I say/think to myself it's here I stand once again, now which direction do I take and my answer...I'm not going to walk away this time.

LIE, CHEAT, AND STEAL
November 16, 2005

The late Owen Hart once said, ~I find too often in the wrestling business, you just wrestle, get to the hotel, make your money. Sometimes I have to stop and remind myself to enjoy my life and not just rush through.~ The world of professional wrestling is a business that goes all year round and unlike sports such as baseball, basketball, football, etc. there is no off season. Essentially when you decide to become a professional wrestler you sign up to be away from home months at a time, which is a big sacrifice to make for not only yourself but also for your family. Primarily, you have to love what you do in front of millions of people, if you don't then you're in the wrong business.

In a business, fans, like myself, can make or break a wrestler by simply responding to a particular wrestling character that determines either longevity or back to the drawing board, so to speak. For those who aren't wrestling fans, you don't really have an understanding as to why fans like myself go nuts overgrown mature adults wearing ridiculous looks and hitting each other over the head with chairs. From a fan's perspective, its mainly the entertainment aspect of it all as you can go through so many emotions such as anger, happiness, shock, spite. etc. and yet know that these guys are giving you an awesome show even though at times they may or may not be feeling that good emotionally, as well as physically.

As said before, pro wrestlers don't get an off season and the injuries they suffer over the years take their toll. Its the price they pay for doing what they love to do and oftentimes the injuries they suffer happen while in the ring. Though I haven't seen it live, I witnessed on television wrestlers such as Eddie Guerrero break their arm or Triple H suffer a serious possibly career ending leg injury and despite that they continued to to wrestle until the match has ended, which shows how devoted these guys are to their craft. Whether it's bruised ribs, torn up knees, broken necks, or the simple bumps and bruises, these guys play hurt and yet they work past the pain to try to give awesome performances day in and day out.

Personally speaking, I have been a wrestling fan for almost 21 years, and I grew up watching wrestlers such as Hulk Hogan, Ric Flair, Sting, The Legion of Doom, and many more. I couldn't see any other profession that these guys are suited for other than wrestling, how about you? Undeniably, wrestling fans aren't stupid because we know that it's scripted, not fake but despite that fact we watch anyway because its pure entertainment. In what business can you kidnap a person's wife or try to run someone over with a car and not get arrested for it. It's the passion they give for the wrestling business that keeps us watching and wanting more every week.

In retrospect, when you speak of passion for the business Eddie Guerrero had tons of passion burning within his heart to where he was known as Latino Heat. He grew up in the wrestling business and wrestled with his own demons as well. E.G. passed away Sunday, which shocked not only fans but his friends/wrestlers and family as well. He was humble, had charisma, talent, personality, but most of all he had a big heart. I'm going to miss seeing the three amigos, the frog splash, the way he tried to get the upper hand, but most of all I'm going to miss him coming out in the lowriders. In the end, Eddie Guerrero stole all our hearts, which is fitting in a way for a man who lived by a creed that will live on forever for every wrestling fan and that creed was to lie, cheat, and steal.

BY THE NUMBER
November 18, 2005

Adolf Galland once said, ~Sometimes numbers are the telling factor.~ For some, most, or all of you who have read a number of the Yodaisms that have been sent out. If you've read my early one's compared to the one's you've been reading recently there is a definite change in the overall structure but conceptually the ideas are still the same. Just to refresh your memory the title, quotes, and mood are the three key ingredients that bring it all together. Yet, the question remains, how many quotes have been used, which author(s) have been used and or quoted the most, which Yodaism would I like to redo, what three subject matters have been primarily talked about, and most importantly, which particular subject matter has been thought about the most.

In the early stages of writing these Yodaisms there wasn't any use of quotes because they were basically short thoughts. But as time progressed the Yodaisms started to progress as it got more and more on a deeper level in which it made you think, as well as use your imagination. In my own thinking, the right quote is essential and authors such as Charles Dickens, Rainer Maria Rilke, William Shakespeare, Mark Twain, E.E. Cummings, Robert Louis Stevenson, C.S. Lewis, Leo Buscaglia, and Ralph Waldo Emerson were instrumental in making a Yodaism come together. Primarily 206 quotes have been used and when it comes to the author quotes most, 6 times, it comes from my favorite author Ralph Waldo Emerson.

Without a doubt, every Yodaism that I have written I have felt content in the finished product. However, there is one particular Yodaism that didn't really sit too well with not only myself but also other people as well. It was a Yodaism entitled Apple Of Your Eye in which that special someone was like an apple on a tree and the basic premise was asked how far are you willing to climb to be with that particular guy or girl of interest. It had the best intentions in being an ok Yodaism but it entirely went off into a totally different tangent. If I had to do it all over again, I would still use the same quote, but give it a new concept, as well as a new title "The Core" which may be done later down the road.

If you have been an avid reader of the Yodaisms that I sent out and/or posted, you get three subject matters that are either from my own personal experience or what I observe around me on a semi-daily basis. The first subject is life and each one of us goes through certain situations in life that are either similar or parallel to each other's lives. The second subject is love and/or relationships that every person can relate to a little bit or a lot, which one can sympathize with because you may be going through what I tend to talk about. The third subject is my job at the Youth Center otherwise known as The Insane Asylum, which has given me some of the greatest material to talk about when it concerns "my kids".

In retrospect, there have been countless friends who have read the Yodaisms that I have sent out to and they in turn have sent them to their friends. For there have been a number of people who have emailed me saying that certain Yodaisms have gotten them through the toughest of times. In any case, the total number of Yodaisms, which includes this one, comes to 306 and the number will continue to rise because there are many untapped subject matters to talk about such as Karma. Ultimately, the subject of my job has been talked about 26 times, love and/or relationships 132 times, and life about 148 times. So, in the end, when you look at it by the numbers the subject of life wins out just a bit over love and far surpasses what I see/do at work.

THE BROKEN ROAD
November 20, 2005

Someone once said, ~It's a long road when you face the world alone, when no one reaches out a hand for you to hold. You can find love if you search within your soul, and the emptiness you felt will disappear.~ If you think about it, our own heart can be considered a road in which each of us are traveling a metaphorical journey to find and/or meet that someone special who will permanently stop us from getting lost within it, not just physically but emotionally as well. For its when we all travel the proverbial highways and byways within our own heart you experience the highs and lows of love or the feelings you have that lead up to falling in love. Let me ask you this question, how long have you been traveling the lonely road within your own heart?

Without a doubt, it can be a lonely road as one hears and feels the bumps on the road of life, which oftentimes seems as if it's going on forever or around in circles. Depending on how big those bumps are they can be considered a representation of the moments of happiness/contentment one feels when meeting someone new and is inevitably interested in. It's those particular bumps, whether its brief or long term, that can give your heart a reason to beat faster as it hears and feels the beat of someone else's heart who is knowingly or unknowingly traveling the lonely road alongside with you, which may or may not truly be felt from someone either within an instant, within days, within weeks, within months, and/or within years.

Unfortunately, there are times where you will encounter potholes that can most definitely make one's travel complicated, difficult, and/or uncomfortable. If you think about it, those so-called potholes represent the times your trust and heart were broken to where there are pieces left scattered on the side of the road, so to speak. For its those broken pieces on the side of the road of life are the love/feelings that were once held by/for a particular someone but are now left untouched and unused, which is a sad situation indeed for a guy or girl who doesn't deserve that kind of hurt. A hurt so painful that you lose all feeling, emotion, and love to where you forget what it's like to experience it all over again in your heart.

However, every so-called pothole that is left on your heart will eventually lead you to that long-lost dream you've been wanting to come true. In some aspect, the signs have pointed or are pointing to where he or she is, but for reasons known or unknown you simply missed it, which happens or has happened to every person. Initially, we continue to go through the same emotions and feelings to the point of frustration that you so desperately want to experience something new and exciting. In a sense, your bad past relationship or relationships are compared to northern stars pointing/leading you by hand to that special someone. For the question can be asked, do you know who that one person is who is asking/wanting you to take his or her hand?

Ryan Erickson said, ~The road to finding the "the one" is paved with a bit of promiscuity.~ In retrospect, on the road of life you will meet individuals who have that certain something that you enjoy and appreciate such as a sense of humor, a warm, kind heart, honesty, and many other character traits. In any case, we're never really traveling alone because God is our companion/guide and even though you can't see Him you simply have to close your eyes, look deep within your soul, and He's there. In the end, it's by the grace of God that He blessed the broken road that leads you or already has led you to that one person who is everything you ever wanted and more. Plus, it's a song by country music group Rascal Flatts.

IN A HEARTBEAT
November 22, 2005

Crystal Rose once said, ~Love is a magical dream, existing forever in our minds.~ Without a doubt, love can be considered magical due to the fact that even though you don't know how it works, you just somehow know when meeting someone either for the first time or the second time around. The magic within something so simple and yet so complicated makes you want to truly experience someone who has that so-called magical energy surrounding him or her. An energy that can oftentimes be felt in a vibe, a look, a conversation, and/or a touch such as with a handshake or a kiss. It's that unexplainable energy you feel that can't be described with only words and you either go with it or deny it.

Let me ask you this question, is there anybody in your life that is sending/giving you that so-called magical energy that you have felt before but it somehow feels different? However, due to past relationships you don't want to accept the feeling for the simple reason of not wanting to get your expectations high and your heart broken all over again. In any case, that magical energy can be revealed in the body language one knowingly or unknowingly shows/reveals to a potential relationship in the making. Body language such as the turn away/look back glance, way you smile, and the lean in while talking to that person are signals you quietly give off to someone but absolutely speaks volumes to others who see it clear as day.

Unfortunately, there are certain people who believe love is nothing more than a word that has absolutely no feeling or meaning behind it. In other words, a myth/illusion that was created in order to make men and women feel better so that you could hold on to that one tangible thing called hope. They further argue that love is not a feeling or an emotion but rather a decision he or she makes and companies such as Hallmark are pulling on our so-called heart strings to make the decisions for us. For it's our own self-esteem that tends to play a key factor as "experts" say that because love is about making everybody happy, then love should make you happy and in turn your self-esteem grows. For the question can be asked, do you actually believe this?

When it comes to the magic of love, there comes a point where there is an inner struggle to keep your heart closed and to let it go freely. A struggle in which a sometimes difficult decision to either do what is easy and what is right for your own well-being. Undeniably, its would be quite easy to just completely shut off the feelings you have for a person who potentially may be "the one" who will make you happy for a lifetime because, in your own mind, it's better to not fall in love than to have your heart broken again. However, on the other side of that coin, you have to do what is right for your heart in order for it to heal and its just a matter of letting the right person who your heart genuinely and truly feels a gradual magical connection with.

In retrospect, every person wants love to be a magical story book dream that never ends to where we always have a happy ending. Yet, that isn't how love works and you simply have to learn the hard way rather than the easy way, which some, most or all or you have. Eventually, the nightmares of past relationships will fade as you meet that special someone who is truly worth dreaming about. Ultimately, the happiness and/or love you seek started as a lingering dream which has or will become a reality for you. In the end, the one place where that dream guy/girl is truly real is not found in one's eyes, not in a touch such as handshake or kiss, not in a smile, but found in a heartbeat and when you feel it, it honestly beats with love for you.

TO GOD BE THE GLORY
November 24, 2005

Ray Stannard Baker(David Grayson) once said, ~Thanksgiving is the holiday of peace, the celebration of work and the simple life... a true folk-festival that speaks the poetry of the turn of the seasons, the beauty of seedtime and harvest, the ripe product of the year - and the deep, deep connection of all these things with God.~ Let me ask you this question, what does Thanksgiving mean to you? Without a doubt, it's a holiday that some, most, or all people enjoy as we spend quality time with family you have or haven't seen for quite some time. A family that is normal as can be when visiting separately, but when brought together craziness and hilarity ensues.

When it comes to past Thanksgivings, what made the festive holiday such an enjoyable experience for you and your family? If I could venture to guess it would be the endless amounts of food to gorge on would be the number one answer, second would be family time as you get the 411 on each other's lives, and watching sporting events would be the third, which would be mainly for the guys. Undeniably, when getting together with family that you haven't seen for a while, there is a certain energy level that tends to rise when family is brought together as you see/hear it by the loud laughter and big smiles among the faces that you don't get to see on a regular basis.

As said before, the endless amount of food is mainly what each of us look forward to. For some, most, or all of us we prepare our stomachs to gorge/stuff ourselves with such traditional foods like Turkey, Ham, sweet potato pie, pumpkin pie, mashed potatoes, and if you're a vegetarian that doesn't eat meat then you get Tofurkey. Being a Filipino, the asian flavor is added into the mix with Filipino foods such as lumpia (egg rolls), pancit, chicken adobo, and many more mouthwatering delights. For the question can be asked, is reading this particular Yodaism making you hungry to the point you're thinking about taking a small piece out of the Thanksgiving meal planned for tonight? If so, be careful and if you're caught don't blame me.

If you think about it, the one place that tends to be strictly off limits before or during Thanksgiving is the kitchen. In the cook's or cooks' mind, the kitchen is considered the central military command and if anything important is needed someone will be sent out with specific orders to retrieve said items or items. Depending on who's cooking the meal, the kitchen is considered off limits to so-called unauthorized personnel who are lingering about to get a bit or at least a taste of something, which is a bad idea trust me on this. We've all tried to sneak a bite/taste and end up being whacked upside the head with a particular kitchen utensil such as a wooden spoon, spatula, a wooden rolling pin, whatever the object may be for you.

In the beginning of this Yodaism, I asked the question: what does Thanksgiving mean to you? For me personally, Thanksgiving means giving thanks to God for all the things has done for me in the past, present, and will do for me in the future. He provides me with food to eat every day, a job to pay my expenses as well as a place where I get to spend time and have fun with "my kids." BUT most of all He provided me with family and friends who love and care about me. Ultimately, I am thankful for the prayers that he has answered and for those unanswered prayers, I know He will answer them in due time. In the end, on this day of thanks I simply say to God be the Glory, great things he hath done for me and hopefully for you as well.

~HAPPY THANKSGIVING EVERYBODY!~

TIMES LIKE THESE
November 26, 2005

Someone once said, ~Total self-esteem requires total and unconditional acceptance of yourself. You are a unique and worthy individual, regardless of your mistakes, defeats and failures, despite what others may think, say or feel about you or your behavior. If you truly accept and love yourself, you won't have a driving need for attention and approval. Self-esteem is a genuine love of self. Stop all adverse value judgments of yourself. Stop accepting the adverse value judgments of others. Purge yourself of all condemnation, shame, blame, guilt and remorse.~ Let me ask you this question, did any past relationship(s) cause your self-esteem to a major blow to where you hide within yourself and keep the feelings you have for someone close to you.

Essentially, a person's self-esteem is one of the most fragile next to one's own heart which carries your feelings and emotions. When it comes to past love and/or relationships one's self-esteem can be metaphorically beaten up to the point where it's left black and blue, so to speak. It's a sad situation indeed when women, more so than guys, have their self-esteem toyed with/chopped down to size by a guy or guys who don't know how to treat them the right way. For any woman to experience that kind of degradation/humiliation which, in some ways, is like having the sun go down on you and you're left alone in total darkness to stumble around within their own feelings, emotions, and heart.

If you think about it, when one's self-esteem is lost/misplaced, you permanently or temporarily lose parts of yourself that are considered unique, special, and beautiful. Undeniably, it takes a special someone who is honest and genuine to gradually liven up one's self-esteem to where it will hopefully be fully intact. It's that particular guy/girl who brings to life, as well as gives back something that was initially taken away, metaphorically speaking of course, from you. For the question can be asked, is there someone like this who is not only helping your heart heal but also gradually helping your self-esteem heal to where it eventually will be at 100% capacity.

For a woman, there comes a point where one's smile will return also that was temporarily lost within not only your heart but also your self-esteem as well, which inevitably be felt and seen by those close to you. It's that unmistakable smile that brings out not just one's physical beauty but also one's inner beauty that gives you that proverbial kick in your step. In a sense, the darkness in which you were stumbling around within your emotions, feelings, and heart is now bright as you are given a brand new day to where you can truly leave past hurts behind you. For it's a clean slate within your emotions, feeling and heart as you walk the road of recovery side by side with someone who will potentially give you that fresh start.

In retrospect, when you suffer heartbreak that affects your self-esteem you tend to feel sorry for yourself for suffering through that kind of pain. For you have to keep in mind though that it wasn't your fault to begin with, it was primarily that person's fault for putting you through your own emotional rollercoaster which you truly didn't deserve in the first place. In the end, it's times like these that you're happy to know there is or will be someone special that will in a way help you learn to live again, learn to give again, and ultimately learn to love again within your own feelings, emotions, as well as heart which is a song by the late 1950's Blues Recording artist Peppermint Harris." When or if you have the time, listen to it and enjoy.

IT'S ABOUT TIME
November 28, 2005

Dorothy Canfield Fisher once said, ~if we would only give, just once, the same amount of reflection to what we want to get out of life that we give to the question of what to do with a two weeks vacation, we would be startled at our false standards and the aimless procession of our busy days.~ Let me ask you this question, how long have you worked at your particular place of employment? Let me ask another question, when was the last time you took a well-deserved vacation from the 9 to 5 daily grind, which can most definitely raise your stress level, as well as probably make you go completely off the deep end or come close to it?

If you think about it, every person has a job that is considered stressful and depending on what type of job you have it merits a much-needed vacation. Whether it's a police officer/fire fighter where they risk their lives to serve as well as protect people like us. Soldiers in the military who swore an oath to protect our country from foreign invaders. Air traffic controllers who are consistently responsible for the safety/well-being of said number of passengers that are flying several thousand in the air. One could also say that waste management/disposal can be a stressful jon and you have to respect those workers who basically have to catch crap all day long which is funny because it has a double meaning...or not.

Without a doubt, the job of President of the United States is tough because the whole world has their eyes on you. It can absolutely be difficult to not only try to please the American people but also people around the world as well as those who are constantly critiquing your every move and decision such as reporters, Senators (Republican and Democrat), foreign delegates, the White House Staff, etc. It takes some real thick skin and patience to be bombarded with so much negativity seemingly every day at all once that any normal person would either resign on the spot and appoint the VP President or take a vacation the first week in office.

Undeniably, there are jobs other than police officer, fire fighter, air traffic controller, waste management, President, etc. who need a much-needed vacation. One could say teachers/professors, who spend their time molding young students' minds, need the time off as they oftentimes don't get the respect and pay they want/deserve. The role of being a mother is unquestionably a job that every woman would love to have a vacation from for at least 6 months to a year away from their kids and just have time for yourself to relax, as well as, have "me" time. For the question can be asked to all the mothers out there, would you add your name to that sign-up sheet?

Working at the Youth Center otherwise known as The Insane Asylum, I have spent the last 9 years working and going to school in the process. I never once took a vacation, which tells you one thing right there...I am a dedicated moron. In the past 9 years at the asylum, I've been hit in the head by every ball imaginable, almost been fired 4 times for doing something stupid, had arguments with 3 former employees, broke down 1 time due to stress, and been part of an employee rally to change things at the Asylum. After 9 years of working there I'm finally taking a vacation to get away from the insanity that "my kids" have given me to go spend time with family in Los Angeles, CA and you know what I have to say about that...it's about time.

I'LL BE

December 2, 2005

Someone once said, ~When you love someone, say it. Say it loud. Say it right away, or the moment just passes you by.~ Without a doubt, the three words that can make the biggest impact and mean so much are I LOVE YOU. It can most definitely stop a person from what one is doing as it pierces his or her heart not only personally but also emotionally as well. Let me ask you this question, who was the last person who said those three very deep meaning words to you (besides mom and dad) and did you say it back to that special someone who means so much to you? Essentially, when it comes to saying I love you there is a growing debate as to who should say first: men, women, or whoever feels it the most in his or her heart?

From a guy's perspective, times have now changed where the girl can say I love you to the guy. You have to look at it from our point of view as we're basic/simplistic and let's be honest here we're also stupid. As a guy, we will wonder if that woman of interest actually cares for us deeply to where or when or if she says it we will do something totally off the wall such as do flips, scream out loud, hug/high five total strangers, or do all of the above. Let me tell you something ladies, there is so much going on in our heads that it's impossible to focus on one complete thought let alone other thoughts concerning you that it actually hurts our heads and you wonder why there are so many guys messed up in the head out there.

Yet, from a woman's standpoint, it's the guy who should say I love you first. Why? In their minds, it's the guy who should ask the woman out, the guy who should ask the woman to marry him, and most definitely it's the guy who should ask the woman's father for her daughter's hand in marriage, which is tradition and that's what I will do someday. In a woman's mind, it means so much more that the guy says for the simple reason that you want to know how he truly feels for you and genuinely means it, which can be an unknown for some, most, or all women. However, it really depends on the guy who is considered to be "too good to be true" for you and you are in amazement that he is in your life or you want that guy personally in your life, as well as, in your heart.

When it comes to saying I love you, there are those who believe that whoever feels it the most in his or her heart should say it first. In their own thinking, if you truly, madly, deeply love someone you should say/speak it from your heart and soul only if you've known that guy or girl for several months/years rather than days/weeks. For the most part, it doesn't even have to be the actual words I love you. As a matter of fact, it can be something heartfelt such as you captured my heart, you're my world, I think I'm falling in love with you, etc. whatever the case may be. It's all in how you convey those words and how you look at him or her that makes the "L" word so powerful to so many people who are in love.

George Jean Nathan said, ~A man reserves his true and deepest love not for the species of woman in whose company he finds himself electrified and enkindled, but for that one in whose company he may feel tenderly drowsy.~ In retrospect, that is how love oftentimes is for both men and women as you eventually find that one special person who you can be open with about everything and not be afraid. In my honest opinion, it doesn't matter whether a man or woman says it first, if it's true love between both of them then he, she, or both will say to each other, I'll be loving you forever and its song by Westlife which I am dedicating to those couples, married or dating, who are truly in love.

MORE THAN MEETS THE EYE
December 6, 2005

Khalil Gibran once said, ~Your children are not your children. They are thes sons and daughters of Life's longing for itself. They come through you but not from you, and though they are with you, and yet they belong not to you. You may give them your love, but not your thoughts. For they have their own thoughts. You may house their bodies but not their souls. For their souls dwell in the house of tomorrow, which you cannot visit, not even in your dreams. You may strive to be like them, but seek not to make them like you. For life goes not backwards, not tarries with yesterday.~ When or if you ever get a chance to visit the asylum, you will see us interact and have fun with the kids, but it's what you don't see that makes our job such a challenge.

For some, most, or all people working as a youth program specialist, a fancier term than saying recreational aide, is considered to them an easy and fun job where you can basically goof off, as well as reconnect with your inner child. To a certain extent that's true but a lot of hard work goes on behind the scenes, so to speak, as there are many facets of the job not too many people get to see and/or experience when one either signs up to work at the insane asylum or just merely an observer and/or parent. For if the asylum were given the opportunity to show the other side of the spectrum like in a documentary type setting such MTV Diaries, we would do it to show the so-called "outsiders" that it's not always fun and games.

Without a doubt, a person will experience the full force of insanity once you are thrown to the wolves so to speak, and when I mean the wolves, I mean the kids. However, that is just a small taste compared to the hours of required training, cpr/first aid classes, weekly meeting, making daily schedules, finishing modules which can be oh so fun and yet if you have the right staff attending, a potentially boring situation turns into hilarity and mischievousness. Its within those hours of training we brush up on apsects of the job such as health preparedness, customer relations with kids and adults, spotting child abuse, and let me tell you something there are countless stories can be told concerning child abuse that can make you angry or cry.

Yet, the question remains what do you do when all the training you have received doesn't prepare you to hear news that a child who attended or once attended the asylum passed away. Personally speaking, it can truly be a tough situation for not only us as their counselors to take that bit of news, but also to their friends as we have to be the bearer of bad news. It's at that point where the training goes out the window and you are there for them as just a friend to have a shoulder to cry on or simply talk to if they want to. In some ways, you lose a piece of yourself as they take a piece of you to a better off place, but you know you'll see that child again someday.

In retrospect, when you become part of the asylum family you basically play a small part in the lives of the kids who you see on a semi-daily basis. I often refer to "my kids" as "children of the corn" which I use as a term of endearment, but they do grow on you as they show you love and you reciprocate that love back. There have been many days where I have felt absolutely crappy and its "my kids" who have picked me up and put a smile on my face when I needed one. Its these same kids who at times don't listen, talk back, and have temper tantrums seemingly every day. Ultimately, even though they aren't my kids, they will always be "my kids" in my eyes no matter how old they are. In the end, if you're an "outsider" looking in, there is more than meets the eye going on when you think/see it's just an easy job that we have fun at.

ONE WISH
December 9, 2005

Someone once said, ~When you think about it, life is strange. Some people believe in preordination, although I don't. Still, you grow up knowing that somewhere out there is a person you are going to fall in love with. You wonder what the person will be like. How she will look. How she will walk, talk, and what she will think. How she will smile. How will she laugh? There's no way of knowing of course, until you meet her. The realization that you finally met her comes as a wondrous discovery, a peek into the works of life. This person is in your thoughts most of the time-all the time actually. You see her when you close your eyes, when you look off into the distance, and when you pause from what you are doing and take a deep breath.

Without a doubt, life can be strange when it comes to eventually meeting that special someone you will fall in love with for a lifetime. As a guy, you tend to walk through life telling/thinking to yourself that not having anybody special in your life is the best way to go for many different reasons which may or may not have merit. Oftentimes those reasons can turn into excuses and one of those excuses is that you're too busy so there is no time to pursue a relationship or to be in one for that matter. However, the strange thing about using that excuse is it's not true and yet you can start to believe what you're saying for so long that it sounds true in your own mind, but in reality, you're just scared.

When it comes to falling in love or liking a particular female of interest, it's always scary particularly for the guy. Why? You have to look at it from the guy's perspective. It's that intimidation factor combined with trying to figure out what she is thinking added with those two words every guy hates to hear which are "just friends." that makes it such a lethal 1-2-3 combo. From our standpoint, we can hear so many failed attempts at trying to cross over from "just friends" to more than friends that there comes a point where you just give up ever attempting to follow your heart to potential happiness. It's not until you meet that one woman you realize she's the one who is truly worth conquering your fear for

The question can be asked, how many guys can truly say they have someone truly special right in front of them and hopefully not mess it up for themselves? The answer is not many, and you can bet there are guys out there who are beating themselves up, as well as, regretting what they did or said to the one that got away. Undeniably, women can truly appreciate the fact that they have a guy who is all that she ever expected and more. For a woman it's that certain kind of magic that has the same familiar feeling and yet they experience something totally different from someone that is not like any other guy they've met, which is a rarity these days.

In retrospect, every guy will meet a woman who can make you lose your mind and yet can make you totally focused. A woman who can make you act all weird and yet can make you calm beyond belief. A woman who can paralyze you with a smile and yet can make your heart melt at the same time because of that smile. A woman who you can make you feel weak in the knees for and yet can make you stronger every time you are around her. A woman who can make you forget how to breathe and yet can breathe new life into you. In the end, with Christmas being around the corner, my one wish is to meet this woman and you know what, I may already have.

BEHIND THESE EYES
December 11, 2005

Ralph Waldo Emerson said, ~He who is in love is wise and is becoming wiser, sees newly every time he look as the object beloved, drawing it with his eyes and his mind those virtues which it possesses.~ Essentially, every person has looked either at a drawing or a painting but let me ask you this question. When you look at a drawing or a painting what do you see? For some, most or all people they just see what's on the surface but for others they see something much more meaningful that's behind the painting itself, which keeps you interested. When it comes to love, whether you're a man or woman, it takes a person to continually see with fresh eyes the love you have within your heart, which never grows old no matter how old both of you get.

Without a doubt, the human body can break down to where certain areas of the body don't work like they used to or not at all. One particular part that usually goes is a person's vision and whether you're far sighted or near sighted, glasses or contacts are needed. In a sense, when there is confusion in a person's heart as to whether he or she is in love, one's vision can be impaired to where you don't know which direction your heart is going. Every person has gone or is going through this and let me tell you something, it's no picnic to experience. For it takes someone real special to metaphorically put glasses on your heart to see clear as day to who you want to be with.

When it comes to relationships, potential and/or significant, every person sees their significant other, but does he or she actually see him or her? Let me give you this challenge, ask your significant other to describe you and vice versa, but here's the catch: you can't go by the physical features. Why? Primarily, it's what a person usually goes by first and, in my opinion, in order for a potential and/or significant relationship to flourish you have to see beyond the person. In other words, look past the painting and see what makes that person special, unique, and worth loving. As with a painting, it takes a lot of time and patience to see what's there and when you truly see what's in front of your eyes, you won't be disappointed.

If you think about it, love is like a painting as it starts off as a blank canvas and in some aspect, two people's hearts can be that way as well. As two people meet the colors on the palette of life start to be placed and as they get to know one another the friendship grows to where the colors are mixed together. Inevitably, that friendship turns from like to love and before you know it that metaphorical paintbrush has turned several brush strokes into something both can look back on and smile because no words can oftentimes describe what's been created. You can only just stand back, pray, and be thankful to the Master Painter, GOD, for painting a perfect portrait that you get to see and spend time with every day.

Someone once said, ~Love is like a painting in the beginning its only an idea, but over time, it is built up through errors and corrections till you have a breathtaking work of art for all to see.~ In retrospect, love can be frustrating as you can just stand there looking at a blank canvas for months or even years. It's not until you meet someone that totally inspires you that ideas will form to where something will be created from that inspiration. For the question can be asked, who is your inspiration that keeps your blank canvas constantly colorful? In the end, its when you look at that person you love and say, it's behind these eyes that I see something new every day that nobody else can to where it's love at first sight each time I see you.

THAT'S COOL
December 15, 2005

Sheila G. Flaxman once said, ~Children engage in such (free) play because they enjoy it--it's self-directed. They do not play for rewards; they enjoy the doing, not the end result. Once they get bored, they go on to do something else--and continue to learn and grow.~ When it comes to play back in the day, we ask kids never to get bored doing what we did unlike the kids of today who get bored too easily because it's not entertaining enough for them. Let me ask you this question, what did or do you enjoy doing that is considered fun/entertaining to where it's a learning experience and made you grow as a person?

Personally speaking, working with kids for the past 9 years is truly entertaining and fun...most of the time. It's these kids who have endless amounts of energy as they run around to their hearts content like miniature energizer bunnies as they keep going and going and going. You oftentimes forget what it's like to be a kid and not have so many responsibilities placed on you, as well as things to worry about. What's to worry about at 7 years old? I say nothing because their carefree attitudes about life that makes you envious to switch places just for a moment or two to where doing something so childish to someone such as repeating every word or mimicking every movement would be an absolutely liberating experience.

Without a doubt, the funnest part about my job is the one-on-one interaction with "my kids" because you get to know each of them on an individual basis. As you get to know them you get to know their likes, dislikes, temperaments, weaknesses, strengths, etc. Essentially, you become something more to that child or group of children than just a person who simply clocks in, does one's job, and then clocks out. It's that connection you have with children doesn't happen overnight, but sometimes it does and kids know immediately if they dislike you or welcome you with open arms. For it takes someone who genuinely likes being around kids to show others someone that there are people who still care about the youth of the nation.

However, it's not only the connection you have with the kids that makes what I do awesome, its the connection you have with the parents as well. When it comes to parents or a parent they see the impact/influence you have on them to where they thank you personally for being part of his or her life. In a way myself and my fellow co-workers/ friends are second as an extended family member, though not blood related because they talk about us at home. For it's that type of gratitude from a parent that makes all the headaches we go through well worth it all because you are making a difference in his or her life even if it is for several hours each week.

About a month ago, one of my 6- & 7-year-old girls invited my best friend and I to her birthday party on Saturday, which coincided with us seeing the movie Aeon Flux earlier that afternoon. By the way, it was an excellent movie that I highly recommend going to see and buying when it comes out on DVD. Anyways, when we arrived and walked through the door her face lit up bright as can be and in that short time, we spent with her it made not only her day but her mom's as well, which she thanked us for. We gave her a gift, wished her a happy birthday, and took a picture with her. In retrospect, you never really know how big or small of an impact you make on children until you personally hear and/or see it firsthand and to me that's cool.

WAX ON, WAX OFF
December 17, 2005

Gichin Funakoshi said, ~You may train for a long time, but if you merely move your hands and feet and jump and down like a puppet, learning karate is not very different from learning to dance. You will never have reached the heart of the matter; you will have failed to grasp the essence of karate.~ When it comes to learning martial arts there is a lot of time, patience, and discipline that is involved in a graceful but deadly artform. Whether it's Kung Fu, Tae Kwon Do, Judo, Tai Chi, Aikido, Ninjitsu, Ju Jitsu, Kickboxing, Capoeira, etc. Whatever style it may be it should be taken seriously and not use what you were taught for personal vendettas or to start fights.

For the most part, every guy growing up learned martial arts the fun and old-fashioned way, which was by way of osmosis through old classic dubbed kung fu movies. Movies that when you came out of the movie theater you started imitating the movies, jumping off the furniture, kicking/chopping whoever is near you like your own brother, and making sounds/noises like every guy's favorite martial arts legend Bruce Lee. As a guy, my favorite movie of his is Enter the Dragon with Game Of Death a close second. Undeniably, he was, is, and will always be THE MAN that every guy idolized and wanted to be as a kid including myself.

Without a doubt, there wouldn't be any other guy like him as his style, mannerisms, and philosophy were both unique, as well as one of a kind. For those that preceded him have their own styles that make each of them unique to where hypothetical battles would be thought up to see who people think would win. Such names that would always be thrown into the proverbial hat are Jackie Chan, Jet Li, Marc Dacascos, and of course the legend himself Bruce Lee. A dream battle between these respected men that have been debated on can oftentimes turn into arguments as to who can kick whose butt. My personal opinion, my pick is Jet Li because he has the speed and quickness to kick butt within a blink of an eye.

Personally speaking, my brother and I took Tae Kwon Do for several months but I had to quit due to hyperextending my left knee, which hasn't been quite right since. On the upside, I can tell what the weather will be like by feeling my knee and to be perfectly honest it can be either wrong, right, or somewhere in the middle. Even though I quit, my brother didn't as he won several trophies in tournaments and made all the way to red belt before he decided to venture into something more challenging such as Kung Fu. Let me tell you something, as adults my brother and I have never gotten into a physical fight, but if we did, I would get my head knocked off.

On Thanksgiving Day, Pat Morita died leaving behind many fans who grew up watching him, like myself. Even though he didn't teach martial arts off screen he was considered a true sensei on screen. He was and still is the quintessential television icon who will be best remembered as Mr. Miyagi the teacher/mentor to Ralph Macchio's character Daniel-san in the 3 of 4 Karate Kid movies. It was the character of Mr. Miyagi that kids back in the day, me included, learned the crane kick and karate moves by doing a simple task like painting the fence. In the end, for me anyways, it all started with 4 words that became a classic catch phrase and those for words are wax on, wax off.

STICK WITH YOU
December 18, 2005

Sigmund Frued once said, ~The great question...which I have not been able to answer, despite my thirty years of research into the feminine soul, is what does a woman want? So what does a woman want? That is the single most toughest question guys have been trying to figure out the answer to for years and the answer is ever changing. As far as I know, what a woman wants when it pertains to that so-called perfect guy is honesty, a sense of humor, intelligence, thoughtfulness, a caring heart, notices the little things, etc. Let me ask you this question ladies, have you met this guy who makes you feel good, makes you feel happy, and makes you feel absolutely special in your heart, mind, and soul or are you still waiting for him?

Every woman wants a guy that will make her feel good inside to where the proverbial butterflies in her stomach will always be there. It's that warm and fuzzy feeling within one's heart that each time you it beats, it beats with for him every time you see, hear, and/or touch him. Unfortunately, that feeling is at times temporary due to the fact that certain women can have it and then lose it with just a snap of a finger like the waste of paste billionaire princess Paris Hilton. For it takes a real, special, genuine guy to keep that feeling alive in one's heart and soul to where it's considered love at first sight every time you see him.

Love and happiness go hand in hand to a woman who finds a guy that will not only make her smile on the outside, but on the inside as well. It doesn't take a lot to make a woman happy because all a man can ever give is himself and what women will get is something far more than she ever bargained for. For the question can be asked to you ladies, which kind of happiness would you rather have? The love of a man that will make you happy for a lifetime or the happiness that money can bring to where you buy such material possessions such as jewelry, clothes, and/or clothes related accessories? Pick wisely because one will truly make you happy and the other will make you temporarily happy to where all you left is an empty void in your heart.

Without a doubt, there is a guy who makes you feel absolutely special each time you are around him and if you haven't met him yet...you will just be patient. If you want a description, he's the guy that will call for no reason just to say hi, send you flowers for appreciating your company, call you beautiful when you don't feel like or don't see it, will see how you are doing when you don't feel that well, will make you laugh when you are down just to see the smile on your face, and most of all he is the guy that will be there for you when you didn't even ask as a friend as he lends an ear to listen to you or shoulder to cry on.

In retrospect, when it seems like everybody around you is breaking up there is one constant and he is standing right there beside you. When it seems as if everyone is breaking up and throwing their love away, he is the one that will stay by your side, not give up on you, and love you always. When it seems as though hearts are crashing and burning to the ground around you, he is the one that will take your heart far beyond the clouds. In the end, it's a rare thing indeed to find/meet a guy who meets every expectation and then some; but when it does finally happen you will look him in the eyes and say I love you and I going to forever stick with you.

BYE BYE BYE
December 27, 2005

An old Irish saying says, ~May the road rise up to meet you, may the wind be ever at your back. May the sun shine warm your face and the rain fall softly on your fields. And until we meet again, may God hold you in the hollow of his hands.~ Although we're not going anywhere, 2005 is and there have been many events this past year that have affected us either individually or as a whole. Its these particular events you would either gladly leave behind or keep with you depending on the event or events in question. For the most part, each of us have an event in mind and whether or not you want to keep it is up to you when 2006 ushers in a new beginning.

Politically speaking, 2005 was filled with some very newsworthy stories that either made you cry, angry, confused, confrontational, uplifted, or all of the above. One such tragedy is Hurricane Katrina that caused many people to not only lose their homes but their lives as well. Unfortunately, the immediate response to help was heard but the aide arrived a little too late to where the blame game pointed fingers at the Bush Administration and to former FEMA director Mike Brown, who will forever be considered a douchebag. Despite the controversy, we as a nation either welcomed many of the displaced families into our homes or provided them with food, clothing, and/or health related products which were so badly needed.

For some, most, or all of us who are sports fans, there were some events that happened that were either disappointing, awe-inspiring, or both. As many of you know, the Chicago White Sox won the 2005 World Series after 88 years, which vindicated them from a scandal where several players were accused of throwing the World Series against the Cincinnati Red back in 1919. On a side not, one of those men accused was baseball legend "Shoeless" Joe

Jackson, who even though was acquitted of all criminal charges he received a lifetime ban from playing professional ball. Initially, what happened to them in the past was disappointing, but it paid off big in the long run which kind of parallels their color counterparts the Boston Red Sox.

Personally speaking, there are two events that I will always remember and will keep not only in memory but in my heart as well. The first was opening the asylum doors and meeting the kids of Hurricane Katrina which, as said before, was a truly humbling experience. For myself and my best friend were given the opportunity to spend several hours with these kids. What we gave back to them, for a few hours anyways, were smiles and laughter which I will never forget as long as I live. The second event was meeting a woman who unknowingly would give me two things back that I thought I lost years ago which were faith and hope in my own heart. As I tip my hat to you, I simply say thank you from the bottom of my heart.

In retrospect, there are many other events that happened in 2005 that touched the lives of many. The deaths of Pat Morita, Peter Jennings, Bob Denver, Johnny Carson, and comedy legend Richard Pryor were people who not only I grew up watching but you as well. Whether its Kanye West telling what he thinks of President Bush on live tv, voting in Iraq, the Tsunami, hurricanes in Florida, Lance Armstrong winning his 7th Tour De France, or Rafael Palmero getting his 3,000 hit but then lying to Congress about using steroids, these were some of the events that happened in 2005. In the end, we can collectively say welcome to 2006, but for 2005 three words come to mind...bye, bye, bye.

THE PERFECT GIFT
December 21, 2005

Someone once said, ~The joy of brightening others lives, bearing each other's burdens, easing other's loads and supplanting empty hearts and lives with generous gifts become for us the magic of Christmas.~ Without a doubt, you can feel in the air as there is excitement and anticipation on an upcoming event that not only brings children joy but also the little kid inside every grown adult as well. You can't help but love Christmas as we all look forward to giving and receiving gifts for/from family, friends, a significant other, co-workers, and/or acquaintances. Let me ask you this question, when it comes to gift giving is money no object for that person or persons?

Essentially, every person knows what to get that certain someone who he or she has known or worked with for quite some time. It's just a matter of picking up on the clues as to what that particular person's interests are or are interested in and working your way from there. Personally speaking, there have been two people that I work with who have been at the Asylum since I started, and I know them pretty well to give them gifts they both would like. My best friend is a huge Miami fan and anything that involves Miami is his cup of tea, so to speak. My mentor, who taught me everything I know, loves Dr. Suess and anything that smells good such as incense, perfume, candles, soaps which she has already gotten by way of the kids of the Asylum.

Here's a little-known fact, did you its toughest to shop for men that it is for women. Why? Well, men tend to get the same gifts when it falls either under their birthday, Father's Day, or Christmas, which are clothing such as ties or tools. If you think about its hard to shop for a man that sometimes says he doesn't want anything and for you just to save your money when you really need it, which gives that much more of an incentive to get dear old dad something that shows the family he is greatly appreciated. Whether its a BBQ grill the size of the Titanic or the George Foreman Grill show the man in your life how you truly care about him.

Women, on the other hand, are typically easy to shop for because much of the products are advertised either on billboards, tv, movies, the internet, as well as magazines. As a guy, you can't go two steps without something hitting your peripheral vision on what a woman would like. One of those things that usually gets every guy's attention in commercials pertains to a woman's best friend, which are diamonds. It would be safe to say that when I immediately said that every woman's eyes immediately lit up with a smile and every guy, who may be reading this beside her, just slapped themselves on the forehead. Sorry guys, my bad.

In retrospect, gifts can come in all shapes, forms, and sizes to where the price tag is from reasonable to downright ridiculous. So ridiculous that you either have to put your house up as collateral or be a very rich person like Donald Trump. However, the best gift you can ever receive or give doesn't cost anything due to the fact it comes from your heart to people or that special someone. It's a gift that shows you're thinking about him or her and that you truly care enough that you simply gave of yourself. This Christmas 2005 give the gift that keeps on giving, for that gift is love, which is, in the end, considered the perfect gift.

BELIEVE
December 23, 2005

Someone once said, ~The joy of brightening others lives, bearing each other's burdens, easing other's loads and supplanting empty hearts and lives with generous gifts become for us the magic of Christmas.~ Without a doubt, you can feel in the air as there is excitement and anticipation on an upcoming event that not only brings children joy but also the little kid inside every grown adult as well. You can't help but love Christmas as we all look forward to giving and receiving gifts for/from family, friends, a significant other, co-workers, and/or acquaintances. Let me ask you this question, when it comes to gift giving is money no object for that person or persons?

Essentially, every person knows what to get that certain someone who he or she has known or worked with for quite some time. It's just a matter of picking up on the clues as to what that particular person's interests are or are interested in and working your way from there. Personally speaking, there have been two people that I work with who have been at the Asylum since I started, and I know them pretty well to give them gifts they both would like. My best friend is a huge Miami fan and anything that involves Miami is his cup of tea, so to speak. My mentor, who taught me everything I know, loves Dr. Suess and anything that smells good such as incense, perfume, candles, soaps which she has already gotten by way of the kids of the Asylum.

Here's a little-known fact, did you its toughest to shop for men that it is for women. Why? Well, men tend to get the same gifts when it falls either under their birthday, Father's Day, or Christmas, which are clothing such as ties or tools. If you think about its hard to shop for a man that sometimes says he doesn't want anything and for you just to save your money when you really need it, which gives that much more of an incentive to get dear old dad something that shows the family he is greatly appreciated. Whether its a BBQ grill the size of the Titanic or the George Foreman Grill show the man in your life how you truly care about him.

Women, on the other hand, are typically easy to shop for because much of the products are advertised either on billboards, tv, movies, the internet, as well as magazines. As a guy, you can't go two steps without something hitting your peripheral vision on what a woman would like. One of those things that usually gets every guy's attention in commercials pertains to a woman's best friend, which are diamonds. It would be safe to say that when I immediately said that every woman's eyes immediately lit up with a smile and every guy, who may be reading this beside her, just slapped themselves on the forehead. Sorry guys, my bad.

In retrospect, gifts can come in all shapes, forms, and sizes to where the price tag is from reasonable to downright ridiculous. So ridiculous that you either have to put your house up as collateral or be a very rich person like Donald Trump. However, the best gift you can ever receive or give doesn't cost anything due to the fact it comes from your heart to people or that special someone. It's a gift that shows you're thinking about him or her and that you truly care enough that you simply gave of yourself. This Christmas 2005 give the gift that keeps on giving, for that gift is love, which is, in the end, considered the perfect gift.

WELCOME ABOARD
December 25, 2005

Socrates once said, ~Man must rise above the Earth--to the top of the atmosphere and beyond--for only thus will he fully understand the world which he live in.~ Without a doubt, air travel is the single most exhilarating experience that can bring joy, excitement, frustration, wonderment, anxiety, and fear all in one package. If you think about it, there's something about an airplane, whether you're looking at one up in the air, sitting in the runway as you look at it from the terminal, or sitting in one that brings out the little hyperactive kid inside you. Let me ask you this question, do you feel the same way I do or is it just my dorky and geeky self?

For some, most, or all people the anticipation of getting ready to take off can be considered such an adrenaline rush. Yet, we've all had experiences where one's plane took seemingly forever to start its departure and there comes a point where you start to get a bit edgy. Edgy, not in the sense of going ballistic to where you get beat up by the passengers, but edgy in the sense that you want to be in the air amongst the clouds, birds, stars, etc. In any case, when you do finally depart you feel somewhat like Superman or Supergirl as you gradually rise up up and away into the wild blue yonder minus the cape and the tight-fitting uniform, of course which wouldn't look good on someone like me...trust me on this.

Essentially, when you're in the air up there all your problems are left on the ground, but unfortunately they'll be waiting for. Anyways, when you look down at something so amazing from 30,000 ft or more, you see so much more than when you are on the ground. For the question can be asked, would you rather fly during the day or during the night? Personally speaking, I would rather fly during the night because at night you witness something so spectacular and beautiful as the bright lights illuminate the ground below. In those brief hours you spend in the air, your problems are insignificant as you enjoy the entertainment outside and the in-flight entertainment inside.

Being a military kid, flying was part of the routine and without failure I would sit next to or near the wings. Before leaving Pensacola, the weather was rainy and there came a point where in the back of my mind I wanted to do something that was considered mischievous and a little bit twisted, but I didn't do it, due in part to the passengers may beat me up for it. Now, if you're a fan of the Twilight Zone, you may remember the airplane episode with William Shatner and then later updated with John Lithgow. Yup, you guessed it as I wanted so badly to jump up out of my seat/scream out loud or tap the passenger sitting next to me and say that there is a monkey on the wing.

In retrospect, you are never too young or too old to enjoy flying on an airplane. Despite security checkpoints, passengers taking their sweet time putting their baggage away, people kicking your seat, mediocre meals, crying children, children who every ten seconds peek over the seat, waiting a lifetime to get your bags in the terminal, etc. it didn't take away from the fact that you were flying without wings. How many of us can truly say that we didn't have a smile on our face when we sat down in our seats, buckled our seatbelts, and waited with bated breath to take off. In the end, you're not officially flying until the captain comes over the loudspeaker, greets the passengers, and says these two words which are welcome aboard.

MY LIFE
December 29, 2005

Someone once said, ~Being single has meant that I am free to take risks that I might not take. Being single has given me freedom to move around the world without having to pack up a household first. And this freedom has brought to me moments that I would not trade for anything else the side of eternity.~ When you're single, you tend to live your life thinking/worrying only about yourself to where it can be perceived as somewhat selfish. Selfish, in the sense, that one wants to feel free in taking risks as you meet someone new and not form any kind of attachments within your heart for a particular guy or girl. Yet, it only takes one for you to form an attachment and risk it all with your own heart.

Without a doubt, single life has given many of us the freedom to like/dislike a particular guy or girl. Whether one's reasoning is valid or completely shallow, it's that person's preference as to what peaks his or her interest. As it has been said so many times before, it's not what's the power he or she has on the outside that determines if you love someone, it's the power one has within one's heart that shows how strong and real a person is. For the most part, you don't know if the feelings, emotions, and/or words are truly believable and yet you have to trust your instincts but most importantly trust your own heart as to where or not you will take a trip around the world with him or her, so to speak.

Being a single person, one's heart can absolutely be taken on a trip of a lifetime. If you think about it, there have been people in one's past or present who metaphorically have taken or are taking your heart to the highest reaches of a mountain such as Mt. Everest. Its up at the highest point you feel like you've finally reached something totally unreachable as you look into that person 's, hear his or her voice, or feel one's heartbeat in a warm embrace. It's at the top where seemingly you can breathe easier, the air smells so much sweeter, and when you look down life just makes a bit more sense. For all the worries that were bothering you mentally, physically, and/or emotionally, simply fade away as you take/breathe in all what you see before you.

Unfortunately, there also have been times as a single person, you were literally, as well as, metaphorically taken on one bad trip. A trip where you came back not quite the same person mentally, emotionally, and/or physically due in part to losing or having your heart disappear as if it went into the Bermuda Triangle and never was seen from again. Essentially, its that natural curiosity each of us have as a single person to go into the unknown knowing that we may never be the same person coming out, which is a risk a person like myself is now taking. Let me ask you this question, are you risking your own heart as you head into that so-called "Bermuda Triangle" to someone special?

In retrospect, when it comes to the human heart, it can either step forward and be heard/noticed or it can simply be another "face" in the crowd that doesn't speak out. When you're single, sometimes fearing the unknown will take over your life and that's when you have to say to yourself, you have to live sooner or later. In some aspect, breaking through that roadblock, which is keeping you from the vast open highway within your own heart, may or may not pay dividends..who knows really except for you. In the end, when it comes to one's heart, you have to say to yourself I'm going to live as I'm going with what I feel and I will see who my heart leads me or already has led me to because in the end, it's my life.

JUST A THOUGHT (LAST YODAISM OF 2005)

December 29, 2005

Henry David Thoreau once said. ~As a single footstep will not make a path on the earth, so a single thought will not make a pathway in the mind. To make a deep physical path, we walk again and again. To make a deep mental path, we think over and over the kind of thoughts we wish to dominate our lives.~ If you think about it, each time we metaphorically step foot into our own heart the inner mind games begin. A game in which our own thoughts start bouncing around in our heads to where its like we're playing a game of ping pong as we try to keep certain thoughts flowing and not let them fall off the proverbial ping pong table of life so to speak.

Without a doubt, ping pong is a sport of skill/technique/stamina but where it all starts is with the proper grip of the paddle. We all have our own way of gripping the paddle and for the most part, one usually sticks with what works for one's self. In some aspect, the paddle we all metaphorically hold in our hand is our heart and with each thought, we either let it bounce off the table or return it back to that particular person. For we all can be mentally fatigued at trying to keep one's thoughts steadily flowing and not letting those thoughts get to you, which can be a tough task indeed for anybody. Let me ask you this question, what type of grip do you have on your paddle as we speak?

When it comes to your "opponent", you don't want to be careless as to not notice certain key shots and let them slip by you. Men, more so than women, tend to miss those signals that can initially have one lose points rather than gain them. Yet, it's those shots that can sometimes be misconstrued as mixed signals by way of a look, touch, or a said word or words. For a person like myself whose job it is to observe, you notice things that a particular person is serving to you, to where you return it back, but not in a forceful way. For it's a similar return, but you hold back a little to see what you get back, which inevitably becomes a type of mental stamina for two minds.

In the game of ping pong it's true that you shouldn't be careless; but careful, but too careful. It's a situation where a person can become overconfident and make mistakes both mentally and physically. Such mistakes that can be made are mentally messed up by overthinking situations that it becomes a problem to a point where the service from that particular guy or girl is returned with such force that it stuns him or her to where it leaves you totally or somewhat embarrassed. For the question can be asked to each and every one of you, how many times have you been in that particular situation, whether it was in the past or present?

In retrospect, when it comes to the human heart each step we take is carefully made as thoughts and feelings are served to that particular person. Whether he or she returns those feelings is unknown, but that doesn't mean one isn't answering those serves. For it can be a nonverbal return, which you have to notice in order to keep the ping pong match that is between two people alive. Ultimately, you have to make sure each and every shot you make count and when you see your shot take it. You see, I've taken my shot with a particular someone and hopefully I've made each shot count because in the end, all this started several months back with just a thought.

TIME OF YOUR LIFE (1ST YODAISM OF 2006)

January 3, 2006

Francis Lucille once said, ~Everything is created from moment to moment, always new. Like fireworks, the universe is a celebration and you are the spectator contemplating the eternal fourth of July of your absolute splendor.~ Let me ask you this question, when it comes to experiencing memorable moments on the road of life are you considered the driver or are you simply the passenger? Its a question that is either difficult or easy to answer because there is no in-between answer because the road of life is unpredictable as it will turn a driver into a passenger and vice versa. Essentially, each moment we live there is a possibility of a once in a lifetime opportunity that may or may never be experienced again.

Whether those particular moments you experienced were voluntary or not, you have to admit it was an experience that stayed with you. For its when you reflect back, it seems like only yesterday that it happened as you look over old "war" wounds and treasured mementos that not only bring a smile to your face but tears as well. We all have something that is connected with that particular moment in time such as something worn, tattooed on your person, looked at such as pictures one hid/put away in a special box, which you take out every now and then to look at. Without a doubt, it's those celebrated moments that you will someday share with one's own grandchildren, if those particular stories/item(s) are/were G rated, of course.

As said before, on the road of life you are either the driver or the passenger. When you are the driver, you have complete and total control of the wheel with the knowledge of where you are going and what is going to happen…most of the time. With the wind in one's hair, the tunes blaring, the asphalt beneath your tires you set course for your intended destination, and anticipate the repercussions of what might happen afterwards. For the most part, it's that adrenaline rush one gets as you are in control of your destiny, but with one turn of the wheel its a new destination just like that. Inevitably, life will lead or has led you to a particular turnoff that you really didn't prepare yourself to be on and its at that point you as the driver become a passenger.

As a passenger, you have a totally new perspective as you are no longer in control of the wheel, which yields the so-called "power." For the question can be asked, how many of you found it awkward to be a passenger after you yourself were the driver for quite some time? Such descriptions would be weird, strange, not a good feeling, but go with it because something or someone was coming your way. In the whole scheme of things, we all think we're in the driver's seat, but in reality we're merely passengers on the road of life giving our own perspective at what one sees on our own personal travels. When it comes to being the passenger just live in the moment and as/when you look out your car window, tell me who or what do you see?

In retrospect, New Years is one memorable moment that every person around the world shares together and becomes a spectator as fireworks light the night sky celebrating another year gone by. For some people they celebrated within the comfort of their own home, but others they celebrated in such places like New York's Time Square or in Sin City otherwise known as Las Vegas, which is where I spent ringing in 2006. It was truly a memorable moment for me as it was my first time being there and I can honestly now say I've been there, done that, which I can now check off my list. In the end, wherever you spent ringing in 2006 I hope you had the time of your life because I know I did.

NO PLACE LIKE HOME
January 6, 2006

Someone once said, ~Home is where friendships are formed and families are grown, where joy is shared and true love is known; where memories are made and seeds of life are sown. This is the place...that people call HOME.~ During the past two weeks of a well deserved vacation, Los Angeles and San Diego, were considered home as families who haven't seen each other for quite some time, reconnected to where laughter, joy, as well as, singing were experienced by all. However, it wasn't just about family, as time was also spent consuming mass quantities of food, shopping, and site seeing, where plenty of pictures were taken.

Without a doubt, Los Angeles offered a plethora of eating establishments that absolutely makes one's mouth water depending on what type of taste one has to the particular food(s) in question. In a week and a half, places such as Damons' Ocean Seafood in Chinatown, Goldilocks(a Filipino restaurant), and the Thai BBQ were sources of contentment. Its those four particular places that I highly recommend for those who are planning to visit Los Angeles but leave one thing behind and that is your belt because your full stomach will keep your pants up. Let me tell you something, I surprisingly still weigh the same leaving L.A. at 155lbs...it must be my metabolism.

Let me ask you this question, when it comes to hanging with family you haven't seen in quite some time, do you remember their names and how you're related with him, her, and/or them? When it comes to my family, you literally need a scorecard as to who is related and how we're related to each other, which shows that I have a big family. In any case, when it comes to family there's always surprises to be found and I found mine which is that I'm grandfather...yes you read it right. For I had to confirm it more than twice and it's true

I have a granddaughter, which blew my mind. Hey, I'm already a Godfather, a father-type figure to "my kids" at the asylum, now a grandpa, all I need to do now is become a father and I complete the package deal.

Essentially, a person can't go home empty handed without taking pictures and doing a little shopping, which was very profitable. Profitable in the sense that I was able to have a picture taken at not only Bruce Lee's Star at the Hollywood walk of fame but also at the Hollywood sign itself. Of all the places to shop in Los Angeles, Chinatown was the best, but you had to haggle with the vendors to get a fair and reasonable price. Ultimately, the one place that was the highlight of my two-week vacation was spending New Years in Vegas, which I can now mark off the list of things I wanted to accomplish and even though I didn't gamble or drink I had fun being that it was my first time.

In retrospect, a great ending to a great vacation was looking over brightly lit Los Angeles at night with a friend at Griffith Park. In the two weeks I was there, many memories were shared/made and they will never be forgotten. Ultimately, L.A. was a great place to visit as one witnesses the fast-paced life of people who actually dress up to go out and when I mean dress up, I mean dress up. However, I'm an easy/slow-paced kind of person and dressing up to go out for me is putting on jeans, sneakers, shirt, shades, and a hat...nothing too flashy. In the end, as we landed in Pensacola today, the immortal words of Dorothy from the Wizard Of Oz came to mind in which I said these 5 words...there's no place like home.

NOTHING TO LOSE
January 8, 2006

Erica Jong said, ~Do you want me to tell you something really subversive? Love is everything its cracked up to be. That's why people are so cynical about it. It really is worth fighting for, being brave for, risking everything for. And the trouble is, if you don't risk everything, you risk even more.~ Let me ask you this question, do you believe love is everything it's cracked up to be as you meet that one person who brings you to life within your heart and soul each time you talk, see, or are around him or her? It's that person who "haunts" not only your innermost thoughts but also every room within the chambers of your own heart to where the mention of that person's name or talking about him or her puts a smile on your face.

As it was said in the quote above, people can become cynical when it comes to love. Why? With so many happy relationships/marriages breaking up and not lasting more than a couple years it makes you rethink going for it with a certain someone who made a big impression not only in your life but in your heart as well. We've all at some point heard through the proverbial grapevine of two particular people, whether its acquaintances, friends, and/or celebrities hooked up to where one responds by giving them a certain time frame on how long both will last. If you think about it, we as a society have become more pessimistic rather than optimistic when it comes to love/relationships and yet the question remains which category do you fall under?

Inevitably, there comes a point where every cliche in the book about love comes to fruition when it happens to you. Such cliches are: he's my prince charming, she's one that fits the glass slipper, its love at first sight, it hit you like a ton of bricks, you've fallen head over heels, etc. Depending on if its immediate or gradual it will happen or already has happened to you to where you either fight the feeling and run away from that person or embrace the feeling and walk towards that person. For the question can be asked of you, when it pertains to a potential and/or significant relationship are some, most, or all of the cliches about him or her are true and if so, which ones?

Without a doubt, love is worth fighting for, being brave for, dying for, and risking everything that you put your heart, as well as your soul for. Personally speaking, how many times has your heart been in the battlefield that is love? How many times has it become a casualty of war, so to speak? How many times have you returned to the battlefield knowing that old wounds may open up in your heart? How many times have you continually trusted yourself in opening up yourself and your heart to someone only to have that trust betrayed? Essentially, when it comes to love you have to take risks with your heart and if you don't take them, you risk not ever getting truly shot in the heart by someone who is absolutely worth giving your own life for.

The Greeks, who are known for epic battles, asked only one question after a man dies which is, "Did he have passion?" Passion in the sense that a man believes in everything he said/felt within his own heart and soul to where one metaphorically and/or literally keeps fighting until the end. In the past several months, that passion that was thought to have long burned out in my own heart years ago has started to slowly burn brighter and bigger. Personally speaking, I'm risking everything to follow my heart to where if I die in the battle, I die with passion. In the end, I have nothing to lose and with that mindset, I could quite possibly gain something very valuable in return…her heart.

FOR YOU I WILL
January 10, 2006

Friedrich Von Schiller once said, ~Love is at the same time the most generous and the most egotistical thin in nature; the most generous because it receives nothing and gives all--pure in mind being only to give and not receive; the most egotistical, for that which he seeks in the subject, that which he enjoys in it, is himself and never anything else.~ When it comes to falling in love or being in love, the so called power it exudes makes you want to become not only a better person for one's self bit also for that particular guy or girl as well. For it essentially brings out the hopeless romantic in each of us, which oftentimes displays are own selfless acts of kindness/generosity without expecting anything in return.

Without a doubt, it's a rarity these days for both men and women to meet someone whose generosity comes straight from within that person's heart and soul. For a woman, its difficult to truly find a true gentleman who you can genuinely trust. What he says/does for you is true and yet you end up finding a "gentlemen" in sheep's clothing, in a manner of speaking. A "gentlemen" whose generosity has ulterior motives that oftentimes leaves a woman in tears, as well as, emotional and physically used. For its not only women who experience this, but guys as well who are being taken advantage due to their "nice guy" status that it makes a guy want to turn in his "Mr. Nice Guy" membership card and step over to the dark side, but I digress.

Let me ask you this question to both men and women, when it comes to selfless acts of kindness/generosity for a potential and/or significant other, do you do it because you have to or do you do it because you want to? As a guy, calling a particular female you're interested in to simply say hi or leaving messages to hopefully brighten her spirit and day, or having flowers delivered to her just show that person is in your thoughts are considered gambles due to the fact you have no idea what type of effect, if any, it's going to have on her. It's that unknown, which makes any guy out there willing to be perceived as a love struck fool than to be a fool who didn't at least try and follow one's heart towards that special someone.

As said before, love can be considered the most egotistical thing in nature, which means that a person can have that somewhat Steve Urkel mindset. A mindset in which the thoughtful phone messages left and the flowers sent for a reason or no reason at all to that particular female flips on a metaphorical light switch in one's brain, as well as, heart to where he or she immediately falls in love with you, runs into your arms, and a happy ending/beginning for both. It's an egotistical way of thinking, but you have to admit we all have been in that mindset which shows a level of confidence that shows you are optimistic but not overly optimistic to where one gets his or her hopes up and becomes disappointed when things don't turn out how one planned.

In retrospect, when you meet that special person, questions will be asked that one wants answered which eases your own heart and soul. Such questions are: Will you always be there for me through the tough times no matter how close or far I am? Will you always be there to protect me physically and emotionally? Will you be the person who will always light my way like the sun in the sky? Will you be my hero as you shield me and protect me from harm to the point you give up your own life for me? Will you be my strength when I feel weak and most of all will you fight for me? In the end, it's that person who will look you in the eyes and say to you from one's heart and soul...for you I will, which is a song by Monica that reflects this particular thought.

DO THE RIGHT THING
January 12, 2006

Erynn Miller said, ~It takes a lot of understanding, time, and trust to gain a close friendship with someone. As I approach a time of my life of complete uncertainty, my friends are my most precious assets.~ Without a doubt, friendships can be tested especially between men and women when that proverbial line appears to where there is no turning back at the decision(s) one makes when it concerns him or her. For its a decision that will truly test one emotionally, mentally, as well as personally. Whether one passes or fails it's a learning experience as you find out there are limitations and/or boundaries when it concerns a particular guy or girl who you are interested in.

The funny thing about the friendship between men and women when the so-called line is about to be crossed or is crossed is that one will be emotionally tested. Oftentimes there is a proverbial litmus test as to whether one will either fall apart or keep one's composure due to that person. You may ask yourself, what is the litmus test? Well, there are several such as certain scenes in movies/tv shows but mainly it's the songs on the radio, which can make you sick and tired of hearing them. Yet, for some reason you can't turn on the radio when songs such as So Sick by Ne-Yo play on the radio seemingly every minute of the day, which can be considered cruel and inhuman torture, but I digress.

Essentially, when it comes to mentally understanding the possibility of establishing a relationship with someone your friends with you start rationalizing in your mind whether or not it was a mistake to move forward. It's that unpredictability of it all as one reveals thought, but what's tricky about it is how much to reveal because too much can most definitely make that person feel uncomfortable, which one didn't intentionally intend on doing. For some, most, or all people have been or are in this type of situation with a particular someone to where one jeopardizes the friendship, and the best alternative is to leave it be and not take any further action that causes an even greater rift.

In any case, there comes a point where a person realizes they became someone one always said or told himself or herself would never be. It's that someone who gets emotionally attached and it takes either a reality check such as a slap upside the head or looking in the mirror to see yourself to where one severs the attachment, which is the best thing if one wants a friendship to last. If you think about it, you never really see it coming until you find yourself doing or saying things that you apologize for in hopes that balance is restored in a friendship that was built through time to where trust is eventually gained again.

In retrospect, life is a test and even if one fails you pass because life brings you surprises that you never expect to happen like true happiness. For the most part, there is a sense of frustration when it comes to wondering when one's time of uncertainty will be over when it involves a guy or girl. In the meantime, it's just a matter of keeping yourself busy and hanging out with friends that you can come to in order to ask the right advice about matters of the heart. In the end, a friend summed it up best with this statement: ~In order to keep a great friendship one must do the right thing and that's not to live within your heart but instead just live as you continue on living life with great friends right alongside you.~

CLASS DISMISSED
January 13, 2006

Richard Bach once said, ~Learning is finding out what we already know. Doing us demonstrating that you know it. Teaching is reminding others that they know just as well as you. You are all learners, doers, and teachers.~ On any given day we are bombarded with information that may or may not be relevant in our own lives. With media such as word of mouth, television, books, magazines, radio, and the internet we as a society attain quite a bit of knowledge stored in our ole' memory banks. Whether you've let it go through one ear and out the other or learned through osmosis, you soak in some, most or all the information like a sponge. So kids, take your seats as class begins and please pay attention and no talking...just kidding.

Oftentimes you learn things by accident, which can inevitably benefit others, depending on if they actually respond to what one found out. Personally speaking, I found out that if you have a stuffy nose due to a cold or the flu, just stick your head in the freezer and breathe in the cold air. I know it seems highly unorthodox and totally ridiculous, but when you keep breathing in you will find yourself breathing through your nose easier. Why? The cold air you breathe in shrinks the blood vessels thereby opening the airways in your nasal passages. Let me tell you something, friends of mind have tried it and it worked for them, so what do you have to lose except being perceived as weird by people who catch you doing it.

Without a doubt, there are certain television shows that helped in one's learning process, but they also demonstrated how to implement what was built/made. One such show that you would never really think of being an educational type show is MacGyver.

The main premise of the show is one man using his mind instead of weapons to get out of sticky situations. It's in this show you learn that everyday items such as a Hershey bar and a stick of chewing gum can be made into an explosive device. Plus, it also made a simple adhesive popular and it was practically used in every show...duct tape. Hey, you not only learned something, but you also got a lesson in chemistry, science, and physics as well.

Growing up there was one show that kids, as well as adults watched, and it involved painting with a man that sported the biggest afro for a white guy. The Joy of Painting with Bob Ross partly influenced many kids' lives including my own when it came to choosing art as a subject to focus on in the future. Of the many painters in life, Bob Ross was one of a kind as he taught you to paint in a soft, exuberant tone which pulled you in. It's with that type of speaking voice that, in a way, mesmerized, which is the reason his show was popular back in the day. We've all at least tried to paint with him or like him and to be perfectly honest, it never turned out quite right when I did it. In any case, it was not only a learning experience but fun to watch as well.

In retrospect, life is one big classroom as we learn things that are either trivial, semi-important, or really important that it may or may not help you grow personally, physically, and most of all intellectually. Essentially, you would be amazed at the knowledge each of us has attained over a period of time to where it sticks in our minds. Whether it's knowing the migratory patterns of the Water Buffalo watching the Discovery Channel or learning that country music calms a group of hyperactive kids you use that knowledge to unknowingly teach others. So, if anybody wants to share anything interesting the floor is open to you and if not, then class dismissed.

YOUTH OF THE NATION
January 15, 2006

Kahil Gibran once said, ~The teacher...gives not of his wisdom but rather of his faith and lovingness. If he is indeed wise, he does not bid you enter the house of his wisdom but rather leads you to the threshold of your mind.~ Let me ask you this question, who in life is considered to be your mentor? For it's that man or woman who guided, molded, sought advice from, and helped you become the person you are today. Whether it was in your personal or professional life that person was always supportive and never gave up on you even though you may have given up on yourself. In a sense, he or she is your Yoda who seemingly has some, most, or all the answers when the questions to the answers you seek are hard to come by.

Working in the childcare profession, you're not just considered their friend to many kids but you're also considered a teacher. For the knowledge we have attained over the years has been passed on too many other kids and whether or not the particular information given is valid, one goes with what he or she knows. For we've all been in a situation where a child or a group of children asks you a question and you either have no idea, try to answer it with the best of your knowledge, or ask someone who you might possibly know. For it can be a comical situation when nobody knows the answer and that's when it's left in the capable hands of his, her, or their parent(s).

Speaking of parents, you truly get a sense of a child's upbringing by how a parent rears him, her or them at home. This may not apply to you directly if you have kids, but there are particular parents that I have seen who treat their own kid(s) as second-class citizens to where a no loving, lack-luster greeting is given when picking him, her, or them up. Its like that parent sees their child/children as a necessity rather than a joy to see and granted they just worked long hours, but show some love instead of barking orders to get one's things to leave immediately, which gives us insight and teaches us there is a reason as to why certain kids act out the way they do be it strict rules and/or lack of attention at home.

Without a doubt, each of us is the product of how we were raised and taught by our own parents or parents. Inevitably, you learn a lot from being around kids, especially how they act in the presence of their parent(s) and then left in the hands of childcare professionals such as myself. For their whole persona, attitude, listening skills, and most importantly manners are essentially gone as soon as that parent steps foot out the door. Don't get me wrong, not all kids fall under this demographic as it is certain kids who need direction and an attitude adjustment but done with loving wisdom that one has been taught to use. Yet, the question remains: does it work? My answer… sometimes, but you don't give up at it.

Whether you know it or not, January is national mentoring month and all across the nation people are encouraged to mentor a child. In other words, become a big brother/big sister or be a part of The Boys and Girls Club of America, which is affiliated with the Youth Center that I work at. For three questions can be asked to you: 1.) Were you ever in the big brother/big sister program as a kid? 2.) Do you still keep in contact with him or her? 3.) How many of you are now a part of the big brother/ big sister program? Ultimately, mentoring kids is a great thing because the positive influence you give will hopefully be received back. In the end, they're not just the youth of the nation, they're our future.

BRAND NEW DAY
January 17, 2006

Hammad Chhipe once said, ~Love is just like life. Its is not always easy and it does not always bring happiness...but when we do not drop living, why should we drop loving?~ Without a doubt, life can be considered hard to grasp at times, but when it comes to love that's even harder to grasp. Like life, one oftentimes thinks he or she has the mystery of love solved but unfortunately there are more questions within the answers you find. In a sense, it's like going through an endless cycle of questions and answers to where you end up at the same question you began with. Essentially, when it comes to life and love, there are several inherent truths that we all end up facing and accepting.

Truth #1: No matter how much you try to avoid drama in your life, it finds you depending on if one intentionally or unintentionally looks for it. Every person has at least been a part of or witnessed people being involved in what I like to call the six degrees of Kevin Bacon drama-go-round where one person likes another but that person doesn't like him or her in that way to where you end up with hurt feelings, which makes reconciliation between friends not an easy task to fix. It essentially makes a person laugh not in a funny humorous way but rather in frustration, why is this happening in all kinds of ways?

Truth #2: When it comes to finding the right guy, women want a man who will just love her instead of adore her. Its that proverbial litmus test which helps a woman choose and yet there is a difference in the two as adore is defined as to like very much; worship whereas love is defined as a deep, tender feeling of affection toward a person. It can oftentimes not be easy for a guy to distinguish the two because it can intertwine to where a guy will mistakenly have blind adoration for a woman rather than love and vice versa. Undeniably, women are smart enough to pick up on this and unfortunately it takes a while for guys to figure this out, but hey we learn until we get it right.

Truth #3: Love is the most simplest thing and yet it can become complicated to where we mess it up on our own. How? People spend money on books and talking/listening to so called "experts" that one's brain can be filled with so much information that it can most definitely confuse you. Confuse you in the sense the answer is staring right in the face and yet, you tend to not see it at first. For it will truly mean a great deal to that particular person and you'll have less to think about. For the most overlooked aspect of love is friendship where just sharing a simple smile or a laugh means much more and far surpasses every other moment that is deemed memorable.

Someone once said, ~Love emanates from truth and truth emanates from love; one does not exist without the other. Truth is an internal current and love is its external flow.~ In retrospect, it's never easy facing the truth when it comes to both life and love, but we never stop living or loving. Continually living each day to where you focus on the more positive aspects of your life while spreading the love you have wherever you can, but not to one person but to people you meet along your own personal journey. If you think about it, love moves in mysterious ways to where the truth of love shows you everything you've ever prayed for and because of it you look forward to spending a lifetime as each brand new day always brings something new never before experienced with that special someone someday.

ANYTHING BUT ORDINARY
January 19, 2006

Someone once said, ~Love and relationships are truly one of the most paradoxical aspects of being human. For it is in love that we find the greatest of strengths and the deepest of sorrows. Love can seem to be so fleeting and unachievable yet it remains well within our reach if we only learn how to embrace its power. To experience true love, we must be willing to open ourselves up and sacrifice part of our heart and part of our soul. We must be willing to give of ourselves freely, and we must be willing to suffer. It is only when we expose our inner selves to the white hot flame of rejection, that love can burn so brightly as to join two souls, melding the two into one, creating a bond that joins forever. It is from this bond that we draw strength eternal and power everlasting. It is in this thing that we call love that we find the means to achieve greatness, both in ourselves and in our lives.~

One of the most frequently asked questions people ask is how do two people, who are traveling different paths in life, end up together? If you think about it, we as human beings try to understand each other especially when it comes to men trying to figure out women and women trying to figure out men. Men and women want the enjoyment of each other's company and yet we still keep that part of ourselves that enjoys solitude as well. For it's the frustration, craziness, confusion, anger, pulling out hair etc. that describe the male-female relationship and despite that fact you wouldn't have it any other way because it makes spending time with that person much more enjoyable.

When it comes to love and relationships you can't have one without the other. For its love that is the source of strength that builds a strong relationship and yet it can be considered a weakness to where it completely falls apart. All too often a person can be selfish and forget it's not the happiness you seek for yourself but rather the happiness you seek unselfishly for that person. In its purest form love is honest, real, an unbreakable bond, a calm yet turbulent passion to where you are willing to wait patiently on the needs/desires of that particular person. In all intents and purposes, love is the source that breathes life into love and inevitably into a relationship.

Without a doubt, love is a scary thing as you allow yourself to open up to someone who you're comfortable enough with to actually let him or her care about you. It's a matter of letting go of the control you have and trusting that person to catch you. The fall can oftentimes hurt but it's a good kind of hurt that gives you the freedom and confidence to express how you truly feel? However, the question can be asked, do we limit ourselves on how much love we give and/or receive? I don't think so because for some, most, or all people paid their dues to where one finally receives true happiness and if not for yourself then for someone who is truly deserving.

In retrospect, you have to expect the unexpected when love comes your way. For it will show you that you truly don't have to do anything amazing or spectacular but be yourself. For it also shows that you'll love who you are when you're with a particular person that brings out the best in you. Let me ask you this question ladies and gentlemen, how many of you have found that guy or girl that loves you just for being who you are and its the best relationship you have ever been in? In the end, the love that every person truly deserves has found you or will find you someday and it's a love that is anything but ordinary, for it's absolutely extraordinary.

BEST LAID PLANS
January 22, 2006

Someone once said, ~In life, love is never planned, it does happen for a reason, but when the love is real it becomes you plan for life and your reason for living.~ There are many areas in life that we all make plans for either socially and/or professionally, but the one area that tends to not to be planned is in our personal lives and that is in the area of love. When it comes to love, it's unexpected, unplanned to the point it's considered life altering and changes not only your attitude, but also your whole outlook on life. Nobody ever plans to fall in love and yet it happens without warning and whether or not it's true love...well you just have to find out for yourself.

Without a doubt, when you don't plan on falling in love with someone it gives you a sense of determination and/or purpose in life. It's that thing called love that throws one's intended plans, whether it's professionally or personally, all out whack that one tends to question the timing of it all, which is a mistake to do. You just have to go with the flow, so to speak, and inevitably the questions you always wanted to know about love are answered. Although you don't get all the answers right away, which nobody ever really does, they gradually come through time as you figure them out either the hard way or the easy way.

As said before, nobody ever plans to fall in love, it just happens and the same can be said for falling out of love as well. It can truly be a tough situation indeed for two people to no longer feel the love shared in their relationship. A relationship that was at one time built on trust, honesty, and communication. For emotions such as humiliation, frustration, confusion, anger, resentment, bitterness, denial, and acceptance are just some of what a person may go through when falling out of love. A person can absolutely feel defeated and if or when it happens more than once it can be a miserable experience to where you feel all hope is lost at ever having true happiness.

Let me ask you this question, are you the type of person who generally has everything planned out when it comes to potentially meeting the right person? Women, more so than guys, tend to have a set plan from the time their young in which they aim high for as they try to have all their i's dotted, and all their t's crossed in hopes that their goals within one's plans come true. Meeting the right guy, falling in love with him, getting married, having kids, the proverbial white picket fence house, a successful career, is the basic diagram that each and every woman wants for herself, but it doesn't necessarily mean some, most, or all of it will come to fruition.

Former Beatle John Lennon once said, ~Life is what happens to you while you're busy making other plans.~ In retrospect, life has a funny way of showing you that a person just has to stop making plans, continue living, and let God take control of your love life as He has someone planned for you and me. Don't be too concerned with the plans you have such as meeting and falling in love with someone because you'll miss out on something much more special...life itself. Sometimes, the best laid plans are those that you don't prepare for as it's left in God's capable hands because in the end, when you do finally meet that special someone, He will say with a smile on His face I love it when a plan comes together.

CAN YOU HEAR ME NOW?

January 24, 2006

Rachel Naomi Roman once said, ~The most basic and powerful way to connect to another person is to listen. Just listen. Perhaps the most important thing we ever give each other is our attention…A loving silence often has far more power to heal and to connect than the most well-intentioned words.~ If you think about it, one of the five senses we use the most is our sense of hearing. On any given day, we open our ears and listen to something or someone to where we either have some, most, or all our attention focused on that person or sound at hand. Essentially, a person who has great listening skills is not simply nodding or making hmmm sounds every other second/minute, but actually listening to every word you're saying.

Without a doubt, each and every woman is looking for a guy who will actually listen to what she has to say. Oftentimes, a woman will encounter a guy who hears what she is saying but isn't actually listening at what she is truly saying to him. For its these types of guys who have a hard time accepting the fact that she isn't interested in him to where she will politely try to brush him off with words that are kind instead of ones that are harsh. Typically, the harsh words women try to avoid saying to a guy are that you're an immature, egotistical, hardheaded jerk, who doesn't know when to quit or something to that effect. Let me ask you this question ladies, when was the last time you encountered a guy like this?

When you have the opportunity to work in the childcare profession, part of your job is listening to kids who always have something to say whether its a conflict with another child, a certain request one wants/needs, or simply someone to talk to. More often than not children want to be heard or at least someone to talk to due to the lack of attention he or she may not be receiving at home. Granted, what that particular child may be saying to you makes no sense at all, is hard to understand, or has no point whatsoever but just wants to talk and despite that fact you are giving him or her you full, as well as, undivided attention which pays off big dividends as they appreciate you for lending an open ear.

When it comes to the power of prayer, one wonders if the requests that you specifically want to be fulfilled are being listened to by God. We've all at some point in our lives thrown our hands in the air, looked up, and asked God if He is truly listening at all to what you've been saying to Him in one's prayers. Depending on what you are actually praying for is considered either non-important, semi-important, or truly important; it all comes down to how patient you are and how long you are willing to wait until one's prayer requests come to fruition. For the question can be asked, have any of your prayers been truly fulfilled which leads you to believe that God is truly listening to you.

Brenda Ueland said, ~Listening is a magnetic and strange thing, a creative force...When we are listened to, it creates us, makes us unfold and expand. Ideas actually begin to grow within us and come to life..When we listen to people there is an alternating current, and this recharges us so that we never get tired of each other...and it is this little creative fountain inside us that begins to spring and cast up new thoughts and unexpected laughter and wisdom...Well, it is when people really listen to us, with quiet fascinated attention, that the little fountain begins to work again, to accelerate in the most surprising way.~ In the end, whether its listening to kids, woman wanting guys who will actually listen to them, asking God to listen and grant one's prayers or whatever it may be we're all considered the Verizon Wireless dude as this question is asked by each of us many times over...can you hear me now?

IT'S A SMALL WORLD
January 26, 2006

Deepak Chopra once said, ~When you live your life with an appreciation of coincidences and their meanings, you connect with the underlying field of infinite possibilities.~ Let me ask you this question, do you believe in coincidences that are considered either strange, unusual, and/or unbelievable? We all have been through situations where we're unknowingly connected to someone by way of a complete stranger, acquaintance, co-worker, mutual friend, family member, significant other, whatever the case may be. Every person has a story to tell not just from their point of view but also the point of view from others connected to you as well, which can oftentimes give a better perspective on the particular situation at hand.

In some cases, coincidences happen when it concerns friendships that involve a third party that is connected somehow to one's own circle of friends. For it's that person who you talk to on a semi-daily basis as he or she shares info about a guy or girl that one met. We've been in that particular situation where we don't necessarily pay full attention to the description of him or her, which can sometimes be a complete exaggeration, the opposite of how you actually know that person, or right on the money. It may take either that very moment, several days, months, or even years before ever finding out that you actually know the person that he or she is speaking of and it can come as a complete surprise not just for you but for the two other people as well.

Without a doubt, a person has unfortunate coincidences that can dramatically affect one's life either for better or for worse. One such unfortunate coincidence involves Amber Frey, who was unknowingly connected to the death of Scott Peterson's wife and unborn child. Whether you've been living under a rock for the past year or so Scott Peterson was married to Laci Peterson who on December 23, 2003, went missing and the witness to the prosecution had the so-called trump card to bring down Scott Peterson, which can in the form of Scott's former mistress Amber Frey. Essentially, her life will never be the same as she will be forever connected with a man that killed not only his wife but an 8-month unborn child as well.

When it comes to significant relationships, there can most definitely be a coincidence in meeting one's future wife/husband. Every married couple has a story to share of how they eventually met, and it oftentimes involves a roommate that either set them up together or he or she dated or was trying to date that roommate and it didn't work out. For it can be a comical situation when points of views are shared years later by each person to where things are revealed that you never knew and/or always wanted to know. For the question can be asked for you married folks out there, has this particular situation happened to you and do you still keep in touch with your former roommate?

Personally speaking, I've experienced several coincidences that involve co-workers such as going to the same middle school with my future best friend and not finding out till years later or finding out that someone you're related to is next door neighbors with my mentor at work, which I found out at a funeral for her grandfather. Hey, it's a funny thing about life as we meet people that may or may not be connected to each of us in a six degrees of Kevin Bacon kind of way, where possibly a celebrity and/or sports figure is involved in the mix, in a manner of speaking. In the end, it's when you find out about these certain things that you tend to say out loud to someone or to yourself…wow, it's a small world.

RIGHT HERE WAITING
January 28, 2006

Someone once said, ~True love is waiting an eternity for one moment, one kiss, one smile. True love is wanting anything and everything for that person, whether you can't give it to that person or not.~ In a metaphorical sense, life is like an airport where millions of people each day come and go. Essentially, there is one constant when it comes to being in an airport and that is we wait. Whether its waiting to board, unboard a plane or waiting for a particular passenger or passengers, that's what we do in life, especially when it comes to love. For if life represents an airport, then each gate is a representation of love possibly walking through those gate doors for every person and yet the question remains which gate is it?

Which gate is it? Answering that particular question is easier said than done as every person asks themselves questions in which they not only want to know where but when will that special someone arrive? If you think about it, it's when one looks up into the bright or starry filled night sky you metaphorically look at the schedule times of when and where that person may be arriving. For we all can stare up there all we want but the fact of the matter is it doesn't accomplish anything, and it can cause you to explore other areas in life that you haven't seen and/or experienced. Essentially, it's when you do explore other areas in the airport of life you encounter interesting people who start out as strangers then become your friends

As with any airport, delays are expected which can make one's wait unbearable to where a person can become somewhat or extremely anxious. It's within those moments of anxiousness that a person will go through a rollercoaster of emotions such as frustration, confusion, yearning, and anger. When I mention anger, it's not due to that person's absence; but rather the emotions you put yourself through, which is totally unnecessary and can somewhat border on the melodramatic. We've all witnessed someone go through it and whether or not you want to admit or not you have to admit it's mildly entertaining to watch as you see people's reactions when they finally see the person or person's he, she, or they have been anxiously waiting to see.

Let me ask you this question, how long have you been waiting for that unknown passenger to walk through the gate that leads straight into the terminal of your heart? Without a doubt, it can truly be uplifting as you see men and women smile as their special someone walks through the gate doors that they've been standing in front of and into his or her arms. However, it's when you stand in front of the gate you think he or she may be coming out of, you can become disappointed as you end up basically staring into a long barren tunnel, which is a representation of your own heart, hoping he or she is the last one to come out. it's at that point you either give up waiting or continue waiting because you still have faith and hope that he or she will show up.

In the movie The Terminal starring Tom Hanks the main premise is about waiting. Waiting to go to New York to fulfill a promise for his father; waiting to go back to Krakozhia, and most of all waiting for love. In some aspect, we're all considered a Viktor Navorski as each of us are waiting in front of a gate with flowers in hand for that special someone. Yet one has to keep on living and/or exploring the airport of life with people that you befriended along the way. In the end, that special someone will someday walk through your gate but in the meantime, you telepathically say to him or her my heart will always be right here waiting for you to give. Plus, it's a song by Richard Marx that tends to reflect this thought.

TOUCHED BY AN ANGEL
January 31, 2006

Someone once said, ~Angels are the guardians of hope and wonder, the keepers of magic and dreams. Wherever there is love, an angel is flying by. Your guardian angel knows you inside and out, and loves you just the way you are. Angels keep it simple and always travel light. Remember to leave space in your relationships so the angels have room to play. Your guardian angel helps you find a place when you feel there is no place to go. Whenever you feel lonely, a special angel drops in for tea. Angels are with you every step of the way and help you soar with amazing grace. After all, we are angels in training; all we have to do is spread our wings and fly!~

Let me ask you this question, do you believe in angels? Let me ask you another question. who do you consider to be an angel? Personally speaking, I honestly believe in angels as they are all around protecting and keeping us from harm. Though you may not see them, you tend to feel their presence in times of strife. For it's not only the angels you don't see, but also the ones you see every day who are considered angels and it's just a matter of truly opening your eyes. Essentially, an angel could possibly be a small child who runs up and gives you a hug, a total stranger offering to give you directions when you're lost, or most definitely a friend who touches your heart with uplifting words of encouragement.

We've all at some point in our lives felt that life has us on the ropes and yet, in some sixth sense sort of way, someone either calls you just to see how you are doing or emails you something that was very much needed at that particular moment in one's life. In some aspect, he or she is considered an angel and even though you may not see the wings or a halo above his or her head, the light that exudes from within that person's heart and soul shows that he or she is a blessing from God who you have been initially been praying for when life itself becomes difficult and/or confusing. Hey, for all you know I could be an angel, which is highly unlikely, but you never really know.

Without a doubt, there are certain people in our lives that are Heaven sent by God and yet, it's that one person He sends who is considered an angel of light. For its one's angel of light that may potentially hold some, most, or all of your dreams to where they magically come true, but not all at once. A person can be truly lucky to meet someone that personally touches you and that gives you a new perspective on the way one sees life through his or her own eyes. However, it's hard to imagine a guy or girl who will always keep your heart and soul brightly smiling and that you will absolutely never feel alone even though you may feel it at times.

In retrospect, angels can take many different sizes, shapes, forms, and skin color. For they are masters of disguise as he or she can be either a total stranger, a friend, or even your own worst enemy. If you think about it, they're not always dressed in flashy looking clothes who stand out but rather dress casually and look like your average joe and jane on the street. Oftentimes, it's when you need help the most, an angel will be there answering your call and the line is never busy because all you have to do is pray. In the end, I ask you this question, when it comes to you everyday life have you been touched by an angel?

SHOW ME THE MONEY
February 2, 2006

Donald Trump said, ~Money was never a big motivation for me except as a way to keep score. The real excitement is playing the game.~ Without a doubt, money is considered a big incentive when it comes to being an athlete, actor/actress, and most certainly a musician. When it pertains to musicians, particularly those in the area of rap/hip hop, money is the name of the game to where one can make a name for himself or herself depending on the sales of their records. It can truly be staggering how much these "artists" make as we all read, see, or her them buy lavish material possessions such as houses, cars, clothes, and most definitely.

Let me ask you this question, have you ever thought to yourself when you're looking at a certain rap artist that they're really overdoing it with all the bling? In a sense, they can literally be on the cusp of being the next Mr. T in the making, which is a description not meant to be considered flattering. Yet, it's not so much the quantity of bling but the or ice, as it is otherwise known, it's the size of bling one wears that amazes you that person is actually standing upright due to sheer mass and weight of it. It's no wonder they need bodyguards not just because of their fame but rather the millions of dollars they're displaying and oftentimes flaunting around their neck, wrists, fingers, on their ears, and even on their teeth.

You truly know when someone has too much money when they start putting diamonds, gold, and/or platinum coverings for their teeth or otherwise known in the urban lingo grillz. For the most part, it's been done in the past before rap/hip hop exploded into the mainstream, but it was more toned down back then. Now, you have rappers with diamond/gold/platinum encrusted braces or teeth guards which have become popular with "artists" such as Paul

Wall who sported them on Nelly's recent music Video Grillz. In my honest opinion, they're nice for show but they'll end up cutting the inside of your mouth and talking is a total impossibility.

Essentially, when it comes to the bling you know there are people out there who are bold enough to try to jack their jewelry. It's a given because the price tag of a particular rapper's bling they wear can reach millions, which in all intents and purposes can pay for not just my house but my friend's houses especially the bling in their mouths as well. Undoubtedly, potential robbers may not be just going after the usual things such as wallet, the earrings, necklace, rings, but also taking what's in their teeth, which makes it funny to think about as a rapper is trying to describe what one's teeth looks like to the police, but I digress.

In retrospect, money can be considered a double-edged sword to where it's considered survival of the fittest. When money plays a part in the music industry, it can either make or break you in album sales. It helped rapper 50 Cent's and it probably helped sales when people heard he was shot 9 times and lived to tell about it. You have to admit though we as a society thrive on building people up to where they make it big and jump off the proverbial bandwagon once that person falls i.e. M.C. Hammer. In the end, when potential rappers think they've got what it takes, get signed to a label, and start buying things such as jewelry, just know it all began with a single thought that became a driving force which was...show me the money.

SAY IT WITH A SMILE
February 4, 2006

Lydia M. Child once said, ~Flowers have spoken to me more than I can tell in written words. They are the hieroglyphics of angels, loved by all me for the beauty of their character, though few can decipher even fragments of their meaning.~ You have to admit, one of the gifts that a woman most likes to receive, other than jewelry, are flowers. With Valentine's Day being just around the corner there will most definitely be a rise in sales of flowers, particularly roses. Valentine's Day is a chance for people, mainly guys, to show our romantic/softer side with a particular female or group of females and what better way to show appreciation than to personally give or have flowers delivered to show her or them we care.

Without a doubt, when guys like myself have no idea what to say we let flowers do all the talking. Flowers can express a plethora of emotions that can convey passion, respect, congratulations, friendship, appreciation, and regret when someone wants to apologize for something one might have said or did to get the proverbial cold shoulder. Thinking about it, flowers are considered the perfect gift for a special someone or potential special someone in one's life as it can not only brighten her day, but also put a smile on her face to where it makes her feel special. Let me ask you this question ladies, when was the last time you received flowers and who was the guy that sent them?

For some, most, or all guys the standard flowers to give women are red roses and yet they can sometimes grow seemingly tired of receiving the same thing to where a guy can be considered predictable in the flower department. For the most part, its just a matter of changing it up not only with the colors but also the type of flowers to give, which shows women that guys are actually taking their time to think what flowers to get and not just picking the first cheesiest flower he sees. It's a mistake that guys tend to make and, in a sense, for a woman, the right flower can either break a guy; but if he takes the time to find out what her favorite flower is then he might have a chance and there is a big emphasis on the word MIGHT.

For those particular people who may not have a Valentine this year or previous years, giving flowers or Valentine related gifts are something to be avoided. However, you can still give without having any kind of personal attachments. Personally speaking, I don't have a Valentine but that doesn't stop me, as well as my best friend from giving flowers as gifts to our female co-workers of the insane asylum/Youth Center. For the past several years, we've been doing it because we wanted to and it inevitably has now become a tradition every year to buy them and give them personally to each lady depending how many ladies, we both buy them for. By now, they're expecting us to deliver and let me tell you something we both don't want to disappoint them.

Someone once said, ~To see a flower of beauty is such a special thing...The petals wrapping around the stem, it can make you want to sing...Fragrant smells of roses, carnations and the such...You want to reach out to the petals, with just a small soft, touch...The colors of the rainbow, so bright and vibrant are they...We take for granted the flowers, each and every single day...So stop and smell the roses, carnations and the such...Revel in the beauty and make that small, soft touch...Remember that the flowers are a treat, they surely are a treasure...Remember this whenever, the flowers bring you pleasure.~ In the end, every guy will give a someone special or a close friend flowers and as its personally handed to that certain someone Happy Valentine's Day will be said and they will most definitely say it with a smile.

UNBREAKABLE
February 6, 2006

Lois Wyse once said, ~A good friend is a connection to life-a tie to the past, a road to the future, the key to sanity in a totally insane world.~ If you think about it, the connection each of us have with one's friends oftentimes can't be described with just mere words. Essentially, there is an unseen bond in which you clique with someone that a friendship is formed either in an instant or gradually. It's these same friends who keep life interesting, exciting, and laughable to where its never dull being around him, her, or them. Without a doubt, each one of us have great memories shared with certain friends and it's the connection with a particular moment in time with him, her, or them that will always be considered special.

When it comes to our friends, past or present, something will inevitably connect him, her, or them to you. Though the connection may be different with each person individually you still keep that balance of friendship level as can be so as to not disturb the harmonious flow that's been established in one's inner circle. Yet, you can't help but hang out more with a particular number of one's inner circle, which doesn't necessarily mean you don't enjoy their company. It's due in part to the length of time one has known the person or persons, as well as interests that may be shared with you. Let me ask you this question, who in your inner circle have you known the longest and how well does he, she, or they know you?

Essentially, there are moments in one's past with a particular friend or friends that either a secret or promise is shared. In other words, a pact that is made between friends to where a certain situation is kept under wraps that only some, most, or all know and whether or not that particular secret will be tight lipped depends on how strong the friendship is. OR its a pact where friends, who may have gone their separate ways, come together to fulfill a promise that was made in the past. For it's a pact in which an agreement sealed it tight such as a pinky swear, spit handshake, a speech, or whatever the case may be for you and your inner circle past or present.

In any case, there comes a point where a friendship that was long forgotten in the past surprisingly steps back into the present. What do I mean? With this being an updated and ever-growing technological age, we can find/stumble on friends that one grew out of touch with back in the day. With such websites as Myspace, Friendster, and classmates.com, a person can find old friends if he, she, or they are on there. Personally speaking, I've kept in contact with a few of my friends who I went to school with overseas. For they were and still are family, being that it was a military base, and the funny thing is that you will meet them again where you unknowingly find yourself working with that person or people.

In retrospect, the faces may change but the spirit of friendship is never lost as we all connect with people on a semi-daily basis. Whether it's in person or online in websites such as Myspace and Friendster, you form an initial bond even though you may not know him, her, or them personally. In this totally insane world, the connection we have with our totally insane friends who, in some aspect, keep us sane shows that no matter what comes between a friendship that breaks it apart something happens to bring it back together. In the end, the road of life will always connect us to friends in the past and present to where they will someday meet in the future because in the end, that unseen bond friends share with each other is truly unbreakable.

HEAVEN ON EARTH
February 8, 2006

Neil Gaman once said, ~Have you ever been in love? Horrible isn't it? It makes you so vulnerable. It opens your chest and it opens your heart and it means that someone can get inside you and mess you up. You build up all these defenses, you build up a whole suit of armor, so nothing can hurt you, then one stupid person, no different from any other stupid person, wanders into your stupid life...You give them a piece of you. They didn't ask for it. They did something one day like kiss you or smile at you and then your life isn't your own anymore. Love takes hostages. It gets inside you... It hurts not just in the imagination, not just in the mind. Its a soul hurt, a real-gets-inside-you-and-rips-you-apart-pain.~

You have to admit, it would truly be a wonderful world if you didn't have to go through the pain and suffering that comes with love such as rejection. Every person, whether one wants to admit it or not, has been rejected by someone who he or she was initially interested in/in love with or vice versa. Depending on the type of rejection and the number of times, it can affect a person to where one can have his or her heart turned on and off like a proverbial light switch, which sounds cold, but you have to look at it from their perspective. For it would be so much simpler if the things that complicated love like rejection would be taken out of the equation, but one can only dream of that every happening.

When it comes to love, we all metaphorically wear a suit of armor to protect ourselves from seriously getting hurt especially from within our heart. Yet, no matter how thick one's armor is or how well protected you are, somehow someone who you didn't intend to fall for, pierces through our armor and into our heart. We've all been in or are going through that particular situation to where you completely let down all your defenses, which leaves you totally vulnerable not only in your heart but your soul as well. Essentially, you consequently open yourself up to him or her but unfortunately that someone of interest may not, which leaves you without a parachute to safely float to the ground, in a manner of speaking, as you take that leap of faith.

As was said before by Nel Gaman, all it can take is either a kiss, smile, or something to wake your heart up. Its that so-called wakeup call that gets inside your head to where you want to know more about that person not in a stalking, creepy sort of way; but rather in a genuine fondness way. As a guy, you want to know what her favorite flower, color, smell is and not only that you want to genuinely get to know her by finding out her hopes, dreams, likes, dislikes, as well as plans for the future. I know for all women, it's a rarity these days to meet a guy who takes the time to get to know you inside as well as out and for a woman, that guy is considered a dream come true.

In retrospect, a person can spend a lifetime waiting for love that can make you happy and yet miserable at the same time, but in a good way. It's the happiness deep down in your soul, the happy misery that you've always wanted and yet it's not fixable when things don't work out as you expected. Yet despite the pain, suffering, and rejection you, as well as your heart kept getting back up after being knocked down. Ultimately every person has made this statement: ~When I fall in love I want it to last forever.~ In the end, it will or has come true for you to where it always feels like heaven on earth and a song that reflects this thought comes from the movie Sleepless in Seattle entitled When I Fall In Love by Celine Dion & Clive Griffen.

WALK THE LINE
February 11, 2006

John Myers once said, ~What makes a man a Man? A friend of mine once wondered. It is his origins? The way he comes to life? I don't think so. It's the choices he makes. Not how he starts things, but how he decides to end them.~ As a guy, one's manhood can be called into question when it pertains to certain areas of life such as relationships, love, marriage, etc. Without a doubt, every guy has been told to be a man when something or someone affects us that it totally changes the fabric of our being either for better or worse. For its how a man deals with the particular situations placed in front of him that essentially defines not only his character but also his heart as well.

Every man starts out with the adolescent innocence of a small boy and for the most part some, most, or all grow up and become the man he was born to be. For its through proper training and guidance from one's parent(s) who instill in him criterias in life to either follow or not follow, which in turn gives a woman insight into how he was raised and the values he holds close. The combination of a nurturing, caring, loving mother mixed with a no-nonsense, stern, sometimes stubborn father gives a woman the man that stands before her. Yet, results can vary depending on the man's family situation growing up and the atmosphere surrounding his upbringing.

Without a doubt, all men have an ego to where if that ego is bruised, foolish pride sets in and every guy, whether he wants to admit or not, has made a fool of himself when it came to following his heart. A man's ego and his heart, two things that continually clash as it begins and ends with a woman, who may or may not be "the one" that not only makes him crazy for a lifetime but also truly brings him to life. For some, most, or all men, its the choice to swallow his pride/apologize for things right or wrong that may end up embarrassing her and ultimately severing a plutonic/potential/significant relationship, which is truly becoming of man.

Let me ask you this question ladies, when it comes to encountering conflicts with the man in your life, does he leave things unfinished to where resentment is felt, or does he stay by your side and talks things through until the situation is resolved? That is the determining factor in any relationship for any woman to find a guy who will not run away or avoid the conflicts that fester over time and if not dealt with they'll explode to where there will be no survivors left standing. Every woman has been in this type of situation and there is still a bit of resentment towards a particular guy who not only did you wrong, but left things unfinished which left you scar that hasn't healed within your heart.

Personally speaking, I have to ask this question: what makes me a man? Is it how my mom taught me to always say yes sir, no sir, yes ma'am, no ma'am, plus please and thank you. Is it how my dad, who was an officer in the Navy, taught me to respect women and never lay a hand on them. Or is it how both my parents taught me to always be a true gentleman, which is seriously lacking in the guy department. What it comes down to are the choices made in the beginning and seeing them all the way through. In the end, I continue to walk the line my parents set me on and even though I've made mistakes with the choices I've made, they will always be proud of me as the man I am now and also the man I will become in future.

MY VALENTINE
February 14, 2006

Pierre Teilhard de Chardin once said, ~Love alone is capable of uniting living beings in such a way as to complete and fulfill them, for it alone takes them and joins them by what is deepest in themselves.~ Powerful, mysterious, giving, selfless, understanding, painful, patient, are just some of the verbal descriptions of what love can bring/give to two people who are truly in love with each other. Yet, it's the happiness you find within love that you can never really describe with words to someone who either has never been in love or doesn't know the true meaning of what love is. Let me ask you this question, have you found that indescribable love that completes you in so many ways?

Without a doubt, there are three absolutes you know about in life, and they are you're born, you pay taxes, and then you die. It's a given and yet there is one thing that you will never be able to know about which is who are you going to fall in love with? It's the unpredictability of love that matches two people together who may be of a different race, color, creed, size, shape, opinions, political stance, whatever the case may be that when you see both of them together you say to yourself or to others they absolutely fit together. Though some may not see it from a visual standpoint, it's what a person "sees" within the heart of those two people that can truly open his or her eyes.

If you think about it, love is synonymous with patience because it takes a lot of patience to continually be in love with someone who can also get on your nerves. Essentially, its not until you're completely comfortable with each other enough that one's habits will start to present themselves. Every couple has at least one or two things that annoy each other such as cracking knuckles, cutting one's toenails and leaving them where they are, saying a certain word/phrase over and over again, etc. Despite those annoying little quarks, which can drive you crazy, you still love him or her and learn to look past it because that is what love is as you accept that person for who he or she is, faults and all.

In a sense, the love that two people share has a universal language all its own that flows deep within each other's heart to where only you and that particular person can understand it. Though the way the message being sent is different for some, most, or all couples, the message itself is the same, true and true. For its that oftentimes unspoken language that can give a woman, more so than a guy, a sense of peace within her heart and soul that she is actually being heard without ever speaking verbally to the man she loves. For the question can be asked to you ladies, does the man in your life hear you loud and clear when you are sending him unspoken messages?

In retrospect, knowing the love you have deep within your heart is not considered a burden to carry around but rather a gift to share with that one person who sees how big of heart you truly have. It's when that person takes some of the load of your heart and places it in his or hers that you finally see the face of unselfish love. For that person is your best friend for all time who shares with you tears of joy and sadness, which is something special to behold. In the end, for those who are single, you will someday meet or have already met that special someone who you've dreamed a lifetime for and as you give your heart to him or her you will say to that person you are, as well as, forever will be my valentine, which is a song my Martina McBride.

YOU DA MAN
February 16, 2006

Someone once said, ~Depending on the imagination of the man proposing, a marriage proposal can be the most romantic even in a woman's life. Its the time to express profound love and a commitment to mutual deviation.~ Did you know that is 85% of women have been "disappointed" in the way they were proposed to which shows that many guys don't take the time to plan out the proposal or if it was planned out it fell apart before, during, and/or after the special event. Without a doubt, being proposed to for a woman is considered one of the greatest events she will ever be involved in, as well as remember for all time. Let me ask you this question to the ladies who are engaged or married, how did your man propose to you?

Essentially, what makes a proposal such a momentous occasion for any woman is the particular place that she is being proposed at, which may or may not have any importance to. One such place that is oftentimes used as a romantic backdrop for a proposal of marriage is at the beach either at sunrise where everything is peaceful or at sunset when the stars are about to shine in the sky. For the most part, sunset rather than sunrise is because the sound of the ocean combined with the moon reflecting off the water, as well as, shining brightly above gives it sort of a spotlight feel for a guy. In some aspect, the beach is the stage and once that spotlight hits its showtime folks for a future to possibly begin together.

When it comes to special occasions such as Valentine's Day the setting is right for getting on bended knee because you can sense it in the atmosphere and smell love in the air. In a poll conducted by Diamond Information Center, 10% of the reported 2.3 million couples who get engaged do it on Valentine's Day. Any woman can truly appreciate the time, effort, and planning of something so simple as a proposal because it shows how much a guy is willing to give from within his heart and soul. Whether it's elaborate or simple, as long as a guy finds the words to her how much he loves and means to her by asking for her hand in marriage then it's forever a special memory.

Countless stories can be told of romantic engagements in places such as on The Eiffel Tower, but how about in a cemetery? Well, it's a true story and involves a couple who have been dating for several years and the woman's father passes away who she is very close to. One day, he plans a visit to where her father is buried and when they arrive he tells her to wait. He walks over, kneels down on one knee, and prays in front of her father's tombstone. Afterwards, he(still kneeling) motions for her to come over and when she does she asks what he was doing he said, 'I was praying to your father for your hand in marriage.' Touched by his answer, she asks what he says? His response, 'Take care of my daughter' and he proposes to her right there.

Jean Diruni said, ~The greatest risk with proposing to someone is that they might say yes.~ Why? In the back of every guy's mind there is that small seed of doubt to where she says no, which one readily prepares for. But when the answer is yes, all the pressure leading up to that moment is a heart attack waiting to happen as a simple answer seemingly takes forever. Whether it's on the beach, on Valentine's Day, or in a cemetery, asking a woman for her hand in marriage is the most nerve-racking moment any guy will go or has gone through. Ultimately, it's when you hear romantic stories of how a particular guy proposed to his future wife you just have to stand up, give him props, and in the end say to him you da man!

NEVERMIND
February 18, 2006

Mark Twain once said, ~Never do tomorrow what you can do the day after tomorrow.~ Let's be honest with ourselves people, we all are at times a bunch of lazy, procrastinating people. We can't help it because it's part of our nature and it's how God made us to have faults that we inevitably need to work on. In our hectic daily lives we put certain things or people on hild for the simple reason of either not having time, not wanting to deal with the drama, or starting and/or finishing a certain task that needs to be dealt with/accomplished. Let me ask you this question to each and every one of you. Is there something, whether it concerns a relationship or something else, that needs to be taken care of that you have been putting off?

Without a doubt, when it comes to schoolwork kids, as well as adults, will put it off either until tomorrow or until the last minute to finish something fairly or majorly important. Working with school age kids for the past 9 years, you witness kids starting or finishing homework that he or she should have done the night before or over the weekend. It's not just kids that fall victim to this, college students will pull all-nighters to start or finish research that was given weeks/months in advance, but it wasn't until the night before it was due that one will risk losing sleep to finish it. We've all done it and it is me or does your printer seemingly not work when something important such as a research paper needs to be printed out?

When it comes to fighting, there comes a point where a person just becomes lazy about it and realizes that it's just not only a waste of time, but also just plain stupid, especially if it's amongst brothers. Speaking from experience, physically fighting with your own brother can be considered one of the most exhausting experiences mainly because when you're young you want to know who's the man, in a manner of speaking. However, when you get older the physical aspect of it all is replaced by talking smack to each other, which is by far a much more immature way of settling things. Hey, it's a guy thing and it saves trips to the hospital because bones don't heal like they used to when you're younger.

Oftentimes, in a significant relationship such as in a marriage there are certain things that a man, more so than a woman, can become lazy about due to the number of years they both have spent together. One such thing that a husband can do for his wife is to show how truly lucky he is to have her as his wife is taking her out on a date. Whether it's a simple moonlit stroll on the beach at night, a movie she would like to see, or going shopping with her which all men dislike doing but they'll have to bite the bullet. Essentially, it shows that a husband still got what it takes to romance the woman he loves after many years of marriage. For the question can be asked to married women, when was the last time your husband took you out on a date?

In retrospect, well all will have our own spurts of laziness from time to time which can either work for us or against us. For some, most, or all people they thrive on the pressure of doing things at the last minute because, in a sense, to that person it's considered another challenge that life has placed in front of him or her. Yes, others can be a quality which can really hurt a person even when it pertains to a dating or marriage relationship. Ultimately, the responsibility falls squarely on our shoulders to get off our butts and take care what's needed to be done like starting a research paper that I have been putting off so.....eehhhhhhhhhhhhhhh....nevermind....I'll do it tomorrow.

BROKEN
February 20, 2006

Albert Einstein once said, ~ The most important human endeavor is the striving for morality in our actions. Our inner balance and even our very existence depends on it. Only morality in our actions can give beauty and dignity to our loves.~ In the whole scheme of things, life is about having an equal balance of highs and lows and yet at times it seems as if the lows outweigh the highs. If you think about it, we all go through the same lows even though the situation may be different for each of us. Situations such as people talking behind your back, starting rumors, and/or being accused of something you didn't do stem from a lack of maturity in which some, most, or all people haven't grown out of. Do you agree or disagree?

Essentially, that lack of maturity is oftentimes aimed in your direction because quite frankly people have nothing better to do with their own lives but to see others suffering, which is amusing to them. The mistake would be responding back because it only fuels the fire and the more drama, as well as anger you put on the fire the flames are going to get higher to the point where it's out of control. It's just a matter of knowing the truth of the particular situation or people or persons involved which is considered the water that puts out the fire that can totally burn not only you but those around you that care about you. Though it may not be in an instant, it will gradually die down once the truth is revealed.

Without a doubt, we all want to see the good in people and yet they can have two sides to them. In other words, a proverbial Dr. Jekyll and Mr. Hyde persona and it's this persona that will have you inevitably re-evaluate friendships and probably adopt a new attitude because of it. We all must draw the line at some point when it concerns the people in our lives and say enough is enough that it affects your outer balance, as well as the inner balance to where its been pushed way beyond its breaking point. It's at that point you either start cleaning out your closet, so to speak, of one's inner circle or adopt a new attitude that initially will cause you to be either labeled the "B" word or an a**hole, but that's the price you have to pay.

There comes a point where we begin to ask ourselves questions concerning the balance of life not only outwardly but also inwardly too. Questions that concern life to where you ask the following: How do you keep going when people around let you down? How do you deal with being hurt emotionally within your heart and yet still keep going on? How do you know whether or not to stick with certain friends or give up on them completely? Who do you go to when the friends you turn to aren't there for you? It's these particular questions and many others you may have that ultimately have one answer which will always come up time and time again…God.

Someone once said, ~It's easy to get discouraged when things go bad. But we shouldn't lose heart because God is at work in our lives, even in the midst of pain and suffering. Remember, the next time your little hut is burning to the ground it just may be a smoke signal that summons the grace of God. For all the negative we have to say to ourselves, God has a positive answer for it.~ In retrospect, the life each of us lives is not an easy one but we continue to wake up and thank God we have one even though it may stink at times. In the end, it's when you feel like you've been broken both inside and outside, it's God who has the power to heal, as well as bring back balance to your life. A song that somewhat reflects this thought is Broken by Seether ft. Amy Lee.

THE REAL THING
February 23, 2006

Will Smith's character Hitch said, ~Life is not the amount of breaths you take, it's the moments that take your breath away.~ If you think about it, throughout life there are moments where we hold our breath with anticipation when it concerns a certain special someone who you either have met already or haven't met yet. In a metaphorical sense, since the time of our birth each of us has been holding our breath waiting for the right guy or girl to walk into our lives and finally tell us to breathe. For it's in that moment of exhaling you breathe out times of frustration, heartache, anger, confusion, and/or disappointment, which has been building up and its been a weight on not only your heart but also on your soul as well.

Let me ask you this question, have you truly met someone who honestly and genuinely takes your breath away and with good reason. Essentially, you've waited all your life for a person who makes you smile from ear to ear no matter how your day was, bad or good. A person who makes you laugh at the things one says or points out that seem insignificant, which shows he or she has a sense of humor that is never failing. In other words, one who can turn a negative into a positive. For this person is considered a blessing from God and yet at times you feel like you aren't deserving of him or her to where you think that person should be with someone else, but that particular thought is quickly squashed.

Without a doubt, when you finally do meet that person who leaves you breathless, he or she seemingly makes breathing easier for you. Of course, there have been those in the past who you thought would absolutely keep you breathing in and out sighs of fulfilling relief, but was it considered premature sighs of relief that caused you to hyperventilate? What do I mean? To simply put, sometimes you can get so excited in a relationship that you choose to overlook certain things he or she does. Unfortunately, its those particular things, whatever they may be, that will turn initial excitement into heartache to where you breathe into a paper bag due to the number of emotions that will overwhelm you, which we've gone through at some point in our lives.

Oftentimes, there comes a point where you will ask yourself questions when it concerns that special someone. Such questions are: Does this person bring out the best in me to where he or she challenges me to reach my greatest potential? Does this person have that north star quality to point and guide my way back to where I got lost in my journey of life? Does this person have a hero/storybook quality and that even though I may have stopped believing in Superman, Cinderella, Prince Charming, Knights in shining armor, etc. it's nice to know that someone is looking out for me. Finally, does this person have the qualities to be my best friend for life who knows me inside and out that he or she is not afraid of who I am, which can be scary.

Someone once said, ~Falling in love with someone is, in essence, not a conscious thing. You can wake up one morning, madly in love with someone, without any inkling how, when, or where your heart decided to beat in his direction. Falling in love is like breathing. You don't plan to do it, but something in your anatomy dictates that you should. That, plus the fact that consciously trying not to will only make you choke and turn blue. But it doesn't mean you won't continue doing it anyway...~ In retrospect, the love you find with that one person will bring/already has brought to your heart true happiness that when you savor each breath when you're around him or her you absolutely know you have the real thing.

I'M FREE AT LAST
February 28, 2006

Ralph Waldo Emerson once said, ~Debt, grinding debt, whom iron face the widow, the orphan, and the sons of genius fear and hate, which consumes so much time, which so cripples and disheartens a great spirit with cares that see no base, is a preceptor whose lessons cannot be forgone and is needed most by those who suffer from it most.~ Essentially, each one of us have debts to pay that we knowingly put ourselves in to where it may take days, weeks, months, years, or even decades to get out of it. Hey, it's part of being a responsible adult and oftentimes a reality check is needed to wake a person up. Let me ask you this question, when it comes to owing money, how minor or major are you in debt?

We've all borrowed money from people or vice versa and depending on the amount of money borrowed you primarily want it to be paid back. Thinking about it, you truly know who your friends are when one finds himself or herself in financial difficulty, but because of our pride you refuse to accept help. It's those particular people in your life that you thank God for love, support, friendship, and act of selflessness towards not only you but your family as well. It can truly be a sad, but sometimes comical situation when one owes or is owed money that a person will either make excuses or try to avoid him or her at all costs, which can test the limits of one's patience.

Without a doubt, being a college student you can inevitably rack up some major debt as the cost of living in one's particular college of choice can bite you in the butt. Paying for you classes, food expenses, phone bills, etc can all add up to where it all seems hopeless that it may or may not get paid. Whether or not you yourself are paying for it by working or having your own parents for it, the education you received will be well worth it as you are handed your diploma. For the question can be asked of you, have you paid off any past college debts or are you still paying them? Personally speaking, I'm about a couple weeks shy of paying off a college debt that has lasted seven years, and I'm going to be when I make that last payment.

If you think about it, there are some debts that we all as human beings can never pay back because we continually owe this person our lives. For this debt we owe is a debt of gratitude to God Almighty for sending his Son, the Lord Jesus Christ, to die on the cross for us and pay for our sins even though we did not deserve it. As we continue to give thanks in prayers for his self-sacrifice, we owe it to Him to spread his message and save others that are lost in sin. We are all sinners in the eyes of God and if you have not accepted Jesus as your personal savior now is the chance to get on your knees, pray to God, and accept him in your heart. Trust me, you'll be glad you did.

In retrospect, in this day and age people easily get themselves deep into financial debt due to enticing offers and too good to be true deals. Whether it's spending too much with one's credit card or gambling to the point that you lose not only yourself but also your family and friends there will come a point that you will hit rock bottom. What it comes down to is managing your money wisely and for those who have experience on one's side they learned it the hard way to where the knowledge is passed to those that need to hear it. In the end, it's when you finally come to the point where you do get out of the red, so to speak, you can say yourself or out loud I'm free at last.

A SOUL THING
March 4, 2006

Ray Charles once said, ~What is soul? It's like electricity, we don't really know what it is, but its a force that can light up a room.~ Let me ask you this question, when you think of the word soul when it pertains to music, who do you immediately think of? Personally speaking, names that come to my mind are Aretha Franklin, James Brown, Stevie Wonder, Eric Clapton, B.B. King, Fats Domino, Luther Vandross, Bo Diddley and of course the late great Ray Charles. It's these particular people who have an essence to their soul that they not only breathed life into their songs but also they moved you both physically and metaphorically to where it brings out certain thoughts, feelings, and/or emotions as well.

Without a doubt, music touches the soul to a point where you can literally get lost in the melody and lyrics. Sending you to a far off distant world thinking about a moment of happiness or sadness in your life, depending on which song it was of course. Every person, at some point in life, has stopped what they were doing, closed their eyes, and listened to a song that would take them on a journey. Although they weren't physically going anywhere, they were most certainly going somewhere mentally, as well as, emotionally to a point that you actually were tired from the journey afterwards. Whether it was your first kiss, first dance, the day you got married, when your child was born, etc. your soul was moved by that particular song playing on the radio.

If you think about it, there is an absolute truth and beauty when something or someone stirs your soul to the point where it changes you. Most definitely, there is absolute truth and beauty in a song especially the ones that you keep close to your heart and soul because they're a link to someone special or particular event in your life either in the past, present, or future. In a sense, a song defines who we all are as individuals and it brings to life something within one's soul that when you hear a particular song you can't help but be captivated by not only the lyrics but also the person singing those words.

For the question can be asked, who have you seen or heard lately on the radio that exudes soul today? Not many come to mind because certain artists tend to bring out one single emotion rather than a plethora of emotions such as joy, laughter, sorrow, aggressiveness, anger, heartache, heartbreak, and anger. An artist, such as Ray Charles, had that underlying presence and energy to bring out those emotions and feelings to where you continue to feel the soulful meaning within every word he sings to this day. It's a rarity these days to hear a person now-d-ays whose presence leaves a lasting impression on not only you but also people around you as well.

American Idol has graced our presence once again and one simple questions needs to be asked, 'Does anybody have soul?" Among thousands of people, Taylor Hicks, has become the definition of soul and he's a person who not only has it, but also brings with him a certain, presence, likeability factor, and an energy that is electrifying many people across the world, which hasn't been felt in music in quite some time. A throwback of Ray Charles and Joe Cocker, with a bit of Michael McDonald mixed in. When it comes to the fans of Mr. Taylor Hicks, it's not about an obsession thing or a popularity thing, it's not even a rivalry thing with over fans; in the end, what it basically comes down to is a soul thing.

A TOUCH ABOVE THE REST

March 18, 2006

Edwin Hubbel Chapin once said, ~Every action of our lives touches on some chord that will vibrate in eternity.~ You have to admit, the power of a touch whether its metaphorical, physical or emotional can make a big difference in a any person's life that it can personally affect you. For a simple touch can trigger the senses that it will have you reflect back to the who, what, where, when and sometimes why of that particular person and/or event in one's life. Let me ask you this question, who or what in your life has touched you in such a positive way that you will always have a smile on your face.

If you think about it, there is something special in a certain look that is given by or received from a potential and/or significant other, which can pull/touch the proverbial heartstrings. Essentially, it's that nonverbal communication that can absolutely speak volumes to where you can actually see two hearts touching and connecting together. Yet, does that look stand the test of time 10, 20, 30, 50 years down the road? My answer is yes because even though my parents have had rough times the look is always there between them, which shows that the nonverbal communication of love continues to touch both of them even when they are angry at each other.

When it comes to the physical aspect of being touched, in a positive way of course, it's like a greeting or goodbye that you feel good within your heart. For guys, a welcomed greeting such as a handshake can turn into a well-choreographed routine of hand gestures and though it looks stupid it brings enjoyment, as well as a sense of cohesiveness for a group of guys who made their own personal greeting for each other all their own, which nobody can take away from them. Women, on the other hand, are more affectionate and personal with their greetings and goodbyes to where hugs are shared and tears are shed as if they may not see each other again, which shows that there is a bond between women that totally confuses guys, but I digress.

Without a doubt, a person can be emotionally touched within one's own heart and soul. Music, considered chicken soup for the soul, can touch every emotional button by the lyrics being sung by a particular artist or group. It's the lyrics in a particular song that can convey how you feel now or back then that can bring out certain emotions such as anger, confusion, sorrow, bitterness, happiness, contentment, etc. Each and every one of us has a song growing up that when you hear it you smile as you flashback to your childhood. Personally speaking, the song Bear Necessities from The Jungle Book always brings a smile to my face to where I still find myself moving to the beat of the song and I will continue to do so long into my golden years.

In retrospect, the actions each of us take when it comes to our own heart will reverberate and hopefully touch someone who sees how truly special you are. For the question can be asked though, when it comes to one's own heart, has there been a guy/girl who truly looked within your heart, touched it to the point your heart smiles, and ultimately gave you a song within your heart that lasted a lifetime? For those of you who have never experienced being fully touched in your heart, you will someday meet or already have met that special someone who touches every part of your heart and you know what, in the end it's considered a touch above the rest.

GIRL POWER

March 27, 2006

Jeffery Bernard once said, ~Women should have labels on their foreheads that say, 'Government Health Warning: Women can seriously damage your brain, genitals...and good standing among your friends.'~ Without a doubt, women are considered the most beautiful creatures on the face of the plant and yet can also be considered the most dangerous force to be reckoned with, which many a man out there have experienced firsthand. As a guy, you have to always proceed with caution when approaching a woman or even a group of women because you never know if you'll be greeted with open arms or a right hook to the jaw.

When it comes to psychological warfare, women know how to get in our heads to the point that we're seriously messed up mentally. Women have that innate ability to make guys so crazy that we end up literally tearing out our own hair because of how they can affect us in either a positive and/or negative way. Positive in a way that you always have a goofy grin on your face when you're thinking about a particular female and negative in a way that you start doing/saying things that you wouldn't normally never do, which makes a guy look/sound foolish. Let me tell you something, I've been messed up in the head several times because of a particular female, but I've ended up coming out of it okay...for the most part.

Essentially, being physically hurt by a woman, whether intentionally or by accident, really really hurts. Every guy for whatever reason has either been hit in the arm, punched in the face, slapped upside the head, pushed, slapped in the face, and/or kneed in the walnuts, etc. for doing/saying something stupid or doing/saying absolutely nothing, which from our standpoint is considered a lose-lose situation. Though I haven't personally been slapped/punched in the face or kneed in the walnuts *knock on wood* I know some guys that have and to those particular guys out there I simply say this to you, I feel your pain.

Oftentimes, a woman can cause friction between a man and his friends due to the amount of time he spends with her rather than with them. It can be a proverbial tug of war, in a manner of speaking, to where an ultimatum is given by the woman to either choose either his heart for her or his friendship with them, which is a touchy decision to make indeed if you're looking at it from a guy's perspective. On one hand he wants to be happy within his heart, but on the other hand he doesn't want to turn his back on the friends who he's known for quite some time. However, think about this ladies, if a man's friends or truly his friends they will tell him to choose you because they will always be there for him no matter what happens in the relationship.

In retrospect, women will always be around to make guys crazy, hit them physically in some kind of way, and cause friction between their friends. Thinking about it though, it's because of women that they make life that much more interesting even though we may suffer brain damage from them. In a funny way men need women because without them guys all over the world wouldn't know which direction to go, how to dress, and constantly be reminded how moronic we are at times. Ultimately, no matter how many times guys swear off women because of bad experiences, we continue to dust ourselves off and get back in the game because they have that certain power over us which I can only simply describe as girl power.

AND THE WINNER IS...
April 2, 2006

Kenneth Boulding once said, ~The future is bound to surprise us, but we don't have to be dumbfounded.~ Let me ask you this question, if I had told you that Marshall Mathers, otherwise known as Eminem, would one day win an oscar what would your response have been? First you would probably have laughed, then thought I was out of my mind, and then would say the chance of Eminem winning an oscar is the day that Arnold Schwarzenegger becomes Governor of California. SURPRISE! Eminem indeed did win an oscar for best song entitled Lose Yourself from his hit movie 8 mile and The Terminator himself Arnold Schwarzenegger is Governor of California. I'm telling you, it's a matter of time when a rapper wins for best actor. Mark my words.

50 Cent, Bow Wow, Snoop Dogg, Mos Def, T.I, Andre 3000, Big Boi, Ludacris are just a handful of rap artists who have transitioned themselves from rappers to actors of either the small and/or big screen. Whether it's action films, screwball comedies, horror flicks, dramas, whatever the case may be, it's considered for them not only a steppingstone to something possibly even greater but it's also a learning experience to fine tune their acting skills...if any. Essentially, the films many rap artists star in today have done quite well such as 50 cent's starring role in Get Rich or Die Tryin, Ludacris' supporting role in Crash, Mos Def's supporting role opposite Bruce Willis in 16 Blocks, and Andre 3000 in movies such as Be Cool and Four Brothers.

However, its those particular rap artists who should give credit where credit is due as their predecessors paved the way for them such as The Fat Boys, Kid'N Play, Tupac Shakur, L.L. Cool J, Ice T, and Ice Cube. When it comes to Actor/Rapper Ice T, he has done very well for himself as a legitimate actor with many film credits under his belt. Yet, it's his role as Det. Odafin "Fin" Tutuola in the widely popular television show Law and Order: Special Victims Unit that has playing opposite some of the great actors such as John Cullum, Mary Stuart Masterson, Samuel L. Jackson, Cathy Moriarty, and Martin Short. Like Ice Cube, they are considered to be in my opinion the standard at which all rappers should look up to and learn from.

Speaking of Ice Cube, he too has also done quite well not only in the rap game but also in the film industry as well. Like Ice T, he has established himself as a legitimate actor working with big names of the big screen such as Willem Dafoe and Samuel L. Jackson in Triple XXX: State of The Union; George Clooney in Three Kings; Jon Voight In Anaconda; and Dan Akroyd in Christmas with the Kranks. BUT, it's his work as Doughboy in the movie Boyz In The Hood in which his character has been in and out of institutions since childhood and now sits on his porch with a forty in his hand and a pistol in his waistband. In my opinion, that role defined him as an actor and it's not too shabby either if you play opposite a future academy award winner by the name of Cuba Gooding Jr.

This past Academy Awards, 3-6 Mafia won the Oscar for best song entitled It's Hard Out Here For A Pimp in the movie Hustle And Flow starring Terrence Howard. It was also on that particular night Crash won for best movie and even though Ludacris didn't win anything, he was part of an ensemble cast in a movie that won best picture betting odds on favorite Brokeback Mountain. Without a doubt, rap artists are making noise in Hollywood to where it's being heard loud and clear. I started this thought by saying a rap artist will win best actor or even best supporting actor and I'm sticking to my word. For it initially began with Eminem then passed on to 3-6 Mafia and who knows maybe next year or the year after that, but one day the envelope will be opened, and these 3 words will be said....and the winner is: (insert rap artist name here).

THE GIRL NEXT DOOR
April 11, 2006

Dave Matthews once said, ~Where you are is where I want to be. And through your eyes all the things I want to see. And in the night you are my dream. You're everything to me.~ Without a doubt, every guy hopes to see, meet, get to know, then fall in love with, marry, and ultimately spend a lifetime with a girl who, in some ways, reminds you of Wonder Years' character Winnie Cooper. A girl who is sweet, unassuming, and yet truly doesn't know how beautiful she truly is. For some, most, or all guys know this type of girl and whether one hangs out with or sees her on a semi-daily basis she is not only special in her own unique way, but also exudes beauty both inside and out.

If you think about it, as a guy it's impossible not to be like this type of girl who in some ways places a hypnotic spell for the right reason of course. A spell that tends to fly under the radar so to speak as the beauty she exudes shines forth from within her personality, which can oftentimes be overshadowed by the physical beauty of certain girls. It's because she flies under the radar, she has an unexplainable, mysterious charm to her that guys tend to be attracted/drawn towards. In other words, it's this type of girl who any guy would love to be in a relationship with and if not in a relationship, then just as a friend one would enjoy hanging around.

Let me ask you this question, have you ever wanted someone to see you not just with their eyes, but with their heart as well? As a guy, you always tend to wonder as to what a girl sees through her own eyes and what's going on within the complexities of her mind as she looks for Mr. Right. Yet, time after time you see her tend to pick Mr. Wrong to where guys ask the standard question which is what does she see in him? If it were ever possible, you want her to see through your eyes a guy who has all the qualities she is looking for in Mr. Right and he is or has been standing right in front of her the whole time.

Every guy, in some metaphorical/Steve Urkel kind of sense, has been chasing or is chasing their own so-called dream girl. For some guys, they've caught her and never let go, but unfortunately for others that particular dream irl is seemingly out of reach. For those guys in particular, they tend to be considered quite delusional due to the fact that in some people's minds no one fits a complete description of the qualities one is looking for and you never will. However, there is a saying that goes never say never because there is a girl who fits all the qualities that a guy, like myself, is looking for and one day that particular girl will step out of my dreams and become a reality.

In retrospect, the qualities that a guy like myself is looking for in a girl are the following: down to earth, strong, witty, smart, funny, sweet, shy, simple, loyal, reserved, talented, pretty, serious, patient, soulful, sophisticated, innocent, womanly, caring, gracious, dependable, nurturing, protective, generous, wacky, etc. It's these particular above-mentioned qualities that mean a lot to me and thinking about it, this type of girl is a rare jewel to find, and you have to admit any guy would love to live either near or next to her. Ultimately, the type of girl I'm looking for is what I like to describe as the girl next door.

STAND BY ME
April 20, 2006

Someone once said, ~Don't stand in front of me, I may not follow. Don't stand behind me, I may not lead. Just stand beside me and be my friend.~ Without a doubt, a friendship should be established before love ever happens between two people who have a gradual or instant connection. Yet, when it comes to love one can get ahead of himself or herself to the point where you're left not only standing either slightly or majorly embarrassed, but you also jeopardize a friendship as well. Hey, it's part of life as we all knowingly meet that special someone while on our own individual journey. Let me ask you this question, when it comes to potential love and friendship between you and a certain someone do you absolutely know where you stand?

Essentially, every person is standing or has stood in front of a certain someone whose friendship means so much but every so often you just have to follow your heart and see where it takes you. When one does follow his or her heart one ends up metaphorically standing afar off raising it above your head towards that particular person, which is kind of similar to what John Cusack's character Lloyd Dobler did in the movie Say Anything. In some aspect, we all can be considered a Lloyd Dobler and even though we may not have a boombox blaring a Peter Gabriel song, one has the next best thing, which is a beating heart that is blaring one's feelings loud and clear.

Where do I stand with you? If you think about it, it's a question that has been asked so many times over by so many people to a certain someone. For it's a heart pounding experience as you stand in front of that person with absolute vulnerability and wait for the possibility of a decision from him or her…if any. However, the decision is primarily left up to that person and that person alone and you can't force it or manipulate the situation in your favor, which is not how love works. What it all comes down to is patience and when the decision is eventually made one will reach out and ask that person will you take my hand and follow me?

Like life, love has a proverbial crossroads where the decision that one makes will determine whether he or she takes several steps back due to fear, doubt, and/or reservations or step forward straight into excitement, happiness, and/or contentment, which is a place every person wants to be in within their own heart. For it is in that place where a person is truly real and the things you say or do while standing in front of that person cannot be faked. Ultimately one leaves it to chance and even though you can't guarantee what lies ahead in the future, you know you want to guide that special someone mentally, emotionally, physically, and spiritually in the right direction.

Someone said, ~Love is like standing in wet cement. The longer you stay, the harder it is to leave. And you can never go without leaving your shoes behind~ In retrospect, every person deserves someone to truly love and be your best friend. That certain someone is unlike any other as he or she metaphorically is standing within one's soft and tender heart to where his or her so-called footprints leave deep and lasting impressions. For it those impressions within your heart that give you a sense of calm when situations around you fall apart. In the end, when you look into the eyes of that special person you say you with loving confidence as long as you stand by me everything will be alright. A song that tends to reflect this thought is Ben E. King entitled Stand By Me.

BLAZE OF GLORY
April 30, 2006

Plato once said, ~Laws are partly formed for the sake of good men, in order to instruct them in how they may live on friendly terms with one another, and partly for their sake of those who refuse to be instructed, whose spirit cannot be subdued, or softened, or hindered from plunging into evil.~ If you think about it, American Idol is a lot like the old west and the contestant each week are in a showdown with each other but instead of six shooters their voices are the weapon of choice. Like any "town" it must have its resident peacekeepers laying down the law in this so-called High Noon type setting where sound or unsound criticism either sends them to an early grave or live to fight another day.

For the most part, the "town" of American Idol has had its share of memorable gunfighters, but none has created more buzz around the world than a gray-haired cowboy named Taylor Hicks otherwise known as the Silver Fox. A man who not only made his presence known when he walked into town in Nevada but also brought something along with him that inevitably became a force to be reckoned with and that is soul. Since then, there has been a following of mass proportions to where the mention of his name causes a disturbance in a positive way of course. Yet, that positive disturbance hasn't been sitting well with one of the three lawmen who has taken upon himself to take him down any way possible and his name is Simon Cowell.

Without a doubt, Simon Cowell is considered one of the meanest and toughest hombres who's quick to judge attitude branded the Silver Fox an outlaw due to the fact that he does not fit what he thinks an American Idol should be thus making him a wanted man, in a manner of speaking. His unique and one-of-a-kind style of gunfighting, so to speak, has not only wowed the crowd to the point of bringing them to their feet but it has also brought tears to the eyes of the female population as well. In Simon's "town" he's branded public enemy #1 and the barrage of flying criticisms have consistently been aimed towards the Silver Fox, which has wounded him deep but as the saying goes what doesn't kill you makes you stronger.

Essentially, the Silver Fox has taken off the gloves so to speak and is not going to comply with laws that have been set before him, which has subdued the once gray-haired stranger that America, as well as the world grew to love back in Nevada. The Silver Fox is considered a free spirit and the apparent refusal to no longer play by the rules that have been set forth shows that he's going back to what brought him to the dance, in a manner of speaking. In a sense, Taylor Hicks is bringing everything he's got in his arsenal for a showdown of a lifetime. A showdown that may in fact turn either good, bad, or ugly and by the end of the night it will hopefully be the gray-haired cowboy who will be the last man standing

In retrospect, Simon Cowell considers Taylor Hicks a serious threat because he's such an unpredictable and dangerous foe. Tuesday night, The Silver Fox is heading into a fight and right behind him is his posse who has been with him every step of the way with itchy dialing trigger fingers locked and ready to dial. Most certainly a tombstone marked with not only his name but also the names of each and every member of the soul patrol posse too. In the end, two days from now The Silver Fox is prepared to walk in six shooters firing at all cylinders and in the end I ask you this question Soul Patrol, are you prepared…are you ready to go down in a blaze of glory, which is a song by Jon Bon Jovi from the movie Young Guns II.

YOU'LL BE IN MY HEART
May 11, 2006

Someone once said, ~If I could be given a chance to decide my destiny, I would choose your heart because that's where I want to spend the rest of my life.~ If you think about it, we're all given chances to fulfill a destiny within our own heart when it comes to the matter of true love. A destiny that can be instantly changed as you meet that special someone who gives one reason to follow his or her heart. Essentially, it's a person who even though you may or may not know the identity of, you have that innate feeling of his or her presence within your heart and soul. Let me ask you this question, do you believe true love can change the course of one's own destiny?

Without a doubt, true love changes the course of one's own destiny by the choices each of us make to follow what one's heart is saying/telling you. We've all been or are now at that proverbial crossroads when our heart wants to either walk away or walk towards someone that only makes you smile but you also have fun being around him or her. In some universal sense, it's as if you and that particular person were destined to meet but there have been circumstances that have prevented it from ever coming to fruition. Circumstances such as he or she is currently in a relationship or is hesitant to be in a relationship because of what happened to that person in the past. Which can put your heart in true love limbo.

Oftentimes, it's difficult to know what the future holds with someone who you truly see growing old with. We've all been in a situation, past or present, where the things you said or did presumably put you on a path towards that particular person's heart but instead left you lost not knowing what to do or where to go next. Essentially the future can be ever changing as one look, one word, one touch can completely change the direction of where your heart is going. For the question can be asked, are you in a position where life is giving you an all or nothing chance to go with how you feel about someone, and it simply takes one step that will hopefully change the rest of your life.

In any case, we've all heard the expression you're destined for greatness when it pertains to one's professional life as success(fame and/or fortune) are metaphorically written in the stars for you, so to speak. When it comes to your own heart, it deserves happiness with someone who, in a way, makes you feel forever rich, and no amount of money can ever buy what two people share together that is deemed special. It's when you share something that is considered to be the most valuable commodity that can't be bought or sold, you and that person will truly have success in the relationship regardless of fame and/or fortune. Think about this, good things happen to you all the time, but great things happen to you all at once if you are truly deserving of it.

Someone said, ~As we make our journey through life, sometimes fears get in our way and detour us down a different path. I say walk into the face of fear with eyes wide open. Remember you only live once, and it's ok to be afraid, just don't let fear change your "Destiny". Some of us feel we need to walk alone, others don't. Which one are you?~ In retrospect each of us hold our very own destiny within the palm of our hand. That destiny comes in the form of true love, which is lying in wait for you to reach for it and holding it tightly. In the end, it's through destiny that we meet people, but it's from our own heart that it will ultimately say to one person now and forever you'll be in my heart, which is a song by Phil Collins that reflects this thought.

GO REST HIGH
June 1, 2006

Ecclesiastes 3:1-2 says, ~To every thing there is a reason and time to every purpose under the heaven; A time to be born, and a time to die; a time to plant and a time to pluck that which is planted.~ Without a doubt, there are two things we know for certain and that we live and die. Most certainly, we all have the living part down pat, but when it comes to death nobody can ever really be prepared to hear or witness someone who you know, care about, and/or love pass away. For the things that go in between birth and death is what each of us make of it as the decisions/choices one makes will inevitably have you be remembered either in a good or bad way.

For some, most, or all people the good times rather than the bad times are essentially remembered for someone who was part of your life either on a personal or professional level. Depending on the particular person's situation, one should always reflect on the positives, which keeps not only you smiling but also everybody around you smiling as well. Although it's a time of sadness, it's a time of celebration as well for that person who enjoyed life with a passion with the people he or she cared about and loved. We've all been in this particular situation, and it unfortunately doesn't get any easier as time goes on, but as the saying goes you keep on keepin' on the best you can.

If you think about it, the one question that tends to get asked over and over again is why? Why him/her? It truly is hard to rationalize why good people are taken away too soon and in the prime of his or her life no less. When it pertains to that person, it is oftentimes a difficult situation to try to change a certain routine that involves him or her such as saying high to each other in passing or whatever the case may be for you. Yet, one eventually accepts the fact that the person who you either woke up next to, see every day at work, were classmates with, were best friends with, etc. is no longer there in the physical sense, but is absolutely with you in the spiritual sense.

As I've said before in the past, you form attachments to the kids in the asylum who you spend almost every day around. Over the past 10 years, I've been privileged enough to see many kids grow up before my eyes and it's within those 10 years several kids have passed away. For me personally, even though they aren't your kids you feel like you are and hearing that type of news can affect you in some way, shape or form. For it's tough to handle and yet it's doubly tough when you have to tell his or her friends that their friend is gone. Let me tell you something, after 10 years whether its a child or even the parent of the child, it increasingly becomes harder rather than easier to handle because of the bond that has been established.

About 2 weeks ago, one of "my kid's" parents, who I've known for several years passed away due to breast cancer, which she successfully beat. What made it so tough to hear that news, which shocked not only me but also my best friends, was that we both saw her the previous week at a local popular eating establishment, and she was happy as can be. In any case, we learned that she didn't suffer as she passed on in her sleep and as I stood a couple of feet away to pay my respects, I said to her you can now go rest high on that mountain where the Lord Jesus Christ has already welcomed you with open arms. A song that best reflects this thought is Go Rest High by Vince Gill.

MY TIME
June 13, 2006

A woman said, ~He is the person I go to when I need to laugh, and he is always ready for me with something hilarious to say. He is the one I go to when I want to share my good day, and he asks all the right questions, knowing all the answers anyway. He is the one I can cry to and not scare away. He's by my side; he's in my mind, and he's here to stay.~ Without a doubt, any woman is truly lucky to meet a guy who is everything she ever wanted and more, which in all intents and purposes is the man of her dreams. For is this so-called dream guy that exhibits three main qualities which are a sense of humor, intelligence, and caring sensitivity.

It has been said laughter is the best medicine when it comes to one of the many qualities that a woman looks for in a guy. Being able to tickle her proverbial funny bone is a characteristic that is considered attractive, but the type of humor presented determines either a look of loving happiness or a look of utter disgust. It's merely a matter of questionable taste as to what is just plain funny or just plain crude, which a woman truly takes note of with her eyes and ears. Like that first initial kiss, women know that if a guy genuinely makes her laugh then he's the one and if he is able to make you laugh to the point of changing your undergarments then he's most definitely a keeper.

For some, most, or all women they want a guy with intelligence and when I mean intelligence, I mean is he able to put the toilet seat down every time after only being told once, but that's a whole other subject saved for a later Yodaism. Anyways, when it comes to intelligence a woman wants a guy who's not dumb as a doornail and yet doesn't want a guy who is a pompous intellectual that supposedly knows everything. In other words, a guy whose intellect is somewhere in the middle and to a woman being able to have a meaningful stimulating conversation means so much because it gives her a chance to find out if he will be able to give her the answers that she has been searching for when it comes to love.

Caring sensitivity is a character trait that is rare indeed these days for a woman to find in a guy, especially when life isn't going as planned to where tears are being shed. I'll be honest with you; guys don't necessarily know what to do when there is a woman crying in their presence because we have no idea the nature of the problem that caused the waterworks to start a flowin'. Yet, as a guy it's our gentlemanly duty to give the proverbial shoulder to cry on, let her vent, and not say a single solitary word to where she feels better. In a sense, it just doesn't take an open ear to show that a guy cares, it also takes an open heart to metaphorically catch those tears to show her that he's going to stay by your side and not run away.

This past Saturday, a woman who I have only known for 4 days got married to a friend of mine for several years. It's this same friend that I got to go experience traveling to and from Ohio facing near death experiences...twice, as well as, characteristics that really got under my skin, which I tended to look past being that I'm never around him on a daily basis. Yet, as I stood only a few feet back I could see she absolutely loved him no matter what with all her heart and soul. In the end, my time will someday come to be the guy who the woman in the beginning quote described plus a whole lot more and a song that tends to reflect this thought is Someday by Vince Gill.

THE WAY IT IS
June 16, 2006

What is a hottie? It's a question that essentially has many different answers when it concerns either a guy or girl who supposedly has the total package going on. An athlete, actor, actress, musician, comedian, soldier, etc. are just a plethora of people who tend to be given the prestigious title. A title that can be given to someone solely on the basis of superficiality or given to someone that has something more than what's beyond the surface. Now it would be safe to say that for those who are reading this you may already have someone in mind. Let me ask you this question, who do you consider to be, whether you know this person or not, a hottie?

As a guy, several names stand out as the term hottie refers to someone of the female persuasion. Such names that come to my mind are Angelina Jolie, Jessica Alba, Heidi Klum, Halle Barry, Maria Sharapova, the lead singer of the Pussycat Dolls, Rachel Hunter, Heidi Klum, etc. the list goes on and on. Yet, it doesn't stop at celebrities as guys very well know certain females who one sees on a regular or semi-daily basis who are considered smokin'. Personally speaking, I know and/or am friends with certain females who I work with, have worked with, classmates with, chatted online with, and hung out with who I considered to be hotties; BUT unfortunately, I will not divulge who those particular females are...sorry.

When it comes to the male side of the spectrum, guys don't necessarily sit around and talk about who's considered a hottie. However, women do to the point they talk all day about it to the point polls, fan clubs, as well as, websites are created in honor of the gentlemen they've picked to be the hottie of the minute, hour, day, week, month, and/or year. Such names that I have overheard who are deemed hotties are Johnny Depp, Brad Pitt, Paul walker,

Orlando Bloom, Usher, Justin Timberlake, Taylor Hicks, etc. and the list goes on and on. More often than not its their appearance that tends to get their heads a turnin', their eyes a poppin', and hearts a poppin' to the point that a cold shower is needed to cool them down.

For the question can be asked though to the ladies, can someone who is in his golden ages still be considered a hottie? Is the hottie status reserved just for those of the younger generation? For there are plenty of distinguished gentlemen who still got their mojo going and are considered hotties in their own right according to a certain number of women across the world. Such names who still have the capacity to make women's hearts go pitter patter are Sir Sean Connery, Clint Eastwood, Paul Newman, and Robert Redford. Whether it's 007, Dirty Harry, or two guys who will be forever known as Butch Cassidy and the Sundance kid its these guys who still have that certain something to which I tip my hat to them out of respect.

About 2 weeks ago a female friend of mine said that I am a hottie and though I was flattered I responded with a resounding no I am not. Why? I don't see myself as a hottie because I've experienced that ever so popular 5 word statement that I tend to hear which is you're a nice guy but. That "but" has been the proverbial bullet with my name on it and I've unfortunately hit many times with it. Being the so-called cute guy with dimples who is considered to be "just friends" material is who I feel that I am and if it seems that I sound a bit angry\/frustrated…well I am. In the end, that's the way it is and no amount of convincing me otherwise to prove me wrong will help.

I'M STILL STANDING
June 21, 2006

Someone once said, ~There is within each and every one of us the ability to love somebody with all of our heart. And although our hearts may get broken, it is only through heartache and pain that we learn how much love we really can give.~ Think about this, the most resilient part of the human body is a person's heart because of how much punishment it can endure. In some aspect, love is the ultimate test to see how strong and/or tough one's heart can become when you deal with feelings, as well as emotions that can physically and metaphorically break you. Let me ask you this question, when it comes to love, how strong do you think your heart is?

Within every person's heart there holds a love that is mysterious, gentle, funny, tender, nurturing, soulful, and most certainly passionate. For it truly takes a special person to awaken those certain attributes that are hidden away/left dormant to not ever see the light of day, so to speak. It's when you meet that special someone those particular attributes shine through bringing out the best in you, which can be seen by those around you. That love within your heart by no means makes you weaker but rather it makes you stronger as you find yourself showing other attributes you didn't know you had in you, which can surprise not only yourself but also the one you love.

In any case, it would be safe to say that many of you have felt heartache whether by being lied to, cheated on, or whatever the case may be. In a sense, it's like being stabbed in the heart and whether or not it has repeatedly happened to you it's an experience one doesn't want to live through again. Those betrayals of supposed love can twist the knife in one's heart to where the pain can linger on for months, years, or even decades. Nobody ever wants to be reminded of a painful past love, which can open back up those particular wounds and yet they are, in a way, a driving force to grow stronger not just in the physical sense but also in the emotional sense within your heart.

When it comes to love there are many lessons to be learned and one of those lessons is that loving someone with all your heart is difficult. What it comes down to is having respect for that person and showing that he or she is truly important to you not just as bf/gf/husband/wife but as a friend. However, if respect is not reciprocated back the time and effort put into that relationship falls apart. In my opinion, in order to earn respect from the one you love you have to give respect by appreciating and acknowledging all that he or she does with kindness, love, and compassion. For the question can be asked, do you have this person in your life right now who is considered the source of your strength in your heart.

In retrospect, pain and heartache will always be synonymous with love because without it life wouldn't be that interesting. Each time you experience it, you essentially learn from it and hopefully grow into a better person. For the metaphorical scars and bruises you suffer from being hurt can be considered badges of honor that have inevitably led you to meet the one who you're going to spend the rest of your life with. In the end, when you look back at past hurts that have knocked you down you not only see how far you've come but also you see the strength and resiliency you have within your heart to keep getting back up to where you say to yourself or outloud to those who wronged you I'm still standing.

FEARLESS
June 26, 2006

Aminda M. Phillippe once said, ~I can jump off a cliff and be scared for thirty seconds. But I can look love straight in the face and be scared for the rest of my life.~ One of the scariest experiences a person will face is that moment where one takes that leap of faith in the name of love. It can truly be a scary situation indeed as you risk the mortality of your own heart for that special someone. For those that jumped before you have either found themselves continually falling happily or unfortunately felt the sudden impact that they didn't want to see coming. Love, it's considered an exciting adrenaline rush that lasts a lifetime and yet the question remains why be so afraid of it?

When it comes to love you totally commit yourself wholeheartedly to jump without ever really thinking about the consequences you may suffer. At first, you feel that initial rush of excitement running over your entire body to where you have that feeling of flying like Superman. It's a feeling of strong confidence as you feel absolute invulnerability and yet that same strong confidence can be gone in an instant leaving you vulnerable within your heart. For the control you thought you had is slowly lost and is replaced with extreme doubt as you find yourself thinking, saying, or screaming out loud have I completely lost my mind?

Essentially, every possible thought concerning that certain someone can/will go through your mind to where you're rationalizing reasons why jumping was clearly a big mistake. Such reasons that come to mind are: Am I even ready for love? Am I going to be able to give this person all that he/she wants and/or needs? Am I truly worthy enough to be part of this person's heart? Am I strong enough to be there for this person both physically, spiritually, and emotionally? Did I actually make the right choice in jumping? It's these questions and more that can scare you senselessly to a point where you start to grab on to anything to either slow down or stop. For the question can be asked, are you now or have you been in this particular situation?

Without a doubt, there is nothing safe about love and no matter how hard you try to protect yourself from being hurt you can't. In a sense, love is like kryptonite, and it inevitably saps your strength both physically and emotionally each time you get hurt or when getting closer to someone. If you think about it, saying I love you to that certain someone opens you up to reveal your true self that holds emotion and feelings you don't want to show. Why? By admitting to yourself that you love someone the pain and heartache will become much greater to the point where the freefall grows increasingly faster.

Someone said, ~I'm scared to fall in love, scared to fall fast, because every time I fall in love…it never seems to last.~ In retrospect, when you fall in love there will always be risk involved as you jump in hopes that you don't become another so called victim of love and yet the biggest risk is holding back the love you have for that certain someone. Ultimately, you just have to keep jumping and risk all that you are, as well as all that you have in your heart to conquer your fear. In the end, when you do find that special someone who you would risk falling forever for even though you're scared out of your mind then my friend you truly are fearless.

EYE OF THE TIGER
June 30, 2006

Michael Jordan once said, ~I just feel that my competitive drive is far greater than anyone else that I've met and I think that I thrive on that I think that is my biggest motivation in life...to completely find different competitions in certain things in life and try to overcome that, be it positive or negative.~ We all have, whether you want to admit it or not, have that competitive spirit/drive inside to where you don't like to lose at certain things. Depending on the level of one's competitiveness, experiencing loss or defeat can sting to the point where it can stay with you for a short or long period of time. For it can not only affect adults, but it can also affect kids as well.

Without a doubt kids have that competitive drive especially when it's against each other. Younger kids, more so than older kids, tend to have that competitive drive which can be switched on and off like a light switch. We've all witnessed kids play/create fun and/or interesting games at the spur of the moment to where the rules, that oftentimes are made up, can be changed at any moment. For it when they are losing at that particular game the rules either change to suit their advantage or quit and play a completely different game. Hey, it's what each and every one of us did back in the day and even though it was what your friends made, they still were your friends at the end of the day...most of the time.

When it comes to competition between kids and adults the results can be taken personally not by the kids but by the adults. As an adult, our ego and pride can take a big hit when one goes head to knee with someone who can't stay up past 8.p.m. As I said, nobody likes to lose and when you lose to a kid it can be a humbling experience as you not only have to endure the gloating from him or her, but also endure biting your tongue so that you do not say something you may regret or get fired. Of course, if the situation were reversed the gloating would be reciprocated back, which I have done plenty of times to kids at the asylum and I don't apologize for doing it.

Essentially, the will to win is something that all adults want to achieve as it is a competitive out in the real world. Whether it's business, academics, sports, etc., a person will be in competition in some kind of way, shape, or form with someone or something. For it truly is a dog-eat-dog world as you want to be the best at what you do despite all the obstacles one may face. One such name that comes to mind that personifies competitive drive while faced with obstacles is Lance Armstrong. Facing cancer and critics, he beat both to not win 7 Tour De Frances, but he also beat the critics who accused him of using performance enhancing drugs to win, which he did not.

As we all know July 4th is just a few days away and there will be competitions galore in celebration of it. One of those competitions is the annual 4th of July Hot Dog eating contest, which has been won by, in the past 5 years mind you, by Takeru "Tsunami" Kobayashi. For he owns the world record in 2004 for scarfing down 53 1/2 hot dogs and let me tell you something I get full after eating only 3 of them. For the question has to be asked, will Takeru "Tsunami" Kobayashi continue his win streak this 4th of July? In the end, it's just a matter of having that one thing which when you see it you know that the competition is on and that is the eye of the tiger.

OUT OF THIS WORLD
July 2, 2006

Josh Brand once said, ~Gravity. It keeps you rooted to the ground. In space, there's not any gravity. You just kind of leave your feet and go floating around. Is that what being in love is like?~ In my own thinking, love is like a rocket ship/space shuttle that blasts you up to the final frontier where the vastness of space allows you to do miraculous things, which you normally wouldn't do in the confines of Earth's atmosphere. Without a doubt, love can bring you to new heights within your heart that you haven't quite yet seen to the point you're amazed at what you see. Let me ask you this question, when it comes to love, are you prepared for the ride that your heart is going to take?

If you think about it, when it comes to love and your heart there can be a metaphorical countdown as to when one's time of liftoff with someone special will come. For it can be either a short or long wait depending on whether or not certain things will call for delays such as fear. Its just a matter of patience as you want so badly to have that clock countdown to zero in order to be at a place where it's just you and that person circling Earth forever. In any case, there is a friend of mine who I've been in contact with that is personally on his countdown to potentially establishing a new relationship amongst the stars to which I say to him good look and safe travel.

Oftentimes, a person can feel like an outcast as those around him or her seem to be launching into new relationships. In a sense, it's like they're looking down from the inside-out of their own heart to those on the ground whereas you are looking up from the outside-in waving back. It can truly be a lonely feeling as if you're the only person left behind, in a manner of speaking, as friends and acquaintances experience something that is considered to be a thrill of a lifetime. A thrill of a lifetime that you would gladly experience over and over again just with that one person who finally gives you the opportunity to like inside-out from within your heart.

For the question can be asked, is there someone in your life who gives you that feeling like you are rocketing towards the stars above? It's a feeling that you don't want to lose because, for the most part, it frees you from pain, heartache, tears, and the fears you have that can most certainly weigh you down to the point where you fall to the ground. For its that freedom within your heart and soul to not be afraid of how you feel about that certain someone who you would travel to infinity and beyond for. Let me tell you something, how often does this feeling come along to where you look down from the heavens above and be given a totally new perspective that just takes your breath away.

In retrospect, true love gives you a chance to experience weightlessness that can make you flip and spin. It can make you so excited that the anticipation of it all can make you absolutely sick in the stomach. It can metaphorically take you around the world and places in the universe, as well as in the stars, that have never been charted. For some, most or all people are experiencing this right now and they're loving every minute of it. Unfortunately, for a person like myself my feet are still planted on the ground, and I don't yet have a reason to travel into space, so to speak. In the end, when I do finally have that reason to boldly go whether others before me have gone then it will be something truly out of this world.

YOU'LL THINK OF ME
July 6, 2006

Someone once said, ~I die inside because I've finally realized the fact the time arrived when you don't want me back. But you're the one who did the heartbreaking, so why do I do all the heartaching? I guess because I'm the only one of us who can see that I never meant to you what you meant to me.~ It would be safe to say that there are countless people, whether it's guys or girls, who have felt the stinging effect of being burned by a particular someone. Yet, how long one felt or has been feeling the effects of being burned is primarily determined by the guy or girl in question. Let me ask you this question, is there one person who totally burned you to where it left a scorch mark within your heart that hasn't really gone away?

More often than not, women are more likely to become so-called burn victims than guys because of the emotional attachment they can have with those certain gentlemen in question. I use the term gentlemen loosely as there are guys out there who say and act like the proverbial handsome princes but then end up turning into fire breathing dragons. For they can say the right words, as well as do the right things to genuinely win one's heart as it makes them feel like a princess but unfortunately those words and deeds can become meaningless to the point it just turns into a bunch of steaming hot air.

For guys or girls, being burned is in a sense like being Punk'd and your heart is considered the main target. Oftentimes, you can see it coming but there are times where you can't, and you just get blindsided by those four words...we need to talk. Without a doubt, you don't know what is about to happen and yet you prepare yourself to stop, drop, and roll, in a manner of speaking. Once one hears those words he or she has been dreading there's not only an initial shock but also complete disbelief that it's actually happening to you. However, unlike the end result of Punk'd it's no laughing matter as your heart is left humiliated and betrayed.

For the question can be asked, can being burned by someone be, in the long run, a good thing? I believe so because as I said before the most resilient part of the human body is a person's heart. Though you may think the love you have within your heart will burn you, you'll find that it will heal you as you meet someone who inevitably removes that scorch mark within your heart. A female friend of mine experienced an unfortunate break-up but surprisingly she is in good spirits about it because she saw it coming. Essentially, she didn't suffer any permanent burn marks within her heart and to make a long story short she has met someone new who has given her a reason to smile both inwardly and outwardly.

Someone said, ~So what do you do when somebody you're so devoted to suddenly just stops loving you and it seems they haven't got a clue of the pain that rejection is putting you through. Do you cling to your pride and sing 'I Will Survive, do you lash out and say 'How dare you leave this way', or do you hold on in vain as they just slip away?~ In the end, when it comes to being burned a person can take back words of love, as well as, material things that mean something special, but what you can't take back are the memories you shared together to where you say to that person even though you've moved on with your life with someone else you'll think of me, which is a song by country recording artist and newly married man Keith Urban.

NEVER FORGET
July 9, 2006

Fred Savage's character Kevin Arnold from The Wonder Years once said, ~In your life you meet many people. Some you never think about again. Some of you wonder what happened to them. There are some you wonder if they think about you, and there are some that you wish you never had to think about again...but you do.~ If you think about it, throughout our own lifetime we meet so many people that it's sometimes impossible to remember the names that go with the faces. Yet, its those certain people that tend to stick in our minds whether it's on a conscious or subconscious level. Let me ask you this question, has there been someone you've been thinking about who you haven't seen in quite a long time?

Where are they now? That is a question that tends to pop up as you look through old pictures, as well as yearbooks back in the day. For it's your former classmates that you find yourself asking the following questions concerning certain people. Questions such as: Is he/she single? Is he/she married? Does he/she have any kids? If so, how many? Is he/she still the same person that you knew him/her as or has he/she changed? Essentially, it's these questions and more that lay dormant in your mind until you bump into him/her/them years later or stumble upon him/her/them in a popular website such as Myspace, which can be a nice surprise indeed.

In any case, you can sometimes wonder if there are certain people from your past that ever think about you. Depending on whether or not you're a person that made a positive impression on people it would be safe to say you would be an unforgettable person. Though egotistical as it may sound, you would be considered flattered that there is someone out there from your past who not only remembers your face but also remembers your name as well. It can be especially touching if that particular guy or girl who's been thinking of you was a person you had a close, special relationship with or was at one time in a significant relationship with that ended on good terms.

Speaking of relationships. there are certain ones that you most definitely don't want to look back on when it concerns an ex. The arguments, jealousy, mistrust, being overbearing, domineering, lack of showing appreciation, etc, whatever the case may be are aspects of the relationship that you don't want to ever think about and if you do they bring you to tears. Without a doubt, there have been many women, as well as men, who have cried themselves to sleep because someone totally did them wrong. For the question can be asked, can you think of a past ex that just the mere thought or mention of that person's name sends chills up and down your spine...in a bad way of course.

In retrospect, we all will continue meeting people in the present who will be part of our past, to where they possibly may be part of our future. Unfortunately, you have to take the bad with the good as there are those who will not have our best intentions in mind when it comes to friendship or love, and you inevitably leave their memory in the past where it belongs. However, every once and awhile you meet someone that just brings joy to your life and you continue to smile, as well as laugh when you think about him or her. In the end, even though your mind may forget the names and faces of people from your past who are considered special and/or important, it's your heart that keeps on remembering to where it will truly never forget.

X MARKS THE SPOT

July 13, 2006

Herbert Otto once said, ~We are all functioning at a small fraction of our own capacity to live fully in its total meaning of loving, caring, creating, and adventuring. Consequently, the actualizing of our potential can become the most exciting adventure of our lifetime.~ Let me ask you this question, have you ever wanted or thought about what it would be like to be a pirate? Living life to the fullest by doing what you wanted, taking what you wanted, taking who you wanted, and most of all not letting any kind of set rules hold you down? With that said, wouldn't it be interesting if true love were like that where absolutely nothing stood in your way to capture someone who truly stole your heart.

Thinking about it, any guy would jump at the chance to be a pirate because it gives us a chance to be the bad guy. As the so-called bad guy we would just swoop in unannounced with one's trusty sword in hand take the proverbial fair damsel away. Let me tell you something, every guy has had that thought of taking a particular female they either knew or a complete total stranger, whisk her away over one's shoulder, sailing off into the sunset, and have her eventually fall in love with you. Only in our dreams I know and besides one would truly suffer the consequences with jail or prison as the charge of kidnapping would put somewhat of a damper on establishing a relationship with the damsel in question.

Without a doubt, it's a woman's fantasy to be taken by a pirate, who would otherwise be known as the proverbial bad guy. Why a pirate? To be perfectly honest I have no earthly idea but my best guess is that there is a mysterious, romantic, arrogant, charm mixed in with a carefree, take no prisoners attitude that can cause any woman to be mesmerized to the point of being attracted to him. Respect must be given because even though a pirate is considered a dirty, rotten, scoundrel, he's a free spirit who loves the open sea with a passion. Unfortunately ladies, whether or not he resembles Captain Jack Sparrow a.k.a Johnny Depp will probably be best left in the fantasy of your own imagination.

As I've said before, true love is considered the greatest adventure two people can ever be on as you have the thrill of the chase for the guy and the thrill of being chased for the girl. Most definitely, countless stories can be told of men forever capturing their future wife and yet even though the chase is over the adventure still continues to go on. In any case, there are guys like myself who are still out there sailing the high seas, in a manner of speaking, chasing that unknown fair damsel. The same can be said for any woman who is still waiting for their unknown swashbuckler to sail in, give chase, and forever capture her heart.

In retrospect, we all metaphorically hold a map that leads to the greatest treasure a person can ever find...the human heart. Oftentimes, one's metaphorical map can take you in every direction but the one you want to go to the point that you find yourself lost sailing the high seas within your own heart, so to speak. It's at that point you try to figure out the next course/heading within one's internal compass, which can either take days, months, or years. Ultimately, when it comes to the map of true love there are those who are fortunate enough to find the greatest treasure connected to that special someone and in the end, x marks the spot for those who haven't given up the chase to find what truly does exist.

ALL FOR LOVE
July 16, 2006

James Baldwin once said, ~Love does not begin and end the way we seem to think it does. Love is a battle, love is war, love is growing up.~ If you think about it, when it comes to true love it can initially start off small but then it eventually steamrolls into something much bigger than anyone can ever imagine. When it comes to battle for true love a person can predict a possible outcome when it pertains to a certain someone in the beginning stages but unfortunately the end result is sometimes not what one predicted. Despite that, one must remain with the proverbial battle plan established within your heart, which holds the following three things: courage, faith, and determination.

Without a doubt, it takes courage within your heart to head into something that you have absolutely no idea as to what will happen next. Once a person makes that decision to step on the field of battle, so to speak, there is no turning back and most definitely an overwhelming sense of fear will be felt. Yet, it's that same sense of fear that drives you, as well as motivates you to keep moving forward even though you're scared out of your mind. If you think about it, its when you're truly scared that you find within yourself the courage to not be afraid of the feelings and emotions that repeatedly hit you to where you remove the bulletproof vest you metaphorically wear, which protects your heart from being hurt.

True love not only takes courage, it also takes faith as well. Faith you put not only in yourself to make the right decisions, but also in God to help protect and guide you through the so-called warzone. For it can be a tough situation indeed as you can easily be distracted from all that is happening in, to, and around you to where you lose focus. It's when you lose focus the faith you have in God and in yourself slowly turns to doubt, which happens when one's heart and mind clash. In order to bring that focus back you have to pray and faithfully trust that God is leading you or already has led you to someone who will have/has complete faith in you to protect and guide him or her to a place that is absolutely calm and peaceful.

Essentially, every person comes face to face with one's heroic nature which is shown by the determination yielded in his or her heart. The determination to fight for what is honest, pure, as well as, true and even though you may not have the physical, mental, and/or emotional strength you keep on fighting, which shows how much heart you have. Thinking about it, falling in love is just half the battle because the other half of the battle is staying in love and if you don't run away from it you show signs of growth. In a sense, when you fight for someone who you would give your life for then you truly know the meaning of true love to where you're all grown up and the boy/girl you started out to be is now gone as you now become a man/woman.

Someone once said, ~Love is fighting for what you want and always working to make it better. So, if you fight for what's in your heart you're likely to receive love back.~ In retrospect, true love gives you a fighting chance to not ever give up on someone special who will most definitely not ever give up on you. It's just a matter of fighting with all your heart and whether you win or lose, you fought with honor. In the end, when you find someone who also has the same courage, faith, and determination to join you in the greatest battle two people will ever face together it's all for one and all for love, which is a song from the movie Three Musketeers by Bryan Adams, Sting, and Rod Stewart.

MY FINAL THOUGHT
July 18, 2006

Someone once said, ~The end is never as satisfying as the journey. To have achieved everything but to have done so without integrity and excitement is to have achieved nothing.~ There comes a point where the intellectual journey one has been traveling on becomes mentally exhausting. The time and effort put into something that takes either hours or days to write takes just several minutes to read for those who not only become an avid reader but dare I say a fan as well. For it can be a tough situation indeed to keep subjects such as love fresh because quite frankly what can be said about it that has already been said.

When it comes to the subject of love you can make so many comparisons, as well as, observations about it that you may very well repeat yourself. Without a doubt, it's a subject matter that can be considered difficult to comprehend and yet there are so called experts out there who not only have PhD's but also written books on the problems, complexities, and solutions of love, which can be confusing if you ever have time to read them. Let me tell you something, I don't consider myself an expert, but I do consider myself to be a people person who listens, observes the bigger picture, and sees what others are not able to see by putting my own personal twist on it.

Essentially, within each and every Yodaism I've hopefully achieved a certain amount of integrity to where I've earned the respect from my peers. For there has always been a moral code to treat subjects such as heartbreak with tactfulness and dignity that it truly deserves to those who experienced it. However, when it comes to the subject of sex, I tend to leave it well enough alone. Why? It's primarily something special that should remain private to where it shouldn't be shared and/or described by having it read in detail by friends and/or total strangers. It's just not my style and so far I've been able to not break what I stand for, as well as who I am as a person.

Personally speaking, it's been a blast sharing what I've learned and/or experienced with many of you who have, in turn, shared your experiences with me. It shows trust as you get to know the person behind the person finding out things that touch not only the heart but the soul as well. If you think about it, there are those rare moments where you meet someone who you find totally intriguing to where you deem him or her a one-of-a-kind person who can never be replaced or duplicated. For the question can be asked, am I that person? With that said, I tip my hat to each and every one of you who was ever able to get the message within the message, which was a thrilling and exciting challenge for me.

In retrospect, life is about creating challenges for yourself that can help test you mentally and/or physically. For nearly a decade, I've challenged myself mentally by trying to figure out what life and love are all about. It's through either personal experience, word of mouth, or witnessing it firsthand you've read it all coming from the perspective of a guy. Whether you agreed or disagreed with what I said on a particular subject matter, I challenged you to think and if you are a person who hates thinking I'm sorry. In the end, after writing 373 Yodaisms that have challenged me to think I ask myself is this my final thought and my answer...not a chance because I'm just getting started.

DIRTY LITTLE SECRETS
July 21, 2006

Gilbert Parker once said, ~In all secrets there is a kind of guilt, however beautiful or joyful they may be, or for what good end they may be set to serve. Secrecy means evasion, and evasion means a problem to the moral mind.~ Let me ask you this question, do you have any secrets that you may be hiding from your own family, friends, and/or significant other? Secrets that can possibly hurt not only yourself but others around you, blackmail worthy, or simply embarrassing for anyone to know. Hey, it's a part of life as one chooses not to reveal certain pieces of information from your past and depending on the type of person you are it can either be an easy or tough situation to keep on the down low.

Oftentimes, a particular secret one holds concerning his or her health can hurt both emotionally, as well as physically, when it involves food. Eating disorders such as Anorexia or Bulimia are no laughing matter and more often than not women, more so than guys, go through it because of the pressure to be thin caused by either guy, society, the media, or Hollywood. It's a sad situation indeed when a woman sees herself as overweight and takes dangerous measures to lose weight such as throwing up the food she ate, which she can hide for months or even years. Let me tell you something, it truly boggles my mind as to why perfectly healthy and beautiful women put themselves through that kind of torture to where they risk losing their own life.

When it comes to keeping a secret such as infidelity it can most definitely hurt not only the one, he or she supposedly loves but it can also hurt those who are closely connected as well. Families can be torn apart to the point that the kids, if any, are caught up in the middle in a proverbial tug of war. Why do it in the first place? One reason that comes to my mind is being bored in the marriage and that thrill of meeting someone new makes trying not to get caught red handed, so to speak, is considered an adrenaline rush. For the question can be asked of you, whether you're married or in a significant relationship, have you ever thought or actually cheated on the one you loved behind their back?

Essentially, when you talk about keeping secrets on the down low there is one place that should automatically come to each and every person's mind. Las Vegas, otherwise known as Sin City, is a place that has countless untold stories by people who have sworn absolutely secrecy to never utter a word about their exploits or particular events that he/she/they may or may not possibly remember due to the quantity of alcohol one consumed during one's time there. Yet, pictures can say much more than words ever could as a person can be blackmailed by one's own friends, which they hold over your head for many years. Hey, as the saying goes, what happens in Vegas, stays in Vegas.

In retrospect, people all over the world probably have secrets that are considered to be a skeleton or skeletons in one's closet that he or she doesn't want to be opened ever again. It's those particular skeletons in one's closet that can most definitely wreak havoc on a person's life such as using drugs, giving up a baby for adoption, having an abortion, changing one's gender, coming out of the closet, having family/ancestors who are/were criminals and/or murderers, or whatever the case may be. Ultimately, secrets can most definitely hold power over you depending on what type of secret it is. In the end, I ask you this simple question: do you have any dirty little secrets, which is a song by the band All American Rejects.

BREAK THE WALLS DOWN
July 23, 2006

Candice A. Land once said, ~Each time my heart gets broken or trust is lost, its like a wall is being built around my heart and my brick wall is almost done.~ If you think about it when you experience heartbreak, a broken trust, or even loneliness for that matter within your heart you can most definitely feel like the walls are not only closing in on you but also getting higher to the point you're in complete darkness. It can be a scary situation indeed as you metaphorically can't see what's in front of you and the only sign of light, depending on how high one's wall is, is directly above you. Its at that point, a person can experience or have that feeling of claustrophobia even though one's not in or around any enclosed spaces.

Let me ask you this question, are you now or have you ever felt claustrophobic to the point you're own heart couldn't even breathe, so to speak? It's when you're in that metaphorical dark confined space you find its gets harder and harder to breathe. Why? In a sense, it's like the surrounding darkness grabs hold of your heart, doesn't let go, and slowly squeezes it. No matter how hard you try to struggle and fight, it becomes more difficult to escape as its hold grows increasingly tighter to where you start to slowly lose your own sanity. In order to regain back one's declining sanity, the only logical and reasonable thing to do is climb up and out of the darkness that will inevitably turn you completely insane.

Without a doubt, the climb up can be tough, time consuming, as well as, dangerous and yet it won't stop you from reaching for the light above. In a way, that is how getting through heartbreak is as you begin at rock bottom and then you try working your way out of the sadness, anger, bitterness, loneliness, and/or confusion that one deals with. One has to be reminded though, you can't climb up too quickly because one wrong move will send you tumbling back down to that deep, dark, and seemingly cold abyss, which nobody ever wants to be in. Slow and steady is what it comes down to as you don't want to make any mistakes and oftentimes it truly makes a difference when you eventually reach the top.

Essentially, once you reach the top and sit on the edge you take in all that you see before you as you're able to breathe easier. One can feel victorious at the effort put in and yet sitting there on the edge you, in some ways, feel like the nursery rhyme character we've all sang about as little kids. In some aspect, we can all relate to Humpty Dumpty because every person has experienced a great fall to where it left you and your heart broken and in several pieces. However, unlike the ending to Humpty Dumpty, you and your heart can be put back together again. For the question can be asked, is there someone in your life who has been right by your side every step of the way helping you heal with tender, loving care?

In retrospect, when it comes to heartbreak, a broken trust, and/or loneliness you can feel like you will never be able to get out from within those four walls to where you feel trapped. A person can spend so much time screaming and yelling for help that all you hear is the echo of your own voice bouncing off the walls. It can truly be a frustrating and scary situation for any person in not knowing who will come to their rescue and save them from slipping into madness, in a manner of speaking. In the end, when it comes to the walls that surround you in complete darkness someone special will hear you and break the walls down so that you see, as well as feel his or her bright, shining love.

REALITY BITES
July 26, 2006

Someone once said, ~Sometimes its hard to face reality. You feel the greatest feeling every time you're with them. You can't sleep just because you'll see them tomorrow. Every time you're with them its like a moment in heaven. Soon enough the magic disappears. Your heart is breaking and tears constantly come. Every beat of your heart hurts from all the pain. You wish you were hidden from all the world, and maybe all the pain would go away. Sometimes, its hard to face reality. Love - its not always what it seems.~ When it comes to love, as well as, matters of the heart, there comes a point where a person needs to or must be given a reality check that is considered harsh, ugly, brutal and yet its truthful.

If you think about it, there is a twisted narcissistic element hidden within love to where a person will play on certain emotions to basically stroke their own ego and pride. Its that all about me mentality that can have the person who supposedly loves/loved you actually manipulate you with words that are either knowingly or unknowingly harsh. For its these knowingly harsh words "you don't love me anymore" that can truly hit below the belt, so to speak, as he or she plays on the guilt one may be feeling. Yet, he or she knows how truly devoted you are/were as you spent countless nights crying over him or her. Let me ask you this question, was that ever said to you and can you remember the person who said it?

Without a doubt, love is a beautiful thing and yet it can turn ugly to where it's dark, dreary, and most of all depressing, which people choose to ignore. Unfortunately, you can't ignore what is always going to be there no matter how hard you try to suppress or hide it. The anger, hate, bitterness, resentment, etc. that you may have locked away within your heart from an extremely bad past relationship can crossover into a seemingly great one. Its those unresolved issues that haven't been dealt with can be like a dark cloud hovering over you to where it's starts to build up each time a certain problem is ignored until something big or little happens that unleashes the storm of the century, in a manner of speaking, that is not only ugly but nasty as well.

As I've said in the past, love is a battle worth fighting for that can leave you both metaphorically and emotionally scarred, which is worth it. However, a person has to face a brutal reality concerning love and that is sometimes it really isn't worth fighting for. Essentially, a person can have all the courage, faith, determination to keep fighting, but it's considered a losing battle to where you simply have to stop, turn around, walk/run away. Even though your heart is in it, in your mind you know you have to give up. A female friend said, ~Some guys...relationships...some love is really not worth fighting for. That's when faith and determination need to be kicked to the curb...and all you need is the courage to get the hell away.~ Do you agree with her?

In retrospect, looking back at past Yodaisms about love I've come to realize that maybe I've been living in a dream world. Initially, there is always a sense of hope that true love will not only bring closure, but true happiness within one's heart. However, no matter how close you are to finding/meeting true love, it seems that he or she will always be just out of reach and for the most part, it doesn't always have a happy ending either. Love can quite honestly be brutally harsh to a point that you can't stand to look at it because of how ugly it can make you or the person who loves/loved you. In the end, when it comes to the realities of love, I've got only two words that best sum up this thought and they are reality bites.

BRING ME TO LIFE
July 29, 2006

Someone once said, ~Of all the forces that make for a better world, none is so indispensable, noe so powerful, as hope. Without hope people are only half alive.~ In some aspect, there is within hope a pulse that keeps a strong and steady beat, which gives a person assurance that one will someday find/meet true love. When it comes to true love, hope is the one solid thing you tend to hold on to as it gives you a reason to keep on fighting to live, so to speak. Yet, there comes a point where the hope that pulsates with your own heart starts to slowly fade and you're inevitably left hanging on by only a single thread. Let me ask you this question, how strong is the hope you have pulsating within your veins and can you feel it?

For the most part, the hope you have pulsating within your veins when it pertains to true love can start out faint to where it eventually grows stronger as you potentially meet someone new. For it can truly be felt as one's palms become sweaty, nervousness sets in, and one's pulse goes absolutely haywire, in a manner of speaking, to the point of suffering a heart attack, which of course is a good thing in this particular situation. However, experiencing the absence of meeting that special someone or facing constant disappointment for that matter can put one's pulse from somewhat faint, to strong, to nearly unreadable to where you don't know whether or not you're dead or alive?

As said in the beginning quote, without hope people are only half alive and when you add the absence of true love you feel like you're dying or dead inside. One can have that cold, empty feeling not only in your heart but also in your soul as well. It's within one's self imposed tomb you, in a sense, feel as if you're wandering/sailing around in your very own sea of dark emotions somewhat like the River Styx from Greek mythology where the souls of the dead are transported across to the underworld. Whether or not you pay a toll, which is one obol(coin), to the cloaked skeletal ferryman Charon would primarily be best left up to your own interpretation of this particular thought.

In any case, without hope people are not just half alive but their also half themselves. If you think about it, you don't have a real identity as you struggle to keep from ceasing to exist all the while trying to find the one who truly completes you in every way. Oftentimes, a person can lose one's self as the hope he or she holds on to can essentially strip away the remaining identity you have left to where it completely destroys you and leaves you just a mere shell of your former self. Without a doubt, hope can be considered our greatest ally that keeps one's pulse beating but unfortunately, it's that same hope that is also considered to be our greatest enemy as it can slowly kill you mentally bit by bit.

In retrospect, a person can put so much faith in hoping true love will come one's way that one risks killing it completely and the stress that you can put yourself through can cause it to die off in a slow, painful death. It's a sad situation indeed when one tries to resuscitate hope that is metaphorically dying to the point of either shocking it with a defibrillator or putting it on life support, which is just plain foolish. It's that proverbial fool's hope, which if one monitors it with an echocardiograph, shows its pulse slipping away to the point of flatlining. In the end, it's on your so-called death bed that you pray for a miracle to walk through the door as you find yourself screaming out loud these words bring me to life, which is a song by the band Evanescence.

IF YOU'RE NOT THE ONE

July 31, 2006

Someone once said, ~Do you know how confusing you are? You are the most confusing person in the world. Sometimes you confuse me so much, I get confused about why I'm still crazy about you.~ Without a doubt, the life each of us are living is considered to be at times confusing, but when you potentially meet someone or are with someone who touches your heart, as well as, your mind it gets even more confusing. For it's truly and utterly amazing how one person can instill in you a plethora of feelings and emotions that when you experience them individually or all at once it can only be quite confusing, it can drive you nuts just thinking about to the point of going completely insane.

Let me ask you this question, are you interested in or with someone who makes you so confused that it drives you crazy? Crazy in the sense that even though its frustrating and difficult to deal with how you feel about that certain someone who may not share the same feeling as you do and yet despite that you're thankful that person is part of your life. For it truly takes patience to be around or with someone who does or says things that sometimes make no sense whatsoever and yet you can't help but laugh about it. It's what relationships, whether they be friendly, potential, and/or significant, are all about because to be perfectly honest love or true love for that matter would be absolutely boring.

Essentially, there comes a point in all the craziness and confusion that goes on within your heart, thoughts of why you're such a loser begin to creep into your mind. You begin to wonder what's wrong with you that you start deconstructing yourself and it inevitably leads you spiraling down towards anger, bitterness, and resentment, which is something that a handful of people have experienced. Thinking about it, every person has probably at some point in their lives done that and has had those thoughts to where they've initially looked back at one's past relationships or attempts at relationships that you've become convinced that you're not only a pathetic loser but also a failure as well.

In any case, it's oftentimes hard to understand why we feel the way we do when it pertains to someone who not just makes you smile but also makes you want to pull your own hair out. Why? Maybe for the first time in your life you find something that feels so real that its scares you to death to fully experience it. It's a sad situation indeed when you go through constant heartbreak that when you truly have /find something special and real in someone you're scared to let everything go. Instead, you hold back/keep inside what's in your heart, which makes you miserable every time you think about him or her. For the question can be asked, as confusing and crazy as this may sound who makes you miserable that it feels good?

In life, someone comes along that just turns one's already crazy and confusing world upside down even more than usual. For that person gives you the chance to say or at least let him or her know how you really feel. It's with genuine honesty that you say that when you are in my thoughts my head hurts because it brings up all the feelings for you that make my heart spin out of control, which makes me absolutely miserable. Miserable in a good way and you know what, I've waited all my life to feel this way. Now that it's happened/happening I'm terrified, but the crazy thing I don't want the feeling to ever go away. So, I stand before no longer confused as I know you are the one for me, BUT if you're not the one then I ask you who is? A song that best reflects this thought was written and sung by Daniel Bedingfield.

ABOUT THE AUTHOR

Dante Abundo Jr was born in Subic Bay, Philippines. He grew up with a military father who is happily retired from the Navy and has been spending quality time with his wife of 48 years. Dante lives in the Sunshine State of the Florida Panhandle. When he's not working, he enjoys in his spare time a number of activities such as drawing, traveling, playing video games, watching anime, and writing. You can find him on social media: Facebook, Instagram, Twitter, YouTube etc.

Visit The Inner Sanctum:
http://yodaisms.blogspot.com

www.ingramcontent.com/pod-product-compliance
Lightning Source LLC
Chambersburg PA
CBHW070310240426
43663CB00038BA/1295